The Teaching of Instrumental Music

SECOND EDITION

RICHARD J. COLWELL
Boston University

THOMAS GOOLSBY
University of Washington

Prentice Hall, Englewood Cliffs, N.J. 07632

Library of Congress Cataloging-in-Publication Data

Colwell, Richard.
  The teaching of instrumental music / Richard J. Colwell, Thomas
Goolsby. -- 2nd ed.
    p.   cm.
  Includes bibliographical references and index.
  ISBN 0-13-892688-3
  1. Instrumental music--Instruction and study.   I. Goolsby,
Thomas,   . II. Title.
MT170.C64 1992
784'.07--dc20   91-19210
                                                        CIP
                                                        MN

Acquisitions editor: **Bud Therien**
Editorial/production supervision and
  interior design: **Jordan Ochs**
Copy editor: **Carole Brown**
Prepress buyer: **Herb Klein**
Manufacturing buyer: **Patrice Fraccio**
Cover designer: **Patricia Kelly**

 © 1992, 1969 by Prentice-Hall, Inc.
A Simon & Schuster Company
Englewood Cliffs, New Jersey 07632

Printed in the United States of America

10 9 8 7 6

ISBN 0-13-892688-3

Prentice-Hall International (UK) Limited, *London*
Prentice-Hall of Australia Pty. Limited, *Sydney*
Prentice-Hall Canada Inc., *Toronto*
Prentice-Hall Hispanoamericana, S.A., *Mexico*
Prentice-Hall of India Private Limited, *New Delhi*
Prentice-Hall of Japan, Inc., *Tokyo*
Simon & Schuster Asia Pte. Ltd., *Singapore*
Editora Prentice-Hall do Brasil, Ltda., *Rio de Janeiro*

Contents

Preface

The second edition of a book is always a pleasure for the author. The fact that a second edition is needed means that the first has been successful, and, in addition, the author has a chance to mend what he has come to recognize as deficiencies in the earlier text. This book originally grew out of needs encountered in teaching elementary and high school pupils, and subsequent work with college students preparing for instrumental music teaching. The current interest in school reform has heightened the need for comprehensive guides for teachers, and this new edition contains new information, updated information, and a slightly revised organization. The trouble-shooting charts at the end of the chapters on instruments are seen as a useful addition.

As before, the book combines material relating to teaching of the instruments—woodwind, brass, and percussion—with a thorough discussion of the problems related to work with instrumental ensembles, large and small, in the school situation. Almost all instrumental teachers in the public schools play a dual role: They give private or class instruction on the instruments themselves, and they teach music through band or orchestra rehearsal. Because their responsibilities are so broad, they often need information and guidance. This book does not pretend to be exhaustive; one of its strengths is the selectivity exercised that facilitates the use of the book as a text. However, lengthy references are offered on each subject so that the user can pursue a topic further.

No single school of thought is represented in the instrumental chapters. The most widely accepted viewpoint is given on each problem, and often two or more views are presented where each seems to have widespread support. This is particularly true of the chapters on general principles of brass, rehearsal techniques, and classroom procedures, where numerous suggestions and ideas are offered from which the reader may choose.

In the first edition, students in instrumental methods class at the University of Illinois offered frank, helpful reactions to the material. For this edition, detailed critiques of the instrumental chapters were made by some of the nation's leading pedagogues, among them: Dr. Wayne Bowman, Dr. Alan Dilly, Dr. Frank Fenley, Dr. Mark Fonder, Dr. Wayne Gorder, Dr. Martha Henriksen, Dr. Joseph Koob, Dr. Karel Lidral, Dr. James Madeja, Dr. Charles McAdams, Dr. Ann Miller, Dr. Ross Miller, Dr. Kate Rushford Murray, Mr. Raymond Pettit, Dr. John Pherigo, Dr. George Townsend, Dr. George Weimer, and Dr. Jerry Young. The thoughtful suggestions made by these experts greatly enhanced the value of the chapters on which they commented.

Two chapters have been added: general principles of woodwinds, and the baritone-euphonium (which in the previous edition was treated with the trombone). The marching band receives greater emphasis in the administrative chapter and in the percussion chapter.

Many of the photos taken for the first edition by Mr. James Wilcox have been retained. New photos are by Mr. John Chenault. The authors would also like to extend their gratitude to Jennifer and Abigail Pack. The painstaking editing without which the book would have been much less readable was again accomplished by Dr. Ruth Colwell.

RICHARD J. COLWELL
THOMAS GOOLSBY

1

The History of Instrumental Music

A knowledge of the history of instrumental music is not essential for success as a band or orchestra conductor. Still, it seems appropriate to begin a book on musical instruments and instrumental music teaching with a brief historical survey. Besides the intrinsic interest history holds for us, there is practical value in the perspective gained from a knowledge of history. One can develop an awareness of trends; observe the ways in which things were done in previous times; learn about objectives, procedures, and methods; and gain a greater understanding of the reasons behind present practices and present situations. One hopes that such knowledge would help the teacher plan using sound bases, avoid mistakes of the past, and shape the future intelligently.

THE DEVELOPMENT OF THE ORCHESTRA

The earliest common use of instruments, recognizable ancestors of our modern woodwinds, strings, drums, and brasses, dates to several thousand years B.C. Instrumental ensembles may be traced to groups of flutes and lyres used at the time of the Greek dramas of Aeschylus and Sophocles, although Eastern music may have used grouped instruments at an even earlier date. Little development of group instrumental music occurred until the close of the sixteenth century, when the modern orchestra saw its beginnings with the creation of opera. The orchestra grew in size and importance as opera became more and more a public favorite. In one of the first operas, Monteverdi made an important contribution to the orchestra when he used instrumental tone colors to portray mood and character, perhaps the first such use of instruments for their unique, individual qualities. Rudimentary in nature, the early orchestra used imperfect instruments and had no set instrumentation.

For the public school teacher, the relevant history of bands and orchestras begins with the development and use of relatively modern instruments and instrumentation. Since the violin is the heart of the orchestra, the modern orchestra was inconceivable until the seventeenth century, when the great Italian violinmakers perfected their craft and created master instruments. The first good orchestra is considered to be the Twenty-Four Violins of the King, in the service of Louis XIII of France, which reached its peak of excellence some forty years later under Lully, during the reign of Louis XIV. Lully, a great conductor who demanded perfection (he conducted with a cane to ensure rhythmic unity), created a balanced ensemble of violins, flutes, oboes, bassoons, and double basses. While in France at this time the orchestra was a vehicle for the private entertainment of the nobility, the first recorded public concert by an orchestra took place in London in 1673.

By the time of Corelli a generation later, the modern violin had taken precedence over its competitors as the heart of the orchestra, and viols, vielles, and lutes were thereafter rarely used except as solo instruments or for special effects. Corelli, a noted performer as well as composer, is often given credit for originating the practice of matched bowing for orchestra. Alessandro Scarlatti increased the importance of the operatic orchestra, often dividing the strings into four parts and balancing them with the winds. The brasswinds became a legitimate part of the orchestra in about 1720. Thus, the French and Italians had developed the orchestra into a well-established entity before the time of Bach. During the time of Bach they continued to increase the orchestra's importance. It was therefore capable of a high level of technique and emotional expression before Germany became the primary musical center in Europe.

Bach himself was a master of orchestral writing, and contributed to the orchestra his unique voicing of the instruments, in which each is treated as a solo instrument. Handel also, though perhaps to a lesser extent than Bach, used instruments for their individual timbre, obtaining novel effects. The cello became important as both soloist and orchestra member; the full range of the bassoon was exploited; kettledrums were used for a solo part in *Semele*; and the oboe, until this time a military instrument, was often featured for its hauntingly beautiful tone quality.

Any list of individuals important to the development of the orchestra must include Gluck. He not only made innovations in the use of instruments, but, more significantly, he radically changed the type of music played by the orchestra. He introduced the clarinet, omitted the harpsichord, and gave the orchestra music that was genuinely expressive and dramatic, mirroring the scenes and action of the opera. With Gluck the orchestra discarded its role as simple accompaniment and became an independent dramatic force.

The Classical period of Haydn and Mozart created the balanced instrumentation and the musical forms that have for the past few hundred years made the symphony orchestra the chief of musical structures, most popular with the public and most challenging to the composer. During the nineteenth century, the number of orchestras multiplied rapidly in Europe and were established in America as well. The first symphony orchestra to be organized was the London Philharmonic in 1813. The New York Philharmonic, formed in 1842, is still one of the world's major orchestras; and the Boston Symphony and the Chicago Symphony, founded in 1881 and 1891, respectively, have also thrived to the present.

Several events gave impetus to the orchestral movement. One of these was the visit of the Jullien Orchestra to America in 1853–54. Jullien was a spectacular showman whose antics not only fascinated audiences but also made a real and positive impact on the American public.

Jullien was always dressed in an extravagantly embroidered shirt front, glistening white waistcoat, with a great black mustache and lavishly bedecked in gold chains, rings and pendants. He stood on a crimson platform edged in gold, tapestried with crimson velvet. He had white kid gloves brought to him on a silver platter before conducting Beethoven. Before the Firemen's Quadrille commenced, the audience was warned that something unusual might happen. Jullien loved to spring a surprise but a lot of fainting women might be too much of a good thing. Wiping his brow with his gorgeous silk handkerchief, he arose and faced his men. The piece started quietly like a nocturne or lullaby. A hush through the house made the suspense more thrilling. Then the music picked up a bit, the violins fluttered as they told of the awesome mystery of darkness. You could almost see ghosts. Suddenly the clang of firebells was heard outside. Flames burst from the ceiling. Three companies of firemen rushed in, dragging their hoses behind them. Real water poured from the nozzles, glass was broken. Some of the women fainted, and the ushers were rushing here and there yelling that it was all part of the show. And all the while the orchestra was playing at a tremendous fortissimo.

When Jullien thought they had had enough, he signaled for the firemen to go, and in a glorious blare of triumph the orchestra burst into the Doxology. Those of the audience who were conscious joined in the singing.[1]

---

[1] John Tasker Howard, *Our American Music*, pp. 230–231. New York. Thomas Y. Crowell Co. 1931, as quoted in T.F. Normann, *Instrumental Music in the Public Schools* (Bryn Mawr, PA: Theodore Presser Co., 1939), p. 51.

Of more lasting value and genuine artistic merit was the work of Theodore Thomas, who toured the United States with his own orchestra in 1863. He served as inspiration for the founding of the Boston Symphony and he founded the Chicago Symphony. His interest in education led him to start a school in Cincinnati for the training of professional musicians.

THE DEVELOPMENT OF THE BAND

The growth of the band movement is much less clearly defined than that of the orchestra. In the late sixteenth century, Venice was the center of a group of composers who wrote for brass ensembles, primarily trombones and cornets, that performed principally in the church. These groups were succeeded by other brass groups throughout Europe in the seventeenth and eighteenth centuries, usually civic or military bands, whose only similarity to present-day bands was that they used wind rather than string instruments. The typical instrumentation was oboes, clarinets, horns, and bassoons. Considering the state of these instruments at the time, one would expect that their sound was primarily useful for battle signals rather than as musical entertainment. Bands as we know them today seem to have stemmed from the formation of the forty-five-piece band of the National Guard in Paris in 1789. This band was conducted for one year by Sarrette. In 1790, its number was increased to seventy, and François Gossec became the conductor. Two years later the band was dissolved, but its members eventually became the nucleus of the French National Conservatory, founded in 1795.

America has been a leading country in the formation of bands, with groups that antedate the Paris Band of the National Guard by more than a decade. (For an excellent treatment of this subject, see Richard Franko Goldman, *The Wind Band*, Boston: Allyn and Bacon, 1961.) Josiah Flagg, often known as the first American bandsman, was active as early as the 1770s. The Massachusetts Band, formed in 1783, later became the Green Dragon Band, then the Boston Brigade Band. In 1859, this band acquired a twenty-six-year-old conductor, Patrick Gilmore, who changed its name to Gilmore's Band, took it to war, and made it famous. The Allentown Civic Band, formed in 1828, still performs today. The usual size of these early American bands was between eight and fifteen players, comparable to that of the U.S. Marine Band, founded in 1798, which at the turn of the nineteenth century was composed of two oboes, two clarinets, two horns, a bassoon, and a drum. Bands soon increased in size, however. Beethoven wrote his Military March in D (1816) for a minimum of thirty-two players, an average-sized group for the period. To honor the visit of the Russian Emperor Nicholas to Prussia in 1838, Wieprecht combined the bands of several regiments and conducted more than one thousand winds plus two hundred extra side drummers.[2]

Of major significance to the band movement was the invention for brass instruments of the valve by Blumel (c. 1813) and the subsequent improvement of the piston by J. P. Oates in 1851. These two events coincided with the rapid improvement of European bands in the first half of the nineteenth century, which reached a peak with the international contests in the 1860s and 1870s. Perhaps the greatest band contest of all time was that held in Paris in 1867, with nine nations competing. According to Goldman, the pieces played included the Finale of the *Lorelei* by Mendelssohn, "Fantasy on the *Prophet*" by Meyerbeer, *William Tell* Overture by Rossini, the "Bridal Chorus" from *Lohengrin* by Wagner, and a "Fantasy on the *Carnival of Venice*."[3]

The cornet, vastly improved by the invention of the valve, assumed the same role in American bands that the violin held in the orchestra. Many of the conductors were virtuoso cornet soloists. In fact, the band in America was for the three decades prior to the Civil War primarily a brass band. This can be attributed at least in part to the influence of the Dodsworth Band, one of the first professional bands and perhaps the best band in New York prior to Gilmore's heyday. In 1853, two New York bandmasters, Kroll and Reitsel, began to use woodwinds with the brasses, which greatly expanded the band's musical potential as well as its repertoire.

Bands increased in importance during the Civil War years, but while most of the members of the regimental bands enlisted together, they were mustered out in a year and the bands were dispersed. The real impetus to the band movement came from an event in 1864 designed to celebrate an inauguration, stemming from the inventive genius of Gilmore. This event, for which he formed a "grand national band" of five hundred army bandsmen and a chorus of five thousand school children, whetted his appetite for massed festival performances. Accordingly, in 1869 he organized the National Peace Jubilee, in which a band of one thousand, an orchestra of five hundred, and a chorus of ten thousand were brought together. The event appealed to patriotism, education, and Gilmore's spirit of business enterprise. Its immense attraction may be gauged by the fact that members of Congress, the entire Cabinet, and President Grant himself attended. Three years later, a World Peace Jubilee was organized on an even grander scale. The performing groups were twice as large as those of the national event, and many of the finest musical organizations of Europe participated. Not only did these huge festivals attract the public and popularize better music, but they also served to raise American performance standards—the visiting European groups dazzled the audiences with their skill; it was obvious that American bands and orchestras were no match for them.

[2] R. F. Goldman, *The Wind Band* (Boston: Allyn and Bacon, 1961), 28.
[3] Ibid., 28–30.

American professional bands improved rapidly after the jubilees. Gilmore took over the leadership of the 22nd Regimental Band in 1873 and directed it until his death in 1892. He was succeeded by the unlikely personage of Victor Herbert, whose well-loved melodies seem to have been little influenced by the military march. From 1880 until 1892, John Philip Sousa conducted the Marine Band and gave it a national reputation. Sousa and Gilmore toured extensively, bringing fine performances of both great music and popular music to audiences who otherwise had little opportunity to hear professional concerts. Many fine local bands sprang up whose repertoire included transcriptions of orchestral favorites, music written especially for band, and virtuoso solos with band accompaniment. For millions, local bands represented the only avenue to good music of any sort.

The size and scope of the band movement would not have been possible without the British band libraries. Published arrangements had become possible due to the standardized instrumentation encouraged by Kneller Hall, the Royal Military School of Music. British firms such as the Boose Journal and Chappell Army Journal were able to publish band arrangements of generally high quality, which stimulated and influenced the course of band music in both Great Britain and the United States.

Standardized instrumentation in the United States came about through the influence of band leaders such as Herbert L. Clarke, Albert A. Harding, Frederick Stock, John Philip Sousa, E. F. Goldman, Taylor Branson, and C. M. Tremaine. When band contests became popular in the mid-1920s, the Committee on Instrumental Affairs of the Music Supervisor's National Conference, which formulated the rules for band contests, instituted severe penalties for those organizations that did not have the recommended instrumentation, thus assuring standardization.

THE GROWTH OF PUBLIC SCHOOL MUSIC

The year 1925 marks the end of the Sousa era, and with it the abrupt decline of the professional band, although the Goldman Band and a few radio bands did maintain their popularity. Many factors contributed to this decline. The advent of radio, the phonograph, the moving picture, even the popular-priced automobile diverted attention away from the bands. Two musical trends may also have contributed to the lessening of interest in bands. One was the rise of the symphony orchestra, perhaps itself brought about by the increased desire for good music that the band era had inspired. The second was the increasing excellence and popularity of public school performing groups. School music seems to have gotten its impetus from the Peace Jubilees of Gilmore, and as public education broadened, so did school music organizations. Freeport, Illinois, schools have had a continuous orchestra program since 1864, when an individual was hired specifically for this task.[1] An extracurricular, student-run orchestra was formed in Aurora, Illinois, in 1878. Around the end of the 1800s, the outstanding instrumental work of Jessie Clark in Wichita, Kansas (1890), and Will Earhart in Richmond, Indiana (1898), was evident.

Despite the impact of the professional band movement in the last third of the nineteenth century, school bands were generally started after the orchestras. Freeport, Illinois, for example, had no band until several decades after the inception of its orchestra. By 1910, some one hundred school orchestras existed, and while there are references to school bands at this time, the primary exponents of band music around the turn of the twentieth century seem to have been the civic boys' bands that flourished in nearly every town.

It was in the first fifteen years of the twentieth century, however, that several notable instances of real pioneering in music education may be found. A few schools with vision and foresight were far ahead of the general public in adopting instrumental programs. In Los Angeles in 1904, grade school orchestras were formed to provide good players for the high school organizations. In 1905, A. A. Harding came to the University of Illinois to begin the college band that set the standard for bands in the next half century. A few years later, around 1912, A. R. McAllister instituted in Joliet, Illinois, a band program whose reputation for excellence continued for half a century. School boards as far apart as Oakland, California, and Rochester, New York, allotted $10,000 each to purchase band and orchestra instruments for every school in their systems (this in the years 1913 and 1918 when that amount of money was a princely sum). Such instances were the exception, but they provided the leadership and inspiration for others.[5]

The rapid increase in public school bands after World War I has often been attributed to the war and the attraction of the military band during this period. It was believed that musicians who returned home after playing in military bands created an abundant supply of teachers for the schools. This is only partially true. School orchestras and bands abounded before the supposed influx of teachers; a survey of 375 schools in 1919 showed that three-fourths of them had orchestras and one-fourth had

[4]"In 1864, Miss Francis Rosebraugh was called by the Freeport Board of Education from New York, where she had just completed two years of work in mathematics in a small up-state college. It was understood that in addition to her classes in mathematics she was to form an orchestra which would be the official group for plays, operettas, commencement exercises, etc. Our first orchestra consisted of two violins, one cornet, one clarinet, and a piano. The orchestra gradually grew in size and ability through the years until in 1913 some of the boys . . . petitioned the principal to form a school band. This he granted on provision that the string players buy their own band music. From that year on our band has flourished along with our orchestra." (Excerpts from a letter to the author written in 1967 by Mr. Ernie Seeman, Director of Music Education, District 145, Freeport, Illinois.)

[5]Edward Bailey Birge, *History of Public School Music in the United States*, (Boston: Oliver Ditson Co.; 1928), Chapter 7.

bands. Numerous other factors contributed to the sudden growth that had begun prior to the postwar period.

The same cultural changes that affected the decline of the professional band contributed to the rise of the school band. Schools broadened their outlook to take in a number of vocational, athletic, artistic, and recreational activities not previously within their scope. Music became important to competitive athletics, for public relations purposes, and for civic advertisement. Service clubs experienced a sudden growth, the National Band Association was formed, and the Cardinal Principles of Secondary Education were proclaimed by the National Education Association—all of these directly and advantageously affecting the school band. Young people were changing; they were staying in school longer, and the band appealed to them with its color, group spirit, military apparel, and the chance for recognition.

Bands have always marched. The primary purpose of the military band was to march into battle or to perform for those who were marching. The first college bands were small military organizations supported by the military departments in the land-grant institutions. When these bands became associated with schools of music, their size increased; and with A. A. Harding's initiation of homecoming and the integration of band shows into it, the growth of the marching band was assured. Music and showmanship combined to fill an important niche in American culture. Bands increased in size from the twenty-nine-piece military band to two hundred or more players accompanied by squads of flags, rifles, twirlers, pompons, and other visual pleasures. The public's interest in football shifted the focus of the marching band from street marching to performances during the half time of the football games. These performances included dancing, acrobatics, marching routines, and theme shows using music that ranged from marches to popular music, jazz, and an occasional classic. Today, band as a subject is offered in more schools than any other subject, save English, being available in 93 percent of American high schools.[6]

Although America in the first quarter of the twentieth century still looked to Europe as its mentor in things musical and artistic, the rise of music in the schools was not directly influenced by European practices. No such school instruction existed on the Continent; the skilled professional musicians of Europe either did not know how to teach groups of children or did not care to do so. One exception was the Maidstone movement in England around 1908, which presented instrumental instruction to children. This movement was studied by the supervisor of music in the Boston public schools, who introduced its principles and methods into the schools of that city around 1910.

[6]James A. Keene, *A History of Music Education in the United States.* (Hanover, NH: University Press of New England: 1982: Washington: U.S. Office of Education, 1986.)

With the introduction of music into the curriculum came the problem of credits. The members of the very early groups, from the Farm and Trade Band of Boston Harbor in 1858 to those existing at the end of the nineteenth century, usually met after school and received no academic recognition or credit. As far as we know, the first instance of students receiving credit for school music was in Richmond, Indiana, in 1905, where students gained one-half credit for playing in the orchestra, which met after school. The following year, McConathy in Chelsea, Massachusetts, secured school credit for students who took music lessons after school from private teachers. In 1920, Charles McCray in Parsons, Kansas, gained both school time for the orchestra and credit for the students.

The next major innovation in school music occurred in 1923, when the instrument manufacturers sponsored a national band contest in Chicago as a promotional device. As with Gilmore's jubilees, the commercial venture proved to be a powerful influence, and the success of the contest was unquestionable. The manufacturers wisely turned the management of future contests over to the schools. State contests were held in Kansas in 1912, and by 1925 they were coordinated by a Committee on Instrumental Affairs of the Music Supervisors National orchestra. The first school-sponsored national contest was held in 1926 in Fostoria, Ohio. The immediate success of contests was ensured by the competitive spirit of the American people. As with athletic competition and debate tournaments, the American community was given a chance to test its superiority against its neighbors in a music contest. The history of the contest became the history of the school band.

At almost the same time, school orchestras received more impetus from a different source, the formation of a national high school orchestra. Joseph Maddy, who made an outstanding reputation as a high school orchestra conductor in Kansas, New York, Indiana, and Michigan, and who started orchestral tryouts and high school vocational music programs, took his orchestras to conventions where they could be heard. The response to the Parsons, Kansas, orchestra at the Music Supervisors National Conference in 1921 inspired him to form a National orchestra for Detroit in 1926. Accordingly, he advertised in music journals, and from 400 applications he selected 238 students for the orchestra.[7]

The program for the conference was of such quality that Maddy was invited to form a second national student orchestra to play for the 1927 Dallas meeting of the Department of Superintendence, the official national organization of school superintendents. The audience was highly impressed by the orchestra's performance and passed this resolution: "We would record our full appreciation of the fine musical programs and art exhibits in connection with this convention. They are good evidence that

[7] Norma Browning, *Joe Maddy of Interlochen* (Chicago: Henry Regnery Co., 1963), 178.

we are rightly coming to regard music, art, and other similar subjects as fundamental in the education of American children. We recommend that they be given everywhere equal consideration and support with other basic subjects."[8]

This resolution resulted in the initiation of hundreds of instrumental programs in schools across the country. Music was the "new thing" established as a worthwhile area deserving both school time and credit. Maddy organized a third national orchestra for the 1928 Music Supervisors National Conference in Chicago. Administrators at all these conventions were impressed by the healthy experiences of students working together, the excellent discipline (much of which Maddy had learned from T. P. Giddings), and those byproducts of citizenship, health, and useful recreation that were considered so important at the time. Thus, the success of Maddy's orchestra coincided with the proper cultural and social conditions of the time to bring about music's firm establishment in the schools.

Superintendents and music supervisors returned home from the conventions to find that administrative problems were involved in setting up instrumental programs. In the smaller schools there were too few students to support both a band and an orchestra, instructors who could teach both were scarce, and financial support for two instrumental groups added a sizable amount to the budget. Since the same musical and extramusical values were claimed by both, the band took precedence over the orchestra partly because of its greater flexibility, usefulness to the community and athletics, and appeal to youth. Bands therefore became the dominant school music group, and orchestras failed to get a major start.

The influence of the band instrument manufacturers and the uniform companies on this trend should not be overlooked or discounted. When the town bands declined, these businesses provided temporary funding for school band directors' salaries, and they offered attractive instrument rental and purchase programs. In addition, they actively supported contests, supplied financial aid to Joseph Maddy in the founding of the National Music Camp at Interlochen, Michigan, and later established yearly conventions that offered conductors new ideas and new materials to help build successful band programs.

A new literature for school bands was promulgated with the formation of the Eastman Wind Ensemble by Frederick Fennell in 1952. Ensembles playing original music written for winds sprang up at the University of Illinois and Northwestern University, and were quickly emulated by other colleges and the larger public schools. The idea of one-on-a-part wind instrument experiences enhanced the educational arguments for school bands; and extensive lists of excellent, usable literature were collected by

David Whitwell and Robert Gray. With this, the dominant influence of the marching band in schools was balanced in the last half of the twentieth century by the wind ensemble, and, to a certain extent, a renewed interest in the British brass band.

REFERENCES

BIRGE, EDWARD BAILEY. *History of Public School Music in the United States*, 172–205. Boston: Oliver Ditson Co., 1928. Reissued by Music Educators National Conference, 1966.

FENNELL, FREDERICK. *Time and the Winds: A Short History of the Use of Wind Instruments in the Orchestra, Band, and the Wind Ensemble*, Kenosha, WI: G. Leblanc Co., 1954.

GOLDMAN, RICHARD FRANKO. *The Wind Band: Its Literature and Technique*. Boston: Allyn and Bacon, 1961.

GRAHAM, ALBERTA. *Great Bands of America*. New York: T. Nelson, 1951.

KEENE, JAMES A. *A History of Music Education in the United States*. Hanover, NH: University Press of New England, 1982.

SCHWARTZ, H. W. *Bands of America*. Garden City, NY: Doubleday, 1957.

WHITE, W. C. *A History of Military Music in America*. New York: Exposition Press, 1944.

Supplementary References

ADKINS, H. E. *Treatise on the Military Band*, 1–10. Rockville Centre, NY: Belwin, 1945.

BERGER, KENNETH. *The March King and His Band: The Story of John Philip Sousa*, 9–62. New York: Exposition Press, 1957.

BIERLEY, PAUL. *John Philip Sousa. American Phenomenon*. New York: Appleton-Century-Crofts, 1973.

BROWNING, NORMA. *Joe Maddy of Interlochen*. Chicago: Henry Regnery Co., 1963.

FARMER, H. G. *Military Music*. New York: Chanticleer Press, 1950.

———. *The Rise and Development of Military Music*, 7–10 and Chapters 4 and 5. London: W. Reeves, 1912.

GOLDMAN, RICHARD FRANKO. *The Band's Music*, Part I. New York: Pitman Publishing Co., 1938.

———. *The Concert Band*, 18, 19 and Chapters 2 and 3. New York: Rinehart and Co., 1945.

HAZEN, M. H., and R. M. HAZEN. *The Music Men*. Washington: Smithsonian Institute Press, 1987.

HOTZ, EMIL A., and ROGER JACOBI. *Teaching Band Instruments to Beginners*, Chapters 1 and 2. Englewood Cliffs, NJ: Prentice-Hall, 1966.

LINGG, ANN. *John Philip Sousa*. New York: Henry Holt and Co., 1954.

NORMANN, THEODORE. *Instrumental Music in the Public School*, Chapter 1. Bryn Mawr, PA: Theodore Presser Co., 1939.

PRESCOTT, G. R., and L. W. CHIDESER. *Getting Results with School Bands*, 3–13. New York: Carl Fischer, Minneapolis: Paul A. Schmitt Music Co., 1938.

SUNDERMAN, LLOYD. *School Music Teaching: Its Theory and Practice*, 1–5. New York: Scarecrow Press, 1965.

WHITWELL, DAVID. *History and Literature of the Wind Band and Wind Ensemble: Northridge California Winds*. 9 vols. Northridge, CA: University of California Press, 1982–1984.

WRIGHT, A. G. and S. NEWCOMB. "Bands of the World." *Instrumentalist*, Vol. 16 (no. 1), 1971, 12.

2

Objectives

To speak of objectives in education has become fashionable. But while every teacher knows objectives are indispensable to good teaching, these objectives now have to be categorized as behavioral and experiental, program or unit, and so on, from a galaxy of similar terms. Emphasis on goals, aims, and objectives, however, often amounts to no more than lip service, ignored in the practical business of organizing the materials of teaching. Theory and practice often diverge when one moves away from the printed page or the symposium to the daily routine—teachers still teach as they were taught, not as they were taught to teach.

The instrumental teacher may say, "My objectives are to teach as much good music as well as possible—the music is my goal!" What does this mean? Great music is rarely written for the sake of teaching, and players cannot perform it adequately without first having learned much in the way of skills, understanding, and specific knowledge. Serving up good music is not like serving up food—there is no "instant Beethoven" or "Johann Sebastian Bach mix." Instruction books and teaching materials must be used for learning, and the teacher needs objectives to help select the most satisfactory of these. Objectives are a device to bring the fuzzy purpose of activities and experiences into the sharp focus of learning.

Objectives provide a structure for the music program. It is in terms of objectives that the teacher decides what shall be taught, when, and how. It is in terms of objectives that the teacher asks. "Is this worth knowing or doing? What difference will it make in the lives of the students? What difference will it make to them as adults?" Only through the careful construction of goals can music instruction become meaningful.

To be of value, the aims of music education must be specific, clearly stated, and attainable in the length of time allotted for music instruction, whether the time period under consideration is one class period of fifty minutes, one year's instrumental class, six years of grade school general music, or three years of high school orchestra. Unless the teacher clearly knows where she is going, she cannot know how far she has progressed toward her goals. These goals must lie within the goals of the school, but the school's broad objectives for the total life of the student—citizenship, literacy, moral responsibility, critical thinking, and skill in problem solving—say very little about planning the music program.

Two basic objectives seem prominent in today's schools. One is to fit the student into the complex, twenty-first-century American form of democracy and life, as citizen and individual. The other is to prepare him for some form of activity after graduation, either further education or a vocation. The school has the continuing problem of balancing these two broad aims—personal development and mastery of subject matter. Each of these goals' appeal has fluctuated to reflect changing social demands since 1900. At present, the pendulum has swung rather sharply in the direction of subject matter after an era in which personal development was emphasized. Music contributes little to either goal by itself, and what it cannot do it should not attempt. But music seems well fitted for developing a number of nonmusical values, and if these can be included without detriment to musical learning, so much the better. Good posture can be developed in music as in physical education. Music can also teach about other peoples, countries, and cultures in a direct and vivid way. Because music integrates so well with a variety of other areas, the teacher may lose sight of his own goals while pursuing these secondary values. Administrators may champion music because of its important secondary contributions, requiring the teacher to work within this framework; and if so, it will be hard to stress the unique values of music. Because music has rarely been justified on its own merits in the public schools, teachers fear to do so now. With today's emphasis on subject matter, however, music educators should speak up for the quality of content within their subject.

At the same time, the effectiveness of the extramusical values must not be underestimated. Consider the history of instrumental music. Though the orchestra came into the public schools first, the marching band has been the vehicle through which the instrumental music program has flourished, obtaining equipment, music, building space, professionally trained teachers, and public attention in a manner impossible for the concert band or the orchestra. Music has found a fairly secure place, not because it has caused a noticeable upgrading of musicianship in society or in the school, but because the marching band has publicized the school, created excitement and spirit for competitive athletics, and made patriotic holidays more colorful. Second, the contest, with its often nonmusical but clearly defined goals, has been one of the primary sources of support for the entire music program. Hence, the teacher must utilize the colorful, attention-getting facets of the music program, but she must also learn to keep them in proper relationship to the actual teaching content of music. He should remember as well that some secondary goals are compatible with musical goals; for example, discipline, cooperation, leadership, fellowship and individual responsibility.

AREAS OF OBJECTIVES

The unique characteristics of music amplify the problem of selecting objectives that cover all facets of the subject. Music is an art, an experience, and a skill. In the public school, it is also an activity, and this must not be discounted, for it has brought music to its present place in the curriculum. Objectives for music education must encompass all four of these areas.

Music as an Activity

The Cardinal Principles of Secondary Education were formulated in 1918 by a commission of the National Education Association. They are outmoded in today's educational thought but are not quite out of style. Books and curriculum goals written in the past have offered as the *raison d'être* of music its ability to contribute to health, command of fundamental processes, vocation, responsible home membership, worthy use of leisure time, civic education, and ethical character. With this reasoning, music is usually thought of as being extra- or cocurricular. Some of the attractions of music in the schools are that it promotes informality, makes use of physically healthful activities, and involves some interrelationships with the student's home life. Music can provide the benefits of teamwork, yet it has an advantage over competitive athletics in its utilization of larger numbers of students and wider ranges of ability. Compared to the first ten players in basketball, the "first-string" band contains a larger number of students, many of whom have not developed skills at all comparable to the first-string basketball team. Still, they may derive the same feeling of accomplishment from concert and competition, even when sitting last chair. And while music is often a "team sport," it can also be an individual sport—the player can enjoy her skills alone as well as with the group, which allows for the possibility of continued enjoyment from music after graduation. The fact that music can accommodate groups of widely varying size with a wide variety of ability and interest levels is strongly in its favor. In addition, one of the most important benefits the successful player acquires is a self-imposed discipline in developing the skills that allow music to be an emotional outlet and a means of self-expression.

In formulating objectives, some account should be taken of the goals of personal development and how these can be forwarded within the music program. If our aims are more than musical, we can accept the student who is not particularly talented, knowing that she will have an opportunity to develop by interacting with her peers even if she does not progress very far musically. A place will be found for her, though maybe not in the best performing group, so that she can have the experiences music offers to help her grow as an individual and a member of society.

The potential of music to create ideals and alter attitudes must be reflected in the instrumental program. The value of the marching band as a device for public relations and a source of enjoyment for students is a reality the director cannot ignore, regardless of how much he prefers the concerts of the symphonic band or the wind ensemble. The marching band must have objectives and must be skillful—both in marching and in playing. The director cannot afford to feel that marching band is an inferior part of the year's activities and one simply to be tolerated. The marching band is the student's first introduction to the year's activities. To wait for enthusiasm and interest to flourish with the first concert is hazardous—the group may by that time reflect a carelessness and negativeness produced by the chore of weekly football shows under an indifferent director.

In addition, the marching band, though not strictly a playing organization, plays enough so that there are opportunities to teach some music, technique, range, breathing, endurance, and understanding. Good and bad arrangements can be compared, marches can be learned well enough to improve fingers and ears, and the quality of the music played in field shows can be discussed for comparison with other kinds of music.

Music as an Experience   *activity-specific objectives*

Two thoughtful educators, Elliott Eisner and Robert Stake, have advanced the idea that a distinction should be made between an activity and an experience. Selected educational experiences, such as attendance at a band concert or sightreading music by Lutoslawski, are worthwhile, even though they defy behavioral formatting. Every student should have the experience of attending a live production of an opera, but to list expected behavioral outcomes from a class of ninth graders would be sheer folly. Limited resources may prohibit the ensemble from performing great contemporary music to any reasonable standard, but the experiences of reading, studying, and practicing the music may be needed in a well-balanced program.

Whether these objectives are called "experiential," "expressive," or "nonbehavioral" is not important; these objectives, which are often interdisciplinary, are of enormous value to the educational program. The problem of including experiential objectives is not in trying to justify them, but rather that they are often unclear and unspecific, the product of the instrumental teacher's fuzzy thinking.

The best teaching in instrumental music is marked by teacher clarity and the establishment of understandable objectives that challenge each student intellectually and musically. Students can be excellent critics of their own progress toward attaining the objectives of the instrumental program; thus it is important that they understand the differences between behavioral and experiential objectives. Excellent applied music instruction is based almost entirely on the attainment of impeccable musical skill, whereas to perform music from all major style periods or to compose may require an incredible amount of work for which time is unavailable. The result is a shoddy product. Focused work required by performing or composing distinguishes an experience from an activity. In addition, an experience is directly related to becoming a musically educated individual.

Music as an Art

Music's firm position in the school curriculum may be due primarily to its power as an activity, but its basic essence is art. Public school music may seldom reach the level of art, yet it retains the drawing power of art—the ability to symbolize the feelings of humankind that cannot be put into conventional language. Like most adults, children are not aware of the symbolic quality of music, but they react to it. In recent years, leaders in the field have focused attention on music as art, as an aesthetic experience. Any teacher of the arts must be concerned primarily with guiding the student's growth in aesthetic sensitivity and understanding—in helping him learn the principles of that particular art, what the artist is trying to do, and how to find meaning in the great works of art.

Teaching for aesthetic growth is not simple. It is seldom accomplished by using vague terms to describe the beauty of a work to students. It can be accomplished by helping students recognize what they hear in a composition—balance, contrast, tension, relaxation, form, texture, color, mood—and then leading them to understand how these are related. The teacher's purpose is to develop in the student the ability to hear music and understand it, which means to understand the structure that enters into every detail of the composition and to know whether the work he has heard is on the level of great music, good music, or trivial music, and why. Such teaching requires teachers who can really hear music and understand it well enough to explain it.

This approach has as its objective music appreciation in the genuine sense—not appreciation as it denotes a course in which many compositions are heard, their composers discussed, and their dates pinpointed in a time continuum, but instead, meaning careful attention to a few compositions. Music being performed or studied should be examined to hear how it is put together, how melodies interact, how harmonies create tension and resolve, how instruments blend and stand out, how phrases return and lead to other phrases. Aesthetic growth means that the student should learn what makes the quality of Schubert's music better than that of John Williams's—

the student should hear for himself the difference, not simply be told of it—and why he should be at least respectful if not loving in the presence of Bach.

To teach music as an art is the most difficult of the four approaches because it requires more skill and preparation on the part of the teacher. Directors of performing groups tend to slide over this area presuming that, as students play more music and play it well, they will acquire understanding and appreciation. This is simply not so. The third horn player, struggling with her part, does not pay much attention to the principal themes and perhaps not even to the harmonic structure of which she is a part. The oboe player knows melodies he himself plays and probably hears more than the third horn player because he is accustomed to listening for the soprano line that is often the melody. But hearing the melody is not tantamount to listening with understanding. How many players are aware of the harmonic structure of the music they play—recognize where key changes occur, where unusual chords appear, and how these unexpected harmonies heighten the tension or create an element of suspense in the music? How many players know what to expect from a minuet or a passacaglia, a rondo or a fughetta? Can they recognize the thematic material when it appears in an inner voice or altered form? Do they understand how the composer uses motives and themes to hold the work together and at the same time give it contrast and variety? Since these things differ in every musical work, the teacher must talk about the music itself as well as about the fingering for fifth-line F-sharp. Students will play better when they know how their own parts fit into the work.

At times students should listen rather than play. Recorded versions of the music they are working on or compositions with similar form or style can broaden understanding. But one does not become aware of all the things happening within a complex piece of music simply by sitting passively and listening—the process is active and takes expert guidance. This is part of the teacher's job, whether she is an instrumental director or a grade school music teacher.

Music as a Skill

Music depends upon skill. Around the turn of the century, when choral music was required and was taught as an academic class, the skill of reading music was emphasized to the exclusion of other facets of the art. The movable *do* system, with its chromatics up and down, was drilled into every pupil. Some students learned to read music fairly well but often opened a songbook for the last time at the graduation exercises. Overemphasis on music-reading ability has long since been replaced by "pleasure in music," "experiences with music," "discovering music," and "music for every child." To deride the philosophy of pleasurable experiences in music is easy, but the philosophy has much to recommend it. We would never return to the older drill method that recognized so little of the joyous, free response to music that is part of the child's nature, nor limit ourselves to the narrow use of materials and activities that the singing classes exemplified. The rich variety of approaches to music that the five-fold program and its successors brought into being is taken so much for granted that we fail to appreciate it. Singing, rhythmic activities, listening, instrumental and creative activities all serve to keep children interested and actively engaged in music, preparing them for the band and orchestra programs as well as for the choral groups in the later public school years.

The five-fold program grew out of the effort to find experiences suitable for all children. Musical activities became varied because of the widespread belief that all children do not necessarily respond to the same musical stimuli. Diversity, however, proved to be a mixed blessing. The activities themselves rather than the learning they embodied tended to become the focus. Today we do rhythmic activities but learn little about rhythm. We sing but do not grow in reading skills nor in the beauty of singing quality. We use rhythm instruments but have little conception of the patterns we create or the rhythm symbols that denote these patterns. We sing two- and three-part harmony but do not learn what a major chord or a tonal center is. We listen to music as if it were the background score for an imaginary television drama instead of catching the return of themes and the building of climaxes. As we pass from elementary into secondary school, we are forced to become more specialized. There may be a choice between performing groups, music appreciation, and music theory. The performing groups expect skill, but in varying degrees. The choir singer may learn all parts by rote, although there are usually a few trusty stalwarts who shoulder the burden of music reading. It is no secret that performing levels are uneven in bands and orchestras. The sad truth is that children exposed to ten to twelve years of music are badly lacking in tangible skills.

Valid music programs need skill-oriented objectives. The student needs mental skills, aural skills, physical dexterity on the instrument, and musical understanding, which must be developed in the same manner as a skill. Knowledge of key signatures, time signatures, clefs, and tempo indications is not enough. The player must also hear the notes as he sees them on the page; he must listen intelligently to hear and understand key centers and modulations as well as meter changes, return of previous thematic materials, and changes of mode and texture in the music. He must be able to look at his part in the score and play it somewhat musically, with thought for line and phrase. He must manage the technical requirements of his part—if not the first time through, then with a little practice. He should be able to concentrate sufficiently on a short three-minute piece of music to keep his mind on it actively from beginning to end. He ought to have sufficient tonal memory to retain obvious themes after he has heard them a few times. The fact that music is for all does not invalidate teaching musical skill in the public school. Any student making music is a performer, and performers possess skills. Students who do not wish to make music should have other choices that will develop other skills—listening skills, for instance. The student who wishes to play but not to develop any musical skills should be guided rather than accommodated. The purpose of the school is to change the individual into something more than he is now.

The experience of skillfully performing a piece of music should not be overlooked. Skillful group performances are important both for the thrill they offer and for the high standard they set. Playing music badly is a waste of time. A polished performance of concert music encompasses a majority of the important goals of music: good tone, correct notes, technical skill, knowledge of musical symbols and terms, awareness of the style and form of the music, control of tone quality and intonation, and ability to follow the conductor. Each student must excel on his part, even though it may be simple; the necessity for excellence from everyone in the group is the primary reason why performance is of such value for learning.

The fact that performance does hold so many values creates the problem of balancing it against other areas of musical experience. Excellence of performance is a chief emphasis of every instrumental teacher. No book can allocate the distribution of time for performance or for any other aspect of learning; the teacher herself will have to decide how much emphasis is to be placed on developing skills and the basic understanding of music, and how much of the year's music should be performed with the goal of perfection in mind. If flawless performance alone is the goal, students tend to become mechanical wonders who can play with precision but often without musical independence. On the other hand, the goal of excellent performance is both the inspiration and the chief learning vehicle of the music program.

In formulating objectives, therefore, the music teacher must realistically consider music as an activity, an experience, an art, and a skill. She must reconcile all four when they seem to be disparate, for she really cannot sacrifice any one of them. Students try to make everything an activity rather than a course. But—and this is often overlooked by the popularity-conscious teacher—students like to learn and like to progress in knowledge; their pride in achievement is spontaneous and great. Parents and the rest of the community look tolerantly on musical skills but are really interested in participation; many parents view skills as a means to this end. The music teacher can understand this view while not subscribing to it. Regardless of how specific the objectives are, they are only a list of good intentions. Any number of bad music programs possess good objectives. Each objective must be a minimum standard representing a specific accomplishment toward which the pupil's energies and efforts are directed.

LEVELS OF OBJECTIVES

To arrive at proposed goals by the time the learning period is over, be it one year or twelve, the goals must be separated into different levels. To conclude that the areas of skill and aesthetic development are basic and that experiences and personal development are important byproducts is not enough. Belief in the importance of these four areas must be transformed into (1) broad program objectives, (2) course objectives, (3) yearly objectives, and (4) objectives for a semester, a grading period, a week, and a day.

The instrumental teacher must be concerned with all levels of objectives. The broad program objectives are her concern, for she must fit her classes and courses into them. She must decide how the ensemble fits into the accomplishment of his broad goals and she must formulate aims for the ensemble that are consistent with the aims of the total program. The music she selects, the activities she plans, and the concerts he schedules must all be chosen on the basis of what the students need to learn to add to their knowledge and move toward the total objectives of the program. If she makes his selections on the basis of fancy, whim, or even the demands of her concert schedule, she may be neglecting large areas of learning that students need.

Often the high school director does not consider her groups a continuation of the music program at the lower levels, and she does not feel any necessity to make the performing groups a vehicle for progress built on previous attainment. When she thinks about the music program at the lower levels, she is inclined to complain about what her students failed to learn instead of taking responsibility for these objectives and making the process a continuous one. The high school band and orchestra share the same broad goals as the kindergarten and fourth-grade music classes and the high school appreciation class. Instrumental teachers might do well to visit grade school music classes occasionally, talk with elementary teachers and music supervisors, help with rhythmic or preinstrumental activities, and discuss common goals and how to reach them.

With the objectives of the instrumental program and the potential of each experience in mind, the teacher can formulate goals for the year. From the year's objectives, one can derive weekly, monthly, and sometimes even daily goals. When written down, they become a blueprint for teaching. If a director skips lesson plans, this usually indicates a focus on the performance of music rather than on music as a vehicle for learning. The music used must be partially determined by objectives; not every class is based entirely on specified objectives, but every successful class is based on a well-formulated plan. The intensity with which any particular composition is rehearsed will depend upon what it offers in terms of objectives, and whether a festival is attended or ignored will depend upon how it fits into the objectives for the group. The amount of drill, section rehearsal, listening to records and/or marching practice will also be determined by the objectives.

To formulate a set of objectives for the total program and then to derive different levels of objectives applicable to the various phases of music is a large task. But a careful formulation of objectives is the best starting point for productive teaching, and frequent reference to the objectives is the best method for evaluating the quality of the teaching.

OBJECTIVES FOR INSTRUMENTAL MUSIC

If the teacher is to reach toward objectives that include music as an activity, experience, art, and skill, she must plan the program and her daily work to include all four areas. It is probably impossible to teach music in the most efficient manner at all times, because emphasizing one area of objectives will result in the temporary neglect or abandonment of other areas. The second band and other lesser groups need objectives as badly as the top organizations—perhaps more so, if they are to produce results and retain students' interest. Objectives unquestionably share in contributing to student achievement at every level. Challenging objectives stretch the teacher's abilities as well as those of the students. In fact, the term *lesser groups* should not be used any more than labeling freshman English a "lesser" course than senior English.

The teacher must also be concerned with individual differences, for the progress of each individual within her groups will depend on the individual's background, aptitude, interest, private study, and home cooperation, perhaps more so for music than for any other course in which the student engages. In spite of his desire to keep students in her groups, the teacher must be honest in evaluating their progress and reporting it to them and their parents. The common practice of giving everyone As and Bs will help to keep some students in performing groups, but if it is accompanied by low aims and low standards, it will quickly breed contempt.

Finally, the director must be willing to work cooperatively with a number of groups who want her services but who do not contribute to her program objectives. To deal with administrators, athletic directors, and civic leaders who wish to have bands and orchestras perform for various school or community functions, the instrumental teacher has to sacrifice some orderly, logical scheduling of learning experiences. Curriculum specialists are beginning to advocate a sequential curriculum based on the discipline of music. Some advocate a sequential curriculum within high school bands and orchestras, with twelfth grade students undergoing different experiences than ninth graders. The theory of asking each student to work to her fullest potential throughout high school is sound, as is the concern for pedagogically based programs to develop musical skill and understanding. The best music may not have been composed with instruction in mind, and eleventh graders are likely to differ widely in their musical needs. We support the philosophical goal; however, because performance is such excellent motivation, the program may not lose greatly in accommodating itself to the demands of the community. Performance, however, must be kept within reasonable bounds if it is not to become a burden and handicap to other objectives.

REFERENCES

ABELES, HAL, CHARLES HOFFER, and ROBERT KLOTMAN. *Foundations of Music Education*. New York: Schirmer, 1984.

HOFFER, CHARLES. *Introduction to Music Education*. Belmont, CA: Wadsworth, 1983.

LEONHARD, CHARLES, and ROBERT W. HOUSE. *Foundations and Principles of Music Education*, Chapter 6. New York: McGraw-Hill, 1972.

MAGER, ROBERT F. *Preparing Instructional Objectives*. Palo Alto, CA: Fearon Publishers, 1962.

SWANWICK, KEITH. *Music, Mind, and Education*. London: Routledge, 1988.

TAIT, MALCOLM, and PAUL HAACK. *Principles and Processes of Music Education*. New York: Teacher College Press, 1984.

Supplementary References

GARRETSON, ROBERT L. *Music in Childhood Education*, 7–9, 237–43. New York: Appleton-Century-Crofts, 1966.

HERMANN, EDWARD J. *Supervising Music in the Elementary School*, Chapter 2. Englewood Cliffs, NJ: Prentice-Hall, 1965.

HOFFER, CHARLES R. *Teaching Music in the Secondary Schools*, 3rd ed., Chapter 2. Belmont, CA: Wadsworth, 1983.

HOUSE, ROBERT, W. "Curriculum Construction in Music Education." In *Basic Concepts in Music Education*, edited by Nelson Henry, 242–45. NSSE Yearbook LVII, Part I. Chicago: National Society for the Study of Education, 1958.

———. *Instrumental Music for Today's Schools*, 15–17, 21–25. Englewood Cliffs, NJ: Prentice-Hall, 1965.

KAPLAN, MAX. *Foundations and Frontiers of Music Education*, Chapters 3 and 4. New York: Holt, Rinehart and Winston, 1966.

KUHN, WOLFGANG. *Instrumental Music: Principles and Methods of Instruction*, 86–91, Chapter 4. Boston: Allyn and Bacon, 1962.

LEEDER, JOSEPH A., and WILLIAM S. HAYNIE. *Music Education in the High School*, Chapter 1, 100–101. Englewood Cliffs, NJ: Prentice-Hall, 1958.

NORMANN, THEODORE F. *Instrumental Music in the Public School*, 32–36, 212. Bryn Mawr, PA: Theodore Presser Co., 1939.

REIMER, BENNETT. *A Philosophy of Music Education*, 2nd ed. Englewood Cliffs: Prentice-Hall, 1989.

————. *Towards a Transformation of Music Education*. New Zealand Society for Music Education Yearbook for 1985. Christ Church: New Zealand Society, 1986.

SINGLETON, IRA C. *Music in Secondary Schools*, 273–276. Boston: Allyn and Bacon, 1963.

VAN BODEGRAVEN, PAUL. "Music Education in Transition." In *Perspectives in Music Education, Source Book III*, edited by Bonnie C. Kowall, 29–41. Washington: Music Educators National Conference, 1966.

WILSON, HARRY ROBERT. *Music in the High School*, Chapter 2. New York: Silver Burdett Co., 1941.

3

Evaluation

Evaluation is the keystone of the teaching process, yet it is an area largely neglected by the music teacher. Too often the teacher thinks of evaluation in terms of pupil selection, identifying those students best fitted for instrumental instruction or for advanced groups or ensembles, as a means of motivating students by giving grades, or as an administrative necessity. Though important, these uses are minor when compared with the real purposes of evaluation. As defined by Norman Gronlund, evaluation is "the systematic process of collecting, analyzing, and interpreting information to determine the extent to which pupils are achieving instructional objectives."[1] This definition implies more than paper and pencil tests. It includes not only measurement, but also the use of any number of other sound methods for arriving at an accurate appraisal of the student's progress and for improving instruction and learning.

DEFINING EVALUATION IN MUSIC

Good teaching that includes evaluation is illustrated by the private music lesson. This form of instruction has always been, and continues to be, the most effective vehicle for teaching music as an art and as a skill. The chief activity that distinguishes a private lesson from other music teaching is evaluation: The teacher continually evaluates the student's performance, making suggestions, changes, and assignments based on his appraisal of the student's progress. The objectives of the private lesson may seldom be

[1] Norman Gronlund, *Measurement and Evaluation in Teaching*, 5th ed. (New York: Macmillan, 1985.) p. 5

stated or carefully thought out, but they are made clear to the student by the teacher's concern for specific strengths and weaknesses in the pupil's performance. At the end of each lesson and, indeed, within the lesson, teacher and student know what the student can do well and what needs attention. Evaluation is consistently made in terms of the music, the present or past assignment, and the student's ability. If classroom teachers would spend a similar proportion of time on evaluation, they would soon make sound improvements in methods, materials, and approaches. However, the classroom teacher, busy keeping a roomful of pupils actively engaged in music making, tends to forget that activities can be meaningless without knowledge of intent and constant appraisal of results.

In the classroom, evaluation is facilitated by a precise definition of the objectives, stated in behavioral terms when possible. Good teaching can happen without stated objectives, but it is just that—a happening. These chance occurrences of exemplary teaching appear throughout the public school system, but are seldom permanent. Without objectives that can be verbalized, good music programs and good bands and orchestras come and go with the director. Music teachers give grades and counsel students without a consideration of the objectives, and in so doing, their grading and counseling are ineffective if not harmful. In music as in other areas, evaluation, recommendations, and advice should be as accurate as the science of music teaching allows. Evaluation can prescribe the objectives, but it should not. The teacher's and the school's philosophy dictate what is important in music and what should be taught.

Evaluation is often thought of only in terms of what the teacher does to the student—the kind of test created, the tryout or challenge system used or the point system enforced. However, one of the greatest benefits of evaluation is how it works *for* the student. Louis Thorpe states in the NSSE Yearbook, "Learning to play an instrument or to sing proceeds with greatest effectiveness when the individual periodically is provided with clear knowledge of progress made toward his goal."[2]

Any student can relate to the importance of evaluation. The first question asked by students in a new course is, "How many tests and what kind?" Equal to her anxiety over a grade is the student's own pleasure in recognizing progress and a desire for structure in the learning process. The knowledgeable teacher uses this interest and concern to motivate learning. There is little doubt that most students work best under slight pressure, so that those activities not evaluated tend to be neglected, even if valued, under the demands of the educational process. Thus, evaluation when used for motivation is more than the mere giving of grades.

Measurement and evaluation are not synonymous. Measurement, the use of tests and scales that produce a specific grade, is a part of evaluation.

[2] Henry, Nelson, Ed., Basic Concepts in Music Education, Part I. *The 57th Yearbook of the National Society for the Study of Education*, Chicago, University of Chicago Press, 1954, p. 192.

Evaluation, however, encompasses a host of other factors and tools, including observation, interviews, checklists, and subjective appraisal. The giving of grades, so often considered the sum total of evaluation, frequently depends on a single act of measurement, one test or one tryout. This is not only unfair to teacher and pupil, but it is a complete misrepresentation of the role of evaluation.

Most important, to be effective, evaluation must be systematic as well as comprehensive. Frequent, carefully planned steps will give the most accurate and complete appraisal of the teaching–learning situation. In music, with its many subjective judgments, the need for frequent, organized, evaluative procedures is great.

EVALUATIVE TOOLS

The use of standardized or formal tests is important even with ensemble teaching, but other valid evaluative techniques as well must be used to ensure the improvement of learning and instruction.

1. Measures of musical aptitude have value. The effectiveness of teaching can best be measured in terms of a student's potential. The job of the teacher is to develop each student to her fullest potential, to cultivate the aptitude a student possesses for a subject. The teacher who helps the slow and average students to achieve deserves respect, but he does not fulfill his responsibilities unless he also provides the talented students with appropriate challenge and opportunity.

The *Seashore Measures of Musical Talents* and Bentley's *Measure of Musical Abilities* measure some skills expected of all good musicians. The *Musical Aptitude Profile*, (the *Primary Measures of Musical Aptitude* providing similar results for children under the age of ten) and the *Standardized Test of Musical Intelligence* by Wing provide in a different manner an indication of a student's potential. In addition to standardized indicators of musical aptitude, the teacher can obtain indications of talent from private instructors, from the level of the student's performing ability, from the classroom teacher, and from the student's past achievement. All indications of talent should be recorded so they may be retained for future use.

2. Measures of music achievement, both standardized and teacher constructed, should be used. Achievement test scores will reflect not only aptitude, but also motivation, hard work, interest, good teaching, and a host of other known and unknown factors that contribute to success in instrumental music. Measures of musical achievement are listed in the references. Teacher-constructed achievement tests are of value only when based on principles of good test construction and some knowledge of successful testing procedures.

3. Audio and video tape recorders, including interactive video, are good evaluative tools. Like the proverbial picture, recorded sound can be worth a thousand words. Used with rehearsals and classes as well as with concerts, tapes provide an opportunity for the teacher to examine at leisure the strengths and weaknesses of any performance. Often sections that sound good in rehearsal contain flaws when heard in retrospect, and those that were annoying in the stress of drilling may have improved enough to be acceptable. The video tape recorder allows students and director to see as well as hear themselves, and to alter actions and habits accordingly.

4. Students can judge themselves and judge each other. Making critical decisions about one's own performance or that of another provides a means for motivation, for developing values, and for increasing aural attention to the details of performance. Often, students set higher standards for themselves than those set by the instructor. The effectiveness of group opinion and peer standards is well known. The ability to make critical judgments is a central component of Arts Propel, the evaluation component of Project Zero: The student's performance is recorded, and he critiques the performance and makes suggestions for improvement. The critique idea is expanded to allow the student to reflect on the performance of her section and the entire ensemble, and how individuals and groups can improve.

5. Computers can judge performance in pitch and rhythm to whatever degree of precision is desired. The computer is patient, and there is no opportunity for personal embarrassment when a machine judges and provides the feedback.

6. The music contest or festival can furnish an ideal evaluation situation. To do so, however, both teacher and pupil must view it as an opportunity to learn rather than as the glorification of a cause. Adjudicators are always hurried and sometimes biased, but they usually offer some suggestions of value. These either reinforce the viewpoint of the teacher or offer a new insight. In either case, the adjudication sheet or tape should be pondered carefully before it is revealed with pride or destroyed in anger.

7. The private lesson, as previously discussed, is a fine vehicle for evaluation. When possible, the private teacher's opinion should be solicited and compared with other data on the student's progress. Whether information from private teachers is obtained by interview or written inquiry, a definite set of questions should be formulated in advance. General statements seldom offer enough details to be of value as an evaluative tool.

8. Interviews with students can reveal special strengths, interests, background, and environment, as well as prejudices, weaknesses, and dislikes. Although time may not be available to interview all students, an interview can be a valuable device for evaluating students who are not responding favorably to the present teaching process.

9. Student logs can be used to discover the range of the student's musical activities outside the classroom. The log is a record maintained by

the student of her musical experiences and her reactions to them. To be most helpful, the log should include both formal and informal encounters with music: concert attendance; television, videocassette, compact disc, or radio performances heard; and participation in organized groups such as church or club ensembles and in unorganized happenings such as campfire singing, combos, and family music making. The log may be handled as a routine daily or weekly report, or it may be filled in monthly, thus reflecting only those items significant enough for the student to recall. Either way, it must be systematic and regular.

10. The critical-incidents test is a successful tool for measuring a student's perception of musical situations. The test consists of having the student describe the best and the worst moments of yesterday's concert or Friday's football show. Although the teacher should also take such a test, he must remain open-minded to students' reactions and to their degree of understanding.

11. Attitude scales are used in many areas of education to discover how students feel about something. The attitude scale is usually a list of statements, each reflecting a slightly different point of view, to which the individual responds with "strongly agree," "agree," "no opinion," "disagree," or "strongly disagree," or a similar set of choices. In the most carefully constructed attitude scale, each statement is given a numerical weight that indicates the negative or positive value of the attitude it reflects. A score can then be determined. Less objective scales reveal information by the type of answers given and the number and degree of negative and positive statements on the scale. Scales may take the form of open-ended statements to be completed by the student, matching of pictures to feelings, or essays for which the student answers a set of questions. A valid scale is one constructed so as to not reveal the attitude being sought, as students usually prefer to make the "right" response rather than the honest one. Statements must be of sufficient variety, contain different viewpoints, and offer an occasional "distractor" to conceal the purpose of the scale. Having the student complete the scale in homeroom or some other neutral situation also helps elicit honest responses.

12. Preference scales are easier than attitude scales to construct and are of value. In this scale the student ranks in order of preference such items as school classes, recreational activities, musical compositions, recording artists, tone quality, and others. As with attitude scales, in order to minimize attempts to give the "right" answer, preference scales should be completed in homeroom or other neutral situations with sufficient distractors to disguise the purpose of the scale.

13. Practice cards on which the student records the amount of daily practice on her instrument can be useful. They do not reveal anything concerning the student's achievement, but when filled in honestly, they are an indication of interest and effort. They are more likely to be honest when unaccompanied by pressure of grade or placement within the organization.

14. Sectional rehearsals provide the instructor with an opportunity to evaluate individual performers. In the full rehearsal, it is often difficult even for conductors with highly trained ears to know who is participating wholeheartedly, playing accurately and musically, and paying attention. When sectionals are student led, the teacher has an even better opportunity to observe and judge. Whenever ratings are made in sectional rehearsals, full rehearsals, private lessons, or other learning situations, they must be systematic, analytical, and complete. Superficial observations often lead to erroneous conclusions that hinder rather than aid the learning process.

15. Student demonstrations, whether spontaneous or planned, afford opportunities to evaluate skill and understanding. Spontaneous demonstrations occur when correct performance of some musical passage or pattern is requested of individuals or sections by the director. Planned demonstrations of technique, tone, or timbre, performed in public or rehearsal, are an effective device for motivation and learning. The teacher must observe these demonstrations carefully and record his reactions objectively.

16. Point systems are effective for motivation and evaluation. As an evaluative tool, the point system is most valid when it is broadly inclusive, covering as many aspects of student development as possible.

17. Checklists ensure greater objectivity and more adequate coverage of all factors of musical performance. Checklists are applicable to all forms of evaluation, including self-evaluation by the teacher. One common use of a checklist might be to rate the student's performance on any number of items such as tone, articulation, expression marks, phrasing, pitch accuracy, rhythm accuracy, rests, keys, breathing, practice routines, and style. Self-evaluation, the checklist filled out by the student, peer evaluation, and section leader evaluation can be effective uses of this tool.

18. Teacher-constructed tests seem to be most successful when used to measure knowledge. Specific items that have been taught and emphasized in class or rehearsal are appropriate material for paper and pencil tests. Of course, many items are difficult to measure, but those that are measurable should be tested. A danger occurs when recall tests become speed tests; in other words, when there are more questions than the slowest student can do in the time available. The faster student can then score higher than the slower student who knows just as much.

Collecting data on student achievement must always be done with reference to objectives. Frequently, tests or other evaluative tools are selected that do not reflect the actual objectives or content of the music class. The result is that the test shapes the content of the course. If a tool is genuinely appropriate for a music program, it must enhance progress toward the accomplishment of objectives already determined. The purpose of instruction is not to provide material for testing; rather, the purpose of testing is to provide information for the improvement of instruction.

Idealism should be reserved for teacher inspiration. Sound judgment must be used in setting up appropriate expectations for student growth. Valid measurements will be of little value where objectives are not commensurate with the situation. Objectives must be attainable within the time allotted.

In closing this section, it must be emphasized that evaluation requires a careful, systematic approach. Inspection of only the final test scores will seldom improve the teaching–learning process; one must evaluate and record findings throughout the process to determine whether the instruction is as effective as intended. Use of any one or all of the suggested tools will not in itself ensure good evaluation. It must be carefully planned, frequent, varied, and objective. Spurious judgments harm both the student and the program.

PRINCIPLES FOR EVALUATION

In one sense, all teaching can be looked upon as an experiment, a continual process of improving learning through more effective materials and instruction. But simple trial and error is neither good teaching nor good experimentation. The knowledgeable teacher approaches instructional problems with some insight and can reject many approaches without trial in the classroom. Effective teaching, like effective experimentation, cannot take place without tools for determining the success of the endeavor. Once proven successful, methods and materials should be retained, but with the recognition that each combination of learning experience and student potential is new. The alert teacher must observe daily the results of the teaching situation.

Evaluation is dependent on objectives and, similarly, objectives cannot function without evaluation. The importance of this statement cannot be overstressed, but it has had little visible effect on the teaching profession. Objectives are still often considered by themselves. Unfortunately, they serve little purpose when stated in such general terms that progress toward them cannot be evaluated. A common objective in music circles is "awareness," but it is like the pot at the end of the rainbow, vague and unattainable. Although broad program objectives cannot be systematically evaluated each day, some reasonable indication of their success or failure must be found.

Goals for the band or orchestra must primarily be those taught and reasonably attainable. One common set of objectives for all school situations is not feasible due to the students' different backgrounds. Evaluation must be based on a realistic appraisal of what is possible. The concept of a sequential curriculum in band and orchestra would be more difficult to implement than in any other subject. Not only are students different, but the demands of the parts in any piece of music differ in complexity and requisite skill. The most successful music program considers the student and his instrument in formulating objectives and conducting systematic evaluation.

Evaluation cannot begin after the learning process has started. It must be a part of curriculum planning, taking place at every stage. Teachers tend to teach and emphasize favorite materials, ones they enjoy teaching, rather than base content on an objective appraisal of student needs. Ensemble directors can often be typed by the kind of music performed and the manner of performance. With acceptable means of evaluation, these materials and methods can be appraised by experts, other faculty, and administrators, as well as by the teacher, to shape course content and keep it in line with student needs. Proper planning and frequent evaluation can minimize the need for radical revision later.

Evaluation in music must take into consideration the influence of noncurricular factors. Because music has entertainment and activity value, much learning takes place outside of school. The effect of private music instruction, church or club music groups, performance in a combo or ensemble, and the exposure to music in the home environment must be accounted for before the school can take credit for student achievement. The factors that impact student evaluation also affect teacher evaluation and to a lesser extent program evaluation.

It has become educationally fashionable to compare students, schools, teachers, buildings, and even states with respect to school achievement, and it is incumbent on all teachers to have data indicating that students are learning what they should know. The public seems to accept football shows, exciting concerts, and contest victories as evidence of a solid music program. Most teachers and thoughtful school board members will require additional evidence if music teachers claim to be teaching musical understanding, appreciation, ability to read music, and knowledge about music, in addition to those skills needed for a successful performance. The best plan is to establish the objectives for the year cooperatively with students, administrators, and parents, and for the teacher to provide data at the end of the year that reflects the extent to which these goals have been met. One cannot expect that 100 percent of the students will meet the goals established for the ensemble or class; a more reasonable expectation might be that 70 or 80 percent of the students will meet the standards established by group consensus.

Some schools have adopted a "gain score" approach to evaluation. The objective is to pre-evaluate all students and judge adequacy of the program on the year's gain. Although such a plan has obvious strengths and can be used to the teacher's advantage, sufficient weaknesses render it inappropriate as the sole evaluative criterion. Gain depends on the students' initial ability and achievement level. Students could show marked gain and remain below acceptable standards or show little gain and be among the nation's finest. And with high ability it is more difficult to demonstrate gain in raw scores or in percentages; the most advanced artist may spend months to improve the most subtle interpretations.

Much damage to music programs has come from those who insist that what they teach, the arts, cannot be evaluated. Such statements lack credibility. Any subject and its subdomains of art, skill, and activity, if it can be systematically taught, can be systematically evaluated. "Experiences" as such, which are not taught but are prepared for, are the one component that is difficult to evaluate, yet even these can be tabulated and reported at the end of the year. We may not know what each student has learned from attending a concert of the New York Philharmonic, but we are still accountable for providing that experience for all students whose music education has been assigned to us.

EVALUATING MUSIC AS AN ACTIVITY

Music as an activity involves participation, attitude, and habits. Because students may also acquire knowledge in an activity, some measure of this is appropriate.

Participation

1. Is the student dependable and punctual? Full participation in a musical group requires regular attendance.
2. Does the student participate wholeheartedly in rehearsal activities? Reading books, doing assignments, and gossiping during rehearsal are negative indicators of participation. Evaluation may indicate whether the fault lies with the student or with a rehearsal that lacks challenge, interest, or musical satisfaction.
3. Does the student use her music skills in leisure activities?
4. Does she participate in civic and church music organizations?
5. Does she take full advantage of school music offerings?
6. Do the good habits of group participation carry over into her everyday life?

Participation can be evaluated by student logs, checklists, interviews, critical-incidents measures, practice cards, and point systems, the method of evaluation dependent only on the imagination and desires of the instructor.

Attitude

1. Does the student participate fully and willingly?
2. Where does music rank in the student's preference for school subjects? In his preference for recreational activities?
3. What selections and kinds of music does the student prefer?

Attitude can be appraised using the questions under participation and by sophisticated attitude scales. Degrees of agreement with statements of preference can be obtained. Students can be asked to caption pictures, to supply nonexistent subjects for described situations. Attitudes can be changed by effective lecturing, reading, and relating of interesting facts and similar devices, but change is most effective when the student, through participation, discovers for himself how satisfying experiences with good music can be. The major task of the instructor is to provide skills and knowledge, including reading, ear training, and performance skills, and to provide musical experiences in large and small ensembles, where attitude formation and change can be expected to occur.

Habits

1. Does the student have a regular daily practice routine?
2. Does she consistently warm up or warm down properly?
3. Does she routinely take care of her instrument?
4. Does she regularly participate in community music or informal groups outside of the school?
5. Is concert attendance and record buying habitual within her means?

Good habits do not spring automatically from a good music program. Like transfer of training, habits must be specifically taught by insistence on schedule and routine. In habit formation, regularity is more desirable than spontaneity. In the same way that habits are hard to break, some are hard to form. They are generally reached gradually through the careful attention and dogmatic insistence of the instructor rather than through inspired teaching.

EVALUATING MUSIC AS AN ART

To acquire an understanding of music as an art is far more difficult than to participate in music as an activity. Yet music is from first to last an art; activity and skill are only facets of learning this essential quality. As art eludes definition, it eludes evaluation. Most appropriate in instrumental music is to differentiate among the various kinds of learning that assist aesthetic development, and to evaluate them. Such learning may also fit into the category of skills, because certain skills are required in the aesthetic response. The learning related to understanding music as an art includes factual knowledge; discernment; understanding of style, orchestration, and structure; and listening skills. For the director who is teaching music through participation, it may be impossible to objectively measure the student's awareness of music as an art. Evaluation devices can be used, however, that are pertinent to the understanding of music from the listener's viewpoint.

Factual Knowledge

Measurement of factual knowledge is relatively easy. The problem is not testing for knowledge but preventing knowledge tests from becoming the only type of evaluation used. Too often a hastily constructed knowledge test is given in order to have a grade for semester reports, a practice that has little place in either good teaching or evaluation. Some factual knowledge is related directly to growth in musical skills—key and time signatures, pitch and rhythm symbols, tempo and expression terms. These are found on the musical page, and must be understood for skillful performance of the piece. They relate only indirectly to growth of musical understanding, however. The type of knowledge essential to musical understanding is that concerning the music itself, including its historical place and significance, form and structure, style, instrumentation, and social or extramusical connections. The more the student knows about the way music is put together, the people who put it together, the way "putting together" differs in various historical periods and countries, and the reasons for those differences, the greater will be his musical understanding.

The type of paper-and-pencil test with which to measure such knowledge is the teacher's option. Recognition tests (multiple choice), recall tests (short answer), essay tests, and occasionally a true–false test can accurately measure factual knowledge. Of greater importance is measuring the student's ability to apply his knowledge when listening. For this, the test may consist of listening to a short composition one or more times and answering questions directly related to that piece of music. The piece may be familiar, perhaps one the group has been rehearsing, or it may be unfamiliar, depending on the teacher's purpose. Questions asked may pertain to such items as form, style, possible historical period, possible composer, instruments used, tempos, dynamic levels or texture. This test of applied knowledge is usually more useful than a test demanding only recall or recognition.

Musical Discernment

Discernment is more than recognition of tunes or moods. It indicates the ability to follow the music as it unfolds, to distinguish great music from good music, to recognize the style of the composition, to understand the composer's message as reflected in the structure and style of the work, and to evaluate accurately the quality of the performance. Evaluation can take the form of the critical-incidents test, in which the student listens to music and answers questions about it. Or the student may be asked to listen to two or more compositions, and state which is the superior piece of music and why. In creating such tests, the teacher needs to be certain that she herself understands the music well and has included questions that truly reveal the acuity of the student's listening.

Recognition of Style and Structure

Recognition of style and structure is a part of both factual knowledge and discernment. It is mentioned separately because of its importance in understanding music as an art. The essence of an art object is its structure or form, and the style through which the form is displayed alters with each historical or cultural period. Therefore, the knowledgeable listener must know what to expect from a piece of music. He must not be bored or displeased when a Classical symphony sounds different from late nineteenth century, large-orchestra, "movie-mood" music. After he has become familiar with the Baroque concerto style, Classical chamber music style, or a contemporary style, he will then be free to follow the form, to set up expectations as to what will happen in the music, and to take pleasure in how the composer fulfills or alters his expectations.

Tests in this area may take several forms. First, the simple objective test may be used, in which the student lists the characteristics of an art period, selects the correct answers from a given list, or answers true–false questions. The same can be used to test knowledge of form by asking the student to identify, label or define certain musical forms such as *rondo*, *sonata*, or *tone poem*. These tests give no indication of her ability to apply the knowledge to her listening, however. A more revealing tool is the single-line score test. The student follows the score of the melody as she listens to a composition and indicates in the appropriate measures items that reveal style or form. She may be asked simply to check the measures where important things happen in the music, or she may be asked to describe what is happening in certain important measures. A single-line score test can be as simple or as complicated as the situation requires; the teacher's responsibility lies in selecting a composition that can elicit good answers and in developing complete answers by which to evaluate the student's responses. A third type of test for this area is that described in the previous section, in which the student listens to a work and answers specific questions about it, having no score to read from.

Listening Skills

Because music is primarily a listener's art, listening skills are a necessary part of music participation. The relationship between seeing and hearing music is so close and intricate that to mentally hear what is seen in the score and to visualize what is being heard are usually the marks of the skillful listener. However, some auditory skills can be developed without any accompanying visual skills: The student can learn to hear scales, key center and key changes, mode and mode change, meter, common chord progressions dynamics, and tempo without being able to read music. Teachers can measure skill in these items the same way the items are taught, by playing examples and asking for identification. When the student is able to identify these elements, the hearer has made progress toward musical understanding.

Auditory–visual skills are commonly measured by tests requiring the student to follow short musical items (usually four or eight measures) in a score and to determine where the score differs from the musical items played. There are standardized tests of this type, as well as of the type measuring only auditory skills. These are discussed in detail in the following section.

EVALUATING MUSICAL SKILLS

In the majority of public schools, music was for many years thought of primarily as a skill, and usually in the narrow sense of a performance skill. This is natural, since music depends on performance; but other skills must also be developed if performance is to lead to a long-lived interest in music. Chiefly, these other skills fall into two categories: reading skills and auditory–visual skills.

Performance Skills

Any number of vehicles exist for evaluating performance skill. The most familiar of these are private lessons, section rehearsals, daily rehearsals, tryouts or challenges, student demonstrations, concerts, contests, and festivals—in short, any type of student performance. These vary in value because group situations of any type increase the difficulty of objective measurement of individual performance skill. In order to avoid a subjective judgment, the teacher should use a list of specific objectives. For example, objectives for performance include the following: production of a good tone throughout the pitch range and the dynamic range, the ability to change tone quality to suit the music, accurate intonation, a pitch range sufficiently wide for the level of music played, a dynamic range from pianissimo to fortissimo, and accurate and rapid use of fingers. Each of these objectives could be measured on a point scale, ranging from 1 to 25 or more. When ratings are made using terms such as *poor, good, excellent,* and *superior,* the student can more easily see improvement.

Surprisingly, performance skill, which receives much teaching emphasis, has had little attention from test makers. Only one test is in print, the *Watkins–Farnum Performance Scale,* which is available for wind, string, and percussion instruments. Fourteen graded melodies, sixteen bars each, are given to the performer to play. These range from the easiest type to one of near-professional grade. The performer is graded on the number and type of errors she makes.

Reading Skills

Reading skills are the key to pleasure in musical participation. When the player can understand the musical page by himself without direction from the teacher, he can learn new music on his own, play in ensembles, enrich the family music circle, and in general enjoy musical freedom. Any good sightreading test will follow somewhat similar lines of construction as the Watkins–Farnum test. In sightreading, the student should see more than the notes. Evaluation should include awareness of the key signature, all accidentals, dynamic markings, accents, phrase and tonguing (bowing) markings, and a recognition of the phrase so that proper articulation is observed. A teacher-constructed test can include a single piece of unfamiliar music or exercises of graded difficulty, as long as it contains a sufficient variety of musical elements for the teacher to check each item to be evaluated.

Auditory–Visual Skills

The third area of skill is auditory–visual discrimination. This includes those skills that depend basically on the ear and its relationship to the eye; the ability to visualize what is being heard and to hear inwardly what is seen on the musical page. It differs from sightreading in that an instrumentalist may successfully sightread by allowing the notation to indicate what fingers to put down rather than hearing inwardly what she reads—she may have to play a melody before she knows how it sounds. Auditory–visual skill is what the sight singer uses, for he must hear the music inwardly before he can sing it accurately. Objectives for auditory–visual skill include ability to visualize simple melodies heard and, conversely, to inwardly hear simple melodies seen in a score. They also include the ability to recognize the tonal center and modulations, and commonly used chords and unexpected harmonies; the ability to remember melodies adequately for following simple formal structure; the ability to follow parts other than the principal melody; and the ability to recognize timbre and texture.

Four standardized tests are available for measuring auditory–visual skill:

1. The *Aliferis Music Achievement Test* is available as a college entrance test, and The *Aliferis–Steckline Music Achievement Test* as a midpoint or end-of-the-semester test. Either form of the test may be given from a tape. Each has three sections, measuring melodic, harmonic, and rhythmic discrimination. The student selects from three or four multiple-choice items.

2. The *Music Achievement Tests* I, II, III, and IV are primarily tests of auditory ability, although one section in Test II and one in Test IV are auditory–visual tests. Other sections measure pitch discrimination, interval discrimination, auditory–visual discrimination, mode recognition, melody recognition, musical style recognition, instrument recognition, chord and cadence recognition, and musical texture.

3. The *Farnum Music Tests* have a similar format to the auditory–visual section of Music Achievement Tests.

4. The Australian Council for Education Research publishes three tests, two of which require the ability to read and understand music. Although lengthy, the tests are interesting and employ a wide variety of music.

REFERENCES

ANASTASI, ANNE. *Psychological Testing*, 6th ed. New York: Macmillan, 1988.

COLWELL, RICHARD J., *Musical Achievement Tests*. 84 Fuller, Brookline, MA 02146, 1968–70.

CRONBACH, LEE. *Essentials of Psychological Testing*, 4th ed. New York: Harper and Row, 1984.

LEHMAN, PAUL. *Tests and Measurements in Music*. Englewood Cliffs, NJ: Prentice-Hall, 1968.

Supplementary References

BOYLE, J. DAVID, and RUDY RADOCY. *Measurement and Evaluation of Musical Experiences*. New York: Schirmer, 1987.

COLWELL, RICHARD. *The Evaluation of Music Teaching and Learning*. Englewood Cliffs, NJ: Prentice-Hall, 1970.

GRONLUND, NORMAN. *Measurement and Evaluation in Teaching.* 5th ed. New York: Macmillan, 1985.

HOLZ, EMIL A., and ROGER JACOBI. *Teaching Band Instruments to Beginners,* Chapter 11. Englewood Cliffs, NJ: Prentice-Hall, 1966.

HOUSE, ERNEST. *New Directions in Education.* London: Falmer Press, 1986.

————. *School Evaluation.* Berkeley, CA: McCutchan, 1973.

LEONHARD, CHARLES, and ROBERT W. HOUSE. *Foundations and Principles of Music Education,* 2nd ed., Chapter 11. New York: McGraw-Hill, 1972.

National Interscholastic Music Activities Commission of the Music Educators National Conference, *NIMAC Manual,* Chapter 7. Washington: Music Educators National Conference, 1963.

Tests (In Print in 1991)

ACER and University of Melbourne Music Evaluating Kit. 1976. Jennifer Bryce and Max Cooke. Beginning of secondary school. 7 parts, 105–140 minutes. 157-page handbook. Uses cassette tape. Australian Council for Educational Research. Hawthorn, Victoria, Australia 3127.

Advanced Measures of Music Audiation. 1989. Edwin Gordon. G.I.A. Publications, Inc. 7404 South Mason Ave., Chicago, IL 60638.

Aliferis Music Achievement Test (College Entrance Level). 1954. James Aliferis, 28-page manual. Order from John E. Stecklein, 1988 North Wheeler St., St. Paul, MN 55113.

Aliferis–Stecklein Music Achievement Test (College Midpoint Level). 1962. James Aliferis and John Stecklein. 36-page manual, includes administrative instructions and scoring instrument. Uses cassette tape. Order from John E. Stecklein, 1988 North Wheeler St., St. Paul, MN 55113.

Audie: Toddler's Musical Game. 1989. Edwin Gordon, G.I.A. Publications, Inc. 7404 South Mason Ave., Chicago, IL 60638.

Aural Skills Training Series: Melodic Ear-to-Hand Skills Program. 1987. James O. Froseth. All cassettes and packs include student progress monitoring logs and content outlines. G.I.A. Publications, Inc., 7404 South Mason Ave., Chicago, IL 60638.

Australian Test for Advanced Music Studies. (ATAMS). 1974. Doreen Bridges and Bernard Rechter. ACER Grades 13–16. Measures developed aural abilities and general musical intelligence. 3 Parts: "Tonal and Rhythm Memory and Musical Perception;" "Aural/Visual Discrimination, Score Reading and Understanding Notation;" and "Comprehension and Application of Learned Musical Templets." ATAMS, P.O. Box 210, Hawthorn, Victoria, Australia, 3127.

(Bentley) Measures of Musical Abilities. 1966. Arnold Bentley. 7-page manual. Research data from his 151 page book. Uses a cassette. NFER–NELSON Publishing Company Ltd., Darville House, 2 Oxford Road East, Windsor, Berkshire, England SL4 IDF.

Farnum Music Test. 1969. Stephen E. Farnum. 15-page manual. Uses a record (includes record, manual, correction key). Bond Publishing Company, 787 Willett Avenue, Riverside, RI 02915.

Farnum String Scale, The. 1969. Stephen Farnum. 28-page manual, 3 pages contain instruction and development of the test. Four trial editions were used, each with a few students. A grading chart is furnished based on 14 of 17 exercises given to 50 violinists in different sections of the country. No additional data are furnished. Instruments are required. Hal Leonard Music, Inc., 960 B Mark Street, Winona, MN 55987.

Group Tests of Musical Abilities. 1988. Janet Mills. 22-page teacher's guide, answer sheets. Uses a cassette. NFER–NELSON Publishing Company Ltd., Darville House, 2 Oxford Road East, Windsor, Berkshire, England SL4 1DF.

Indiana–Oregon Music Discrimination Test. 1965. Newell H. Long. 16-page manual. Uses a record. Midwest Music Tests, 1304 East University Street, Bloomington, IN 47401.

Instrumental Score Reading Test. 1987. James Froseth. Complete kit (pre- and post-test, manual). G.I.A. Publications, Inc., 7404 South Mason Ave., Chicago, IL 60638.

Instrumental Timbre Preference Test. 1965. Edwin Gordon. Includes a cassette. G.I.A. Publications, Inc., 7404 South Mason Ave., Chicago, IL 60638.

Intermediate Measures of Music Audiation. 1983. Edwin Gordon. A music aptitude test for grades 1–4. G.I.A. Publications, Inc., 7404 South Mason Ave., Chicago, IL 60638.

Iowa Test of Musical Literacy (ITML). 1970. Edwin Gordon. 6 levels. Revision in progress, G.I.A. Publications, Inc., Chicago, IL 60638.

Musical Achievement Tests (MAT). 1968–69–1979. Richard Colwell. 36-page administrative and scoring manuals for each of tests 1–4. A 143-page interpretive manual for tests 1–2, 254-page interpretive manual for test 3–4; scoring templets. Uses a record for each test. MAT, 84 Fuller St. #1, Brookline, MA 02146.

Musical Aptitude Profile. 1965. Edwin Gordon. 113-page manual. Uses cassette tape. Houghton Mifflin Co., Boston, MA.

Primary Measures of Music Audiation. 1979. Edwin Gordon. A music aptitude test for kindergarten through grade 3. 107-page manual. Uses 2 cassette tapes. G.I.A. Publications, Inc., 7404 South Mason Avenue, Chicago, IL 60638.

Seashore Measures of Musical Talent, The. 1960 revision. Carl Seashore, Don Lewis, and Joseph Saetveit. 11-page manual. Uses a record or tape. The Psychological Corporation, 555 Academic Court, San Antonio, TX 78204.

Standardized Tests of Musical Intelligence, The. 1968. Herbert Wing. Most technical data contained in Tests of Musical Ability and Appreciation, 2nd ed. Cambridge University Press, Cambridge, England. In this reference the test is also entitled Wing Musical Aptitude Test. Uses a reel-to-reel tape. National Foundation for Educational Research (England and Wales). The Mere, Upton Park, Slough, Buckinghamshire, England.

Watkins–Farnum Performance Scale, The. 1954–62. John Watkins and Stephen Farnum. 40-page manual. 33 pages containing music for the test. Requires wind and percussion instruments. Hal Leonard Music, Inc., 960 B Mark Street, Winona, MN 55987.

4

Motivation

A successful music program is one in which participation results in musical learning. A good teacher is one whose basic musicianship and knowledge enable her to produce good performances of good music, and whose grasp of pupil psychology helps her produce enthusiastic participation leading to greater skill in and positive attitudes toward music. These qualities are essential for good teaching. Without musicianship and technical knowledge, the teacher may produce participation but little student achievement; without an understanding of her pupils, the teacher may develop a program that involves only the highly motivated few, depriving many others of the enjoyment of participating in music as adults.

It is simply not true that good music in itself furnishes sufficient motivation for public school pupils. For the more advanced pupils, good music can and should be the strong central attraction. For the beginner or the pupil of limited ability, however, other factors influence his participation and affect his learning. Even for the advanced pupil, teacher personality, classroom atmosphere and organization, as well as teaching and learning procedures are of crucial importance.

The importance of motivation to learning is well established. Since any teaching, whether of an individual or a group, has as its aim the development of musical knowledge, good practice habits, technical proficiency, and musical understanding, the suggestions for motivation given here can be applied to either individual or group situations, although some will, of course, be more appropriate for one than for the other. The ideas presented in the next few pages fall into two categories. First, those pertaining to long-range planning, representing intrinsic values; and second, those relating to day-by-day, immediate goals, representing extrinsic motivation. When used together, these two kinds of motivation can do much to promote interest and stimulate better performance and learning.

Although motivation in school is directly related to the student's goals, both short and long term, the teacher should remember that motivation is also based on the student's preferences, feelings, and values. These human characteristics determine the extent of the student's personal investment in any subject or experience. Instrumental music is almost always an elective experience, and students give up many other alternatives to participate in it. Success in instrumental music may sometimes represent the attainment of a dream; when this is the case, other motivational factors such as pride in the group effort become much less important.

Whether the characteristic of fun is intrinsic or extrinsic, the study of music must be fun. The fun of being in band or orchestra may be the student's goal—and the student determines whether the fun and enjoyment of performance justifies the extensive study and practice. The list of motivational factors presented in the following pages should help ensure that enjoyable experience.

INTRINSIC MOTIVATION

1. Use good music. The music itself should be the central motivating force for any musical learning, though it is rarely the only factor. To furnish genuine motivation, music must be of high quality, for poor music soon becomes tiresome and boring. Also, it is so easily available to the student on tape or television that she does not need to participate in school music groups in order to find it. Teachers are tempted to make one of two mistakes regarding the quality of the music to be used. The first is that of using popular commercial music on the ground that it will interest the student. The fallacy in this approach is that the basic goal—that of developing a love of good music—can never be reached, even though the student may acquire considerable performing skill.

The second mistake is to set unrealistically high standards for the music to be used. To use good music does not necessarily mean to use only great music. The skillful teacher begins where the student is—selecting music that will appeal to her at her present level of understanding—and gradually introduces her to better music as she becomes ready for it. A variety of types of music is more satisfying than a steady diet of one kind and can teach the student to judge between varying qualities. As long as the music is well written, challenges the student with something new, has genuine musical worth, and is not trite or shallow—in short, as long as it broadens the student's appreciation—it is good music and should be used.

2. Use a wide musical repertoire. New music is the most obvious way to maintain interest. Even if the individual or the group is not able to

perform the old music perfectly, there comes a time when a change is necessary. Nothing brings on boredom faster than working continually on the same few pieces or trudging wearily over the same exercises until all is perfected. If a long period of time is needed to learn a piece well, the selection is probably too difficult. The use of much music of varied levels not only helps maintain interest but also contributes to the sightreading skill of the learners. This principle holds for both individual and group instruction. Many music teachers seem to feel that only one instruction book or one solo should be used at a time. Limiting a student's musical experiences in this way contributes to a loss of interest.

3. Have a goal. Each student should know why he is practicing and what his objective is. Similarly, the teacher should make clear in rehearsals what she is trying to lead the group to do. Like the proverbial carrot in front of the donkey, the goal should be visible. Unlike the carrot, it should be attainable. The teacher must have long-range goals that shape her planning and programming, but short-range goals are also necessary.

For the greatest effectiveness, a goal must be fairly specific. If the group is working toward a concert performance, they will put forth more effort if the date has been set and the numbers selected. When time is given to drill, to sightreading, to listening, or to factual or technical learning, the students will respond more readily if they know what the purpose of the activity is.

4. Relate technical drill to real music. Scales, studies, and exercise material should be used in anticipation of the difficult spots in the music being learned. Until the student encounters a particular technical problem in a piece of music, he will see no reason for practicing exercises designed to give him that facility. Treat technical studies like vitamins: they are to be taken as needed, but never as the main ingredient of the diet.

This is not to suggest that technical studies be omitted—far from it. Because technical drill focuses on particular kinds of learning, it can help the student become technically proficient much more rapidly than if he works on musical pieces exclusively. Drill needs to be meaningful and relevant, but if omitted altogether, the individual and the group will suffer.

5. Develop musicianship skills and factual knowledge. Factual knowledge about music and the ability to perform some of the musicianship skills, such as transposing, reading several clefs, and improvising, are both goals of the music program and real motivators. Like good music, knowledge and skill are of intrinsic value and furnish one of the most valid ends of motivation. Students like to know, for instance, the problems that double-reed players have with reeds—how difficult they are to make, how scarce good cane is, and how much adjustment is necessary. They can be interested and inspired by details about composers and about music itself—how a fugue is put together, the background of a Wagner composition, or the type of social system in which Haydn lived and worked. The more the

student knows and the more she can do in any area, the more she is likely to retain a lively, active interest in it.

6. Develop a tradition of excellence. Music programs with a reputation for quality provide a momentum that motivates students to practice and minimizes discipline problems. When there is an established standard to measure up to, students usually accept the challenge.

High school students are idealistic, and they take pride in doing things well, even though they often talk to the contrary. They can derive satisfaction from meeting high standards, whether in personal or group achievement; they develop loyalties toward organizations and individuals who expect much from them, and enjoy living up to those expectations.

A tradition of excellence is not established overnight. If a teacher moves into a school without such a tradition, she must build it by starting with the younger students. Older players unaccustomed to high standards will resist drastic reforms and may retain their habits of sloppy practice or halfhearted participation. Such students may respond to the challenge from younger players who begin to surpass them and occupy first-desk positions. Sometimes the best way of dealing with these students is to be patient and let them graduate.

7. Help the student to arrange enjoyable, independent musical activities other than the private lesson and the large-group rehearsal. Try to arrange schedules and assignments to make it possible for students to work together toward a common goal. Practicing alone can be boring and take considerable inner discipline, whereas working on parts with other students is much more enjoyable. This is especially true for students who play such nonmelody instruments as tubas and horns. Two or three students practicing together, all on the same part or each on a different part, can increase the pleasure of each participant and also help to develop musicianship.

Also supply duets, trios, and other kinds of ensemble music to interested students. Whether the group remains together for a long period or simply reads through the music a few times, such activity should be encouraged. A good library of ensemble music representing a variety of instrumental combinations and levels of difficulty is a must in a good instrumental program.

8. Encourage the establishment of small ensembles. The small chamber group presents the greatest musical challenge, the best training, the heaviest individual responsibility, and the highest musical pleasure of any activity. Some special problems are involved in establishing small ensembles; these include scheduling, grouping students of similar levels of ability, and helping the groups become independent of teacher supervision. To create an ensemble of students whose levels of ability are comparable is perhaps possible only in a large school. In smaller schools, the group will usually be uneven, and the more capable students will have to wait for the

less capable players or even help them with their parts. This in itself can have learning advantages if it is properly handled so that no resentments or antagonisms occur. The learning derived from small-ensemble work is likely to be more valuable if the teacher does not have to supervise ensemble rehearsal regularly, and the saving of time to the teacher will be great. It is therefore important to promote an atmosphere in which independent rehearsal is desirable and expected. Whether small ensembles perform in public, go to festivals and contests, or play only for their own pleasure is the decision of the individual teacher. However, performances for appropriate community groups bring added motivation and also strengthen public relations.

9. Select music in which supporting players can star. The second-desk baritone player and the third snare drum are likely to lead humdrum existences musically. When it is possible to do so, the teacher should use music that gives solo passages to the little-heard supporting players. Such music may be short on artistic value, but it is long on psychological value. Even a short solo passage may offer incentive for additional practice, and the chance to be heard is something every player deserves.

10. Hear good performances. Players should not play all of the time. They should occasionally listen. Listening should include both live and recorded performances, amateur as well as professional. Older, advanced players may perform or demonstrate for younger players. Pupils are always interested in performances by groups of their own age level, whether these are semiprofessional or simply outstanding public school organizations. Some students will be more encouraged by virtuoso displays and master performances. An occasional poor performance on record or tape may serve as an opportunity for intelligent criticism. Opportunities to hear an occasional professional concert, informal presentations by adult members of the community whose skill would be an inspiration, and exchange concerts with other schools—these live performances can supplement the recorded ones.

11. Obtain good equipment and facilities. Much has already been said on this point. Good tools help to produce good results. Poor instruments affect both the group and the individual; an inferior instrument handicaps the student and may embarrass him as well. The teacher should see that both school-owned and student-owned instruments are of the best quality the financial situation will permit. Lack of practice areas or a good rehearsal room can also be a handicap. The players of large instruments such as the tuba, string bass, or drums especially need an in-school practice room, and these rooms may be a great convenience to other students whose schedules would permit practice time within the school day.

Regardless of the physical facilities in which the teacher and students work and learn, a room that is efficiently arranged, neat and ready for work provides a certain motivation. A room in disarray sends a message of laxness and lack of concern. If a room presents the impression that efficiency and industry are the rule, the liklihood of this being true is enhanced.

12. Develop favorable attitudes. Students will accomplish little without the proper attitude. Attitudes are contagious—especially among teenagers—and so the attitude of a few may set the pattern for the group. The teacher needs to communicate to the students a sense of responsibility for their own individual parts in the organization, together with a pride in the organization and a desire to work for it. The student needs to feel that his practicing is important, not only for his own improvement but for the improvement of the group as a whole. The teacher can instill a sense of responsibility by taking notice of those students who are responsible, commending sections that have improved, pointing out areas that are weak, and helping students who need extra practice find the time and place to do so. Pride in the organization can be encouraged by stressing honestly the achievements of the group, by planning attractive activities, and by reporting to the group any commendations that come from the community, the student body, or school officials.

13. Build esprit de corps. Pride and responsibility are least successful when they spring solely from teacher inspiration, though in the beginning it may be necessary for the teacher to be the main source of inspiration. A group spirit of unity is the best source for control; the desire to belong and be accepted will lead a student to adopt the ideals of the group. If the group is included in appropriate decision making, a spirit will be fostered that will spread to new members coming into the group. Because high school students are not yet mature adults, group spirit can be strongly influenced by such extrinsic values as uniforms, contests, social affairs, and good publicity, as well as by successful performances.

14. Use student leaders. Esprit de corps can be enhanced through the selection of the right student leaders. In addition, some of the less talented students can find recognition and satisfaction in performing organizational tasks or becoming student officers. Student government not only aids in developing esprit de corps but also in lessening the load for the director and providing a chain of command through which the teacher may channel authority and needed regulations. Some positions are best filled by popular election while others should be appointed by the director.

15. Treat all students and their ideas with respect. Students need to feel that their ideas contribute to the selection of music, procedures, organizational rules, and even the amount of practice expected of every member.

It must be clear that the director makes the final decision in all matters but that she is also a good listener. If the atmosphere is such that all students believe that they and the group can improve, the students will usually establish higher standards and expectations of themselves, often exceeding even those of the director.

16. Plan a sensible schedule. The schedule should make it possible for students to practice and to attend all extra rehearsals. Performance goals should be reasonable so that the students are not discouraged. If too many events are scheduled, there may be continual frantic effort to prepare for the next performance or activity, and students may be deprived of participation in other worthwhile activities. Always present is the danger of exploiting the talented student. Often she is capable in many areas, and many teachers wish her to participate in their particular fields. Because of this, such a student can become accustomed to doing rapid, superficial work and forget the importance of sustained effort. The teacher must be willing to think of the student's welfare first, to help her acknowledge her limits and budget her time wisely.

17. Take into consideration the motivating force of the teacher. The teacher is the decisive element in providing inspiration, motivation, and learning. Much has been said about what the teacher does; of more basic importance is who the teacher is. Her level of musicianship, technical facility as a performer, command of musical knowledge, and depth and breadth as a human being can inspire students to imitation and emulation. The necessity to be both musician and teacher has already been discussed; the inspiration that comes from a fine musician and a fine teacher is the point here.

In addition to being timely, motivational goals and activities must not be too specific. Teachers should apply the Goldilocks principle and pursue programs that are "just right." Students do not study instrumental music because it is a medium for the creation and expression of beauty or because they sense their aesthetic needs are unfulfilled. Neither do they enroll in instrumental music to learn more about the music of Francis McBeth or Gustav Holst or to learn the relationship of key signatures to the circle of fifths. "Just right" programs and goals are understandable, meaningful, and attainable.

The foregoing suggestions are of a long-range type; they are based primarily on a belief in the motivating force of good music and in the importance of psychology in working with students. These suggestions should be the basis of the teacher's planning and decision making. A second group of suggestions related to motivation is most pertinent to temporary or short-term goals. These suggestions alone would never be adequate to provide a healthy atmosphere or a firm basis for musical learning, but they can serve to create temporary inspiration and day-to-day interest. Many of them do not relate directly to music; thus they provide extrinsic rather than intrinsic motivation.

EXTRINSIC MOTIVATION

1. Praise is effective when properly used. Most students will respond to a deserved compliment from a teacher whom they respect, and they will

work to earn one. Praise can be directed at the entire group or focused on one section or individual. The praise must be honest and must not be so frequent as to become meaningless. Students should not be led to think that their work is better than it is, but improvement and effort as well as good performance can call forth praise. The teacher should be careful that her praise does not always fall on the same heads, but that the little-noticed plodders are also given credit.

Praise and approval can come from other sources than the teacher. The commendation of the administration and the student body are important in forming a group's opinion of itself, and such commendation is a legitimate goal for which to work. One excellent way in which to see that a music group receives deserved recognition is to publicize its activities. Newspaper, television, and radio publicity of group activities fosters both school and public awareness, and encourages the student to take pride in her organization.

2. Criticism and disapproval also have a place in motivation. Being inspirational should not imply that the teacher is the Good Humor Man. She should use praise liberally when it is merited but be firm when the situation demands it. Since psychologists have spent years sending animals through mazes and giving them electric shock treatments, it is fairly well established that punishment as well as reward is effective in learning. Many successful teachers create a lasting enthusiasm for music while at the same time arousing a certain amount of apprehension at the weekly lesson or the daily rehearsal. When the student can relax without fear of criticism regardless of what she does, the atmosphere no longer contains that creative tension in which learning takes place. Remember, however, that as a general rule, sarcasm, ridicule, and other unfair practices have no place in good teaching, and criticism and disapproval need not be couched in these terms. Students respect firmness and want to be challenged to meet high standards. Respect for the teacher may often be based on the number of mistakes she identifies and the helpfulness of the suggested corrections. And it may be that at the immature level, mild fear is the strongest motivator.

When offering criticism, teachers need to know whether performance failure is due to lack of ability or lack of effort. Mild punishment works wonders when the problem is a lack of effort; however, when the student is doing everything she can but lacks ability, criticism and punishment lead to discouragement.

3. Keep parents informed regarding practice requirements and objectives. Enlist parents' support, but never allow home practice to be used as a form of punishment for their children. Many directors send a periodic progress report to parents in order to maintain a close relationship between the music program and the home.

Emphasis on a regular time for practice may help serve as a kind of motivator for the student. If he feels that practice is important enough to be done at a particular time each day, with this time to be sacrificed only under exceptional circumstances, an aura of significance develops around the practice hour. Since consistent practice is of great intrinsic value, the teacher need not hesitate to support it in any way she can.

4. Grades are as valid in music as in other areas. Although some teachers recommend grading as a disciplinary measure—that is, the student who manages to avoid breaking the rules receives a high grade—it seems more psychologically sound to accept the traditional view of grading as a reward for good work. Many systems of grading are used in music programs, including the following:

a. *Practice charts.* Students are required to practice a specified amount each day. Those who exceed the minimum get higher grades. The drawback to this approach is that it rewards effort rather than results. Also, it is difficult to be certain that practice reports are accurate.

b. *Progress charts.* Students are graded for completing specified objectives. Such a chart has the advantage of establishing definite goals and of rewarding actual attainment rather than time put in. It gives the teacher an impartial and objective vehicle by which to determine grades and places music on the same plane with the more academic subjects, in which grades are determined objectively on the basis of work accomplished.

c. *Point system.* Like progress charts, the point system rewards achievement and in addition may cover a wide range of other accomplishments. Point systems may also be useful to determine annual awards for members of the organization. Some teachers object to the clerical effort involved in keeping an accurate record of earned points for each student, but student help can be successfully used in keeping records.

One of the important values of a systematic grading procedure is that the student can examine his progress and see his results. He can see a graphic illustration of progress for the year, the relationship between work and achievement, and can make a personal evaluation of this progress.

5. Competitive seating plans are an excellent stimulus. When there is a competitive seating plan, the better players are encouraged to work for the honor of retaining their positions as first-desk players, while those beneath them strive to catch up. For this plan to be effective, the teacher needs to schedule tryouts at fairly regular intervals. The importance of the first-chair position for every part should be stressed (e.g., first chair, third clarinet), not simply the solo chairs. Whether tryout times are announced ahead of time or scheduled without notice is the teacher's decision. Each has its advantages. Some teachers feel that announced tryouts stimulate more energetic practicing, while others have discovered that their students practice more consistently when they have to be ready for unannounced tryouts.

6. Challenge systems are a corollary of the competitive seating plan. Students of the lower ranks may aspire to the higher chairs through testing the occupant in a fair match. The director should make the challenge

system as democratic and as fair as possible, probably by including students on the judging committee and by having a clear challenge procedure that will also serve to produce added practice. In order not to spend too much class time on challenging, it is better to have a set time or schedule in which challenges may take place.

7. Tryouts for chair positions or ensemble membership are important. As in other subjects, the music teacher should make specific assignments and then test all students on the preparation of the assignments. Such testing may take place at rehearsals, sectional practices, or at lessons; but regardless of the method, students should be expected to do the work assigned and be graded accordingly. Whether such tryouts affect seating is up to the teacher.

Some teachers succeed in holding tryouts during regular rehearsals, calling on individuals to play the assignments in front of the group. The director should use discretion and not force unwilling students to submit to such a practice if it seems too harsh. Once the routine is established, however, it may encourage students to be well prepared in order to avoid making a poor showing before their peers.

8. Competition on technical proficiency has a place. Students can derive a great deal of fun and inspiration from an occasional contest for sheer technical proficiency—players compete to see who can play the greatest number of scales correctly, play the fastest, hold notes the longest, and so forth. Such contests should not be considered a serious part of any evaluation but be used simply to stimulate interest and challenge students to greater technical mastery.

9. An occasional written test may be of value. Tests of musical learning, used infrequently, may result in extra effort from students. Such examinations may test knowledge of music fundamentals: terms, keys, scales, and tuning. While these tests give no indication of the student's playing ability, they help to emphasize the importance of basic musical knowledge. Written tests take up valuable time, but even in performing groups an occasional written test can provide motivation for learning and give the teacher some valuable insights.

10. Various methods of evaluation may add to the perceived importance of the group and its goals. Public performance evaluation, properly handled, can contribute both to the level of motivation and to musical understanding. For example, an outside critic may be employed during the regular rehearsal period to listen to individuals and sections, to comment to the group on the performance, and to offer suggestions for improvement. Or students may perform their parts for the entire ensemble, identify their weaknesses, and suggest how they will improve their parts by tomorrow or by next week. Such an activity can be great fun, constitute public testimony of intent, and act intrinsically and extrinsically as a motivator for musical excellence. In addition, members may comment on their section's progress toward the overall goal and what they need to do to improve. The more

specific the suggestions, the more helpful this activity will be. Comments like "take our parts home and practice" may be on target but lack sufficient specificity to ensure meaningful improvement. Comments about how better or more intelligent use of warm-ups and home drill and practice can improve the intonation, balance, or musical line of the performance can be especially worthy.

11. Membership standards for all groups, beginning through advanced, are desirable. Although there must be some flexibility in selecting members for each group, students should have a fairly accurate idea of what must be accomplished in order to gain membership in the group. A clear set of standards is one way to encourage practice and achievement. In addition, standards can help dispel any feeling that the teacher is partial or unfair. Published rules must be followed; the fewer exceptions made, the more important these rules will become in the eyes of all members. Moreover, there is a natural desire to be a member of those groups having an aspect of selectivity. The Marine Corps, Phi Beta Kappa, and Who's Who would lose their appeal if open to all comers. Musical organizations should not be exclusive, cliquish bodies, but membership in them should imply that certain standards have been met and that each member is characterized by a certain level of achievement.

12. Awards provide another stimulus to effort. They may take the form of letters, medals, sweaters, service stripes, or certificates. An award has no intrinsic value of its own and is important only as a means of promoting greater musical growth. Even so, students often prize an award highly, taking pride in earning it and pleasure in others' recognition of it. As with membership standards, a definite system for giving awards should be established that the group knows and understands. If the point system or competitive chairs are an accepted practice, the awards system should be related to these and to other administrative practices. To be most effective, awards should be presented in public, with at least a modicum of ceremony.

13. Scholarships are an even more effective incentive to achievement. The scholarship should relate to the music program—for instance, a scholarship to an outstanding summer music camp. This kind of award may be used to sustain the interest of the best students in the organization. Funds for scholarships may be secured through money-raising projects by the group itself or by a parents' group; or they may come from one or more civic groups or from private individuals. To be most effective, the scholarship should be publicized throughout the year and be awarded at the close of the year.

14. Section rehearsals are a necessity for all good bands and orchestras. They have been discussed at some length already. Sectional rehearsals not only help the student with specific difficulties but provide some additional incentive for outside practice. When the whole group always rehearses together, the student may not hear his mistakes or realize how important it is that he perform his part correctly. If scheduling makes extra

section rehearsals impractical, the director should consider using some of the regularly scheduled large-group rehearsal time for concentrated work with various sections. Where feasible, several sections might be scheduled at the same time with responsible students in charge.

15. Summer music camps offer students a chance to improve their musical skills in new and stimulating surroundings. The inspiration of a music camp comes from excellent teachers, the outstanding ability of other students, and a high level of performance. The director should encourage any student who can attend summer camps to do so. A local summer camp can often be organized with successful results. The staff may consist of college music students, teachers with free time, or guest conductors from college campuses or other school systems. If an actual campsite is available, the experience will be enhanced, but even without an outdoor atmosphere the local music camp can be worthwhile.

16. New instruments provide a reward for work well done. The teacher should encourage her students to own the best instruments they can afford. When a new instrument is obtained, the teacher should make the acquisition known to the group and help the student attract attention to his new possession.

17. Tape recordings and videotapes allow students to hear and see their efforts and point up shortcomings as well as achievements. Problems of intonation, wrong notes, and poor attacks and releases often show up more vividly on tape than in actual rehearsal. An impending recording session furnishes another incentive for additional work and is in this sense a close kin to the live performance.

18. Social activities can be a way to develop greater interest. Special dances, banquets, and trips foster a spirit of unity and help maintain interest. These events also provide a welcome change from the routine of daily rehearsals, concerts, and sports events. In addition, they help the director become acquainted with her students on a different basis.

PERFORMANCE

Theoretically, the music program does not exist for the sake of performance. In practice, however, most of the efforts of both teachers and students have performance as the conscious or unconscious goal; the opportunity to perform represents the greatest single motivating factor. This is natural; music is a listening art, and the greatest satisfaction comes when performers feel their music has reached a listening ear. Therefore, the instrumental music teacher finds occasions for a variety of kinds of performances, knowing that the opportunity to perform will stimulate more conscientious and concentrated practice, prompt interest in concomitant musical learning, provide an outlet and a reward for students, and serve as a demonstration of the accomplishments of the music program.

The danger is that this last consideration will take on undue importance and that performance will become the goal of the program rather than a vehicle for greater learning. In considering performance and motivation, one should remember that performance is encouraged primarily because of its motivation power, not the reverse. On the other hand, the group that does not perform at least once a semester will almost always be a dying organization. Students need to be challenged to do their best and to attain what is possible; with most music groups that means a reasonably active performing schedule.

Performance can take several forms. Contests and festivals are a common and valuable form of public performance. In some instances, these occasions are the only times groups play good music. The challenge to compete successfully is strong, so that the music for contests and festivals is learned more thoroughly and played more adequately than that for any other occasion. If the pressure to succeed in the competition is too great, however, the psychological negatives can outweigh the pluses. It is the teacher's responsibility to see that the efforts of the group are focused on excellence for the sake of excellence and for the sake of the music, not for the sake of winning the highest rating.

Concerts hold a place of equal importance and nearly equal intensity to contests and festivals. Here again, the music should be carefully chosen for its value and played as well as possible, as long as rehearsals do not become drudgery for the sake of unattainable perfection. The music chosen should be well within the ability of the group, so that a satisfactory performance does not demand an unreasonable amount of preparation.

Exchange concerts have all the advantages of regular concerts, with the addition of the value of competition—the students' desire to excel in comparison with another group, school, or town. The teacher should not make competition a major consideration, and should be careful to emphasize good and bad features of both groups so that the students profit both from their own playing and from listening to the exchange group.

Special performing events are another form of motivation. Bringing in a guest conductor or guest artist to work with the group, hearing an artist perform, attending a clinic, or playing in select groups such as all-state or all-city organizations can result in great inspiration for a young player. Such opportunities are probably greater now than ever before.

Tours, though often viewed with dismay by teacher and administrator alike, have high appeal for students. Performing tours are probably never worth the agony involved, but great values are to be gained from them even if not an adequate return for effort expended. The kind of "professionalism" gained from performing well day after day is a fine experience for the student. However, the teacher must decide whether she can justify the expenditure of time and effort for value received.

Solo, small-group, and large-group performance before civic organizations has been emphasized. The more students who participate in such programs, the more value for the students and the more interest promoted in the entire music program. When one or two highly touted groups are sent out exclusively, these tend to become exploited, the learning values diminish for them, and other deserving students are barred from the opportunity to perform.

This chapter has put forth sound educational principles translated into terms and situations applicable to the instrumental music program. The casual reader may feel that these principles are things she can take or leave, utilize or ignore. Sound motivation, however, is not simply something with which the music program is better, but which it can do without. Motivation is the *sine qua non* for learning, musical or any other kind. The teacher cannot take or leave it as she desires, for if there is no motivation there will be no learning, and where there is thoughtless or misguided motivation there may be negative learning. Motivation comes from within, but the teacher can provide day-to-day situations that are as desirable as possible so that the student's interest grows and he becomes motivated to develop in those areas that are the teacher's goals. Basically, every individual is motivated by her own needs. The psychological and physical conditions that hold promise of answering these needs can stimulate her to respond.

Motivation, however sound, is not in itself educational. Even the best motivation does not necessarily lead to learning. In music, we often forget that not all experience is educative, just as not all experience is motivating. To be educative, experience must be purposeful. Psychological studies have indicated that people attending lectures or reading material gain widely differing information from what they read or hear, depending on what they expect to gain. Sometimes their impressions vary so greatly that one person's bear no resemblance to another's. When purposes differ, the resulting learning also differs. To apply this to music is not difficult; merely practicing or reading through music or drilling perfunctorily on exercises is not educative. A purpose must be present, the student's purpose as well as the teacher's. Instrumental teachers continue to teach primarily in the "drill" fashion; the paucity of results attests to the failure of this method. Kurt Lewin said, "It seems easier for society to change education than for education to change society."

REFERENCES

MAEHR, MARTIN, and LARRY BRASKAMP. *The Motivation Factor*. Lexington, MA: Lexington Books, 1986.

5

Administration

ORGANIZATION

The orchestra director couldn't find his baton—again. His small (but appreciative) orchestra waited patiently for him to locate the missing baton. He was an excellent musician. He just couldn't get organized.

Across the hall in the band room the director stepped up on the podium, and his band snapped to attention with military precision. Today they were going to play the latest band overture.

And so it goes. We might imagine a musical seesaw with the perfect musician on one end and the perfect administrator on the other. To stay on an even keel, a balance must be struck between music and administration. At times one must clearly be more administrator than musician, and, fortunately, there are many other times when one can be foremost a musician—the resulting combination equals a "music teacher." One director thinks of administration as forms, record keeping, inventories, and bids; another thinks that objectives, evaluation, and curriculum development are the essence of administration. Neither aspect should be neglected.

Though it is often said that good musicians are poor administrators, this is not so. Music educators have spent many years developing high-level skills for making music, but attention to administrative tasks is often learned on the job. The teacher who understands how to run his program with the maximum of smoothness and the minimum of fuss has more time for making music, for selecting and learning scores, and for organizing his teaching. Record keeping does not have to be a full-time job. A stockpile of good ideas has accumulated over the years based on the successful routines used by good teachers. A director should know the tricks of administration and select from them. Nevertheless, he does not need to use all of them to keep his musical house in order. The prospective music teacher should begin to collect his own private store of good administrative techniques: sample seating plans, records, forms, and the like. Numerous computer programs are available to help keep records and for other tasks such as organizing the band library, the instrument inventory, and uniform inventory/assignments. Such programs save both time and space.

The first item required for organization is a calendar. It is useful for the director to carry a pocket calendar, have a "master calendar" on his desk, and post a large wall calendar on the wall of the rehearsal room. One of the first tasks for new directors is to contact the state music educators association or district "bandmaster" or "orchestra division" president in order to join the organization and receive a calendar of the year's events. These events should be placed on the calendars of the instrumental teachers at all levels.

From this schedule, the instrumental music teacher can plan his concerts, band camps, recruiting activities, and any other events (such as trips) that vary from year to year. Each of these dates should be cleared with the principal and coordinated with other music teachers. All possible performance dates should be mailed to students' parents in the summer with a note to contact the director immediately if these dates conflict with previously scheduled family activities. Such early notification can help prevent many scheduling conflicts.

Coordination between music teachers is important. In school systems that have a music supervisor, coordination may present few problems. In systems having no designated "chair" of the music program, the high school band or orchestra director should simply assume the role of coordinator by asking the other music teachers for their schedule of activities. If other teachers have not planned ahead, the director can simply provide them with a list of his dates (i.e., whoever is most organized gets to be the chair). The high school orchestra and band directors should also work with the middle school and elementary teacher(s), since these individuals can make or break the program.

One of the most difficult tasks is to encourage the middle school director to set his goals and expectations beyond the middle school level. Occasionally middle school directors—who work only with sixth, seventh, and eighth graders—can become limited to goals attainable by eighth graders. They may not look beyond that level or motivate students to excel beyond that level. In short, sometimes the ultimate goal of middle school instrumentalists is to earn a superior rating playing Grade III music at a concert band festival, with no thought toward a higher level of musicianship. Yet, it is the middle school director who shapes the attitudes that students have toward the high school music program.

It is virtually impossible for an instrumental music teacher to accomplish all the administrative chores needed for a band or orchestra to function smoothly (unless the program is small or not very active).[1] Many responsibilities can be handled by students, parents, and even local service clubs. Students may be elected to positions of president, secretary (to check roll), quartermaster (to oversee uniform distribution, collection, and storage), property manager (to keep track of and maintain marching band equipment, stereo system, video cameras, etc.), and treasurer; students may be *appointed* by the director to the positions of student conductor, librarian, publicity chairman, section leader, and drum major. Other positions that may be appointed are especially useful during marching season; for example, squad leaders can assist the director in teaching drill after they have attended a summer training session or a band front camp.

Students assuming positions of responsibility should have their names printed in programs, announced over the public address system at football games, or awarded special ribbons, medals, or chevrons. Students often put great value on a "letter" or other badge of distinction.

Parents' organizations can handle a variety of tasks such as helping with concerts, trips, fund raising when necessary, and chaperoning.

All of the effort put into administration will be enhanced by the practice of consistently keeping the principal informed.

BUDGETING AND PROPERTY

One of the most difficult aspects of being an instrumental music teacher is the budget, or lack thereof. Few schools in the country have all the financial resources they need. With the rise in popularity of marching bands in the 1970s, the need for more money also rose. New percussion equipment, color-guard equipment, and travel all required more funds. As many programs grew in size and sophistication—for example, using five tonal bass drums, three quintuplet tenor drums, six snares, three pairs of cymbals, and another four students playing assorted mallet and trap instruments—they outgrew the teaching ability of the director in terms of both time and skill. Naturally, very few schools were able to fund these marching machines, so parents took up the slack. In some instances, the additional funding was necessary and easily justified as it allowed more students to participate in the instrumental music program (even if they did not play an instrument, e.g., rifles). In a few cases, however, it led to an elitism that rejected students who could not afford to pay their fair share of the expenses. And in a few cases, due to the need to justify the expense and the extra staff to help with the "teaching," marching band became a year-round activity—the primary component of the instrumental music program.

[1] Carrol M. Butts. *Troubleshooting the High School Band: How to Detect and Correct Common and Uncommon Performance Problems*. (West Nyack, NY: Parker Publishing Co., 1981), 195–197.

Most comprehensive instrumental music programs have a good marching band. The degree or extent to which the marching band is "good" depends first and foremost on how well the instrumental music teachers teach music, and second on the community's, students', parents', and administrators' definition of "good" and their willingness to finance the program. For example, a good marching band requires a good visual element in addition to good music; this visual element depends on a variety of aspects that may lie beyond the skills and training of a music educator. This extramusical element is enjoyable, but it requires ancillary equipment and training in order to be worthwhile.

Budgets are provided to the instrumental music program on a yearly basis. If additional funds are not requested, additional funds will not be appropriated; if parents are willing to make up the difference between the required funding and that allocated by the principal or board of education, then the administration will be less inclined to provide additional funding.

Instrumental music programs are more expensive to operate than any other program in the high school curriculum (athletics are considered as extracurricular), especially the outlay for equipment that may be useful for only five to eight years (e.g., marching band percussion and uniforms). If the band and orchestra have a good history of retaining their membership, and if the ensembles and individuals perform as frequently as possible for as many people as possible, then the community and politicians will feel they are getting their money's worth.

Ideally, every dime used for the instrumental music program should come from the board of education. In the 1980s, as taxes became a major political issue, taxes were not raised even though the cost of education continued to rise; and in some areas of the country they were actually lowered. Yet bands, for the most part, continued to do what they were doing—participating in contests and traveling. These activities in the face of status quo or reduced budgets reinforced the notion that increased funding was not necessary for the instrumental music program to flourish. As the nation approaches the twenty-first century, increased emphasis and focus are on basic education, so it is even less likely that additional funding will be allocated to instrumental music programs.

This dilemma has been resolved in various ways by instrumental music teachers. Some have gone into fund raising as a profession; those who in the mid-1970s foresaw the growing needs of marching band programs have been financially successful. Some teachers have thrown up their hands in despair, worked their eight-to-four jobs, and let the chips fall where they may, leaving everyone the poorer. And some—perhaps most— have simply taught music well, supplementing the resources they had with required fund-raising.

When budgets are inadequate, it is very easy to exploit parents' organizations, or even the students, to constantly raise funds. The better approach is to continue to seek funds from the principal, letting the parents raise money only for those items the director *knows* the school cannot afford. As a worst case scenario, if the school will not purchase new uniforms and the director has tenure, the band can always wear T-shirts and jeans—in which event it is likely that the community will apply pressure on the board of education for new uniforms. . . .

Budgets are usually presented to the principal each spring for the following school year and take effect on the first of July. New teachers should ask to see the budgets for at least the three previous years to determine any growth or reduction and to know on what items the funds were spent. Most school systems use a numbered code to denote what the funds were used for (equipment will have a number, instrumental supplies a number, office supplies a number, additional staff or assistants a number, and so on). The beginning teacher should learn these codes in order to present his budget in as orderly and accurate a fashion as possible. All teachers must discover the process by which money is spent, that is, to whom they submit their requests for purchases. And most important, teachers must determine to whom the funds are allocated. Site-based budgeting has changed the rules of the game. In some systems the upper administration will directly provide the instrumental music program with a budget; in others, the principal is provided with a budget and she allocates it based on school priorities.

The budget request should be as exact as possible, using round figures only on items that are impossible to determine precisely (such as instrument maintenance or telephone calls). A short explanation justifying each request can help facilitate a principal's decision, and attaching bids indicating that the director has done his homework also helps. For example, in the budget request under the item *educational equipment*, the figure may represent the total sum for a bass clarinet, a student-line oboe, a euphonium, and two marching mellophones (plus tax and shipping). Attached to the budget request should be a paragraph listing how that sum breaks down and a sentence or two about why each instrument is needed, including how long the instrument will last.

Middle school and high school budgets are usually divided into supplies (expendable items that normally do not last more than a year or so), equipment ("permanent supplies"), music (which may fall into either of the previous two categories), instructional staff (clinicians, honorariums, color guard instructors, arrangers, or director's pay for summer band camp—although putting the instrumental music instructor on an eleven- or twelve-month contract seems to be an increasingly common practice), and instrument maintenance (for yearly overhauls of selected school-owned instruments and minor repairs for numerous other school-owned instruments).

The director must attempt to prevent items such as file cabinets, stereo and recording equipment, and office furniture from being part of the yearly budget. These "once-in-a-decade" purchases should be from funds other than program funds. It is better for the director to bring a kitchen chair from home than to sacrifice a needed instrument.

Early on, all new teachers need to create a wish list, numbering each item in order of priority. This list should be submitted annually and updated as items are acquired and new needs identified. Such a list is helpful in long-term planning, and every teacher must approach his job as a long-term career. Be sure to explore means other than purchasing when acquiring items on the list. It is tempting to place items such as computers near the top of the list, when use of the school's computer labs is a more realistic solution. Similarly, stools for the trumpeters in the jazz band or stools for the double bass players in orchestra can usually be obtained somehow from the chemistry laboratory.

The new teacher should check last year's inventory and immediately delete missing items, school-owned instruments that are not worth repairing, and those instruments that have been stripped through the years to create two or three playable instruments.

A time-consuming task for the band director is to list the missing scores and parts. The first year's appropriation for music may be spent on missing first trumpet parts and needed flute parts, resulting in no new music being purchased.

PURCHASING

Valve oil, cork grease, violin strings, reeds, tape for repairing music and scores, "pop" tunes for basketball games, and a host of other supplies that the school does not stock and that need to be on hand should be purchased as soon as the new fiscal year begins. Otherwise, the director will have a quadruplicate form to fill out the day of a performance or each time he wants a roll of adhesive tape.

The most economical method for school instrument purchase is to advertise for bids. The disadvantage of doing this is that it may not be possible to obtain the exact instrument desired unless the bid is drawn up to indicate that only one specific brand and model will meet the requirements. The teacher who does not draw up the bid carefully and neglects to obtain several bids harms the program. Occasionally, a company may try to substitute a less expensive item for the one specified, omitting certain features or making what it considers to be relatively unimportant changes in the specifications. Usually, however, instrument companies are eager to have their quality instruments in the schools and cooperate in providing competitive prices. If a trade-in is involved, it is even more important to see that multiple bids are obtained, for trade-ins are more valuable to some firms than others.

The greatest disadvantage in bidding for instrumental purchases is that tax dollars may not flow to local merchants. These businessmen feel, with some justice, that they support the schools and that the schools should in turn support them. The director may thus be forced to choose between saving money and gaining goodwill, and is hardpressed to know which is more precious. Many school boards have a five-percent rule for just this reason. The rule states that out-of-town bids must be more than five percent less than the local bids in order to be considered. Other tactics include local purchase of music and all miscellaneous items. A major advantage of dealing with local businesses is that they can rescue one in an emergency. For example, if the school gives a local dealer its business, then the director is much more likely to be able to "borrow" a drum head to replace the one broken hours before Friday evening's performance.

A bid should specify make, model, key, finish, special features, accessories, case, acceptable standards (provision for rejection of shipment), acceptable alternates, desired method of shipment (if important), latest date for delivery, and possible trade-ins.

A long-range purchase program helps the school board determine the reasonableness of the music department's requests.

Sometimes it is possible to completely outfit a band or orchestra through a lease–purchase plan. If the director can convince the administration of his long-term commitment, using statistics from the beginning and feeder programs, indicating trends in rising costs of musical instruments, and sharing his priority list and how it has been followed and revised, then he may be able to attain all of the much-needed instruments in one year—allowing the school to pay for them over three to five years. The director must then strive to secure sufficient funds in his repair budget.

A major purchase from year to year is music. Band directors must be careful to purchase a balance of marching band music, light works, and serious works for concert band (knowing that arrangements of popular music become quickly dated). Orchestra directors must purchase a balance of arrangements and compositions for string and full orchestra, both light and serious works. Undoubtedly the most neglected music is that for solos and small ensembles. Although this music is fairly inexpensive and absolutely essential to the program, band and orchestra directors are usually most familiar with good large-ensemble works, as they hear new ones at conventions, on demo records distributed by publishers, and at other band and orchestra concerts. However, selecting brass quintet, string trio, and woodwind quintet music at appropriate levels for different students is more foreign and requires additional learning on the part of most instrumental music teachers.

As with instruments, a wish list for music is useful, aiding long-term planning, budgeting and purchasing. Music should be categorized by type (e.g., light, festival, marching, pep band, string quartet, etc.) and briefly described (e.g. "requires good oboists"), then purchased as funds become available.

Accountability

The director needs to be cautious about accepting money for any purpose. Some music companies expect to give the teacher a percentage of new-business sales. For this reason it is best not to handle student or school money. Money collected in school for fees or assessments of any kind should be paid directly to the business office or collected by a band parent and deposited in the school account.

Once acquired, an inventory of equipment must be maintained. As with all public property, the teacher is responsible for the equipment in his area, so he must always know who has what. He should be able to account for stands, normal classroom furniture, instruments, uniforms, music, and stereo and recording equipment—those items that are part of his standard paraphernalia and that are movable. Commercial aids are manufactured to help the director perform this part of his duties, and computers are wonderful for it. Most schools have several computers, and the instrumental music budget need only cover the software. Numerous companies have marketed very inexpensive software programs designed for administration of instrumental music programs. These programs are available for organizing and maintaining music libraries, equipment inventories, and uniform distribution and maintenance, but none has been developed for selling band candy. A yearly inventory is a good idea and, of course, a necessity when assuming a new position or leaving an old one.

School-Owned Instruments

Keeping records on instruments can become very extensive, but making duplicate copies is not difficult, especially with the availability of paper that does not require carbons for producing multiple copies. Thus, the teacher can have sign-out cards for all equipment filed alphabetically by student, maintain a file by instrument indicating those checked out and those still available, give a copy to the student so that the student knows what she is responsible for, and have a copy available for the business office or other interested parties. The same applies to a bond, which in elementary or junior high schools is more common than a sign-out card because the parents are usually the responsible parties.

Some practical suggestions pertaining to record keeping are:

1. The record should have the student's name, address, phone number, and ID number (in computerized schools). A complete description of the instrument, including all of its parts and its replacement value, is a *must*. A statement that sets the limits of responsibility and the uses prescribed for the instrument is also desirable.

2. It is a good legal precaution as well as good psychology to have both the parent and the student sign for the instrument. Both will then feel responsible for its care.

3. The form should tell whether the school or the user is obligated to pay for normal repairs during the year, and it should give a monetary limit.

4. The same form may be used to record the repair work done on the instrument: the date, cost, type of repair, and a yearly depreciation record showing percentage of depreciation each year and the present value of the instrument. If it seems more desirable to use separate forms for signing out the instrument and for recording its year-to-year history, a note on the sign-out form stating the present value of the instrument is important.

5. If rental fees are charged, the form should include a statement of the fee and show payments. Rental of instruments is not always a first-rate idea, however. To most people, rent of any kind, whether house, lawnmower, or musical instrument, implies that the owner assumes the cost of all repairs. This often entails having to render judgments throughout the year such as: Did that pad fall out as the result of use over the years or through the fault of the present user? A rent-free system, one making the user responsible for repairs during the time he has the instrument and obliging him to return the instrument at the end of the period in as good condition as when he received it, means fewer problems for the director and may be just as feasible economically.

6. If rental fees are charged, the director can save himself many problems by having them paid directly to the business office, even if they go into a general fund rather than into the music fund. If the business office assumes responsibility for collecting fees and issuing bills when necessary, hours of teacher time will be saved. It is possible in most situations to have the rental funds deposited into a specific account for yearly repairs.

7. A good suggestion often made but worth repeating is that the signing out of all school property, including that of the music department, should be handled by the school office. When this route is taken, the instrumental teacher's sole responsibility is to fill out an authorization slip indicating who is to have which instrument. The school office may then decide on the necessary forms or bonds and make decisions about rentals, deposits, and repairs for damages as well as rules for use of the instrument.

Other records on instruments may include any of the following:

1. A record of repairs for each instrument allows a systematic approach to overhauls and helps avoid serious last-minute repairs. To wait until

the instrument breaks down completely is no wiser than to ignore preventive maintenance on a car. Keeping track of what has been done helps the director decide what should be done to maintain the instrument in good working order. A long-range schedule can be based on a revolving system, in which two or three instruments receive an extensive overhaul every several years.

2. A repair list on each instrument furnishes valuable information about which brands and models have given the best service. In addition, it may be used as a guide for the purchase of new instruments, since it can show at what date it would have been cheaper to invest in a new instrument rather than repair the old one.

3. A checklist for student maintenance of the instrument is helpful. Some directors set aside a class period twice a year in which the energy of all students is devoted to a thorough cleaning job on every instrument—whether it needs it or not.

4. A standard method should be followed for taking school instruments to the repair shop and picking them up when repairs are completed. The director should see to it that he does not have to do this himself: the duties can be delegated to some responsible student or to someone in the school administration.

5. Instruments and cases should be marked. The manufacturer's serial number is the best and easiest way to keep track of the equipment; it is already on the instrument, it is not easily removed, and it will probably not duplicate any other number. A school number can be put on the case, neatly and in small-sized numbers, by use of a stencil and an aerosol paint can.

School-Owned Uniforms

Uniforms are probably the most difficult item for the director to handle efficiently. Each separate part of the uniform should be numbered for record keeping. A set of records by number should be maintained so that if a shortage is discovered (belt #45 is missing, for example) a check can easily be made. However, it is just as necessary to have a record of every part of the uniform each student is using—Freddie Jones has coat #32, trousers #39, plume #67, and so on. The director also likes to know what sizes he has available, so a master sheet should be posted stating the size and number of every item. Size labels are not too reliable, however, as most students have alterations made initially and again as they change shape in the course of their school years.

A tailor is more practiced in judging which basic sizes can be successfully altered to fit any particular individual. Since it is important to get the largest possible number of students fitted well, having a tailor do the fitting and the major alterations will be a wise expenditure of time and money. A tailor shop will often issue uniforms for a school in return for the alteration and cleaning business.

Having the student maintain his own uniform is often unsatisfactory. Some parents are more frugal than others, so that while one mother carefully "spots" the uniform and presses it, another sends it to the cleaners before every appearance. At the end of the year, one uniform is darker from having dirt pressed into it and the other is lighter from excessive cleaning. For this reason, many schools keep the uniforms at the building; students change immediately before and after the performance and never take the uniforms home. Cleaning is paid for by the school or by charging the students.

When uniforms are left at school rather than kept at home, two other problems are avoided, the first being that after a concert or a sports event students often begin to shed their uniforms bit by bit, thus creating a sloppy impression of the band. The second is the problem of students arriving with part of the uniform missing—"I thought you said no belts tonight!" Keeping the uniforms at school may also help minimize the game of trading for a better fit, which wreaks havoc with the most careful record keeping.

In some school situations parents sign bonds for the uniform just as for the instrument, and often, damage deposits are charged. There are other situations in which use of the uniform is entirely free; and in some places the student is required to purchase the uniform for the period of time he is in band—from one to four years—and sell it back to the school at the end of that time at its depreciated value. In four years' time a new uniform depreciates perhaps 40 percent; the student absorbs this loss.

MUSIC LIBRARY

As any professional librarian can tell you, there is practically no limit to what can be done in the library routine. Besides listing the music by composer, a cross-filing system by titles is useful, and this can be expanded to cross-filing by filing numbers, type of composition, required instrumentation, date of publication, date of last performance, and on and on. Library work is one area in which the job expands to fill the time available.

In organizing the instrumental music library, two areas must be considered: music in the library and music in the hands of students.

Music in the Library

In the library, it is absolutely necessary to have a system that allows the teacher or ensemble librarian to go to the files, find the desired composition quickly, and know that all the parts are there. The teacher may not always know just what composition he wants but may have only a set of stipulations in his mind (especially when pulling a selection for sight reading). Therefore, two items are essential: (1) a means for storing music so that browsing is facilitated, and (2) a listing of the holdings by composer. Band and orchestra music should be kept separate, not stored in the same area or listed in the same card file.

Nothing has yet replaced a heavy manila folder and a regular filing cabinet for storing music—the music is placed in the folder, on which is printed the title, composer, and file number, and the folder is put in its numerical place in the filing cabinet. The filing drawer can be filled as tightly or as loosely as one wishes, but it must support the music upright in a way that its name is easily seen. Music is often stored in paper envelopes, but this method has disadvantages: It is less accessible for browsing; the top corners of the music get ragged, bent, and illegible; and the temptation is always present to try to squeeze in that last single piece of music without taking the envelope out of the file. With the use of folders, instrumentation can be printed on the folder or on a separate sheet inserted in or stapled to it.

Narrow shelves are also often used for storing music, but they waste space. The shelves are either too narrow to accommodate the thick symphonic parts of larger works or are too wide to be well utilized for the thinner numbers.

Filing cabinets built for march-size and for octavo-size music can also be obtained. Music should be filed by number as it is acquired, rather than alphabetically. The latter is too time consuming, since it means rearranging almost every drawer and changing the labels on the outside of the drawers when a quantity of new music is purchased. New music can be given the next higher number above the last acquisition and placed behind it in the newest file. The card file can easily tell where the composition is to be found, simply by its number; for example, "4–A–12" means cabinet 4, drawer A, folder 12.

A separate filing system should probably be set up for chamber music, jazz-band music, and small-ensemble music. These should be cross-indexed according to ensemble type: woodwind quintet, woodwind quartet, string quartet, brass sextet, stage band, and so on. Percussion ensembles are best filed by the number of players used, for example, trios or quartets.

Every piece of music must be stamped with the name of the school to establish ownership. Stamping should be done in an obvious spot and should be neat—straight with the page and not smeared.

A library should be equipped to mend, file, and distribute music. A paper cutter, a large-carriage typewriter, tables and sorting racks are minimal. The distribution of music should be done from a movable folder cabinet that can be placed inside the rehearsal room.

Music in the Hands of Students

It is easier to identify folders and to pass out music when the small shelves on a folder cabinet are labeled with an individual's name, part assignment, and a number (shelves should be arranged in score order). Folders (supplied as advertisement by music dealers) protect the music and are useful any time music must be taken outside of the classroom. Many directors forbid students to take single pieces of music from the folder, stipulating that the entire folder must be taken by the student who wants to practice at home. The object of this rule is to prevent lost and mutilated parts of music.

Less important, but contributing to efficiency, are these practices:

1. Keeping music in a certain order in the folder, separated by size and arranged perhaps numerically, will save rehearsal time when the folder contains a number of selections.
2. In putting music in the folders, the librarian should leave a note in the folder when a part is missing so that the player does not have to hunt or ask for it, taking rehearsal time to settle his problem.
3. If the performing group has an instrumentation requiring extra parts beyond the publisher's normal set, give the local music dealer a list of these additions. She can see that these parts are included in the order, saving time that would be wasted by treating each order as a unique request.

FACILITIES

Most of the time a director doesn't choose the physical characteristics of his rooms—he inherits them and either suffers with or enjoys them. Knowledge of the ideal specifications for rehearsal and practice rooms is important, if only to determine how far from the ideal one's own conditions are. The MENC has published an excellent pamphlet on the subject, covering the number of cubic feet per person, types of acoustical treatment, the height of ceilings, and the use of windows.[2] When a new rehearsal room is being built or an old one remodeled, the director can get the most accurate information about acoustical materials and their sound-absorbing qualities from a basic acoustics book. Architects are not always well informed on the subject of acoustics, so the director should know what he wants by doing some research himself.

[2] Harold Geerdes. *Music Facilities: Building, Equipping, and Renovating*. (Reston, VA: Music Educators National Conference, 1987).

If the rehearsal room is not carpeted, it may be possible to solicit used carpet from someone in the band parents' organization. A parent who is a banker or businessperson may be aware of a store or office that is being remodeled. A carpeted floor is among the most essential acoustical treatments of a rehearsal room. Air conditioning is also frequently a necessity so that doors and windows can be kept shut to prevent rehearsals from disrupting other classes.

Permanent risers have both advantages and disadvantages. The disadvantages are chiefly that they severely limit flexibility of seating, and they make coping with changes in the size of a section difficult. They also discourage experimentation with seating effects. In addition, they make small-ensemble arrangement troublesome because they are usually not wide enough to permit the V- or U-shaped seating of quartets and sextets. In rooms without satisfactory ventilation, players on the top risers may be playing in a tropical climate, adding to intonation problems and encouraging sleepiness. On the other hand, permanent risers are an asset for two reasons. First, they make it possible for both students and the director to see and be heard. If risers are used in concert, it makes good sense to use them in rehearsal. Second, they discourage use of the room for meetings and academic classes scheduled during the room's free hours. Since such meetings can leave the room in a state of chaos, this advantage should be given serious consideration. Risers should have an approximate 6-inch increment and be deep enough to get all the necessary equipment and players on, allowing for breathing space.

Most instrumental music rooms are built with adjoining practice rooms. These are costly to build and must be used if their expense is to be justified. Not many students find it possible to practice during the day, and when the practice rooms are not used they tend to become storage places and eyesores. Administrators should be aware before having practice rooms built that they will be used largely before and after school rather than during the school day. If other classrooms can be made available for small groups and for individual practice before and after school, one should consider seriously whether practice rooms are really advisable. The advent of programmed learning such as the Temporal Acuity Products rhythm and pitch machines and computer-assisted instruction may increase the opportunity for individual study and the use of practice rooms during the school day.

Other rooms included in the ideal situation are a director's office with a soundproof glass wall into the rehearsal room; a library with sorting racks, work tables, and files; a small repair shop; and a uniform storage room. Others could be added, but these offer the most in efficiency and usefulness.

Equipment for the rehearsal room can be extensive and expensive. It can also be excessive if not properly used. Among the articles that have been useful to most instrumental groups are the following:

1. Numbered chairs with a straight back and with metal or rubber tips on the legs.
2. A sufficient number of music stands of the pneumatic type.
3. An electronic tuner.
4. A quality tape recorder with high-grade microphone.
5. A high-fidelity stereo system.
6. Music cabinets, storage, reed supplies, basic repair items, and other daily needs such as valve oil, pencil sharpeners, and a metronome.
7. A movable chalkboard or dryboard and a bulletin board.
8. Stands for large instruments such as sousaphones and baritone saxophones. Lockers or cabinets for all instruments, including the percussion.
9. A piano.
10. Indirect lighting or lighting from the rear.

PUBLIC RELATIONS

Publicity through newspapers, radio, and television is an important way of strengthening community relations. Any band or orchestra activity is of potential interest if the announcement is attractively written and accompanied by well-chosen pictures; for example, activities of parents, groups, trips, fund or membership drives, work with other departments such as drama or athletics, twirlers, and new instruments or new uniforms. Unique features of the group may furnish material for a story: examples might be rare instruments, an unusual library collection, a musical family with members in the band or orchestra. The director should take the time to submit a short press release on individual band or orchestra students' accomplishments, even if these achievements are not related to the music program. Headlines such as "High School Bandmember Is National Merit Scholar" can do wonders for public relations. Publications designed to help the director with publicity are available.[3]

Press releases should be short and to the point. (Most newspapers like to create their own "catchy" headlines.) Several short paragraphs indicating who, what, when, where, how, and why are all that is needed. Students' names and grade levels should be included.

[3] For example, Kenneth L. Neidig, *Music Director's Complete Handbook of Forms* (West Nyack, NY: Parker Publishing Co., 1973). and Guy S. Kinney, *High School Music Teacher's Handbook: A Complete Guide to Managing and Teaching the Total Music Program* (West Nyack, NY: Parker Publishing Co., 1987).

Some directors shy away from writing press releases because of the time involved and because the director believes that he does not write well. This task, however, cannot be ignored. Publicity is required to make the community aware of these activities, especially those citizens who do not have students in school.[4]

One of the most important benefits of good public relations is to prevent administrators or boards of education from neglecting or overlooking the instrumental music program in their attempts to conduct the school's business. If the public is unaware of the numerous and varied activities of the instrumental music program, boards of education are more likely to take funds from this "expensive" activity to fund other areas.

When photograph sessions are scheduled, everything should be ready when the photographer arrives—including the human elements. This is especially important for large groups. Many a photographer has wasted her time and lost her temper waiting for the orchestra or band to collect itself. It is better to spend group time beforehand than to waste a paid professional's time. The position of every chair on the stage should be marked in advance, and the players in their positions. This seating arrangement should enable every player to be seen. Chairs should be placed so that proud parents can spot their child playing third sax or fourth horn.

Optional Activities

The teacher should consider the values of a scrapbook. If well kept, scrapbooks give pleasure to alumni, present players, and interested townspeople as well as material for publicity.

An up-to-date list of the alumni of the organization can be useful. To have alumni appear at concerts and rehearsals sparks interest, provides for publicity, and heightens the prestige of the organization.

Displays in store windows, for concerts and for recruitment, arouse interest. The displays—usually posters, but even a mannequin dressed in a high school band uniform—must look good. When the director has posters he is proud of, he should assign responsible students to ask permission of merchants to place them in their windows. Of equal importance is poster pickup after the event.

RELATIONSHIP WITH PARENTS

The relationship with parents can be the difference between a smooth or a thorny path for any teacher. A director cannot handle all of the details of trips and performances; he needs either a parents' organization or the

[4]Guy S. Kinney, ibid, 71.

cooperation of individual parents. Contests, trips, housing, food, festivals, games, fund raisers, the problems of uniforms, instruments, stands, and music, to say nothing of props for half-time shows are part of a director's everyday work. The best ways to gain parental cooperation are (1) to earn the admiration of the students and (2) to keep parents well informed.

Policies and procedures governing uniforms, practice, attendance, regulations on instruments, grades, point systems, merits and demerits, and rental fees, as well as a brief statement of objectives, will be welcomed by parents. For each performance, the parents should be informed what time the student is to arrive and at what place, what uniform is required, how long the performance will last, and whether the public is welcome. Parents should not simply be invited to attend a rehearsal—they should be requested to come. Their attendance is an opportunity for them to see what the director does in a class period.

Music parents' clubs are not essential; they are helpful except for an occasional one that definitely belongs in the "how-to-waste-time" category. Parents' organizations must always have a project. Parents' clubs can be actively involved in recruiting, in organizing trips, and in publicity and money raising, but they *should not* expect to have a part in formulating objectives or running the program.

Though there are obviously views to the contrary, money raising and fee collecting for special events should not be necessary. Students should not be expected to pay extra fees for contests or for all-state festivals of any sort. If these events are educational experiences, the school should be willing to underwrite them; if they are less educational than staying in school, then students should not be allowed to go.

When uniforms or expensive instruments cannot be purchased out of school funds, or when a trip is deemed worthy of the time expenditure but not the money expenditure, the music parents' group can be used to organize money-raising projects.

RELATIONSHIP WITH STUDENTS

First and last, the success of the director's program depends on student response. While his ability as a musician and teacher is decisive for the achievement of his objectives, he must be able to enlist students and keep them interested before he can ever teach these objectives. One of the most difficult tasks necessary to accomplish this is realizing that the band or orchestra is not the most important thing in his students' lives—it often is in his life, but it is his job, not theirs.

The basic relationship between the director and the band or orchestra should be the typical student–teacher relationship. Since the high school band or orchestra director has the same students for four years (and possibly in the elementary or middle school before that) and extra time is spent in working/rehearsing, most directors develop special relationships with students. This relationship must be all business whenever the director is on the podium but can be more relaxed when off. Directors should take an interest in students' activities outside of band or orchestra, but listening to students talk negatively about other teachers or other students is never appropriate. The director should *never* speak negatively about other students, parents, administrators, or other programs. He should be careful to say only those things that he does not mind having spread throughout the entire community. Every director must strive to give the same attention to every student, even to those with little promise—acceptance is important to adolescents and lack of acceptance is the most common and most serious threat to a student's self-esteem.

And remember, respect is a bit like smiling: When one gives a little, the recipient reciprocates.

Student Responsibility

One cautionary note: When student responsibility and efficiency are emphasized, a complex, military structure can evolve, with superiors and subordinates, fines and prizes, demerits and awards, and rules and regulations for everything. Students are extremists about most things, and if sold on an idea they will carry it as far as the director allows. He must know, then, just what kind of atmosphere he wants, and patiently but firmly work for control where he wants it and relaxation where he wants it.

If there seem to be only a few rules that the teacher wants enforced, a single page containing instructions may be sufficient. These instructions should be given to every student so that no pleas of ignorance are possible. Most instrumental teachers will find, however, that much more than a single page is necessary, in which case a band or orchestra booklet is excellent.

Rather than a list of rules, the booklet should contain procedures. For example, behavior at a football game should be a procedure ("this is what we do") rather than a list of "don'ts." Behavior at games is a good illustration of what can be included. What are the procedures for getting up to buy food and soft drinks? Students do not always appear to be in their right minds at athletic events; the quiet, hard-working oboe player in the concert band goes wild with her cymbals at a basketball game. Some written procedures may help to curb her enthusiasm and outline what is expected.

The delineation of the authority of the officers is another important area that should be clearly spelled out so that they and the rest of the students know the limits of their authority. Doing so saves many complaints such as "John fined me five cents last night for doing . . . and I was really only . . . just like you told us to!" If the delineation of authority is not clear, the director becomes a full-time adjudicator rather than one preparing for adjudication.

Travel

Travel is the student's great delight and the bane of the teacher's existence. Even for a short trip to a neighboring town for a game, there are so many things to load and unload that a check sheet of some sort is standard equipment. For a long trip there are additional considerations, such as meals, lodging, chaperones, loading crews, and schedules, to mention a few.

Lost among the many details may be the need to attend to adequate insurance coverage in case of accident, plus the need to have full administrative approval of every detail so that the teacher himself will not be liable. If a student rides across town with the teacher to pick up an instrument from a repair shop, the director and the school are assuming responsibility. All types of releases have been required of parents by school districts in the case of travel; however, no release will stand up if some negligence can be proved. Recent court decisions have found schools liable to the extent that the legislators in many states are passing laws to cap the amount of liability. The teacher cannot be too careful nor overinform the administration.

Students should never be allowed to come to an event by school transportation and return home by other means. The only exceptions to this should be if they are going home with parents, and this only when the proper release has been executed before the trip begins. Even if the student's parents have given him permission to ride home with someone else, he should not be allowed to do so. The best policy is to allow no exceptions to the rule, even to parents. Always use a school bus (even if it may be only partially filled) or commercial transportation, so that all students come and go by the same means.

RELATIONSHIP WITH ADMINISTRATORS AND COLLEAGUES

One element in developing and maintaining a good relationship with the school principal is that every act discussed in the preceding sections should be cleared with the principal's office. In matters of curriculum, discipline, budget, scheduling, and giving permission, most authority for important decisions lies with the principal. Simply stated, it is virtually impossible for the instrumental music teacher to provide too much information to the principal. The principal should be kept well informed of every aspect of the total program.

The first point to clarify is the amount of school time allowed for extra appearances such as pep rallies, team send-offs, and similar spontaneous outbursts of goodwill toward defenders of the school's honor. Administrators must be informed that when a pep rally is scheduled for the last fifteen minutes of the school day, the band must be called out fifteen or twenty minutes earlier so that equipment can be readied and some coordination with the cheerleaders can take place. In addition, the band and orchestra director should send memoranda to other teachers giving as much advance notice as possible of any activity for which students must miss class, and closer to the event reminders should be sent out.

Rehearsals must end on time. Occasionally band directors are tempted to do "one more run-through" during marching season. When students are late for class, relations are damaged.

Among the more important items about which to keep the administration informed on a yearly basis are objectives, breakdown of instrumental enrollment by beginning, intermediate, and advanced students; use of school-owned instruments; equipment inventories; a schedule of the year's programs; musical activities; and a financial report. Other items that make a good impression on the administration include publicity releases, contest–festival reports, number of appearances of all large and small groups and soloists, results of group election of officers, and any compliments on the music program—particularly if they come from some official source. Administrators may also be interested in the drop-out rates in the music program, class sizes, and the percentage of the total student body participating in instrumental music. When superintendents and school boards know the actual number of students an instrumental teacher contacts each week, they may become more sympathetic to a balanced program.

REFERENCES

Butts, Carrol M. *Troubleshooting the High School Band: How to Detect and Correct Common and Uncommon Performance Problems.* West Nyack, NY: Parker Publishing Co., 1981.

Ernst, Karl and Charles Gary. *Music in General Education.* Washington, DC: Music Educators National Conference, 1965.

Garofalo, Robert. *Blueprint for Band.* Portland, ME: J. Weston Walch, 1976.

Geerdes, Harold. *Music Facilities: Building, Equipping, and Renovating.* Reston VA: Music Educators National Conference, 1987.

Glesso, Neal E., William B. McBride, and George H. Wilson. *Secondary School Music.* Englewood Cliffs, NJ: Prentice-Hall, Inc., 1970.

Guidelines in Music Education: Supportive Requirements. Washington, D.C.: Music Educators National Conference, 1983.

HOFFER, CHARLES R. *Teaching Music in the Secondary Schools.* Belmont, CA: Wadsworth Publishing Co., 1964.

HOFSTETTER, FRED T. *Computer Literacy for Musicians.* Englewood Cliffs, NJ: Prentice-Hall, Inc., 1988.

HOUSE, ROBERT W. *Instrumental Music for Today's Schools.* Englewood Cliffs, NJ: Prentice-Hall, Inc., 1965.

INTRAVAIA, LAWRENCE J. *Building a Superior School Band Library.* West Nyack, NY: Parker Publishing Co., 1972.

KINNEY, GUY S. *Complete Guide to Teaching Small Instrumental Groups in the High School.* West Nyack, NY: Parker Publishing Co., 1980.

_____. *High School Music Teacher's Handbook: A Complete Guide to Managing and Teaching the Total Music Program.* West Nyack, NY: Parker Publishing Co., 1987.

KINNEY, RICHARD. *Handbook of Rehearsal Techniques for the High School Band.* West Nyack, NY: Parker Publishing Co., 1976.

KUHN, WOLFGANG E. *Instrumental Music.* (2nd ed.) Boston: Allyn and Bacon, Inc., 1970.

LABUTA, JOSEPH A. *Teaching Musicianship in the High School Band.* West Nyack, NY: Parker Publishing Co., 1971.

NEIDIG, KENNETH L. *Music Director's Complete Handbook of Forms.* West Nyack, NY: Parker Publishing Co., 1973.

OTTO, RICHARD A. *Effective Methods of Building the High School Band.* West Nyack, NY: Parker Publishing Co., 1971.

ROBINSON, WILLIAM C. *The Complete School Band Program.* West Nyack, NY: Parker Publishing Co., 1975.

SNYDER, KEITH D. *School Music Administration and Supervision.* (2nd ed.) Boston: Allyn and Bacon, Inc., 1965.

WEERTS, RICHARD. *Developing Individual Skills for the High School Band.* West Nyack, NY: Parker Publishing Co., 1972.

6

Recruiting and Scheduling

Recruiting students for the instrumental program is the responsibility of all instrumental teachers, not a task assigned solely to the elementary school teacher. To attract new members, the instrumental staff should cooperate to: (1) provide a successful program; (2) develop positive relations with other teachers, administrators, the community, and parents of present students; (3) meet the needs of the local community and the objectives of music education; and (4) work hard in a planned recruiting program.

Recruiting styles vary with the personality and preferences of the teacher. Visiting grade school classes, appearing at grade school assemblies to talk about the music program, or performing for the youngsters may be effective for one teacher, while another has more success when high school students talk, perform, and demonstrate. A third scenario might find last year's beginners involved in the demonstrations.

Letters to parents, summer music programs, instrument displays in elementary school buildings, advertisements in local music stores, enthusiasm created by visiting bands or orchestras, news of high school group activities (e.g. tours and honors), involvement with arts advocacy groups, publicity of individual and group achievements—all are legitimate ways of capturing interest.

Making the instrumental program visible is important. Many activities compete for students' time, including sports, church and clubs, required and elective school subjects, MTV, computer games and goofing off. Marketing is a part of even the youngest students' lives, and they expect to be given choices and to be persuaded. If a student with low initial interest and high talent is recruited, he is likely to remain in the program throughout school. If recruiting is successful, and a high demand for membership in the performing ensembles is developed, instrumental music will have administrative and community support and will not be affected by the vagaries of financial and curricular support.

PRELIMINARIES TO SUCCESSFUL RECRUITING

First, recruiting is not just a one-shot (one week or one month) event that takes place in fourth grade. Recruiting is a year-long endeavor and can be effective at any age level. Students' interests, abilities, and sometimes aptitudes change rapidly. Second, recruiting requires energy and an enthusiastic approach to music education. Enthusiasm is contagious; excitement about what is being accomplished in the instrumental music class influences students' attitudes and provides motivation. Third, the maxim "Nothing succeeds like success" is true in instrumental music as well as business. Peer acceptance of the program is important; having large numbers of students participating encourages other students to enroll. When one has recruited half the students in a classroom, getting another 25 percent may be almost automatic.

WHEN TO BEGIN

Students in elementary schools should be allowed to begin studying a musical instrument at any time during the school year. Most elementary music programs have a "pull-out" arrangement so that students leave their regular class to participate in instrumental music instruction, allowing for flexibility of initiating study. The research of Ed Kvet and James Littlefield indicates that being excused from class has no negative impact on a student's academic course work.[1] Even reading class need not be sacred; reading is taught in small groups and thus may be one of the classes least impacted by a student's being absent for twenty or thirty minutes. On the other hand, an established beginning time is also effective; group psychology works with youngsters following an effective recruiting program, and most students will start around the same time. Instrumental rental pro-

---

[1] Kvet, Ed, *Excusing Elementary Students from Regular Classroom Activities for the Study of Instrumental Music: The Effect on 6th grade Reading, Language, and Math Achievement.* Unpublished DME dissertation, Cincinnati, U of Cincinnati; 1982. Also, Littlefield, James, *An Analysis of the Relationship between Academic Achievement and the Practice of Excusing Elementary Students from Class for the Study of Instrumental Music.* Unpublished thesis for the Specialist in Music Education degree: Atlanta, Georgia State U., 1986.

grams and teacher scheduling make it advantageous to have established starting dates for classes.

There is no best time of the year to begin instrumental music instruction. State aid may be available to pay for the teacher's summer salary, and though family vacations will interrupt, third, fourth, and fifth graders often have time for practice and for lessons in the summer. Fall is an equally good time to begin classes, as rental periods end about Christmas, an appropriate time for a first public appearance and for the purchase of the rental instrument as a cherished Christmas present.

Recruiting intensifies as students enter third grade. Students can successfully begin instruction on most instruments when eight or nine years of age, and most are ready by fourth grade, although a few may not catch the fever or be sufficiently mature until fifth grade. The 1989 American Music Conference data indicate that 79 percent of Americans began their study of instrumental music when they were between the ages of six and eleven.[2] Piano teachers and Suzuki specialists have demonstrated that preschoolers can successfully participate in beginning instrumental music classes. With proper parental support, it is almost never too early to begin the study of music. When the physiological and psychological attributes of a child indicate readiness, let instruction begin.

RECRUITMENT DEMONSTRATION

The instruments available for starting wind and string players should be brought to an evening meeting to which parents and students are invited. This event should be preceded by plenty of hype and classroom discussion. Top players from the high school band should be at the meeting. These students, dressed in their concert or marching uniforms, can demonstrate the instruments and help with other details.

Time should be allocated for students and parents to ask questions of both the director and the high school students. Parents are part of the decision-making process, and parent and child join the program together. A positive impression can be made on prospective band parents by soliciting parents of students from the high school ensemble for assistance: setting up chairs for the audience, displaying the various instruments, making coffee, and most of all, being available to answer questions from the experience of having a child in band or orchestra for four to six years.

Registration forms for parents to take home, complete, and return within the next week should be provided at the meeting. Registration forms should be accompanied by complete information about the instru-

[2]*Music USA, 89,* American Music Conference, Chicago 1989.

mental program: costs, obligation, grading practices, and rules, regulations, and expectations.

The most burdensome decision concerning recruiting meetings for parents is whether to ask retail instrument companies to send representatives or to have the music teacher provide all the information concerning instruments. This controversy has resulted in numerous lawsuits in at least ten states since 1975.[3] In most cases, the courts have ruled that the band director has the prerogative to choose a music company for the demonstration if invitations are extended to all interested companies and selection is based on factors such as quality of instruments sold and rented, prices, inventory of the companies, repair services, whether or not the companies pick up and deliver instruments for repair, as well as assistance offered by each company. Being involved, together with your principal and/or superintendent, in a lawsuit can ruin a perfectly good day. If there are no space restrictions, allow all interested companies to participate.

TESTING

Testing a student for musical aptitude is an important part of recruiting. The no-testing approach is a no-recruiting approach. If the student and the parents are given evidence that the student has sufficient talent to make the effort worthwhile, these students will likely enroll. Instrument manufacturers learned the importance of aptitude testing some fifty years ago, and most of the manufacturers publish their own talent test. All of these tests are limited in their ability to determine musical aptitude, but most are based on common sense and are preferable to no test at all.

INSTRUCTION

In many elementary schools, the instrumental music teacher instructs the general music class on songflutes or recorders for a month or six weeks. The results of this instruction are helpful in recruiting: some basic experience is given to students, and the teacher has the opportunity to identify potential talent. Songflutes and recorders are useful for teaching basic music reading skills, developing finger dexterity and coordination, and generating interest. A final recorder concert may be part of demonstration night for the parents or may be used as a separate recruiting event. The disadvantage to teaching the six-week program is the time involved for the

[3] *Greer Music House* v. *McFadyen Music Company and Florence Co. Schools* (South Carolina), *Laporte* v. *Escanaba Area Public Schools* (Michigan), *Ken Stanton Music* v. *Board of Education City of Rome* (Georgia), *Davidson-Nicholson* v. *Pound* (Georgia), *Dickinson* v. *Cunningham* (Alabama), and *Leeper* v. *State* (Tennessee).

instrumental teacher, whose other duties may be in the middle school or high school.

A truthful and honest recruiting program is the only way to the long-term success of a music program. Any misconception of instrumental music as all fun, trips, uniforms, concerts, and immediate success will bring negative reactions as soon as the child is into the program. The recruiting program is directly affected by how well the teacher relates to the members of the band or orchestra; how well she deals with the parents; how well she works with the administrators at the various levels of the school hierarchy; how well she instills in students, parents, and administrators a feeling of pride, accomplishment, and *value* with regard to the instrumental program; and how well she articulates the objectives and benefits of the program.

RETAINING MEMBERS

Retention of membership is, of course, a broader issue than recruiting. A high attrition rate is always a negative reflection on the instrumental music program. While students should be provided every opportunity to join the program, it is important that students *and* their parents understand that instrumental music is a long-term commitment. Music classes can and should be fun, but instrumental music should not be treated as a home video game to be shelved as soon as the student becomes the least bit bored. Every music program will have times when at least some of the students will be bored, and virtually every student will at one time or another encounter frustration. Parents and students must be convinced that frustration is part of life and that the instrumental music program can help students in an "extramusical" way, teaching students to deal with the less glamorous as well as the glamorous periods of any experience. A high dropout rate is a major concern of the music industry, school officials, and music teachers, as expensive, unused horns in a community contribute negatively to recruiting. Long lists of reasons for dropouts have been prepared by industry and graduate students, and each begins with loss of interest as the primary reason for a student dropping out. Use of the ideas in this book and showing concern for every student are the most effective methods of retaining students in the program.

SCHEDULING

One of the most important administrative tasks facing the instrumental music teacher is scheduling. The task is not only important but also difficult due to the limitations imposed by available facilities, the size of the instrumental staff, and demands on student and faculty time. The time factor has been a major concern in virtually every school system since 1985, when a strong emphasis on basic education began to be felt in all fifty states. The resulting curriculum changes have limited students' electives, have caused a greater concern for academics (a positive development and one that should enhance instrumental music rather than threaten it), and in many instances have brought about cutbacks of music staff in order to hire faculty in new or expanded areas of the curriculum.

The problems and suggestions presented in this chapter are organized in terms of elementary, middle, and high school programs. Because much of the schedule depends on that of the high school instrumental music teacher, the three levels will be discussed in reverse order, beginning with the high school.

HIGH SCHOOL

Curriculum reform in the secondary schools has had a major impact on instrumental music programs. The "back-to-basics" and "arts are basic" movements often lump all the fine arts together, making little distinction among them. The practice has become to require students to take at least one course in the arts, but to leave little room for electives that would enable students to participate in band or orchestra on a continuing basis.

The highest dropout rate among band and orchestra students occurs when they transfer schools. There is a natural concern for the unknown: Will the next grade or school be more difficult? Will I still have time to practice? Increased high school graduation requirements and the same number of periods in the school day make decisions more difficult. Pressure on teachers to improve education has often resulted in more homework and higher standards.

The recently expanded requirements and the focus on academic excellence need not damage the instrumental program. Parents and students will not readily abandon programs of proven worth and high visibility. Successful band and orchestra directors have long realized that the quality of time spent in rehearsals is more important than the quantity of time. High school music teachers should use the increased focus on excellence to strengthen their position, as band and orchestra along with athletics are the only courses that truly challenge all students. No known criticism of the instrumental music program has been raised during the reform movement except in those few communities where the teachers were not earning their pay. In states that mandate a year of the arts for high school graduation, careful planning and negotiating (and *initiative*) on the part of the instrumental music teacher may result in additional staffing rather than cutbacks.

One basic fact remains—as long as there are football and basketball in high schools, there will be high school bands. And as long as there are bands in high schools, there will be (99 percent of the time) some way to schedule band.

Summer Programs/Private Lessons

In addition to summer high school marching camps, school systems schedule six-week summer programs for beginning and younger students, grouping them by ability level or by instrument. Summer music camps available on college campuses provide wonderful experiences for high school and middle school players. These programs may provide students with the initial encounters with music theory and history. Students can benefit from intensive private lessons in the summer and year-round.

Honors Courses

One trend growing out of the educational reforms of the 1980s has been honors or advanced placement courses. The argument is made that some courses based on their greater difficulty or greater requirement of time and preparation are deserving of more units of credit than other courses. In school systems that use some form of course weighting, the ambitious and bright students may feel they have no choice but to drop out of music in order to attain the highest grade point average. Students can, and do, drop band or choir in order to take study hall and improve their overall GPA (since an A in music can count 3.5 quality points while study hall does not assign a grade). Countering negative feelings toward scheduling and grading practices requires both initiative and patience.

One plan that has met with success is the use of several course numbers for each grade level of the high school band or orchestra. Under this system, students are allowed to sign up for band as a "traditional-type" band class and receive fewer quality points, or they may register for band under a different course number requiring additional work such as solo preparation, small-ensemble participation, participation in regional bands, the completion of computer courses in music theory, term papers, and other options associated with a comprehensive program. The band is the same under both course numbers, but the "courses" and weight of the grade are different.

Avoiding Conflicts

Instrumental music teachers at the high school level need to ensure that scheduling of the large ensemble(s) causes the fewest possible conflicts. High school bands and orchestras are among the few completely cross-sectional classes in the school, including students from ninth through twelfth grade. Scheduling requires convincing the principal or guidance counselors that completely cross-sectional classes should be scheduled first, partial cross-sectional classes (those with only one section) should be scheduled second (e.g., the school newspaper or third-year German), and the remaining classes scheduled around these. The instrumental music teacher needs to present his case in such a way as to make clear that band or orchestra is not the most important class but simply is cross-sectional and thus requires being scheduled first.

The principal must be aware of the need for students to remain in the program each year and not be forced to drop music for an academic requirement. She should understand that it takes time to establish a solid and well-rounded program and that the older, more experienced students are perhaps just reaching a level of musical understanding that enables them to most benefit from the program. Those persons who do the scheduling must understand that both student progress and the instrumental program are in jeopardy when students drop in and out of the program for a quarter, semester, or year.[4]

Elective Courses

As the course requirements for high school graduation become more stringent and student schedules more difficult to manage, schools are adding periods to the school day. The extra period may be a zero period beginning an hour or so before school technically begins or an additional period after school. An extra period may be created by lengthening the school day by thirty minutes and borrowing five minutes from each of the regular periods.

Each scheduling option depends on a number of factors. When a band program is fairly small, it may be advantageous to schedule a single band class with a separate class for beginners. With a band program that has a strong tradition of concert playing and less emphasis on marching, two separate bands may be scheduled during the day, with the marching band comprised of volunteers or auditioned personnel from both groups meeting two afternoons each week.

The quickest way to improve the top band at a high school is to start a second band. The improvement is due to the resulting pride, practice, esprit de corps, and general attitude as much as to the grouping together of the most proficient players. By the same token, the second band is improved by the existence of a third, beginner/remedial band.

The purpose of a second band is to prevent the weaker players from

---

[4]Guy S. Kinney, *High School Music Teacher's Handbook: A Complete Guide to Managing and Teaching the Total Music Program,* (West Nyack, NY: Parker Publishing Co., 1987), 35–41.

becoming buried in the third clarinet section or relegated to a four-year tenure on third cornet. In the second band, students who would normally find themselves at the bottom of a section play first parts and provide leadership.[5]

One final point about scheduling a first and second band: Students, parents, and administrators should know whether students will be selected according to an audition process by which students scoring below a set standard will be assigned to the second band, or if standards will vary according to instrumentation. Scheduling two different bands during concert season usually requires some type of double standard; that is, a weaker student may qualify for symphonic band if he plays bassoon but not if he plays flute. This practice has only limited validity. Directors should avoid placing unreasonable demands on weaker players simply because the instrument is needed in the ensemble.

Small Ensembles

One of the most effective components of the high school instrumental music program is small ensembles that rehearse on a regular basis before or after school. Small ensembles place more technical and musical demands on individual students than do large ensembles in which players can become swallowed up, and they promote better music-reading skills.[6]

The instrumental music teacher should assign students to at least one ensemble and carefully avoid assigning the best players to more than two. Students should be grouped according to ability levels. For example, first-chair players may form a woodwind quintet that can perform far more challenging music than is possible in duets and trios. Players of average ability and those sitting toward the bottom of sections can benefit greatly from small ensembles in which each player covers a single part and is unable to depend on the better players. Allowing students to form their own groups can cause problems, as the groups may become cliquish.

Mixed small ensembles have a distinct advantage over ensembles of like instruments because through them players can generally learn more about balance and blend. Furthermore, a duet, trio, or quartet of like instruments offers a lead part and one or more accompanying parts, and students can still be followers. In a small ensemble, performance errors and

---

[5] Band directors differ over whether or not the second band should be expected to perform with the same standards as the top band. Many directors believe that a second group cannot be expected to play with as good tone quality, as accurate intonation, or as cleanly as the top band because the players are weaker and there are no outstanding players for them to emulate. However, because the second band plays less demanding music, there is more time to devote to tone production and intonation; the only justification for a lower-quality ensemble sound is incomplete instrumentation.

[6] Guy S. Kinney, *Complete Guide to Teaching Small Instrumental Groups in the High School*, (West Nyack, NY: Parker Publishing Co., 1980), 21.

intonation problems are immediately apparent, and aural skills are developed more quickly. Also, it is easier for students to perceive and comprehend style when only four to eight players are trying to achieve a uniform style. Players can thus quickly become sensitive to the necessity of uniform interpretation (e.g., articulation, nuances, and tempo). In a large band, three or more players on the same part often results in students not listening.

Extra Rehearsals

Extra rehearsals are often required. Sectionals, small ensembles, and individual lessons are almost always scheduled as extra rehearsals. With proper planning, extra rehearsals can be kept to a minimum. When they are scheduled, it is essential that they end on time. Ending the rehearsal early can cause parents to be concerned, while holding students beyond the scheduled time causes inconvenience and irritation. Remember that when extra rehearsals are called, parents are affected as well as students.

MIDDLE SCHOOL

A good band or orchestra program is based on continuity between schools; hence, the quality of middle school programs can make or break the high school program. The most formative instruction takes place at the middle school level. Here, attitudes toward band and orchestra are shaped, and parents' perceptions and expectations of the instrumental music program are formed.

Advanced Band and Orchestra

Advanced ensembles should be scheduled on a daily basis. The middle school director will not need to hold extra rehearsals, except when a combined honors group is formed from the best students in the several grades. Block scheduling in the middle school is a major problem solvable by inserting an extra "block" into the school day for instrumental music and similar subjects or insuring that the schedule contains a school period for co-curricular subjects that remains throughout the school year.

Many students in middle school develop a close relationship with their band and orchestra director. When she takes an active part in the high school program, security is provided for students making the transition to high school. The middle school director should send a form home to parents encouraging enrollment in the high school instrumental program and a sample schedule of courses students can take that combines the college preparatory program with music. These forms should be signed and showed to the high school principal to encourage proper scheduling.

ELEMENTARY SCHOOL

The best time to start instrumental music is in the fourth grade. Students beginning instruction during middle school immediately encounter many new and varied aspects of life, class-to-class movement after each period, interest in the opposite sex, use of makeup, body consciousness, and the other phenomena that accompany puberty. Life in elementary school is far more relaxed.

Starting instrumental music in the third or fourth grade gives students ensemble experiences to look forward to during their final year at the elementary school. Instrumental music classes at the elementary level are usually a pull-out program; students leave their regular classes, often on a rotating schedule, to attend a group instrumental music class.

Ideally, beginners in elementary school would all receive private lessons. The second-best situation is for like instruments to be scheduled together.[7] The next most advantageous scheduling, and one of the most frequent, is grouping beginners by families—woodwinds, brass, strings, and percussion.

HONOR/COMMUNITY ENSEMBLES

An all-city band or orchestra composed of the best players from each of several groups rehearsing once a week on a regular basis throughout the school year offers many rewards. Such honor groups provide experience with more complete instrumentation and more challenging music than any one school can offer, as well as constituting an additional source of pride for the community. The school conductors who provide students for the group should take turns conducting, as the group can provide an inspiration for teachers as well as the students.

Honor groups provide additional motivation for string players, since string programs have traditionally been smaller than band programs. The increased learning attained in such groups will enhance each band and orchestra program.

---

[7]Some authorities extol the virtues of this type of schedule to the extent that one meeting a week is sufficient for beginners if the trumpets, for example, are kept together. Carrol M. Butts, *Troubleshooting the High School Band: How to Detect and Correct Common and Uncommon Problems* (West Nyack, NY: Parker Publishing Co., 1981).

REFERENCES

ERNST, KARL, and CHARLES GARY. *Music in General Education*. Washington: Music Educators National Conference, 1965.

FROSETH, JAMES. *NABIM Recruiting Manual*. Chicago: G.I.A. Publications, 1974.

GAROFALO, ROBERT. *Blueprint for Band*. Portland, ME: J. Weston Walch, 1976.

_____. *A Guide to Successful Recruiting*. Durham, NC: Pearson Music Company (n.d.).

KINNEY, GUY S. *Complete Guide to Teaching Small Instrumental Groups in the High School*, West Nyack, NY: Parker Publishing Co., 1980.

_____. *High School Music Teacher's Handbook: A Complete Guide to Managing and Teaching the Total Music Program*. West Nyack, NY: Parker Publishing Co., 1987.

KLOTMAN, ROBERT. *Scheduling Music Classes*. Washington, D.C.: Music Educators National Conference, 1968.

Music Achievement Council. *A Recruiting Guide For Band and Orchestra Directors*. Carlsbad, CA: The Music Achievement Council, 1986.

WITT, ANNE C. *Recruiting for the School Orchestra*. Elkhart, IN: The Selmer Co., 1984.

7

Rehearsal Techniques

The word *rehearsal* is familiar to musicians. It comes from the Old French word *rehercer*, meaning "to harrow again" (also from which the word *hearse* was eventually derived). Interestingly, one of the definitions of *harrow* is "to torment." A more positive note is that harrowing is, of course, used to prepare the field for seed, part of the process of producing a good crop. However, there are rehearsals that do not harrow in either sense. They are satisfying enough to the student but are not effective for learning; among those are the ones that drill endlessly on a few contest selections, that simply entertain the students, and that prepare to entertain the public. In this chapter, which examines the rehearsal as preparation, consideration will be given to:

1. Rehearsal planning and score preparation
2. Intonation
3. Tone, balance, blend, and instrumentation
4. Tempo, meter, and rhythm
5. Phrasing
6. Attacks and releases
7. Musical independence
8. Interpretation
9. Selection of music for concerts
10. Classroom management

The rehearsal depends on the conductor. Ideally, she has the following qualifications. First, as a good musician who reads the full score with an understanding of transpositions and terms, she knows how to get at the subtleties of the music once the major technical problems have been over-come. Second, as a good teacher, she is acquainted with bowing, fingering, and the unique problems of each instrument. Third, as a good conductor, she can use the baton to help her group understand what she wants from them. Fourth, as a receptive human being, her mannerisms, appearance, and attitudes do not alienate her from students. She must be receptive to the mood of the group and be able to use that mood, she must be able to establish a rapport with most of her students, and she must understand the importance of the group's sense of acomplishment.

PLANNING THE REHEARSAL

Many successful directors maintain a master schedule. Starting with con-certs and working backward it is possible to outline the rehearsal schedule for every day of the school year. One can indicate which piece(s) will be rehearsed each day—match warm-ups and technical drills with these pieces and include sight reading selections and time for listening activities.

Most teachers can sight read the score faster than the students and can get by with selecting a piece of music at the last minute to fill some rehearsal time. Alternatively, the period can be spent drilling on a difficult number from start to finish. But the effective rehearsal will be planned to include a variety of activities selected with a *goal in mind*. With good planning, the teacher can include in one rehearsal period some sight reading, technical drill, form and style recognition, and intensive work on one or two concert numbers, with a few minutes for "fun music," old favorites, or a listening period.

The primary work of the band or orchestra director takes place before stepping onto the podium. If the director waits to learn the score in rehearsal, she wastes time. Because a large part of the rehearsal is devoted to correcting errors, knowing the score is essential.

Rehearsal time is a precious commodity. To use the time most effec-tively, the director must (1) plan each rehearsal and (2) establish a routine. The routine includes any necessary preparation of the rehearsal room (setting up chairs, distributing folders, turning on the appropriate lights, etc.) and the routine for the rehearsal itself, announcements, warm-up (including individual warm-ups), technical drill, working on concert music (the primary portion of the rehearsal), sight reading, and playing through previously prepared music (old favorites) or a listening activity.

Administrative tasks are also part of the routine: making announce-ments, checking attendance, having students get their music in order, and other tasks. The music teacher can waste copious amounts of rehearsal time in administrative tasks. It is far more efficient to make only the most essential announcements (that is, reminders of the most immediate activities) and communicate other items by a bulletin board and a large calendar. A minute or two of each rehearsal should suffice to remind students of activities for that day and week.

The attendance roster can be checked by the band or orchestra secretary during the first few minutes of rehearsal. A chalkboard in view of the students should have on it the important announcements for the day and selections for the day's rehearsal. A cabinet or a separate section of bookshelves should be used to store folders and to pass out new music. Students collect their folders and new music as they enter the room. This efficient system depends on planning *before* the rehearsal hour.

The playing portion of the rehearsal should always be directed toward clearly defined objectives as discussed in Chapter 2. The overall purpose of each rehearsal is to develop musicianship, the secondary purpose is to prepare a concert; focusing on the first will make the second much easier.[1]

Because effective use of the rehearsal is dependent on the objectives, these must be reasonable. The director must write out a plan and follow it, then after the rehearsal, review and evaluate it. She may realize, for example, the need for more warm-ups or more technical drill based on the results of rehearsing the concert music. Many directors fail to realize that if twenty minutes or so of the rehearsal is spent on concert music, it is perfectly fine to spend it all on one piece (depending on the length of the work and other factors discussed below). These directors believe that the group will become bored if twenty minutes is spent on one four-minute piece, so they rehearse two or three selections. Trying to cover so much ground in so little time is usually *not* efficient use of rehearsal time. Evaluation of each and every rehearsal will and should aid in subsequent rehearsal plans.

Warm-Up

When students enter the bandroom for rehearsal, they should assemble their instruments and begin to warm up individually. Individual warm-ups are important, and all students must be told and reminded how to warm up. Brass players should buzz on the mouthpiece alone, play a few scales in the middle register, and gradually expand the range of these scales downward and upward with frequent resting. Woodwind players should do scales and long tones. This period of several minutes for individual warm-up is also important in focusing students on music, but while it can be a beneficial segment of the rehearsal, it may become a chaotic waste of time and energy. The director should stand by the podium (not *on* the podium

[1] Wolfgang E. Kuhn, *Instrumental Music: Principles and Methods of Instruction.* (Boston: Allyn and Bacon, 1966), 144–48.

until silence is desired) to assist students with their warm-ups and with problems and questions such as requests for music, reeds, and valve oil. (These latter items are necessary for the rehearsal; the band librarian or quartermaster can handle such requests.) The important point is that all students need several minutes of individual warm-up and time to check their equipment, but they must be taught *how* to warm up, tune, and get ready for the rehearsal

After three or four minutes of individual warm-up, the director signals for quiet by stepping onto the podium—this part of the rehearsal routine will also take practice. The essential announcements should be made, then the ensemble warm-up should begin immediately. The purpose of this warm-up is to learn the basics of ensemble playing; it is an extension of the individual warm-ups (to warm up the instruments, embouchure, fingers, tongue, and brain). Chorales provide excellent ensemble warm-up material. Because the notation of chorales is fairly simple, students are able to concentrate on following the conductor and on listening for and adjusting intonation, balance, blend, and tone quality. The best chorales consist of long, sustained chords allowing students to watch the conductor and to listen to the ensemble. Again, students must be told what to listen for and how to interpret the conductor's actions.

Chorales are important teaching tools for attacks and releases, for ear training, for shaping phrases, and for developing flexibility and alertness. The director should instruct students to quickly memorize a phrase and then watch her for tempo and dynamics—the director may conduct at a variety of tempos, with constant changes, and shape the phrase in a variety of ways.

In short, there is little or no reason for students to become bored if chorales are used with imagination. During the five or six minutes of rehearsal time devoted to a chorale, the group may work on only a single phrase, as it is more important that the ensemble perform a single phrase of the chorale well than play through the entire chorale several times. Students must be reminded of the purposes of this portion of the rehearsal: to listen and watch; to concentrate on following the conductor; to work on intonation, balance, tone quality, blend, attacks, releases, control of dynamic levels, and articulation—the stuff of which music is made.

After marching band season, the group may benefit by spending more time, from ten to twelve minutes, on daily chorale playing—not because a marching band should sound different from a symphonic band, but because show music seldom requires the ensemble to follow a conductor to the extent that concert music does. Also, marching band music is seldom as slow as chorales, and slow, controlled ensemble playing is much more demanding than fast, technical passages.

One last point regarding chorales: A chorale with the same key signature as the major portion of the day's rehearsal can simplify the teaching during the rehearsal. For example, if the concert music is primarily on the soft, controlled side, the chorale may be played very softly with control; if the concert music to be rehearsed is primarily loud and full, the chorale can be preparation for that sound; if the rehearsal is to be predominately brass-oriented, or is to emphasize the woodwinds, then the director may ask the brass or woodwinds to perform selected phrases of the chorale soli.

Technical Drill

Four or five minutes of technical drill should follow, in which the director drills on the most common technical problems in that day's music. This is the time when a uniform style is sought; for example, articulations, marcato passages, use of the bow. To be meaningful, the material covered during the technical drill must be applicable to what follows.[2]

Rehearsing technical problems with the full ensemble is not as efficient as individual drill, but it increases evenness of technique and other elements of precision for the group. While it may be appropriate for middle school groups to drill on scales and arpeggios to learn fingerings and bowings, high school players will benefit more from fast articulations, multiple tonguings, or light, staccato playing at a loud dynamic level.

Junior high bands and orchestras may need to devote more time to this portion of the rehearsal than high school groups. It is also important to remember that repetition is required. This means that most rhythms and articulations or bowings will be drilled many times.

The most useful technical drills are those from drill books and those created by the teacher. The advantage of books is that each member has clear, precise notation, already transposed and in the proper clef; their disadvantage is that the director must skip about the book selecting those items most beneficial to the rehearsal.

Drill on isolated rhythms and articulations can benefit listening and playing by ear if the director drills the group simply by telling each section their beginning note and asking them to echo the pattern she gives them.[3] It is essential that the students *see* how the rhythm is notated in addition to hearing how it sounds.

For high school students, drill can be used to teach transposition, functional harmony (triads), and interpretation of notated articulations. Students will not become bored if they find meaning and usefulness in what is drilled.

[2] Ibid., 121–25.
[3] Daniel L. Kohut, *Instrumental Music Pedagogy* (Englewood Cliffs, NJ: Prentice-Hall, 1976), 219–20.

Though technical drill is the shortest portion of the rehearsal period, it is necessary for continued improvement of individual technique and for uniformity of style. Some directors have been successful in using specific spots in the concert music for drill, but seldom do all students have the same rhythm in the same spot of the music, so part of the group sits idle. Sectionals before or after school should be used instead of drill time to work out technical difficulties in the concert music.

It is tempting to occasionally eliminate the technical drill from a rehearsal; it is also very easy to put a drill book in students' folders and randomly select an exercise when writing the rehearsal order on the chalkboard. Careful planning coupled with patience, however, will result in drills that steadily improve the ensemble's playing throughout the school year as well as benefit each day's rehearsal.

Rehearsal of Concert Music

Rehearsing (learning, cleaning up, and polishing) a familiar but "unfinished work" will constitute the major portion of each rehearsal.[4] This is the time when a work that has previously been sightread is prepared for performance. Normally, several musical works at various stages of preparation are in students' folders. Those pieces that are most prepared will be polished during the rehearsal, while the works that are less prepared will be approached in greater detail.

Overall, each work should be approached as a whole, followed by attention to a variety of problems in various sections. All the various sections are then put back together to form a better whole, and this whole is polished by the director adding or drawing more subtle elements to or from the work.

Objectives should be stated at the outset of the twenty to twenty-five minutes devoted to concert music. The director's responsibility is to stay on task. If, for example, the objectives include cleaning up a technical section of the music, the director should not stray off into blend and balance unless and until the technical problems are overcome.

This portion of the rehearsal should end with a run-through of the entire piece or a large section of the piece, to help "lock in" what was rehearsed.

Students should always have pencils and develop the habit of marking in their music anything that will help them play better, for example, difficult spots to watch for and practice at home, accidentals, breathing places, added nuances, expression marks, intonation, and special attacks

[4]Kuhn, op. cit., 120–22.

and releases. A uniform procedure for marking, such as illustrated here, should be used.

1. legato
2. semilegato
3. detached
4. breathe
5. no breath
6. space

7. pitch (if too flat)
   (if too sharp)
8. peak note
9. release on count 3
10. release on count 1

Directions should be given clearly, with a consistent system, so that the group always understands what it is to do. When giving directions for starting other than at the beginning, the director should state them once—twice at most—and begin. When directions are repeated several times, students fall into the habit of ignoring the first two or three statements and listen only the last time, if then.

Most rehearsal time is spent working with music that will be performed for parents, friends, and interested citizens of the community: audiences who hear fewer flaws and expect less from school musicians than the director usually assumes. The teacher should strive for the best the group can produce, but not at the expense of the teaching-learning objectives. Since good teaching in the long run results in good performances, the long-term is a better view, and sufficient time devoted to musical learning will result in an adequate performance without requiring all the rehearsal time. *It is the good musicians who are the good performers.*

The final two portions of the daily routine are a period of daily sight-reading and a period in which previously learned music is played—either "fun" music or music rehearsed sometime during the previous few days and played straight through to reinforce what was learned.

Sightreading

One of the most frequently discussed objectives of music education is perceiving and performing music from notation. A daily session for sight-reading leads to this objective and numerous others; for example, sight-reading is the best way to acquaint students with a wide variety of musical forms and styles, keys, and so on, since the ensemble is limited in the number of works that can be prepared for performance. Sightreading is the means by which all the learned skills, aural, technical, and cognitive, are used.

Music for this part of the routine can be compiled before school starts. The director should go through the music library or the card catalog and list music by form, key, style, and difficulty. These lists should then be ranked from easy to difficult in each category, the number of categories depending on the size of the instrumental music library.

On Monday of each week, the director should distribute five pieces for sightreading purposes. In the fall, these should be the easier tunes in each category, gradually progressing to the more difficult pieces. The easier selections are normally shorter, thus leaving more time for warm-up and technical drill earlier in the year when it is most needed. A number of the sightreading pieces, especially those more difficult, should be read through several times and pulled out other days for analysis by the director (e.g., to illustrate sonata-allegro form). For each sightreading, students should be allowed a minute or two to scan the piece, and the director should point out changes of tempo and key.

Previously Learned Music

It is important to end a rehearsal on a positive note (the oldest pun in the profession), and the easiest way to do so is to play through music the ensemble enjoys and plays well, often allowing students to select the final piece. The teacher should be cautious not to criticize the students' preferences or musical tastes (after all, at all other times she asks them to perform the works she selects). Their favorite selection in the folder is frequently the least musical piece; as this trend changes, it is a positive reflection on the teacher's effectiveness.

When playing through partially prepared music, the director can make mental notes of what needs attention, which selections sound good, and how to plan for an upcoming rehearsal. The run-through should be of a piece other than the one rehearsed that day; it may, however, be a play-through of the piece rehearsed the previous day.

Directors must also be aware of when the group is becoming tired. It is, however, well and good for students to feel tired at the *end* of the rehearsal—this is a result of work and accomplishment.

SCORE PREPARATION

There is no single "best" procedure to prepare a score for sightreading and rehearsals. All conductors, however, will agree that the director must be familiar with a work in order to rehearse it efficiently, and the extent to which the director is familiar with the score basically determines how much she can accomplish. This is the conductor's first responsibility, but all too often administrative details interfere and she resorts to sightreading. When the conductor is in a position of having to "discover" elements of the work when she is already on the podium, planning for the rehearsal is impossible. Even with the best musicians, score preparation makes the rehearsal more effective.

Usually the score is learned and prepared in various stages. First the score is perused to determine if it is useful for sightreading, then it is examined for overall form and overall style. As the work is studied for subsequent rehearsals, more and more details are found. The process of learning the score, depending on the artistic magnitude of the work, will continue until the score is virtually memorized, and the better the musical work, the more detail and effects will be discovered through study of the score. Also, the ability to "hear" a score (audiation) will improve with experience.

Audiation and study of the score are enhanced by use of a metronome. While the metronome may be set at a tempo slower than that desired for performance, the steady beat will help the director determine the overall flow, rhythm, and direction of the work. It will also help the director determine which rhythms, technical passages, or articulations may cause the ensemble to stumble—and hence are candidates for technical drill. During such study the director should try not to stop, but continue through the entire work or until the metronome must be stopped or the beat changed (such as ritardandos, accelerandos, or other tempo changes, and passages in an odd meter).[5]

During this initial study, harmonic analysis is unnecessary, as is detailed analysis of isolated rhythms or articulations. With the metronome maintaining a constant tempo (not too fast or too slow), the director should follow through the score with her eyes moving from line to line attempting to audiate the ensemble playing. Although few new teachers will be able to hear in their "mind's ear" exactly what the score sounds like, it is important to read through the score and gather from it as much as possible. As the director becomes more experienced, these initial perceptions will become more accurate. While the metronome forces one through the score during the initial study, the director may attend primarily to an underlying, driving rhythmic accompaniment in the low brass rather than the melodic figure in the upper woodwinds—this is fine as subsequent study will disclose other musical features.

The eye will soon explore more elements in the notation (and the mind will "hear" more elements) and the form of the work will gradually be outlined in the mind. The next stage is to go through the score mentally

---

[5] Francis W. McBeth, *Effective Performance of Band Music: Solutions to Specific Problems in the Performance of 20th Century Band Music* (San Antonio, TX: Southern Music Co., 1972), 12–25.

and aurally, humming or singing various lines of the score in different sections. For *many* new directors, this stage of humming the melodic lines is needed before the formal sections of the music can be identified and outlined (i.e., before larger sections and smaller sections, periods, and phrases within the periods can be determined).[6] Postpone listening to recordings or using an instrument to play the melodic lines. The director should first sightsing the lines and only use an instrument later to check accuracy.

As the director becomes more comfortable with it, the score is then studied and analyzed bit by bit, including the rhythmic elements, the melodic elements, harmonic elements, texture, and orchestration. The director should examine and if necessary mark in pencil any tempo changes and meter changes. The relationship between tempos of large sections and whether these tempos are used to help establish a specific mood (such as a driving rhythmic figure used for a slower melodic line) should be observed. Changes in the tempo, such as ritardandos and accelerandos, should be noted with respect to "where they are going," the quickness of the change, and their effect on any established mood.

Common meters normally present little problem for ensembles or directors. Any odd ($\frac{3}{8}$ or $\frac{4}{8}$) or asymmetrical ($\frac{5}{8}$ or $\frac{7}{8}$) meters may require practice by the director. The score should also be examined for rhythmic devices relating to the bar line (such as displaced accents or the use of hemiola), syncopation, diminution or augmentation, ostinato, grand pauses, fermatas, or an unusual and perhaps clever use of silence.[7]

Melodic aspects of score study include locating the primary melodies and countermelodies and identifying the instruments playing them. In addition to the overall form, each melodic section will have a form, tonality, and style.[8] The contour of the melodic lines is also important to phrasing and style, and the overall contour of the entire work is basic to interpretation. The variety of ways the composer develops the melodic material should also be identified.

Garofalo recommends beginning harmonic analysis by determining the tonal centers at the beginning and end of the work's large sections. The next step is to identify the harmonic basis of the various sections (i.e., major, minor, modal, chromatic, twelve-tone, atonal, polytonal, etc.). Each section is then analyzed in terms of the harmonic motion that gives the music its momentum and direction (the most common cadences are perfect, half, plagal, and deceptive, but a large number of works for band are twentieth-century music and make use of more modern cadential devices). The structure of individual chords is also important to observe (for exam-

---

[6] Ibid., 12–25.

[7] Robert Garofalo, *Blueprint for Band* (Portland, ME: Weston Walch Publisher, 1976), 30–36.

[8] Ibid., 30–36.

ple, most jazz chords are the result of adding the sixth or seventh and/or ninth to the basic triads).[9]

Together, the melodic and harmonic components of the work will determine dynamic levels. The dynamic levels notated should be observed, and any special effects (such as *sfz*) should be marked for special treatment and possible technical drill. The director will add nuances beyond those indicated in the score as suggested to her by the melodic contour, instrumentation, and underlying harmony.

Texture is generally the result of the combination of melodic and harmonic elements. All music students are familiar with the concepts of monophonic, polyphonic, and homophonic music. Most band and orchestra works are predominately homophonic, occasionally interspersed with polyphonic sections. Study of the texture helps determine which instruments carry the primary melodic material and which are performing a supporting role—and, equally important, which instruments are playing secondary melodies or countermelodies that when handled properly make the music come alive. In most works for school ensembles, tone color shifts constantly as different instruments move in and out of the foreground, middle ground, and background. This change of texture may be subtle and gradual, or it may be sudden for noticeable contrast.

Related to the idea of texture is instrumentation. A primary focus of many conductors in preparing the score is how to compensate for the group's less-than-perfect instrumentation. Often, study of the score will reveal that important lines carried by missing instruments are doubled in other parts, and that many times a solo is cued for another more common instrument. However, study of the score may instead indicate that sections of the work need to be altered or rewritten. For example, analysis of a band work may indicate that the basses, bassoons, baritone saxophone, and contrabass clarinet all play an important rhythmic ostinato in unison, but the band does not have a bassoon, baritone saxophone, or contrabass clarinet, and has only one tuba. Further study of the score may indicate that the work is not appropriate for this band beyond sight-reading experience. If the work is appropriate for performance, the section in question may need rewriting; instead of the tuba simply playing louder, the part may be doubled with trombones, baritones, or even horns.

Analysis of instrumentation may reveal passages too difficult for weaker sections of the ensemble, and these too can be rewritten. Analysis may also reveal passages that are suitable for challenging key individuals or key sections. Further information obtained may include unusual equipment or methods of playing (e.g., mutes, multiphonics) for which the director needs to alert sections. And finally, analysis of the score can help determine those portions of the music that are more efficiently rehearsed in sectionals.

[9] Ibid., 30–36.

The director should practice conducting just as she expects her students to practice their parts. The only aspect of the score that may be determined on the podium is the final tempo of the piece. Tempos will vary from group to group just as they vary from interpretation to interpretation. After the score has been learned, listen to good recordings of the work, especially of transcriptions recorded in their original medium.

When practicing conducting a work, one frequently practices giving cues, especially when conducting a record. As the conductor learns the work, it is easier to give more cues; as the ensemble learns the work, however, there is less need for cues. Giving too many cues minimizes musical independence as well as distracts the audience at a performance.

SELECTION OF MUSIC

A number of factors go into the selection of music. The director should not just select music for performances, but carefully choose music appropriate for teaching musical concepts and for sightreading as well. While everything placed in the folder should have some educational value, it is good to include some music that is "fun" even if it has less aesthetic value. Since band and orchestra directors have an extensive background in music and a deep appreciation for serious music, they may be tempted to select "heavier" pieces over "lighter" ones. To some extent, the director should select music with the students, audience, and administration in mind; it may prove just as easy to teach accents and marcato playing "Highlights from *Phantom of the Opera*" as a transcription of Liszt's *Les Préludes*. There is no way to please everyone all the time, but including a variety of works on a concert can bring some musical enjoyment to each member of the audience. As the public receives training in music appreciation, the audience and administration will also come to appreciate a wider variety of music. In addition, the strongest and best aspects of the ensemble should be considered when picking music for performance, while the music for rehearsals should be expanded to meet all objectives of musical learning.

When planning music for a concert, the director should consciously select opening and closing pieces that will appeal to the majority of the audience. Longer selections should be toward the beginning of the concert and multimovement works can follow those. Few concerts can be too short.

When music is selected for skill development, a number of skills can become the focus (either separately, or more commonly, jointly). Technical skills are those most frequently considered, since music is generally graded according to fingerings and rhythms. Too many school groups play music so technically challenging that little time is left to devote to other aspects of musical learning. For example, aural skills are often ignored when directors choose music—yet one of the most common flaws among school performing ensembles is intonation. Another good reason to actively develop aural skills is that the majority of students who graduate and leave the program will encounter music with their "ears" rather than with their "fingers."

Ideally, directors will select music that will challenge and ultimately improve performance skills (sightreading, aural, *and* technical) in a context that provides useful information *about* music, that is, historical and structural information. Orchestras have traditionally had a broader range of quality literature from various historical periods to choose from than bands. And band directors created their own limited repertoire in the 1970s by avoiding anything but original wind music. Such a policy ignores a tremendous volume of fine transcriptions and denies students a valuable component of their music education. Rehearsing, listening, and comparing music from various historical periods is an important lesson for wind as well as string players.

Equally important is the use of music written in different forms. The vast majority of music for wind bands has been written since 1950 and is in an ABA format. To develop an understanding and aural recognition of forms such as sonata-allegro, rondo, fugue, and larger forms such as the symphony and dance suites, transcriptions of music from a variety of mediums must be used.

Techniques for studying a score for purchase are similar to studying a score for rehearsal. The teacher should determine the key, the grade level, and if the work requires instruments not in the ensemble. The teacher should carefully observe the ranges for each instrument; the rhythmic complexity and tempo; the type and style of bowings or articulations (for example, must the trombones double-tongue, or are there outrageously fast staccato passages for saxophone?); the dynamic range in the context of register, articulation, and the group's instrumentation; and any awkward technical passages. An important consideration often ignored by band and orchestra directors is the piece's length; not only should one note the overall length of a selection that places great demands on students' ability to concentrate, but also the length of phrases and the "musical line." For example, there are several band transcriptions of Ralph Vaughan Williams's *Linden Lea*; while the overall piece is fairly short and easy with regard to technical proficiency, it is demanding due to the lengthy phrases and the consistent requirement to give each line direction and momentum.

CONCERTS

For every concert, there should be at least one rehearsal in the performance auditorium. While it is important to use this rehearsal to adjust balance, check blend, and listen for any unexpected problems, it is also important to emphasize and practice concert poise. Every school band and orchestra has new students in it each year. Although every director has many aspects of the performance on his mind, each group needs to at least discuss in detail how they will enter the stage, how they will exit if another group is performing, and what the behavior should be during the concert.

Small details such as clean and polished instruments (and shoes), proper dress, and good posture make a group look good. The famous band director Herbert L. Carter has personally been responsible for the improved appearance of literally hundreds of male conductors by simply suggesting that they keep their jackets buttoned. While at first this seems somewhat restrictive, it presents a much cleaner appearance than does a floppy suit coat. Another small detail that is a wise investment is a classy looking program that will present the proper image and reflect the hard work put into the concert.

Concerts can be outstanding, wonderful, and extremely enjoyable—they will never be perfect. The concert is the natural outcome of rehearsals, and as Wolfgang Kuhn has pointed out, it can have a maximum education-al value only to the degree that it leads toward the development of the musicianship or music appreciation of the performers *and* the listeners. It must be of artistic quality regardless of the selections programmed.[10]

INTONATION

Frederick Fennell had two signs in the Eastman Wind Ensemble rehearsal room. One, No Smoking, was required by law; the other said, in larger letters, LISTEN. If anything should be added, it should be Listen and *Think*; good intonation requires concentration.

Among conductors, there are those who champion *listening* for more accurate tuning and those who make use of pitch measuring devices such as the Korg electronic tuner. Actually, there is no conflict between the two groups, for in either approach the objective is the same: to develop con-sciousness of pitch and improve intonation. Whereas *tuning* is the process of adjusting one's instrument to the correct length of tubing, *intonation* is the process of playing the instrument with a pitch that matches those of others.[11] For example, when tuning, a trumpeter should only lip up or lip down to find the correct pitch and then adjust the tuning slide appro-priately. When playing, the process of lipping a note is used continually for good intonation. The trumpet player can rarely leave his slide in the same position and lip-up every pitch. Use of an electronic tuner holds the risk that students will come to consider intonation as a visual thing. Therefore, the director must repeatedly explain what the task is and how to achieve

[10] Kuhn, *Instrumental Music*, 158–59.
[11] McBeth, *Effective Performance of Band Music*, 2–5.

it—what to listen to, why, and what to do about it. Equally short-sighted is the director who uses her ears only to tune a group.

Although pitch varies with temperature, dynamic level, mechanical equipment, individual physiology, register, and scale temperament, general agreement can be reached on what is approximately in tune. When a group reaches this general agreement, it produces a clear sound; without agreement it has a muddy sound, ranging from annoying to blood-chilling. Tuning each instrument to a single pitch is generally a waste of time, although occasional random checks using an electronic tuner can ensure that individuals are at the agreed-on pitch standard. A little knowledge is a dangerous thing, and pitch is an area in which many have only a little knowledge. It is amusing to hear some directors assure a visitor that they tune their group to A-441, to observe that the room temperature is 85 degrees, and then to hear the group. What is needed is less pseudoscience and a great deal more listening, starting with the beginning instrumentalists.

No one would seriously argue against good-quality instruments, but it is misguided to try to *buy* good intonation. No instrument can be purchased that will play with perfect intonation in all registers at all dynamic levels. Only the performer can do that.

The initial process of tuning should utilize chords, unison scales, and sustained intervals. A loud, fast march is fun to play but useless for tuning. The best music for tuning is usually a chorale, a harmonized scale, or a chord study used for technical drill. Many students, it seems, have never considered that they have to do anything special to play with good intonation, and they must be helped to learn the pitch tendencies of their own instruments. In general, brass instruments and flutes tend to go sharp and clarinets flat during crescendos. In diminuendos, the opposite generally occurs. Other instruments vary according to the player and the register in which the instrument is being played. Individual instruction or section rehearsals can include training in pitch adjustment. Ask students to sing a simple triad, then to play it on their instruments. If they are typical, after the initial giggling, the singing will probably be more in tune than the playing. Simply asking students to adjust pitch is not enough—teach them how to adjust their fingers or lips to alter pitch.

Individual players may need extra work with the electronic tuner or with a well-tuned piano to become conscious of pitch. Players may be paired so that one plays intervals and scales while the other observes. Playing with good pitch on a wind instrument also depends on proper breathing, which is discussed in Chapter 8, "An Overview of Woodwind and Brass Instruments".

Rather than creeping up or down to the correct pitch, students need to learn what "too sharp" and "too flat" mean. Psychologically, most players would rather play sharp, and invariably the average player thinks he is playing flat when the director says she is out of tune. A trick for practicing tuning, well known to band directors, is to tune three or four players to the different pitches of a triad using an electronic tuner. After the students play the chord several times to hear what the in-tune chord sounds like, the director moves two or three of the students' tuning devices so that they are slightly out of tune. She then directs them to adjust their lips and airstream so as to produce the original in-tune sound. After the exercise is finished, they may readjust their tuning devices. The object of this exercise is to stress the importance of lip adjustment for intonation—initial tuning should, of course, be as close as possible. Many students are constantly wiggling tuning slides to make microscopic adjustments in tuning, or so they think (it does indicate, however, that they are conscious of intonation). When the instrument's length matches the tuning pitch as closely as possible, adjustment of the embouchure must take over.

For intonation purposes, many students find perfect fourths and fifths easier to hear than octaves. It is especially difficult for bass instruments to adjust to higher-pitched instruments because the lowest instruments set up a series of overtones for each note that sound in the range of the notes played by the higher instruments. If the low instruments are only slightly out of tune, the effect is multiplied, as their upper partials clash with the pitch of middle- and high-range instruments. The most useful remedy is, therefore, to tune the group in relation to the lower instruments, first checking these against the electronic tuner. A simple tuning method is to use a chord with the basses sustaining the tonic pitch and the upper instruments alternating on the third and fifth. Tuning on chords may be done without music or by using chords from the ensemble's chorale books; each chord should be sustained until it is as in-tune as the players can get it. On the second try, those upper voices that had the fifth should play the third of the triad, and those who had the third should play the fifth. Obviously, students must know what a fifth and a third sound like; this they learn by singing or playing arpeggios. Another useful technique when tuning to chords is to have the full ensemble crescendo and decrescendo after they have tuned, trying to keep the chord in tune throughout, which requires embouchure change for many instruments and proper breathing for all instruments. When playing dissonant chords, students should hear the chords alone, on the piano, or on a recording, so that they understand the dissonance.

The composer Francis McBeth advocates improved intonation through appropriate balance. This relationship is similar to that between good intonation and tone quality, both depending as they do on proper breathing, a good embouchure, and careful listening. However, the two are not interchangeable; often young musicians are in tune according to an electronic tuner but sound like a chainsaw cutting through a vat of mashed potatoes. McBeth's approach adds one more avenue to achieving good intonation.[12]

In McBeth's theory, pitch problems cannot be solved until balance problems are resolved. At any given dynamic level, the higher-pitched instruments should be playing softer than the lower-pitched instruments. McBeth illustrates this concept with an isosceles triangle resting on its base and the two equal sides pointing upward to a point over the center of the base. The width of the triangle is the measure of volume, so the higher the voice, the softer the sound; and the lower the voice, the louder the sound, for proper balance. The ensemble is divided into four groups: Group 1 would include the first trumpets and clarinets, the flutes, and the oboes; Group 2 would include the second and third trumpets and clarinets; Group 3 would include horns, alto and tenor saxophones, alto clarinet, and first trombones; and Group 4 would include the second and third trombones, baritones/euphoniums, baritone saxophone, bass clarinet, bassoons, and tubas.

To demonstrate this concept, McBeth suggests playing a chord at pianissimo and crescendoing to fortissimo. Then do it again, but this time Group 4 does the same full crescendo while Group 3 plays three fourths of the crescendo, Group 2 plays one half of the crescendo, and Group 1 one fourth. Finally, the band plays the chord once again, but with the balance reversed: Group 1 playing a full crescendo and Group 4 playing one fourth of the crescendo. When students hear a recording of this their first or usual crescendo will sound more like the third one with its reversed balance than like the pyramid-type balance. It is also likely that the second (balanced) crescendo will sound like a superior level band. It may also be useful to use this procedure with woodwinds alone and with the brass alone.[13] The director should point out that multipart sections such as the clarinets and trumpets should use this type of balancing within their individual sections as well.

When proper balance is achieved, players are able to *hear* the lower voices. If each individual is playing softer than those playing lower pitches and louder than those playing higher pitches, then he is able to tune the bottom of the chord. Consequently, instead of more time spent tuning the soprano-voiced instruments, as is the norm, more time should be spent tuning the lowest-voiced instruments.

Poor tone quality is sometimes mistaken for faulty intonation. The bad tone, like the out-of-tune player, stands out in the group. Students do not always understand that quality may be adjusted to suit the music; an abrasive tone may at times be more suitable than a smooth, glowing sound.

[12] Ibid., 9–11.
[13] Ibid., 3–5.

Some group intonation problems require editing the music. Knowledge of the individual instrument's tuning problems is vital to such editing, of course. Excessive doubling is not good, and all-purpose scoring in which, for example, alto saxophones and third clarinets play the same parts, will create intonation problems. The best cure for this is to thin out the ensemble. Marking danger spots in the parts is sometimes useful; for instance, brass players should be reminded to adjust pitch downward for sustained tones with 1–3 and 1–2–3 valve combinations. Many woodwind passages can be improved by using fewer players on the upper parts. Passages scored for clarinets above high C, for instance, are hard to get in tune even with advanced players, so the most satisfactory solution is to have some of the players tacet. As a rule, young oboe players should not attempt to play in unison.

Daily practice contributes to good intonation. Many offenders in sour-sounding groups are students who see their instruments only at rehearsal time. Tired embouchures lead to poor intonation. Players with dirty instruments, leaking pads, and worn-out reeds must be prodded into correcting these faults.

A few suggestions conclude this discussion of intonation. A good idea is to occasionally use an electronic tuner when practicing long tones. Many players will be surprised to have visual proof of their inability to sustain a tone at a constant pitch, especially when changing dynamic levels. An awareness of the most common alternate fingerings will help woodwind players improve intonation in their performance. Listening to recorded performances of outstanding bands and orchestras can help the entire group develop concepts of good intonation and tone. And the tape recorder is perhaps the single most effective tool in alerting the group to their strengths and weaknesses and to those musical passages that are in particular need of improvement.

Players of double-reed instruments should obtain reeds of the proper length to get the best intonation from their instrument. Bassoonists should have a bocal of the correct length. Clarinet players should insert tuning rings in the barrels of their clarinets or obtain new barrels if excessive pulling is necessary. Their intonation problem is usually related to embouchure or the high temperatures in the rehearsal room. Clarinetists should not leave marching-band lyres on their instruments indoors, since the lyres can cause tuning problems.

Brass instruments are most efficiently tuned to their open or first-position tones. Woodwinds should be tuned to tones produced near the mouthpiece of the instrument: for example, clarinets should be adjusted first to open G or thumb F, then tuned to tones that use more of the tube. Specific intonation adjustments for each instrument are discussed in subsequent chapters.

TONE, BALANCE, BLEND, AND INSTRUMENTATION

Music teachers are fond of claiming that a beautiful tone is the most important single factor in good playing. Most musicians agree with this, but the public does not seem overly concerned about beauty of tone, judging by the best-selling compact discs, television programs with high ratings, and famous-name performers. Loud and distorted guitars, a bass with no tonal center, raucous saxophones, and edgy-toned trumpets abound. Department and record stores are more likely to stock the selected specialties of Ernest Ernie and his Twelve Tub Thumpers than they are flute solos by Rampal or cello concertos by Yo-Yo Ma.

Before players can play with a good tone, they must hear examples of good tone. This is an excellent reason for believing that listening time is well spent in the rehearsal period. Records, tapes, and compact discs can be used to develop the students' mental concept of beautiful tone. The director may be an accomplished instrumentalist, and hearing her illustrate types of tone will be valuable to the students, but she cannot adequately illustrate the entire range of instrumental sounds nor the total sound of a fine band or orchestra.

If all the players had a good tone and all sections blended internally, the battle would yet remain unfinished; the overall tonal blend and balance of the organization would still have to be worked out.[14] This is a problem for the teacher more than for the individual players, as the teacher must adjust the components of her human instrument (the ensemble) to match her mental conception of the desired sound. Such adjustments are easier said than done, since many variables interfere: instrumentation, scoring, acoustics, and strengths and weaknesses in sections, not to mention subjective judgments by conductors. The conductor listens constantly to judge the balance and blend of the group, but when she is on the podium close to the group, she may get a very different impression from that obtained several yards away. Occasionally, rehearsals in a larger hall enhance the sound, and the players as well as the conductor will hear the difference. The conductor should turn the baton over to a student director and move back into the hall to listen for intonation, blend, tone quality, and balance. What she hears may be revealing, especially if rehearsals are ordinarily held in a bright room in which the sound runs together.

---

[14] Balance generally refers to the degree that some section or "voice" in an ensemble dominates over others. In a well-balanced chord played by an orchestra all instruments are heard equally well and no note of the chord sounds louder than the others. Blend indicates the quality of individuals' and sections' fitting together inseparably. At times the brass should blend into a *brass* sound rather than a sound that is distinctly trumpet, horn, trombone, and tuba; an individual player with a substandard tone quality will not blend and will hurt his *section's* blend.

Balance does not mean that every section plays at the same dynamic level. The music will partially determine which sections need to predominate at any given moment, with the melodic parts usually being of more interest than those that are strictly accompaniment. Since each musical composition is different, it is useless to elaborate on the point except to remind the director that the trumpets will not always be dominant, and everyone in the ensemble will not play at precisely fifteen decibels.

The instrumentation necessary to achieve a satisfactory balance requires planning. An ideal instrumentation is impossible to achieve in most situations, but some general rules can be followed. First, one seldom hears a band or orchestra criticized for having too many clarinets or too loud a clarinet section. The woodwinds in an amateur group sound better when there are enough to produce a balanced sonority without being forced to overblow in defense against the brass section.

Second, for bands, balance will not be possible if the brass section is equal in number to the woodwinds. At the same time, most young brass players will not have the mature volume of tone heard from professional groups using one on a part. The solution is to judiciously double the parts. Doubling of the lower parts is especially useful for a good ensemble sound. Ideally, there should be more third trumpets than first trumpets (although the demand on lead players may require doubling to assist).

Third, having capable players on all the parts will contribute to the balance, rather than placing the best players on the first parts with the poorest on the third parts. To put all the best players in the first chairs and the poorest players in the last chairs may be good for competition but not for musical results. Few bands or orchestras have enough good players to form an ideally matched ensemble, but judicious distribution of talent is one way to balance the group. Musicianship, technical ability, personality, temperament, and experience should be considered. The director might alternate players with strong and weak sense of rhythm, good and poor bowing, good and poor technique, and accurate and inaccurate intonation, so that the better players can help the weaker ones.

Fourth, the size of the saxophone and percussion sections in the band should be kept reasonable. Four saxophones can be heard in a large band (ten saxophones can be heard at the starting line of the Daytona 500). Two weaker players may be used to do the job of one strong player, but given a choice, one strong player would be better. As for the percussion section, there is really no need to have eight or ten players standing around hoping to get to thump a drum now and then. One snare drummer usually suffices for a large symphony orchestra. Modern school bands and orchestras can surely get by with four or five players to beat, rattle, and shake things while the rest of the group tries to cut through the resulting wall of sound.

Fifth, school purchases should be planned over a long-term period to make possible a complete instrumentation with bass and contrabass clarinets, oboes, English horns, violas, bassoons, bass trombones, piccolos, mallet percussion, and so forth (leaving alto clarinet at the bottom of the priority list or perhaps just above an ophicleide). It is true that one may substitute a baritone saxophone or muted euphonium for a bassoon, a muted trumpet for an oboe, a mellophone or alto saxophone for a horn, a parade snare drum for a concert snare drum, a tenor saxophone for baritone horn, and a baritone or trombone for second or fourth horns. Such substitution is necessary if that is the only way the group can perform the music, but it should not be the final word. Composers and arrangers cannot be expected to produce music that will sound good with an arbitrary mixture of instruments.

To help the instrumentation it may be necessary to switch students to new instruments. Common transfers include flute players to oboe, saxophone, and percussion; saxophonists to other saxophones, oboe, bassoon; trumpeters to horn, baritone, and tuba; and baritone players to trombone, tuba, and trumpet.[15]

Sixth, seating arrangements should be changed until the most acceptable pattern is found for the group. The conductor who keeps the same seating arrangement from year to year isn't listening to her group. Good seating arrangements are determined by considerations of appearance, balance, precision, and practicality. Seating, planned to enhance the weaker sections and subdue the too prominent ones, contributes to a blended sound. Remember that some instruments, such as trumpets and trombones, are directional—they project their sound mostly in front of them. Other instruments, such as clarinets and strings, are nondirectional and radiate sound all around them. The instruments on the outside edge of the group are easier to hear, and those that produce the least volume should be placed there. Horns should always be seated so that the first horn plays into the rest of the section (i.e., at the left end of the section) and the bells of the horns are facing away from the audience. The acoustical features of the stage and concert auditorium will also enter into the seating plan. The existence of curtains that absorb sound sent in a particular direction or a shell that sends the sound out into the audience will help determine the placement of the stronger and weaker sections.

The seating charts shown in Figures 7-1 through 7-9 are presented only as suggestions; they illustrate that great variety is possible while maintaining good seating.

When instrumentation and seating are adequate, work can be done in the area of blending. Good blend is the result of listening and matching one's tone to that of the section. There is no room for individualism here. Controlling the kinds of instruments and mouthpieces used is helpful.

[15] Carrol M. Butts, *Troubleshooting the High School Band: How to Detect and Correct Common and Uncommon Performance Problems* (West Nyack, NY: Parker Publishing Co., 1981), 153–55.

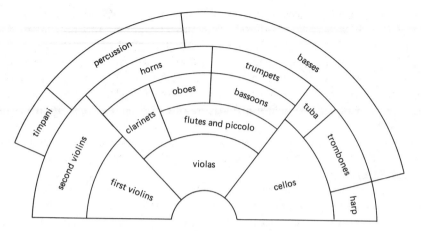

Figure 7-1   Symphony Orchestra #1

Brass players should have a mouthpiece that will produce a characteristic, legitimate brass sound rather than a special super-double-cup high C mouthpiece. Woodwind players can achieve both better tone quality and better blend by matching mouthpieces and by properly selecting and adjusting reeds. String players need to use quality strings on their instruments. School-owned instruments must also be equipped with good mouthpieces and good strings. Periodic inspections and insistence on quality instruments should prevent mechanical problems from ruining tone, pitch, and blend in a section.

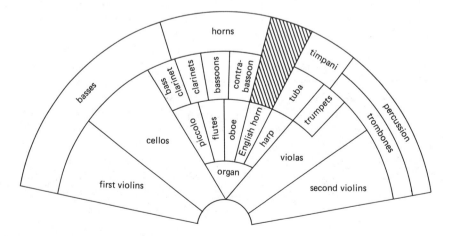

Figure 7-2   Symphony Orchestra #2

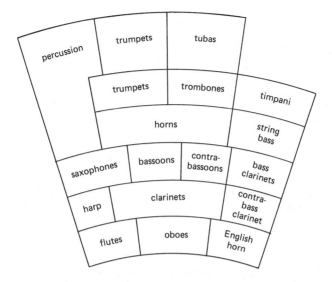

Figure 7-3   Eastman Wind Ensemble, Frederick Fennell, Conductor

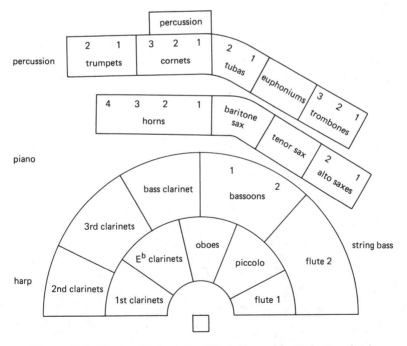

Figure 7-4   Boston University Wind Ensemble, Eric Rombach, Conductor

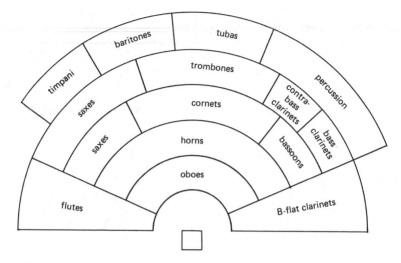

Figure 7-5   University of Minnesota Symphonic Band, Frank Beneriscutto, Conductor

TEMPO, METER, AND RHYTHM

A composition need not be played at its performance tempo during rehearsal, especially when the ensemble is sightreading the work. Most conductors practice music at tempos slower than those to be used later, at least until problems of technique and facility are under control. A minority of

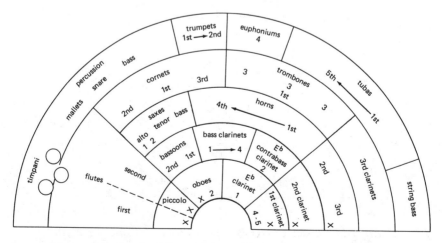

Figure 7-6   Seating chart of Symphonic Band, John Paynter, Director

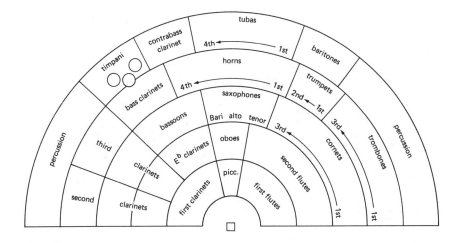

Figure 7-7   University of Illinois Symphonic Band, Harry Begian, Conductor

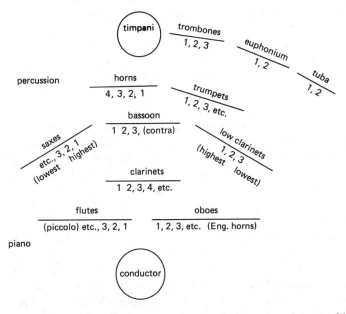

Figure 7-8   New England Conservatory of Music Wind Ensemble, Frank Battisti, Conductor

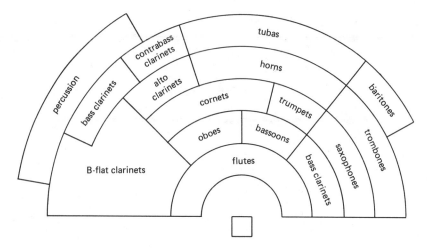

Figure 7-9   University of Michigan Symphonic Band, William Revelli, Conductor

conductors argue, however, that musical values are often lost when pieces are rehearsed continuously at slower tempos; linear, metrical, and rhythmic aspects and interpretation can become mechanical and wooden. Playing music slowly has no particular inherent virtues; instead, it is a way to help conductor and student locate and refine those portions of a composition that require technical corrections. It is fallacious, however, to imagine that there is a single, correct tempo for a composition—compare, for example, recorded versions of the Beethoven symphonies as performed by Bernstein and by Boulez. Bernstein was often criticized for his fast tempi, but there is a range of acceptable tempi for music of all styles. Tempo is determined by each conductor's interpretation and sometimes constrained by the technical abilities of members of the ensemble.

Maintaining a tempo is nearly always difficult because of the tendency of amateurs to rush through passages with lots of rapid notes and to drag passages with fewer notes. Loud parts of compositions usually bring out the speed impulse, soft music the instinct to lag. The conductor is responsible for making the musicians obey her tempo indications. Players must be able to see the baton as well as their music. They should adjust their music stands at a proper height and alignment to make both visible. The conductor can encourage closer attention during rehearsals by intentionally beating time erratically on occasion. By adding a fermata here and there and by changing tempo, she can ensure that players are paying attention. This technique is especially useful when playing the warm-up chords, during which every eye is focused on the conductor rather than on the notation. The size of the beat should vary inversely with the control demonstrated by the players; that is, a smaller beat, not a larger one, should be used to gain precision. (Try going immediately to a smaller beat pattern when a group is dragging instead of beating a larger pattern). Some stunts that seem to help include beating a series of short downbeats, each one indicating a separate attack to which the group responds on a repeated tone or on tones in an ascending scale. This kind of practice may be refined still more, so that the conductor indicates rhythmic patterns for the group to interpret from her baton without benefit of written music. Such practice is fun, ensures close attention from the players, and forces the conductor to give clear signals.

Players need to develop the habit of holding back rapid passages and pressing forward in places where the music might drag. Most rushing of fast passages stems from lack of command of fingering and articulation. Often the necessary facility can be better developed by playing through the passage with altered rhythms than it can through mere repetition.

One of the most difficult obstacles in late twentieth-century literature for winds, percussion, and strings is the more frequent use of asymmetrical meters. Most beginning method books and junior high literature are limited to $\frac{4}{4}$, $\frac{2}{4}$, $\frac{3}{4}$, and $\frac{6}{8}$ meters, so the first time a group encounters $\frac{5}{8}$ or $\frac{7}{8}$ they flounder like beginners. Asymmetrical meters should be introduced *before* they are encountered in the music by incorporating them into the portion of the rehearsal routine devoted to technical drill. The meter $\frac{7}{8}$ can easily be learned by playing scales (ascending and descending at varying tempos) in unison, since there are seven different pitches in the scale. Different notes of the scale can be stressed depending on the subdivision of the $\frac{7}{8}$ measures (that is, 2–2–3, 2–3–2, or 3–2–2).

The director should explain that $\frac{5}{8}$ is simply a lopsided $\frac{2}{4}$ and $\frac{7}{8}$ is a lopsided $\frac{3}{4}$ (with one of the beats having an "extra" half of a beat). She will conduct the $\frac{5}{8}$ and $\frac{7}{8}$ like a two or three pattern with a delay after the "long" beat equal to the "extra" eighth note—most directors will help themselves and the group by counting aloud "one and, two and, three and, and."

A performing group is united by its perception of the metrical pattern of a composition. This perception is based on what each player knows, hears, and sees. The relationship between meter and tempo, and what the conductor does is worthy of attention at every rehearsal. No march or waltz accompaniment, for instance, can be perfected without training players to feel the underlying pulse of the music within the framework of what the conductor indicates.

Spacing notes properly is important to maintaining tempo. The habit of rushing is common whenever afterbeats or repeated dotted figures appear. When the tempo is fast, a useful rule is to require a space after any longer note that is followed by a shorter note, as in the rhythm shown in Figure 7–10.

written

played

Figure 7-10 Spacing

When this figure is played slowly, however, the longer note should be held full value. This is a basic aspect of style that all players should learn.

Accuracy of rhythmic interpretation is a major bugaboo for professional as well as amateur groups. The recorded rehearsals of such great conductors as Bruno Walter and Robert Shaw show infinite care being taken to obtain rhythmic correctness, even with the very best professional musicians. For the public school conductor, the problem is multiplied. Singing, speaking, and clapping rhythms are the most effective ways to achieve precision and unity. Singing is closer to the real music in question, but speaking or chanting can create more vitality in rhythm practice, and clapping can get the feel of the rhythm into the muscles. Probably all should be used, even on the same problems. Many teachers shy away from singing and so do their students, although it should be natural enough for musicians to be able to sing as well as play their instruments. The way to get a group of students over self-consciousness of this sort is to sing, speak, or clap the rhythm for them and tell them to respond similarly. If the teacher acts natural, the students will also.

Perhaps the most common rhythmic inaccuracy occurs in the playing of dotted eighth-sixteenth patterns: ♩. ♪ ♩. ♪. Many players (and teachers) treat these as if they were § time: ♩ ♪ ♩ ♪. When this happens, dividing the quarter note beat into four equal parts is an effective antidote. This may be done by counting "1–2–3–4" during each quarter; or by playing four sixteenths first, then thinking four as the correct rhythm is played. Players may have to be reminded each time this pattern recurs, but at least they will have learned a handy tool with which to correct the mistake once it has been called to their attention. The opposite problem arises when groups attempt music in the popular style, for which the precise rendition of ♩ ♩. ♩ ♩ sounds square and stilted and the § ♫ ♩ ♫ ♩ | ♩ sound, is closer to the ideal.

A part of the problem of rhythmic correctness is the distribution of "weight" on the tones. Sometimes the pattern indicates equal weight but is played with one tone stressed too much, actually lengthening out the stressed note and cheating others, ♫♫ or ♫♫ when it should be ♫♫. Rhythms such as ♫ | ♫ ♫ are more easily spaced when the sixteenth note is played as a grace note to the next beat rather than on the "last fourth of the beat"—its association with the following beat rather than with the previous one will result in greater precision and may prevent rushing. Students must understand that a quarter note equals four sixteenths, but computing fractions while trying to play a musical instrument may not bring about rhythmical clarity. Treating the sixteenth as a pick-up to the next beat is more natural, more musical, and usually more stylistically correct.

Reading the whole rhythmic pattern rather than individual notes can aid in precision. Using words to represent the rhythmic feeling is helpful as an illustration (Figure 7–11), if the words do not become a crutch.

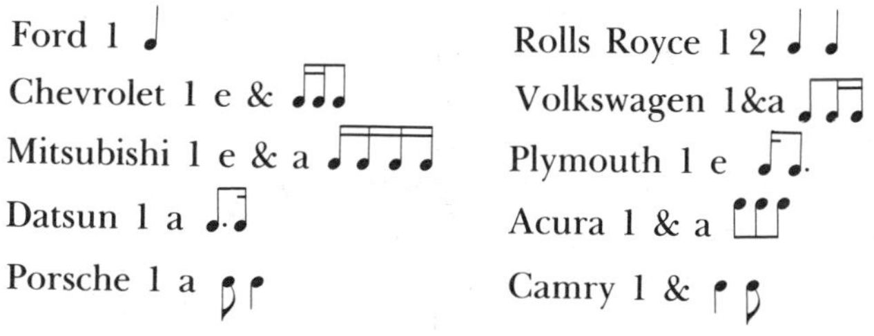

Ford 1 ♩	Rolls Royce 1 2 ♩ ♩
Chevrolet 1 e & ♫♪	Volkswagen 1&a ♫♪
Mitsubishi 1 e & a ♬♬	Plymouth 1 e ♫.
Datsun 1 a ♪. ♩	Acura 1 & a ♬♪
Porsche 1 a ♪ ♪	Camry 1 & ♪ ♪

Figure 7-11   Rhythmic Patterns

The entire basis for rhythm is the subdivision of the beat. Experienced directors are aware of the difficulty students have in keeping a steady beat, often initially realized by players during their first confrontation with a metronome. Subdividing an unsteady beat moves one step farther away from precise rhythm. Lack of a uniform tempo, uniformly subdivided, results in a muddy ensemble sound. The ability to maintain a tempo and accurately subdivide the beat is what the director does in score preparation with the metronome ticking, and what the ensemble practices in technical drills. The entire problem is compounded when articulations by the various instruments are considered. One difficult skill is to hear who in the ensemble is not subdividing correctly. This skill improves with experience and can be improved more quickly by recording rehearsals, then diligently studying the recordings with a metronome handy.

Style is dependent on the interpretation of rhythm and the articulation of rhythm. Butts observes three causes of style problems: (1) inaccurate interpretation of rhythms, (2) lack of knowledge of basic styles, and (3) lack of rehearsal time devoted to achieving this uniformity of style.[16] The director must be aware of basic rules of interpretation; for example, eighth notes are generally detached at a fast tempo and have full value at a slow tempo (unless otherwise marked). An example of this can be demonstrated by having the ensemble play a strain of a ⁶⁄₈ march with all the eighth notes played full value, then again with the quarter notes played shorter. Most students will agree that the second style sounds better, or more appropriate. Such elements are determined by tempo, notated articulations and style markings (e.g., *marcato, pesante, scherzando, grazioso,* etc.), and the general character of the music (the first item assessed in the initial reading of a score).

While the above example of quarter notes may be fairly obvious, other style aspects are not so obvious. When most bands play marches, it is usually the percussion that holds the tempo, with the tubas slightly behind the beat. The reverse, however, should be true—the basses should play on top or even ahead of the beat. Other style characteristics of traditional

[16] Ibid, 182–86.

marches include an effervescent first strain, followed by a dramatic second strain (with brasses in the background and woodwinds playing with power in the foreground); a lyrical, singing trio (often enhanced by having brass *and* percussion tacet the first time); and a martial, marcato break strain (when the brass finally get to open up).[17]

Students should know basic differences in style, especially from a historical point of view, for example, the lightness of a Baroque dance suite compared to the heaviness of a Romantic overture. Listening to recordings of professional groups can aid in rhythmic awareness, rhythmic accuracy, and style. As with tone quality, getting the sound of precise rhythm into ear and brain is one of the best ways to improve.

Finally, the director must be patient in rehearsals. Some students have more innate rhythmic ability than others. All students, however, require instruction in style and the performance of rhythms beyond that required for reading rhythmic notation.

PHRASING

Melody

A musical phrase is the natural division of a melodic line. It is demarcated by a cadence, but more than this it is musical movement from a point of rest. Musical phrases are analogous to sentences in language; they are made coherent by having climactic points and cadences, which act like punctuation marks. For example, the perfect authentic cadence functions as a period, while half, deceptive, and imperfect cadences function as commas, semicolons, and so on. The separate phrases of the composition must be considered in relation to the whole, so that there is an overall peak or climactic point of the piece. Playing with awareness of the phrase means that the music *goes somewhere* and the performer gives a line direction— each note leads to the next. Examine the single phrase; tension points are often higher in pitch than other parts of the melody, since there is a relationship between high tones and tension. Upward movement seems to imply a strain or struggle against a downward pull. The way this upward pull appears in music is extremely varied. In general, the single highest note is usually the point of greatest tension within the phrase, and the performer should move toward this point. From the point of greatest tension, the phrase then continues to a point of rest, indicated by a cadence. (The term *cadence* is from the Latin infinitive *cadere*, "to fall.") The tension point may be created by rhythmic intensity rather than melodic height. An unexpected change in the rhythmic flow—faster melodic move-

[17] McBeth. *Effective Performance of Band Music*, 4–5.

ment or a sudden slowing—can produce the focal point of the phrase. To talk about the high point of the phrase is complicated, but hearing it is usually easy.

Whether or not every musician expresses his ideas about tension and release in music in exactly the same way is not so important as the fact that phrasing is concerned with melodic movement or direction, and the location of cadences. The conductor and the performers must understand where cadences appear if they intend to phrase the music artistically.

Students should mark phrase or breath points in their parts with a small comma. Long phrases in the wind parts may call for staggered breathing, that is, for students on each stand to take a breath at different places in the phrase so that the section as a whole may sustain it. Whenever possible, the peak notes of a phrase should be located and marked. Students should visualize the shape of each phrase and be helped in performing with a feeling of direction, which will instill vitality into their playing. Conducting should be done according to the phrase structure and the overall shape of the composition. The dynamic markings in edited music should be regarded with skepticism if they seem to contradict the musical structure; the editor may not have been adequately aware of phrase structure and meaning.

As the phrase rises and falls, the intensity and/or volume of tone should rise and fall. Sustained tones should not remain at the same level, but must also increase or decrease in intensity. These rules apply not only to the melody, but also to the accompanying parts of the music, so that *every member of the group should be playing with a consciousness of the phrase*. Repeated notes in a phrase, unless very rapid, should not be identical in weight but should vary dynamically. Finally, phrase endings should be smoothly tapered, since the tension is usually reduced at cadence points. Phrase endings should be sustained for their full value.

Harmony

Harmony and melody are so interwoven in music that one may hardly consider them as separate elements except for purposes of discussion. The interaction of melody and harmony is especially noticeable at cadence points, where a moment of relaxation in the melody is paired with a harmonic feeling of rest. The kinds of cadence differ in their finality, a half cadence indicating only a pause compared to the degree of completion implied by a I_4^6-V_7-I cadence. Language is like music in this sense, because it uses punctuation in writing and vocal inflection in speech to indicate its cadences. When one ends a sentence, the voice drops to a lower pitch. A question is expressed with a rising inflection.

Harmonic structure has bearing on the feelings of tension and relaxation in the music and helps determine how a phrase should be played. The tonal center and the tonic chord represent release or relaxation—the absence of tension—so that the farther away the harmony moves from the tonal center, the greater the tension is produced. The more sudden and unexpected the harmonic movement, the greater the tension. A brief summary of the way in which harmony helps create movement would include these elements:

1. Cadences are points of relaxation; cadences not on the tonic imply continuation, while cadences on the tonic produce finality.
2. Movement away from the key center creates tension; the more distant the movement, the greater the tension.
3. The return of the key center releases tension.
4. Modulation to a new key requiring a decisive cadence in the new key, not just the appearance of an altered chord or a secondary dominant, is an expressive device, signaling greater tension.
5. Chromatically altered chords produce tension, and the altered tones require more stress, followed by relaxation as they resolve.
6. Dissonance is relative, and the style of the music will determine the consonance or dissonance of any particular chord.

Our modern ears are jaded from over-frequent exposure to music and to key relationships that were less common in music of the past, so it is not surprising that the emotional effect of a modulation may not strike us unless we are alert for it. Knowledge about the music is necessary for the conductor who wishes to approximate the composer's intentions. A chord highly dissonant in the music of Mozart could be quite tame in the music of Schoenberg. That which appears dissonant in Classical music is often consonant in Romantic music, and may be completely innocuous in contemporary music. It is not so much the inherent tension of a particular chord that need concern us; rather, we should consider the level of tension of that chord relative to the other chords in the composition.

Players are often vaguely aware of the harmonic movement of the music without understanding it or without listening specifically for it. If the teacher will talk about the chord structure and what it does in developing phrase and climax, she can greatly increase the pleasure students take in listening and also increase their ability to play musically.

Dynamic Levels

Changes in dynamic levels, whether notated or not, can help phrasing. A general rule of thumb is that every note that receives more than one beat should either increase or decrease in volume. Ensemble players should be able to perform with good tone quality and control (while maintaining balance and blend) at least six separate and distinct dynamic levels: *pp, p, mp, mf, f, and ff.* Control of the sound beyond these levels should be an objective of many warm-up sessions.

While direction in music is largely established through the written pitches, rhythms, and harmony, it would be virtually impossible to notate all dynamic changes. Composers and arrangers generally notate only a general outline of the dynamics or notate special effects that are accomplished with dynamic changes (such as *fp, sfz*). To enhance the direction inherent in the melodic line, harmony, and rhythm, of every musical composition, the director should outline crescendo and decrescendos throughout the entire score and also mark the score in such a way that the ensemble with its unique instrumentation is balanced. For example, a melodic line played by the trumpet section may build from piano to mezzoforte, while the horn and trombone accompaniment should simultaneously build from mezzopiano to forte.

ATTACKS AND RELEASES

Satisfactory playing of the phrase demands not only that the group understand musical direction and respond to it, but also that students begin and end the phrase precisely together. Within the phrase, notes to be attacked or released will not produce the desired effect unless the attacks and releases are clean and accurate. Good attacks depend on several things:

1. The instrument must be in playing position.
2. The player's finger position, bowing position, or breathing must be prepared.
3. She must be watching the conductor.
4. The conductor must have a definite, clear preparatory beat and downbeat or cut-off that the player understands.

None of these things is hard to achieve, but constant attention must be given to them until the group has formed the habit of clean attacks.

Interestingly, while most directors are adept at identifying sloppy attacks and will drill repeatedly for precise ones, relatively few bother much with releases. If there is one single aspect of performance that separates Division I from Division II bands and orchestras, it is precise releases. A precise release at the end of a tapered phrase with a slight ritard, followed by resumption of tempo at the next phrase, is no less important than breathing.

Releases are difficult to execute with precision unless the players have agreed on a procedure for counting. Since releases are not always indicated by the conductor, they must be carefully counted, and the player must know where they come. Most quarter-notes are released at the beginning of the second count. A system of penciling a check mark with a number on it slightly behind a note can be useful for marking releases (see page 97). When the conductor signals the release, she must use a clear gesture of baton or hand so that the precise instant of release can be seen. When groups have trouble with clean releases, the problem may be with the conductor and not with the players. Baton technique is easily checked in front of a mirror. For notes played staccato or marcato, the conductor should make clear how long the notes are to be, then illustrate, drill, and correct them until the group plays with precision.

Not one band or orchestra in a hundred plays with precision, yet it is the easiest problem to detect. Aspects of ensemble performance such as intonation, tone quality, phrasing, balance, and blend are more subtle and exist in performance to varying degrees. With precision, however, a group either "has it or doesn't." The group that has rhythmic precision and plays with clean attacks and releases is such a surprise and joy that many other sins can be forgiven.

Most of the causes of sloppy playing can be corrected by an attentive director. It is essential that players follow the conductor, especially when playing slow music. When players do not follow, the conductor should stop immediately and start again, demanding accurate response. When groups are sloppy and slovenly, it is not because they lack ability. The conductor is to blame and had better face up to the fact. If she values precision and asks for it, she will get it. In fast music such as a march, the conductor is seldom needed to keep time; the basses and percussion help serve as a metronome, leaving the conductor free to adjust dynamic levels, style, balance, and blend.[18]

Directors often have a tendency to over- or underconduct; it is difficult to find a happy medium. Many baton techniques such as releases, cutoffs, and changing of dynamic levels are learned in conducting class. The director needs to be consistent, always using the same gestures when she desires a specific effect.

MUSICAL INDEPENDENCE

Instrumental teachers will recognize this situation: The orchestra has just played a familiar warm-up number with good tone and intonation and fair balance; now they are going to play scales. They begin. Surprisingly enough, they are quite accurate and play with a fair degree of technical skill. As they play in different rhythms and move to different keys, they sound commendably competent. With scales completed, they begin to

[18]Butts, *Troubleshooting the High School Band,* 191–98.

rehearse their concert music. Suddenly the group sounds like a parody of itself. The playing is out of tune, the woodwind and brass players are overblowing, and the conductor is struggling to be heard above the din. It is obvious that she knows what the piece should sound like, but her group appears less certain. They stop, and she listens to various sections alone. The errors she finds seem incongruous, considering the time spent on technical drill. Students are missing key signatures, seem unaware of tonality and balance, and fail to understand basic musical principles; for instance, no one in the clarinet section remembered to carry an accidental through the entire measure. However, the director has infinite patience and corrects each mistake she finds, no matter how painstaking the process. The orchestra begins again, and the chaos is slightly less. Some of the errors the director pointed out have been reduced. But with the next new composition, the cycle begins all over again.

Is this exaggerated? For many bands and orchestras, it is not. The solution is to teach more music through music, and to teach less pure technique. If difficult numbers cannot be mastered without sacrificing musicianship training, then the difficult numbers should be replaced with simpler ones. Time spent on sightreading, ear training, listening, and drilling on musicianship rather than technique may in time produce musicians capable of the more difficult numbers, if the conductor has patience. If the conductor does envision a developmental program of musical learning for the band and orchestra, she must be unequivocally committed to planning, because learning comes only through logical steps that proceed in orderly fashion from the simple to the complex.

Musicianship cannot be learned unless it is taught. Drill is necessary to develop musicianship skills, so ways must be found to make drill attractive. Contests between groups can be fun, especially if the groups are selected in whimsical ways: blondes against brunettes, talls against shorts, low instruments against high, and so forth. Augment the drill with all possible opportunities for application and transfer. No new piece of music should be attempted without first considering its key, meter, form, rhythmic problems, melodic problems, accidentals, dynamic markings, and the meaning of terms. This is the stuff of music—time must be taken to teach these things.

With middle school groups, the director must realize that their ability to concentrate and stay with the task is usually less than that of high school students. Furthermore, younger students do not always have the physical strength to play for a full hour. Time must be allocated for physical rest, and it is during these periods that other tasks can be introduced. For example, as the students begin to show signs of fatigue, observant middle school band directors will continue to work on the music by having the students clap rhythms, sing parts or even scales, listen, or do other activities. This approach is far more beneficial than a listening activity at the beginning of the period followed by forty minutes of playing.

Musical independence can also be promoted through the way a director corrects mistakes. Performance errors *will* occur—and it is essential that directors demonstrate their understanding of this to students. If the students did not make mistakes they would not be wasting their performance skills in school. Clearly, a successful director corrects the most glaring and obvious problems first. As the correction process continues in preparation for a concert, the director should involve the students in the process of making musical decisions as well as in the identification and correction of technical problems.

Generally it seems much faster to the director for her to stop the group and quickly give directions to improve the performance. However, if time can be taken to lead a discussion on how to shape a phrase or where a crescendo might be added to make a section of the music "prettier," to ask the clarinet section leader to devise an "easier" fingering, or to ask the tuba section if they feel the percussion are rushing, more learning will occur, more critical observation and listening will take place, musical judgments will be made, in short, musical independence will be developed. Students seldom make mistakes on purpose (well, maybe the trombones)—but it can become habit-forming for students to plod along, satisfied with their own mediocrity, if the director doesn't prod them to greater alertness. Encouraging students to analyze a problem and devise a solution leads to musical independence. Musical independence leads to a group of musicians. And working with a roomful of musicians is a genuine pleasure. Students can help determine *why* a mistake was made, and often they can determine *how* to fix it. They should not always need a director to point out the mistake and tell them how to fix it. They *never* need a director to embarrass them in the process.[19]

It is essential that young people realize that mistakes are a part of learning. Ensembles strive for perfection, but perfection is a goal that can never be reached. Students can learn to anticipate errors and avoid them (often simply by paying attention), and with time the director can establish herself as a source of information and guidance to help them reach *their* goals—not as a tyrant who rules "her" band with an iron fist and every mistake results in personal humiliation.

Musical independence is an overall goal of the entire program, during every rehearsal. A positive attitude helps tremendously to accomplish this goal. No one enjoys falling below a teacher's expectations. Success should be met with reward; limited success should be met with limited reward. *Success gives rise to success.* The director must provide opportunities for every student to meet with some degree of success or sense of accomplishment.

Finally, musical independence is demonstrated in part by students'

[19] *Holz and Jacobi*, 1966, 46–50.

individual practice. In today's busy adolescent life, students have difficulty making time for practicing their instruments. Being talented helps a student achieve, but efficient and consistent practice helps more.[20] Students need to learn to practice, however. The ability to practice is no more natural than the ability to finger an oboe—both require instruction.

Students on each instrument in the ensemble must be taught an appropriate warm-up, the daily exercise of playing scales, arpeggios, slurs, and so on. Forming the main body of the practice session will be solos, ensemble music, etudes, and isolated problems such as multiple tonguing for brass, a new rudiment for percussion, or crossing from one register to the other for woodwinds. A bit of sightreading, then running through a favorite piece (especially a lyrical piece) can conclude the practice session. The most difficult aspect for students to master in their individual practice is the ability to listen critically to their own tone quality, articulation (style), intonation, and rhythmic accuracy. Each repetition of a passage *must* have a purpose. The use of recording devices is so beneficial to ensemble and individual practice that it is hard to imagine how students in the early part of the century practiced without them.

Students must also be convinced that practicing a difficult passage slowly is prerequisite to playing it fast. The simple saying "If you can't play it slowly, you can't play it fast" is true; more important, to play something technically correct at a fast, even, and controlled tempo almost *always* requires practicing it slowly. Every student has some innate feel for rhythm. The problems seem to emerge when rhythms do not look the way they sound. Drills in rhythm during the technical drill section of each day's rehearsal should emphasize first listening to a rhythm, then the chalkboard should be used to show how its notation looks.

Sectionals

Because drill with individual sections during the large rehearsal runs the risk of losing the attention of the rest of the group, most of such work is best relegated to scheduled sectional rehearsals. Some work with individual sections will always be necessary during large rehearsals, but it should be kept to a minimum. The sectional rehearsal offers a chance to iron out difficulties and rectify errors that may not even be heard in the large rehearsal. Sectionals should be scheduled on a regular basis. When reliable student leaders are put in charge of the sections, the leaders gain valuable experience, and the section develops independence from the teacher.

[20] Richard K. Weerts, *Handbook of Rehearsal Techniques for the High School Band* (West Nyack, NY: Parker Publishing Co., 1976) 9–17.

INTERPRETATION

Every year at contests and festivals, adjudicators undergo one or more experiences like this: The band uses as a warm-up number a traditional march played very straight, with all proper notes and most of the rhythms played correctly; the tempo slows slightly at the trio and continues to slow to the end as the band tires (the result of getting used to a tempo variation in rehearsal). The orchestra selection is a Vivaldi sonata in fugue form, chosen for its difficulty and played very slowly, because the strings have not mastered it well enough to play it at the proper tempo. The winds play also, although the work is really designed for strings alone. The band performs an arrangement of a movement from a Brahms symphony, playing all the notes all at the same volume, regardless of whether the notes are melody, countermelody, harmonic support, or snare drum part added by the arranger. The adjudicators are forced to mark the band down. When interpretation of the music is lacking or erroneous, technical accuracy and precision cannot take its place.

Interpretation includes everything that is not strictly technique—tempo, rhythm, tone, balance, line dynamics, phrasing, attacks and releases—in short, that which makes notation musical. Interpretation must be appropriate to the style of the music and must conform to the accepted practices of the period from which the music comes. Interpretation means observing all the movement within the music and playing in such a way as to enhance it. The movement of melodic lines, motifs, harmonic progressions, countermelodies, and counterrhythms is the stuff of which music is made. Bringing these out effectively so that they are heard in proper balance, from the smallest passing tone to the total formal design, is interpretation. This can be done only when the players recognize movement and can hear how their parts fit into the whole. Players learn this through explanation and example from the conductor and also from guided listening to records. To explain what the inner voices do, to subordinate a countermelody to the principal melody (but not too much), to show how contrasting tone colors help produce motion, to help bring out the altered note in an altered chord, to trace the melody and all its variations through the composition so that they may be emphasized is time consuming, but it teaches the player about music as nothing else can.

Most music teachers get a smattering of knowledge about style from their college courses, especially in their applied music lessons, but this must usually be augmented by listening to authoritative performances. The form of the piece also has bearing on interpretation: a Baroque fugue is played in strict tempo, while a Baroque toccata has continual tempo changes; a Romantic song is relatively contained and intimate, while a Romantic tone poem can run the gamut of dynamic variety. Contemporary music may be lyrical or austere; Classical music may be serious or filled with humor. The conductor must know which is appropriate.

Command of a variety of tonguing and bowing styles, from legato to staccato, is necessary for appropriate interpretation. Command of a wide dynamic range from pianissimo to fortissimo and a tonal range from dry to lush is also necessary. Emphasis on interpretation must not wait until these things have been mastered, however. Interpretation can furnish an incentive for greater control of tonguing, tone, and dynamics (and all other musical factors), because it is what makes the music alive and worthy of the effort.

Style might be thought of as the way the music flows. Everyone remembers the scene in *Hamlet* in which Hamlet directs the actors to "Speak the speech, I pray you, as I pronounce it to you, trippingly on the tongue. But if you mouth it, as many of our players do, I had as lief the town crier spoke my lines." Hamlet cautions the actors to be moderate in their delivery and not to "tear a passion to tatters." "Be not too tame neither; but let your own discretion be your tutor." Amateurs are bound to experience some difficulty in "speaking the speech" as it is intended. In musical terms, delivery is in part a matter of understanding legato and staccato as opposites. March style, for instance, is usually characterized by vigor and a light, detached kind of delivery, with each strain in a specific style.

Style has been mentioned throughout this chapter. One of the primary aspects of style subject to interpretation is articulation. There may be as many different interpretations of *marked* articulations as there are conductors. This is partly due to the different ways articulations are executed on different instruments (resulting in clarinetists, for example, interpreting a marking slightly differently than a trumpet player) and due to early wind-music composers borrowing markings from strings (especially in the transcriptions that constituted the majority of band literature from 1910 through the 1940s). McBeth has pointed out the problems resulting from wind composers borrowing from string markings: "off the string" markings, for example, give a shorter, lighter effect, but the string still vibrates; wind players either blow the air or don't (unless striving for a poor sound), so when winds separate the notes there is silence between pitches.[21]

If students are to learn to play legato, music selected to illustrate it should be used in rehearsals. Grainger's *Irish Tune from County Derry*, for instance, could be used to teach a singing legato. Most of the great wind soloists of the past claimed they learned how to "sing" on their instruments by studying the performances of great singers. Today many successful instrumentalists learn more about phrasing from Dietrich Fischer-Dieskau than from any instrumental players.

Rather than skipping over this thought casually, ask if your group can play any simple song in a truly musical style. The point is that we overlook the problems that are fundamental to music most of the time, while we

[21] McBeth, *Effective Performance of Band Music*, 16–25.

Figure 7-12.   Range of Markings, from Detached to Connected

worry about eight-to-five on the football field or whether to tune to a Pythagorean scale in the concert hall. In his book *How I Became a Cornetist,* Herbert L. Clarke recalls that the great Patrick Gilmore required him to play a ballad, "The Last Rose of Summer," as part of his audition to join Gilmore's band.[22] From the purely physical standpoint, legato playing is connected and smooth with a continuous flow of tone. True legato is probably one of the most difficult problems for wind players.

Staccato should be considered separated, not short, since the space between tones varies with tempo and music. Students should be able to differentiate between the degrees of separation, ranging from the most detached to the most connected, and to recognize the markings for these degrees (see Figure 7–12). The conductor indicates style through her baton technique, and the players should learn to respond to the baton instead of depending on a verbal reminder to play staccato or play legato.

It is important that students are encouraged to mark their music in pencil. Simple markings along with codes devised by the students themselves will help them remember how an accent mark is to be played in one selection and how it is played in another.

Baton technique and conducting per se are beyond the scope of this text. They are covered in other courses and "perfected" in the field. One point to be made is that the diagrams in conducting texts use arrows to indicate the direction in which each beat goes; however, when one observes good conductors he will usually notice that the beats themselves are all in the same place (or very close), and that it is the preparatory actions that follow the directions of the arrows.

No director, however, can expect the band or orchestra to perform beyond what she conducts. If she expects a band to play marcato, she must conduct that way; if she expects the group to play *grazioso,* then she must conduct that way. She can either stop and explain these differences to the group (which will have an impact for a few measures), or conduct appropriately, which will save time and obtain the desired effects.

CLASSROOM MANAGEMENT

The final section of this chapter is devoted to classroom management. A number of texts and methods advocated in college education courses deal

[22] Herbert L. Clarke, *How I Became a Cornetist* (St. Louis, MO: Joseph L. Huber, 1934), 71.

specifically with discipline. This short section is comprised of a few concepts that may benefit new band and orchestra directors. Because bands and orchestras consist of volunteers who have worked hard to get in, there is no reason for any conductor to be plagued with discipline issues. Students will normally behave as the director expects them to.

Directors should enforce the rule that absolutely nobody speaks when *anyone* is on the podium. If a director desires to use a similar rule and demands that when she raises her hands or baton, instruments are supposed to go to the embouchure, then it is essential that the director not talk after she raises her hands. It is an excellent habit to indicate by a raised baton that "things are fixin' to happen"—but when that expectation is broken by a comment, the rule is broken. Some unfortunate directors will use the "raised-baton" trick to get students' attention in order to make announcements—such tactics will work for about a week.

Classroom management or discipline is the result of respect. If the teacher expects to be respected, she must show respect. Tactics such as referring to students by name, chatting with them off the podium, frequent and genuine compliments during rehearsal, all indicate interest in the students as individuals. Compliments to individual players reinforce the self-esteem and self-respect that instrumental music programs instill in the participants.

In a rehearsal, students should play as much as possible instead of having to listen to the director's talking. With fewer stops, the director can establish the attitude that her comments are important and worthwhile. Successful directors know before they stop what they are going to say; they then stop, say it, and continue.[23] Comments should be to the point. Instead of "trumpets, you're flat," a comment such as "trumpets, when the line ascends in the first phrase at letter A, keep the corners of the embouchure firm and blow a fast, pencil-thin jet airstream" achieves much more.

Prompt termination of the rehearsal is just as vital as a prompt beginning. Time is needed to disassemble instruments, wipe them out, put them in cases, put music away, and maintain general good housekeeping in the rehearsal room. No teacher has the right to expect the students to be punctual when she is not; and while she usually thinks in terms of starting on time, students and parents often think in terms of ending on time.

The rehearsal is the core of most instrumental music programs. What the conductor-teacher does with her rehearsal time may spell the difference between success and failure. It is not possible to summarize the chapter on rehearsal techniques, as a rehearsal calls forth all the administrative, personality, and musical abilities in a teacher. One can only emphasize the need for explicit and cogent directions, careful workmanship, and a high level of musical understanding.

[23] Kuhn, *Instrumental Music*, 125–127.

REFERENCES

AMMER, CHRISTINE. *Musician's Handbook of Foreign Terms.* New York: Schirmer, 1971.

BUTTS, CARROL M. *Troubleshooting the High School Band: How to Detect and Correct Common and Uncommon Performance Problems.* West Nyack, NY: Parker Publishing Co., 1981.

DART, THRUSTON. *The Interpretation of Music.* London: Hutchinson's University Library, 1954.

DORIAN, FREDRICK. *The History of Music in Performance.* New York: W. W. Norton, 1942.

GALAMIAN, IVAN. *Principles of Violin Playing and Teaching.* Englewood Cliffs, NJ: Prentice-Hall, 1962.

GAROFALO, ROBERT. *Blueprint for Band.* Portland, ME: J. Weston Walch, 1976.

HOLZ, EMIL, and ROGER JACOBI. *Teaching Band Instruments to Beginners.* Englewood Cliffs, NJ: Prentice-Hall, 1966.

KELLER, BLAINE. *Symbolization and Articulation.* New York: W.W. Norton, 1965.

KELLER, HERMANN. *Phrasing and Articulation: A Contribution to the Rhetoric of Music.* New York: W.W. Norton, 1965.

KINNEY, GUY S. *High School Music Teacher's Handbook: A Complete Guide to Managing and Teaching the Total Music Program.* West Nyack, NY: Parker Publishing Co., 1987.

KOHUT, DANIEL L. *Instrumental Music Pedagogy.* Englewood Cliffs, NJ: Prentice-Hall, 1973.

KUHN, WOLFGANG E. *Instrumental Music: Principles and Methods of Instruction.* Boston: Allyn and Bacon, 1966.

LABUTA, JOSEPH A. *Teaching Musicianship in the High School Band.* West Nyack, NY: Parker Publishing Co., 1972.

LISK, EDWARD S. *The Creative Director: Alternative Rehearsal Techniques.* Syracuse, NY: Onondaga Music Co., 1989.

McBETH, W. FRANCIS. *Effective Performance of Band Music: Solutions to Specific Problems in the Performance of 20th Century Band Music.* San Antonio, TX: Southern Music Co., 1972.

MERCER, R. JACK. *The Band Director's Brain Book.* Evanston, IL: The Instrumentalist Co., 1970.

RASMUSSEN, RICHARD. *Recorded Concert Band Music, 1950-1987: A Selected, Annotated Listing.* Jefferson, N.C. McFarland and Co., 1988.

RIGHTER, CHARLES B. *Success in Teaching School Orchestras and Bands.* Minneapolis, MN: Paul A. Schmitt Music Co., 1945.

WEERTS, RICHARD K. *Handbook of Rehearsal Techniques for the High School Band.* West Nyack, NY: Parker Publishing Co.; 1976.

8

An Overview of Woodwind and Brass Instruments

TONE QUALITY

First and foremost, the brass or woodwind player must have a good sound. No matter how well developed her other musical skills are, if the student plays with a bad tone, all else is of little concern. Tone quality is determined by a number of factors. Those covered in this chapter are breathing, vibrato, and warm-ups. The other important elements of embouchure and articulation are discussed in the general chapters on brass and woodwind as well as in the chapters on specific instruments.

Breathing

Teachers often use the term *proper breathing*. Proper breathing refers to the method of breathing that maximizes the amount of air drawn into the lungs to support the tone, and the actual process of exhaling to support the tone.

Posture. Establishing good breathing habits is more successful when the performer maintains good posture. Though the position for playing a wind instrument may appear unnatural, the body need not and should not be strained. The neck, throat, shoulders, chest, and arms must be free of tension; the upper part of the body should rest naturally on the lower part, and the player should be alert but relaxed. Good posture is difficult if the student has used the wrong muscles for years or if he has come to band from a class in which he has been hunched over a desk for an hour.

The "rag doll" approach is frequently used to eliminate tension so that the right muscles for playing can take over: Flop over from the hips, let the top of the body fall in a limp, rag-doll fashion, rotate the head around in as large an arc as possible. This exercise can be used as part of the warm-up with beginners. Exercises to loosen facial muscles, such as dropping the jaw and taking deep, relaxed breaths, will further aid relaxation. Encouraging relaxation techniques as the first item of business in rehearsals and lessons can establish good habits.

For all the winds, the correct playing position is based on moving the *instrument to the player*, the mouthpiece to the face and lips. In no case is it desirable to bring the player to the instrument or to adjust the head and shoulders to the position of the mouthpiece. The player should sit or stand tall; the spine should be straight. The notion of a string attached to the top of the head will help create a posture in which the air column is not constrained at the throat or by the rib cage.

Correct posture while seated should include ensuring that the back is not supported by the back of the chair, spine is straight, and shoulders down. Feet should be on the floor with one usually forward of the other to give a better sense of balance. Elbows should be held comfortably away from the rib cage. The instrument should be held with the hands, not propped on a leg or chair (except for the tuba).

Diaphragm.   Proper breathing is done with the diaphragm as well as with the chest. With hands on the waist just below the rib cage, thumbs in front, and fingers in back, one can feel movement all around the lower torso when breathing properly. If the diaphragm is drawing in the maximum amount of air, this area will expand in the back as well as in the front. It is impossible to expand the back of the abdominal cavity without expanding the front, but it is possible for the front to expand without the back expanding.

The diaphragm is a rather large, flat muscle located in a plane parallel with the floor (Figure 8-1), separating the upper body from the lower. When the diaphragm is relaxed, it assumes a dome shape over the abdomen. When the muscle contracts, it flattens to create a vacuum, which draws air into the lungs and displaces the organs in the abdomen resulting in a slight projection of the abdominal wall. Due to the fixed nature of the abdominal viscera, there is a limit to how far this projection can extend; consequently, full and deep breaths should also result in the rib cage expanding.

Proper breathing will *not* raise the shoulders. Encourage students to inhale *downward*—to draw air toward the waist, a practice that eliminates raising the shoulders and helps ensure the proper use of the diaphragm. The feeling for a deep breath can be developed by taking a sudden inward gasp, with the fingers positioned to feel the expansion of the lower back

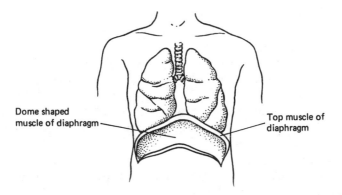

Figure 8-1. The diaphragm.

and stomach, then shouting "hey" in a deep voice and feeling what happens to the muscles. Practicing Santa Claus belly laughs or panting like a tired puppy on a hot day can reinforce these sensations.

Controlled breathing is inhaling sufficient air and then exhaling it under pressure. Many players run out of air because they force it out too fast, an almost universal problem with beginning flute players. The player who can sustain a long phrase is one who has (1) a good embouchure that enables an economical use of air and (2) good control over the muscles used for exhaling. The following devices are helpful for teaching the student to inhale correctly.

1. Imagine stepping into a cold shower on a hot day. The result is a sudden gasp as the air rushes deep inside, seemingly to the stomach.
2. Imagine taking an unmannerly "slurp" of soup. Actually make the sound, *then* duplicate the sound silently.
3. Sit in a chair and lean forward with the chest touching or almost touching the knees and the arms extending beside the legs to the floor. Breathe as deeply as possible. In this position it is difficult to inhale incorrectly.
4. Inhale several short breaths in sequence. For instance, before playing a whole note, inhale on the four preceding counts.
5. Stand with the heels and shoulder blades touching the wall. Inhale without moving the shoulders or chest.
6. Lying on a rug on the floor, inhale slowly—the small of the back will touch the floor. The more relaxed the muscles around the lower back are, the easier this becomes.

While these exercises communicate the feel of proper breathing, it must be noted that in actual performance the majority of breaths must be taken very quickly. Therefore, breathing exercises should also be practiced rapidly.

While most students can learn to inhale properly, the process of exhaling correctly has the most direct effect on tone quality, pitch and intonation, and range. To exhale properly, try the following:

1. Hiss in imitation of a teakettle (being careful to make sure that the sound is produced by air rushing by the tongue and not produced by a tense, tight throat).
2. Blow up a balloon.
3. Whistle a note in a comfortable register and sustain it as long as possible without diminuendo.
4. Blow a stream of air against the hand, holding the hand a few inches in front of the lips (ask students to exhale air as hot as possible, then exhale air as cold as possible—the process used for blowing cold air is that required for playing a wind instrument).
5. Repeat the preceding exercise, but blow the air through a mouthpiece (several instruments will not work with the warm air technique—the oboe for example).
6. Sustain a pitch on the mouthpiece, holding the free hand a few inches from the end of it. If the tone remains steady, the airstream will hit the hand evenly and continuously.

Below are additional exercises that may speed the development of proper breathing habits.

1. Inhale as though yawning.
2. Inhale as in a relaxed gasp.
3. Inhale rapidly.
4. Pretend to blow out a candle.
5. Pretend to blow out the candles on the birthday cake at your one hundreth birthday.
6. Inhale while the teacher counts aloud to four, then exhale hot air in four counts at the same tempo.
7. Inhale while the teacher counts aloud to four, then exhale cold air in eight counts.
8. Inhale while the teacher counts aloud to four, then exhale while hissing for twelve counts.

A helpful concept is to think of blowing the air *through* the horn, *through* the stand, and *through* the wall. The idea of projecting air through the instrument rather than just into the mouthpiece will help with both inhaling and exhaling and will help create a more intense tone.

A common breathing problem is caused by tense throat muscles that constrict the throat and the passage of air. Symptoms of a closed throat include raised shoulders, tense neck muscles, slightly protruding tendons and blood vessels in the neck, a pinched upper register, a weak lower register, and the inability to tongue rapidly. A closed throat may result from attempting to play in the upper register before the necessary muscle development has taken place (usually to satisfy the demands of the performing situation, often in jazz and marching band). For players with this problem, the remedy lies in such exercises as pretending to yawn, relaxed gasping, and fogging a mirror while saying "ah" (i.e., slower inhalation and exhaling a warm airstream). While correcting a closed-throat problem, the student should avoid the upper register, concentrating on the registers in which playing is comfortable, relaxed, *and* sounds good.

Attempting to play with the teeth together (a problem with young brass players), blocking the air passage with the tongue, and failure to exhale completely also create breathing difficulties.

The quantity of air required for good tone quality varies with the different instruments. Among woodwind instruments, the oboist requires the least amount of air, the bassoonist and clarinetist the most. With the brasses, the air required is proportionate to the overall length and diameter of the various instruments: the tuba requires the most, the trombone more than the trumpet, and the horn the least. Note that the *quantity of air* should not be confused with the *speed of the airstream* (air pressure), as both the oboe and the horn demand a fast airstream for good tone quality.

Vibrato

Vibrato is a pulsating of the tone by slight variations in pitch, intensity, or both. It should not be used constantly. Its use in lyrical passages gives a warm, voicelike quality to the tone.

Knowing *how* and *when* to use vibrato is an essential part of instrumental training. Classical and preclassical music seldom require vibrato, although many musicians like to use some as long as it is subtle and unobtrusive. Contemporary music often demands a perfectly even, "straight" tone. The music that usually requires the most vibrato is that of the Romantic era, and jazz and popular music. We hear more Romantic music than any other kind of serious music, and what we hear is often played with exaggeration; thus the student naturally tends to play with exaggerated vibrato, dynamics, and rubato. Musicianship should be taught along with instrumental techniques by introducing the student to many examples of wellplayed music, both live and recorded.

Vibrato is produced in a number of ways. Sheer fright is the least recommended. Among the methods most frequently used for producing a controlled vibrato are use of the hand, the diaphragm, or the jaw. Head vibrato, most often used by jazz performers who desire a broad range of vibrato for special effects, usually causes a tightening of muscles that should remain relaxed, such as the throat and base of the tongue. Vibrato produced by opening and closing the throat usually results in variations of tone quality as well as pitch and also should be avoided.

Jaw vibrato is used frequently, although opponents believe that it interferes with maintaining a proper embouchure, causes bad articulation habits (e.g., "chewing" notes), and becomes so habitual that a straight tone is impossible. Advocates disagree, maintaining that this technique actually helps in developing a good embouchure, reduces excessive pressure from the mouthpiece, constantly redistributes pressure created by a fast-moving airstream behind the embouchure, and is more natural. When used mostly by players of the larger brass instruments, jaw vibrato is produced by a slight muscular movement of the jaw, controlled by the muscles at the corner of the mouth and in the cheek, as if vocalizing "ya-ya-ya-ya" without moving the lower jaw more than necessary.

Hand vibrato is commonly used by trumpet and trombone players. For this type of vibrato, the right hand makes small back-and-forth movements while pressing down the valves or holding the slide. For the trumpeter, this vibrato increases and decreases pressure on the lips. To develop an even vibrato of this type, the student should begin by practicing slowly, with pulsations at about eighth note speed, increase them to sixteenth note speed, and on to a speed as fast as possible with control (most authorities advocate striving for seven pulsations per second). The hand should move from the wrist, not from the finger joints. At first, practice should be with long tones and the vibrato metered in rhythm. Hand vibrato is not successful for the player who uses excessive lip pressure, as it depends on forcing the mouthpiece slightly against the embouchure to produce the higher pitch, the "top side" of the vibrato.

Diaphragm vibrato is the most widely accepted method of vibrato, although it is the most difficult to learn and to control. Diaphragm vibrato is favored by woodwind players and is occasionally used by brass players. To produce diaphragm vibrato, the student should begin by panting, a "ha" or "ho" done slowly to give the feeling of the diaphragm moving up and down. This should be practiced on long tones, with four or eight pulses to each pitch. When the player has established a controlled, steady rhythm, he should attempt to speed up the pulses and diminish their size. Rhythmic, metered vibrato should be practiced until he has mastered slow and fast, and wide and narrow pulses. Only then should he stop counting the pulses and let the diaphragm work in a less controlled, more natural manner.

The normal rate of vibrato is about seven pulses per second. It should be smooth and regular, but not mechanical. Faster vibrato enhances intensity, slower vibrato gives a more relaxed quality. For most musical styles, the fast vibrato should become narrower and the slow vibrato broader, though certain musical climaxes will dictate an intense vibrato that is both fast and wide.

Warm-Up

A daily warm-up should be part of every woodwind or brass player's routine. It should include brief relaxation exercises (including breathing exercises), finger exercises, tonguing exercises using a variety of tempos and articulations, long tones (crescendoing and decrescendoing), and interval practice (slurred and detached). Exercises for the brass should include lip slurs and those for the woodwinds, wide slurs.

For beginners, the warm-up is a period for daily embouchure training, during which habits can be established. The routine of long tones, lip slurs, technical exercises, and lyrical playing will accelerate development.

A warm-down period is especially important. The instrumental music teacher should allow two to five minutes at rehearsal's end for a brief warm-down. Players should play softly and relaxed, working their way to the lowest register of their instruments. For brass players, this will include pedal tones when possible. During a demanding rehearsal or practice period, muscle tissue in the lips is destroyed and blood circulation is restricted. A relaxed warm-down gets the blood flowing properly and prevents the embouchure from being stiff the next time the student plays.

INTONATION

Closely related to tone quality is intonation, the degree of agreement about what frequency level a notated pitch should sound. Intonation is dependent on equipment, embouchure, and listening. It is most of all dependent on the airstream, since this is what produces a well-focused, centered sound. Although the teacher can go to great lengths to tune the student's instrument to an electronic device, all efforts are fruitless unless the student maintains control of the airstream while listening to her playing.

There is a distinct difference between the *amount* of air passing through the embouchure and the *speed* of that air. *The quantity of air determines the volume level, and the speed of the air determines the pitch of the note.* These two aspects are often confused by young players. Beginning students frequently blow more air when they should be blowing the air faster. The steadiness of the airstream is crucial both to good tone quality and to good intonation. Thinking the correct pitch before playing is the final step before playing.

REFERENCES

Woodwind and Brass Instruments

BLACKWOOD, ALAN. *Musical Instruments*. New York: Bookwright Press, 1987.

BROWN, FRANK. *A Band Director's Handbook of Problems and Solutions in Teaching Instrumental Music*. Lebanon, IN: Studio P/R, 1979.

CURTIS, TONY. *Musical Instruments* (revised ed.), Galashiels, Scotland: Lyle Publications, 1978.

DARLOW, DENYS. *Musical Instruments* (revised ed.). London: A. and C. Black, 1980.

DONINGTON, ROBERT. *Music and Its Instruments*. London: Routledge, Chapman and Hall, 1982.

ENGEL, CARL. *Musical Instruments*. Wolfeboro, NH: Longwood Publishing Group, 1977.

FENNELL, FREDERICK. *Time and the Winds*. Kenosha, WI: G. Leblanc Co., 1954.

HAYES, GERALD. *Musical Instruments and Their Music: 1500–1750* (2 Vols. in 1, reprint of the 1930 ed.). New York: Broude Brothers, 1969.

HAZEN, MARGARET and ROBERT HAZEN. *The Music Men: An Illustrated History of Brass Bands in America, 1800–1920*. Washington: DC: Smithsonian Institution Press, 1987.

KELLY, EDGAR S. *Musical Instruments*. Wolfeboro, NH: Longwood Publishing Group, 1980 (reprint of the 1925 text).

PORTER, MAURICE. *The Embouchure*. London: Boosey and Hawkes, 1967.

RASMUSSEN, MARY. *A Teacher's Guide to the Literature of Brass Instruments*. Durham, NH: Brass Quarterly, 1964.

REINHARDT, DONALD, and DONALD MATTRAN. *A Teacher's Guide to the Literature of Woodwind Instruments*. Durham, NH: Brass Quarterly, 1966.

REMNANT, MARY. *Musical Instruments of the West*. London: Batsford, 1978.

SAWHILL, CLARENCE, and BERTRAM McGARRITY. *Playing and Teaching Woodwind Instruments*. Englewood Cliffs, NJ: Prentice-Hall, 1962.

SWEENEY, LESLIE. *Teaching Techniques for the Brasses*. Rockville Center, NY: Belwin-Mills, 1953.

THOMPSON, KEVIN. *Wind Bands and Brass Bands in School and Music Centres*. New York: Cambridge University Press, 1985.

THORTON, JAMES. *Woodwind Handbook*, San Antonio, TX: Southern Music Co., 1960.

TIMM, EVERETT. *The Woodwinds: Performance and Instructional Techniques*. Boston: Allyn and Bacon, 1964.

WEAST, FREDERICK. *Brass Performance: An Analytical Text of the Processes, Problems, and Technique of Brass* (2nd ed.). New York: McGinnis and Marx, 1965.

WESTPHAL, FREDRICK. *Guide to Teaching Woodwinds*. 4th ed. Dubuque, IA: W. C. Brown, Co., 1985.

WINTERNITZ, EMANUEL. *Musical Instruments and Their Symbolism in Western Art*. Cambridge, MA, Yale University Press, 1979.

General Instrumental Music

ADAIR, AUDREY. *Musical Instruments and the Voices: Fifty Ready-to-Use Activities*. Englewood Cliffs, NJ: Prentice-Hall, 1987.

CAHN, MEYER. *The Instrumentalist's Handbook and Dictionary.* San Francisco, CA: Forman Publishing Co., 1958.

CARLTON, MALCOLM. *Music in Education: A Guide for Parents and Teachers.* Totowa, NJ: Woburn Press, 1987.

GALLO, STANISLAO. *The Modern Band: A Treatise on Wind Instruments, Symphony Band and Military Band.* Boston, MA: C. C. Birchard and Co., 1935.

GOLDMAN, EDWIN. *Band Betterment, Suggestion and Advise to Bands, Bandmasters, and Band Players.* New York: Carl Fischer, 1934.

GOODMAN, A. HAROLD. *Music Education: Perspectives and Perceptions.* Dubuque, IA: Kendall-Hunt, 1982.

HARRIS, ERNEST E. *Music Education: A Guide to Information Sources.* Detroit: Gale Research Company, 1978.

HOUSE, ROBERT. *Instrumental Music for Today's Schools.* Englewood Cliffs, NJ: Prentice-Hall, 1965.

JONES, ARCHIE. *Music Education in Action: Basic Principles and Practical Methods.* Boston: Allyn and Bacon, 1960.

JONES, LLEWELLYN. *Building the Instrumental Music Department.* New York: Carl Fischer, 1949.

KOHUT, DANIEL. *Instrumental Music Pedagogy.* Englewood Cliffs, NJ: Prentice-Hall, 1973.

KUHN, WOLFGANG E. *Instrumental Music.* 2nd ed. Boston: Allyn and Bacon, 1970.

KUPPUSWAMY, GOWRI and M. HARIHARAN. *Teaching of Music* (2nd ed.). New Delhi: Sterling, 1980.

LABUTA, JOSEPH A. *Guide to Accountability in Music Instruction.* West Nyack, NY: Parker Publishing Co., 1974.

LAWRENCE, IAN. *Music and the Teacher.* London: Pitman, 1975.

MOORE, E. C. *The Band Book.* Kenosha, WI: G. Leblanc Co., 1953.

Music Teacher Education: Partnership and Process, The Task Force on Music Teacher Education for the Nineties. Reston, VA: Music Educators National Conference, 1987.

NEIDIG, KENNETH. *The Band Director's Guide.* Englewood Cliffs, NJ: Prentice-Hall, 1964.

PETERS, DAVID and R. MILLER. *Music Teaching and Learning.* New York: Schirmer, 1982.

PHILLIPS, HARVEY. *Play Now.* Morristown, NJ: Silver Burdett Co., 1968.

PRATT, ROSALIE. *Music Education for the Handicapped: Second International Symposium.* Van Nuys, CA: Alfred Publishers, 1983.

PRESCOTT, GERALD, and LAWRENCE CHIDESTER. *Getting Results with School Bands.* New York: Carl Fischer and Minneapolis, Schmitt Music Co., 1938.

READ, GARDNER. *Contemporary Instrumental Techniques.* New York: Schirmer, 1976.

WALKER, ROBERT. *Music Education: Tradition and Innovation.* Springfield, IL: C. C. Walker, 1984.

WEERTS, RICHARD. *Handbook for Woodwinds.* Kirkville, MO: The Simpson Printing Co., 1966.

ZINAR, RUTH. *Music in Your Classroom: An Activities Program for Music Skills, Appreciation and Creativity.* Englewood Cliffs, NJ: Prentice-Hall, 1982.

Elementary Instrumental Music

BAYLESS, KATHLEEN, and MAJORIE RAMSEY. *Music: A Way of Life for the Young Child.* 3rd ed. Columbus, OH: Merrill, 1987.

BEALL, GRETCHEN. *Music as Experience: Structure and Sequence for the Elementary School.* Dubuque, IA: W. C. Brown, 1980.

CRADOCK, EVELINE. *Musical Appreciation in an Infant School.* London: Oxford University Press, 1977.

HACKETT, PATRICIA. *Musical Classroom: Models, Skills, and Backgrounds for Elementary Teaching.* Englewood Cliffs, NJ: Prentice-Hall, 1979.

HOFFER, MARJORIE, and CHARLES HOFFER. *Music in the Elementary Classroom.* New York: Harcourt Brace Jovanovich, 1987.

HOLZ, EMIL, and ROGER JACOBI. *Teaching Band Instruments to Beginners.* Englewood Cliffs, NJ: Prentice-Hall, 1966.

KONOWITZ, BERT. *Music Improvisation as a Classroom Method.* New York: Alfred Publishers, 1973.

LANDON, JOSEPH. W. *The Music Lab: Individual Activities for Music Education.* Fullerton, CA: Music Education Publications, 1982.

NELSON, ESTHER. *Musical Games for Children of All Ages.* New York: Sterling Publishing Co., 1981.

NYE, ROBERT, and VERNICE NYE. *Music in the Elementary School.* 5th ed. Englewood Cliffs, NJ: Prentice-Hall, 1985.

PEERY, J. C., IRENE W. PERRY and THOMAS DRAPER. *Music and Child Development.* New York: Springer-Verlag, 1987.

REGNER, HERMANN. *Music for Children.* (Orff-Schulwerk: Vol. 2). London: Schott, 1977.

SWANSON, BESSIE. *Music in the Education of Children.* 4th Ed. Belmont, CA: Wadsworth, 1981.

WIRTH, MARIAN, and VERNA STASSEVITCH. *Musical Games, Fingerplays & Rhythmic Activities for Early Childhood.* Englewood Cliffs, NJ: Prentice-Hall, 1983.

Secondary Instrumental Music

BENNER, CHARLES. *Teaching Performing Groups: From Research to the Music Classroom.* Vol. no. 2. Washington, DC: Music Educators National Conference, 1972.

DUVALL, CLYDE. *The High School Band Director's Handbook.* Englewood Cliffs, NJ: Prentice-Hall, 1960.

HOFFER, CHARLES. *Teaching Music in the Secondary Schools* 3rd ed. Belmont, CA: Wadsworth, 1983.

KOHUT, DANIEL. *Musical Performance: Learning Theory & Pedagogy.* Englewood Cliffs, NJ: Prentice-Hall, 1985.

LABUTA, JOSEPH. *Teaching Musicianship in the High School Band.* West Nyack, NY: Parker Publishing Co., 1972.

MERCER, JACK. *The Band Director's Brain Book.* Evanston, IL: The Instrumental Co., 1970.

PIZER, RUSSELL. *Instrumental Music Evaluation Kit: Forms and Procedures for Assessing Student Performance.* Englewood Cliffs, NJ: Prentice-Hall, 1987.

History of Instruments

BAINES, ANTHONY. *Musical Instruments Through the Ages.* New York: Walker and Co., 1975.

CARSE, ADAM. *Musical Wind Instruments: A History of the Wind Instruments Used in European Orchestras and Wind Band, from the Later Middle Ages up to the Present Time.* 2nd ed. New York: Da Capo Press, 1965.

GALPIN, W. A. *A Textbook of European Musical Instruments: Their Origin, History, and Character.* New York: J. DeGraff, 1956.

GEIRINGER, K. *Musical Instruments: Their History in Western Culture.* 3rd ed. New York: Oxford University Press, 1978.

SACHS, CURT. *The History of Musical Instruments.* New York: W. W. Norton, 1940.

URBAN, DARRELL. *The Enigma of the Tromba Da Tirarsi.* Fullerton, CA: F. E. Olds, 1968.

Tuning and Acoustics

BACKUS, JOHN. *The Acoustic Foundation of Music.* New York: W. W. Norton, 1969.

BENADE, ARTHUR H. *Fundamentals of Musical Acoustics.* New York: Oxford University Press, 1976.

_____. *Horns, Strings, and Harmony—The Science of Enjoyable Sounds.* Garden City, NY: Anchor Books, 1960.

BROADHOUSE, JOHN. *Musical Acoustics: Or the Phenomena of Sound as Connected With Music.* 4th ed. London: W. Reeves, 1980.

CAMPBELL, D. W. AND CLIVE GREATED. *Musician's Guide to Acoustics.* New York: Schirmer, 1987.

CULVER, C. A. *Musical Acoustics.* 4th ed. New York: McGraw-Hill, 1956.

HALL, D. E. *Musical Acoustics: An Introduction.* Belmont, CA: Wadsworth Co., 1979.

HUTCHINS, CARLEEN. *Musical Acoustics: Violin Family Functions.* 2 Parts. New York: Academic Press, 1976.

KENT, EARLE, ED. *Musical Acoustics: Piano and Wind Instruments.* Stroudsberg, PA: Dowden, Hutchinson and Ross, 1977.

RIGDEN, J. S. *Physics and the Sound of Music.* New York: Wiley, 1977.

Repairing Instruments

BRAND, E. D. *Band Instrument Repair Manual.* 4th ed. Elkhart, IN: Erick D. Brand, 1946.

NILLES, RAYMOND. *Basic Repair Handbook for Musical Instruments.* Fullerton, CA: F. E. Olds, 1959.

SPRINGER, G. H. *Maintenance and Repair of Wind and Percussion Instrument.* Boston: Allyn and Bacon, 1976.

TIEDE, CLAYTON. *The Practical Band Instrument Repair Manual.* 3rd ed. Dubuque, IA: W. C. Brown, 1976.

WEISSHAAR, OTTO H. *Preventive Maintenance of Musical Instruments.* Rockville Center, NY: Belwin-Mills, 1966. The text is also available in separate publications for flute & piccolo, oboe & English horn, clarinet, saxophone, bassoon, piston valve instruments, rotary valve instruments, and percussion instruments.

Jazz/Stage Bands

ABE, K. *Jazz Giants.* 2nd ed. New York: Billboard Publications, 1988.

BOGART, MAX. *Jazz Age.* New York: Macmillan, 1969.

BERENDT, JOACHIM E. *The Jazzbook: From New Orleans to Rock and Free Jazz.* New York: Hill and Wang, 1966.

BURNETT, MICHAEL. *Jazz.* New York: Oxford University Press, 1986.

CARR, IAN, DIGBY FAIRWEATHER and BRIAN PRIESTLY, *Jazz: The Essential Companion.* Englewood Cliffs, NJ, Prentice-Hall, 1988.

CHARTERS, SAMUEL. *Jazz: New Orleans 1885–1963.* New York: Da Capo Press, 1983.

CHARTERS, SAMUEL and LEONARD KUNSTADT. *Jazz: A History of the New York Scene.* New York: Da Capo Press, 1981.

CLAYTON, PETER, and PETER GAMMOND. *Jazz A-Z.* New York: Sterling, 1987.

COKER, JERRY. *Improvising Jazz.* Englewood Cliffs, NJ: Prentice-Hall, 1964.

————. *The Jazz Idiom.* Englewood Cliffs, NJ: Prentice-Hall, 1975.

————. *Patterns for Jazz.* Lebanon, IN: Studio P/R, 1970.

COLLIER, G. *Jazz.* New York: Cambridge University Press, 1976.

CRITTENDEN, VICKY L. *Jazz: A Case Study.* Reading, MA: Addison-Wesley, 1986.

DANKEWORTH, AVRIL. *Jazz: An Inntroduction to Its Musical Basis.* New York: Oxford University Press, 1968.

FINKELSTEIN, SIDNEY. *Jazz: A People's Music.* New York: Da Capo Press, 1975.

FRANCIS, ANDRE. *Jazz* (Roots of Jazz Series). New York: Da Capo Press, 1960.

GAMMOND, PETER and CHARLES FOX. *Jazz on Record: A Critical Guide.* Westport, CT: Greenwood, 1978.

GERARDI, JESS. *Factors Associated with the Rise of the Stage Band in Public Secondary Schools of Colorado.* Fullerton, CA.: F. E. Olds, 1962.

GITLER, IRA. *Jazz Masters of the Forties.* New York: Da Capo Press, 1982.

GIUFFRE, JIMMY. *Jazz Phrasing and Interpretation.* New York: Associated Music Publishers, 1969.

GLASER, MATT and STEPHANIE GRAPPELLI. *Jazz Violin.* New York: Oak Publications, 1981.

GODDARD, CHRIS. *Jazz Away from Home.* New York: Da Capo Press, 1987.

GOFFIN, ROBERT. *Jazz: From the Congo to the Metropolitan.* New York: Da Capo Press, 1975.

GOLDBERG, JOE. *Jazz Masters of the Fifties.* New York: Da Capo Press, 1983.

GRIDLEY, MARK. *Jazz Styles: History and Analysis.* 4th ed. Englewood Cliffs, NJ: Prentice-Hall, 1991.

GRIFFIN, CLIVE D. *Jazz.* London: Dryad, 1988.

HADLOCK, RICHARD. *Jazz Masters of the Twenties.* New York: Da Capo Press, 1988.

HALL, M. E. *Teacher's Guide to the High School Stage Band.* Elkart, IN: Selmer, (n.d.).

HARRIS, STEVE. *Jazz on Compact Disc: A Critical Guide to the Best Recordings.* New York: Harmony Books, 1987.

————. *Jazz on LP's: A Collector's Guide to Jazz on Decca, Brunswick, London, Felsted, Durcretet-Thomson, Vogue Coral, Telefunken, and Durium Long Playing Records.* Westport, CT: Greenwood, 1978.

HEFELE, BERNHARD. *Jazz Bibliography.* Munich: Saur, 1981.

HENTOFF, NAT. *Jazz Is.* New York: Random House, 1976.

————. *The Jazz Life.* New York: Da Capo Press, 1975.

HENTOFF, NAT and ALBERT MCCARTHY. *Jazz: New Perspectives on the History of Jazz.* New York: Da Capo Press, 1974.

HOLMES, LOWELL and JOHN THOMSON. *Jazz Greats: Getting Better with Age.* New York: Holmes and Meier, 1986.

JAFFE, ANDREW. *Jazz Theory.* Dubuque, IA: W. C. Brown, 1983.

JONES, TIM. *The Educational Validity of Stage Band Literature in High School Music Education.* Fullerton, CA: F. E. Olds, 1962.

LEVEY, JOSPEH. *Jazz Experience: A Guide to Appreciation.* Lanham, MD: United Press of America, 1987.

MCCALLA, JAMES. *Jazz: A Listener's Guide.* Englewood Cliffs, NJ: Prentice-Hall, 1982.

MEADOWS, EDDIE. *Jazz Reference and Research Materials: A Bibliography* (22 vol). New York: Garland, 1981.

PINCKNEY, WARREN R. *Jazz: A Guide to Perceptive Listening.* Dubuque, IA: Kendall-Hunt, 1986.

REISNER, ROBERT G. *The Jazz Titans: Including "The Parlance of Hip".* New York: Da Capo Press, 1977.

SARGEANT, WINTHROP. *Jazz, Hot and Hybrid.* 3rd ed. New York: Da Capo Press, 1975.

SAUNDERS, LESLIE. *Training the School Dance Band.* New York: Chappell, 1956.

SHAPIRO, NAT. *Jazz Makers: Essays on the Greats of Jazz.* New York: Da Capo Press, 1979.

SHAW, ARNOLD. *Jazz Age: Popular Music in the 1920's.* New York: Oxford University Press, 1987.

STANTON, KENNETH. *Jazz Theory: A Creative Approach.* New York: Taplinger, 1982.

STEWART, REX. *Jazz Masters of the Thirties.* New York: Da Capo Press, 1972.

TANNER, PAUL, MAURICE GEROUT and DAVID MEGILL. *Jazz.* 6th ed. Dubuque, IA: W. C. Brown, 1988.

TIRRO, FRANK. *Jazz: A History.* New York: W. W. Norton, 1977.

VULLIAMY, GRAHAM. *Jazz and Blues.* London: Routledge, Chapman & Hall, 1982.

WILLIAMS, MARTIN. *Jazz Masters of New Orleans.* New York: Da Capo Press, 1979.

————. *Jazz Tradition.* London: Oxford University Press, 1983.

WISKIRCHEN, GEORGE. *Building a Stage Band.* Kenosha, WI: G. Leblanc Co., 1964.

WHITMAN, PAUL, and MARY MCBRIDE. *Jazz.* New York: Arno Press, 1974.

Conducting

GREEN, ELIZABETH. *The Modern Conductor.* 4th ed. Englewood Cliffs, NJ: Prentice-Hall, 1987.

KAHN, EMIL. *Conducting.* New York: The Free Press, 1965.

————. *Workbook for Conducting.* New York: The Free Press, 1965.

RUDOLF, MAX. *The Grammar of Conducting.* 2nd ed. New York: Schirmer, 1980.

Marching Bands

GORE, W. C. and CONNIE BRITTON. *Promoting a Successful Marching Band Contest.* Nashville, TN: Arrangers Publishing Co., 1985.

HOLSTON, KIM. *Marching Band Handbook: Competitions, Instruments, Clinics, Fund-Raising, Publicity, Uniforms, Accessories, Trophies, Drum Corps, Twirling, Color Guard, Indoor Guard, Music, Travel, Directories, Bibliographies, Index.* Jefferson, NC: McFarland & Co., 1984.

HOPPER, DALE. *Corps Style Marching.* Oskaloosa, IA: C. L. Barnhouse Co., (n.d.).

————. *The Drill Designer's Blue Book.* Macomb, IL: D. Hopper Music, 1988.

MEHAN, JACK and WAYNE DOWNEY. *Ensemble Techniques.* Volumes 1 and 2. New Berlin, WI: Jenson Publications, 1982.

PETERS, SHARON. *Marching Band Mystery.* Mahwah, NJ: Troll Associates, 1985.

RAXSDALE, BILL. *Contemporary Color Guard Manual.* New Berlin, WI: Jenson Publications, 1980.

————. *Contemporary Show Design Manual.* New Berlin, WI: Jenson Publications, 1981.

————. *The Marching Band Director.* New Berlin, WI: Jenson Publications, 1985.

RYDER, DAN. *Marching Band Drill Design: A Complete Manual.* New Berlin, WI: Jenson Publications, 1987.

SHELLAHAMER, BENTLEY, JAMES SWEARINGEN and JON WOODS, *The Marching Band Program: Principles and Practices.* Oskaloosa, IA: C. L. Barnhouse Co., 1986.

SNIDER, LARRY. *Developing the Corps Style Percussion Section.* Oskaloosa, IA: C. L. Barnhouse Co., 1979.

————. *Total Marching Percussion.* 3 vol. Oskaloosa, IA: C. L. Barnhouse Co., 1982.

SNOECK, KENNETH M. *Contemporary Drill Design.* Oskaloosa, IA: C. L. Barnhouse Co., 1981.

VINSON, JOHNNIE B. *Arranging for the Marching Band.* Lebanon, IN: Studio P/R, 1981.

VOSE, DAVID. *Developing Musicianship in the Contemporary Marching Percussion Ensemble.* Lebanon, IN: Studio P/R, 1981.

WELLS, JAMES. *Marching Band in Contemporary Music Education.* New York: Interland Publications, 1976.

WRIGHT, AL. *Marching Band Fundamentals.* New York: Carl Fischer, 1963.

9

Principles
for Woodwinds

The various woodwind instruments are not as similar to each other as
are the brasses. There are exceptions to virtually every common denomina-
tor. For example, all woodwinds are (or were) made of wood—except the
saxophone. All use a wooden reed as a tone generator—except the flute.
All overblow the octave for their second register—except the clarinet. All
of the upper woodwinds have one register key—except the oboe. All are
based on the acoustics of a pipe closed at one end—except the flute. All are
found with open tone holes that are covered with the fingers—except the
saxophone. All behave acoustically as a conical bore instrument—except
the clarinet. All are suitable for beginners—except the bassoon. All have
bells—except the flute. . . . and so on.

All woodwinds make extensive use of their fundamental pitches and
use their second partial for their middle registers. The various pitches are
sounded by shortening and lengthening the vibrating air column. Keys are
used to uncover tone holes in order to raise the pitch. Six tone holes
are uncovered one at a time to produce a seven-note scale. The upper tonic
of the scale is played by covering all the tone holes again and overblowing
the fundamental frequency to sound the second partial—this point between the first and second registers is called "the break." Additional tone
holes and keys are added and manipulated by the little fingers to extend
the range downward and to play the chromatic scale.

The second register is made accessible by use of an octave or register
key that opens a vent hole near the mouthpiece. Many teachers and
students believe that this vent hole forces the vibrating air column to
double in frequency to produce the second partial. What the octave or
register key actually does is make the lower register (fundamental pitches)

impossible to sound, because the opened vent hole changes the instrument's resonant frequency. In short, the octave key does not facilitate the second register, it simply makes the lower register much more difficult, or impossible, to play. For all woodwinds, the left thumb is used to operate the register key(s).

ACOUSTICAL CONSIDERATIONS

Like the brass instruments, woodwind instruments produce sound from the longitudinally vibrating air column contained inside the instrument. These sound waves are labeled *standing waves*, since they are stationary between points called *nodes* (points where the longitudinal motion is reversed). Air enters a woodwind instrument through the mouthpiece (which in combination with the reed serves as a tone generator) and forces the air already inside the instrument to vibrate. The air molecules move longitudinally back and forth between nodes at a frequency equal to the pitch being played.[1]

The length of the longitudinal motion is determined by the length of the instrument (which can be shortened or lengthened by opening or closing the tone holes). There is always at least one node present when the low register is played on any woodwind; it forms near the bell or the first open tone hole, where the change in air pressure is sufficient for the pressure wave to be reflected. As tone holes are uncovered, the node moves up the instrument to the highest open hole; the air column is thus shortened and the pitch is raised accordingly. The sound is projected through the first open tone hole and makes the air surrounding the instrument vibrate, carrying the sound to the listener.

Flute

The sharp outer edge of the flute embouchure hole splits the airstream. This split is not as clean and neat as one might expect, with one half of the air going into the flute and one half blowing across the top of the embouchure hole. The airstream is split in such a way that almost all of it is directed into the head joint, which fills with air in milliseconds. The airstream is then deflected out of the embouchure hole and "across the room," until the air pressure in the head joint is lowered again and the

---

[1] For a more detailed explanation see John Backus, *The Acoustical Foundations of Music* (New York: W. W. Norton, 1969); Arthur H. Benade, *Horns, Strings, and Harmony* (New York: Doubleday Books, 1960); or Everett Timm, *The Woodwinds: Performance and Instructional Techniques*, 2nd ed. (Boston: Allyn and Bacon, 1971).

airstream is pulled back down into the head joint (again, taking only milliseconds). This "up-and-down" motion across the sharp edge of the embouchure hole creates turbulence that triggers one of the flute's resonant frequencies (depending on how many tone holes are covered and the speed of the air). Usually, one of the fundamental pitches will sound.

Increasing the speed of the airstream will cause a slight rise in pitch (but only within the confines of the length of the flute's bore). A greater increase in the air speed with a slight change of direction of the airstream will cause the vibrating air column to double in frequency and the second partial (the second octave) to sound.

This principle of a sharp edge splitting the airstream to produce a sound is how a recorder works, and an even simpler example is that of the whistle used by a football referee. On the recorder, the performer blows through a rectangular chamber that controls the direction of the airstream and the amount of air allowed to reach the sharp edge (consequently determining the tone quality, the volume level, and to an extent the pitch). The flute embouchure serves the same function as the recorder mouthpiece but, without a fixed chamber to direct the airstream, allows the performer much greater freedom to alter the tone quality, the volume level, and the pitch.

Like all other woodwinds, the flute has six primary tone holes that are closed and opened by the first three fingers of each hand. These tone holes sound a D scale when raised one at a time; when all six are raised a C-sharp is sounded. The tone holes are then covered again and the velocity of the airstream is increased to overblow the instrument and cross the break to the second partial, the second octave D, and the second register.

Other keys are added to facilitate the complete chromatic scale and to correct intonation flaws. Additional tubing is added to the flute to extend the range down to C.

Reeds

The other woodwinds use a reed as the primary element of tone generation. All use the fundamental and second partial as their first and second registers and also use six primary tone holes (the first three fingers of each hand) for their basic scale.

The reeds used on woodwind instruments are flexible slivers of wood carefully carved to vibrate at the appropriate resonant frequencies. Because reeds are considerably less flexible than brass players' lips, woodwind players cannot manipulate pitch as much as brass players can. Whereas a brass player can play seven to ten pitches without changing the valve or slide combination, the woodwind player can play only one pitch (sometimes two and rarely three) using the same fingering.

Single Reeds

Single reeds are attached to the mouthpiece by a clamp called a *ligature*. The ligature is designed to hold the reed firmly in alignment with the mouthpiece yet allow it to vibrate freely. The tip of the reed is aligned carefully against the tip of the mouthpiece, which curves slightly away from the tip of the reed. This "lay" of the mouthpiece creates a small opening between the reed and the mouthpiece through which the air moves.

The mouthpiece is placed in the performer's mouth so that the reed is against the lower lip. The player presses this lip against the reed to partially close the opening at the tip. When the air is blown, the resonant frequency determined by the fingering is set in motion and the instrument responds. Since the reed itself has a resonant frequency, care must be taken not to allow it to sound (this happens when the player bites it). Some beginners with incorrect embouchures allow the reed to vibrate at its own frequency, resulting in a squeak.

The single reed mouthpiece behaves similarly to the flute head joint in the way the air pressure in it fluctuates. As the air pressure inside the mouthpiece builds, it forces the flexible reed to bend open to allow more air to enter the mouthpiece, but only if the air pressure in the performer's mouth is greater than that inside the instrument and mouthpiece. This puff of air forces the "high pressure area" inside the mouthpiece and down through the instrument, which in turn creates lower pressure in the mouthpiece. The low pressure acts as a vacuum to pull the reed toward the mouthpiece, sealing off the player's airstream. This oscillation of the reed is very fast, considerably faster than the frequency of the pitch being sounded by the instrument itself.

Two factors make it difficult to play softly on a reed instrument. First, the frequency of the reed must be faster than that of the instrument's air column (which requires a fast airstream). And second, any slight drop of the performer's air pressure will force air into the mouth rather than into the instrument. Both factors require the player to blow a steady, supported, fast airstream into the mouthpiece.

Clarinet

The clarinet is the most nearly cylindrical instrument found in the band or orchestra. One limitation of cylindrical pipes closed at only one end is that they produce only the odd-numbered partials of the overtone series. If a trumpet were genuinely cylindrical throughout its length, it would require several additional valves to close the gap between those playable notes of the overtone series. Instead of missing a maximum of six half steps between playable notes of the overtone series, it would be missing eighteen half steps between the first and third partials.

This is precisely how a clarinet works. The basic six-tone-hole scale is a G scale; tone holes and keys are added to extend the range down to an E and up to add the G, G-sharp, A, and A-sharp above. To play the next B, all the tone holes are covered (as if fingering the low E) and the fundamental is overblown to the third partial (a twelfth). The second partial, or octave, will not sound.

The second register is assisted by pressing the register key that opens an additional vent hole near the mouthpiece and destroys the resonant frequencies for the fundamental pitches. For some of the higher notes in the second register and for notes in the third register, additional tone holes are opened to serve as additional vent holes.

Saxophone

The saxophone uses a single reed like a clarinet but is the most obviously conical-shaped instrument in the woodwind family. It overblows the octave with the help of a register key that opens a vent hole on the neck. Its basic six-tone-hole scale is D, like the flute, but it has additional tone holes and keys to extend the range down to B-flat and to provide the chromatic scale.

Due to the size and stiffness of the saxophone reed, coupled with the instrument's lack of resistance, the saxophone is among the easiest of instruments on which to produce a sound but among the most difficult to control.

Double Reeds

The tone generator for double reeds is the reed itself. While the area inside a single-reed mouthpiece acts as the vibrating chamber, the double reed's vibrating chamber is the area between the two curved reeds, and so is much smaller in size. The two flexible reeds vibrate toward each other and then away from each other to create the same effect as that produced by the single reed and mouthpiece. This vibrating chamber does, however, allow the performer to have more control over pitch, volume level, and tone color than a single-reed player does.

Oboe

The oboe is a conical-shaped instrument. The basic six-tone-hole scale is D to C, with keys to extend the range down to B-flat. The octave key destroys the resonant frequencies of the lower octave. To play some notes in the second and third octaves, additional octave keys are required. To compensate, the oboe is provided with several vent holes and also uses a half-hole technique to provide a small vent for some pitches. Other pitches are played with upper tone holes opened while lower tone holes are covered to provide yet a third type of vent hole (these fingerings are called "fork fingerings," and they can frequently also be used to improve intonation in the lower octave).

Bassoon

The bassoon is also a conical-shaped double-reed instrument. Its total length is about 100 inches (over 8 feet), doubled up to position the six primary tone holes and keys within reach of an average-sized adult hand. Even in this position the fingers must stretch for certain keys.

The double reed attaches to the bocal, which is inserted into the wing joint. The wing joint derives its name from the shape of wood used for it. The first three tone holes are positioned in this joint, and if they were positioned in the proper place in the bore of the joint, they would be too far apart for the first three fingers of the left hand to cover all three. Wood is added to this joint to make it thicker, allowing the tone holes to be cut at an angle so that the hand can cover them, but so that they open into the bore of the instrument with the correct distance between them.

The basic six-tone-hole scale is G to F. The range is extended down to a low B-flat with the addition of more keys and tone holes. Because the tube is so long, there is no way for one vent hole to serve as an octave key for all pitches.

EMBOUCHURE

Each of the woodwind instruments requires a different embouchure. Although the clarinet and saxophone embouchure, for example, may appear similar, fundamental differences between them are essential to good tone quality. All beginning woodwind players must devote their concentration and most of their practice time developing the embouchure. Tone quality, pitch, range, endurance, and articulation depend upon the embouchure.

TONE QUALITY

As has been said, tone quality and intonation are dependent on each other. Tone is the basic stuff of music; beautiful tone is the basic stuff of beautiful music.

Woodwind players have more difficulty developing a good tone quality than do brass players, largely due to woodwind players' dependence on the reed, and the instrument's unforgiving reliance on a proper embouchure.

Woodwind beginners should be instructed in homogeneous classes. Beginning woodwind players in heterogeneous classes often attempt to play as loudly as brass players, resulting in poor tone quality. At the high school level, homogeneous ensembles such as woodwind choirs, clarinet or flute choirs, and saxophone quartets can promote better intonation, balance, and blend, as well as tone quality.

Most beginning woodwind players will benefit from long-tone studies. The student should play long tones as softly as possible, crescendo to a full sound (without overblowing, letting the pitch change, or moving the embouchure), and then decrescendo to silence. If the young woodwind player attempts to crescendo to the same decibel level as a brass instrument, the embouchure will be affected for the worse. Long tones should be combined with scales for constant tone quality between notes. Tone quality becomes important when students cross the break to play in different registers.

Because the reed is such an important factor in tone production, reed players must receive instruction on care and maintenance of the reed fairly early on in their instruction (another advantage to homogeneous classes). It is probably not worth the time and trouble for single-reed players to bother making their own reeds; double-reed players will, however, benefit from learning how to finish reeds that have already been cut, gouged, and shaped.

Most new reeds are playable straight from the box, but they can usually be improved and adjusted to respond better. Basic care and adjustment of the reed should include instruction on sanding the back of the reed to make and keep it flat, lightly sanding or rubbing the beveled portion of the reed to close the pores, and clipping the tip. Unfortunately, accurate reed adjustments take a great deal of experience; it is likely that most students will produce many more poor reeds than good reeds in the process of learning this skill.

Students should be instructed to know when a reed is past its prime. Many students continue playing on a worn-out reed only to develop bad embouchures in trying to make the reed respond. Since most reeds wear out gradually, it is easy for a student not to notice the difference until harm has been done.

INTONATION

The player is responsibile for learning to play in tune by listening and adjusting the instrument or his embouchure. The teacher's responsibility, however, is to teach how this is done.

Intonation is a basic element of performance, therefore dealing with intonation problems should not be ignored in the beginning classes. Many teachers postpone discussion of intonation, believing that the students' embouchures must be better developed in order to make adjustments and keep the pitch under control. Using the embouchure to control intonation, however, is an excellent way to encourage its development. Students in a fifth-grade beginning woodwind class can determine with ease which of two pitches is higher than the other. All they lack is the knowledge of how to raise the lower pitch or how to lower the higher pitch and the *opportunity* to practice and gain experience making these corrections.

Students are expected to do their practicing at home. It is impossible, however, to practice at home the procedures for playing in tune in an ensemble. This aspect of performance can be learned and practiced only in the classroom; instrumental music instructors should include this goal in their lesson plans. Students can, and should, practice playing in tune with themselves at home (through slow scale practice). Tendencies of instruments to change pitch, such as clarinets going sharp on soft passages while flutes and oboes go flat, can also be remedied and controlled through home practice.

A good warm-up is essential for good intonation. Woodwind instruments require a few minutes of playing to reach the proper temperature and humidity to perform with a constant pitch. Also, woodwinds, due to their straight shape (unlike the coiled brass) have a tendency to cool-off during rests in the music or during lengthy explanations by the teacher.

TECHNIQUE

Woodwind players are expected to be able to play lush, lyrical passages and fast, technical passages equally well, and with proper style and precision. The clarinet and trumpet are both pitched in B-flat, but due to the clarinet's ability to play lower and higher, and also to play larger intervals with ease, the music considered idiomatic for each is quite different. Because one trumpet can easily play louder than one clarinet, bands should have more woodwind players than brass, making greater demands on precision in the woodwind section.

Fast passages with many notes are found more frequently in woodwind music than in brass music. And while brass players can resort to double- and triple-tonguing when rapid articulations are required, reed players must learn to single-tongue at very fast tempos. Consequently, technique is an element of woodwind performance that is constantly practiced and improved. Since technique is a psychomotor skill not unlike a sport, woodwind players must continually work toward faster fingers and a faster tongue, all with control and precision.

Technique is the synchronization of the embouchure, the fingers, and the tongue with the brain. The way the instrument is held is essential to finger dexterity. Almost all beginners initially find the woodwind position awkward. In the early stages of instrumental instruction, the exercises do not require many finger changes, so it is easy for students to seek more secure but incorrect means of holding and supporting the instrument. Each of the woodwinds has a proper place for the left thumb and all four fingers of each hand to rest. These hand positions must be maintained from the outset, since subsequent fingerings will make use of them.

Scales and arpeggios are the basis of at least 90 percent of all finger technique required in school bands and orchestras and form the foundation of all exercises intended to improve finger dexterity. Even if the entire eight-note range of a scale has not been learned, students can practice the first four or five notes, striving for even notes, smooth changes between notes, and evenness of tone quality between notes.

Scales should be practiced systematically in all major and minor keys (plus chromatic scales). A tempo should be established at which the student can play evenly and accurately with good tone quality and intonation. Scales are best practiced in a cycle beginning on the tonic, playing up to the highest note learned (or possible) in that key, then down to the lowest note learned (or possible) in that key, and back up to the tonic.

Due to the way pitches of woodwind instruments are raised, by uncovering tone holes, adjacent notes are often different in tone color. This is especially apparent when the break is crossed. Practice on scales is essential to maintaining good tone quality throughout the range of the instrument.

Arpeggios are excellent means for practicing raising and lowering simultaneously more than one finger at a time. Arpeggios also help develop the embouchure, secure good tone quality across registers, and train the ear.

While practicing both scales and arpeggios, the student should concentrate on maintaining a good embouchure and proper breath support. Eventually, these elements of performance will become automatic, allowing the player to concentrate on notation and the expressive elements of performance.

One characteristic unique to woodwind performance with which students must deal is the movement of keys. When a finger is lifted to change notes, the new note is heard as soon as the finger moves. When a finger is lowered to change notes, the new note is not heard until after the finger moves the distance necessary to close and seal the tone hole. As a result, the instrument responds slightly quicker on ascending passages than on descending passages. The note will respond at the same instant that the finger arrives at the downward location, but the note will respond *before* the arrival of the finger's upward position.

REFERENCES

BACKUS, JOHN. *The Acoustical Foundations of Music*. New York: W.W. Norton, 1969.
BAINES, ANTHONY. *Woodwind Instruments and Their History*. Rev. ed. New York: W.W. Norton, 1963.

BARTOLOZZI, BRUNO. *New Sounds for Woodwinds.* 2nd ed. London: Oxford University Press, 1982.

BENADE, ARTHUR. *Fundamentals of Musical Acoustics.* New York: Oxford University Press, 1976.

————. *Horns, Strings, and Harmony: The Science of Enjoyable Sounds.* Garden City, NY: Anchor Books, 1960.

CARSE, ADAM. *Musical Wind Instruments.* New York: Da Capo Press, 1965.

GILLESPIE, JAMES E. *The Reed Trio: An Annotated Bibliography of Original Published Works.* Detroit, MI: Information Coordinators, 1971.

HOVEY, N. *What to Look for When You Choose Your New Woodwind Mouthpiece.* Elkhart, IN: The Selmer Co., 1978.

KIRK, G.T. *The Reed Guide: A Handbook for Modern Reed Working for All Single Reed Woodwind Instruments.* Decatur, IL: Reed-Mate Company, 1983.

MATHER, B. and DAVID LASOCKI. *Free Ornamentation in Woodwind Music 1700-1775.* New York: McGinnis and Marx, 1976.

MERRIMAN, LYLE. *Woodwind Research Guide.* Evanston, IL: The Instrumentalist Co., 1978.

NEDERVEEN, CORNELIUS. *Acoustical Aspects of Woodwind Instruments.* Amsterdam: Frits Knuf, 1969.

OPPERMAN, KALMEN. *Handbook for Making and Adjusting Single Reeds.* New York: Chappell and Co., 1956.

PETERS, HARRY B. *The Literature of the Woodwind Quintet.* Metuchen, NJ: Scarecrow Press, 1971.

RIGDEN, JOHN S. *Physics and the Sound of Music.* New York: Wiley, 1977.

SAUCIER, G.A. *Woodwinds: Fundamental Performance Techniques.* New York: Schirmer, 1981.

SAWHILL, CLARENCE and BERTRAM McGARRITY. *Playing and Teaching Woodwind Instruments.* Englewood Cliffs, NJ: Prentice-Hall, 1962.

STAUFFER, DONALD W. *Intonation Deficiencies of Wind Instruments in Ensemble.* Washington: Catholic University of America Press, 1954.

THORTON, JAMES. *Woodwind Handbook.* San Antonio, TX: Southern Music Co., 1963.

TIMM, EVERETT. *The Woodwinds: Performance and Instructional Techniques.* 2nd ed. Boston: Allyn and Bacon, 1971.

VOXMAN, HIMIE and LYLE MERRIMAN. *Woodwind Ensemble Music Guide.* Evanston, IL: The Instrumentalist Co., 1973.

————. *Woodwind Solo and Study Guide.* Evanston, IL: The Instrumentalist Co., 1975.

WEERTS, RICHARD. *Handbook for Woodwinds.* 3rd ed. Kirksville, MO: Simpson Printing and Publishing Co., 1966.

————. *How to Develop and Maintain a Successful Woodwind Section.* West Nyack, NY: Parker Publishing Co., 1972.

WESTPHAL, FREDERICK. *Guide to Teaching Woodwinds.* 4th ed. Dubuque, IA: W. C. Brown, 1985.

WHITWELL, DAVID. *Woodwind Anthology.* Evanston, IL: The Instrumentalist Co., 1972.

10

The Flute

The flute is the soprano instrument of the wind family, together with the C piccolo which uses the same fingerings as the flute and sounds one octave higher. Both are used for coloring effects. Pitched in C, the flute is nontransposing. Other flutes include the E-flat flute which is pitched between the regular C flute and the piccolo, the alto flute pitched in G and which is becoming ever more popular in jazz, and the bass flute in C pitched one octave below the regular C flute.

HISTORY

The flute has the longest history of any of the wind instruments. There are in existence two flutes taken from Egyptian tombs and believed by scholars to date from about 2200 B.C. Amazingly, both are in playing condition. Wall drawings and paintings from this period show flute players at various court and religious functions. Around 1300 B.C., a double- pipe instrument related to the flute existed, each pipe with three finger holes. By A.D. 79, the art of music had advanced to the extent that a fifteen-hole instrument was in use fitted with silver bands which slid or twisted to cover the holes not being played. Most of the ancient flutes were not transverse but were held vertically, and the vertical flute, in its familiar form as the recorder, was popular through Bach's time. However, transverse flutes also existed in ancient times, and pictures of them are found on Japanese monuments dating from about 50 B.C.

During the 1600s, the flute began to take on its modern aspects. The first key, the D-sharp key, was added about 1600; the bore was changed from cylindrical to conical in 1680; the round embouchure hole was re-placed by an oval one in 1724. In the early 1700s, the flute became very popular. During this time many keys were added. The innovations and alterations of Boehm that made the flute what it is today came about one hundred years later. In 1832 Boehm invented a ring-key flute; in 1847 he changed the conical bore back to cylindrical; and in 1851 he added covered, open-standing keys.

SELECTING THE INSTRUMENT

Most student-line flutes manufactured by reputable companies are fine for beginners; those made by Armstrong, Artley, Emerson, Gemeinhardt, and Yamaha have been of consistently good quality for years. The majority of these flutes have a bore that starts at 17 millimeters at the cork end and is graduated to 19 millimeters at the joining end. A combination of conical head joint and cylindrical body allows for better intonation in the upper register.

Various aspects of new flutes can provide evidence of the quality of craftsmanship. Those aspects include the keys, tone holes, post mountings, and optional keys. A good student-line instrument has forged keys as opposed to cast ones, appropriately shaped trill keys and D-sharp key, "pulled" tone holes as opposed to soldered ones (soldering is found only on expensive models), and posts mounted on ribbing rather than directly on the body of the flute.

Optional keys may be added to the flute to mitigate technical difficulties such as an awkward fingering or trill. The options are, however, seldom used by young flute players. Perhaps the easiest to justify is the low B key, which is seldom used but adds resonance and enhanced tone quality to the lower notes (shown on the flute in Figure 10-2). Other keys such as the split E key (to make the high E easier to play) and the C-sharp trill key are used by the medium to advanced middle or high school player. Other optional keys should be avoided except by advanced players. Adding keys complicates mechanical adjustment problems.

One aspect of flute construction that is of interest to parents is the material used for plating. Silver plating is priced about the same as the more commonly found nickel plating. Retailers prefer to rent the nickel-plated models, however, since these instruments will still look shiny when returned. Silver plating is preferable for timbre and has the advantage of being less slippery than nickel. The silver will begin to tarnish after a few weeks or months, and students must be reminded to wipe off the instrument after playing. Silver polish is not used to clean the finish.

The closed-hole plateau instrument is easier to master in the early stages than is the open-hole French flute. It is also less expensive. The tradition of advanced flute players "moving up" to an open-hole model is coming to an end as most of the advantages of open-hole instruments are now available on closed-hole models. The primary advantages of the open-hole flutes are (were) that (1) the player can control the intonation more exactly by partially covering the holes with his fingers (some avant-garde music requires pitches played by partially covered holes) and (2) the open-hole promotes proper hand position; in fact, it cannot be played successfully *without* good hand position.

Adjusting screws are used to ensure either that keys activated by pressing other keys are fully closed or that open keys remain open the proper distance. The adjustment screws also assist in realigning keys when a pad is replaced. Beginning students should not tamper with adjustment screws; adjustments of screws are usually necessary only when the uneven strength of the player's fingers cause uneven wear on the keys and pads. A number of companies have eliminated these adjustment screws.

Used flutes should be inspected for common signs of use such as worn pads and for indications of abuse such as damaged keys and rods, and dents or scratches. These may indicate more serious neglect or excessive wear. Furthermore, the prospective buyer should make sure that the outer edge of the embouchure hole is still sharp, that the keys are in alignment and the pads seat properly, that the cork in the head joint is tight (if the crown can be turned easily with the fingers, the cork may be too loose), and most important, that the instrument fits together easily but not too easily. Although minor repairs may be inexpensive, too many repairs may warrant the alternative of buying a new instrument.

The piccolo is similar to the flute, and all accomplished flutists should also be able to play the piccolo. It has the following distinguishing characteristics:

1. Low D is the lowest note because the piccolo has no foot joint; otherwise, the piccolo plays the same range and notes as the flute, but sounding an octave higher. The piccolo cannot go beyond high C.
2. Although the C piccolo is almost universal today, the D-flat piccolo is scored in older march music and transcriptions. The ability to transpose up a half step is useful.
3. The piccolo lacks the pitch flexibility of the flute.
4. The wooden piccolo, more sonorous than the metal, is more desirable for orchestral playing. The metal piccolo is easier to blow and more brilliant in quality.
5. The piccolo requires firmer lips and more pressure on the extreme high notes to overcome the instrument's tendency to sound flat in this register; hence, it is more tiring to play than the flute.
6. Because there is greater resistance, a smaller quantity of air is required, but the airstream must move much more rapidly.

7. Piccolos are made with either a cylindrical or a conical bore. Most flute teachers recommend the cylindrical-bore instrument for marching band and the conical-bore instrument for professional and orchestral players.

An advanced flutist with good intonation is the best candidate for playing the piccolo. Students with small, dexterous fingers and thin lips are usually the most successful.[1]

ASSEMBLING THE FLUTE

Although assembling the flute is a simple matter, a few precautions may help establish good habits that contribute to playing technique and to keeping the instrument in good repair.

The flute consists of three pieces: the head joint, which includes the embouchure hole, the embouchure plate, and the cork; the body of the instrument; and the foot joint, which contains three tone holes. The flute should have a cleaning rod in the case. Correct alignment is important. The head joint should be grasped between the embouchure plate and open end with the left hand; with the right hand, the body of the flute should be picked up gently, without grabbing the key mechanism any more than necessary. The two pieces are twisted together, not pushed or wiggled. The center of the embouchure hole in the head joint should align with the center of the line of keys. Student-line flutes are often made with an engraved mark on the head joint and a matching mark on the body. If the embouchure hole is turned in, a slightly covered sound and flat pitch result. If the hole is turned out, higher pitch and better projection are obtained. The correct alignment allows complete finger freedom, proper balance, and the embouchure hole parallel with the lips.

The foot joint is grasped in such a way that the keys will not be damaged, then gently twisted onto the body of the flute. The rod on the foot joint should bisect the D key on the body of the flute. In correct position, with the fingers of the right hand on the keys, the little finger of the right hand can drop to the low C key without the right wrist having to move. If the foot joint is turned in too far, the little finger will hang over; if out too far, the little finger must poke at the key rather than depress it.

The student must adjust his embouchure to the correct alignment, not the alignment to his embouchure. After a player has acquired considerable skill, he may turn the head joint slightly one way or the other, but experimentation should be postponed until the student has had considerable experience playing with the conventional alignment.

---

[1]See Thomas Rainey, Jr., *The Flute Manual: A Comprehensive Text and Resource Book for Both the Teacher and the Student* (Lanham, NY: University Press of America, 1985), 141.

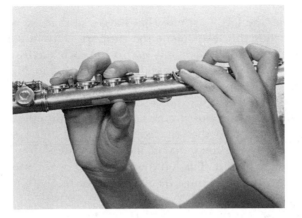

Figure 10–1   Hand Position for the Flute

The head joint is not pushed all the way in, but is pulled out from 1/8 to 1/4 of an inch, to allow for tuning with other instruments. The tenons, the ends of the joints where the pieces fit together, are somewhat delicate and can bend easily if assembled carelessly. The flute should be assembled with a smooth, circular movement, pushing and turning the parts together. If the flute is difficult to assemble, clean *only* the tenons with a mild silver polish. Using a lubricant causes the tenons to attract dirt and grime.

HOLDING THE FLUTE

Most students are uncomfortable when first attempting to hold the flute. The fingers must rest properly on the keys. The size of the hand determines the hand position that will allow the fingers to do this. The flute is supported primarily by the base of the left forefinger and the thumb of the right hand, with the right little finger adding balance. The lips also serve to balance the instrument.

The right thumb supports the flute from below and should be placed *approximately* underneath the F key, or between the right index and middle finger (Figure 10–1). The thumb does not extend under and past the flute; it should be bent so the side of the thumb, not the underside of the knuckle, supports it. The right wrist should not bend; it should be held straight with the fingers slightly curved, the hands forming a C. The pads of the four fingers should rest on their proper keys (rechecking the alignment of the foot joint is advised). A number of Suzuki-oriented flute teachers have proposed that one teach the right-hand position by asking the student to pretend to hold a glass; then pour out the contents. When the hand has turned 90 degrees and the glass is "empty," the correct hand position has been formed.[2]

[2]Takahashi, *Takahashi Flute School* (Suzuki Method) Vol. 1 (Evanston, IL: Summy-Birchard), 7.

In general, the left wrist must be curved, so that the base of the left forefinger touches the instrument for support. The fingers of the left hand, especially the forefinger and less so for each successive finger, are curved more than those of the right hand to allow easy manipulation of the proper keys. The left hand has a tendency to turn out, in which case the fourth finger must stretch for the G-sharp key, thus hindering technique. The fingers must be kept close to the keys. The left thumb is placed on the B key at a slight tilt so that the edge of the thumb presses the key. Beginners often have a tendency to slide their thumb too far under the instrument to help hold it. The left thumb should not be used primarily to support the instrument; it must be able to move freely to manipulate the B-flat key.

Initially, this position may feel somewhat unnatural. The teacher should check frequently to see that the player has not relaxed into habits that feel more natural but are incorrect. Fingering is done by the pads of the fingers. The instructor must watch that the fingers do not overlap the keys, a practice that not only reduces finger dexterity but could cause uneven wear of the pads.

The position for playing the flute is shown in Figure 10–2. The flute is held approximately parallel to the line formed by the lips, that is, the embouchure hole should be parallel with the embouchure both horizontally and vertically. Proper position results from keeping the flute almost parallel to the floor—with the end joint a little lower than the rest of the flute (no more than a 20-degree tilt for the instrument). A slight tilt to the head is appropriate as long as it is not due to poor posture and does not restrict the airstream.

The right elbow is raised until the muscle in the upper part of the arm begins to pull. The correct position is when the elbow is dropped to a point where pulling ceases. Beginning students may try to drop the right arm to a

Figure 10–2   Position for Playing the Flute

more comfortable position, but this cramps the hands, flattens the fingers, and hampers technique.

When playing while seated, the feet are kept flat on the floor with one slightly in front of the other, the body is erect, and the back is away from the chair. The arms must be kept free of the body, not draped over the chair. The student should stand part of the time, during lessons and during practice. Proper upper body position does not change for a standing position. For beginners, maintaining correct playing position may cause some fatigue, therefore the beginning flutist should practice only for short periods of time.

A possible option for the flute is the curved head joint available from several manufacturers. This option makes good hand position easier while still enabling a satisfactory tone. As the student grows physically, this head joint should be replaced with a standard one.

THE BEGINNING STUDENT

The beginner should start on the head joint alone so that he can concentrate solely on adequate tone and correct embouchure. He should be asked to relax his lips as if vocalizing the syllable "em" (this keeps the teeth apart and lips together). Remember that the head joint is placed so that the embouchure plate is parallel with and centered on the lips. Until proper holding position becomes a habit, the student can place the embouchure plate below the lower lip in the curve of the chin and roll the head joint up to center it.

The correct flute embouchure is illustrated in Figure 10–3. The embouchure hole of the flute generally rests on the spot on the lower lip where the clearest tone is produced. This spot will be higher for students with thick lips than for students with thin lips. For most beginners it is safe

Figure 10–3 Flute Embouchure

to position the inner edge of the embouchure hole where the red of the lip meets the facial skin, the lower lip covering approximately 1/4 of the embouchure hole. The player may need to move the head joint up and down, raising and lowering the flute on his lip to find the best spot. Experimenting with very slight movements will help.

With the head joint closed by the palm of the right hand, the student should be asked to blow air as if vocalizing "pee" (syllables such as "poo" cause the embouchure to pucker too much and should be avoided). This small puff of air should produce second-space A; when the hand opens the head joint, an octave higher is sounded. Beginning students often use more air than is required and become dizzy when playing their first tones. Students should be encouraged to focus the airstream, keeping the aperture of the embouchure a small oval. Never should the width of the embouchure opening exceed the width of the embouchure hole.

The airstream should cross the embouchure hole at the very center of the embouchure plate. A tell-tale sign of where the airstream is crossing the plate is the trail of condensation formed by the breath. The trail should look like a small triangle with the base at the far edge of the embouchure hole.

The use of a "pee"-type articulation can help the student produce the beginning sounds on the flute, but its use should not become automatic because the syllable "pee" uses a burst of air to open the lips, whereas the player should form the embouchure opening prior to blowing the air. The Suzuki flute teacher Takahashi advocates that students "spit out one grain of rice at a time" to establish the embouchure. This task keeps the aperture of the embouchure small and the corners firm (but not too firm), and a burst of air pressure is required to send the rice flying. This technique can give the student the appropriate feel of the aperture of the embouchure and the corners of the mouth. (It can, however, also lead to the habit of tonguing between the teeth if not corrected.)[3]

When the student can sustain the two As on the head joint for three or four seconds without fainting, he should be guided to focus the airstream by making the aperture in the embouchure slightly smaller and blowing the air more toward the outer edge of the embouchure hole. He can accomplish this by moving his jaw forward slightly while maintaining the "spitting-rice" embouchure. This change should produce the third harmonic, high E, when played on the closed head joint. In his first attempts, the student may blow *more* air rather than a *faster* airstream. The player should instead try to produce the upper harmonic by blowing *less* air faster.

[3] Nancy Toff, *The Flute Book* (New York: Scribner's, 1985), 214–215.

EMBOUCHURE AND REGISTER

Factors affecting tone are (l) the quality of the instrument, (2) the player's embouchure, (3) his breath support, and (4) his facial structure. Since accuracy of intonation and beauty of tone depend on proper embouchure, more needs to be said concerning the embouchure than any other facet of flute playing.

First of all, *the flute is not played like a soda pop bottle.* This approach, taught all too often, results in a hollow sound. The air should be directed primarily *across* the embouchure hole, although somewhat downward for the low register and slightly upward for the upper register. In general, the player blows more directly into the embouchure hole for louder sounds.

Basically, the flutist's embouchure has these characteristics: (1) The corners of his mouth are stretched back rather tightly, firm but not pinched or clamped as tightly as a brass player's; (2) the corners of his mouth are straight or even turned down rather than in a smiling position; (3) his lower lip is drawn back just enough to allow his upper lip to protrude over it slightly. If the lower lip is too far back, the air column will be directed straight down; if it is even with the upper lip, the air column will go straight out as when blowing out a candle.

The player may want to try two versions of a correct embouchure to see which works best. Some players use both.

1. The upper lip is relaxed while the lips are held in an even position. Only enough pressure from the corners of the lips to smooth out the wrinkles in the lower lip is used. The lower lip will cover approximately one fourth to one third of the embouchure hole, and the column of air will be blown just inside the outer edge of the embouchure hole.
2. The upper lip is stretched tight against the teeth. This embouchure can be thought of as being long, straight, and thin, rather than round and open. Playing is done by blowing over the moist inner surface of the lower lip (such as vocalizing "pee" with the corners of the mouth held firmly). While playing in the upper register, the student relaxes his lip and covers more of the hole.

With either approach, the lower register will require less of the embouchure hole covered and more of the air directed into the flute. The upper register requires the flutist to direct the air toward the outer edge of the embouchure hole and cover more of the embouchure hole with the lower lip.

The size and shape of the embouchure opening will also change depending on the register. For the low register, the mouth should be open about the width of the embouchure hole; the mouth opening becomes narrower and more oval in shape for the middle register, and a smaller oval is used for the upper register. The mouth aperture should not be round. An opening that is too wide produces a coarse, breathy, and inflexible tone. If the opening is too small, which seldom happens, the tone will be small and thin. As the player develops, he will find that lower notes respond more easily with a wider, flatter embouchure, and the higher notes are more responsive using a more oval-shaped, focused embouchure. He will also notice that intonation improves with these embouchure changes. Knowing this will help the player only if he practices in front of the mirror at least a few minutes each day.

Initially, the smaller the lip opening the better. It makes for more resistance to the airstream, enables production of a better tone, and helps avoid dizziness.

Correcting the Embouchure

If too little of the embouchure hole is covered, the tone will be breathy and require more air. If the lips are too tight and too far away from the hole, the air striking the sides of the aperture will cause extraneous vibration in the upper lip. The air column may not be focused, resulting in a thin tone with poor intonation. To improve focus, the student should cover more of the embouchure hole with his lip, turn the flute in slightly by lowering his head, and while not changing his hand position, pull his jaw back, or a combination of these.

If too much of the embouchure hole is covered, the tone will be small and thin, there will be a limited response to the attack, legato playing will be more difficult, dynamic range will be limited, and flexibility will be impaired. To correct this, the student should turn the flute out slightly by raising his head, pushing his jaw forward slightly, or tightening his lips. Sometimes the solution lies in moving the flute up higher on the lower lip so that less of the lip covers the embouchure hole. This can, however, alter the intonation, because with less of the embouchure hole covered, intonation will be sharper; and with more of it covered, it will be flatter. To remedy this, the player will need to turn the head joint in.

Variations in facial structure that affect the embouchure are:

1. A relaxed or receding jaw, which results in a spread, unfocused tone. To correct, the student should bring the lower lip out or turn up the corners of his mouth.
2. A protruding jaw, which produces a breathy tone or no tone at all. To correct, roll the head joint in more.
3. An overhanging upper lip, which causes the mouth opening to be too wide and the lower lip to cover too much of the hole, letting air strike

the sides of the embouchure. Use the same solution as for a receding jaw.

4. Thick lips, which can be compensated for by placing the flute higher onto the red portion of the lower lip.

5. A slight dip in the center of the upper lip, which can be accommodated by keeping it raised and supported by the upper teeth. The student with a very pronounced dip may meet with some success by playing off center; the aperture of the embouchure, however, should be centered on the embouchure hole.

INTONATION

Flute players are notorious for their intonation problems. Because the instrument's range is in the upper register of the grand staff (see Figure 10–4), the wavelengths are shorter, and pitch variations among players cause interference between the several close sound waves. The points of interference occur two, three, or four times per second faster than for other instruments and are thus more easily heard. The result is considerably more annoying than when four tuba players play slightly out of tune.

Generally, the flute has these intonation problems: the low register is flat, the middle register is in tune, and the upper register is sharp. Both middle and upper registers, however, change with volume—flatter when soft and sharper when loud. The flute player deals with pitch by applying two rules: (1) covering the embouchure hole or directing more of the air *into* the instrument, which lowers the pitch; and (2) uncovering the embouchure hole or blowing more air *across* and out of the instrument, which raises the pitch. These two methods are explained to students in a variety of ways, including "raising or lowering the head," "directing the air to the floor or wall," and the most common, "rolling the flute in and out" (which usually results in poor hand position and should be avoided).

The flute tends to be flat in cold temperatures. The instrument should be thoroughly warmed before tuning by gently blowing air into the instrument with all keys closed. The flute can cool down so quickly that most flutists need to warm it by blowing warm air prior to making an entrance after long rests.

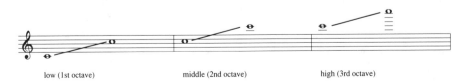

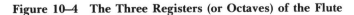
low (1st octave)　　　　　　middle (2nd octave)　　　　　high (3rd octave)

Figure 10–4　The Three Registers (or Octaves) of the Flute

The A or B-flat without vibrato are good tuning notes, but one well-tuned pitch does not ensure correct intonation on all notes. Particular notes on the flute have their own intonation problems, as shown in Figure 10–5. The biggest offender is C-sharp in the staff, and to a slightly lesser extent the C-sharp above the staff. To correct sharpness, the player must lower the jaw very slightly to direct the air more into the embouchure hole. F is usually tested after tuning, as it is usually flat. If higher notes sound flat in relation to lower notes, the cork (the stopper at the end of the head joint) is too far from the embouchure hole and needs adjusting. Notes may also be flat when the embouchure plate is too low on the lip.

The rules on how to raise and lower pitches on the flute can be applied to a single note or to an entire register, as mentioned earlier in this section. To bring a tone down to pitch, the player must drop and pull back the lower jaw in order to blow more directly into the embouchure hole. Bringing flat tones up to pitch calls for the opposite approach. As the student gains more technical and listening skills, he will discover the best methods for correcting out-of-tune notes.

Flute players have a tendency to go flat at the ends of phrases and sustained notes because the breath support diminishes. To counteract sagging pitch, the player can raise his head slightly and protrude his jaw at the end of a note, directing the air more toward the outer edge of the embouchure hole. Diminuendos require special care to keep the pitch from going flat. The player should bring his jaw forward, close his mouth, cover less of the embouchure hole, and blow more across the embouchure hole. For crescendos, the opposite actions are used.

The greatest flutists disagree about whether the flute goes sharp or flat as the volume increases. When other factors are held constant, an increase in volume raises the pitch; but seldom are all other factors held constant. The player usually tightens his embouchure when he increases the volume, to prevent the flute from skipping to the next octave higher, and focuses the airstream more directly into the flute. As the air pressure builds, the pitch rises, and the player must blow more directly into the tone hole to compensate for the higher pitch. The instruction "lowering the head to compensate" should be avoided, however, as the student may cut off breath support and close the throat rather than merely drop the jaw. Some flutists drop the lower jaw rather than turn the head down. To keep forte playing from being sharp, the player needs to open or relax the

Figure 10–5   Intonation Characteristics of the Flute

throat, lips, and jaw. Blowing the air in an arch that follows the contour of the mouth and is aimed at the outer edge of the embouchure hole will help maintain an open throat and mouth. In soft playing, the lips must be stretched to bring the pitch up.

Windy tones, caused by not enough air going through the flute, are usually sharp. Insufficient air going through the flute may result from the player having uneven teeth or very thick lips, or from pads that do not completely seal the tone holes. When the fault lies with the teeth or lips, the player should try playing with the lips pushed out slightly. Pad problems call for immediate repair.

Loss of pitch control may be due to jaw movement or tired lips. Overpracticing and playing with tired lips are unwise. When the lip muscles become strained, several days of rest from playing are required. Shorter practice periods are the rule until the lips become strong. If the lips are not tired, the jaw is probably being kept too far back. The student should bring his lower lip out, turn the corners of his mouth up, or if possible bring his jaw forward. If his jaw is too far forward, he should reverse the process. Practicing exaggerated jaw movements may aid in controlling the jaw's movement.

The cork, at the end of the head joint, controls intonation. It should not be tampered with once it is set. Moving the cork makes the pitches at both extremes harder to control. The mark on the swab stick/tuning rod, about 17 millimeters from the end, is used to check the position of the cork. That mark should appear in the center of the embouchure hole when the tip of the rod touches the cork. Adjustments are made only when necessary and then by a repairperson who unscrews the crown cap and moves the cork to the proper position. The possibility of adjustment is best kept a closely guarded secret from beginners and their parents.

In summary, to *lower* pitch on the flute:

1. Direct the airstream more into the flute.
2. Cover more of the embouchure hole with the lower lip.
3. Drop the lower jaw or lower the head.
4. Pull the corners of the mouth back and down slightly.
5. Roll the flute inward (then adjust the head joint if necessary).

To *raise* pitch on the flute, do the opposite.

TONE QUALITY

Dazzling technique can be impressive, but phrasing, tempo, dynamics, pitch, and rhythm are also important. Beautiful tone quality, however, is more cherished than any other single aspect of a player's performance.

The interdependence of tone quality and intonation has been emphasized in previous chapters. Technical skill is enhanced by a beautiful tone, and without a beautiful tone the music does not satisfy.

Good *tone* is dependent on: (1) proper breathing, (2) good posture and proper position of the instrument and (3) embouchure formation.

Some fortunate flutists produce an excellent tone naturally and easily. For others, numerous approaches to improve the sound exist. A student should recognize good flute tone, from both recordings and local experts. It is difficult for students to achieve something that they cannot even imagine.

A good flute tone is round and full-bodied, not thin, shrill, or breathy. As for all instruments, the tone should be well-centered and focused, not spread. The embouchure plays an important role in flute tone. It controls the size of the airstream—as small and focused as possible but more open in the lower register.

Here are some common tonal deficiencies and means of correcting them:

1. A stuffy tone. The flute is probably turned in too much.
2. An open and fuzzy tone. It may be improved by pulling the lips back sideways, then stretching them forward and apart at the center, curling the lower lip down and the upper lip up. This sounds more complicated than it is.
3. A hard and thin tone. This may be caused by hardness of the lips around the embouchure hole or by playing too much on the outer surfaces of the lips rather than on the moist inner surfaces.
4. A hard upper register. This may indicate that the lips are too tense; practice flutter tonguing and tonguing past the lips.
5. Dropping down into the lower octave or producing double stops. Bring the lower jaw forward and cover more of the embouchure hole with the lower lip. Using more breath support also helps.
6. Low tones are breathy. The lips are probably too open; direct the airstream down, more into the embouchure hole.
7. Weak low tones. The lips may be too tense. Practicing soft low tones, flutter tonguing, and tonguing past the lips can improve the volume and fullness of the lower register.
8. Cracked tones in the middle register. These are not serious. One of the idiosyncrasies of the flute is that it has weak resistance in the middle register, and the player must learn how to adjust to it.

One of the best ways to improve tone quality on all wind instruments is to practice long tones. Long tones are especially difficult for beginning flutists. The need for the player to create his own resistance in order to use the air efficiently is a skill learned over a period of time. Playing long tones can result in frustration and boredom for the beginning flute player, so they should instead practice on simple melodies, attempting to increase their phrasing ability until they can sustain a line or note for some length. Most beginning method books start the young instrumentalists in the key of E-flat. However, this is not the best key for flute. Supplemental material in the low register, in the key of F, will help beginning flute players develop their embouchure, efficient use of the airstream, and their finger/articulation technique more quickly.

B above the staff is one of the best notes for developing embouchure, and practicing long tones in the key of G centering around B is helpful. To develop richness and focus, the student should work for more drive or projection in the tone. One good exercise to practice is taking deep breaths, using diaphragm support, then getting rid of all the air in eight beats. When working for drive in the tone, the player must avoid the windy-sounding tone that comes from relaxing the cheeks and the corners of the mouth. The same embouchure and support are used for loud, driving tones as for softer tones.

The greatest difference in tone quality between adjacent pitches on the flute is found between fourth-space E and fourth-line D. E is a dark tone, D is bright. For a legato passage in which these notes occur in succession, the player must adjust his embouchure so that the tones will match as much as possible.

A "sweet" tone is not necessarily a good tone. It may be the result of covering too much of the embouchure hole with the lip or turning the flute in too far. Either of these habits limits the player's development, for both make lip slurs difficult and produce a delay in attacks.

Vibrato

Vibrato is essential to musical playing on the flute, but it should not be used all the time. The flute sound is easily turned into a saccharine, overly sentimental one if vibrato is overdone. The flute can also have a pure, classical, crystal sound. The student should understand these opposites, learn how to produce both, and use each with discrimination.

Diaphragm vibrato is preferred by most flutists. The teacher introducing vibrato to his student for the first time will get the best results by having the student practice a very slow alternation of loud and soft. For example, the student may play whole-note scales with a metronome set to 42 beats per minute then push on the airstream every beat, sustaining each note eight beats.

Development of diaphragm vibrato may be benefited by having the student vocalize "ha–ha–ha–ha," gradually turning it into: "a–a–a–a," while still using the diaphragm. Gradually, the speed of the alternations should be increased until an even and real vibrato results. The slow vibrato should be practiced with a definite difference between the loud and soft; then as the speed increases, the vibrato should become narrower until the flutist is able to produce both fast and slow vibratos, either wide or narrow. The normal vibrato is about seven pulsations per second.

TECHNIQUE: ARTICULATION AND FINGERING

Articulation for the flute player is similar to the tonguing technique used by brass players. The section on articulation in Chapter 15, "Principles for Brass," should be consulted, with "tee" syllables substituted for "duh" or "doo." The flute player has available a great variety of articulations including double-, triple-, and flutter-tonguing.

Articulation is more than just tonguing and slurring. Articulation is the joining of notes together, and the ending of the notes is as important as the beginning. Flute players have difficulty with the endings of phrases, because the natural tendency to taper notes by lessening the air pressure causes the pitch to go flat. To compensate, the flutist must raise the airstream at the end of the phrase, directing more air toward the outer edge of the embouchure hole, and pushing the jaw forward.

Tonguing is best taught to the young flutist by having him "hoot" the first few exercises, that is, use no tongue while playing the exercises. As the embouchure and playing position become more natural, tonguing is introduced by having the student vocalize "tee" while playing. The student should sustain a tone, holding a pitch steady for as long as possible, then repeat the tone while disrupting the steady airstream at a slow, regular pace. This is done by striking the roof of the mouth with the tongue, placing it in the same position as for the syllable "tee." "Dee," "kee," "lee," and "gee" syllables are useful; but some syllables such as "doo" or "loo" should be avoided because they may adversely affect the student's embouchure. As discussed earlier in the section, "The Beginning Student," use of a "pee" articulation is helpful in producing the first sounds on a flute, but delays setting the embouchure and ensures that the initial attack will be uncontrolled.

Problems to be avoided are the habit of tonguing on the back of the upper teeth, tonguing between the teeth, and not retracting the tongue quickly enough. In learning staccato, players should not stop the note with the tongue; this creates a pitch change, leads to breathing problems, and makes it more difficult to control the next attack. Staccato is achieved by stopping the air by the diaphragm, not by blocking the airstream with the tongue.

The flute is the only woodwind on which it is possible to double- and triple-tongue without faking. The advanced flutist can demonstrate dazzling technique beyond the ability of other student woodwind players. The flute player double-tongues by rocking the tongue inside his mouth, alternating tongue placement for each note between the syllables "tih–kih, tih–kih" or "tuh–kuh, tuh–kuh"; a more legato double-tongue uses the syllables: "dih–gih, dih–gih." Triple-tonguing is achieved by rocking the tongue back across the roof of the mouth as though vocalizing: "tih–dih–kih, tih–dih–kih." Flutists are also called upon to flutter-tongue on occasion; this is done by rolling the tip of the tongue on the roof of the mouth as a child may do when pretending to be a motorboat.

Single and multiple tonguing should be practiced slowly and gradually increased in speed. For multiple tonguing, one must give special attention to the "second" and "third" syllables, practicing them individually as if single-tonguing.

Good flute technique depends first on good flute position. Bad position may not become apparent until the student undertakes passages that require great technical facility. For example, young players often slip their right little finger under the G-sharp key to help support the instrument. It is also common in practicing whole notes or repeated notes on the same pitch for students to raise the fingers far above the keys. Furthermore, young players often use incorrect fingerings. An example of the latter is fourth-line D. Although all beginning method books show the correct fingering, it is possible to "come close" while leaving the left index finger down, leading to problems in pitch and tone quality. Another example involves the D-sharp key. This key should be used for most of the notes played on the flute. One of the notes for which it is often omitted is fourth-line D. Most method books start on top-line F and move down so that this D is the third note encountered. As the little finger is usually the weakest finger, many youngsters soon discover that the D-sharp key can be avoided completely.

Young flute players should be encouraged to practice scales or even parts of scales. These may initially be written out, but soon should be learned by ear. Technique should be taught as coordination between the fingers, tongue, and brain. Evenness is far more desirable than speed and should always be a prerequisite to speed.

WHAT TO PRACTICE

Tone quality is the most important aspect of performance, and intonation and tone quality go hand in hand. Long tones should be omitted from the flute player's daily practice until the economical use of the air supply is learned, which is facilitated by playing simple melodies. When long tones are first introduced, they should be played in the middle and lower registers. Long tones played while crescendoing and decrescendoing may follow as the player begins to develop control.

Scales including the chromatic scale should be part of the daily routine, as should tonguing exercises at various tempos and in various styles. The different flute registers have different tonal characteristics, and even within one register the notes at the extreme ends have different timbres. Students should play a scale with the objective of not letting the "audience" know where the change in timbre takes place. Such a task is more difficult when playing arpeggios. Eventually larger and larger intervals are to be practiced.

Flexibility studies should be included in every flute student's daily routine. From the first day when only the head joint is played, flexibility is stressed. The control of airspeed and embouchure will promote flexibility. Unlike brass players, the flutist intent on improving flexibility is *also* confronted with the task of changing the direction of the airstream *and* using the jaw to cover and uncover the embouchure hole. The reason that low notes on a flute are so difficult to play is that, due to friction, the air has a tendency to "run out of steam" before reaching the entire length of the flute.

The second harmonic is played by adjusting the embouchure so that the air entering the flute is traveling much faster in order to halve the wavelength. With the air moving faster, a change in the direction of the airstream is required so that the sharp outer edge of the embouchure hole "flips" less air into the instrument and more air is expelled from the instrument. More advanced flute players should play the overtone series in various orders as part of their daily warm-up. Figure 10–6 indicates the notes that can be played by fingering a low C on the flute.

The student should not blow harder when attempting to move the pitch upward. Instead he should direct the airstream by raising and dropping the lower jaw, making the aperture in the embouchure wider and rounder for low notes, with more focus for higher notes. Understanding the acoustics of the flute helps one to understand why the C and C-sharp are always so sharp; the air does not travel very far down the tubing of the instrument, and these pitches are played with more air than is actually required. Performance of C, C-sharp, and D in the staff, for example, involves a significant change in the distance that the air travels. Ideally the

Figure 10–6   Harmonics Based on Low C

performer should increase the air flow for the D, at the same time playing these notes smoothly as a line.

CARE AND MAINTENANCE OF THE FLUTE

The bore of the flute should be swabbed and dried frequently during and after each playing, primarily so that dust does not accumulate in the damp interior. An old silk handkerchief is fine for a swab cloth; linen or cotton is also adequate. Most flute cases are equipped with a swab stick that also serves as a tuning rod. Swabbing should be done with care to avoid damaging the tenons or scratching the inside of the instrument. When swabbing the head joint, care must also be taken to avoid poking the metal covering of the cork located inside.

The exterior of the flute does not need elaborate care. In fact, silver polish on a metal flute may damage it; all the finish needs is to be wiped off after each playing. Care should be exercised in wiping the head joint since the outer edge of the embouchure hole may be dulled by excessive rubbing.

The head joint should be cleaned two or three times a year with hot, soapy water, followed by thorough rinsing and drying. The body and foot joint should not be washed.

Sticky pads cause a delayed response when a finger is lifted from a key. To clean, the pad should be closed lightly over a clean piece of lens paper, which is then withdrawn. Even a piece of tissue paper can be used if the pad is closed over it and held while the paper absorbs moisture. A simple item of preventive maintenance to teach flute players from their first day is to hold the instrument with the pads up when not playing, thus preventing moisture from collecting in the tone holes and being absorbed by the pads.

The pivot screws should be oiled at least once every four months to ensure that they work properly. Occasionally these screws must be loosened using a jeweler's screw driver, oiled, then retightened.

If the tenons become dirty and sticky, they can be cleaned with denatured alcohol or with silver polish (the latter will remove a very slight layer of the finish as well as the grime). Protector rings for the end joints are frowned on for two reasons: they make it more difficult to keep the ends clean, and they add wear with the frequent removing and replacing. This wear can result in distortion of the dimension and parabolic construction of the head joint. In the days of wooden instruments and poorly constructed cases, protector rings were necessary for the preservation of the cork on the ends, but today there is no longer a reason for them, and most companies no longer make them.

TROUBLESHOOTING

EQUIPMENT

sticky pads

1. Moisture absorbed by pads. If pad is not damaged place lens paper between pad and tone hole, press key, and gently pull paper out; repeat several times pulling the paper out in different directions. As a last resort: Apply a *slight* amount of talcum powder to absorb the moisture, being careful to keep it off mechanism.
2. Bent rods. Have repaired by competent repairperson.
3. Worn springs. Have repaired by competent repairperson.
4. Pivot screw at end of rod through post may need oiling (one drop). Occasionally it may need to be loosened and partially removed, oiled, then retightened.

pads not seating correctly

1. Leaking pads—usually discovered when lower register does not respond easily. If pads are in good shape, readjustment of the adjusting screws may be necessary. Insertion of thin paper "washers" behind pad can be made by repairperson. Possibly bent rods to be repaired.
2. Brittle or hardened pads (replace or have replaced by competent repairperson).
3. Torn pads. Have replaced by competent repairperson.
4. Loose pads. Reheat the glue, seal the pad with gentle pressure.

TONE

breathy sound

1. Too much embouchure hole covered. Move flute up or down to cover one fourth to one third of the embouchure hole.
2. Airstream not centered with embouchure hole. Practice in front of mirror to keep embouchure centered. In rehearsal, roll flute up to lips before attacks and entrances to make sure embouchure hole is centered. If due to physical shape of lip—such as a tear-drop-shaped upper lip—some have success playing off center, many switch to another instrument.
3. Aperture in embouchure is too large or too round. In upper register keep aperture small; in low registers keep embouchure flatter and slightly wider.
4. Not enough air support. Breathe correctly and let air flow, keeping constant pressure behind the airstream. Be careful not to overblow, however, and keep airstream focused.

5. If in upper register, too much of a smile embouchure. Make more rounded.

fuzzy, hollow sound

1. Not enough embouchure hole covered. Move head joint up to cover one fourth to one third of the embouchure hole. Roll flute inward.
2. Flute turned out too far. Correct alignment of head joint or holding/hand position.
3. Misdirected airstream. Blow air slightly more into flute.
4. Airstream not focused or incorrect shape of aperture in embouchure. Aperture should be relatively flat and wide for lower notes and small and round for upper pitches. Physical shape of lip can prohibit focused airstream—attempt to pull upper lip more tightly against teeth.
5. Aperture in embouchure too loose. Focus airstream. Firm up corners of mouth slightly.
6. If in low register, commonly due to too small an aperture. Relax corners of mouth. Pull back and down on corners and attempt to raise center of upper lip.
7. Leaky pads.

thin, strident shrill sound

1. Too much tension in lip around embouchure hole. Try to relax center of upper lip. Focus airstream. Form flatter, wider aperture for lower register, rounder for upper register.
2. Playing on outer surface of lip. Roll lips out to play more on the moist inner surfaces.
3. Blowing too hard. Blow easier yet maintain air pressure. Focus air more.
4. Airstream not centered. Roll flute up and down to center embouchure hole with embouchure. Hold flute so that embouchure hole is parallel with lips. Cover more embouchure hole, pull corners back and down more, roll flute in slightly—or a combination of these.
5. If in upper register—corners of lips too tense (i.e., too much of a smile embouchure). Relax corners. Practice flutter-tongue to loosen mouth.
6. Too much air blowing over and out of flute. Blow more air into instrument.
7. If in lower register, aperture too small. Attempt a wider, flatter embouchure.
8. With poor flexibility—not enough embouchure hole covered. Move head joint down, cover at least one-fourth of embouchure hole, but not more than one third.

stuffy sound

1. Flute rolled in too far. Roll out. Correct alignment of head joint. Make sure right thumb is pressing against left index finger for proper balance.
2. Too much embouchure hole covered. Move head joint up to cover at least one-fourth of the embouchure hole. Roll flute out.

weak sound

1. Not enough air support. Breathe correctly.
2. Leaky pads.
3. Too much embouchure hole covered. Move head joint up to cover at least one-fourth of the embouchure hole but not more than one-third.

difficulty

1. Bring jaw forward and cover more of the embouchure hole with the lower lip centering pitch in upper register.
2. Use faster, more focused airstream.
3. On sharp notes such as C-sharp direct air slightly more downward into embouchure hole or try arching tongue more with roof of mouth then aim air toward outer edge of embouchure hole.
4. Focus and direct air more toward outer edge of embouchure hole with more rounded embouchure aperture.

difficulty w/ lower register

1. Lips too open—direct airstream more downward into the lower register flute.
2. Lips too tense—practice softly, relaxed on lowest pitches. Blow more air being careful not to overblow.

flexibility problems

1. Too much embouchure hole covered. See above.
2. Aperture of embouchure too large. Common problem when playing in low register—keep aperture only as wide and large as necessary.

PITCH

Flat

1. Airstream is directed too much into the flute. Raise head or lower jaw slightly, blow more toward outer edge of embouchure hole.
2. Too much of the embouchure hole is covered. Raise head joint, roll flute out.
3. To avoid going flat when descending into the first octave, uncover embouchure hole while directing more air into the embouchure hole.

sharp

1. Airstream is directed too much toward the outer edge of the embouchure hole. Lower head or jaw slightly, blow more into the embouchure hole.
2. Not enough of the embouchure hole is covered. Lower head joint, roll flute in.

3. In lower register—pull the corners of the mouth back
   and down slightly.
4. A C-sharp is being played. Lip down, fake it, or cough at
   the appropriate moment.

REFERENCES

Texts

ARNOLD, JAY. *Modern Fingering System for Flute.* New York: Shapiro, Bernstein, and
Co., 1963.

BATE, PHILIP. *The Flute: A Study of Its History, Development and Construction.* London:
Ernest Benn, 1979.

BOEHM, THEOBALD. *The Flute and Flute Playing in Acoustical, Technical, and Artistic
Aspects.* (Second English edition by Dayton Miller.) New York: McGinnis and
Marx, 1960. (Originally published in German in 1871.)

————. *On the Construction of Flutes.* Culemborg, Holland: Frits Knuf Buren,
1982. (Reprint/English translation of 1847 original.)

CHAPMAN, F. B. *Flute Technique.* 4th ed. London: Oxford University Press, 1973.

DELANY, CHARLES. *Teacher's Guide for the Flute.* Elkhart, IN: The Selmer Co.,
1969.

DE LORENZO, LEONARDO. *My Complete Story of the Flute: The Instrument, the Performer,
the Music.* New York: Citadel Press, 1951.

DICK, ROBERT. *The Other Flute: A Performance Manual of Contemporary Techniques.*
London: Oxford University Press, 1975.

Flute World—Graded Catalogue. 5th ed. Flute World, P.O. Box 248, Franklin, MI
48025 (n.d.).

GALWAY, JAMES. *Flute.* New York: Schirmer Books, 1982.

HOWELL, THOMAS. *The Avant-Garde Flute: A Handbook for Composers and Flutists.*
Berkeley, CA: University of California Press, 1974.

KINCAID, WILLIAM (in collaboration with Claire Polin). *The Art and Practice of
Modern Flute Technique.* Vol. I. New York: MCA Music, 1967.

PELLERITE, JAMES J. *A Handbook of Literature for the Flute.* 3rd ed. Bloomington, IN:
Zalo Publications, 1978.

————. *A Modern Guide to Fingerings for the Flute.* 2nd ed. Bloomington, IN: Zalo
Publications, 1972.

PHELAN, JAMES and MITCHELL D. BRODY. *The Complete Guide to the Flute from
Acoustics and Construction to Repair and Maintenance.* Boston: Conservatory
Publications, 1980.

PUTNIK, EDWIN. *The Art of Flute Playing.* Evanston, IL: Summy-Birchard Co., 1970.

RAINEY, THOMAS E. *The Flute Manual: A Comprehensive Text and Resource Book for
Both the Teacher and the Student.* Lanham, NY: University Press of America,
1985.

ROESENFIELD, JOAN. *Flute Music.* Sherman Oaks, CA: Caravan Press, 1987.

SHEPARD, MARK. *How to Love Your Flute: A Guide to Flutes and Flute Playing.* Los
Angeles: Panjandrum Books, 1980.

STEVENS, ROGER S. (ed. Ruth Zwissler). *Artistic Flute Technique and Study*. Hollywood, CA: Highland Music Co., 1967.
TAKAHASHI, *Takahashi Flute School. Suzuki Method*. Evanston, IL: Summy-Birchard Co., 1971.
TOFF, NANCY. *The Flute Book*. New York: Scribner's, 1985.

Journals

The Flutist's Quarterly. Quarterly from the National Flute Association. Myrna Brown, 805 Laguna Drive, Denton, TX 76201.
Flute Talk. Ten per year from Flute Talk, 200 Northfield Road, Northfield, IL 60903.
The Flutist. Out of print, published 1920–1929, Ashville, NC.

Studies

Easy—Beginning (elementary or junior high)

ARNOLD, JAY. *Introduction to the Flute* (C. Hansen).
BUCHTEL, F.L. *Elementary Method for Flute* (Kjos).
CAVALLY, ROBERT. *Original Melodious and Progressive Studies* (Southern Music).
ECK, EMIL. *Tone Development for Flute* (Belwin-Mills).
GARIBOLDI, GIUSEPPE. *30 Easy and Progressive Studies*, (Books I and II) (Edwin F. Kalmus).
HART, ARTHUR. *Introduction to the Flute* (Oxford University Press).
KINCAID, WILLIAM. *The Art and Practice of Modern Flute Technique*, Vol. 1 (MCA Music).
LEJEUNE, HARRIET. *Pitch and Sound Search Studies for Flute* (Broude).
———. *A Flutist's Manual* (Summy-Birchard).
MOYSE, MARCEL. *Beginner Flutist (Le De'butant Flutiste)* (Alphonse Leduc).
PARES, GABRIEL. *Daily Exercises and Scales* (Carl Fischer).
———. *Pares Scale Studies* (Belwin-Mills).
PLATANOV, N. *School of Flute Playing* (Leeds).
TAKAHASHI. *Takahashi Flute School* (Suzuki Method), Vols. 1 and 2 (Summy-Birchard).
WYE, TREVOR. *Beginning Books for the Flute*, Vols. I and II (Novello).

Medium (advanced junior high or high school)

ADLER, SAMUEL. *Harobed—7 Studies* (Southern Music).
ANDERSEN, J. *18 Studies for Flute*, Op. 41 (International).
BONA, PASQUALE. *Rhythmical Articulation* (G. Schirmer).
CAVALLY, ROBERT. *Melodious and Progressive Studies*, Books 2 and 3 (Southern Music).

GATTI, GIOVANNI. *15 Studi Moderni* (Edizioni Berben).

KINCAID, WILLIAM. *The Art and Practice of Modern Flute Technique*, Vol. 2 (MCA Music).

KOEHLER, ERNESTO. *20 Easy Melodic Progressive Exercises*, Op. 93, Vols. 1 and 2 (Belwin-Mills).

_____. *Romantic Etudes* (Southern Music).

MOYSE, MARCEL. *24 Etudes Petites Melodious* (Alphonse Leduc).

_____. *Exercices Journaliers* (Alphonse Leduc).

PARES, GABRIEL. *Daily Exercises and Scales* (Carl Fischer).

PORCELIJN, DAVID. *Communication for Easy Flute and Modern Flute*, Vol. I (Zalo Publications).

STEENSLAND, D. (ed. Ployhar). *Studies and Melodious Etudes for Flute*, Levels 2 and 3 (Belwin-Mills).

TAFFANEL, PAUL (ed. Gaubert). *Complete Method for Flute* (especially "17 Daily Finger Exercises for Flute," which is available separately) (Alphonse Leduc).

TAKAHASHI. *Takahashi Flute School* (Suzuki Method), Vols. 3 through 5 (Summy-Birchard).

WYE, TREVOR. *Practice Book for the Flute*, Vols. 1 through 4 (Novello).

Advanced (high school or college)

ANDERSEN, JOACHIM. *24 Exercises*, Op. 21. (Southern Music).

_____. *24 Studies*, Op. 15 (Southern Music).

_____. *24 Technical Studies*, Op. 63. (Southern Music).

BARRERE, GEORGES. *The Flutists' Formulae* (G. Schirmer).

CAMUS, PIERRE. *12 Etudes* (Alphonse Leduc).

DONJON, JOHANNES. *The Modern Flutist* (includes Karg-Elert listed below) (Southern Music).

DROUET, L. *25 Etudes for Flute* (Alphonse Leduc).

GALLI, RAFFAELE. *30 Exercises*, Op. 100. (G. Ricordi).

GATES, EVERETT. *Odd Meter Etudes* (Fox Publishing).

JEAN-JEAN, PAUL. *16 Modern Studies* (Alphonse Leduc).

KARG-ELERT, SIGFRIED. *30 Caprices*, Op. 109. (Southern Music).

KINCAID, WILLIAM. *The Art and Practice of Modern Flute Technique*, Vol. 3 (MCA Music).

MOYSE, MARCEL. *Exercices Journaliers* (Alphonse Leduc).

_____. *De La Sonorite* (Alphonse Leduc).

_____. *Scales and Arpeggios* (Alphonse Leduc).

PLATANOV, N. *30 Studies for Flute* (International).

SCHADE, WILLIAM. *24 Caprices* (Southern Music).

WYE, TREVOR. *Practice Book for the Flute*, Vols. 5 and 6 (Novello).

FLUTE
Fingering Chart

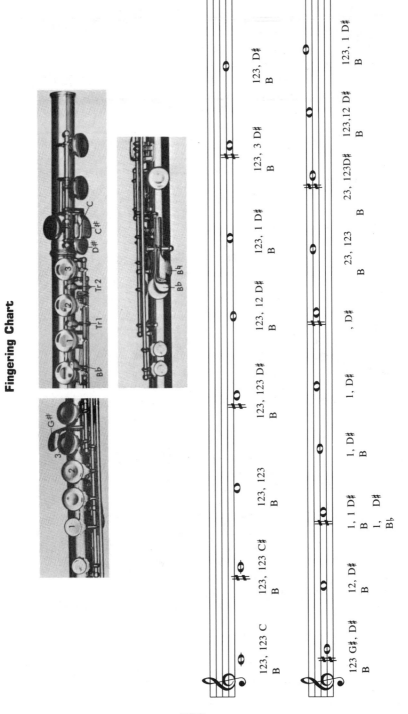

123, 3 D#
B

123,
B

123,123 C*
B

123G#, D#
B

123G#, 123D#*
B

12, D#
B

12, 123*
B

1, 1 D#
B

1,
B♭

13, 123D#*
B

1, D#

13, 12 D#*
B

1, D#

123, 1D#
B

23, 2D#

23, 123C#*
B

23, D#
B

23,Trl D#*
B

123 G#, 123 D#
B

23G#, Tr2 D#*
B

12, 12 D#
B

12, 12 Tr2 D#*
B

13, 1 D#
B

13, 1 C#*
B

13, 3 D#
B

13, 123*
B

123, D#

1, *

123, 123 C#
B

23G#, D#

123G#, 123C#*
(T)

2, 1 D#
B

, 1 Trl
B

13, Trl 23
B

13, Trl 3

1 Tr2

⌐ 8a - - - - -

123 G#, 1(D#)
B

2 G#, 1 C#

3, 12 C
B

123 G#, 1 Trl 3D#
B

12, 2 Tr2

2, 2 Tr2

2 G#, 13 C

3, 1 Tr2C
B

3, 1C
B

3, 1 Tr2 C
B

*harmonic ( ) optional

181

11

The Oboe

The oboe has the most limited compass of any woodwind instrument and seems to resist one's efforts to achieve a good tone. However, when mastered, its unique timbre and its expressive possibilities are ample rewards to the player. When played correctly, it can express humor, satire, calm, mystery, and despair, among many others. Unfortunately, when played badly, it can be downright unpleasant.

Every aspect of the oboe is different from other band and orchestra instruments. Solo and ensemble literature from every historical period is plentiful . The oboe is also a favored solo instrument by orchestra and band composers. A fine oboist is perhaps the single most wished-for individual by band and orchestra conductors.

Many band directors choose not to start beginners on the oboe due to the problems of control. Other teachers do start young oboists, however, and with great success.

HISTORY

Instruments with a double-reed mouthpiece of cane date from 3700 B.C.; the name "oboe" is mentioned as early as 2000 B.C. in the literature of Mesopotamia. Various forms of oboes were to be found in all parts of the East. They were used by shepherds and by fakir snake charmers in the old Turkish Empire, in the harems of Baghdad, and in the temples of Cairo.

The oboe belonged to the Asian world until Europe began to be aware of Near Eastern civilization in the late Middle Ages. About the thirteenth century, the shawm, derived from the Arabian double-reed instrument called the zamr, was introduced to Europe by returning Crusaders. This instrument was called the bombarde by the French, and the pommer by the Germans. Its cousin was the krummhorn, whose double reed is contained within the instrument and cannot be placed in the mouth. It is set in motion by the player blowing into the opening in a way similar to the manner organ pipes are sounded. With the exception of the krummhorn, however, these early instruments were played by taking the entire reed into the mouth, the lips resting against a metal disc.

The oboe had only three or four fingerholes up to about 400 B.C. Collars and half stops were added until the player had to operate as many as fifteen holes. Egyptian oboe players had a unique practice of breathing through the nose while they played, making it possible for them to sustain a tone continuously.

From the high Renaissance through the Baroque period, the oboe became increasingly important. It was a popular member of Elizabethan bands. By the eighteenth century, the descant shawm assumed the present form of the oboe. It was introduced into the orchestra by Lully and was later a favorite instrument of Handel, whose orchestra contained twenty-six oboes, forty-six first violins, and forty-seven second violins. Bach used the oboe d'amore for sprightly and plaintive effects; he was particularly fond of it in combination with the solo voice. By the time of Haydn, Mozart, and Beethoven, the oboe had become a standard part of the orchestra.

SELECTING THE INSTRUMENT

Let the buyer beware. The prospective automobile owner always kicks the tires and slams the doors in an involuntary admission that she doesn't know how to judge the quality of the engine. An oboe is an expensive purchase that one hopes to keep for many years. Knowing what to look for is vital because good oboes are not mass produced, and one cannot always trust name brands.

As for any other musical instrument, the overall sound is the primary guide for selecting an oboe, whether new or used. Oboes differ in tone quality, even those made by the best manufacturers. Unless the instrumental music teacher is herself an accomplished oboe player, she may be unable to evaluate the potential of an instrument. A skilled oboe player should therefore be found to assist in selecting an oboe for the parents or the school.

The conservatory system, based on the innovations and improvements of Boehm, is almost universal, but many different models exist within it. The plateau system has covered tone holes (vented plates with pads). This system was initiated about 1906 by F. Lorée, one of the most famous makers of oboes. The plateau oboe is preferred by the majority of professionals because it produces a rather dark sound.

Since there is such great variance in oboes, a stable reed should be used when checking the overall pitch of the instrument, and individual notes should be checked with an electronic tuner. All notes throughout the registers of the instrument should respond freely, with a good tone quality and a full, resonating sound.

Oboes come with either a semiautomatic or a fully automatic octave key. With a semiautomatic key, the player must add the side octave key to all high notes beginning with A above the staff. With a fully automatic key, the player presses only the octave key on the back of the instrument to obtain the upper octave of any pitch. With the semiautomatic, the player can leave his thumb in position on the instrument. The semiautomatic system is best for beginning students. The fully automatic octave key is not recommended for two reasons: First, it has a temperamental mechanism that is usually in need of adjustment, and second, it makes the harmonics from G-sharp through C and some alternate fingerings impossible.

Of major importance is the low B-flat key. An oboe without this key is not a good purchase. Though school-grade music seldom requires the low B-flat, it must be available when it does appear, and it improves the resonance of low B and C. Trill keys are likewise useful and important to school oboists, although these are usually considered optional.

The F resonance key, also considered optional, is a must. It opens automatically when the forked fingering is used for F, eliminating the need for the E-flat key to be pressed with the right little finger. The standard order of importance for remaining optional keys might be the following: the low B/C- sharp trill, the low C/D trill, the left hand A-flat/B-flat trill, the left little finger F key, and the left hand C/D trill.

Because a musical instrument is expensive to manufacture, ways are continually sought to lower the cost. One of these is to substitute plastic for wood. Experiments with plastic oboes have met with varying success. The quality of tone produced is the determining factor for a successful alternate material. The traditional oboe is made of grenadilla wood, and the quality of the wood is crucial to the quality of the instrument. An instrument should be made of wood with the straightest grain possible. Secondhand instruments should be checked for cracks and for scoring inside the bore.

The reed is almost as important as the instrument and is a favorite topic of conversation among teachers and players. Reeds appropriate for beginners are essential for initial success. They may be purchased from a music retailer, but few of these are considered good reeds by professional oboe players. A better source for reeds is a professional oboist who makes and sells them; these custom-made reeds are usually of good quality, and the professional can make them for various levels of embouchure development. Reeds appropriate for beginners should have a relatively small opening and blow easily without changing pitch between dynamic levels. More advanced students should learn to make their own reeds; this skill should be considered an essential element of any oboe player's instruction and development.

ASSEMBLING THE OBOE

The first task is to soak the reed, an often neglected but necessary part of the beginner's instruction. The reed should soak in about $\frac{1}{2}$ inch of water in a small, clean container for at least five minutes (less if the reed is not thoroughly dried out)—cane end down. If water is not available, the reed may be thoroughly wetted with saliva and set aside to absorb the moisture for ten to fifteen minutes. This moisture is necessary for the two blades composing the double reed to assume their natural curved shape and make an airtight seal at the sides.

The key mechanism of the oboe can be damaged in putting the instrument together or taking it apart, so care should be encouraged from the outset. The oboe has four parts: the reed, the upper joint, the lower joint, and the bell. The beginner should learn to assemble it with careful movements, not by wiggling or forcing it, because: (1) the tenons are thin and easily broken, (2) the cork can be compressed or loosened, (3) the ends of the tenons can become rounded from wear, and (4) the keys can easily be bent. These four factors affect the snug fit necessary to prevent leakage of air around the joints and pads.

To assemble the instrument, first the bell is held in the right hand with the thumb over the pad covering the low B-flat tone hole. The lower joint is held in the left hand, and the two sections are pushed together with a gentle turning motion. The bridge key between the bell and the lower joint is then aligned.

The upper and lower joints are assembled by placing the left hand at the top of the upper joint and the right hand over the rings or pads between the lower joint and the bell section. The keys on the lower joint and bell sections are not depressed when assembling because touching the F-sharp tone hole or C/D trill key raises the bridge key. The two joints are pushed together with another gentle turning motion aligning the bridge keys. The corks at the ends of the joints (the tenons) may be greased slightly to make assembly easier.

The reed is grasped at the cork by the thumb and first finger and inserted in the upper joint with a slight downward push. If the reed is not pushed in all the way, an air pocket is created that affects intonation and tone. Grabbing the cane of the reed while inserting it will damage one or both blades or destroy the fit, causing air leaks. After the reed has been inserted, it can easily be turned so that the blades line up with the rest of the instrument. One of the two blades will always be stronger than the other; as the player gains experience, she will notice that the instrument plays better when one particular side of a reed is up. To identify that side each time, she can place an ink mark on the cork.

HOLDING THE OBOE

The oboe is held with the left hand on the upper joint and the right hand on the lower joint, as shown in Figure 11–1. The fingers are slanted slightly downward toward the bell to facilitate the use of the C and C-sharp keys by the right little finger, and so the left little finger can more easily play the G-sharp, B, and B-flat keys. The thumbs point slightly upward. The fingers should be slightly arched, with the fleshy pad of each finger centered on the tone hole. The little finger of the right hand rests lightly on the D-sharp key and the little finger of the left hand on the B key. The inside edge of

Figure 11–1   Hand Position for the Oboe

the right thumbnail is on the thumb rest. If the thumb is placed too far around the oboe, the right fingers will be cramped and unable to move rapidly. Hand position will vary somewhat according to the size of the hand, however. Freedom of action is the important consideration.

The left thumb rests against the instrument at an angle of approximately 60 degrees (approaching 90 degrees for students with small hands) just below the octave key so that it can activate the octave key by a rolling motion (i.e., not by lifting it and placing it on the key). The index finger of the left hand should be on the first tone hole; the first joint of that finger rests lightly on or over the second octave key. This position enables the index finger to do two things: (1) roll back and forth to half-hole and (2) depress the second octave key with the first joint of the finger while keeping the other fingers of the left hand in place. The teacher must keep a careful eye on beginning oboists to make sure they do not get into the habit of slipping their index fingers under the side keys to help support the instrument.

The oboe should be brought to the head, not the head to the oboe. The instrument should be centered on the embouchure. Movements of the head, body, and instrument are not necessary when playing the instrument and can in fact detract from the playing. When the head is moved, the embouchure is changed and the position of lips on the reed is altered, so control is lost, tone quality distorted, and pitch and response jeopardized.

Correct position for playing the oboe is illustrated in Figure 11–2. The oboe is positioned directly in front of the player whether she is standing or sitting. Her head is kept erect. The oboe is held between 30 and 45 degrees from the body, supported primarily by the right thumb and steadied by the embouchure. Beginning students may try to copy clarinet positions, especially if the new oboists are former clarinetists, in which case the instrument will be held too low. Others may get into the habit of holding their head down, which is the same as holding the instrument too

Figure 11–2 Sitting Position for Playing the Oboe

high. The overall sound will be difficult to control if the air enters the reed at this angle.

BEGINNING INSTRUCTION

For years there has been a controversy over whether beginners should start on oboe or play a year or two on another instrument before switching to oboe. Although a fourth grader is fully capable of beginning on the oboe, there are advantages to starting on another woodwind instrument such as the clarinet. One primary reason is that most beginning method books start with a pitch designed for immediate success on the trumpet, low brass, clarinet, and saxophone. The most commonly used first note is F, which for the oboe is one of the most awkward fingerings used, a forked F. Then follow E-flat, D, and C, all of which are difficult for the oboe. If already familiar with the fundamentals of music reading, beginning oboists can use an oboe book that begins on an appropriate pitch such as middle-line B and extend the range downward and upward. The notes in this register use few fingers, so the oboist is not faced with trying to cover all the keys immediately. With proper guidance and encouragement, however, the oboe can be included with the other beginning wind, percussion, and string players.

    After soaking the reed and assembling the oboe for the first time, the student should practice disassembling it and placing it in its case. The first playing should be with the reed only. The player drops her jaw $\frac{1}{2}$ of an inch and relaxes her lips. The tongue is slightly extended to prevent damage to the reed; the reed is placed on the tongue, which guides it to the center of the lower lip, with the tip of the reed placed about halfway over the lip. At the same time a breath is taken, the lip is rolled over the teeth so that the tip of the reed is inside the mouth about $\frac{1}{8}$ of an inch past the lower lip, and the very edge of the lip is over the lower teeth. Also at the same time, the upper lip closes over the upper teeth and over the top of the reed so that no red of that lip is showing. The lower jaw remains in the dropped position. The corners of the mouth are tightened and pushed toward the reed. Embouchure formation is easier to explain than to do, and much easier to do than to maintain.

    When the air is released, a "crowing" sound should be heard. If there is no response, gently press the reeds together with the thumb and forefinger to slightly weaken the reed, or possibly soak the reed a bit longer. Frequently the new reed is too stiff; beginners should start on a soft reed in order to get an immediate response. Tone quality and intonation will suffer, but the softer reed is easier to blow. As the embouchure becomes stronger and more developed, the student should switch to a stabler, often stronger reed.

    The amount of reed that authorities say should extend inside the mouth (past the lips) varies from $\frac{1}{16}$ to $\frac{1}{4}$ of an inch. One uses more reed inside the mouth when playing in the upper register and less reed when playing in the lower register. Beginners should be encouraged to use the mirror frequently to watch their embouchure.

EMBOUCHURE

The Lips

The correct oboe embouchure is formed by rolling both lips in slightly over the teeth to form a cushion above and below the reed. The facial muscles form a gentle pucker that exerts pressure on the reed from all sides. The corners of the mouth are pushed in toward the reed, and one may have all of the lips over the teeth. A "smile" pucker or "crocodile face" should be avoided. A flat chin, although not as important as on clarinet, usually accompanies an embouchure that surrounds the reed with even pressure. If the corners of the mouth are held firmly and forward *toward* the reed, the chin will remain flat. Air bulges may appear in the cheeks, caused by lack of muscular control: unequal tension between the muscles pulling to a pucker and those pulling to a smile. A fleshy upper lip may only give the appearance of an air pocket; if probing with the index finger disturbs the embouchure, there is, in fact, an air pocket. The correct oboe embouchure is shown in Figures 11–3 and 11–4.

    The oboist's teeth should allow the lips to roll over them and provide a supple cushion for the reed. Extreme overbite or underbite can prevent the player from applying equal pressure to both blades of the reed. Lips should be in a vertical line, usually with more of the red of the lower lip rolled in. The edge of the lower lip (where the red meets the flesh) should be directly over the edge of the teeth. A heavy upper lip usually has an adverse effect on the tone because it restricts control. A thick lower lip appears to be an advantage, as it forms the cushion necessary to avoid nasal quality.

    The tongue rests in the bottom of the mouth with the tip near or resting on the lower lip, which is turned inside the mouth. Keeping the tongue relaxed is essential for accurate and correct articulation.

    With the beginning student, one of these problems usually occurs: (l) Too much of the lip is turned in. Only enough lip so as to control the reed needs to be rolled in. (2) With a clarinet-type embouchure, too little lip is turned in. (3) When the upper lip is short and less flexible, it is often placed too far on the reed. Furthermore, like the brass player, the oboist is confronted with endurance problems resulting from the air pressure in the mouth and depending on the extent to which the facial muscles are developed. Two major differences between oboe and brass players are that the

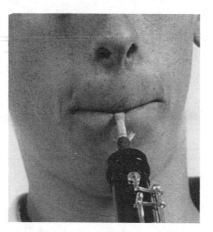

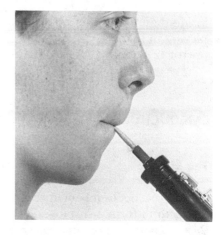

Figure 11–3   Oboe Embouchure   **Figure 11–4   Oboe Embouchure
(side view).**

latter have much less resistance in their instruments and their mouthpiece helps hold the lips in place against the air pressure. The oboe player must gain a great deal of strength in the appropriate muscles before she can play complete phrases or for long periods of time.

The Teeth

The framework of the embouchure is formed by the teeth, whether one rolls the lips over the teeth or keeps the lips just in front of the teeth. The teeth determine the size and shape of the embouchure and must be kept open so that the other elements of the embouchure function properly. Keeping the teeth apart prevents biting into the reed and forces the lips to apply pressure to the reed from all sides. There is no upward bite in the normal embouchure. The lower teeth and jaw drop away from the reed. Control is derived entirely from the lips.

The Reed

Usually the reed is placed in the mouth with about a third to a half of the cane covered by the lips. Or, the tip of the reed is first placed about $\frac{1}{4}$ to $\frac{3}{8}$ of an inch (appearing as $\frac{1}{16}$ to $\frac{1}{4}$ of an inch) on the red part of the lip when the lips are in normal position, then the lips are rolled slightly over the teeth. To check placement, the student should play fourth-line D and slur down one step to C. If she has too much of the reed in her mouth, the C will sound wild and quite sharp in relation to the D. She should then experiment with less of the reed in her mouth until she can play the two-note slur with good intonation and consistent tone quality. If she has too little of the reed in her mouth, which rarely occurs, the C will be flat.

Of the many factors that determine the distance the reed should be inserted, the most important is the tessitura of the music. A different lip cushion is required for each octave. The reed is placed farther in the mouth for the upper register and is moved out slightly for lower tones. A second factor is the type of tone desired. A third is the lip and jaw formation. And a fourth is the reed itself.

The beginner often puts too much of the reed in her mouth in order to play on pitch, particularly on low tones. If she puts the correct amount of reed in her mouth, her intonation will be flat. With too much reed in her mouth, the tone is apt to be strident and sharp. When a skilled player desires a bright, hard tone, she puts more reed in her mouth, but makes adjustments to keep the intonation correct. If the player puts too little reed in her mouth, the tone may be fuzzy and weak as well as flat. As the beginner's control grows, the amount of reed placed into the mouth should change.

The Grip

While there is no biting in a good oboe embouchure, the lips must be firm enough to control the reed. This firmness means that the player's embouchure is "in shape." The grip of the lips depends on the amount of reed in the mouth as well as the register being played. The firmness for the higher registers should not cause the throat to tighten. Tonguing usually tightens the embouchure. Because most method books begin with tongued tones exclusively, the student can start with a rather relaxed embouchure, and it will soon tighten of its own accord. Most teachers urge the student to play initially with too much tension. Regardless of the player's advancement, too tight a grip on the reed will choke off the tone, cut off most of the lower overtones, or make them play sharp. The player should always be able to feel the reed vibrating, even when playing in the upper range of the instrument where the greatest firmness is required. Conversely, if the player relaxes the lips too much on low tones, the reed vibrates excessively and some of the overtones become stronger than the fundamental.

The oboe requires different embouchures in different ranges and for crescendos and decrescendos. The firmness of the embouchure increases for decrescendos and relaxes for crescendos, an approach opposite of that used by clarinet players. In playing crescendo passages, many fine oboists allow their lips to roll out slightly, covering the teeth with somewhat less lip while relaxing the embouchure. This action counteracts the sharpness accompanying an increase in volume.

The Jaw

For most players, leaving the jaw alone is best. The average person's upper lip protrudes slightly over the lower, which is the correct position to maintain when forming the embouchure. The lower jaw is pulled down and slightly back so the lower teeth drop away from the reed, thus forming the pucker. Probably the most common fault of the young oboe player is that she juts out the lower jaw, apparently to create some feeling of needed support from the lower lip. A player with a receding lower jaw should hold the oboe at less than a 30-degree angle rather than push the jaw forward in an unnatural position.

The Angle of the Instrument

The angle at which the instrument is held affects both embouchure and tone quality. The best general position is given on page 189. As a general rule, the lower the instrument is held, the darker the tone; as the angle increases, the tone becomes brighter. The present trend is toward a brighter oboe sound. If the head is held erect and the student sits or stands tall, an angle of approximately 30 to 45 degrees is an excellent one, producing a bright tone and allowing for a faster, lighter tonguing action. When the oboe is lifted too high, the reed is pulled away from the lower lip cushion and the upper lip presses too tightly on the reed. The result is a drop in pitch, particularly in the upper register, and a bright, harsh tone. Holding the oboe down to produce a dark tone with a mysterious, haunting quality must not be carried to the extreme. When the oboe is nearly parallel to the body, the upper lip is prevented from serving its normal function, the sound becomes not only dark but hard, and the tone has a tendency to be sharp in all registers.

In summary, these elements determine the oboist's tone: (1) the distance between the teeth as they form the framework for the embouchure; (2) the quantity of reed placed in the mouth; (3) the relationship between upper and lower jaws and lips; (4) the grip of the lips on the reed; (5) the angle at which the instrument is held; and (6) the quality of instrument, reed, and breath support. The student needs to be reminded of these factors at each lesson.

INTONATION

Although professional orchestras tune to the principal oboist, the young oboist cannot be so confident of correct pitch. She should frequently use an electronic tuner first to check individual pitches and then to adjust her overall tuning. If she finds herself adjusting each and every pitch, it's time to get a better instrument or learn to make reeds.

Intonation on the oboe is related to embouchure as well as to the position of the reed in the mouth. Specifically, sharp intonation is caused by:

1. An embouchure that is too tight.
2. Too much reed in the mouth (especially for the second octave).
3. Too stiff a reed.
4. Holding the oboe at an angle of less than 30 degrees from the body.
5. Too much lower lip turned under.
6. Too much upper lip turned under.

The tone will be flat when the reverse errors occur. When a combination of faults occurs, intonation problems will be difficult to correct as there are so many variables to test. The ear is the key; students must learn to listen carefully and evaluate their pitch in relation to that of other players.

All intonation problems do not lie with the player. The instrument itself, no matter how fine, is never perfectly in tune. Defects in the dimensions of the bore may make the low tones unstable. The very high pitches are often sharp and the low register flat. However, the oboe is by no means the most difficult instrument to play in tune, being considerably easier to control than, for example, the clarinet or flute. Pitch can be altered by the reed itself and by the player's approach to the reed. A higher arch to the tongue raises the pitch and a lower arch lowers it. (The arch should change as one goes from a high to a low register.) The temperature of the instrument and the amount it is pulled at the joints also affect pitch. Figure 11–5 illustrates notes that generally tend to be out of tune on the oboe.

Both the oboe and the bassoon profit from the addition of extra keys. The value of these additional keys varies with the individual instrument, so that experimentation is necessary to discover which keys will improve specific pitches or contribute to tonal resonance. Usually, the ring keys played with the right hand and the low D-sharp, C, C-sharp, B, and B-flat keys of either hand should be tried to see if they improve intonation or enhance resonance.

If the pitch is unstable (some notes going sharp and others going flat within the same register) the player may not be blowing directly into the reed. Both blades of the reed must vibrate equally in order to obtain

Sharp   Flat

Figure 11–5 Intonation Tendencies of Selected Pitches on the Oboe

consistent pitch. The player should try tipping her head up and down or slightly altering the angle at which the oboe is held while listening to the result. While experimenting, the player must play throughout the entire range rather than listen only to one pitch or one register.

A problem known as "flat staccato," is not really related to intonation but to a timbre that makes the pitch sound flat. Flat staccato is caused by having too much reed in the mouth, which forces the tongue to curl into an incorrect position in order to reach the tip of the reed for tonguing. The same term is sometimes applied to the poor tone quality that results when the angle of the reed is too great and there is too little bottom lip on the reed. This situation also impairs the accuracy of the attack and the speed with which the player can tongue. Pitch discrepancies also occur with dynamic changes. Students often open their embouchure to allow more air to enter the reed in order to play louder. Without increasing the speed of the airstream and firming the lips for control, the pitch will go flat; if the velocity of the airstream is increased and the embouchure remains in the same position, however, the pitch will go noticeably sharp.

In attempting to flatten the pitch, the oboist should not pull the reed from the upper joint or pull out each of the joints. If the reed is pulled out more than just the slightest amount, an air pocket will form, causing the instrument to lose response. Low notes will tend to become wild, some will be difficult to attack clearly, fuzzy in quality, or generally uneven in sound.

As a new oboe is broken in, some of the keys will need adjusting to stabilize or correct pitch and enhance finger dexterity. Some pads seat better as the new instrument is used, some fingers are stronger than others, some keys are used more than others, some springs become weaker. Most oboes have at least a dozen small set screws for regulating key height and the evenness of the mechanism. Until students learn to make adjustments with these keys, the music teacher or a competent repairperson should do it. Although the oboe is tremendously difficult to play in tune if it is out of adjustment, having it in adjustment does not guarantee that it will play in tune.

TONE QUALITY

All performers should strive for beauty of tone, the oboe player among them. A good oboe tone depends on four things: (1) the player's concept of tone, (2) breath control, (3) embouchure, and (4) a good reed. The beginner's tone is usually coarse and uncontrolled due to too much wind going through the reed, or else it is dead and unresonant due to insufficient pressure. The abdominal muscles must pressurize the air, and the embouchure must be firm enough to control this pressure; a balance of these forces creates an appealing tone.

A small tone, even when pleasant, is limited in dynamic variety and in carrying power. The reasons for a small tone are biting the reed, too little reed in the mouth, not enough lip over the teeth, and holding the instrument too close to the body. A squawky tone results from the opposite factors.

Sometimes a player becomes accustomed to a nasal tone and even strives to maintain it. The player on any instrument must listen to her own playing and compare her tone with the sounds she would like to imitate.

Harmonics are useful for college-level oboists and advanced high school students. The oboe harmonic is the second overtone, an octave and a fifth (a twelfth) above the fundamental; for example, if the player fingers low B-flat, top-line F will sound. Harmonics are produced by over-blowing—tightening the lips more and using more pressure than necessary for the fundamental tone. Using the low C key with harmonics will help keep them in tune; harmonics are usually flat. There are two uses for harmonics, the more common being tone color; harmonics are particularly useful in quiet orchestral passages and for pianissimo notes. The second use is to correct markedly sharp pitches in the upper registers; played very softly, harmonics offer a workable substitute for the normal fingerings.

Vibrato

Oboe players in some countries disapprove of vibrato. They believe it destroys the characteristic oboe sound and prevents the instrument from blending well. Most players, however, feel that vibrato enhances the sound by adding warmth and expressiveness to the tone. Diaphragm vibrato seems to be preferred for oboe. Throat and jaw vibrato tend to constrict and tighten muscles, producing a disappointing, artificial sound. Lip vibrato may affect the embouchure. Vibrato on oboe is probably not for beginners.

TECHNIQUE: ARTICULATION AND FINGERING

Good tonguing is inseparable from artistic playing. For the oboe, while the tone is being produced, the tip of the tongue touches the lower lip or rests on it slightly with the lower lip turned inside the mouth. To stop the tone, the tongue may stop both blades by touching the tip of the reed with the upper, flat part of the tip of the tongue, or stop the lower blade just under the tip of the reed with the very tip of the tongue. Both techniques are used by experts, but more students find the second method easier. The tongue should move up and down rather than back and forth. The oboist has less success with "doo" tonguing than the clarinetist. A "t" motion gives a sharper, cleaner attack.

Double-tonguing on the oboe is not recommended and is seldom used, although it is possible. The "k" sound required in double tonguing is not successful because it tends to produce a flat tone and a fuzzy, muddy attack. The oboe player should achieve a facile single-tongue and depend on it for fast passages.

Many players twist the reed or the instrument itself slightly to the left, making it possible to tongue on the corner of the reed. This achieves a rapid, clean tonguing action. The standard approach should be mastered first, however, as the oboist plays with the reed horizontal most of the time.

Finger dexterity is developed by practicing slowly, then speeding up what is already learned. Coordinating tonguing with fingering is absolutely essential. The young player should begin tonguing on a single pitch, concentrating on synchronization of the fingers and the tongue. Slow practice will allow time to think about what is happening. Evelyn Rothwell explains the importance of conscientious practice:

> When you play . . . you may sacrifice—consciously or unconsciously—certain details for the effect of the whole. For instance, if you are in an orchestra, other instruments are playing at the same time as yourself and may cover up the imperfections in your own technique of which you may not be aware. You may, even when playing quite by yourself, be too carried away by the musical pleasures of what you are doing to listen critically enough to small technical faults, particularly to careless intonation. The purpose of real practice is to acquire complete coordination and control of the muscles you need, by conscious and concentrated mental discipline. *No* slip or fault, however slight, must be allowed to pass. Train your ears to observe imperfections, and use your brain to put them right.[1]

Scales and technical studies are excellent means for developing finger coordination. Scales help the player attain evenness throughout the entire range, and arpeggios are useful for learning to coordinate several fingers at a time. Études apply these concepts to more musical materials, but scales are basic to the acquisition of the desired aural and physical skills.

WHAT TO PRACTICE

The oboe requires the least amount of air of all wind instruments, but it is not the easiest to blow. On the contrary, when the trumpet player is fatigued and running out of air at the end of the phrase, the young oboist is

---

[1] Evelyn Rothwell, *Oboe Technique*, 3rd ed. (London: Oxford University Press, 1982), 61.

suffering the effects of bottled-up air still in her lungs. The oboist must take deep and proper breaths, learn to "hold back" the air, and expel unused air at the phrase endings before inhaling again.

Most beginners play the oboe with a loud and raucous sound, while the method books used for other wind instruments are instructing them to play softly and with different articulations. In the long run, if the teacher patiently guides and encourages the new oboist to play in tune, the other aspects of control will follow. Playing softly may lead to bad habits and eventually to overall loss of control, for example, less air support, biting or pinching the reed, too little reed in the mouth, too soft a reed, and so on. It is easier to tame a loud sound than to open up a small one.

Like beginners on other wind instruments, young players should practice for several short periods of time a day, extending these sessions as the embouchure and breathing apparatus become more developed. The beginning studies should start with notes in the middle of the staff, which do not require as many fingers, side keys, or half holes. Slurred long tones fluctuating between two adjacent notes are recommended: The student learns to move fingers evenly, to match timbre, and to improve her embouchure. The two adjacent notes should increase gradually to three notes, then four, then five, to finally encompass a major or minor scale.

As the beginner develops her range and tone quality, crescendos and decrescendos should be added to the long tones. At first, scales and arpeggios should be played very slowly, then gradually practiced faster and faster. They should cover the entire range for which the student has learned the fingerings. Scales should always begin and end on the tonic, but the upper and lower notes of the scale need not always be the tonic. Fingers should not be raised too high, but remain relaxed and in their proper positions.

CARE AND MAINTENANCE OF THE OBOE

A well-fitting case is important. It protects the keys of the instrument against damage and it helps prevent extremes of heat and cold from damaging the wood. An outer vinyl or fleece-lined nylon case cover further protects against damage and sudden temperature changes.

Dirt is more harmful to an oboe than to other instruments because the small tone holes are easily clogged. It should be swabbed out after each playing. A swab of soft cloth is satisfactory for the bell and lower joint; for the upper joint, a soft pheasant or turkey feather should be used to dry the bore all the way to the top. The feather should first be washed with soap to get rid of natural oils.

Many oboe players oil the bore to guard against splitting wood. However, most reputable manufacturers now guarantee their instruments against cracking, and preparation of the wood in the factory includes soaking it in oil. If oiling the instrument seems better, a small amount of almond oil should suffice. Too much oil remaining in the bore adds to the accumulation of dirt. The springs of the oboe should be oiled perhaps once a year and very lightly with key oil, which is available with a needle applicator.

Water that collects in the smaller tone holes and the octave keys can be blown out as a temporary solution, and a piece of coffee filter placed between the tone hole and the key, pressed gently, will absorb any remaining moisture. The tone holes should carefully be cleaned regularly with a pin or with the quill of the feather.

The keys and pads of the instrument should be checked frequently. The keys should be wiped off occasionally with a soft cloth. They should not be polished with silver cleaners since the polish may clog the mechanism and destroy the silver plating.

REEDS

The quest for good reeds has forced oboists to make their own; learning to play the instrument includes learning to make a satisfactory reed. The teacher must make the reeds or purchase them for the beginning player. Purchasing reeds does save time, but all reeds need adjustment, even those guaranteed to play. Good oboe reeds are made too stiff for normal playing; minor adjustments are necessary.

The ideal reed is one that responds to louds and softs, highs and lows, and staccatos and legatos with little effort. On it the player can control pitch, tone quality, and dynamic changes with a minimum of embouchure manipulation. "The reed should sound good with no help, so that when there is help, it sounds great."[2]

Every player should have more than one reed ready to play. Clarinet and saxophone players rotate reeds, but this is not necessary for the oboist. It is, however, necessary to have another reed ready and broken in. One should not wear out an oboe reed, since the embouchure will compensate for one that is wearing out.

During the middle and late 1970s, plastic oboe reeds enjoyed a brief popularity. Although these reeds may be more durable than cane reeds, it is absolutely impossible for the young student to produce a good quality tone with one.

Selection of Cane

If students desire to make their own reeds from scratch, the cane can be purchased by the pound in tubes bundled together. Starting this way requires more tools than precut cane. It requires additional skill and

[2] Jay Light, *The Oboe Reed Book: A Straight-Talking Guide to Making and Understanding Oboe Reeds* (Des Moines, IA: Drake University, 1983), 7.

greatly increases the number of things that can go wrong. Most student oboists should purchase cane that has already been split, gouged, and shaped.

In purchasing either cane or ready-made reeds, the appearance of the cane and its pliability are both guides to selection. A shiny golden color to a brownish color with spots indicates sufficient ripeness and curing. Cane need not be spotted—this is not always a sure indication—but if too green it will not make a satisfactory reed.

Pliability and porousness are also considerations. On a ready-made reed, pliability can be checked with the thumb nail; if the nail makes too deep a mark, the cane is probably too soft. Cane that is hard to cut was harvested too late and is not pliable; cane that is too soft flakes off while being gouged and scraped. The porousness of the cane can be tested by wetting the butt end. If it darkens to an orange arc, it is properly aged; if bubbles appear when one blows on the butt end, the reed is too porous.

Selection of Reeds

Since the oboist cannot play a commercial reed before purchasing it, the following points may serve instead: 1. No jaggedness should be observed in the metal staple. 2. The cane should match the staple so that the oval sides of the reed are flush with it, without cracks on the sides. 3. Slivers of cane appearing at the sides of the reed may not be serious unless their removal will leave a crack. 4. Reeds that have a feathered tip usually have faulty workmanship. The craftsman has feathered out a faulty stroke by scraping and sanding to make it appear acceptable. Reeds made with decisive, sure strokes are almost universally superior to those made with short, choppy strokes. 5. Thin reeds make good tone production easier. 6. The cane should fit snugly together all the way up past the staple and somewhat above the fishskin. Fishskin is immediately above the wrapping and aids in preventing air leaks. The sides of the reed do not meet evenly at the tip, but should be slightly offset when the reed is dry; soaking will counteract the shape. 7. If the tips are flat and parallel rather than oval-shaped when dry, too much offset will occur when the reed is soaked. 8. The reed should be held to the light to determine as best as possible that the two sides of each blade are scraped symmetrically and the two blades are symmetric with each other.

The general craftsmanship of the reed is important. These things indicate good piece of work: Is the string even? Has it been waxed? Is there a good invisible knot? Is the fishskin on at the correct spot and evenly applied? So many items can be skillfully hidden that making one's own reeds seems the only certain way to get a good product. On a commercial reed one cannot see how far onto the staple the cane was placed and whether the winding extends too far beyond the end of the staple. The winding should end exactly with the end of the staple, or at most one thread beyond it. (But beauty is only skin deep; the best-looking reed may not play.)

The more advanced player may be able to judge the type of cut that she prefers, whether V-shaped, U-shaped, W-shaped, and so forth; these can easily be identified by the eye (See Figure 11–6).

Care of Reeds

Store reeds in a reed case to ensure proper drying. Plastic cases make it hard to return the reed to the case without damaging the tip; furthermore, they do not allow the reed to dry and may cause it to get moldy. Reeds become dirty very quickly during playing and then tend to play flat. Lipstick clogs the pores, dust and lint cling to the moist reed, small food particles from the mouth become lodged in the reed. A small piece of paper placed between the blades from the top and gently pulled back and forth a couple of times is sometimes used, but must be handled carefully to avoid breaking the delicate tip of the reed.

If the player promptly runs water through the reed each time after playing, the reed stays clean. Dirt is removed more easily when it is fresh.

Adjustments While Playing

Before starting to play a passage one must check the reed opening and adjust it if needed. The player can pinch the reed to obtain the best opening for playing, but a clumsy squeeze, with too much pressure or in the wrong place, may split the blades down the middle. If the reed is too stiff or is not responding, the player may pinch the two pieces of cane together close to the wrapping on the flat of the blade. This adjustment will

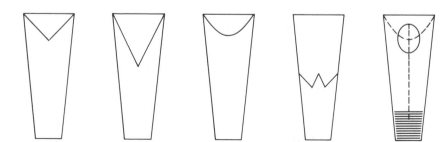

Figure 11–6   Cuts of Oboe Reeds

probably raise the pitch slightly. If the reed is too soft or closing up, press at the sides, where the two pieces join, by putting the fingers in the middle of the blade edges. This is usually only a quick fix, but soaking it longer may be a greater help. Besides pinching, another way of getting the reed to open up is to put more reed into the mouth, down past the beginning of the winding, and alternate between sucking and blowing air through the reed. The fishskin can be tightened to better support the blades if the tip is still too closed.

Use of the Knife in Reed Adjustments

Professional oboists appear to be as opinionated and exacting with regard to the knife they use (type, size, shape of blade, handle, weight, material, and so on) as they are to what to do with the knife. They do agree that the knife should be very sharp. Only a few of the most common adjustments are given here. Each oboist, on reaching the stage of adjusting her reed, should possess three tools: a knife, a mandrel, and a plaque.

Common adjustments for intonation include these: If low C and D are out of tune, open the reed by tightening the fishskin. This will involve inserting the plaque between the blades and scraping the tip of the reed to offset the stiffness coming from a tighter wrapping. If the general pitch is too flat, cut off some of the tip of the reed or trim it slightly on the sides to make it a tiny bit narrower. If the reed is then too stiff, too sharp, or too dull in sound, scrape the tip. If the reed is too sharp, the scraped area should be lengthened or thinned at the lay; sometimes cutting the tiniest bit from the corners helps flatten the pitch. If the player cannot "crow" a C, then the reed is unequally scraped or too thin.

Comparing the pitch of second-line G with the one an octave higher is often used to test the intonation of a reed. The general rule for altering the reed to adjust intonation is this: If the top notes are sharp, more of the reed should be scraped; if the top notes are flat, the tip of the reed should be cut off or the sides of the reed narrowed. A reed that plays sharp can be scraped more, or the grattage (the cut of the reed—the part that is scraped) can be opened from a V-shape to a U-shape. For a reed that plays flat, filing the staple, not the tip, is preferable, but filing the staple should be a last resort. Sometimes "slipping" the reed, that is, moving the blades so that they do not coincide and are slightly offset, will help raise the pitch.

Tone quality, response, and intonation are affected by the various cuts of the reed. If the tone is shrill, bright, and brassy, lengthen the grattage by scraping at the bottom, accentuating a U-form over a V-form, and diminishing the width of the sides toward the opening. Shrillness may also be caused by the winding being too far up the reed. If the top tones are dull and thick, scrape the tip slightly, or sometimes the very end of the tip. Narrowing the sides of the reed will also brighten and harden the sound. If the low notes are difficult to play and are stuffy in sound, thin the bottom of the scrape, particularly at the sides, or else thin both sides of the scrape just below the tip of the reed. Poor response on low notes comes from too short a lay or unevenness in the thickness of the blades.

If the reed blows hard in the upper register, scrape more off the tip. If it blows hard in the lower register, scrape a little at the base near the bark. Whistling may result from unevenness in the thickness of the blades, too short a grattage, or a reed tip that is too thin or too long for balance with other parts of the reed. When the reed seems to be causing uncertainty in attacks yet the cane itself is good, there are probably bumps or unevenness in the scrape.

If a new reed seems hard to play, delay making adjustments until the reed is sufficiently broken in and its opening has assumed its regular shape. New reeds and those not recently used will have wide openings that may decrease with playing. If the opening remains too wide, go lightly over the backbone of the scrape, and lengthen or thin the V at the bottom of the scrape. If the opening is too small, the reed is probably excessively thin or soft and will produce a loose, edgy, thin tone or else a bright, wild sound. The reed can be improved by scraping the sides, with most of the scraping at the bottom of the scrape. In restoring the original length of the lay after trimming the tip, be careful not to make the lay too long, for then the high notes will not respond easily. There is an optimum ratio for each reed; when correcting one fault, don't create a worse one.

Jay Light's 1983 text *The Oboe Reed Book: A Straight-Talking Guide to Making and Understanding Oboe Reeds* is a useful and comprehensive guide to making and adjusting double reeds. It is well written for students new to the art and science of making oboe reeds.

TROUBLESHOOTING

EQUIPMENT

difficulty in assembling

Grease corks on joints, including reed if necessary.

sticky pads

1. Moisture in tone hole(s) or absorbed by pads. If pad is not damaged, place tissue paper between key and tone hole and cover/hold gently for paper to absorb moisture. Do *not* use talcum powder.
2. Bent rods, probably the bridge keys. Have repaired by competent repairperson.
3. Worn springs. Have repaired.
4. Pivot screws at end of rods need oiling (one drop). Occasionally screws may need to be loosened, oiled, then retightened.

pads not seating correctly	1. Leaking pads, usually discovered when the lower register does not respond easily. If pads are in good condition, adjusting of the screws may be required. Possibly bent rods to be repaired by competent individual.
	2. Pads are damaged. Replace or have replaced.
gurgling sound	1. Water collected in tone hole(s) under pads that usually remain closed. Open appropriate key, blow water out of hole and into the bore. Clean with a feather; bore may need oiling.
	2. On low notes—often a tight throat—first overtone trying to sound. Relax throat, drop jaw, blow steady air without forcing.
	3. Too much reed in mouth.

TONE

reedy, nasal harsh, rough sound	1. Head down or oboe held too high. With head erect, hold oboe at 30- to 45-degree angle.
	2. Biting on reed. Drop jaw; lip down and blow faster air to compensate. Use firmer lips/embouchure to control reed.
	3. Jaw protruding. Correct embouchure including jaw.
	4. Reed too hard. Try softer reed or scrape reed.
pinched, small sound	1. Oboe held too close to body. With head erect hold oboe 30 to 45 degrees away from torso.
	2. Opening in reed too small—overall contour or sides too weak. Trim end 1 mm at a time and scrape reed when necessary to reform the tip. Keep lip pressure on sides of reed.
	3. Biting the reed. Drop jaw, use more lip to control reed and blow slightly faster air to compensate for pitch.
	4. Not enough reed in mouth. Place more reed in mouth.
	5. Not enough lip over teeth for reed. Check reed. Use more lip over teeth—less red of lip showing.
	6. Not enough breath support.
	7. First space F-sharp is weak or breathy. Play F-sharp with G-sharp key down. If G-sharp key does not close, replace the G-sharp cork.
unresonant, cold sound	1. Reed too hard. Adjust for free blowing or wrong cut—scrape.
	2. Inappropriate reed cut. Try different brand of reed.
	3. Not enough air. Blow more air after taking proper breath; use proper embouchure to hold the increased pressure.

squawky

1. Reed too stiff. Player attempting to overblow. Adjust reed or replace it with a softer one. Try playing softly, or starting *mf* with decrescendos.
2. Too much reed in mouth.
3. Too much lip over teeth.
4. Reed too open. Carefully close reed between thumb and first finger to reduce stiffness.
5. Embouchure around reed too loose.

trouble with control

1. Oboe too high or too low. With head erect, hold oboe between 30- and 45-degree angle from body.
2. At *pp* volume levels—reed too stiff; biting reed; lips in wrong place for reed.
3. Jaw protruding.
4. Reed too soft. Try harder reed or trim tip.
5. Cheeks puffing. Firm corners to keep chin and cheeks flat.
6. Embouchure around reed too loose.

trouble with flexibility

1. Too much lip rolled over teeth. Let some red show.
2. Too much reed in mouth.
3. Practice overblowing to harmonics. Practice slowly moving from note to note in middle of staff where few fingers are used, gradually adding fingers as range increases up and down.
4. Embouchure around reed too loose.

squeaks

1. Too much reed in mouth.
2. Bent bridge key to bell, pads not seating.
3. Biting reed with lower jaw. Try dropping jaw as if lipping the note flat—increase airstream and firm up embouchure/lips.
4. Oboe held too low. With head erect, oboe should be 30 to 45 degrees from body; experiment for appropriate position.

PITCH

flat

1. Embouchure too loose. Firm up lips, especially corners. Try more lip over teeth, i.e., less red showing. Blow faster airstream.
2. Not enough reed in mouth.
3. Reed too soft. Cut tip 1 mm at a time, scrape when necessary to reform tip to strengthen reed.
4. Head down or holding oboe too high.

5. Too much red showing on bottom and/or top lip. Correct embouchure.
6. Combination of 1 through 5.
7. On individual notes—keys or pads not opening enough. Adjustments to screws to allow for proper opening of pads.
8. Tone holes or vent holes dirty. Clean with feather or needle.
9. Overall with reed inserted all the way. Cut 1 mm at a time from reed, scrape tip when necessary to reform tip—repeat as needed. Reed opening too large—press together with fingers to slightly weaken the reed; soak longer; scrape shoulder of reed. File staple to shorten.

sharp

1. Embouchure too tight. Use less lip over teeth, loosen embouchure, or drop jaw by trying to blow a pitch flat.
2. Especially in second octave, too much reed in mouth. Pull reed out.
3. Reed too stiff. Scrape reed or try a softer replacement.
4. Holding oboe at less than 30 degrees from body.
5. Too much bottom and/or top lip turned in.
6. A combination of 1 or 5.
7. On individual notes—keys or pads may be rising too far. Adjust adjusting screws to open keys properly.
8. Scrape both sides of reed.
9. Pull reed out of mouth.

REFERENCES

Texts

ARTLEY, JOSEPH. *How to Make Double Reeds for Oboe, English Horn and Bassoon.* Old Greenwich, CN: Jack Spratt Publishing Co., 1953.

BATE, PHILLIP. *The Oboe: An Outline of Its History, Development and Construction.* 3rd ed. London: Ernest Benn Ltd., 1975.

BERMAN, MELVIN. *The Art of Oboe Reed Making.* Toronto: Canadian Scholars' Press, 1988.

BEST, ARTHUR S. *The Oboe and English Horn.* Elkhart, IN: C. G. Conn, 1959.

FITCH, WILLIAM D. *The Study of the Oboe: A Method for the Beginner with Previous Beginner Experience.* Ann Arbor, MI: George Wahr Publishing Co., 1960.

GOOSSENS, LEON, and EDWIN ROXBURGH. *Oboe.* New York: Schirmer, 1977.

HEDRICK, PETER, and ELIZABETH HEDRICK. *Oboe Reed Making: A Modern Method.* Oneonta, NY: Swift-Dorr Publications, 1972.

LEDET, DAVID. *Oboe Reed Styles—Theory and Practice.* Bloomington, IN: Indiana University Press, 1982.

LEHMAN, P.R. *Teacher's Guide to the Oboe.* Elkhart, IN: The Selmer Co., 1965.

LIGHT, JAY. *The Oboe Reed Book: A Straight-Talking Guide to Making and Understanding Oboe Reeds.* Des Moines, IA: Drake University, 1983.

MAYER, R.M. *Essentials of Oboe Playing.* Des Plaines, IL: Karnes Music Co., 1969.

MAYER, ROBERT, and TRAUGOTT ROHNER. *Oboe Reeds: How to Make and Adjust Them.* Glen Ellyn, IL: The Instrumentalist Co., 1953.

ROTHWELL, EVELYN. *Oboe Technique.* 3rd ed. London: Oxford University Press, 1982.

———. *The Oboist's Companion.* Vol. I. Bucks, England: Oxford University Press, 1974.

RUSSELL, MYRON. *Oboe Reed Making and Problems of the Oboe Player.* Old Greenwich, CN: Jack Spratt Publishing Co., 1960.

SPRENKLE, ROBERT, and DAVID LEDET. *The Art of Oboe Playing.* Evanston, IL: Summy-Birchard Publishing Co., 1961.

Journals

The Journal of the Double Reed Society. Quarterly of the IDRS. Lowry Riggins, International Double Reed Society Executive Secretary–Treasurer, 626 Lakeshore Drive, Monroe, LA 71203–4032.

Studies

Easy—Beginning (elementary or junior high)

ANDRAUD, ALBERT. *First Book of Studies for Oboe* (Alphonse Leduc).

———. *Practical and Progressive Oboe Method* (Southern Music).

EDLEFSON, WEBER, F. *Student Instrumental Courses: Oboe Student,* 3 vols. (Belwin-Mills).

———. *Tunes for Oboe Technique,* 3 vols. (Belwin-Mills).

FITCH, NILO. *Elementary School* (C. F. Peters).

HENKE, FRED. *Elementary School* (C. F. Peters).

HOVEY, NILO. *Elementary Method for Oboe* (Rubank).

MACBETH, F. *Learn to Play Oboe,* 2 vols. (Alfred).

MAYER, ROBERT M. *Essentials of Oboe Playing* (Karnes Music).

SNAVELY, J. *Basic Technique for Oboe* (Kendor).

Medium (advanced junior high or high school)

BARRET, APOLLON M. R. (ed. Barre). *Complete Method for Oboe* (also available in parts) (Boosey & Hawkes).

Bozza, Eugene. *18 Etudes* (Alphonse Leduc).
Brod, H. *20 Etudes* (Alphonse Leduc).
Dufresne and Voisin, R. *Developing Sight Reading* (Colins).
Ferling, W. *48 Famous Studies*, Op. 31 (Southern Music).
Giampiori, G. *16 Daily Studies* (Ricordi).
Luft, J.H. *24 Studies for Oboe* (Billaudot).
Pares, Gabriel. *Daily Technical Exercise for the Oboe* (Carl Fischer).
Prestini, G. *Collection of Studies for Oboe* (Ricordi).
Rothwell, Evelyn. *The Oboist's Companion*, 2 vols. (Oxford University Press).
Teal, Larry. *Studies in Time Division* (Fox Publishing).
Tustin, Whitney. *Daily Scales* (Southern Music).

Advanced (high school or college)

Bach/Rothwell, E. *Difficult Passages* (Boosey & Hawkes).
Barret, Apollon M. R. (ed. Barre). *Complete Method for Oboe* (also available in parts) (Boosey & Hawkes).
Bassi, F. *27 Virtuoso Studies* (Carl Fischer).
Bozza, Eugene. *Graphismes* (Alphonse Leduc).
Brown, James. *370 Exercises for the Oboe* (Alphonse Leduc).
Debondue, Albert. *100 Exercises* (Alphonse Leduc).
————. *32 Etudes* (Alphonse Leduc).
Ferling, W. *48 Etudes*, Op. 31 (Costallat).
Flemming, Fritz. *60 Progressive Studies*, Vols. 1–3 (C. F. Peters).
Gillet, Fernand. *Studies for the Advanced Teaching of the Oboe* (Alphonse Leduc).
Karg-Elert, Sigfried. *Etuden-Schule*, Op. 41 (Broude).
Loyon, Ernest. *32 Etudes* (Billaudot).
Prestini, Giuseppe. *12 Studies on Chromatic Harmonies* (Belwin-Mills).
Rothwell, Evelyn. *Difficult Passages for Oboe and English Horn* (Boosey & Hawkes).
Tomasi, Henri. *3 Concert Etudes* (Eschig; Associated Music Publishers).

OBOE
FINGERING CHART

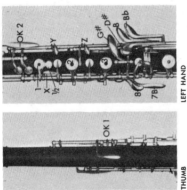

LEFT HAND

THUMB

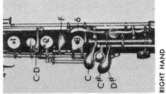

RIGHT HAND

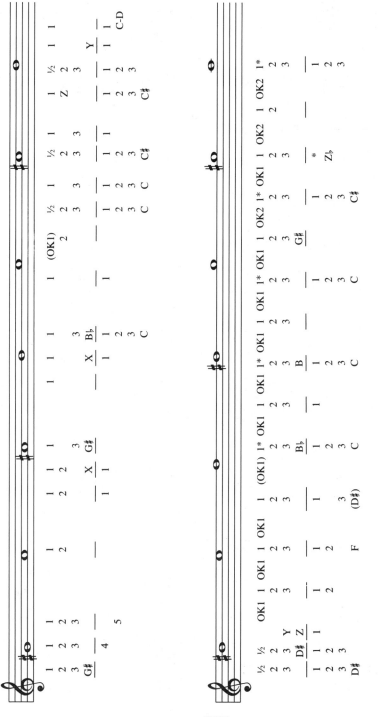

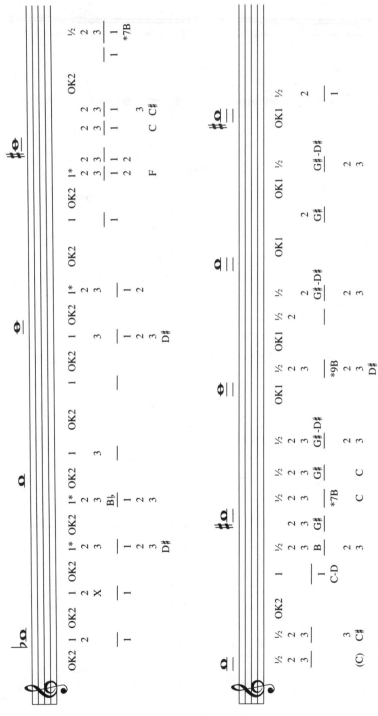

*harmonies
( ) optional

211

12

The Bassoon

HISTORY

The origin of this strange and wonderful instrument is unknown, but it can be traced back to the phagotus that Afranio of Ferrara built in the early sixteenth century. Its name is derived from its resemblance to a bundle of sticks. Another early form of the bassoon was the curtal, or "short wood," which was about 40 inches long. The curtal, also dating from the sixteenth century, had a reed similar to that used today. Its primary function was as an accompanying instrument. It was used in the church as the bass with cornets and trombones. The French bassoon, with its characteristic mellow sound, grew out of this instrument sometime after 1675. Also appearing in the sixteenth century was a dolcian, made from a single block of wood.

The bassoon was a favorite of the composers of the late Baroque and the Classical eras; Bach, Handel, Haydn, and Mozart all used its wide musical resources to good effect. However, the bassoon had gross instability of pitch and could be played in tune only by the most skillful players; it did not become widely used until after 1825 when Carl Almenrader made improvements on it. His innovations improved the pitch but in the process destroyed the instrument's characteristic tone quality. J. A. Heckel in turn improved the bore of the Almenrader instrument until its tone quality was acceptable. The Heckel bassoons appeared in the early part of the nineteenth century. They became common after 1879. The Heckel family still makes bassoons that are considered the finest available. The Heckel system, also called the German system, has become widespread. It is not to be confused with the instruments bearing the Heckel name. French-system bassoons are seldom found in the United States. They are easily distinguished from the German type since they have fewer keys, especially on the boot joint.

Many attempts have been made to refine the bassoon further, but all have resulted in a destruction of the tone quality, so musicians are forced to adapt themselves to its frailties. Nevertheless, with all of its failings, the bassoon is one of the most delightful and beloved instruments, capable of every response from farce to pathos.

The bassoon is the most awkward of all woodwind instruments. It is awkward to manage physically; it is also awkward to play. The bassoon is the only woodwind instrument that authorities agree is unsuitable for young beginners, although success by interested students is not unknown. Physical as well as intellectual maturity is important for the student who undertakes the bassoon. Prerequisite to studying bassoon is experience on another woodwind (or even a brass instrument or piano), through which the student has learned notation, developed finger coordination, and experienced the importance of embouchure formation.

SELECTING THE INSTRUMENT

Since the bassoon is handmade, there will be only general consistency between instruments of the same company, so each bassoon should be checked both by eye and ear. Clearly, most bassoons are school owned, and most music teachers are not bassoon players; hence, the music teacher needs the aid of a professional bassoon player in making such a purchase. A list of things to look for can help in the selection. Although most new as well as used bassoons will be out of adjustment, a good professional player should be able to get the instrument in playable condition quickly in order to evaluate its potential.

Good bassoons are usually made of hard maple stained brown (mahogany) or black (ebony). A quality instrument is indicated by straight-grained wood, carefully made tone-hole edges, and tenons that fit snugly. In examining a secondhand instrument, the wood should be checked for dryness. Clues to watch for are joints that no longer fit, loose keys and key posts, and cracks in the wood. Loose metal protectors on the end of tenons are evidence that the instrument has dried excessively. A crack may not be important at the time the instrument is purchased, but it invariably gets bigger. Some cracks are easily repaired on the bassoon; others are difficult or impossible. If an instrument with a crack seems acceptable in other respects, a competent repairperson should be consulted before deciding on it.

The instrument must be played for tone quality, clarity, and intonation, using an electronic tuner for maximum objectivity. Having the instrument played by a professional makes it possible to determine if the instrument can produce the variety of tone colors one expects from a good bassoon throughout the various ranges of the instrument. The upper register should be clear and in tune. Due to the alternate fingerings possible in this register, it is essential to have a professional opinion. If the intonation between notes is poor, beware.

All used instruments will show indications of wear, especially at the points where the fingers and hands come into contact with the instrument. A worn finish should not affect the tone, intonation, or responsiveness, but it should affect the price—frequently making the purchase of a used, professional-quality bassoon a better buy than a new lower-quality model instrument.

The purchaser has some option regarding the number of keys on the instrument. The full Heckel system is usually considered to be twenty-two keys plus the F- sharp trill key on the wing joint. The addition of one more key, the high D octave key, is very desirable, for without it several upper pitches are more difficult. A lock is advisable between the long and the wing joints to ensure a minimum of damage in assembly. Post locks are standard on most instruments. Metal or rubber inserts that protrude into the bore are often placed on the C, D, and E tone holes of the wing joint in order to prevent an excess of saliva in the holes. The boot collects the most moisture and should be inspected carefully for damage. On many bassoons, the wing joint and part of the boot are lined with rubber or a synthetic material to provide some protection from moisture.

As with all good instruments, the bassoon should offer some resistance to the player, though not to the point that it becomes stuffy, or that some notes are louder or softer than others.

ASSEMBLING THE BASSOON

Proper assembly is one of the principal aspects of caring for the bassoon and must be one of the first things the student learns. Because the instrument is at the same time large and fragile, its assembly is both awkward and delicate. The primary concern is that the keys or rods are not bent.

The bassoon has five parts: the bocal, which holds the reed; the boot (bottom section); the wing joint; the long joint; and the bell section. Using the thumb to press the key that raises the bridge key, the bell is placed on the top of the long joint before the latter is inserted into the boot. Either the wing or long joint may be placed into the boot first and the other fitted carefully next to it with a pushing and slight turning motion without wiggling. A small amount of cork grease on the tenons is recommended for corked tenons, vaseline for wrapped string.

The joints fit tightly and are rarely pulled for tuning purposes. Some bassoonists will use an O-ring on the long joint to lower the pitch in the low register. The last part of the instrument to be put into place is the fragile metal tube, or bocal, often called the mouthpipe or crook, which is inserted into the upper end of the wing joint. The bocal should not be grasped on the curve or on the reed end, but coaxed into place gently by grasping the cork. If forced, the metal may split, and although this can be repaired, the tone is adversely affected. The bocal is usually not pulled for tuning except for very small adjustments. The tiny hole that the whisper key covers is on the bocal, and must fit under the key that extends up from the wing joint.

HOLDING THE BASSOON

The bassoon, played only while sitting, may be held in two different ways: (1) The neck strap that hooks onto the instrument and can be adjusted for comfort may be used with very young beginners. Often used with the neck strap is a crutch or widget that screws into the instrument near the top of the boot joint and serves as a right-hand rest. It impairs right-hand flexibility somewhat and is not practical for bassoonists with short fingers. Without it, the instrument becomes less steady on the open or near-open tones when few fingers are down to help support it. The neck strap can cause poor posture and impaired breathing. (2) The seat strap is used by most professionals and is becoming increasingly popular with younger players. It eliminates the need for the widget, offers maximum flexibility, and yet holds the bassoon firmly. The seat strap either hooks onto the end of the boot joint or is made in the form of a cup in which the end of the bassoon rests. The other end of the strap is held securely at the right length by sitting on it, bringing the lower end of the instrument close to the body. To prevent clothing from catching on the B-flat and F-sharp keys, bassoons should have a protective plate covering these keys. The seat strap has the advantages of taking all the weight off the neck and freeing the right hand from supporting the instrument so that more rapid right-hand technique is possible.

Correct position for playing the bassoon is shown in Figure 12–1. The bassoon is held in front of the player at an angle that allows the instrument to bisect the body of the player from lower right to upper left. The boot rests on the right thigh and the upper portion passes diagonally in front of the player's body, with the left hand almost directly in front of the player's abdomen. One of the most common mistakes is to lean the bassoon out too far, forcing the wrists, the right one in particular, into an unnatural position.

The bassoon is tilted slightly forward so that the mouthpiece enters

Figure 12–1. Position for Playing the Bassoon

the mouth at an angle when the head is held erect. The player should sit on the edge of his chair with both feet on the floor. The head should be only slightly tilted to the left, if at all. The arms should not touch the body. The upper torso should be pulled up out of the hips so that the chest is lifted naturally and there is no cramping of the diaphragm. The bassoon should be brought to the player, not the player to the bassoon. Correct playing posture is made even more important by the whisper key. The player must sit so that he plays comfortably without moving the bocal to either side. Moving it will result in improper closing of the whisper key.

As for all the instruments, the fingers should be slightly curved, with the pads of the fingers covering the keys and holes. With either neck- or seat-strap support, much of the balance of the bassoon is necessarily borne by the left hand. The weight then falls on the base of the forefinger rather than on the fingers themselves. The right thumb rests over the pancake key, the right little finger over the low F key (Figures 12–2 and 12–3). The left thumb rests lightly on the whisper key and the left little finger over the low D-sharp key near the roller to the C-sharp (Figures 12–4 and 12–5). The remaining fingers remain over the holes at all times, never rising more than a half inch or so.

THE BEGINNING STUDENT

As with beginning oboe players, bassoonists should begin with only the reed. Have the student drop his lower jaw about $\frac{1}{2}$ to $\frac{3}{4}$ of an inch. Pulling the lower jaw back slightly while keeping it down, form the lips in a position

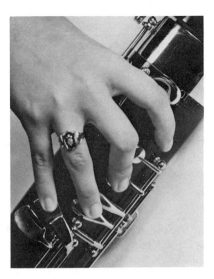

Figure 12–2. Right Hand Position for the Bassoon

as if vocalizing "oooh." The warm airstream will be directed downward. Place the reed (the reed must be prepared for the student) at the center of the student's lower lip and have him roll the lip over the bottom of the lower teeth so that very little red is showing. Have him close the upper lip (it will almost touch the first wire in the reed) and direct lip pressure from all sides toward the reed. The lower jaw should remain "dropped" as much as possible. There will be a slight overbite with the upper lip about $\frac{1}{4}$ of an inch closer to the wire than the lower lip.

Figure 12–3. Left Hand Position for the Bassoon

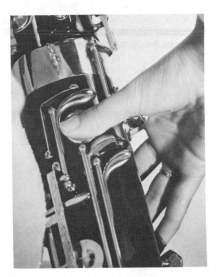

Figure 12–4. Right Thumb Position for the Bassoon

Playing on the reed only, an adequate embouchure for a beginning player can be found by producing a "double crow"—a sound resulting from each of the two reeds vibrating at two separate frequencies. This sound can be produced only when the embouchure is at least very close to correct. One must experiment to determine how much reed is proper for each individual's facial characteristics and the individual reed. Authorities recommend trying to produce a sound with very little reed in the mouth and gradually increasing the amount of reed until the "double crow" is

Figure 12–5. Left Thumb Position for the Bassoon

sounded. The body of the instrument is then assembled as described above, and the first bassoon tones are produced (usually a low C).

EMBOUCHURE

In forming the bassoon embouchure, the player draws his lips over both the upper and lower teeth (with more lip over the lower teeth) to form an ample cushion for the reed. The more lip cushion he provides, the easier he can achieve a full, dark sound. The teeth are apart to avoid biting; his lips support the reed. A small school of bassoon players believes that there is no need for the player's lips to be drawn over the teeth. These players develop their lip muscles to such an extent that their lips support the reed without assistance from an understructure of teeth. Although these players are able to demonstrate this successfully, this embouchure is difficult to achieve and tires more rapidly.

The player should exert all the pressure toward the center of the lips as opposed to forming any type of smile (as is often the case with students who have recently switched to bassoon from another instrument). Keeping the corners of the lips tense (pressure toward the reed) helps to keep the chin flat.

Playing is controlled at the place where the lips touch the reed (with the student aware that it is the airstream that makes the reed vibrate, *not* the lips). The lips are primarily in front of the teeth, rolled over only enough to gain support. The pressure is directed to the center of the lips. The reed is prevented from closing, since the force exerted against the edges is greater than that exerted up and down on the reed.

The jaw muscles should be relaxed. The use of the jaw in bassoon playing constricts the throat and causes biting or pinching. The lower jaw should recede slightly behind the upper, with the reed anchored against the lower lip. The lower lip should be firm and straight with the reed centered on it. About ¼ of an inch of the lower side of the reed goes into the mouth. For at least the first six months of playing, the student should experiment with the exact placement of the reed, in and out, and with the relative positions of the upper and lower lip. A slight change can make a big improvement. The student should not be satisfied with the first acceptable tone produced, for more searching may result in an embouchure that will produce a really fine tone. The most common problem among young bassoonists is a jaw that is too tense—it should remain relaxed and flexible.

With the player's lower jaw behind the upper, the top lip is set on the reed almost to the wire, so that much more of the upper lip than lower lip covers the reed. A very common embouchure fault with bassoon players is not putting sufficient reed into the mouth and not placing enough of the upper lip on the reed. The characteristic bassoon tone is due to the fact that the top half of the reed vibrates slightly more than the lower. The embouchure must encourage this asymmetrical vibration. Too little lip on the reed almost invariably meaning too little upper lip, results in a nasal sound; too much lip, usually too much lower lip, produces a pinched, dark sound. Figures 12–6 and 12–7 show the proper bassoon embouchure.

The teacher will rarely be confronted with a student who is unable to make a sound, unless he is trying too hard, biting on the reed and keeping it from vibrating. The problem is getting the right sound. Although whistling produces a pucker, it is not a good illustration of bassoon embouchure; the lips protrude too much and do not have the support of the teeth. Pronouncing the word "oh" is sometimes used, but this pulls the lips from the teeth. Some fine texts recommend finding the buzz point of the reed and straddling this spot on the reed for the correct embouchure. This can be successful with the teacher who is himself a performing bassoonist, but it has some hazards for students: (1) poor reeds do not buzz or crow; (2) students who do not know what a buzz or crow sound is may get their reeds too far into the mouth, produce a weird sound, and declare that the reed has crowed; (3) the beginning student whose embouchure is undeveloped is inclined to pinch the reed and may have difficulty making the reed crow. It is definitely more difficult to obtain the correct overbite using the reed alone. The feel is different when the instrument is not there to indicate relative position. Any method that will produce the desired results should be used, and what works for one teacher and one student may not work for all.

Flute players and saxophone players probably transfer to the bassoon with the least difficulty. The clarinetist, however, has learned to pull his chin tightly and produce too much of a smiling embouchure. With the bassoon, the lower lip is the anchoring point for the reed and the only place where a constant embouchure is maintained. Thus, the chin has to be relaxed enough to let the sound come from the diaphragm but firm enough so that the chin muscles do not move during tonguing, breathing, or rapid leaps in pitch. If the chin moves, the lip is apt to be forced off its lower-teeth support. The player needs to discover the combination of

Figure 12–6. Bassoon: Embouchure

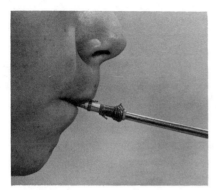

Figure 12–7. Bassoon: Embouchure (side view)

muscles that will make a firm chin but not a stiff one, creating ample support for the reed without biting or tensing the throat muscles. A relaxed and flexible jaw is important.

The bassoon embouchure resembles the oboe embouchure in that it changes with the various registers. In the low register, less lip is required. As the pitches ascend the lip must roll more, taking the reed with it. A similar requirement exists for dynamics: For extremely soft playing there should be less lip and less reed in the mouth; increasing volume demands that more lip be rolled in. The movements should be very slight. They are accomplished by applying a little more or a little less pressure. The player develops lip flexibility for adjusting quickly to large skips or sudden dynamic changes. Flexibility and control are synonymous in this respect, because without the first the second is impossible.

The reed fits onto the bocal in only one position, and the bocal must have a slight downward slant if the reed is to enter the mouth correctly. Players who tilt the instrument forward are forced to lean over it in order to get any semblance of good embouchure. By doing so, they cramp the breathing apparatus and hinder tone.

Although nothing helps develop an embouchure like playing and practicing, overworking will destroy rather than build a good embouchure.

INTONATION

The bassoon is a very imperfect instrument and has many intonation problems; of all the woodwinds, it is the most inherently out of tune. It has twenty-three keys plus five holes that must be placed on a bore over 8 feet in length. It is made from material that changes with the climate, and due to the size, the difference in overall pitch between a cold bassoon and one that has been played for half an hour is greater than for any other woodwind instrument. The doubling back of the bore, the slanting holes, and rods running completely through the instrument all require an exactness of construction difficult to achieve. Tuning may be improved by moving the bocal in or out, but it can be moved only a very short distance without upsetting the relationship of the whisper key to its hole on the bocal.

Bocals affect the sound and feel of the bassoon. Bocals are manufactured in three different sizes to help the bassoonist adjust to ensemble pitch. They are numbered according to size: the No. 0 is for pitches higher than A440, the No. 1 is for standard pitch, and the No. 2 is for flatter pitches and is the longest of the three. School instruments often have only one bocal, depending on which of the two originally with the instrument has become broken or lost.

The bassoon is the least mechanically flexible instrument to tune. In theory, the band or orchestra should tune to the bassoon. The bassoon has flexibility in lipping, but it is not wise to use this method when mechanical means are available on other instruments.

It may be argued that the reed itself makes so much difference in the intonation that any quibble about the bocal becomes unnecessary. The reed is a large factor in bassoon pitch, but all factors must be utilized to make intonation as good as possible—the instrument, the bocal, the reed, and the player. *Improving any one of these will improve pitch, but will not make up for deficiencies in the others.* The following section on reeds offers some details, but the general rules are this: A stiff reed raises the pitch, a soft reed flattens it. Reeds that are old or water–soaked become soft. The reed problem is compounded because the fit of the reed on the bocal is rather inexact. Bassoon reeds are not made on a staple like the oboe reed, but depend on the skill of the reedmaker. There are variations in the size of the butt opening that naturally affect the pitch.

Each bassoon has its own intonation problems, and these display less uniformity than those of other instruments. More of the out–of–tune pitches tend to be sharp rather than flat except in the high register, as shown in Figure 12–8.

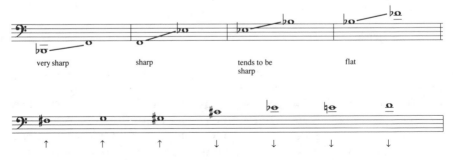

Figure 12–8. Intonation Problems of Certain Notes on the Bassoon

The teacher may suggest the student lower the pitch by:

1. Adding a tuning ring.
2. Half-holing.
3. Dropping the lower jaw (as if trying to bend the pitch downward).
4. Adjusting the bocal.
5. Adding the right little finger.
6. Adding the left-hand C-sharp key.
7. Adding the E-flat key.
8. Opening the reed.
9. Scraping the reed to make the tip thinner or the lay longer.

The player should try these and other ideas to determine which is most effective for his instrument.

Most texts refer to "lipping" a note in tune. Lipping means doing one of several things: drawing back the lower jaw, lessening the tension in the center of the lips, changing the direction of the air, loosening the embouchure, reducing the speed of the air and the amount of breath support, and putting more reed into the mouth. All make the tone flatter. The opposite actions will "lip up" the pitch. A tight throat and a pinched or bunched–up chin make the pitch sharper, as does biting on the reed with the lower teeth. A reed that is too soft or a key too closed tends to flatten the pitch. Furthermore, the bassoon has a tendency to go sharp at louder dynamic levels.

Alternate fingerings and trick fingerings are usually more successful than lipping the pitch in tune because changing the embouchure or airstream can affect the tone quality as much as or more than it can change the pitch. For example, a low C-sharp is usually played much better in tune with the low D key added by the left thumb, the third-space E is improved with the low C key with the right hand, and the E-flat just below it is helped by pressing the low C-sharp key and using the left little finger on low D. In addition, a different fingering may improve not only intonation but tone quality. Bassoons are so individual in character that each one could have its own fingering chart, worked out by a player who explores to see which fingerings are best for each note. Accomplished performers usually develop a set of fingerings for slow passages to produce the best pitch, quality, response, and resonance, then use the more standard fingerings for fast passages where agility is necessary.

TONE QUALITY

The bassoon has an established place in music today despite the same mechanical defects that have long since relegated the ophicleide, sax horn, and serpent to the museum. Its popularity is due to its unique color possibilities. In the hands of an expert, the bassoon can sound as mellow as a cello or as piercing as a trumpet. It can imitate with amazing fidelity the tone of a clarinet, baritone, or horn. It can be shrill, grotesque, pompous, and comical, in short, the clown of the orchestra, but it can be rich and powerful as well.

Good tone is not difficult to teach but it is difficult to talk about or explain in a textbook. Good tone depends on correct training and proper habits. Breath support and embouchure coupled with the reed and the instrument make the sound. If the reed or the instrument are average, good use of breath support and embouchure can produce a bassoon tone that is above average, even exceptional. Good exercises to strengthen embouchure and encourage breath control are sustained tones, slurs in one register, slurs across registers, slow scales that extend over more than one register, and intervals. The player should attempt to match each tone with the preceding one. He must remember, however, that the bassoon has three distinctly different registers. From low B-flat to second-space C is the bottom register, the next octave is the middle register, and the high register is the remainder of the range. Each register in the bassoon range has its own characteristic sound; if it does not, incorrect breathing is the probable cause—the tone is being controlled by the chest or throat and not by the diaphragm.

Not putting enough reed into the mouth, especially not covering the top of the reed with the upper lip, is usually the cause of an unpleasant or buzzing quality. If the lip position seems to be correct but the buzzing quality persists, the reed may be too soft at the tip or the player's lips may be too relaxed. To improve the reed, a very small amount of the tip may be cut off with a sharp knife or razor blade. If the tone quality is not improved, the student might pucker his lips around the reed more firmly, bringing more of the lower lip into contact with the reed. He should not cover more of the reed with his lower lip, but instead make the lower lip firmer.

Poor response and poor quality on the low notes may be due to a closed reed. The reed is easily opened by pressing gently on its sides or edges, although this is usually only a temporary remedy. If the reed is not closed, it may be dried out. It should be moistened well and frequently. If this does not help, the player may be pinching the reed. He should relax his embouchure, particularly the upper lip.

If the player produces a poor tone coupled with irregular response in the higher register, the problem may be with fingerings. He should check alternate fingerings and do some experimenting. His lower lip may be too relaxed, or the reed may be too soft. If only the tip is at fault and the rest of the reed is not overly soft, cutting a bit off the tip can improve the reed and the player's tone quality.

Unsteady pitch on the middle E and F—usually flatness with accompanying bad tone quality—usually indicates that the reed is too soft. The tip may be cut off, one of the temporary cures tried (see pp. 236–237), or the reed replaced.

Another common problem is a tone that cracks on the attack and in the middle register. Cracking may indicate a faulty embouchure: too much pressure from the top and bottom, not enough from the sides. Students who transfer from other instruments whose embouchures require pressure placed more up and down on the reed than into the center may have difficulty applying pressure to the sides of the reed. Cracking is also caused by a plugged hole under the whisper key. Finally, cracking may be due to a flaw in the instrument, and if so the instrument must be humored into a different response. Flicking one of several keys just as the note is attacked often mitigates cracking; it may help to flick the first hole of the left hand to allow a small amount of air in, flick the whisper key, or the D or A key. This requires some concentration until the player gets used to flicking one finger as he puts down other fingers for the desired pitch.

When the middle F-sharp and G respond with poor tone quality or when they crack on the attack, other gradations of the half hole should be tried. The bassoon is temperamental and unpredictable; half-holing with various fine shadings is one of the best ways to conquer the instrument's foibles.

The tones in the low register can be produced best by dropping the lower jaw and applying more pressure to the sides of the reed. The embouchure is not relaxed; the reed is given more freedom to vibrate. If the embouchure is relaxed, the pitch drops. For the upper register, good tone is achieved by altering the embouchure in the opposite direction: more pressure is applied from the top and the bottom, the lower lip and jaw are somewhat more firm, and the corners of the mouth exert less pressure.

As with other wind instruments, a change in the dynamic level must be accompanied by appropriate changes in the embouchure. Forte playing demands a relaxation of the embouchure so that the reed is freer to vibrate; pianissimo playing needs a more careful, restricted, cushioned embouchure (with the throat remaining open).

The bassoonist must learn two skills unique to his instrument: First, he should begin reading the tenor clef as soon as possible. Adjusting to a second or third clef is not difficult, especially for a young pupil whose habits are still forming. The bassoon player should be introduced to tenor clef after playing the instrument for a year or so. Sufficient practice at an early stage of development will prevent the student from having to mentally transpose tenor clef notation to bass clef before playing it. Second, he must have or develop a flexible thumb. Unlike other wind instrumentalists, the bassoonist must play eight or more keys with the left thumb, so he must adjust to this strange situation.

Finally, the instrument must be in good repair, the bocal should not leak, the reed should be suited to the embouchure and in good condition. The student should check his posture and breath support, continually work for a better embouchure, and listen, listen, listen.

Vibrato

There are purists who insist that a really beautiful tone does not need to be enhanced by vibrato, and that vibrato is used only when it fits the musical style. Most musicians, however, seem to agree that a good vibrato adds warmth and humanity. The human voice is the most expressive and personal of all musical instruments, and other instruments imitate its qualities if not its timbre. Of the different ways to produce vibrato, both diaphragm and jaw vibrato are acceptable on the bassoon.

The most consistent use of vibrato is in twentieth-century music and the majority of band literature. The vibrato should normally be fast (about seven pulsations per second) and not very wide. It should always be tasteful.

TECHNIQUE: ARTICULATION AND FINGERING

Tonguing on the bassoon is somewhat different from tonguing on the other reed instruments because the reed lies farther in the mouth, making it impractical to tongue at the very tip of the reed. Only the bottom half of the reed needs to be touched to achieve a clean articulation.

If the player uses the tip of his tongue on the tip of the reed, he will have to place his tongue high in the mouth for contact, tightening the throat and cutting down on the resonance. The better way is to touch the underside of the reed about $\frac{1}{4}$ to $\frac{1}{8}$ of an inch from the tip. When this is done naturally, the part of the tongue that touches the reed is not the tip but an area about $\frac{1}{2}$ of an inch from the tip on the top side of the tongue. The action of the tongue is more up-and-down than forward-and-back. The player must experiment to find the easiest and most natural place for tongue and reed to come together. If his tongue is short, using the very tip of the tongue may facilitate articulation; if his tongue is long or thick, touching the reed at a spot farther back on the tongue may work more efficiently.

Because the tongue moves primarily up and down, young students may develop the habit of "chewing notes"; that is, letting the jaw move with the motion of the tongue. The student must be encouraged to maintain a steady airstream and move only the tongue. This can be practiced extensively without the reed in the mouth, and then in front of a mirror while actually playing the instrument. The embouchure must also remain firm when tonguing— many students develop the habit of altering the embouchure when rapid passages are encountered.

Double-tonguing is looked on with skepticism by most reed players. It is far more advantageous to be able to play with a light, fast, single-tongue.

Many notes require awkward fingerings on the bassoon. Bassoonists and music educators joke about the dilemma encountered by the left thumb, that activates eight or more keys, sometimes as many as four at once. Besides learning the basic fingering for each note, the young bassoonist must also learn *how* to move from one note to another smoothly and without tension, sliding the left thumb instead of letting it jump about. The position for holding the bassoon described earlier is essential for keeping the hands relaxed. If the left wrist, for example, is forced into a tense, angled position, thumb dexterity is hampered.

As with the flute, numerous notes can be played on the bassoon without pressing or lifting all the necessary keys. On the flute, these fingerings affect pitch; on the bassoon these partially-correct fingerings affect not only pitch but also tone quality and control. For example, many notes that should be played with the pianissimo (whisper) key pressed will sound without it, but lack control.

The bassoon player needs to half-hole certain notes, such as fourth-line/space F-sharp, G, and G-sharp. These notes can be played with the left first finger completely lifted, but with poor intonation and a harsher tone quality. Players must learn to listen carefully and make adjustments with the embouchure, alternate fingerings and keys, and the extent to which the first tone hole is opened. The teacher must observe visually and aurally the fingerings used for many of the bassoon pitches. In very rapid passages, the tone hole may be completely opened.

While the thumb is extremely busy for the bassoonist, the little fingers have fewer keys to operate than on the clarinet or oboe. The keys manipulated by the little fingers are used more in alternate fingerings. As students' demands require, the alternate fingerings should be taught and practiced. Teachers should always select the best fingerings for the young player until the student matures to the point where he can make those determinations himself. The fingering chart at the conclusion of this chapter indicates many bassoon fingerings; the first one for each note is the basic fingering, the rest are listed in approximate order of their use.

Coordination of tongue and fingers is of great importance in good bassoon technique as with all the other winds. The bassoon reed takes slightly longer to begin vibrating than do the other reeds. While this delay is only perhaps 200 milliseconds, it is an aspect of technique with which the player must deal. A steady airstream with adequate breath support is essential.

WHAT TO PRACTICE

After the student is able to play a few notes on the instrument and is aware of the importance of a correctly formed embouchure and air support, supplementary material should be the focus of his study. He will probably understand the basics of notation prior to beginning study on the bassoon, so progress will be faster than with most beginners. Initial studies should include long tones and slow, slurred passages to encourage proper embouchure and proper breath support. Tonguing should be introduced later, as the embouchure matures, with legato articulations introduced first to ensure that the student does not develop the habit of tonguing too harshly.

To acquire coordination of the tongue and fingers, students should practice scales and arpeggios along with supplementary studies written for the purpose. Practice must begin slowly, at the speed at which the exercise can be played well, and the tempo should only gradually be increased.

The C scale is normally the first scale practiced. As advocated throughout this book, scales should be practiced in cycles; that is, beginning on the tonic, then to the highest note playable with good tone, back down to the lowest note, and back to the tonic. On bassoon, the C scale should initially begin on low C and ascend only a fifth, to G, then down to low G, and back to the starting note. This partial scale is useful for raising and lowering one finger at a time as well as for crossing the break, fourth-line F—going from all fingers up to five-and-one-half fingers down. The upper octave uses a half-hole fingering as the range is increased.

Long tones are useful and should be practiced for endurance and to develop the embouchure. Since the beginning bassoonist is usually more experienced than beginners on other instruments, long tones can be introduced and practiced fairly early. Good tone quality requires a good mental concept, which for bassoon may prove elusive. Students should be encouraged to listen to recordings and live performances, and then listen to themselves critically, constantly attempting to emulate the best sound.

CARE AND MAINTENANCE OF THE BASSOON

By way of long-term maintenance, keys and pads should be inspected and adjusted at least once a year by a competent repairperson, and the instrument should probably be overhauled every five to six years—an item included in the annual budget.

By way of short-term, frequent maintenance, it is well to remember that bassoons do not work well with bent or dirty bocals, loose reed wires, or an accumulation of dust under the keys. The bocal needs to be cleaned frequently and carefully. It should be carefully blown out after each playing, and warm soapy water run through it occasionally, followed by thorough rinsing and swabbing.

The holes covered by the fingers accumulate grease and dirt from the hands, and because of the holding position of the bassoon are susceptible to moisture from the inside of the instrument. This moisture results in tiny layers of sediment around the edges of the holes that decrease the size of the hole and make the pitch sharper. They should be cleaned with a pipe cleaner, cotton swab, toothpick, or some similar tool. Wiping the wooden surface and the keys keeps the exterior clean and the finish intact.

Swabbing the entire bassoon is not a necessity; neither is oiling the bore. Most bassoons are partially lined with rubber linings or synthetic materials to protect the pertinent areas from moisture. Oil causes these materials to deteriorate, rubber more quickly than synthetics. The non-lined portions—usually the larger part of the boot joint, the long joint, and bell joints—may need an occasional slight oiling, but even a little too much oil aids in collecting dust and dirt. It is better not to oil at all than to use too much. Swabbing does discourage the unpleasant smell that unswabbed instruments inevitably acquire. The wing joint and the boot should be swabbed with a linen handtowel rather than a brush swab, as the latter leaves lint in the instrument. Springs and bearings, joints, posts, and rods need minute applications of oil about twice a year. Use a pin or an instrument screwdriver to apply the oil.

The bottom cap and tube of the boot joint should be cleaned occasionally with soap and water—a task that requires a careful procedure. The cap and the tube should be removed from the joint, then washed, rinsed, and dried before replacing. The gasket should not leak when reassembled, as a leak may affect tone quality and intonation of several pitches.

General care includes keeping the instrument away from excessive heat and avoiding sudden extremes of temperature. When the instrument is cold, allow it to warm to room temperature before blowing through it. Check the spot where the bocal fits into the wing joint, as this occasionally leaks air.

The young bassoonist's education should include not only how to adjust commercial reeds, and possibly reed construction, but also how to adjust the key mechanism to ensure proper playing condition—bassoonists have enough challenges without having to contend with an out-of-adjustment instrument.

As new instruments are broken in, or on older instruments, some pads may not seat properly. Pads may be inspected for leaks by closing the pad over a strip of lens paper and gently pulling the paper in various directions. Each joint can be checked for leaks by closing one end with one hand, closing the tone holes with the fingers of the other hand, holding the open end over the mouth so as to seal it, and gently blowing air. Leaks should be inspected to determine if they are due to damaged or worn pads, keys that require adjusting, bent rods, worn or broken springs, or a rod screw that is too tight. Any of these problems can be remedied by a repairperson, many by the teacher and eventually by the student himself.

Leaks and intonation problems also result from worn corks used for adjusting the connection between bridge keys. Worn corks should be replaced or covered with thin slices of cork, then lightly sanded to the point where all appropriate keys are closed securely.

REEDS

The first weeks of teaching the bassoon to a beginner are often the most pleasant because he has not yet learned how much trouble the reed can be nor how it can enhance his prestige to be able to complain to the trombone player about reed problems. The first sounds come easily from the bassoon, and the player is occupied holding the instrument and finding the right places for his fingers; he knows not the difficulties he will encounter. As numerous bassoon teachers point out, every bassoonist should learn to play adequately on a mediocre reed—then when he comes across a good one, he will appreciate his luck. A teacher who gives the bassoon player too much information about the reed too soon will have a student who spends all his time making and fixing reeds instead of practicing. The student will never play better than his practicing has prepared him for, even though he has a reed worthy of a professional.

No reed lasts forever. When a player has a good reed, he must begin immediately to work on or search for another. Like a good meal, a good reed gives tremendous satisfaction for a while, but in time will be consumed and will need to be replaced. Students tend to believe a good reed is imperishable. As a reed is used it deteriorates, and the embouchure with it as the student tries to compensate for changes in the weakening reed. Soon he will not have a reed, embouchure, or a concept of good tone quality.

Although reeds are usually purchased, the student should learn to make them in order to learn to adjust them. Poor reeds should not be discarded, because they have a use; students can learn from working on them, taking them apart and inspecting previous workmanship. The ideal reed, whether commercial or finished by the student, is one that gives a good tone quality, is easy to blow, responds well, and has good intonation in all registers.

The bassoon's double reed is actually two reeds held together with three pieces of wire and some string. The cane should be golden in color rather than green, neither too soft nor too hard, and the fibers will run the full length of the reed. Cane that is only slightly green may improve if allowed to cure in the open air. Although most players look for a golden shade, various shades of yellow may be satisfactory. So, also, may mottled, spotted cane be satisfactory. Coarse-grained cane does not produce satisfactory tone quality for most players, but it responds easily, leading students to believe that these are the better reeds. On the contrary, a reed with a harder response will produce a better tone. Since no sealing agent is used, the edges must fit all the way to the tip, and the tip opening should be oval or elliptical. The tone quality and response of the reed will be determined by the quality of the cane, the workmanship and evenness of the reed, the shape of the tip opening, and the condition of the edges.

In selecting commercial reeds, several criteria besides the quality of the cane may be considered. Drawing the fingernail over the reed can show how hard the reed is. It should have a springy quality. If it is too hard, the fingernail will leave no mark; if it is too soft, the fingernail will leave an indentation. It is better to buy a reed that is too stiff than to buy one too soft. The stiff reed can be altered without destroying its resistance. Spencer designates the hallmarks of a good reed's appearance as "balance, symmetry of design, and neatness in workmanship."[1] Even the most "beautiful" reed can still be a poor-playing one, but it can usually be adjusted to work well.

The sides should be of equal thickness, without either thick or thin spots, for balance and taper. The tips should be even. The corners should have even shading. One can insert a plaque into the reed to check this thickness and also to check the curve of the blades. Cracks and splits should be avoided, especially deep scoring marks on the butt, because they can extend into the blade with the slightest pressure. If the throat of the reed is not completely formed, the reed will be unsatisfactory. Reeds that are alike in color, shape, thickness, and cut will not necessarily play alike. The workmanship varies and the cane even more so; reeds that look good and have been selected with care may still prove to be unsatisfactory or beyond fixing. The experienced player becomes accustomed to this.

It is always difficult to criticize something that apparently works. The plastic reed works but is not recommended by professionals. It is, however, amazingly durable and difficult to crack; it can be worked and shaved like a cane reed; it is always ready to play without soaking; it has a consistent response regardless of the register, and it costs about twice as much as a regular reed while outliving a dozen. Transfers from clarinet like it because they can master it much more easily than a regular reed, which demands a better bassoon embouchure. Nevertheless, the plastic reed has serious drawbacks. The wide difference of tone colors possible in the various registers cannot be achieved with the plastic reed; in eliminating the undesirable variables the desirable ones have also been lost. Since the bassoon's

[1] William Spencer, *The Art of Bassoon Playing* (Evanston, IL: Summy-Birchard Publishing Co., 1958), 28.

great appeal lies in its tonal possibilities, the plastic reed detracts from rather than enhances the value of the instrument.

There are two specific styles of reed, the French and the German, and two general sizes, long and short. The French reed has less heart than the German reed, visible by holding the reed up to an intense light. The French reed tip is about the same thickness at the edges as at the center, while the German is tapered from the center of the tip to the edges and comes to a point at each side where the two blades meet. This makes the French reed a thicker, heavier reed. Such characteristics make major differences in the tone quality. The French quality is lighter and more reedy, even nasal, while the German quality is darker and more mellow. Beginners and even some advanced players will prefer the wide, thinner reed because it gives a rich, full sound, is easy to control, and is especially compatible with players who have transferred from the clarinet. A narrow, more resistant reed may be chosen by the player whose embouchure is highly developed and who wants to be able to control the upper register, the part of the range little used in school music but prevalent in symphonic literature. Longer reeds are usually preferred over the shorter ones.

Spencer has an interesting picture showing the relative size and shape of ten different bassoon reeds.[2] They vary more than $\frac{1}{4}$ of an inch in length, and show different widths and bindings. They can all play in tune because they are cut with a lay that is in proportion to their length, a fact more essential to the pitch than is the actual length of the reed.

Figure 12–9 indicates the various parts of the reed. The lay is that part of the reed above the wire, thicker in the center, or heart, and tapering out to the edges and the tip. The shoulder is the small ridge where the lay ends and the tube begins. Three wires hold the two sides of the reed together. The throat is that part of the tube lying between the second wire and the shoulder.

Problems of Response

If the upper register is unresponsive, the reed may be either too stiff or too soft. For a low register that speaks only with effort, scraping the tip from the center outward or lengthening this cut toward the back will help. Often new commercial reeds have not had the corners removed. These corners must be clipped or "rounded" to make the reed more responsive in all registers. Only very slight amounts should be removed between testing. If too much is removed from the corners or the tip is scraped too thin, the upper register will become unresponsive. It will also have the effect of making the reed too soft and consequently flat and nasal sounding.

[2] Ibid., 26.

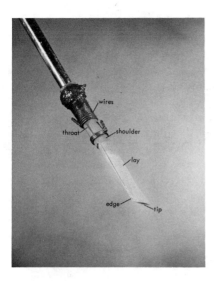

Figure 12-9. Bassoon reed

If the upper register does not respond well, the reed may be too open and can be adjusted by closing the first wire slightly using needle-nosed pliers to press the top and bottom of the reed. This adjustment will immediately affect the lower register if the wire is closed too much. Experience and practice are required to reach a middle ground. Altering the tip opening will also affect control of dynamic levels and tone quality.

If the tip is very thin, the reed may not respond readily in any range; the tip should be trimmed and then scraped from the center toward the sides. If the tip and edges are thin enough, cane in the area of the sides and around the heart should be removed. If cane has been removed at the sides of the reed and the response is still sluggish, one can take a little from the heart, but this must be done delicately and carefully as this area is best not tampered with. If too much is removed from the heart, the reed will be thin and buzzy and impossible to improve. *The smallest change may be sufficient to improve or ruin the reed.*

Pitch Problems

For general problems of low pitch, the tip of the reed should be trimmed. For general sharp pitch, the entire lay of the reed should be lengthened. Lengthening the lay will sometimes simply mean scraping the shoulder back a little, or it may be necessary to rework the entire reed. In selecting reeds or fixing them, C, D, E, and F in the staff are key notes for intonation. Flatness here indicates the reed is too soft, sharpness indicates that it is too stiff.

Specific intonation problems include the following:

1. For sharp low notes, the back and sides of the reed are too heavy.
2. For sharp high notes, the reed is probably too closed and the top wire should be tightened using pliers to apply pressure on the sides.
3. For flat high notes, the reed is too open. Gentle pressure with the pliers on the first wire area of the butt can close the reed somewhat, but the reed must be well soaked and the pliers used carefully or the reed will be ruined. The reed should be squeezed on the top and bottom; squeezing on the sides will serve to open it more.
4. For flat E and F in the staff, the tip of the reed is too long, the heart is too thin, or the reed is old and soggy.
5. When fourth-space G and forked E-flat are very sharp, the reed is too heavy and needs general scraping.

Other rules

1. To improve tone quality, scrape below the tip toward the sides.
2. To increase resistance, scrape the sides of the reed.
3. When scraping one blade of the reed, *always* support the other blade.
4. Sand only a dry reed; scrape a wet reed.
5. A reed with thin spots cannot be repaired.
6. A reed warped at the tip may right itself when soaked, but a wavy tip may indicate the tip has been scraped too thin (it can be trimmed and rescraped as required).
7. If the reed produces a dull tone, thin the tip.

Additional guidelines for adjusting reeds:

1. Reeds become stronger during the breaking-in period. Play only a few minutes a day for the first week or ten days.
2. Make small adjustments and then try the reed; minute differences in scraping, sanding, and clipping can result in the change desired.
3. Do not scrape the reed until it has been well soaked.
4. Wires must always be tight. Tightening the wire takes care and practice; the wire is very fine and a single twist can break it. Wires that are too tight will choke the reed and prevent proper vibration.

The size of the tip opening in the reed should be about $\frac{1}{16}$ of an inch at the center; an opening any smaller will close up in playing, while a larger opening will necessitate too much embouchure pressure. The exact size of the opening will vary from reed to reed, and the player should experiment to see with what size he obtains the best results. Wire adjustments control the size of the opening and change the quality of the tone. When the second wire is squeezed from the sides, a lighter sound results and tonguing will be easier, but there will be less resistance and the reed will tend to close up on forte passages in the low register. If the second wire is squeezed on the top and bottom, the tone is somewhat heavier and the low register easier to obtain. Squeezing the first wire produces the opposite effects. Squeezing the first wire on the top and bottom closes the reed, thins the tone, decreases the resistance, and improves the upper register. Since squeezing the wire usually loosens it, tightening the second wire before adjusting the first wire is recommended in order to keep from loosening the reed and destroying the fit at the edges. A test for proper adjustment of the opening is to tongue low F rapidly—the opening is not too small if low F is in tune and responds normally; play F above middle C—if this note is in tune and responds normally, the opening is not too large.

Tests for a good reed include the following. (1) Put the reed well into the mouth and blow; the reed should crow. If the crow is too high and tight the lay is too short, too thick, or both, and more scraping is necessary. If the crow is too deep the reed is too thin and the lay too long, the tip should be cut off and the reed reworked. If a reed does not crow, it may be leaking or the tips may be too far apart. Try tightening the wires and soaking. (2) Suck briefly on the reed, take it out of the mouth, put a finger over the butt opening and wait a few moments. There should be a "pop" as it dries and the air pressure becomes equal. The reed that does not stay closed is too stiff or too open and needs more work; if the reed stays closed a long time, it indicates softness, for which the remedy is to cut off the tip and rework the reed.

Care of Reeds

Reeds should not be kept in the clear plastic containers in which most commercial reeds are sold, as these are fairly airtight and do not allow a wet reed to dry as it should after use. A Sucrets box can be used for reed holders. The reed is cleaned with a small feather or even a pipe cleaner gently pushed through from the end of the reed and out the tip. A completely clean reed does not play as well as one that has accumulated a little bit of scum inside; perhaps two or three days' worth is about right. This saliva sediment acts as a cushion against excessive vibration and helps produce a darker, clearer tone.

TROUBLESHOOTING

EQUIPMENT

difficulty in assembling   Grease corks on joints, petroleum jelly on threaded joints.

sticky pads	1. Moisture in tone hole(s) or absorbed into pads. If pad is not damaged, place piece of a coffee filter between the key and tone hole and cover gently for paper to absorb moisture.
	2. Bent rods or keys. Have repaired by competent repairperson.
	3. Worn springs. Have repaired.
	4. Pivot screws require oiling. One drop.
pads not seating correctly	1. Leaking pads. Readjustment of mechanism may be required if some keys are remaining open.
	2. Pads damaged or hard and brittle. Have replaced.
	3. Some pads that are worn but not damaged can be reseated by carefully heating the back of the key and pressing the key over the tone hole (being careful to cover the hot key with a soft cloth and realizing that the key may cause other leaks due to its new position).
gurgling sound	1. Water in tone holes. Blow water into bore; clean with feather or pipe cleaner; maintain instrument well—dry out after playing if possible.
TONE	
raucous, loud sound	1. Too much reed in the mouth. Try just a small amount of reed and gradually insert more until the desired sound is produced.
	2. Reed too hard. Try softer reed or scrape and trim as needed.
	3. Cheeks puffing. Firm up corners to flatten chin and cheeks.
	4. Embouchure too loose. Correct embouchure.
	5. Reed too open. Carefully close soaked reed between thumb and index finger to reduce stiffness.
pinched, small sound	1. Not enough reed in mouth. Place more so that upper lip is at least $\frac{1}{4}$ of an inch from first wire.
	2. Chin bunched. Tighten corners of mouth or direct the corners more toward the reed.
	3. Not enough air. Correct breathing, careful not to overblow.
	4. Throat or oral cavity too tight. Try dropping lower jaw; use less jaw, more lower lip pressure.
	5. Biting on reed. Drop jaw leaving lip pressure around contour of reed.
	6. Bad reed, poorly made. Try new reed, perhaps a different cut.
	7. Bassoon held with boot too far back—bad angle for reed. Boot should be by thigh, head erect.

8. Reed not open enough. Trim end of reed a very small amount at a time until the opening produces desired sound.

hard, strident sound

1. Reed too hard or inappropriate cut for embouchure. Try a softer or different cut reed.
2. Biting on reed. Drop jaw, more lip pressure under reed.
3. Not enough breath support. Correct breathing.

trouble with control

1. Not maintaining a smooth airstream. Correct breathing.
2. Biting on reed or poor embouchure. Correct embouchure.
3. Angle of reed entering mouth is too high or too low. Correct holding position.
4. Jaw not dropped or pulled back. Correct embouchure.
5. Reed too soft or too hard. Adjust reed as above and in Chapter 11 on the oboe.
6. Embouchure too loose. Keep firm embouchure around reed.

PITCH

flat

1. Bocal too long. Try different one.
2. Embouchure too relaxed. Correct embouchure with pressure directed toward reed from all sides.
3. Reed too long. Shorten, trim, and scrape.
4. Individual notes—keys may not be opening enough. Have adjusted by competent bassoon repairperson. Or dirty tone holes. Clean with a pipe cleaner or feather.

sharp

1. Problems with bocal. Pull out bocal or try longer one.
2. Embouchure too tight. Occurs with a great deal of back pressure; student may be blowing too hard, relax airstream—"let it flow"—and relax embouchure slightly.
3. Reed too short. Try new, longer reed.
4. Biting on reed. Drop jaw, more lip pressure under reed.
5. Reed too hard. Try softer reed or scrape or trim as needed.
6. Not enough reed in mouth. Place more reed in mouth.
7. Individual notes—keys may be opening too far. Have adjustments made by competent bassoon repairperson. Or adjust embouchure (lipping up or down).

REFERENCES

Texts

Best, A. S. *The Bassoon*. Elkhart, IN: C. G. Conn, 1959.
Camden, A. *Bassoon Techniques*. London: Oxford University Press, 1962.

COOPER, LEWIS H., AND HOWARD TOPLANSKY. *Essentials of Bassoon Technique.* Union, NJ: Howard Toplansky, 1968.

FLETCHER, KRISTINE K. *The Conservatoire and the Contest Solos for Bassoon.* Bloomington, IN: Indiana University Press, 1988.

JANSEN, W. *Bassoon: Its History, Construction, Makers, Players, and Music.* 5 vols., Kinderhook, NY: E. J. Brill, 1978.

HECKEL, W. H. *The Bassoon.* Translated by Langwill and Waples. Old Greenwich, CN: Jack Spratt Music Co., 1940.

KLIMKO, D. J. *Bassoon Performance Practices and Teaching in the United States and Canada.* Moscow, ID: University of Idaho, School of Music, 1974.

LANGWILL, LYNDESAY. *The Bassoon and Contrabassoon.* New York: W. W. Norton, 1965.

LEHMAN, PAUL. *The Harmonic Structure of the Tone of the Bassoon.* Rev. ed. Seattle, WA: Berdon, 1965.

PENCE, HOMER. *Teacher's Guide to the Bassoon.* Elkhart, IN: The Selmer Co., 1963.

PESAVENTO, A. *Design and Adjustment Principles of the Bassoon Reed: A Manual for the Intermediate Player.* Indianapolis, IN: Lang Music Publications, 1972.

POPKIN, MARK, AND LOREN GLICKMAN. *Bassoon Reeds.* Evanston, IL: The Instrumentalist Co., 1969.

SCHLEIFFER, ERIC. *The Art of Bassoon Reed Making.* Oneonta, NY: Swift-Dorr Publications, 1974.

SPENCER, WILLIAM. *The Art of Bassoon Playing.* 2nd ed. Evanston, IL: Summy-Birchard, 1969.

WEAIT, CHRISTOPHER. *Bassoon Reed-Making: A Basic Technique.* 2nd ed. New York: McGinnis and Marx, 1980.

Journals

The Double Reed. Quarterly from the International Double Reed Society. Lowry Riggins, International Double Reed Society Executive Secretary–Treasurer, 626 Lakeshore Drive, Monroe, LA 71203–4032.

The Journal of the Double Reed Society. Quarterly from the International Double Reed Society. Lowry Riggins, International Double Reed Society Executive Secretary–Treasurer, 626 Lakeshore Drive, Monroe, LA 71203–4032.

Studies

Easy—Beginning (junior high)

BUCK, LAWRENCE. *Elementary Method for Bassoon* (Kjos).

HAWKINS, D. *Melodious and Progressive Studies for the Bassoon* (Southern Music).

HERFURTH, PAUL C. *A Tune a Day for Bassoon* (Boston Music).

JANCOURT, EUGENE. *26 Melodic Studies,* Op 15 (Costellat).

LENTZ, DONALD. *Lentz Method for Bassoon,* Vols. 1 and 2 (Belwin-Mills).

MCDOWELL, PAUL. *Practical Studies for Bassoon,* Vols. 1 and 2 (Belwin-Mills).

MCDOWELL/HOVEY, N. *Daily Exercises for Bassoon* (Belwin-Mills).

PARES, GABRIEL. *Scales and Daily Exercises for Bassoon* (Carl Fischer).
SKORNICKA, JOSEPH. *Elementary Method for Bassoon* (Rubank).
WEISSENBORN, JULIUS. *Bassoon Studies for Beginners*, Book I (Cundy-Bettoney and Carl Fischer).

Medium (advanced junior high or high school)

FINK, REGINALD H. *Introducing the Tenor Clef for Trombone (Bassoon) (Accura Music)*.
GAMBARO, GIOVANNI. *18 Etudes* (International).
GIAMPIERI, ALAMIRO. *16 Daily Studies* (G. Ricordi).
JACOBI, F. *6 Caprices* (International).
JANCOURT, EUGENE. *26 Melodic Studies*, Op 15 (Costellat).
KOPPRASCH, C. *60 Studies for Bassoon*, Vols. 1 and 2 (International).
MILDE, LUDWIG. *Concert Studies*, Vol. 1 (International).
_____. *25 Studies in Scales and Chords*, Op. 24 (International).
OUBRADOUS, F. *Gammes et Exercises Journaliers*, Vols. 1 and 2 (Alphonse Leduc).
SATZENHOFER, T. *24 Studies for Bassoon* (International).
WEISSENBORN, JULIUS. *50 Advanced Studies*, Op. 8, Books I and II (Carl Fischer).
_____. *Practical Method for the Bassoon* (Carl Fischer).

Advanced (high school or college)

BITSCH, MARCEL. *20 Studies for Bassoon* (Alphonse Leduc).
BOZZA, EUGENE. *12 Caprices*, Op. 64 (Alphonse Leduc).
GAMBARO, GIOVANNI. *18 Etudes* (International).
GIAMPIERI, ALAMIRO. *16 Daily Studies* (G. Ricordi).
_____. *16 Daily Studies for Perfection* (G. Ricordi).
KLENGEL, JULIUS. *Daily Exercises for Cello* (Breitkopf).
MILDE, LUDWIG. *Concert Studies for Bassoon*, Vol. 2 (International).
_____. *50 Concert Studies*, Op. 26 (Kalmus).
_____. *25 Studies in Scales and Chords*, Op. 24 (International).
OUBRADOUS, F. *Gammes et Exercises Journaliers* Vols. 2 and 3 (Alfonse Leduc).
PIARD, MARIUS. *90 Etudes* Vols. 1 and 2 (Theodore Presser).
SATZENHOFER, T. *24 Studies for Bassoon* (International).
SCHOENBACH, S. *20th Century Orchestral Studies for Bassoon* (G. Schirmer).
WEISSENBORN, JULIUS. *50 Advanced Studies*, Op. 8, Books I and II (Carl Fischer).

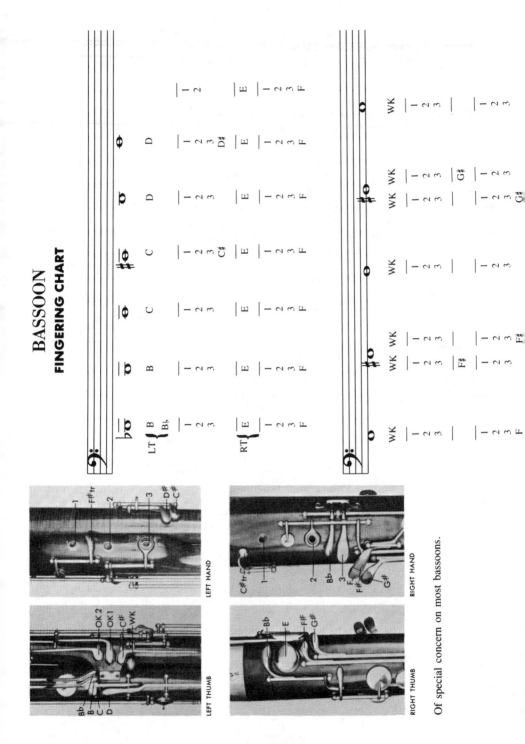

BASSOON
FINGERING CHART

Of special concern on most bassoons.

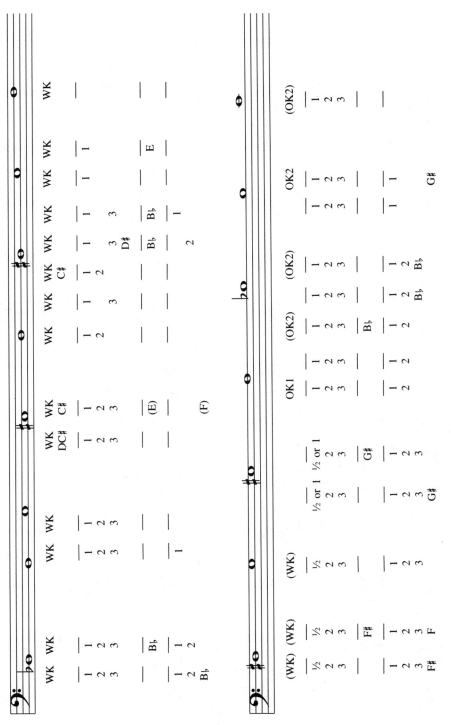

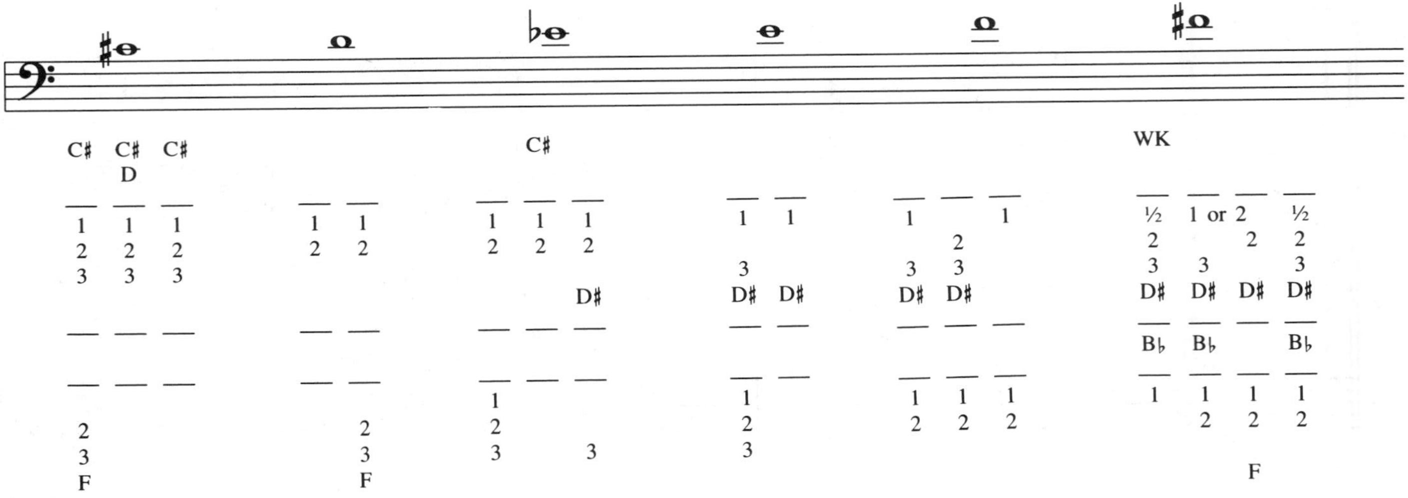
C♯ 1 2 3 2 3 F
C♯ D 1 2 3
C♯ 1 2 3
1 2
1 2 2 3 F
1 2 1 2 3
C♯ 1 2
1 2 D♯ 3
1 3 D♯ 1 2 3
1 D♯
1 3 D♯ 1 2
2 3 D♯ 1 2
1 1 2
WK ½ 2 3 D♯ B♭ 1
1 or 2 3 D♯ B♭ 1 2
2 D♯ 1 2 F
½ 2 3 D♯ B♭ 1 2

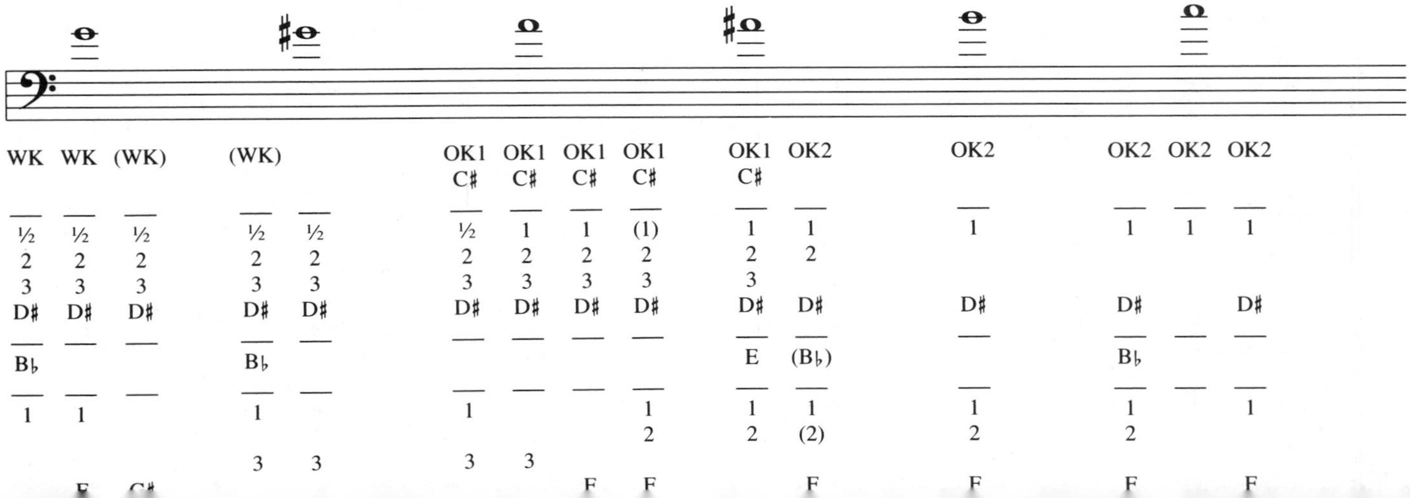
WK ½ 2 3 D♯ B♭ 1
WK ½ 2 3 D♯ 1
(WK) ½ 2 3 D♯
(WK) ½ 2 3 D♯ B♭ 1 3
½ 2 3 D♯ 3
OK1 C♯ ½ 2 3 D♯ 1 3
OK1 C♯ 1 2 3 D♯ 3
OK1 C♯ 1 2 3 D♯ F
OK1 C♯ (1) 2 3 D♯ 1 2 F
OK1 C♯ 1 2 3 D♯ E 1 2
OK2 1 2 D♯ (B♭) 1 (2) F
OK2 1 D♯ 1 2 F
OK2 1 D♯ B♭ 1 2 F
OK2 1
OK2 1 D♯ 1 F

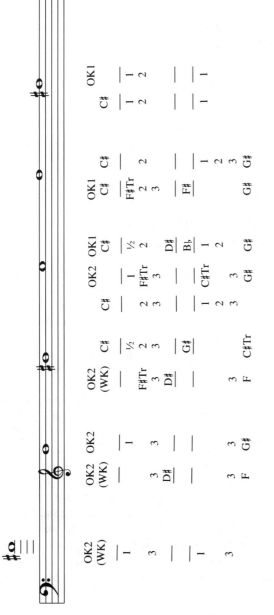

13

The Clarinet

HISTORY

The forerunners of the clarinet, the single-reed instruments, date back to 2700 B.C., when the double clarinet was used in Egypt. A triple instrument dating from this period, the launedda, is used in Sardinia to the present day. A clarinet-like instrument called the jaleika was found in Russia; it also dates from the pre-Christian era. The true forerunner of the present-day clarinet is a Greek single-tube instrument called the chalumeau. This instrument was never as popular as the double-reed shawm, due to problems of mouthpiece construction and a short, incomplete scale that was hard to overblow. The chalumeau increased in popularity during the sixteenth century but was still not favored by the more important composers. Its first real use occurred in two obscure operas written in 1710: Keiser's *Croesus* and Bononcini's *Turno Aricino*. By this time, the chalumeau was already a thing of the past, for in 1690 Johann Christoff Denner had added two keys to create an instrument with a range of two octaves. By 1720, finger keys and the speaker key had been added. This clarinet, using a small reed, sounded a bit like an oboe. The clarinet remained a minor instrument and did not appear in scores until four concertos in 1747, followed by works of Arrein in 1762 and Stamitz in 1765. Muller added a key system in 1810. The clarinet did not become a modern instrument until Klose added the Boehm system in 1843, making it possible to play in all keys. Numerous forms of the clarinet appeared in the nineteenth century with clarinets pitched in C and D, bass clarinets, the bathyphone (in E), and the basset horn, an alto clarinet pitched in F with a narrow bore and thin wall.

Today the clarinet has three chief registers: the low chalumeau register, the middle or throat-tone register, called the clarion or alt because it is loud and brilliant, and the high register. Presently made in five or six different keys, ranging from the small sopranino to the contrabass, the clarinet is one of the most useful instruments. Since the time of Mozart, composers have given the instrument a superior repertoire.

The clarinet is the backbone of symphonic and concert bands. Ideally, the symphonic band has more B-flat soprano clarinets than any other single instrument. The clarinet is popular as a jazz instrument, as a classically oriented solo instrument, and as an essential element in the orchestra. Its range extends almost an octave higher *and* lower than that of the oboe, giving it one of the widest ranges of all the wind instruments.

The B-flat soprano instrument sounds a major second lower than the notes it reads and plays. Other frequently used clarinets include the E-flat soprano (sounding a minor third higher than it reads), the E-flat alto (sounding a major sixth lower than it reads), the B-flat bass (sounding a major ninth lower than it reads), and the B-flat contra bass (sounding a seventeenth lower than it reads). As stated in Chapter 9 "Principles For Woodwinds," the clarinet is the only woodwind instrument with a cylindrical bore (all others are conical) (see p. 150).

SELECTING THE INSTRUMENT

Knowledge of the troublesome idiosyncrasies of an instrument is important to teach or play it well. Clarinets are made of various materials, natural and synthetic; of these, grenadilla wood is the favorite. Several factors enter into the superiority of grenadilla wood: it is easy to work with; it is dense, which minimizes moisture absorption; and it is available in large enough quantities to keep from being prohibitively expensive. The clarinet has been the most successful plastic instrument because the quantities sold have justified the research required to produce a good product. Plastic clarinets, especially the alto and bass, are now made that approach the evenness of scale, the intonation, and the tone quality of the wooden instrument.

Straight-grained wood is always desirable. On older instruments, it is important to check whether the wood has dried out excessively or the posts have become loose. Cracks are not serious if they have been repaired expertly; they can be pinned or banded so that intonation and response are not affected. The appearance of more than one crack may indicate that the wood was not originally aged and seasoned properly. The most important part of a clarinet to check is the joints; any chip in the joints will prevent a perfect seal, allowing air to leak and affecting the intonation. Checking the interior of the barrel is also essential since scratches and scorings there affect intonation and tone.

One should always play an instrument before making a decision about its adequacy—there is no other way to estimate intonation and tone quality. Every clarinet will respond somewhat differently. Pitch should be checked by playing and listening. A good instrument must be tunable. Sometimes one will find clarinets that simply cannot be adjusted to match the ensemble's pitch. At a pitch of A440, the barrel should be pulled about $\frac{1}{16}$ of an inch at 68 to 72 degrees Fahrenheit. This fraction of an inch gives the player freedom to push the barrel in when room temperatures and air density make a sharper pitch desirable. Because warmer rooms raise pitch at different rates for different instruments, the clarinetist needs to be able to match this sharpness when necessary. If a particular clarinet plays under the pitch A440 with the barrel pulled $\frac{1}{16}$ of an inch, a shorter barrel will be necessary.

The individual testing the instrument should play octaves to determine intonation (with an electronic tuner) and then slowly play scales to determine that the intervals are adequately in tune at various dynamic levels. This check for intonation should be made by a professional clarinetist or while using an electronic tuner, as many students become inured to flawed intonation. A professional player will judge the merits of a new or used clarinet based on its potential tone quality, intonation, and response. The evaluation of these items is especially difficult for students to make because tone quality, intonation, and response are all dependent on the reed and mouthpiece as well as on the player. Good tone quality, intonation, and response are the products of a well-matched set of equipment in the hands of a skilled musician.

The quality of the keys should be considered. Keys should be made from a good, forged nickel-silver so they are not easily bent or broken. Bent keys are of special importance on any instrument, because a bent key may not open the proper distance, creating intonation problems. Students will often bend the key back into place, which does not remedy the damage or the intonation problem, but simply makes location of the problem more difficult.

The clarinet is far from a perfect instrument, and many compromises have been necessary in its manufacture. On most clarinets, the register key (not an octave key) and the speaker key for third-line B-flat are the same. To correct the problems caused by this doubling up, it would be necessary to move the speaker key higher on the clarinet and reduce it in size (its present placement results in a flat fourth-line D and fourth-space E). Alto, bass, and contrabass clarinets often have separate keys, one the B-flat key and one the register key.

One common purchase option is the articulated G-sharp, which facilitates playing in keys of more than three sharps but has the serious disadvantage of preventing the fingering of certain notes such as B-flat, D, and F with the first finger of each hand.

A single middle joint would allow a better C-sharp and G-sharp because the hole could be placed lower, but the loss of the option of pulling at this joint for intonation purposes has prevented this design from being adopted on better instruments except for the alto, bass, and contrabass clarinets. The new clarinets manufactured by companies such as Selmer, Buffet, and Yamaha are excellent selections whether one is purchasing a student or a professional-line instrument.

ASSEMBLING THE CLARINET

The various instruments of the clarinet family, ranging from the E-flat soprano to the contrabass, are constructed with similar parts. Precautions that apply to the assembling of one apply to all.

The clarinet has five parts: the mouthpiece (which holds the reed by means of a ligature), the barrel, the upper joint, the lower joint, and the bell. The parts fit together tightly—the tenons, covered with cork, ensure a close fit. The pieces do not slide together easily but must be coaxed. The corks should be greased prior to attempting the first assembly and should remain well greased. The pieces should be assembled by a gentle downward pressure and slight twisting, always in the same direction. They should never be assembled by wiggling.

The left hand firmly holds the lower joint without bending or damaging the keys, and the bell section is attached with a gentle twist. Next, the keys over the tone holes of the upper joint are pressed with the fingers of the right hand and the lower joint is carefully attached to the upper joint so as not to bend or put stress on the bridge keys. The keys can be depressed with the palm, thumb up, giving young students more control. The bridge keys are then aligned. The barrel is twisted on the top of the upper joint; and the mouthpiece, without the reed, is inserted into the barrel.

The flat side, or table, of the mouthpiece is lined up with the thumb hole on the underside of the clarinet, and the ligature is placed over the mouthpiece. The reed butt should be slipped under the ligature rather than the ligature placed over the reed. The ligature screws usually go on the same side of the mouthpiece as the reed. The bottom screw should be tightened enough to hold the reed firmly in place. The upper screw should be tightened only enough to prevent it from vibrating and causing an unpleasant buzzing sound. Stein advocates tightening the *top* screw and leaving the bottom one loose, for *greater* elasticity throughout the entire reed.[1] Caution: if the ligature is screwed too tightly for too long or not loosened after playing, it may cause the mouthpiece to warp when the reed

---

[1] Keith Stein, *The Art of Clarinet Playing* (Evanston, IL: Summy-Birchard Publishing Co., 1958), 6.

becomes wet and expands. When the ligature is placed on the mouthpiece with the screws on top or when the one-screw ligature is used, a great deal of the reed is in contact with the metal portion of the ligature. The object is to provide maximum vibration of the reed and avoid a choked or buzzing tone quality. The Bonade ligature has two metal bars that touch the reed in such a way that no other metal is in contact with it. This is said to allow more freedom of vibration. Many authorities have recommended the use of Velcro or string wound around the mouthpiece to hold the reed in place in order to allow the reed greater freedom to vibrate. For years Pino has used a flat, cloth shoestring as a ligature.[2]

A ligature placed too high on the mouthpiece hinders reed vibration, encourages squeaks, and results in a stuffy tone. When the ligature is positioned too low, the reed has too much freedom to vibrate and the tone becomes harsh. Preferred for reed flexibility is the ligature slightly below the lines marked on the exterior of the mouthpiece.

The reed is placed so that it is centered on the mouthpiece and only a very slight "rim" of mouthpiece is visible when the tip of the reed is gently pressed down. The mouthpiece cap, preferably made of plastic, should be a frequently used item.

HOLDING THE CLARINET

The two general areas that are important in establishing a good position for holding the clarinet are, first, the angle at which the instrument is held, and second, the use of the fingers and the hand position.

The angle at which the clarinet is held should be established first since correct embouchure depends in part on it. The player's posture should be erect whether sitting or standing (see Figure 13–1 for the correct posture when seated). Stiffness should be avoided; neck, shoulders, and arms must stay relaxed with the head erect. Arms held out from the body can create tension in the neck and may cause tenseness in the fingers. One of the first impulses of the beginner is to lower the head to meet the mouthpiece. She should bring the instrument up to her mouth, not her mouth down to the instrument. Depending on her embouchure formation, she should hold the clarinet directly in front of the body at an angle of about 30 degrees from the body. Each student has different posture habits, different teeth formation and lip structure, and the sensible teacher allows for these in determining the angle that fosters the best embouchure.

The student who rests the clarinet on one knee shifts the clarinet to one side and develops an improper embouchure and a rough tone. Some authorities feel that there is little harm in letting a beginner rest the bell on

---

[2]David Pino, *The Clarinet and Clarinet Playing* (Scribner's, 1980), 21-22.

Figure 13–1. Sitting Position for Playing the Clarinet

her knee if she is tall enough. Some clarinet pedagogues even advocate this practice with the belief that this will keep the hands and fingers relaxed and prevent their being used to support the instrument. Resting the instrument on the knee, however, can lead to a misaligned embouchure, the development of the wrong facial muscles, poor breathing habits, and restricted finger dexterity. If a student finds that the clarinet is too heavy to hold without resting it on the knee, she should practice for shorter lengths of time. Proper position may not feel completely comfortable or natural at first, but if the embouchure seems correct and what promises to be a good tone is produced, the student should be encouraged to adjust to the position. Head up, horn down.

If the student's head is lowered or the instrument held too far out from the body, the lower jaw is positioned directly beneath the upper jaw. Instead the lower jaw should be farther down on the mouthpiece. When the lips are equidistant from the mouthpiece tip, the tone is less flexible and more uneven between registers, and the lower lip loses sensitivity. It is better to keep the lower lip about ¾ of an inch from the tip of the reed and the upper lip about ½ of an inch from the tip by holding the instrument at the appropriate angle. This ¼-inch difference contributes to better tone, more flexibility, more consistency throughout the entire range of the clarinet, and a more focused tone. One common rule is that the lower lip should be down as far as possible without squeaking.

If a player has thin lips, she should decrease the angle of the clarinet; if she has thick or full lips, holding the instrument out more than 30 degrees may improve her embouchure and tone quality, but it really depends on the jaw. A player with a protruding jaw must hold the instrument at a greater angle from the body to compensate for increased pressure from the lower jaw. Generally, the smaller the angle at which the clarinet is held, the more shrill the tone. The tone mellows as the angle is increased. A completely dull sound is obtained, however, if the clarinet reaches a 90-degree angle, excluding the rare exceptions such as Benny Goodman and Woody Herman, whose sounds in this position can hardly be described as dull, but are inappropriate for music of a classical nature.

The player should align the clarinet in front rather than holding it to one side. Occasionally students try to hold an alto or bass clarinet to the side like a saxophone, making it difficult to obtain a correct clarinet embouchure. If a dull, fuzzy tone results, adjust the position of the mouthpiece. The floor peg is recommended for the bass clarinet, although for many players a neckstrap suffices.

Correct hand position is shown in Figure 13–2. The thumb rest should lie between the nail and the end joint of the right thumb. The right thumb is responsible for supporting the clarinet, with the left thumb and embouchure only helping to balance or steady it—the right-hand and left-hand fingers cover the holes without gripping the instrument. If the player allows the thumb rest to slip farther back on the thumb, the right fingers curve excessively to fit over the keys, which produces a tense wrist. The

Figure 13–2. Hand Position for the Clarinet

right thumb must be firm but should not push the clarinet into the mouth. Deep teeth marks in the mouthpiece indicate excessive right thumb pressure.

The right hand should slant so that the side keys are easily accessible to the middle of the index finger as the fingertip rests over the fourth tone hole. The left thumb rests below the register key at a 45-degree angle without touching it, and the fingers of the left hand lie almost at right angles to the clarinet. The left index finger is positioned over the G-sharp and A keys. The slant necessary for the fingers to reach the auxiliary keys depends on the size and shape of the hands and the length of the fingers. The tips of the little fingers on both hands should rest on the tips of the F keys.

For dexterity and coverage, the pads of the fingers, not the flat or tips of them are used to cover the tone holes. The fingers should be curved as if holding a ball so that the fleshy pad fits comfortably over the tone hole. Small air leaks caused by insufficient covering of the tone holes can cause large changes in intonation and tone. Students should be able to finger a scale passage without blowing the instrument and hear the scale produced by the popping of the pads on the tone holes.

Students should be encouraged to keep their fingers close to the keys and tone holes, especially the little fingers, which must move directly to the keys without the student peeking. The novice is apt to exaggerate each fingering motion and thereby slow her technique. Some teachers suggest raising the fingers high in order to ensure synchronization of the fingers, but this may cause the student to develop bad habits. From the beginning, students should use as little finger movement as necessary. The problem of synchronizing fingers is more a matter of paying close attention to the finger action than of exaggerating it.

THE BEGINNING STUDENT

Sitting upright, back away from the chair, and with both feet resting comfortably on the floor, the student should drop her jaw about ½ of an inch and form her mouth as if vocalizing "oh." This syllable is useful since it is vocalized by aligning the teeth vertically. The mouthpiece is inserted with the reed against the bottom lip so as to push the lip slightly over the teeth; about ¾ of an inch of the reed extends past the lip into the mouth. The mouthpiece should rest on the lower lip at about the place where the reed and the mouthpiece come together. Approximately one-half of the red of the lower lip should cover the lower teeth—if too much of the red of the lip touches the reed it will hinder vibration and cause the tone to be weak and open. The upper teeth rest on the top of the mouthpiece without biting, and the corners of the mouth are tightened and pulled slightly downward to flatten the chin. The upper lip or teeth cover about ½ of an inch of the mouthpiece. The student should not bite on the mouthpiece, which seems to be a natural reaction; instead, the muscles at the corners of the mouth should be directed toward the mouthpiece—to prevent pushing the bottom lip toward the mouthpiece.

When the air is blown into just the mouthpiece, a tone approximating a high C or D will sound. The student should practice this embouchure formation and use proper breathing until she can maintain a steady pitch for at least five seconds before adding the mouthpiece to the body of the instrument. When producing pitches on the instrument itself the student must adjust the embouchure for the best sound. The final adjustment is based on tone quality; the mouthpiece may be pulled or pushed into the mouth while experimenting with more or less lip over the bottom teeth.

The beginner should not be confronted with articulations until the embouchure formation is reasonably stable. When tonguing is introduced the instructor may explain that the tongue is like a switch that stops the reed and then allows it to vibrate. The tip of the tongue should touch the reed just below the tip and remain in place as the airstream is released. The tongue moves to the bottom of the mouth to let the reed vibrate, then returns to stop those vibrations. The student should be encouraged to try tonguing regular notes evenly at both loud and soft dynamic levels, and while using a "hard" and a "soft" tongue. The soft tongue should merely stop the reed from vibrating while allowing air to freely pass through the mouthpiece and instrument; the hard tongue should almost, but not quite, close the tip of the reed against the mouthpiece completely.

EMBOUCHURE

Clarinet embouchures (Figure 13–3 and 13–4) vary a great deal among students and are described very differently by teachers and professional players. Some teachers prefer more bottom lip over the teeth; others prefer the corners of the mouth pulled downward, or outward, or inward, or simply tightened.

The upper teeth should not bite into the mouthpiece or push down on it; the mouth should simply be closed and the teeth vertically aligned. Many players have a small piece of very thin rubber glued to the top of the mouthpiece to prevent damage from the teeth and to limit the vibrations felt by the teeth.

The corners of the lips are held together so that there is a firm grip all around the mouthpiece. The student should not think of forming a smile. The corners are not drawn back or up, rather the pressure of the lips is exerted toward the center of the mouthpiece. A smiling embouchure produces an undesirable thin, nasal quality in the tone. The chin and jaw

Figure 13–3. Clarinet Embouchure

should be kept as still as possible, since any movement of the jaw tends to raise or lower the pitch causing intonation problems and lack of control.

A successful way to determine how much mouthpiece should be placed inside the mouth is to begin with as small an amount of mouthpiece as possible in the mouth and gradually insert more and more until the best tone quality is produced. Ideally this tone will be produced when the point

Figure 13–4. Clarinet Embouchure (side view)

that the mouthpiece begins to curve away from the reed is directly above the lower teeth, usually ½ to ¾ of an inch.

The pressure on the reed comes principally from the lips. In addition, the need for keeping the chin down has to be stressed often with the beginner, since the sensation is not an accustomed one. Practice with a mirror or with a parent watching can help to keep the chin pointed. Positioning the chin in the proper position is relatively easy, but it tends to return to its natural position as soon as air pressure builds up. Unless the chin is held down and flat, intonation in the high register becomes difficult, the lower register loses some of its carrying quality, and the cheeks tend to puff out. To help flatten the chin, tell the student to think of applying lip balm to the lower lip. With a well-developed embouchure, the clarinet can be held at a lower angle with most of the support on the lower lip, the upper lip encasing the mouthpiece to prevent air leakage and produce the desired tone.

When the player has developed a good embouchure, she should initially take her breath slowly and avoid any disturbance of the embouchure. As the student begins to understand the hows and whys of a proper embouchure, she should be encouraged to breathe through the corners of her mouth, keeping the center of her lips on the mouthpiece.

There should be minimal change of embouchure for different registers and for wide skips up or down. A good exercise is to practice harmonics. If the player finds high E, F, and G difficult to produce, she may not have her lower lip low enough on the reed and should experiment with more of the mouthpiece in her mouth. She may have to stretch the corners of her mouth as the high register is reached, perhaps from about G above the staff. This stretch helps eliminate the "crying" effect so often heard in the high registers. Another recommendation is that the chin be pulled down farther than normal for the upper register without disturbing the basic embouchure. Experimenting is necessary. As the embouchure tires during a rehearsal or concert, more support will be needed to play the upper notes. Proper embouchure formation will prevent damage to the muscles.

When the bass clarinet squeaks in the high register, there is usually too much pressure being exerted from below by the lower lip and jaw, not enough pressure from the upper teeth, or an insufficient amount of the mouthpiece in the mouth. The general rule is that the lower lip and jaw exert less pressure the higher one goes. The upper teeth continue to apply the same or slightly more pressure. Thus the player must take more of the mouthpiece into the mouth, relax the lower lip, drop the jaw, and at the same time slightly increase the pressure on top, pushing the instrument forward so a little more of the upper side of the mouthpiece enters the mouth. This procedure will help remove tension from the lower lip and eliminate much of the problem of high-register squeaking.

A good bass clarinet embouchure (illustrated in Figure 13-5) may enhance one's playing of the B-flat clarinet. A good bass clarinet embouchure requires the player to put more mouthpiece into the mouth and to exert less pressure. When these actions carry over to the soprano clarinet embouchure, the tone quality is usually improved.

Squeaks, one of the continual plagues of the beginning clarinet player, are usually due to, first, having too much of the mouthpiece in the mouth, or second, the player may be using an embouchure that is too tight, biting too much or exerting too much jaw pressure. Squeaks may often be eliminated by a gentler attack on the mouthpiece. Squeaks are also caused by broken reeds, the fingers not covering the holes completely, a leaking instrument, or occasionally, an inferior mouthpiece.

The members of the clarinet family are very similar and most playing techniques apply to the entire family. However, there are some important differences. In playing the E-flat and the B-flat soprano clarinets, the best embouchure is one in which equal pressure is exerted on the mouthpiece from above and below. The higher of these, the E-flat instrument, will be most easily controlled when less mouthpiece is placed in the mouth than that used for the other clarinets, along with a firmer embouchure and more breath support.

The use of the lips helps determine quality and volume of clarinet tone, and the pressure of the lips alters according to the volume desired. For fortissimo playing, the pressure is shifted lower on the reed, farther from the tip; for pianissimo playing, closer to the tip. The embouchure does not change—only the lip pressure is exerted in different areas for different dynamic levels. Adjusting lip pressure affects tone; a relaxed lip results in a bigger, unfocused, more mellow sound, while more pressure against the reed by the lip provides increased intensity of tone.

Figure 13–5. Bass Clarinet: Embouchure

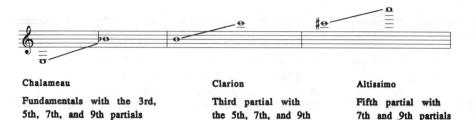

Chalameau	Clarion	Altissimo
Fundamentals with the 3rd, 5th, 7th, and 9th partials present in the tone.	Third partial with the 5th, 7th, and 9th partials present.	Fifth partial with 7th and 9th partials present in the tone.

Figure 13–6. The Three Registers of the Clarinet

INTONATION

Some of the major problems of intonation arising within the band or orchestra stem from the fact that woodwinds playing together present an assortment of pitches for the same note, much of the variation due not to the unskillfulness of the players but to the built-in characteristics of even the best instruments. The director is forced to spend much time on intonation if she is to have a good-sounding organization. The solution is to teach the students to listen and make appropriate compensation.

The clarinet is designed to overblow at the interval of a twelfth when the register key is depressed, rather than the more usual octave. In other words, the fingering that produces B-flat in the low register produces the F an octave and a fifth above the fundamental note when the register key is added. These twelfths are not in tune with themselves. If the lower register that is comprised of the fundamentals is in tune, then the first overtones a twelfth higher will be sharp in some cases, flat in others. Figure 13–6 gives the three clarinet registers.

The clarinet is built slightly sharper than the standard concert pitch of A440. As the clarinet is somewhat inflexible, tuning to it is not out of order. The oboe's pitch is more flexible than that of the clarinet.

Probably the best tuning notes on the clarinet are thumb F and open G, but for best results several notes in different ranges should be used. Changes in temperature and in the density of air affect the pitch; cold and heat, dryness and humidity alter the pitch just as change of volume does. In cold temperatures the pitch will drop, in warm temperatures it will rise. Thin, dry air gives a faster sound wave and a higher pitch, while moist air causes slower waves and a lower pitch. Changes of volume also have an effect: Pianissimo playing will be sharp and forte playing flat (the opposite of the flute) unless the player guards against it.

The clarinet tends to go sharp in the lower register and throat tones, and flat in the upper register, also opposite to the tendencies of the flute. The volume level affects this rule, however. Pianissimo playing will result in a sharp upper register and an exaggeratedly sharp lower register. There is a logical relationship between pianissimo playing and sharpness of intonation. Soft tones should be produced by controlling the airstream with the large breathing muscles, but some players make the mistake of pinching off the air with their lips, thus tightening the reed and producing a sharper pitch. The fact that the tighter lips make a better tone quality in soft playing complicates the problem; the player may have to sacrifice some quality or find other ways to keep the pitch down when playing pianissimo. Try relaxing the right thumb to help bring the pitch down; this effect is probably more psychological than acoustical.

In performances, the clarinet will invariably go sharp as it and the surrounding environment become warmer. While this is the tendency of most wind instruments, unfortunately they do not all rise in pitch to the same degree or at the same rate. The clarinet pitch should be lowered when needed by pulling at the middle joint; the barrel should be pulled primarily to lower the throat tones.

Sharp Tones

Pitches that are particularly sharp when played softly are shown in Figure 13–7. Low E-flat may also be sharp when soft. To correct the sharpness, (l) loosen the lower lip, (2) keep an open throat, and (3) use more breath support.

Flat Tones

Low E and F may become flat in forte playing, even though they are generally sharp in normal and soft playing. The upper register tends to be flat and playing forte increases this tendency, especially among beginners. The beginning player should constantly be made aware of intonation problems so that her ear becomes sensitive to small discrepancies.

Figure 13–7. Pitch Tendencies of Certain Notes on the Clarinet

Adjustments and Corrections

Tightening the lips will raise the pitch slightly. Adequate breath support will keep the pitch from sagging. When the throat is relaxed, the pitch will be steady as well as of better quality; tension in the throat will raise the pitch and adversely affect the tone quality. Any jaw movement will alter the intonation. So will changing the angle at which the clarinet is held. None of these will make large differences in the pitch; for larger differences, the player will have to rely on alternate fingerings, physical changes in the instrument, the quality and the bore of the mouthpiece, and the adequacy of the reed.

Physical Alterations

If the clarinet is consistently sharp, the player should pull out the joints, the barrel, the middle joint, and the bell. If she has tuned the throat tones and the middle register of her instrument and it is still sharp, she might pull the middle joint to improve the intonation of the middle register. Sometimes the intonation in the middle register is so sharp that both the top middle joint and the barrel must be pulled before the pitch is satisfactory. However, pulling too much can add to intonation problems rather than eliminate them; for example, middle-line B-flat uses only ¼ of the clarinet tube as its vibrating chamber, so pulling affects this four times as much as it affects the B-natural one-half step above, which uses all the tube for its vibrating chamber. This register should be tuned at the bell.

Adding tuning discs to correct sharpness lengthens the clarinet without forming air pockets. A shorter barrel primarily raises the throat tones and the left-hand notes. A barrel that is too short produces the same general problems as if the player had failed to pull the barrel sufficiently: Throat tones or the entire register will be faulty and excessively sharp. Conversely, pulling the barrel too much will flatten the throat tones.

Other Factors

Other factors that may affect pitch relate to reeds, position of the instrument, use of the jaw, and others. The most common are these:

1. If the fingers are lifted too high on the six open holes, the resultant pitches may be somewhat sharp.
2. A cheap mouthpiece may play extremely sharp. If the throat tones, G, G-sharp, and A are out of tune, the fault may be with the mouthpiece rather than with the instrument itself. The tone chamber—that part of the mouthpiece which is immediately below the air entrance—is not proportioned correctly for the clarinet.

3. A mouthpiece with a bore slightly smaller than that of the instrument will raise the pitch of notes in the lower register. A mouthpiece bore slightly larger than that of the instrument will lower the pitch of the low notes.
4. The diameter of the barrel also makes a discernible difference in intonation as well as in tone quality.
5. A stiff reed will usually make pianissimo passages sharp in the middle and low register, while a soft reed will make forte passages flat in the upper register.

TONE QUALITY

In the spectrum of instrumental sound, the clarinet's unique contribution is a quality that has both an edge, or bite, and a large, full sound. Those who want to make the clarinet sound only mellow, or who want a personal, romantic sound from the instrument, have failed to appreciate the tonal possibilities of the clarinet.

Each instrument produces the timbre unique to that instrument according to the overtones present and the degree to which they are audible above the pitch being played. Whenever a particular musical pitch is heard on a wind instrument, the related overtones are also heard. With modern technology, it is relatively easy to measure which overtones are present as well as the degree to which they are heard for any and every musical instrument; this has enabled electronic synthesizers to duplicate the sound of virtually any wind, string, or percussion instrument. The clarinet sounds like a clarinet due to the odd-numbered partials sounding. When a low G is played (see Figure 13–8) the second partial, the octave, is not present. The third partial, D, is sounded and becomes the predominate pitch when the register key is pressed, as well as the fifth, seventh, and ninth (B, F, and A) each to a lessening degree as the partials rise. This effect is due to the clarinet's being a cylindrical pipe closed at one end. All other wind instruments are either conical, having the same acoustical properties as open pipes (i.e., sounding all partials), or a combination of conical and cylindrical (such as the brasses) that results in a combination of odd- and even-numbered partials sounding.

Figure 13–8. **The Odd-Numbered Partials Present in the Tone When a Low G Is Played on the Clarinet**

Hearing good clarinet tone is desirable but not always possible in concept formation. D, E, and F at the top of the staff are considered model tones for tone production. Good tone is accomplished by practicing sustained tones, first within a narrow range then gradually enlarging the range as skill increases. An occasional good tone does not constitute good playing. Tone quality must be attractive at all times and in all registers; the chalumeau, clarion, and altissimo registers innately have different timbres. It is far easier for teachers to focus their attention on the more objective elements of performance, such as technique and dynamics, than to work on good tone. Due to facial characteristics, not all students will be able to produce the ideal clarinet tone, but all students with proper instruction on embouchure and breathing can, in time, develop an acceptable clarinet tone.

Variables in good tone production are the instrument and reed, mouthpiece, the player's lip and facial structure, embouchure, breath support, the amount of mouthpiece in the mouth, and the angle at which the clarinet is held. If too little mouthpiece enters the mouth, the tone is unnecessarily thin and small though sometimes sweet and pleasing to the inexperienced student. If too much mouthpiece enters the mouth, the tone will become spread, uncontrolled, and ugly. The instrument will squeak easily under both conditions, especially the latter.

Releasing the air from the lungs through the mouth into the instrument, just as one exhales air in breathing through the mouth, produces the tone. The speed of the air determines the intensity of the tone, and a good tone demands intensity. A small, flaccid tone, less capable of variety, is a result of playing with little air support. The beginner should play with as much air, or as big a sound, as she possibly can. She should learn to control it gradually, to focus it, and to cut down on volume while still keeping the intensity in the tone. She may overblow, causing harsh sounds and incorrect pitches, especially in the high register. If her embouchure is correctly formed, she can use as much air support and pressure as the muscles of her lips and jaw will allow. A harsh tone on the bass clarinet is caused not by blowing too hard but by blowing too fast. The air pressure is not too great, but the amount of air going through the instrument is too great.

An open throat aids in the production of good tone. This is often taught with the help of vowels, an "ah" for the lower pitches and progressing toward "ee" as the pitches rise, with only the tongue moving. The vowel "ee" helps to lift the tongue and compress the space through which the air must travel, thus helping to achieve the rapid air necessary for the high register tones. This vowel change, with its corresponding change of tongue position, can be acquired by practicing slurs of a tenth or a twelfth.

Two other suggestions may help in achieving good tone quality. First, although D, E, and F at the top of the staff are considered model notes as far as tone quality is concerned, practicing from low F to throat-tone G develops a good embouchure and a good concept of tone production.

Second, A. H. Christmann of Juilliard states that the clarinet is always at its best when, for any given degree of intensity, it is as sharp as possible.[3] Others say that the best clarinet tone is the closest thing to a squeak— without crossing that fine line. Therefore, the player should play on top of the tone at all times; the only way to make the pitch any sharper at that degree of intensity should be to tighten the lip, producing a pinched sound, and sacrificing tone quality.

Few approve of vibrato on clarinet. There are times, however, when it is appropriate. Traditionally the diaphragm vibrato has been preferred, with most jazz clarinetists using jaw vibrato.

The Clarinet Mouthpiece

Double-reed players blame all faults on their reeds, clarinet players on their mouthpieces. The average player is advised to buy a good standard mouthpiece and adjust to it. Authorities such as Pino firmly recognize that the clarinet mouthpiece is the single most important piece of equipment.[4] The teacher should know what to look for in a good mouthpiece and what possible troubles may arise from poor or inadequate equipment. Many instrumental teachers request that the local music retailers supply a specific model mouthpiece with all clarinets sold or rented to their students.

A clarinet mouthpiece is illustrated in Figure 13–9. Mouthpieces are made from a variety of materials: crystal, wood, plastics of several kinds, and rubber. Probably the best mouthpiece for the average student is made of hard rod rubber. It retains its shape, plays the most easily, and has the strongest fundamentals and more overtones than mouthpieces made from other materials. The crystal mouthpiece is a good mouthpiece, has stronger fundamentals on the higher notes than the hard rod rubber, but does not have as many partials. Also, it demands great care, being very susceptible to chipping and cracking. Since the slightest chip on the facing ruins a fine mouthpiece, it is not for the careless student. On the other hand, it never warps, is unaffected by temperature changes or moisture, and with care lasts indefinitely.

In selecting a mouthpiece, one should avoid those with shiny inside surfaces. These are usually molded rubber or plastic, which will warp easily. Warping is caused by temperature changes and by the ligature being consistently put on too tightly. Some temperature changes cannot be avoided, but one can avoid washing the mouthpiece in water that is too warm, the most common cause of warping. Tightening the ligature too much is also easily avoided.

Although on an average mouthpiece the width of the window is 11.5

---

[3] A. H. Christmann, "A New Contribution to Clarinet Tuning," *Instrumentalist* (January 1953): 18.

[4] David Pino, *The Clarinet and Clarinet Playing*, 12.

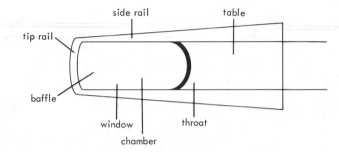

Figure 13–9. Clarinet Mouthpiece

millimeters and the width of the tip 13 millimeters, there is no foolproof formula. A crystal mouthpiece has a different diameter than a rubber one, and so forth; the width of mouthpiece tips varies from 9 to 13 millimeters; one must combine knowledge with experience, instinct, and trial and error.

If the side rails of the mouthpiece, on which the reed lies, are not identical, the clarinet will squeak. This can be checked. If the player has a set of feelers used in checking pad closings, she can put the mouthpiece on a piece of glass and use the feelers to check by pulling them through to see whether there is the same amount of resistance offered by the entire surface of the side rails. Another way of checking the rails and facing is to blow on a piece of glass or mirror so that it clouds over, then place the mouthpiece face down and roll toward the tip. When the mouthpiece is carefully removed from the glass, the points of contact can be checked by the impression left on the glass. The tip rail at the very end of the mouthpiece should be about 1/32 of an inch thick; excessive squeaking may be due to the fact that the tip rail is too thin. On the other hand, if the tip rail is too thick, there will be too much resistance. The tone produced will be a soft, clear tone, attractive to the beginning player, but not a characteristic clarinet tone.

The lay of the mouthpiece determines the amount of opening between the reed and the tip of the mouthpiece; it makes a large difference in the kind of sound produced. A wide variety of lays, or facings, is available because different people prefer different clarinet sounds. Some recommend the close, short, French lay— "short" because the tip of the mouthpiece curves away from the reed a short distance, "close" because the opening that results at the very end of the mouthpiece is narrow. This lay is preferred because it is easier to control and does not require as much pressure.

Such a detailed discussion of the lay may seem unnecessary, but in a mouthpiece the lay itself and its relationship to the bore are the most important factors in sound production. For example, the quicker the mouthpiece curves away from the reed (which usually makes it more open), the harder the reed needed, and consequently, the more difficult it is to control. The advanced player has a broader range of dynamics and articulation at her disposal.

The average mouthpiece is the medium French, with a lay about 18 millimeters long. With a longer lay, the tip should be closer so that a long facing is not combined with too open a tip. A long, open lay would require such a soft reed that good control of the tone would be almost impossible; the sound would be easier to produce, but the tone would have less body. A short, closed lay generally produces a harsh tone quality because a harder reed is required due to limited room for vibration.

The tone chamber at the bottom of the curve of the mouthpiece influences the quality of the tone. A tone chamber with a small bore will tend to have a brilliant tone with an edge, and a pitch that is somewhat sharp. A tone chamber with a large bore produces a still more brilliant tone, but the quality is broader, with less edge. This latter sound is better for band work because it blends well with other instrumental timbres. The typical intonation produced by a large tone chamber is a flat chalumeau and clarion register, and a slightly sharp high register. The small tone chamber, conversely, produces a flat high register and somewhat sharp low and middle registers.

The following list of mouthpiece faults is a guide in locating possible sources of common playing difficulties.

Excessive squeaks may be due to:[5]

1. a vent that is too straight.
2. a thin tip rail.
3. a facing that is too short.
4. a baffle convexed near the tip rail.
5. an uneven facing.
6. an irregular tip rail.
7. a facing that is too open.

Hard blowing may be due to:

1. a wide tip rail.
2. an excessively curved vent.
3. a baffle that is too concave.
4. a baffle that is convex.
5. the pivot in the facing too close to the tip.

A rough tone may be due to:

1. an unduly flat facing.
2. a facing that is too open.

[5] Ralph Ritchie, "The Clarinet Mouthpiece," *Instrumentalist* (November 1961): 66.

3. a facing that is too long.
4. a facing that is both too open and too long.
5. an extremely concave curve in the baffle.

The taper of the barrel may be at fault if the problem is thin tone quality in the upper register or extremely coarse tone in the lower register. If the clarinet appears to be a good instrument, intonation problems most characteristic of barrel trouble are these: a tendency to sharpness in the upper register may indicate that the bore of the barrel is too large at the mouthpiece end for the instrument; if throat tones have a tendency to sharpness, the barrel is probably too small at the end that joins the clarinet body.

TECHNIQUE: ARTICULATION AND FINGERING

Few successful musicians will rate technique as more important to performance than good tone quality and expressive playing. Technique is the control with which the performer manages the mechanized piece of expensive wood that comprises the clarinet. Many young clarinetists are impressed by fast and flashy playing and focus their energy on gaining speed. Rapid practice merely enables students to perform their bad habits more rapidly. Articulations and finger dexterity are useful only to the extent that they can be used to convey the expressive qualities of music. As David Pino observes, the "sound generator" (airstream, tongue, embouchure, reed, and mouthpiece) and "technical system" (the keys, arms, and fingers) are coordinated by "a computer" (the brain) to produce beautiful music.[6] Technique deals with this coordination.

Good tonguing is seldom developed without effort; one must practice to coordinate fingers and tongue. Good tonguing is developed by a gradual acquisition of speed until the tongue is able to handle any tempo demanded of it.

There are two approaches to tonguing. They differ in where the tongue touches the reed and how the tongue is used. In the American method, by far the most popular, the tongue touches the reed about ⅛ of an inch down from the tip of the reed and about ¼ of an inch from the tip of the tongue. In the French method, the very tip of the tongue touches the tip of the reed with short, light strokes, others use the tip of the tongue ⅛ of an inch down on the reed. The length, thickness and flexibility of the tongue, the strength of the reed, the lay of the mouthpiece, and the articulation desired all help determine which kind of tonguing works best for the player.

[6] David Pino, *The Clarinet and Clarinet Playing*, 23-50.

The type of articulation, legato to marcato, depends on how long the tongue touches the reed, while the amount of air determines the dynamic level as well as the style of articulation. Only the forward part of the tongue need move; excessive movement from the tongue or the jaw will reduce tonguing speed and control and can result in a tight throat, further affecting both tonguing and tone quality. The tongue should remain relaxed, resting at the bottom of the mouth as much of the time as possible.

As the player progresses, she will not try to form "t" with each stroke but will relax the tip of the tongue over the tip of the mouthpiece and let the movement itself become more flexible, omitting the hard, time-consuming "t" sound before the vowel.

Heavy, harsh tonguing is a major problem for many players. Directors may inherit these players and need some suggestions for curing their faults. The use of legato studies and legato tonguing is one possibility. McCathren uses a "one-two-three" system to illustrate the process of tonguing: On one, touch the tongue to the reed, blocking the air passage. On two, blow, exerting air pressure against the tongue. On three, draw the tongue away from the reed as if saying "tah," "toe," or "tee." This helps the student understand that tonguing is releasing air into the clarinet, not striking the reed with the tongue.

Technique involves the development of correct, appropriate articulations and the development of accurate fingerings, both at the immediate disposal of the player. The clarinet is designed, for example, so that several notes at the middle of the staff can be played by using keys activated by either the right or left little finger. Students must master both fingerings in order to follow the maxim that the same little finger should not be used for two consecutive notes, a maxim based on the common-sense practice of avoiding fingerings in which a finger must slide from one key to another.[7] Numerous studies and exercises to develop dexterity for these fingerings can be found or designed.

Simple scalewise exercises for finger dexterity can be created by the teacher. Repeating a scalewise pattern over and over (up or down) and starting on different notes of the scale provides practice in lifting one finger at a time and then closing several together (or in descending patterns, vice versa).

Occasionally, however, there is no alternative to the fingers sliding from one key to another. If a finger is raised and then presses another key, a grace note will usually sound or tempo or articulations will be impaired. The most common problem of this sort is playing an F-sharp to an A in the throat register without sounding a G between the two. Little fingers also have the sliding problem unless the clarinet is a full Boehm system.

---

[7] Frederick W. Westphal, *Guide to Teaching Woodwinds.* 4th ed. (Dubuque, IA: W. C. Brown, 1985), 88.

The "diabolus in musica" (the tritone) was the most dreaded element in music in the Middle Ages; today, it can be helpful in teaching beginning clarinetists to cross "the break," that is, to play from the B-flat in the staff to the vast realm of the unknown notes above. Though students are anxious about crossing the break, it is a learned fear. If students are playing confidently in the chalumeau and throat registers, it is merely a matter of pressing the register key with the side of the thumb to play above the break. Having students play in the low register and then activate the register key is a much easier way to cross the break than to approach it scalewise; playing from second-space A to the B requires going from one key pressed with the left index finger to nine holes and keys pressed with eight fingers. After the clarion register is reached securely, crossing between the two can be developed by starting slowly and gradually increasing speed. The right hand can continue to cover the tone holes and keys while playing the throat tones to reduce finger movement.

Many alternate fingerings are possible on clarinet, which the teacher should be able to recommend as the need arises (e.g., to make rapid passages easier and cleaner). The most common alternate fingerings are contained in the fingering chart at the end of this chapter. Alternate fingerings for clarinet are easier to remember if one keeps in mind that fingerings "start over" at middle-line B. The rule of thumb is to move the fewest fingers possible.

The vast majority of the literature for band and orchestra is written in major and minor keys; scales and arpeggios form the foundation of the exercises applicable to improving finger dexterity for this music. Scales should be practiced regularly and systematically in all major and minor keys (plus the chromatic); a tempo should be established at which the student can play evenly and accurately with good tone quality and intonation, then gradually increased. The metronome is useful here. As the clarinetist's range increases, scales can encompass a wider range. Playing, for example, a C scale beginning on low C, up to the top of the range, down to a low E, and then back up to the starting C makes scale practice more applicable to the technical passages found in the literature. Arpeggios are an excellent means for increasing technique by lifting and lowering more than one finger at a time. Technique is coordination, not speed.

WHAT TO PRACTICE

Beginning players must concentrate on embouchure development and hand position almost exclusively during their first few months of instruction; even then, the tone quality will usually be lacking and need years of maturation. Since embouchure development consists of building and using muscles in a new way, it is important that beginners not overpractice. It is much more beneficial for a beginner to practice for three 10-minute sessions than for one 30-minute session.

As has been said, good tone quality is the basis of all musical performance; as the student progresses in her technique, she should also practice slow, lyrical exercises with the goal of improving tone quality. Practice should also include exercises previously learned that the student can play quite well—especially technical etudes—so that, freed from the struggle with notes and fingerings, she can concentrate on tone production.

When tonguing is finally introduced, it should be based on the concept that the tongue is used to stop the vibrations of the reed; the tongue "releases" the reed to allow the air to vibrate it. One approach to fast, even tonguing is to tongue on the first beat of each $\frac{4}{4}$ measure and to rest the tongue on the three succeeding beats without lessening the breath support. The player gradually tongues closer together—on every other beat, then on every beat, and so on as the tongue muscles come under greater control.

The tongue can move more quickly when it is relaxed. Any attempt to tongue short notes by using a "harder" tongue creates tension, reduces control, and will slow the articulations. The tongue does not close off the reed during staccato tonguing; the airstream continues through the mouthpiece. The tongue's movement away from the reed produces the desired effect, not the tongue touching the reed. This concept is especially difficult for students to comprehend when attempting to play accented notes; the tongue touching the reed prevents the clarinet's sound, and the release of the tongue is essential to different types of articulations.

Many authorities suggest the following exercise: The student sustains a soft pitch and tongues the notes very lightly, increasing the force of the tongue for each note; then she plays a louder pitch using the tongue with force approaching that required to close off the reed and then gradually reducing the force of each tongued note. The airstream should flow as if all the notes are slurred.

A warm-up routine is valuable to get the air moving and the reed responsive. Long tones must be part of every student's daily routine, beginning soon after she plays her first notes. Long tones starting on throat G should be played, keeping the tone steady, resting briefly between each note, and proceeding down the scale. Crescendos and decrescendos may then be added. Warm-ups are not limited to long tones; arpeggios, technique exercises, rhythm patterns and awkward fingering passages are all part of a systematic warm-up.

CARE AND MAINTENANCE OF THE CLARINET

All clarinets should be swabbed after each use. Residual moisture will combine with dust and lint particles in the air to form a layer of sediment that gradually builds up in the bore, mouthpiece, and tone holes. This layer of dirt and sediment will make noticeable differences in the intonation of the affected notes and also a noticeable difference in the odor of the clarinet.

Swabbing should not be overdone—too much will wear down the bore of wooden instruments and round the edge of the tenons where the swab enters the instrument. A few times through with the swab is sufficient. Damage can also occur from dropping the metal weights of the swab into the clarinet, which after a while may chip the walls of the bore. Even tiny differences in the bore affect the instrument's response; chips in the mouthpiece are more serious.

Silk, as swab material, keeps the bore shiny. This is of some consequence for tone quality. Silk does not absorb moisture well and may merely spread it around, but if the moisture is spread sufficiently, the danger from cracking will be adequately minimized. Chamois skins are often found in student model clarinets. When chamois is wet it is absorbent, but when dry will tend to spread the moisture in a fashion similar to the silk swab. Chamois retains the moisture in a closed case and helps to prevent the wood from drying out while the instrument is not in use, but being a heavy material, it will be harder on the instrument over a long period of time than the lighter-weight materials. The best compromise is a linen handkerchief, absorbent enough but also hard enough to keep the interior of the bore shiny.

The mouthpiece, the most crucial part of the clarinet, should be treated with special care. A chamois should never be used to swab the mouthpiece, as the sharp edges will wear away with the continual application of the heavy material. Mouthpieces can be cleaned satisfactorily by running lukewarm water through them or by swabbing with a soft linen handkerchief (after first greasing the cork to protect it). The mouthpiece will warp if left lying in the sun or close to a radiator. The reed should never be allowed to dry on the mouthpiece; it should be stored in a commercial holder that allows it to dry properly.

Since swabbing does not rid the tone holes of accumulated moisture, a piece of coffee filter, cigarette, or toilet paper can be kept in the case to blot the water from under the pads. The paper can also be used to clean pads by closing the pad gently on the paper and holding it for a few seconds.

Tone holes should be cleaned every month or so, using cotton ear swabs or a satisfactory substitute. Abrasive materials enlarge the tone hole, causing the pitch to rise.

The advisability of oiling the clarinet is debatable. A well-aged instrument adequately cured during the manufacturing process may never crack from lack of swabbing after use, but there are other reasons why the instrument should be oiled. Moisture from the player's breath penetrates the wood and will in time affect the resonating quality of the wood. Instruments dry out in heated homes during the winter. A clarinet should be oiled more often when new—perhaps as often as every two months, with a minute amount of olive oil or a commercial bore oil. Oiling is accomplished by placing a few drops of oil on the swab and running it through the barrel and through the upper and lower joints and bell. Gradually the oilings can be eliminated; twice a year is probably enough for a clarinet that has had good treatment. The chief disadvantage of oiling too often is that oil may get on pads and rot or harden them; oil may also add to the accumulation of dirt and lint on the key mechanism.

Some shrinkage can be expected to take place that may loosen posts and the rings on the ends of the joints. When the tenon rings become loose they should be tightened by inserting a small ring of cloth or paper under the ring to prevent the instrument from expanding and cracking. One should not be fooled if the bell or other ring has been crimped on and cannot be rotated— this offers no protection if it can be determined that it is loose.

Moving parts of the keys should be oiled very lightly every three to six months, depending on the use the instrument gets. If the climate is humid, a small amount of oil should occasionally be applied to the steel springs to prevent rusting. Springs become weak with time. They can be temporarily rejuvenated by carefully bending them. The cork tenons should be sparingly greased.

Post screws should be loosened and retightened once a year to prevent jamming, so when a pad needs to be replaced, the screw can be unscrewed instead of drilled out.

Cracking can be caused by too much or too little moisture. Climate can have a significant effect on a clarinet.

Equipment in the clarinet case should include: (1) a camphor stick to help control humidity and prevent tarnishing of the keys, (2) cork grease, (3) a small screwdriver, (4) extra reeds, (5) a swab, (6) a pencil, and (7) possibly a lyre. In addition, a handkerchief in the case, spread over the clarinet, will protect the case lining from discoloration due to tarnishing keys and add a layer of insulation for the instrument. An outside covering for the case of any wooden instrument helps preserve the expensive case and offers protection against the effects of extreme temperature changes. When clarinets are brought in out of the cold they should be allowed to warm in the case before they come into contact with the even warmer human breath. A good rule would be to never take a quality wooden instrument outside unless it is in a case.

A check on the condition of the clarinet is to play the chromatic scale through the entire range of the instrument, listening carefully for fuzzy notes caused by swollen pads or keys that have become bent and are opening too far or not far enough. A light or a feeler should be used on each key. An important caveat for clarinetists is that not everyone should feel compelled to be an instrument repairperson.

REEDS

Clarinet players often become as fussy about selection and care of reeds as Stradivarius was about the varnish on his violin. Much of the concern over the right reed is unnecessary; the average student should select a brand and a strength that works well for her and stick with that combination.

It is nearly impossible to tell by looking at a reed whether it has the desired qualities. The generally accepted characteristics marking a good piece of reed cane are (l) straight grain, (2) heavy fibers evenly spaced, and (3) gold or darker color. Green cane will absorb water readily and give a fuzzy tone, yet some artists like cane with a slightly green tint because it offers more resistance. The cane needs to be sufficiently dry, and spotted cane is often selected as indicating dryness. Coarse-grained cane, however, which is golden and spotted, soaks water readily and gives a harsh tone, and is therefore no more desirable than green cane. Mottled or streaked cane is not necessarily bad when these spots are on the bark. Naturally dried cane is preferred; cane that has been artificially dried can be detected by its unpleasant taste and lack of vitality. Holding prospective reeds to the light to find those that have a well-balanced fiber structure is a good practice, but it is virtually impossible to obtain a reed that will be perfect without some additional work. One can wet reeds and expose them to sunlight for additional curing.

After a well-aged, golden cane with straight, even grain has been selected, the next problem is to obtain the proper degree of stiffness. The lay of the mouthpiece influences the appropriate playing stiffness of the reed; for example, a Brilhart No. 4 mouthpiece will need a different strength reed than a Selmer HS, a Stowell B1, or a Woodwind K7; and each reed will have to be placed slightly differently on the mouthpiece. General guidelines can nevertheless be established. Teachers who do not play the clarinet often recommend softer reeds, probably from lack of personal experience, but a stiffer reed (2½ or 3) will produce a better embouchure if used from the beginning. Furthermore, wood can be scraped or shaved from a reed, but cannot be added. The numbers cannot be taken as the sole guide to the proper reed. Some companies use a different numbering system and the strengths vary somewhat.

For the bass clarinet, a slightly softer reed should be used than for the B-flat soprano because of the more relaxed embouchure. A slightly stiffer reed for the E-flat soprano clarinet helps to mitigate intonation problems. Tenor saxophone reeds should not be chosen for the bass clarinet; those for the tenor saxophone are slightly longer and slightly narrower than those for bass clarinet and will be unwieldy when used with the clarinet mouthpiece.

After selecting her reed, the player should be able to make minor adjustments on it. To add life and resistance, a new reed should be well soaked by saliva and immediately massaged by the finger for about 30 seconds, or pressed hard on a piece of glass and rubbed vigorously up and down by the forefinger. The massaging closes the pores and prevents the reed from becoming soaked too quickly.

To determine if a reed is broken in, the butt end of the wet reed is blown on. If it is still porous, bubbles will rise on the vamp and the process should be repeated. A part of the breaking-in process, one that should be more common than it is, is filing down the sides of the reed. Reeds are seldom too wide for the mouthpiece but a very wide reed would hinder staccato playing. The extra width also detracts from the brilliancy of tone. However, filing the sides creates another problem, for it usually will make the reed too thick and hard to play, so it is then necessary to sand the reed down to the proper thickness.

The stock of the reed is about 3 inches long. The tip of the reed is about ⅛ of an inch long and should not have any of the fibers that run the length of the reed. If the fibers or grains come closer to the end than ⅛ of an inch, the reed will tend to have a coarse sound; if they do not extend this close to the end, making the tip more than ⅛ of an inch deep, the reed will not have enough resiliency. The heart extends to within ¼ of an inch from the end of the reed. Parts of the reed are shown in Figure 13–10.

A good reed clipper, one having the same cut as the mouthpiece, is necessary for successful work on reeds. The two cutting surfaces of the clipper must come exactly together—the cutting blade should not pass under the cutting edge but should strike it evenly so that clean cuts occur. Fine sandpaper or garnet paper can be used for sanding down dry reeds; Dutch rush is used when the reed is wet. The end of the rush is used to remove specific spots, or it can be used lengthwise for broader areas.

Before work is done on the reed to correct apparent faults, it should be moved around on the mouthpiece and played in each position. For example, if the lower notes are heavy sounding, the reed may be moved lower on the mouthpiece, decreasing resistance, or it may be moved slightly to one side of the lay. An extremely slight movement is all that is necessary. Shifting the center even minutely changes all the dimensions of the reed. If moving it does not produce satisfactory results, then one can chop and scrape.

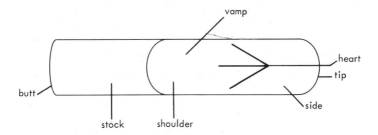

Figure 13–10. Clarinet Reed

The two principal approaches to modifying a reed are scraping to thin the heavy spots and clipping to alter the tip. To determine whether the reed is even or whether it has heavy spots that need to be scraped or sanded, the reed may be flexed on the thumbnail. The following checklist includes reed problems that can be minimized or corrected by scraping.

1. If the sides of the reed are uneven, the player will blow harder because of the stiffer side, making the weaker side vibrate too fast and causing the reed to feel soft. Scrape the stiffer side so that it matches the weaker side. The other approach, recommended by Bonade, is to fix the reed slightly thicker on the left side than on the right, especially in the lower part, farther from the tip. Because the instrument is supported by the right thumb, there is often pull or pressure from this side, and the player bites more on the left side of the reed. If the left side is slightly stronger to accommodate the additional bite, the reed will have somewhat more flexibility and be less likely to choke.

2. Low register: If the reed responds well except in the low register, remove some cane at the beginning of the cut. If the low notes are harsh with proper response, shave the entire reed.

3. High register: If high notes respond but are sluggish, thin the tip of the reed. If high notes fail to respond, work just below the point of resistance.

4. Staccato: If the staccato is poor, the reed is too heavy and should be scraped. If staccato is sluggish there is a hard spot in the tip.

5. If the reed has a good forte but sounds tubby or otherwise poor when played piano, the tip or the left side is probably too thick.

6. If the reed blows hard, go over the entire reed. If it has a good sound but is a little too heavy, work on the lower edge, right side, to thin it down. If the reed gives a poor response, shift it slightly, first to one side then the other to see if any improvement occurs; the poor response may be caused by one side being stronger than the other.

7. If the reed squeaks, one side is too resistant in the heart. Since this reed will have to be discarded if scraping cannot improve it, the player can feel free to work on the heart area to see if she can get rid of the squeak with some judicious scraping. Ordinarily the heart of the reed should be left alone, as faulty intonation will result if too much wood is taken off this area. If a reed causes faulty intonation, the heart is generally the cause, and almost nothing can be done except to discard the reed. If the intonation fault is very minor, lightening the side of the reed may correct it.

8. If the reed is too stiff, scrape the sides near the tip. The tip and the heart govern staccato, freedom of tone production, pitch, and squeaking.

9. If the tones are choked, the reed probably has a rough back. One way of checking this is to see if the imprint of the mouthpiece is visible on

the reed. If it is, some work is in order, as the back of the reed should be smooth and flat, not rounded.

For other problems and reed faults, clipping may be a more effective remedy than scraping, which by no means solves all reed problems. The following defects can be improved or eliminated by clipping the tip of the reed. When using the clipper, have the reed damp and draw it down from the blade of the clipper. After clipping, the tip is often somewhat rough, but this can be smoothed down with garnet paper (grade 8-9) when the reed is dry.

1. The tone is thin and nasal.
2. The reed closes up on high notes, response is stuffy, or generally makes playing the high notes difficult.
3. High notes are flat. Clip the reed about 1 mm at a time, play, and scrape when it becomes necessary.
4. The reed plays too freely. Trim it down and then work it over with Dutch rush.
5. The reed is soft when playing forte passages and too heavy or strong for pianissimo passages. Trim the tip or take some off at the lower left side.
6. The tone is buzzy. Trim the tip at each side slightly. However, buzzing usually indicates that the reed is very old or else split—throw it away.

Rotate reeds daily, keeping from four to six good reeds on hand and using a different one each day. Not only does this prolong the life of the reed, but it keeps the player's embouchure in better shape. When the same reed is used continually, the player tends to adjust her embouchure to it as it gradually alters, so that by the time she is forced to discard the reed, her embouchure may be distinctly different than when the reed was new.

A few things can be done to rejuvenate an old reed. It can (1) be cleaned, (2) have a groove put in its back under the ligature screws and have the ligature tightened somewhat more than normal, and (3) be placed in a hydrogen peroxide solution until the solution stops bubbling, then rinsed in cold water.

Emergencies

If the reed is squeaking during a concert, blowing some saliva into the mouthpiece between the rails and the reed and sucking it out just before the clarinet's entrance in the music will usually eliminate the danger of squeaks.

A partial solution to a soft reed is to keep the head up and the clarinet down—allowing more reed in the mouth and placing the lower jaw farther down on the mouthpiece than the upper teeth. With this change of embouchure, one can apply more pressure without closing the reed.

The placement of the ligature can influence the stiffness of a reed; try raising the ligature if the reed is too stiff and lowering it if the reed is too soft.

TROUBLESHOOTING

EQUIPMENT

sticky pads

1. Moisture absorbed by pads. If pad is not damaged place lens paper between pad and tone hole, press key and gently pull paper out; repeat several times pulling paper out in different directions. Last resort—apply a *slight* amount of talcum powder to absorb the moisture, being careful to keep off mechanism.
2. Bent rods. Have repaired by competent repairperson.
3. Worn springs. Have replaced by competent repairperson.
4. Pivot screws at end of rods may need oiling (one drop). Occasionally they must be loosened and oiled, then re-tightened.

pads not seating correctly

1. Leaking pads. If pads are in good shape, heat back of key with match to melt glue and hold pad down firmly to correctly reseat—use soft rag over hot key. Readjustment of the mechanism may be necessary to align keys. Bent rods to be repaired by competent repairperson.
2. Worn springs. Repaired by repairperson.
3. Brittle, hardened or torn pads. Have replaced.

gurgling sound

1. Water collected in tone hole(s) under pads that normally remain closed. Open appropriate pad, blow water into bore; clean with a pipe cleaner. This can usually be avoided by frequent, preventive swabbing.
2. Consistent water in one tone hole may indicate a path to that key; careful oiling or thorough swabbing may change the path.

TONE

squeaks

1. Reed crooked on mouthpiece. Realign reed.
2. Too much mouthpiece in mouth. Correct embouchure.
3. Tone holes not covered. Correct finger positions.
4. Bent bridge key preventing pads on lower joint from closing. Have repaired by competent repairperson.
5. Leaky pads. Replace or have replaced.

6. Bad reed. Try another reed.
7. Inadvertently pressing side key with hand. Correct holding position.
8. Mouthpiece problems:[8]
   a. a facing (or lay) that is too short
   b. an uneven facing
   c. a facing that is too open
   d. an irregular or thin tip rail

small, pinched sound
1. Biting on reed. Firm lips around mouthpiece while trying to drop jaw as if playing flat.
2. Not enough reed in mouth. Experiment to find the best and most appropriate sound.
3. Throat or oral cavity too tight. Hold shoulders down; keep tongue down inside mouth.
4. Reed too soft. Try a harder reed or clip tip of reed.

squawky, loud sound
1. Not enough lower lip over teeth. Correct embouchure.
2. Lips around mouthpiece not firm enough, especially corners. Correct embouchure.
3. Bad reed. Usually too soft or poorly made.
4. Mouthpiece is too open at tip. Try a different mouthpiece.
5. Too much breath—overblowing. Correct breathing.

hard, strident sound
1. Reed too hard. Try softer reed or scrape reed.
2. Lay is too open or too long on mouthpiece. Try another mouthpiece.

CONTROL

of soft
1. Not projecting a smooth, steady airstream into the instrument. Check and correct breathing.
2. Reed too soft. Try harder reed or clip reed.
3. Mouthpiece too open at tip. Try different mouthpiece.
4. Poorly shaped or too tight embouchure. Work on all aspects of the embouchure.
5. Cheeks puffing. Firm-up corners of mouth to flatten chin and keep cheeks flat.
6. Upper teeth not on mouthpiece. Correct embouchure.
7. On "throat tones." Try adding right-hand keys to notes.

of loud
1. Underdeveloped embouchure—usually too loose or flabby. Do not demand too much too soon; allow development—encourage and provide material for embouchure development.

[8] Ibid., Chapter 7.

2. Overblowing. Do not try to force too much air into instrument.

3. Angle of mouthpiece too high or head too low. Hold head erect, keep instrument no more than 45 degrees from body.

4. Too much mouthpiece in mouth. Correct embouchure.

PITCH

flat

1. Reed too soft. Try harder reed.

2. Clarinet too high or head down. With head held erect, clarinet should be about 30 degrees from body.

3. Not enough mouthpiece in mouth. Correct embouchure.

4. Not enough air. Correct breathing—both inhaling and exhaling.

5. Embouchure not tightening for loud sections. Correct embouchure—lips, especially corners, firm up for loud.

6. Barrel too long. Try shorter barrel.

7. Individual notes:

   a. keys not opening enough. Have clarinet adjusted.

   b. barrel pulled out too far. Push in barrel, pull at middle and bell.

   c. dirty tone holes. Clean with pipe cleaner.

8. Insufficient practice.

sharp

1. Embouchure too tight or biting on reed. Correct embouchure.

2. Reed too hard. Try softer reed or scrape reed.

3. Barrel too short. Try longer barrel.

4. Embouchure not relaxed enough for softer passages.

5. Clarinet held too low. Correct holding position.

6. Individual notes:

   a. keys too open. Have instrument readjusted.

   b. dirty tone holes. Clean with pipe cleaner or needle.

   c. worn corks that determine the opening of keys. Replace or have replaced.

REFERENCES

Texts

BONADE, DANIEL. *The Art of Adjusting Reeds.* Kenosha, WI: G. Leblanc Co., 1957.
————. *Clarinet's Compendium.* Paris: Alphonse Leduc Editions, n.d.

BOWEN, G. H. *Making and Adjusting Clarinet Reeds.* Hancock, MS: Sounds of Wood-winds, 1981.

BRYMER, JACK. *Clarinet.* New York: Schirmer, 1976.

CUMMINGS, FRANK, and CARL GUTMANN. *Director and Student's Band Instrument Repair Manual: Series I, Clarinet.* Berkeley, CA: Don Keller, 1953.

DRUSHLER, PAUL. *The Altissimo Register: A Partial Approach.* Rochester, NY: Shall-u-mo Publications, 1978.

—————. *The Clarinet: Its Evolution, Literature, and Artists.* Rochester, NY: Shall-u-mo Publications, 1973.

EBY, WALTER M. *The Clarinet and Its Care.* New York: W. Jacobs, 1955.

—————. *The Clarinet Embouchure.* New York: W. Jacobs, 1955.

ERRANTE, F. G. *A Selective Clarinet Bibliography.* Oneonta, NY: Swift-Dorr Publications, 1973.

GOLD, CECIL V. *Clarinet Performing Practices and Teaching in the United States and Canada.* 2nd ed. Moscow, ID: University of Idaho Press, 1973.

HEIM, NORMAN. *A Handbook for Clarinet Performance.* Delevan, NY: Kendor Music, 1965.

HOVEY, NILO. *Teacher's Guide to the Clarinet.* Elkhart, IN: The Selmer Co., 1967.

KROLL, OSKAR. *The Clarinet.* Translated by A. Baines. London: B. T. Batsford, 1968.

LEIDIG, VERNON. *Contemporary Woodwind Technique, Manual and Study Guide.* Hollywood, CA: Highland Music, 1960.

MCCATHERY, DON. *Playing and Teaching the Clarinet Family.* San Antonio, TX: Southern Music Co., 1959.

MOORE, E. C. *The Clarinet and Its Daily Routine.* Kenosha, WI: G. Leblanc Co., 1962.

OPPERMAN, K. *Repertory of the Clarinet.* New York: G. Ricordi and Co., 1969.

PACE, KENNETH. *Handbook of Clarinet Playing.* Murfreesboro, TN: Dehoff Publications, 1967

PALMER, HAROLD. *Teaching Techniques of the Woodwinds: A Textbook for the Instrumental Teacher and the Teacher in Training.* Rockville Centre, NY: Belwin, 1962.

PASCUCCI, VITO. *Care and Minor Repairs of the Clarinet.* Kenosha, WI: G. Leblanc Co., 1959.

PINO, DAVID. *The Clarinet and Clarinet Playing.* New York: Scribner's, 1980.

REHFELDT, PHILLIP. *New Directions for Clarinet.* Berkeley, CA: University of California Press, 1977.

RENDALL, F. G. *The Clarinet: Some Notes on Its History and Construction.* 3rd ed. Revised by P. Bates. New York: W. W. Norton, 1971.

RICHMOND, STANLEY. *Clarinet and Saxophone Experience.* New York: St. Martin's, 1972.

SAWHILL, CLARENCE and BERTRAM MCGARRITY. *Playing and Teaching Woodwind Instruments.* Englewood Cliffs, NJ: Prentice-Hall, 1962.

SCHMIDT, ROBERT. *A Clarinetist's Notebook, Vol. I: Care and Repair.* Revised Edition. Rochester, NY: Shall-u-mo Publications, 1978.

SPRATT, JACK. *How to Make Your Own Clarinet Reeds.* Stamford, CN: Jack Spratt Woodwind Shop, 1956.

STEIN, KEITH. *The Art of Clarinet Playing.* Evanston, IL: Summy-Birchard Publishing Co., 1958.

STUBBINS, W. H. *The Art of Clarinetistry.* Ann Arbor, MI: Ann Arbor Publishers,

1965. Presently published: Mrs. W. H. Stubbins, 3040 Exmoor, Ann Arbor, MI, 48104.

————. *The Study of the Clarinet: For Soprano, Alto, or Bass Clarinet.* Ann Arbor, MI: George Wahr Publishers, 1957.

THORTON, JAMES. *Woodwind Handbook.* San Antonio, TX: Southern Music Co., 1960.

THURSTON, FREDERICK. *Clarinet Technique.* 3rd ed. London: Oxford University Press, 1977.

TIMM, EVERETT L. *The Woodwinds: Performance and Instructional Techniques.* Boston: Allyn and Bacon, 1964.

TOSE, GABRIEL. *Artistic Clarinet: Technique and Study.* Hollywood, CA: Highland Music Company, 1962.

WESTON, PAMELA. *The Clarinet Teacher's Companion.* London: Robert Hale and Co., 1976.

WESTPHAL, FREDERICK W. *Guide to Teaching Woodwinds.* 4th ed. Dubuque, IA: W. C. Brown, 1985.

WILLAMAN, ROBERT. *The Clarinet and Clarinet Playing: A Text for Beginners, Advanced Players.* New York: Carl Fischer, 1949.

Journals

The Clarinet. Quarterly from the International Clarinet Society, School of Music, University of North Texas, Denton, TX 76203.

Studies

Easy-Beginning (elementary or junior high)

ALBERT/PARES/HOVEY. *Daily Exercises for Clarinet* (Belwin-Mills).
BUCK, LAWRENCE. *Elementary Method for Clarinet* (Kjos).
CAILLIET, LUCIEN. *Elementary Clarinet Method* (Leblanc).
HOVEY, NILO. *Elementary Method for Clarinet*, Vols. 1 and 2 (Rubank).
————. *First Book of Practical Studies* (Belwin-Mills).
KLOSE, H. *Celebrated Method for Clarinet*, Book I (Carl Fischer).
LESTER, LEON. *The Developing Clarinetist* (Belwin-Mills).
————. *Melodious Studies for Clarinet* (Henri Elkan).
LIEGEL, L. *Basic Method for Clarinet* (Carl Fischer).
OPPERMAN, KALMEN. *Clarinet—Volume I* (Pro-Art Music).
PERIER, AUGUSTE. *La Debutante Clarinettiste* (Alphonse Leduc).
STUBBINS, W. H. *The Study of the Clarinet* (George Wahr).
WALN, GEORGE. *Waln Elementary Clarinet Method* (Belwin-Mills).

Medium (advanced junior high or high school)

ALBERT, J. B. *24 Varied Scales and Exercises* (Carl Fischer).
BAERMANN, C. (ed. Langenus). *Complete Method for Clarinet*, Parts I and II (Carl Fischer).

_____. *Daily Studies* (Boosey & Hawkes).
DELECLUSE, U. *12 Easy Etudes* (Alphonse Leduc).
GAMBARO, GIOVANNI. *21 Caprices* (Billaudot).
GEE, H. *Style Etudes and Technical Exercises* (Southern Music).
HITE, D. *Melodious and Progressive Studies*, 2 vols. (Southern Music).
HOVEY, NILO. *Second Book of Practical Studies* (Belwin-Mills).
JEAN-JEAN, PAUL *Etudes Progressive and Melodiques* (Alphonse Leduc).
_____. *16 Modern Etudes* (Alphonse Leduc).
_____. *25 Etudes Technique and Melodiques* (Alphonse Leduc).
KLOSE, H. *Klose Method for Clarinet*, complete or in 2 parts (Carl Fischer).
LESTER, L. *The Progressing Clarinetist* (Carl Fischer).
OPPERMAN, KALMEN. *Modern Daily Studies* (M. Baron Company).
PERRON, J. *Daily Exercises* (Billaudot).
STARK, R. (ed. Barbarino). *24 Studies in All Tonalities* (Cundy-Bettoney).
STUBBINS, W. H. *22 Etudes for Clarinet* (George Wahr).

Advanced (high school or college)

BAERMANN, C. (ed. Langenus). *Complete Method for Clarinet*, Parts I through III (Carl
    Fischer) or Parts I through V (Cundy-Bettoney).
BITSCH, MARCEL. *Douze Etudes de Rhythm* (Alphonse Leduc).
BOZZA, EUGENE. *14 Etudes* (Alphonse Leduc).
CAVALLINI, ERNESTO. *30 Caprices* (Alphonse Leduc).
DELECLUSE, U. *14 Grand Etudes* (Alphonse Leduc).
FAULX, J. *20 Virtuoso Studies After Bach* (Henri Elkan).
GABUCCI, A. *Dix Etudes Modernes* (Alphonse Leduc).
_____. *26 Cadences en Forme de Prelude* (Alphonse Leduc).
KROEPSCH, F. (ed. by Bellison). *Progressive Daily Studies*, Book III and IV (Carl
    Fischer).
LANGENUS, GUSTAV. *Complete Method for the Boehm Clarinet*, Books 1 and 3 (Carl
    Fischer or Cundy-Bettoney).
LAZARUS, HENRY. *Method for Clarinet*, Parts 1 through 3 (Carl Fischer or Cundy-
    Bettoney).
PERIER, AUGUSTE. *331 Exercises Journaliers de Mecanisme* (Alphonse Leduc).
_____. *20 Etudes De Virtuosite* (Alphonse Leduc).
_____. *21 Etudes Modernes* (Alphonse Leduc).
POLATSCHEK, V. *Advanced Studies* (G. Schirmer).
ROSE, CYRILLE. *40 Studies for Clarinet*, Books I and II (Carl Fischer).
_____. *32 Studies for Clarinet* (Carl Fischer).
STARK, ROBERT. *The Art of Transposition*, Op. 28 (Rahter).
_____. *24 Grand Virtuoso Studies* (Cundy-Bettoney).

CLARINET
FINGERING CHART

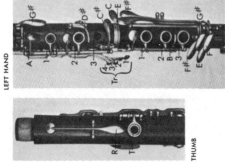

LEFT HAND

RIGHT HAND

THUMB

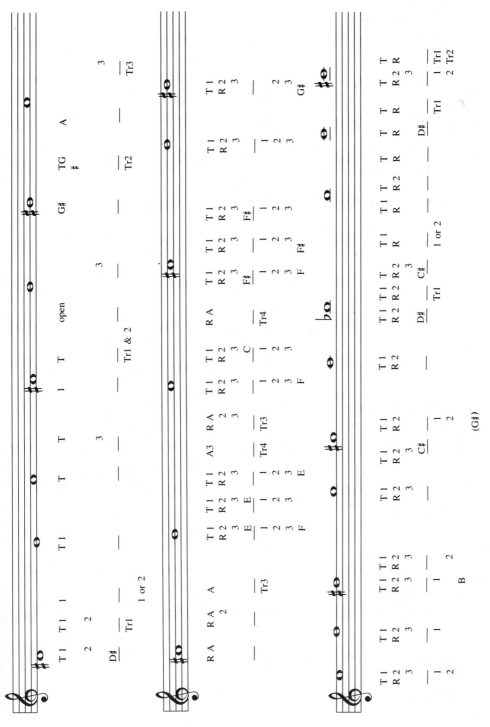

( ) optional

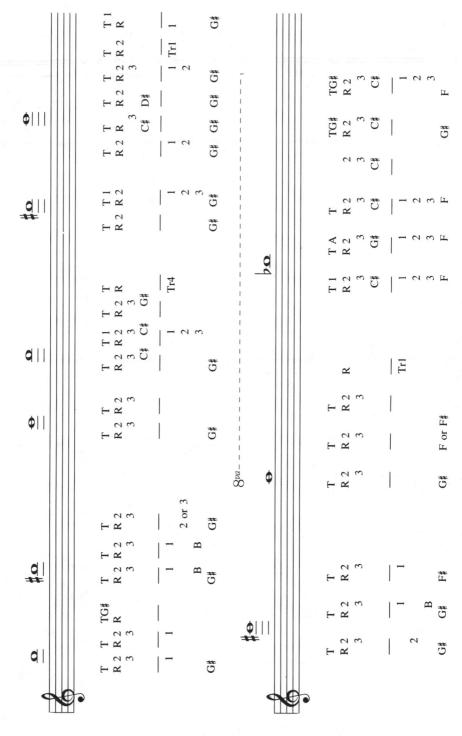

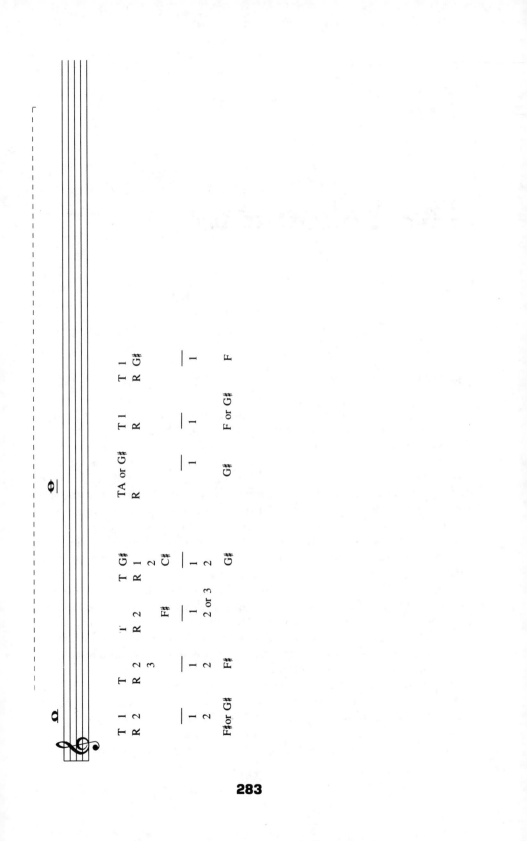

14

The Saxophone

HISTORY

The saxophone differs from the other instruments in that it did not gradually evolve, but was deliberately invented. When Deshontenelles produced a clarinet with a bent mouthpiece in 1807, and Lazarus a tenoroon in 1820, they created the closest predecessors to the saxophone. It is far younger than the other instruments, being little more than one hundred fifty years old, compared to the four-thousand-year evolution of the flute and three-thousand-year history of the trumpet. In 1840, Adolph Sax, an instrumental craftsman of Brussels, set out to combine a woodwind mouthpiece with a brass body that would have woodwind fingering. The saxophone, an instrument similar to one created by Miekle some twenty years earlier, was the result, and except for a few minor changes remains today as Sax invented it. Its original popularity has not faded, due to its extreme dynamic range and the possibility for producing a very personal, intimate, and sentimental tone quality well suited to many kinds of music.

The instrument stands in a class by itself, being neither brass nor woodwind, having a clarinet mouthpiece, oboe fingering, and a brass body.

In America, the saxophone has been associated primarily with jazz and popular music and tends to be somewhat ignored by serious musicians. In some European countries, France in particular, it has been readily accepted as a member of the band and orchestra. French composers often include a double quartet of saxophones as an integral part of the concert band, and compose seriously for saxophone solo and ensemble.

SELECTING THE INSTRUMENT

The entire family of saxophones includes nine instruments (E-flat, C, and B-flat sopranos; alto, C melody; tenor; baritone; and the seldom used B-flat bass and E-flat contrabass), each differing from the others in range, tone, appearance, and playing problems. The most commonly used saxophones include the B-flat soprano, made in curved, partially curved, and straight versions, that sounds one step lower than the notes it reads; the E-flat alto, the most popular and useful of the family, that sounds a major sixth lower than the notes it reads; the B-flat tenor, which sounds a ninth lower than the notes it reads; and the E-flat baritone that sounds an octave and a sixth (a thirteenth) lower than the notes it reads.

A number of companies manufacture excellent-quality saxophones for beginners. Selmer (Bundy), Buffet, and Yamaha are among the best. Other companies make reliable instruments also, but parents who are shopping for a new saxophone for a beginner should be wary of buying "off brands" sold by department and some music stores. These instruments may look beautiful, but a saxophone of inferior quality has numerous disadvantages and is not a good investment.

The principal item to look for is workmanship. The horn should be well machined and of reasonably good quality metal. The pads should be attached well and all should close without leaks. The resonators on the pads should be carefully attached and centered, there should be no noisy keys, and the tone holes should open the same amount. Playing the instrument will show the purchaser the quality of the response and the intonation. New instruments will always respond a little stiffly; this is desirable since saxophones loosen up with playing. Intonation, with the regular fingerings and alternate fingerings, should be checked with an electronic tuner.

A used saxophone should have no air leaks around or under the pads. The action should be even for all keys, with no "bounce" from the keys when they are released. If one spring has been replaced, that key will be stronger than the others and all the springs will require replacment to maintain even action. Though a repairperson can even out the action by bending the springs to various degrees of resistance, this repair is only temporary, and the springs will certainly have to be replaced eventually. Bending springs also weakens them. Any drag in the keys is an indication of bent rods or posts and can be more serious and costly to repair.

Most pads on saxophones are leather and will show signs of wear with any use. Torn or scuffed pads should be replaced by a competent repairperson.

When purchasing any used wind instrument, the prime considerations are tone quality, intonation (with itself), and response. When the guidance of an expert is desirable, saxophone players may not be satisfactory. The majority of professional saxophone players specialize in jazz, and the tone quality appropriate for jazz may not be considered appropriate for wind ensemble playing. Colleges and universities with music departments usually have a number of expert saxophone players, and the music teacher may know a qualified saxophone player who can give good advice. This advice is especially important due to the high cost of good used saxophones.

Special keys such as the low A for the baritone saxophone can be obtained on some saxophones. The standard model baritone saxophone is recommended for school use, although more and more pieces requiring the low A are finding their way into the high school repertoire.

ASSEMBLING THE SAXOPHONE

The saxophone is not as sturdy an instrument as it looks. The three sections, the mouthpiece, the neckpiece, and the body of the instrument, are simple to assemble and care for. Assembling the saxophone involves putting the neckpiece onto the body of the instrument. Like the flute, there is no cork on the joint where the two pieces fit together, so forcing or wiggling can damage the metal and alter the fit. The parts fit easily if placed together with a slight turning motion to get the neckpiece to its seat in the body. The clamp screw must be loosened in order to do this. All too soon adolescent players learn that with a little force the saxophone can be assembled and moved without loosening the screw. The damage this does to the fit, which must be airtight, should be obvious.

Saxophones have an octave key lever that must go inside the octave key ring on the neck; this ring should not have to be bent since it is adjusted before the instrument leaves the factory, but if it does, it should be taken to a competent repairperson. Often a damaged ring is the result of good intentions backed up by the mistaken belief that the key ring should be round. In careful assembling, the octave key should not be depressed; the neckpiece should be put on at approximately the proper angle because turning the neckpiece too much after it is on the body can cause damage.

The cork on the neck should be greased for the mouthpiece to fit. The mouthpiece, without the reed or ligature, is put on straight so that the player's head need not be cocked to either side when playing. The mouthpiece has no regular stopping place on the neckpiece such as a rim or edge beyond which it will not go, so it can be put on a small distance or pushed down nearly to the octave key depending upon the strength of the student and the thickness of the cork. Intonation is directly affected by the distance the mouthpiece goes on the neck, so careful listening and tuning are recommended. An ink mark can be placed on the cork as a starting position for good tuning, but small adjustments will have to be made to accommodate different temperatures and humidities, and to adjust the instrument to the pitch of other instruments. Students generally fail to put the mouthpiece on far enough; the cork on a new instrument is made a little too large in order to allow for wear and shrinkage. Most students, therefore, play on instruments that are slightly flat, and they form bad habits of embouchure when trying to lip the tone up to the pitch of the ensemble.

The ligature is the metal band that holds the reed in its place on the mouthpiece. The ligature screws should be turned only enough to hold the reed centered on the mouthpiece without slipping. Players often turn the screws as far as they will go, which cuts into the reed and limits all vibration, so that any musical quality to the tone is impossible. The reed should fit nearly even with the tip of the mouthpiece.

The placement of the music stand deserves mention. Both beginning flute and saxophone players develop bad habits because of crowded conditions. There are often more beginners than parts or books. When many players share a music stand, the result can be poor posture and playing position.

HOLDING THE SAXOPHONE

Contrary to widespread opinion, the angle of the alto saxophone is correct whether the player is standing or sitting when the instrument is held in front of the body and the player's head is in normal position and his neck relaxed (this position is imperative when standing). When the saxophone is at the side and the bottom crook pulled too far back, tension in the right arm and fingers results, as well as a bad embouchure. It is not incorrect to play the alto saxophone to the side when seated, although the angle must be less than with a tenor saxophone. The mouthpiece must be adjusted so that the head and neck remain in a straightforward, relaxed position. Smaller students can hold the instrument directly in front by sitting on the edge of the chair. The practice of holding the alto saxophone to the side is so widespread that the Selmer Corporation (recently followed by other companies) manufactures its beginner-line saxophones with the keys near the bell positioned on the right side of the instrument to avoid damage from contact with legs or chairs. When the saxophone is held to the side, the chair should be rotated approximately 30 degrees counterclockwise. This chair placement allows rotation of the player's trunk to the right, more closely approximating the front-held position. Alto saxophones should be held in the front unless the performer's trunk is so short that the right wrist would be in a cramped position. Positions for holding the saxophone are shown in Figures 14–1 and 14–2.

The crook at the bottom of the saxophone is normally held farther back than the mouthpiece in order to ensure that the reed and mouthpiece enter the mouth at the proper angle. The right arm is positioned slightly back to keep the right hand and wrist relaxed. The instrument is *preferably* held directly in front of the player, since it is less apt to encourage bad habits of posture and position. The tenor and baritone saxophones are usually held to the side along the leg, but not pulled all the way back to the hip unless the student is very small, in which case he should adjust his holding position as he grows physically. For these instruments, the head remains in normal position with the mouthpiece straight with the player's mouth, not straight with the instrument. These instruments can be held to the side because the neck is a different shape and the mouthpiece will enter the mouth at the proper angle. With the largest instrument, the baritone saxophone, most players will rest the instrument on a stand or on the floor directly in front of them unless they use a thick neck strap that distributes the weight.

The neck strap should be adjusted so that the student's head position is not disturbed. A neck strap that is too short can make the head tilt down. No matter whether the instrument is held in front or to the side, good posture is essential for proper breathing. The head should be held erect as for all woodwinds to allow the mouthpiece to enter the mouth at the angle conducive to articulation and to producing the best tone quality.

Some students, perhaps attempting to emulate jazz saxophonists, hold the instrument too far back when seated, all the way to the hip, for

Figure 14–1 Sitting Position for Playing the Saxophone (saxophone held in front)

Figure 14–2 Sitting Position for Playing the Saxophone (saxophone held to the side)

example, rather than to the leg. This position puts the right arm in an awkward position, creates tension, and forces the head to be buried, restricting the airstream, or making the mouthpiece and reed enter the mouth at an inappropriate angle.

The instrument is held with the left hand on top, right hand below, and fingers placed similarly to the position for oboe, except that the pads of the fingers lie on pearl buttons positioned on the keys rather than on open tone holes. Left fingers lie on the second, fourth, and fifth buttons with the little finger on the G-sharp key (Figure 14–3). The left thumb rests below the octave key on a thumb rest at a 30- to 45-degree angle depending on student size, always touching the octave key. The right-hand fingers rest on the lower buttons with the little finger on the C-sharp key and the thumb under the thumb rest. The fingers should not be flat and hang over the far side of the keys; neither should the hands be drawn away from the instrument so the fingers barely touch the keys. A relaxed arch to the fingers, with the pads of the fingers resting on the keys, will allow the most flexibility and synchronization of movement (Figure 14-4).

Support comes from two areas: the right thumb positioned on a thumb rest on the back of the instrument similar to the clarinet, and a neck strap attached to a ring midway on the back of the horn. The embouchure, with the mouthpiece anchored to the upper teeth, and the left hand serve to steady the saxophone. The right thumb actively contributes to the embouchure and to tone formation by pushing the instrument up and out, and pushing the saxophone forward so the player is blowing through the mouthpiece (or even down into it). The instrument should never hang by

Figure 14–3 Left-hand Position for Playing the Saxophone

the neck strap because it is the right thumb's function to support the horn. The thumb, being active, is able to support the saxophone at the place where it contributes most to comfort, good embouchure, and good tone quality. It is important that the neck strap be adjusted so that no alteration of embouchure or hand position is made because of it.

If the instrument is held too far from the body, not enough of the mouthpiece is in the mouth; if it is held too close to the body, the arms become cramped and tense and pitches are often flat in the low register. A comfortable position is for the horn to be about six or seven inches from

Figure 14–4 Right-hand Position for Playing the Saxophone

the body, depending on the player's embouchure formation. Position does not depend on such items as the length of the player's arms or the size of his hands; the embouchure takes precedence over feelings of comfort or naturalness. Some saxophone teachers advocate an instrument position that allows the tip of the mouthpiece to point upwards, resulting in more facile tonguing than a position in which the mouthpiece is more horizontal. To point the tip of the mouthpiece upward, the player holds the instrument closer to his body. Experimenting is necessary to find the best angle for the best sound with each individual's embouchure formation. Neckstrap adjustment is critical in moving the instrument to the musician, not the musician to the instrument.

The player should sit or stand erect, with his chest pulled away from his lower torso, his shoulders back but relaxed, and his breath support from the depths of his abdomen. Saxophonists often lean forward in a tense, unbalanced position, right shoulder high and right elbow back, the head twisted and the entire upper torso showing obvious strain. This position must be avoided.

THE BEGINNING STUDENT

The saxophone is among the easiest instruments on which to produce a sound but among the most difficult to master. Most beginning saxophonists will choose an alto instrument. A few with sufficiently large hands may begin on the tenor sax, and often that instrument is a school-owned instrument. The student should initially begin with the mouthpiece only so that the embouchure is the sole area of concentration.

Beginners should use a prepared reed that is a bit on the soft side, but no softer than a 2 lest improper habits be encouraged. To establish the proper feeling for the embouchure, the student should vocalize "oh," then retain this general position while opening the mouth a little wider and pointing the chin. The mouthpiece is then inserted with the reed rolling the lower lip over the teeth. An attempt should be made to align the edge of the lip that separates the red of the lip from the flesh-colored part of the chin to a position directly above the teeth. The lips and corners of the mouth close *toward* the mouthpiece from all directions and the teeth rest on top of the mouthpiece about ½ of an inch from the tip. The upper lip should close around the mouthpiece and should be held firmly against the eye teeth.

In general, like the clarinet embouchure, the point where the mouthpiece begins to curve away from the reed is placed directly above the teeth. These details will require experimentation by teacher and student to find the best position for the best sound—a difficult task with beginners. As with the clarinet embouchure, the lower lip should be held firmly against the lower teeth, with a feeling of tautness or "pointing" in the chin. The sound will be thin and nasal if there is not enough mouthpiece in the mouth, and wild and loud if there is too much. Approximately ½ to ¾ of an inch of the mouthpiece should be inserted into the mouth, leaving plenty of reed free to vibrate inside the mouth.

The tongue is also in a sense part of the embouchure. It should be relaxed, low, forward, and well spread. The fact that the lower jaw does not form part of the support cannot be overemphasized; it only provides increasing support as one ascends. The student must not rest the saxophone on the lower lip, or worse, the lower teeth; the teacher should be sure that the student is using his hands (the right thumb) to push the instrument up and out, anchoring it on the upper teeth. The lower teeth remain open, with the lower lip and corners pushing toward the mouthpiece. Lower teeth down, lower lip up.

One of the best ways to check a student's embouchure is by his pitch. When the mouthpiece is played alone, the pitch produced with a correct embouchure and mouthpiece placement approximates A440. If the pitch is too high, the player is probably using too tight a grip on the mouthpiece, usually by the lower teeth. If the pitch is too low, the embouchure is not sufficiently developed; the player has to learn to play with a tighter grip. A bad saxophone tone is often caused by a clarinet embouchure; loosening the tension of the lips and checking for a horizontal pull at the corners of the mouth can help improve the quality. The embouchure for the higher, smaller saxophones is firmer than that for the larger ones, but still not as firm as for the clarinet.

The tongue does not strike the reed to begin a tone, but acts as a valve and pulls away and *lets* the reed vibrate. The tongue maintains contact with the reed prior to the attack. While some air will build up behind the tongue, too much air pressure will produce a harsh attack.

EMBOUCHURE

Although the mouthpieces for clarinet and saxophone are similar, they have slightly different dimensions. These differences along with the different demands of the instruments call for distinctly different embouchures. One can produce sounds on the clarinet by using a saxophone embouchure, but these will not be acceptable clarinet sounds; one can also produce sounds on a saxophone by using a clarinet embouchure, but not acceptable saxophone sounds. Both the clarinet and saxophone embouchures rest the upper teeth on the mouthpiece and both place the mouthpiece in the center of the mouth; there the similarities end.

A correct saxophone embouchure is shown in Figure 14–5. A saxophonist with a good embouchure has his bottom lip firmly against and

Figure 14–5 Saxophone Embouchure

slightly over his teeth. His chin is pulled down rather than bunched up. Too much lip over the lower teeth destroys the resonance. The lower lip provides the cushion on which the reed vibrates, so it cannot be pulled too tightly over the teeth, but too much cushion dampens the vibration. The chin pulled down helps prevent too much lower lip from resting against the reed. When the lower lip is too far over the teeth or too much mouthpiece is in the mouth, the tones will not speak and will lack resonance. With too little lip over the teeth, however, or too little mouthpiece in the mouth, the player is plagued with squeaks and can produce only a tiny, fragile tone. Students have different facial characteristics so each will require a different amount of lip over the teeth to produce the optimum sound. The teacher and student must experiment over a period of time to determine the best mouthpiece placement for producing the best sound possible.

The lower jaw is not part of the support; rather, the upper teeth on the mouthpiece form the anchor, with the instrument pushed up against the upper teeth by the right thumb under the thumb rest. A small piece of rubber is often glued to the mouthpiece to protect the mouthpiece and to prevent the player from being bothered by the vibrations from it. Many young students develop bad habits due to shying away from the mouthpiece with their upper teeth.

The middle of the upper lip stays on the mouthpiece at all times, with little lip visible. The lower lip may be thought of as resting against the reed. The pressure is upward where the mouthpiece pushes against the upper teeth, and not downward where the reed meets the lower lip. Unlike a double reed, the mouthpiece remains stationary for the entire saxophone range; it is not moved in and out to achieve the extreme ranges. The player breathes through the corners of his mouth without removing his upper teeth or lower lip from the mouthpiece. Dropping the jaw often causes the player to lose his embouchure and tends to move the mouthpiece in and out.

With the correct embouchure, the corners of the mouth push toward the mouthpiece and the upper lip is firm against the eye teeth. All pressure must be toward the mouthpiece, because horizontal pull at the corners of the mouth gives a squeezed, tight sound. If the student has a tendency to stretch as well as push toward the mouthpiece, dimples will be apparent in the cheeks.

From the teacher's view, the mouthpiece should appear to be placed about 1 inch in the mouth. From the player's standpoint, the teeth are placed about $\frac{1}{2}$ of an inch on the mouthpiece for the alto saxophone, perhaps $\frac{5}{8}$ of an inch for tenor saxophone, and slightly more for baritone saxophone. The amount of mouthpiece in the mouth has a definite effect on the tone. The sound will be too thin if there is too little mouthpiece in the mouth and noticeably spread and uncontrolled if too much of the mouthpiece is taken in or if the chin is not down.

A good check for proper mouthpiece placement and lip tension is for the student to play octaves on the instrument. If both octaves respond with only the octave key manipulated, then the embouchure is at least close to being correct. If only the upper octave speaks, then the embouchure is too tight or there is not enough mouthpiece in the mouth; if only the lower octave speaks, then the embouchure is probably too loose or there is too much mouthpiece in the mouth.

INTONATION

In listening to school saxophonists, one is often hard-pressed to decide which is the more objectionable, the intonation or the tone quality. The sad part about this is that it is unnecessary; the saxophone is one of the most perfect instruments with respect to intonation and thus easier to play in tune than other instruments. It may be that the instrument is so easy to play initially that the saxophonists are neglected by the instrumental teacher. Poor band scoring also contributes to the problem; experience in saxophone ensembles and jazz groups helps.

Pitch problems depend partially on the instrument itself: how well it is made and cared for. For example, if the keys open too wide, the pitch will be sharp. Alhough the most perfectly in tune of all woodwinds, the saxophone still has built-in flaws in intonation, as illustrated in Figure 14–6.

The soprano saxophone has intonation problems similar to those of the E-flat clarinet; it is a smaller instrument which, even when of good

Figure 14–6 Intonation Problems on the Saxophone

quality, requires more experience. The more common alto, tenor, and baritone saxophones are generally well made by leading manufacturers, and such instruments can be easily controlled when their pitch characteristics are understood.

Basic tuning is accomplished by adjusting the mouthpiece on the neckpiece to lengthen or shorten the instrument. Reeds also affect overall pitch: a harder reed is usually more difficult to blow and control than a soft reed, but has better intonation tendencies. Intonation is controlled by tightening and loosening a properly formed embouchure during performance. The more the mouthpiece curves away from the reed, the more control the player has. Without this control, most young saxophonists will tend to blow flat on loud passages and sharp on soft passages.

The double octave key mechanism makes intonation a series of compromises. The lower octave of the alto saxophone is usually sharp, the upper octave generally flat. The upper octave is especially flat with inexperienced players whose embouchures are not adequate to produce proper intonation; this problem can be at least partially corrected by the use of additional keys. For other flat notes, low C-sharp, low E-flat, chromatic F-sharp, G-sharp, the Sl and S2 keys may be added. Additional fingering changes that may improve intonation are as follows:

1. Third-space C-sharp is always out of tune with the fingering ordinarily suggested for it; use of the low C-sharp fingering makes the pitch quite sharp, and the right-hand keys can be added to lower the pitch.
2. The first-leger-line A-sharp is out of tune and can be improved by the addition of the F-sharp key, third finger, right hand.
3. The following chromatic fingerings are usually fingered for technical ease and not for intonation: (l) F-sharp, use forked F-sharp key; (2) B-flat, use the side key; (3) C, use the B key and the second trill key.
4. In playing the pattern D–C-sharp–D on the staff, intonation will be improved by using the fingering for low C-sharp plus the octave key. Be careful to lip down since both pitches are quite sharp. The timbre of the C-sharp may be stuffy.

In general, closing additional tone holes other than those required to produce a particular note will lower a pitch. At least one tone hole below the lowest one used for the actual fingering must obviously remain open, and the closer the open or closed tone hole is to those used for the actual fingering, the greater its effect on the intonation.[1] These are general rules; listening is the only answer to intonation problems.

Pitch problems can sometimes be corrected by changing the angle of the mouthpiece in the mouth, turning the neckpiece slightly to the right or left, or varying the amount of bottom lip over the teeth. These should be used as a last resort. The same admonition applies to lipping up the pitch—changing it by raising the jaw to tighten the embouchure. The saxophone embouchure does not have the lip flexibility of other woodwind embouchures, and any practice that involves changing the embouchure is not advised. Advanced players may tighten the throat slightly to make a minute adjustment in the pitch, but this usually leads to bad habits, constriction of the throat muscles, and inadequate tone quality. Some players find helpful a mouthpiece with a comparatively open tip because it allows use of a softer reed and a gain in pitch flexibility.

When vibrato is used, instruments are often tuned slightly sharp. This practice is frequently overused, but it keeps the tone from dropping below pitch on the low side of the vibrato.

If the player's embouchure seems correct and still one or more individual notes are out of tune, the teacher should consider the excellent pitch alteration chart in *The Art of Saxophone Playing*.[2]

TONE QUALITY

True saxophone tone, with its own characteristic and beautiful sound, is rarely heard by young instrumentalists. Only since 1950 or so has the instrument been widely accepted as a vehicle for serious music. In 1965, the *Saxophones of Paris* was one of the few recordings useful as a guide to good saxophone sound. Within 20 years, however, many recording artists, both jazz and classical, had contributed greatly to the discography of the saxophone. Listening still has to be selective, for the commercial music on radio and television, as well as many recordings, uses the instrument with an obvious blatant sound. For every instance in which the true sound of the instrument is heard, there are a hundred instances of bad sound. The problem is in retaining that concept teaching students to imitate the good sound rather than the bad one.

[1] Frederick W. Westphal, *Guide to Teaching Woodwinds*, 4th ed. (Dubuque, IA: W. C. Brown, 1985), 142.

[2] Larry Teal, *The Art of Saxophone Playing*. (Evanston, IL: Summy-Birchard Publishing Co., 1963), 66.

The sound of E, F, and G at the top of the staff is most characteristic of the instrument's tone quality, and an acceptable tone should be easier to obtain in this range. One of the universal factors in bad tone quality along with poor breath support is a bad embouchure. The player should work to obtain maximum control, the muscles of the mouth and cheek withstanding additional air pressure, so that a more intense column of air can be sent through the mouthpiece. If the player can produce the same kind of breath support and air pressure used by the trumpet player for high notes, he will be well on his way to a disciplined tone.

The study of harmonics should begin early, as an aid to good tone and successful altissimo performance. Harmonics help to develop breath control and support, a firmer embouchure, and a consciousness of pitch. In addition, harmonics themselves are useful, for they can literally add octaves to the top range of the saxophone.

Many bad habits are formed by beginners who are told to play softly. The student tightens his throat, ignores proper breathing, and finds no reason to work on a firmer embouchure since there seems to be no need for control. These habits stay with him and are broken only with great difficulty. To develop air pressure, the beginning student will have to play loudly and with insufficient control. As saxophone sound is powerful in its carrying power, the beginning efforts of a young player are hard to take.

The following symptoms are clues to the types of problems the student may be developing:

1. A quiver in the tone usually means that the throat muscles are too tight and breath support inadequate. To get the right feeling in the throat for an open, unobstructed flow of air, use the syllable "who." Using "who" must be understood as pertaining to throat relaxation and not to the syllable formed in the mouth. "Who" may be used for any instrument when the player needs a word to help him understand the feeling for throat relaxation.

2. A harsh tone and a low register in which the tones are difficult to produce may mean that the embouchure is too firm or the reed is too stiff; working over the reed or changing to one of less resistance may help.

3. If the sound is deficient in resonance, the problem is usually that the mouthpiece tip is too closed. The lack of resonance may also be due to the player's embouchure: too much lower lip over the teeth.

4. A weak, breathy tone may be characteristic of the beginner who lacks sufficient wind to fill the mouthpiece. He can be helped to develop more air pressure and breath support, of course, but his tone quality can be improved by changing to a more closed mouthpiece. The Meyer 5 with a medium chamber or the Selmer C is of this type and is fine for beginners who have not developed enough air support to cope with a more open mouthpiece.

Vowel formation in the mouth will help produce the type of tone color desired. The more open vowels should be used in the middle and low registers, and the more closed vowels in the upper. An "oh" or "ooou" are often suggested to produce the fuller, rounder sound desirable for Romantic music, with "ay" or "ee" for Classical repertoire because they produce a brighter, less personal sound. For the upper register the "ee" or "i" sound will result in a brilliant yet free tone quality. Frequently the saxophone sound is spread, lacking brilliancy and beauty, with no center or focus to the tone. To obtain edge or focus to the tone is not easy: The player must have a concept of the sound he wants, an open throat with a vowel formation in the mouth sufficient to support the tone, and a well-controlled embouchure and sufficient intensity of air pressure. When these are present the tone takes on a focus and edge that make it beautiful and interesting.

Vibrato

A good vibrato enhances a beautiful tone, but an inappropriate vibrato can make the saxophone tone glaring and vulgar. The straight tone is useful in rapid passages. Vibrato is best used judiciously and adds warmth when needed. The straight tone tends to sound somewhat manufactured except in the hands of a real artist. In ensemble playing, vibrato must also be judiciously used or avoided completely, because vibrato does not blend with other instruments. This is particularly true of saxophones and horns (mid-range instruments), whose range is such that all intervals are hazardous and unisons are frequent and especially obvious.

Unlike other instruments, the saxophone is not at its best with diaphragm vibrato and does make successful use of the jaw vibrato because it can be controlled more accurately. The jaw vibrato is an alteration of high and low pitch rather than of fluctuating intensity and must be handled with care. A definite change of vibrato is required for the high, low, and middle registers. Since the jaw vibrato does alter the pitch, one can readily see why the saxophone is usually tuned sharp enough for the bottom of the vibrato to be up to pitch. The general rule, unless the music dictates otherwise, is a slow and spare vibrato for the low register, faster and narrower for the high register, and of medium pace and width for the middle register. In musical spots that require intensity for a specific musical effect, a fast, narrow vibrato will be required regardless of register.

Because the lower lip is only providing a cushion for the reed rather than support for the embouchure, jaw vibrato can be used without distorting the embouchure, provided the player has both correct embouchure and the correct approach to vibrato. The lower jaw may be moved with discretion to assist proper intonation. If the player's habits are correct and well established, a small movement will be felt by the player but not seen and will not interfere with the embouchure formation.

When should the student begin learning vibrato? Because control is not possible without training, many saxophonists advocate beginning vibrato study by the second or third week, with a few minutes practice a day devoted to vibrato and to strive for evenness. Other practicing to develop a solid embouchure, good breathing habits, and a pleasant and correct tone is done without vibrato. One to three years of playing without vibrato is not uncommon.

The Mouthpiece

The saxophone mouthpiece, like the clarinet mouthpiece, is an important factor in the tone quality of the instrument. The size and shape of the tone chamber, the proportion of the facing, the type of baffle, and the material of the mouthpiece each influences the tone quality in specific ways. Several ways in which the mouthpiece affects tone quality were discussed in the first part of this section. Unfortunately, mouthpiece selection is not simply a matter of determining what type of sound one wants and picking the appropriate mouthpiece to produce that sound. The student's facial characteristics, lip size, shape of teeth, and structure of the jaw must be taken into consideration. A major objective in selecting a mouthpiece is to neutralize those facial characteristics that may hinder the development of tone quality and enhance those characteristics that help in production of good tone. Furthermore, the saxophone mouthpiece affects pitch, dynamics, and flexibility between registers.

The saxophone mouthpiece (Figure 14–7) fits directly onto the instrument, providing a large tone chamber that results in a big and brilliant tone. One style of mouthpiece has a large, round tone chamber allowing a resonant, refined sound. Another type of mouthpiece may have a smaller bore and is elongated for volume, producing a more piercing tone. Experts such as Leeson believe that the player can achieve a completely acceptable

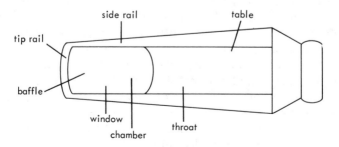

Figure 14–7 Saxophone Mouthpiece

tone on the second type of mouthpiece, while Sigurd Rascher preferred the former, older, larger tone chamber and the resultant more classical sound. A chamber with straight walls produces a slightly more brilliant sound. One with curved walls produces a more subtle, mellower sound.

The baffle, the part of the mouthpiece that lies immediately opposite the opening, influences the volume of the tone and the amount of air needed to produce it. A concave baffle gives a softer sound and requires more air for the tone. The convex baffle gives a louder sound and requires less air. (An extended or elongated baffle produces a very loud, harsh sound and will rarely be desirable.) Of these two choices, one makes a good tone more difficult to produce and the other makes it more difficult to control.

The side rails on which the reed rests may also be found in a variety of shapes. For dance-band work, the usual requirement is straight, flat side-rails similar to those of the clarinet. The siderails that best combine with a large tone chamber will be slightly convex to complement the shape of the chamber.

The facing is the curve on which the tip end of the reed rests, and the curve and length of the curved rails of the facing determine the size of the tip opening. A short facing produces a smaller tip opening, and a long facing produces a larger tip opening. The longer facing requires a firmer embouchure and a softer reed which consequently reduces loud dynamic levels and makes the high register more difficult since more pressure is necessary to close the larger tip opening. With a well-developed embouchure, however, the longer facing provides additional pitch flexibility. At the other extreme, a shorter facing requires less embouchure pressure and a stiffer reed that results in greater control on the part of the player, often a demand that cannot be fulfilled. The medium facing is the most useful unless the player is advanced enough to know his preferences and how to handle a differently proportioned mouthpiece facing.

Mouthpieces come in a variety of materials. Glass mouthpieces exist but are extremely rare. Plastic mouthpieces, formerly avoided because of their tendency to become brittle and crack and because their tone quality was undesirable, have improved greatly and may now be purchased with confidence. They are quite durable as well as inexpensive. Hard rod rubber, or ebonite, is the standard mouthpiece material because it combines high durability with a good tone quality. Metal mouthpieces are also acceptable for the saxophone. Their advantage is that they will never warp under misuse as will plastic and ebonite. Also, they can be made with slightly smaller exterior proportions because of metal's greater strength, which is a true advantage to young, small, tenor and baritone saxophone players who often feel that they are playing with a baseball bat in their mouth. Both metal and ebonite can be retooled and refaced easily.

Range

No discussion of the saxophone would be complete without reference to the octave above top-line F-sharp. This range has only recently been acknowledged, but today all fine saxophone players include these notes in their playing range, and music utilizing them is common. These pitches are all harmonics achieved by a firm embouchure and intense breath support. An advanced player does not necessarily find harmonics easier to obtain; he learns them by specific practice and such practice can be started as soon as the player has established a reasonably good embouchure. Harmonics require experimentation with air pressure, breath support, tongue, lip and teeth pressure, and so on, in addition to much work. The notes are there and the ambitious student should learn to play them if he wants to consider himself competent. Good pitches to start on are the harmonic fingerings for high E and F. Another good exercise is to produce harmonics from the fundamental pitches of low B-flat to first-space F.

TECHNIQUE: ARTICULATIONS AND FINGERINGS

The placing of the mouthpiece in the mouth can help or hinder correct tonguing. If the mouthpiece is in too horizontal a position, the action of the tongue will be impeded; if the tip of the mouthpiece points sightly upward, tonguing will be more easily mastered.

As with the clarinet, the tongue serves as a switch controlling the reed's vibration without closing off the reed and mouthpiece. The force of the airstream and the force with which the tongue touches the reed determine the style of articulation.

There are at least two correct ways to tongue; the best one depends on the individual. The more common way is to use the tip of the tongue to stop the reed, placing it lightly on the reed either at the tip or a little farther down. Rascher, for one, believe in touching the reed a short distance from the tip because it keeps the reed from closing up on the mouthpiece—the vibration of the reed is stopped for an instant but the air going through the mouthpiece is not halted. The tongue action must be as rapid and as slight as possible so that it does not interfere with the smoothness of the tone. Using the tip of the tongue can cause a small movement of the jaw, thus tightening the jaw and altering the embouchure.

The second type of tonguing is to anchor the tip of the tongue at the base of the teeth, at the gum line, and to use the middle of the tongue to stop the reed. The curved mid-tongue makes a small movement forward to contact the tip of the reed, having exactly the same effect as the tip of the tongue in the first method. This position is perhaps possible only with the right kind of tongue and mouth proportions. Those players who can use this method find it to be as fast and as well controlled as the tip of the tongue, with the added advantage that there is no danger of moving the jaw. With either method, the tone is stopped by touching the reed with the tongue to halt its vibration.

Moving the jaw when trying to tongue correctly results in flattened pitches on each tongued note and too much mouthpiece in the mouth. The problem can be helped by having the student tongue the same pitch repeatedly, gradually increasing the speed, while watching the embouchure in a mirror. As soon as the jaw starts to move the student should reduce the speed in order to "lock-in" the proper feel and coordinate the proper tonguing before attempting a faster speed.

Two types of incorrect tonguing can be detected by the sounds that accompany them. A small "thud" with each tonguing action indicates that the player is placing too much of the tongue on the reed, often called a "slap tongue." Besides the unpleasant sound, this kind of tonguing can never be done with much speed or delicacy. The tip of the tongue should be touching only the tip of the reed. The second sound is a small "oink," present when the student is tonguing with the throat. Here, movement in the throat is visible with each tonguing. A player can become so skillful at throat articulations that it is both rapid and quiet, but even so it is far from desirable because the throat action tightens the muscles and inhibits the openness needed for tonal resonance. Tightening the throat is one of the most difficult habits to break once firmly established.

Multiple tonguing can be done on the single-reed instruments, though it is seldom used. The ability to single-tongue very fast and with control is much more important.

Hand position is critical for developing good technique. Young saxophonists often acquire bad habits since they do not have to cover tone holes directly with their fingers. Also, since playing at a fast tempo is not required of beginners, hand and finger positions that "come close" are successful in the initial stages of performance. Playing speed will be enhanced, however, if good habits are formed early. Supplementary exercises should be provided to young students to help develop finger coordination. Fingers must be lifted together, lowered together, and raised and lowered simultaneously. Slurs between certain notes, such as a D-sharp to a G-sharp, help develop the coordination required for complex finger patterns.

As suggested for the clarinet when crossing the break, the saxophonist can leave right-hand fingers down during certain passages, even though the normal fingering does not require them, and other keys such as the G-sharp key can be used in much the same manner. The instructor must determine if a passage is fast enough to mask any intonation flaws that may accompany alternate fingerings.

The saxophonist, like the clarinet player, must pay particular attention to the little fingers, especially on the left hand. Unlike the clarinetist, the saxophonist is not given a choice about which little finger he will use for certain notes in certain passages; he must learn to slide his little fingers from key to key. These notes should be practiced slowly and gradually increased in speed to avoid turning the hand or altering its shape.

The fingering chart at the end of the chapter gives, under each note, the normal fingering that is usually taught to beginners. The fingerings that follow are given in the order that they least affect intonation. Beginners should learn one fingering for each new note. Alternate fingerings such as B-flat, the side key C, and the forked F-sharp should be integrated into the regular fingering patterns. Other alternates can be introduced after the normal fingering is learned.

Basic finger facility is developed by work on scales played throughout the range of the instrument. Control is essential, so scales should be practiced slowly and gradually increased in speed. Students should also practice (*without* raising the fingers too far above the buttons) to coordinate the fingers with the tongue.

WHAT TO PRACTICE

Good tone quality, that most essential element in music, is normally best developed through the practice of long tones. For young saxophonists, however, long tones should be postponed until good habits of mouthpiece placement and lip tension are developed and the player begins to form a good embouchure automatically.

Early development of good tone can be achieved through practice of simple melodies, since the embouchure, if properly established, does not change for register, dynamic level, articulation, or pitch. Beginners should form the correct embouchure, breathe carefully, and play these melodies while maintaining the correct embouchure and a steady airstream, with only the fingers moving. No tongue should be used until correct embouchure formation is secure.

Scales are excellent for practicing tone and intonation as well as finger dexterity. Scales demand use of different fingers and finger combinations and patterns beyond those required in the beginning method books, which are usually limited to the keys of G, C, and D for alto saxophone. Scales can also help develop good intonation, where guidance is provided.

After several weeks of instrumental music instruction, students may still be limited to only the first five or six notes of a single scale. With the right encouragement and use of a fingering chart, assignments to practice "the scale" will lead them to an increased range.

Arpeggios are useful for the development of both intonation and finger coordination. As mentioned for several instruments, scales and arpeggios should be played "in cycle"; that is, each scale and arpeggio should be played over the entire feasible range of the saxophone beginning and ending on the tonic. Six scales will be played to low B, and six scales will be played to low B-flat (or A-sharp).

As good habits of finger coordination and proper embouchure are developed, tonguing is introduced. Practice should include a variety of articulations at various tempos and dynamic levels.

CARE AND MAINTENANCE OF THE SAXOPHONE

Daily care of the saxophone involves: (1) tipping it upside down to drain the excess moisture; (2) swabbing it with a soft, lint-free cloth for sanitation and to extend the life of the pads; and (3) wiping and drying the mouthpiece. Every few weeks the mouthpiece should be cleaned by running lukewarm water through it (hot water will warp it). Not advised is the use of a swab stick or a rough-surfaced object to pull the cloth through the mouthpiece because scratches or nicks on the interior of the mouthpiece can alter tone quality. A simple cloth such as the swab used by most clarinetists is fine. Dropping the mouthpiece can chip the facing. After each playing, the reed should be wiped off and put in a safe place to dry. To be avoided are the cardboard containers in which reeds are usually purchased. Metal or plastic reed holders are better but can damage the heart of the reed if handled carelessly.

The neckpiece tends to collect dirt faster than the lower part of the instrument. The end that fits into the body should be kept clean by wiping with a moist cloth. This makes a good fit easier, as does applying a very thin layer of cork grease to the metal surface. Two or three times a year the posts and pivots should be oiled, first loosening the rods to ensure a more even distribution of the oil. Pads should be checked periodically for air leakage by pulling a piece of lens paper gently through each closed key (if resistance is offered by the closed key it shuts sufficiently to form a seal), or shining a light in the instrument and examining for cracks of light from the closed key.

Periodically, the reed should be given a thorough cleaning with Dutch rush or garnet paper. Beginners should replace the reed every four to six weeks.

Bumper corks adjust the height of the key opening. Two important ones that tend to wear out are the tone hole above the first finger of the right hand for articulated G-sharp, and the forked B-flat fingering.

The exterior requires no particular care, although players who like a shiny surface will polish it with a soft cloth. Wiping off the fingerprints is sufficient.

To prevent damage to the instrument, one should replace the instrument plug when returning the saxophone to the case.

REEDS

Saxophone reeds are adjusted on the same basis as clarinet reeds. The resistance of the reed is the most important single factor to be considered. All saxophones are usually played with a number 2 or 3 reed. The player, the facing of the mouthpiece, and the reed itself vary, so any reed may be too soft or too stiff. If the tone becomes open, flat in pitch, and cuts out completely in the upper register, it is too soft. Other signs of an overly soft reed are these: The lower harmonic is heard when upper register notes are played, biting harder does not produce more edge to the tone, dynamic changes are difficult to produce, attacks tend to scoop, and releases drop in pitch.

For a guide to reed adjustment that presents excellent information in neat, accessible form, specifically for the saxophone but also applicable to the clarinet, the reader may wish to look at the chart in *The Art of Saxophone Playing*.[3]

TROUBLESHOOTING

EQUIPMENT

sticky pads

1. Moisture absorbed by pads. If pad is undamaged, dry by placing tissue paper or small piece of coffee filter between pad and tone hole and closing gently. As a last resort—apply a *slight* amount of talcum powder to pad, being careful not to get on the mechanism.
2. Bent rods. Have repaired by a competent repairperson.
3. Worn springs. Have replaced by a competent repairperson.
4. Pivot screws at end of rods may need oiling (usually these must be loosened to oil—oil sparingly then retighten).

pads not seating correctly

1. Leaking pads. Even if pads are in good shape, they usually cannot be heated and reset like clarinet pads; for a correct repair they must be replaced.
2. Bent keys or rods. Have repaired by competent repairperson.
3. Brittle or "scuffed" pads. Have replaced.

[3] Ibid., 29.

gurgling sound

1. Water has collected at the bottom crook of the instrument or in a tone hole. Dry with a swab.
2. Water in mouthpiece or neckpiece. Swab neckpiece; remove ligature and reed to dry mouthpiece.

TONE

squeaks

1. Worn pads or pads not seating correctly. Have pads replaced by competent repairperson.
2. Too much mouthpiece in mouth. Use less mouthpiece, practice playing soft attacks and decrescendos.
3. Unequal pressure on sides of reed (can especially occur when beginners hold instrument by their sides without adjusting neckpiece and mouthpiece). Correct holding position. If due to leaking pads see #1. under "pads not seated correctly" above.
4. Trying to articulate by biting and releasing reed with mouth. Correct articulation.
5. Inadvertently pressing side key(s). Correct holding position.

thin, pinched sound

1. Biting on mouthpiece. Drop lower jaw; push mouthpiece toward upper teeth.
2. Corners of mouth not pushing toward mouthpiece. Correct embouchure.
3. Not enough lower lip for cushion. Either not enough lower lip over teeth or lower lip is stretched too thin and needs to be "bunched-up" more, or both.
4. Mouthpiece entering mouth at too much of an angle. Hold bottom of saxophone farther away from body or tilt head downward slightly.
5. Not enough mouthpiece in mouth. Insert more mouthpiece, being careful not to put too much inside the mouth.
6. Throat too tight or oral cavity too tight. Drop shoulders. Practice "bending" or "lipping" notes as flat as possible—at least a full step—to open airstream. Keep tongue down except when needed to articulate.
7. Reed too soft. Try stronger reed or clip reed and scrape as necessary.

loud, wild harsh sound

1. Too much mouthpiece in mouth—makes it easier to play loudly. Use less mouthpiece—may require loosening or tightening the embouchure—practice very soft attacks and decrescendos on long tones to reinforce softer tone.
2. Too much lip over lower teeth (pull lip out—try to align the point where the red and flesh meet directly over the lower teeth).

3. Not enough pressure on reed from lower lip. Be careful not to encourage pressure from the jaw or teeth; ask student to tighten and direct muscular force toward reed.

4. Corners or upper lip too loose. Tighten corners and ask student to clamp lips together; upper lip should be firm and press against eye teeth.

5. Mouthpiece too open. Try another, more appropriate mouthpiece.

6. Reed too hard. Scrape reed or try a softer one.

uncontrolled sound

1. Cheeks puffing. Keep corners of mouth firm.

2. Upper teeth not on reed. Correct embouchure.

3. Embouchure too loose. Direct all muscular pressure from lips and surrounding muscles *toward* mouthpiece.

4. Corners of mouth not firm or smiling. Keep corners firm and direct toward mouthpiece.

5. Throat too tight or oral cavity too small. Keep tongue down except when needed to articulate. Keep shoulders down. Practice bending notes down a full step then back to pitch.

6. Too much mouthpiece in mouth. Correct position; try to align the point where the mouthpiece begins to curve away from the reed directly above the teeth.

7. Reed too hard. Try softer reed or scrape reed.

PITCH

flat

1. Reed too soft. Try harder reed or clip reed.

2. Embouchure too loose. Direct all muscular pressure from lips and surrounding muscles *toward* mouthpiece.

3. Saxophone held too far out so that mouthpiece enters mouth almost directly instead of at an angle. Hold head up or pull bottom of instrument toward body.

4. On individual notes: pads over tone holes too closed. Have adjusted by repairperson.

sharp

1. Biting on mouthpiece. Drop lower jaw and compensate by using more lower lip *pressure* against reed. Practice bending notes flat. Push or direct corners of mouth toward mouthpiece. Push mouthpiece up, toward reed. Try a combination of these.

2. Reed too hard. Try softer reed or scrape reed.

3. Mouthpiece at too much of an angle with embouchure. Hold bottom of saxophone away from body more, or tilt head slightly downward.

4. On individual notes: pads over tone holes too open. Have competent repairperson readjust.

REFERENCES

Texts

ARNOLD, JAY. *Modern Fingering System for Saxophone, Including the Register Above High F*. New York: Windsor Music Press, 1950.

BROWN, JOHN R. *How to Play the Saxophone*. London: International Music Publications, 1983.

EBY, WALTER. *Reed Knowledge*. New York: W. Jacobs, 1953.

———. *The Saxophone Embouchure*. New York: W. Jacobs, 1953.

FRIDORICH, EDWIN. *The Saxophone: A Study of its Use in Symphonic and Operatic Literature*. Unpublished doctoral dissertation, Columbia University Teachers College, 1975.

GEE, HARRY R. *Saxophone Soloists and Their Music, 1844–1985: An Annotated Bibliography*. Bloomington, IN: Indiana University Press, 1986.

HEMKE, F.L. *A Comprehensive Listing of Saxophone Literature*. Rev. ed. Elkhart, IN: The Selmer Co., 1975.

———. *Teacher's Guide to the Saxophone*. Elkhart, IN: The Selmer Co., 1975.

LONDEIX, JEAN MARIE. *Music for Saxophone: General Repertoire of Music and Educational Literature for Saxophone*. New York: Roncorp, 1985.

———. *125 Years of Music for the Saxophone*. Paris: Alphonse Leduc and Co., 1970.

OPPERMAN, KALMEN. *Handbook for Making and Adjusting Single Reeds for All Clarinets and Saxophones*. New York: Chappell, 1956.

RASCHER, SIGURD. *Top Tones for the Saxophone: Daily Embouchure Drills and Four Octave Studies*. New York: Carl Fischer, 1941.

RICHMOND, STANLEY. *Clarinet and Saxophone Experience*. New York: St. Martin's, 1972.

SNAVELY, JACK. *The Saxophone and Its Performance*. Uniontown, PA: Heritage Publishing Co., 1969.

TEAL, LARRY. *The Art of Saxophone Playing*. Evanston, IL: Summy-Birchard Publishing Co., 1963.

Journals

Saxophone Journal. Quarterly from the Saxophone Journal, Inc., P.O. Box 206, Medfield, MA 02052.

Studies

Easy—Beginning (elementary or junior high)

CALLIET, LUCIEN. *Method for Saxophone*, Book I (Belwin-Mills).

COUF, HERBERT. *Let's Play Saxophone* (Chappel Music).

EISENHAUER, WILLIAM. *Elementary Supplement Studies for Saxophone* (Alfred).

HEGVIK, ARTHUR. *Modern Course for the Saxophone*, Vols. 1 and 2 (Elkan-Vogel).

HETZEL, JACK. *Hetzel's Visual Method for the Saxophone* (Ditson Company).
HOVEY, NILO. *Daily Exercises for the Saxophone* (Belwin-Mills).
_____. *Elementary Method for Saxophone* (Rubank).
_____. *Practical Studies for Saxophone*, Vols. 1 and 2 (Belwin-Mills).
LINDEMAN, BEN. *Saxophone Made Easy*, Vols. 1 and 2 (Colin).
ROSSARI-IASILLI. *53 Etudes*, Vols. 1 and 2 (Southern Music).
ROUSSEAU, E. *Eugene Rosseau Saxophone Method*, Vols. 1 and 2 (Kjos).
SKORNICKA, JOSEPH. *Intermediate Method for Saxophone* (Rubank).
Medium (advanced junior high or high school)
DEVILLE, PAUL. *Universal Method for the Saxophone* (Carl Fischer).
FERLING, W. *48 Studies* (Southern Music).
HEGVIK, ARTHUR. *Modern Course for the Saxophone*, Vols. 3 and 4 (Rubank).
IASILLI. *33 Concert Etudes* (Carl Fischer).
KLOSE, H. *25 Daily Exercises for the Saxophone* (Carl Fischer).
LONDEIX, JEAN-MARIE. *Les Gammes Conjointes et en Intervalles* (Lemoines).
LOYON, ERNEST. *32 Etudes for Oboe and Saxophone* (Billaudot).
PARES, GABRIEL. *Scales and Daily Exercises for Saxophone* (Carl Fischer).
RASCHER, SIGURD. *Top-Tones for Saxophone* (Carl Fischer).
SELLNER, J. *Etudes*, Vol. I, Elementary (Robert Martin).
SMALL, J.L. *27 Melodious and Rhythmical Studies* (Carl Fischer).
TEAL, LARRY. *The Saxophonist's Workbook* (University Music).
VEREECKEN, B. *Foundation to Saxophone Playing* (Carl Fischer).
VOXMAN, HIMIE (ed. Gower). *Advanced Method for Saxophone*, Vols. 1 and 2 (Rubank).

Advanced (high school or college)

BOZZA, EUGENE. *Twelve Etudes-Caprices* (Alphonse Leduc).
CAPELLE, FERDINAND. *20 Grandes Etudes* (Alphonse Leduc).
CORROYEZ, GEORGES. *22 Pieces of J. S. Bach* (Billaudott).
DEVILLE, PAUL. *Universal Method for the Saxophone* (Carl Fischer).
FERLING, WILHELM. *48 Studies* (Southern Music).
GATES, EVERETTE. *Odd-Metered Duets* (Gornston).
KARG-ELERT, SIGFRIED. *25 Caprices* (Zimmerman).
LABANCHI, GAETANO (ed. Iasilli). *33 Concert Etudes* (Carl Fischer).
MASSIS, AMABLE. *Capriccio-Studies* (Alphonse Leduc).
MULE, MARCEL. *18 Etudes After Berbiguier* (Alphonse Leduc).
_____. *Enseignement for Saxophones* (Alphonse Leduc).
RASCHER, SIGURD. *24 Intermezzi* (Bourne).
SELLNER, JOSEPH. *Etudes*, Vol. I, Elementary (Robert Martin).
VOXMAN, HIMIE. *Selected Studies for Saxophone* (Rubank).

Jazz Materials (high school and beyond)

AEBERSOLD, JAMEY. *A New Approach to Jazz Improvisation*, over 50 vols. (Aebersold Music).
ARNOLD, JAY. *Jazz Styles for Saxophones* (Music Scales).

BAKER, DAVID. *Jazz Patterns* (Studio P/R).

————. *Techniques of Improvisation* (Studio P/R).

BERLE, ARNIE. *Complete Handbook for Jazz Improvisation* (Music Scales).

COKER, JERRY. *A Complete Method for Jazz Improvisation* (Studio P/R).

————. *Patterns for Jazz* (Studio P/R).

DIBLASSIO, D. *DiBlassio's Box Shop: Getting Started in Improvisation* (Kendor).

————. *DiBlassio's Box Shop: The Sequel* (Kendor).

GERARD, CHARLEY. *Improvising Jazz Saxophone* (Colin).

GIUFFRE, H. *Jazz Phrasing and Interpretation* (Associated Music).

HAERLE, DAN. *Scales for Jazz Improvisation* (Studio P/R).

HEJDA, T. *Selected Studies and Jazz Compositions* (Polskie Wydawnictwo).

LACOUR, G. *100 Dechiffrages Manuscripts* (Billaudot).

LA PORTA, JOHN. *Developing Sightreading Skills in the Jazz Idiom.* (Frank).

————. *A Guide to Jazz Phrasing and Interpretation* (Frank).

McGHEE, ANDY. *Improvisation for Saxophone* (Colin).

NIEHAUS, LENNIE. *Basic* (and *Intermediate* and *Advanced*) *Jazz Conceptions*, Books
    1 through 3 (Colin).

————. *Jazz Improvisation for Saxophone* (Colin).

PARKER, CHARLIE. *Charlie Parker Omnibook* (Atlantic Music).

REEVES, SCOTT. *Creative Jazz Improvisation* (Prentice-Hall).

VIOLA, J. *The Technique of the Saxophone*, Vols. 1 through 3 (Berklee Press).

SAXOPHONE
FINGERING CHART

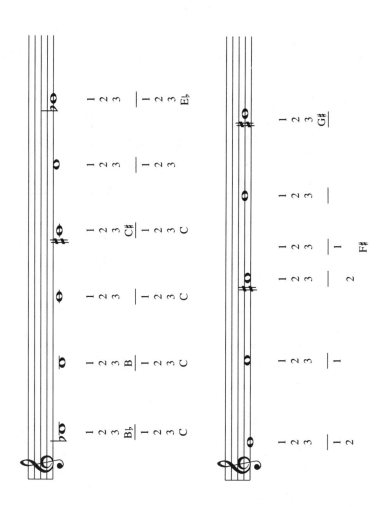

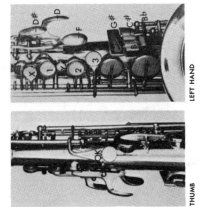

LEFT HAND

THUMB

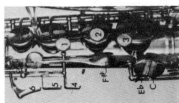

RIGHT HAND

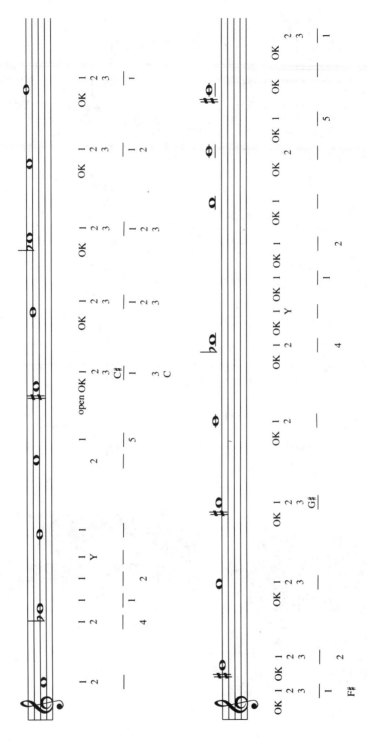

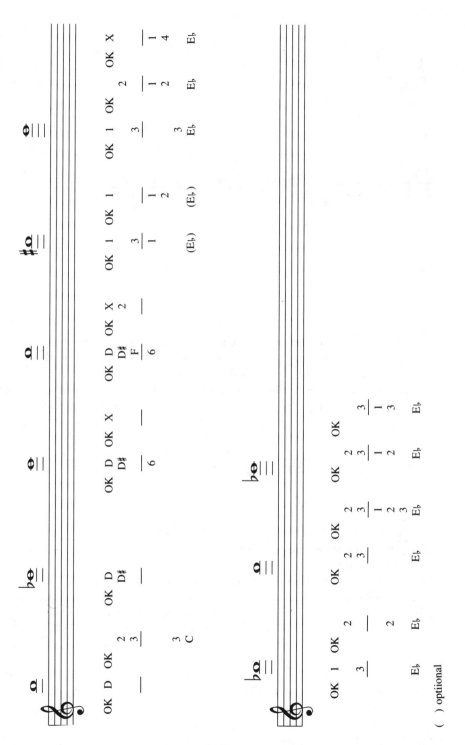

15

Principles for Brass

All brass instruments produce a sound from a vibrating column of air set in motion by the lips. All brass instruments play pitches based on the overtone series and are fitted with mechanical means to play a complete chromatic scale. With the exception of fiberglass used for some sousaphones and the plastic trumpets that were a short-lived fad in the early 1970s, all brass instruments are constructed of a brass alloy.

CONICAL AND CYLINDRICAL BRASSES

Brass instruments can be divided into two classes: those constructed primarily with a cylindrical bore and those constructed of tubing that is almost completely conical throughout its entire length. The cylindrical instruments have a slightly conical-shaped leadpipe (the first section of tubing, before the tuning slide, into which the mouthpiece is inserted) and an exaggerated conical shape forming the bell; roughly two thirds of the total length, however, is cylindrical. Conical-shaped brass instruments have a taper that expands from the mouthpiece to the bell, but about one third of the tubing is cylindrical (the section comprised of tuning and valve slides must be cylindrical so the slide can move for pitch adjustments). The section of greatest difference is in the taper of the leadpipes. Many professionals compare the tone quality of conical brasses to a floodlight and the tone quality of the cylindrical brasses to a spotlight; the acoustical difference is that a conical-shaped standing wave eliminates several of the upper partials from each pitch, resulting in a less brilliant sound than that produced by cylindrical brass instruments. A more rapidly flaring leadpipe enables a brass player to fluctuate the speed of the air more easily—which enhances flexibility. A cylindrical leadpipe necessitates a more constant speed of the airstream, so that flexibility is slightly more difficult or one loses control over intonation just prior to, or after, lip slurs. As a result, flexibility may initially be easier on cornet than the more cylindrical trumpet.

Both classes of brass instruments are available in soprano, alto, tenor, and bass voicings. Although primarily by tradition, the standard full orchestra has utilized two from each family in its brass section.

SELECTING THE INSTRUMENT

One important consideration with all brass instruments is bore size. A medium- or medium-large–bore instrument is the most popular and offers the most immediate success and satisfaction for students, teacher, and parents. The common recommendation that beginners should select small-bore instruments is erroneous. Small-bore trumpets or cornets and trombones may enable the student to produce an initial sound with less effort, but only because the student does not have to breathe properly in order to produce the tone. Small-bore instruments are easily overblown, so that the beginning player finds it more difficult to produce a good tone. The obtained sound is distorted and can be difficult to correct.

At the advanced and professional levels, the size and material of the bell is a matter of concern. The standing wave that produces the sound in a brass instrument is established by the reflection of the pressure wave originating at the embouchure; because this wave is reflected by the change of air pressure created at and by the bell, it is critical to the instrument's tone quality.

The flare of the bell can make a perceptible difference in tone quality. A larger bell is normally indicative of a more flaring bell. The greater flare has the effect of damping the upper partials, thus creating a "darker" tone quality. Less flare tends to project the upper overtones perceptible to the audience. Consequently, the darkest tone is produced by an instrument that has a small bore but a large bell—the more disproportionate this relationship is, the "darker" the sound (e.g., the horn).

Table 15–1. Brass: The Two Classes of Brass with Those Most Commonly Used in the Orchestra Indicated by an Asterisk

Register	Cylindrical	Conical
soprano	trumpet*	cornet
alto	alto horn, mellophone	horn*
tenor	trombone*	euphonium
bass	sousaphone	tuba*

THE BEGINNING STUDENT

Many brass methods, teachers, players, and texts list physical characteristics necessary to learn a brass instrument. Some of these authorities recommend that the teacher inspect a child's teeth, lips, fingers, jaw, arms, hooves, and so on, before allowing her to start a brass instrument. In reality, *interest* is the primary criterion. The only characteristic of the child that the teacher can truly count on is that she will change. Furthermore, all body parts are going to change at differing rates. Any student who has physical characteristics markedly different from the norm should be guided toward that instrument for which she seems suited. Undoubtedly, if Louis Armstrong had started band under the guidance of many band directors, he would have played bass drum. It is often said that Armstrong had the natural embouchure for string bass.

Although some famous trumpet players have suggested that all they do is screw up their lips and blow, there are helpful guidelines for most players. The following suggestions are for starting a student on a brass instrument.

1. Wet the lips, then with the lips alone (and keeping the teeth apart) produce a puttering sound like a child imitating a motorboat. Increase the "speed of the motor" by tightening the corners of the mouth to produce a buzz. Watch for excessive puckering. If buzzing is difficult and the tendency is to "flop" the lips "like a horse," curl the lips under more (so that less red of the lip is showing) and place them closer together. Practice the buzzing until it comes naturally, feels easy, and can be sustained for several counts. At this point, place the mouthpiece lightly to the lips, avoiding any pressure other than the minimum amount necessary to seal off escaping air.

    Some teachers advocate first buzzing with the lips then with the mouthpiece for a week or two before the instrument itself is used. Since this requires unusual patience on the part of the student, this approach is not generally advisable.
2. Place the lips together as if saying "em" (this keeps the teeth apart), firm the corners, add the mouthpiece, and blow until a sound is produced. The student should be cautioned not to pull the mouthpiece back into the lips, but to let the airstream make the sound. Excessive pressure against the lips will prevent them from flexing to change pitches. Excessive pressure is a natural tendency for the beginner, as he is using facial muscles in a different manner than he has before. Unfortunately, excessive pressure is among the more common bad habits for brass players and is the primary reason for poor upper register playing among students at all stages of development. Excessive pressure is usually a symptom of some other problem such as embouchure or air pressure.

3. Have the student gently blow into the instrument without tightening the lips, as if "sighing," then very gradually bring the lips closer together, firming the corners until a pitch is produced.
4. Place the mouthpiece against the lips and release a burst of air into the mouthpiece while simultaneously making a "toe" or "tah" syllable (depending on the instrument) with the tongue touching the roof of the mouth near the teeth. Try the same procedure with the mouthpiece inserted into the instrument.
5. If none of the above helps produce a sound on the mouthpiece, the teacher has several alternatives: (1) Try a brass instrument with a larger mouthpiece, (2) let the student blast to produce the initial sounds, (3) try a woodwind, string, or percussion instrument, (4) send the student to the soccer coach. Brass playing is a vigorous physical activity; in some cases what feels like blasting is exactly what may be required. Blasting is *never* advocated, but it may be worth trying when all other means fail, especially if the term *blasting* conveys the concept of blowing a fast airstream.

When the student can consistently produce a tone with each attempt, he is ready to experiment with raising and lowering pitches by tightening and loosening the corners of the mouth. Playing short melodies with just the mouthpiece is valuable embouchure training; it is also fun, and helps the all-important development of the ear.

EMBOUCHURE

The correct brass embouchure consists of a lip position that uses the muscles to produce both a smile and a pucker. The pucker-type embouchure and the smile-type embouchure both have many successful advocates. Since individuals differ in facial structure, the safest way to help a student develop a correct embouchure is to have her close her mouth, and while keeping the mouth relaxed with the lips touching together (the teeth remaining apart) she should then firmly tighten the corners of the mouth without stretching her lips to a smile (that is, leaving the corners of the mouth where they are and flexing them). The corners of the lips are held tightly (which results in a flat chin), and the center of the lips will be loose enough to vibrate the outgoing stream of air and to maintain the vibration with the continued flow of air. Lip tension is adjusted by slightly tightening or loosening the strongest muscles in the face, those at the corners of the mouth (the corners of the mouth do not clamp on anything but themselves). The process works somewhat like a "zip-lock bag" in that the aperture at the center of the embouchure is closed by tension moving from the outside of the lips toward the inside. The chin is kept flat. This position makes it virtually impossible to puff out the cheeks.

When the velocity of the airstream is increased to play higher pitches, lip tension also must be increased to prevent the greater air pressure from blowing the lips open. The lips vibrate more rapidly when the airstream moves more rapidly. Tension at the corners of the mouth makes the aperture smaller while retaining a similar shape. Initially, students should be encouraged to produce a higher pitch by simply tightening the corners of the mouth or lips. Tightening the corners of the lips will result in the "zip-lock bag" effect, making the aperture at the center of the embouchure smaller but keeping a similar shape, thus increasing the speed of the air and producing a higher sound—*only* if there is no pressure from the mouthpiece against the lips. By "thinking" higher and lower pitches, the player can increase and decrease the speed in much the same way a singer produces higher and lower pitches.

The smile embouchure advocated by many brass players since it initially seems more natural tends to produce lips that are stretched to produce higher pitches, with a resulting thin sound. The pucker-type embouchure creates tension in the center of the lip, which needs to be free to vibrate. The type of embouchure changes the shape of the aperture, which affects tone quality between registers.

The proper embouchure, lips placed together and corners of the mouth tightened, provides a fleshy cushion in the center of the lips that vibrates when the airstream passes through it. The student should experience a sensation of the corners of the mouth gripping slightly while the center almost bunches forward toward the mouthpiece.

Every effort should be made to center the mouthpiece on the lips horizontally and vertically. Though there are many opinions regarding the vertical placement of the mouthpiece, most teachers prefer to have equal amounts of each lip vibrating for trumpet and tuba, and more of the upper lip on the mouthpiece for horn and trombone. A mouthpiece rim or embouchure visualizer is helpful in checking the mouthpiece placement.[1]

When one third of the upper lip and two thirds of the lower lip show from the outside, the placement is closer to half-and-half on the inside of the cup. The lip structure will affect the placement somewhat. If the upper lip is fuller, the mouthpiece may be positioned slightly higher on the lip; if the lower jaw recedes, the mouthpiece will be positioned a bit farther down. The lower jaw should be exactly beneath the upper jaw, with the incisors aligned, making the lower jaw jut out in such a position that it sends the column of air almost directly into the mouthpiece, neither excessively upward nor downward. Most students need to be encouraged to move their lower jaw forward.

Protruding teeth do not affect horn and lower brass embouchures unless they exceed the range of normalcy. For trumpet embouchures,

---

[1] Many mouthpiece manufacturers produce a device that consists of a rim (without the cup or shank) attached to a steel rod or handle. This "visualizer" can be "played" like a brass mouthpiece and allows the teacher to visualize what is normally hidden inside the cup.

however, even moderately protruding teeth may create problems. Although beginning players are encouraged to center the mouthpiece both vertically and horizontally, a slight drift to one side or the other may occur with students who have uneven teeth; this drift should be no cause for alarm. The teacher must maintain a careful watch, however, to make sure the drift does not extend to the point where the mouthpiece placement becomes detrimental to the player.

For most brass players, the direction of the air changes in different registers (more so with larger mouthpieces)—generally, the higher the register the more downward the air is directed and vice versa. The embouchure remains basically the same, but there is a slight shifting of pressure from one lip to the other depending on the register. Upper and lower lips and teeth do not remain perfectly vertically aligned as the lips move into these slightly different positions. The head or the instrument may be pivoted just enough to transfer pressure from one lip to another. The direction of the airstream in conjunction with the degree of lip tension and air speed determines the pitch. In addition, the tongue directs and governs the size of the airstream through the embouchure (generally, articulations such as "doe" are used in the lower registers and articulations such as "dee" in the upper registers; these two vowel sounds require different placement of the back of the tongue but use the same consonant for the beginning of the note).

Both range and dynamics affect the size of the embouchure opening, the embouchure becoming smaller for higher notes and softer tones. Players who resort to a pucker for the lower register and a smile for the higher notes usually experience tension and fatigue. A more satisfactory solution seems to lie in pivoting, that is, in changing the position of the lower lip, since it is not as crucial in producing the "buzz." Pivoting can also be accomplished by raising or lowering the lower lip by rolling it in and out, or in extreme cases, by slightly lowering the jaw.

If the teeth are sufficiently apart, it will be easier to get the right feeling in the lips. One pedagogue says that for trumpet playing the lips should form a small oval resembling the opening of an oboe reed. Beginning players may misinterpret this and open the lips too much, but the visual image of the opening of an oboe reed can help students in properly forming their lips. For the higher brass, the opening is so small that it can hardly be felt by the player but can be seen with a mouthpiece visualizer. An embouchure that is too open is hardly better than one that is too closed, that is, when it allows the air to "spread" and the sound to lose focus. The tone produced by a too-open embouchure will be soft and hollow with no center or resonance; the resulting tone is airy or "fuzzy" sounding. When the embouchure is too closed, articulations will usually be very explosive and the tones choked. For the higher brass, the right opening may be achieved by asking the student to think of the difference in his lip formation between "m–m–m–m" and "f–f–f–f," when the latter is as closed as he can get it (with emphasis on the lips, not on the teeth). For the larger brasses, the opening is greater. Here the ear is the best judge.

A beginning player with a good embouchure who practices every day should develop enough muscle strength to achieve a good tone in six to eight weeks, if not sooner. Practicing in front of a mirror is an excellent way for the student to check his embouchure, mouthpiece placement, position for holding the instrument, and general posture.

Embouchure Faults

Too much mouthpiece pressure is the most destructive fault among trumpet players. Pressure affects the quality of tone, flexibility, and range. When the left hand pushes the mouthpiece into the lips, the sound will be thin and hard with little breath support, or massive and hard with forced breath support. Pressure should be only enough to create a seal between the instrument and the lips. An illustration in *The Art of French Horn Playing* shows the author playing the horn as it is resting on the mantelpiece; his only point of contact with the instrument is his lips on the mouthpiece.[2]

Herbert L. Clarke was famous for his apocryphal stunt of hitting high C with the horn suspended from the ceiling by a string. It serves as a superb illustration of the belief that no mouthpiece pressure was necessary anywhere in the range of the instrument.

Avoiding excessive mouthpiece pressure is also important in building endurance. Pressure restricts the flow of blood to the lips, causing them to become numb and tire quickly. Remove the mouthpiece from the lips at every opportunity, and increase the amount of air. Insufficient air is a cause of mouthpiece pressure, as the player makes her lips vibrate by pulling the mouthpiece back into the lips rather than by relying on an adequate flow of air to create the lip vibration. Research completed in the 1980s indicates that the "best" of brass players do increase mouthpiece pressure with ascending range, especially on the lower lip—but obviously not to the extent that the muscular ability for the lips to vibrate is impaired or the blood circulation hampered.[3]

The player should feel as though the air is pushing the mouthpiece away from her lips rather than pushing them into the mouthpiece. When she pushes her lips into the mouthpiece (pucker), she will attack notes below pitch and scoop upward toward the center of the pitch. The tone will likely be stuffy and dull. The player's lips should have the sensation of being nearly flat across the mouthpiece, not in it. If a correct embouchure is used, the center of the lips will not tire with extended practice, whereas

---

[2] Philip Farkas, *The Art of French Horn Playing* (Chicago: Clayton F. Summy Co., 1956), 66.
[3] John Booth Davies, Patrick Kenny, and Joe Barbenel, "A Psychological Investigation of the Role of Mouthpiece Force in Trumpet Playing" *Psychology of Music* 17 (Nov. 1, 1989), 48–62.

excessive pressure will fatigue the center of the lips. Brass players cannot develop satisfactory tone or range unless they *let* their lips vibrate naturally and properly, which means the center of the embouchure is relaxed. Only the muscles at the corners of the lips should ever become tired.

A more relaxed embouchure is allowable with the lower brasses although tuba players must be careful to prevent the embouchure from "caving in."

Beginners often produce a strange, pinched sound, for which the cause is not readily apparent. A pinched sound may result from keeping the jaws too closed or bringing the teeth too close together. It may be caused by a lack of breath support; the player squeezes her jaws together to keep the pitch up. To get the jaws separated properly, have the student hold a long tone while slowly raising and lowering the lower jaw and carefully listen for the position that gives the best sound. Although one authority says the teeth (not the lips) should be about the width of a nickel apart, the distance between the jaws will clearly differ for the trumpet and the tuba player.

Air in the cheeks will cause the lips to stretch at the center, preventing the muscles at the corners of the mouth from working properly. The smile embouchure will have the same result as air in the cheeks, stretching the center of the embouchure so a good tone is impossible.

Frequently a player starts a session with a good embouchure but in the course of playing shifts the mouthpiece up or to the side. This shifting occurs naturally with many young students who have not developed their embouchure muscles. As portions of the lips begin to tire or become irritated from constant contact with the mouthpiece, the mouthpiece will slip to a new position. As the embouchure develops, the mouthpiece will always fit into the same "grooves" nicely and comfortably. One of Louis Armstrong's unique traits as a trumpet player was his ability to play for hours seemingly without embouchure fatigue. Scholars have observed that this phenomenon was due to his having developed several embouchures. When he felt fatigue setting in, he moved the mouthpiece to a different spot. This may have contributed to the rather unsatisfactory timbre he produced. Arnold Jacobs has demonstrated this ability without notable loss of tone quality.

ENDURANCE

Herbert L. Clarke said that "endurance is 90 percent of cornet playing." On any brass instrument, endurance is the prize for practicing regularly and correctly. As a result of hard work and their natural gifts some performers have unbelievable staying power. Many more are barely warmed up before they are all through for the day. A majority of the brass players believe that endurance and range are the two most difficult aspects of performance. Both require physical and mental skills that are developed over relatively long periods of time.

A student who uses heavy pressure should endeavor to break the habit by relearning the fundamentals of tone production and proper breathing, and temporarily limiting his playing range. An exercise is to support the instrument by balancing it on the thumbs instead of grasping it, or to use the left hand to support the instrument under the valve casings; if undue lip pressure is used, the instrument will slide away from the lips. Daily practice in playing with very little pressure should help the player break bad habits and develop the habit of playing with only the minimum amount of pressure necessary for a clear sound.

Careful practice is practice alternated with rest. The temptation is to do all the practicing at once, but shorter practice sessions spaced out during the day are preferable. The worst scenerios are those in which students who do not practice all week plan to make up for it by practicing four or five hours Sunday afternoon. Those five hours equal one hour of focused practice plus four hours of frustration. During any practice, the brass player should remove the mouthpiece from his lips and rest a few seconds whenever he feels more than a slight strain. Most published exercises do not warn the player to rest after a few lines, with the result that students often force themselves to play an entire exercise regardless of how tired their lips and embouchures are.

The periods of rest can be spent in relaxing the body or in mentally hearing the musical exercises on the page—audiation. The student can test himself by playing the exercises after hearing them mentally, then judging how accurately they were heard. Such "games" incorporated into the warm-up and practice sessions also help improve the ear.

Performance anxiety is also a common cause of poor endurance. Brass performers who do well in rehearsal may find themselves unable to complete the same task under performance conditions. This failure often has to do with the player's inability to concentrate on the right things; if one's mind is focused on the music and the fundamental aspects of brass playing, the tendency to use less air and more mouthpiece pressure will be reduced. Confidence enables the performer to relax and to keep her embouchure set and use the available air more efficiently; correct breathing also helps prevent performance anxiety. A lack of confidence results in loss of mental control over the physical responses to the performance stimuli: physical tension, shortness of breath, and improper use of the embouchure. Teachers should concern themselves with development of the mental as well as physical attributes that enhance endurance.

Increased endurance and the development of a correct embouchure depend on intelligent and conscientious practice. Control and flexibility, so necessary to the brass player, are gained by careful practice.

WARM-UP

Leading brass players agree that the daily warm-up is one of the most important activities of their practice routines. Although the warm-up affects the instrument itself (pitch), its essential purpose is to condition the player in much the same way the athlete's "daily dozen" keeps her in condition—the warm-up increases blood circulation throughout the body and especially the embouchure. For beginning brass players, the warm-up is an embouchure-training exercise. The muscles used in brass playing must be loosened every day before placing the strain of actual performance on them, gently awakening the lips rather than an abrupt reveille. The warm-up not only conditions the muscles for playing, but helps the player coordinate other physical processes before he starts to practice.

As an athlete's calisthenics help her loosen up before a game, they are also building stronger muscles for future endeavors. Similarly, the brass player's warm-up routine is also a muscle-building session that will result in good tone, breath support, tonguing, endurance, flexibility, control, good intonation, and range—in short, almost all the desirable elements of beautiful playing. The word *routine* is important, since the warm-up is a daily process, not a spasmodic occurrence. Furthermore, it must be directed toward a goal and not simply be a mindless series of licks. Individual routines differ, but most include the following daily review, all of which are usually considered essentials: work on long tones, lip slurs, tonguing, finger exercises, and intervals, played in various registers and at various dynamic levels.

Also of importance is the "warm-down." When players have been playing in the upper range for an extended period or exerting physical demands on their embouchure, playing a few warm-up exercises in the low range relaxes the lips to prevent stiffness from occurring, in much the same way that adults exercise to avoid that "morning-after" stiffness. The most common warm-down is to play softly in the lowest register of the instrument (including pedal tones for more advanced players) with *frequent periods of rest* (the mouthpiece off the lips) between short exercises.

Long Tones

Long tones are essential. They provide a daily test of steady breath support, aid endurance, and offer a way to listen for and improve tone quality and intonation. Sustaining a tone without any quiver, wobble, shake, or pitch change is one of the most difficult tasks for a brass player and is attained primarily through the regular, sensible warm-up. When the student can control the long tone, she knows she is making progress. Sustained tones are an excellent way to coordinate breathing action with playing different tones at different dynamic levels throughout the entire register. The player should concentrate on producing and *projecting* an intense tone regardless of how soft the dynamic level is.

Students should strive for a well-focused, centered sound and accurate intonation. The student should also use long tones to improve concentration and listening ability. Long tones can be part of the student's practice period, not simply limited to the warm-up. Like everything else, long tones can be overdone and must be practiced in moderation. Too much time spent in playing long tones, especially those in the upper register, can stiffen the embouchure and limit flexibility.

The electronic tuner can increase the value of the practice of long tones. Playing long tones with the best possible sound and watching the tuner for intonation will help develop aural skills. Use of the tuner (and the ears) while crescendoing and decrescendoing is also excellent for improving intonation.

Lip Slurs

Lip slurs are the technique of changing pitches within a harmonic series by adjusting the embouchure only, without changing slide position or valve combinations. Students should practice lip slurs in all registers, beginning each day with the middle register and gradually extending to the upper and lower registers. Lip slurs help strengthen the important muscles of the embouchure and help coordinate breathing with embouchure change. If lip slurs are difficult for the player to perform successfully, the problem may be caused by (1) failure to maintain a steady stream of air, (2) unconsciously making a break between the two notes of the slur, (3) not enough flesh of the lower lip in the mouthpiece to start the slur, (4) failure to increase the air speed necessary for a higher pitch on the overtone series—often resulting from student's confusion between the speed of the air and the amount of air—and (5) failure to contract the muscles at the corners of the mouth for the upper tone—if there is no contraction, there will be no increase of tension and the increased speed of the airstream will blow the aperture of the embouchure too open. The airstream must increase in speed to slur upward cleanly, and slow down to slur downward; for most beginners this is accompanied by a change of dynamic level from piano to forte and the reverse. As students develop, they should be encouraged to include in their warm-up the use of lip slurs that get softer when moving upward and crescendo when moving downward. Lip slurs are helped by arching the tongue (which can be demonstrated by having a student whistle and "slur" from a low pitch to a high pitch—this can be done only with the tongue), and by moving the lower lip in and out.

CONTROL

Lack of control is such a hazard for brass players that additional ideas must be added to those already given. In the good old days, a trumpet player was judged by his ability to whip through such favorites as the "Carnival of Venice," "Emmett's Lullaby," and the "Grand Russian Fantasia." Today, with the increasing appeal of serious music, amateur performers are required to play what once was left to more advanced groups. The requirements for the "Carnival of Venice" and the trumpet part of a Beethoven symphony are vastly different, but both make serious demands on the performer. The former, with all its flourishes and runs, looks more difficult, but it is just as difficult to play the symphonic part. To play a few isolated notes in various registers with perfect control may be more difficult than to play music that requires dazzling technique. The first measure of Wagner's *Rienzi* Overture may frighten more trumpet players than any solo in the literature. The following suggestions, when used regularly in the daily warm-up, can help in achieving control.

1. Practice single attacks. Learn to play any scale or arpeggio one note at a time, removing the instrument from the lips after each tone. Then preface each single attack with one, two, or three articulated grace notes. Try to acquire the ability to play any pitch in the playing range at any level of volume in any style in tune. This procedure helps develop a "memory" of how the embouchure should feel for various pitches.
2. Practice intervals from any given tone. For instance, begin on second-line G and play a major second, a major third, a fourth, and so on. Practice ascending intervals, descending intervals, and sequences of thirds, fourths, fifths, sixths.
3. Write out a series of unrelated tones and practice them daily. Refer to Farkas's *The Art of French Horn Playing*[4] for an example of this kind of study. Similar studies are available in various books.
4. Work on tones that seem difficult to play accurately. For instance, fifth-line F or G-sharp is difficult on many trumpets.
5. Keep a record of your progress. Try to make fewer mistakes the second time through an exercise. Learn to practice critically. Players who habitually miss dozens of notes in their daily practice sessions are always at a loss to understand why they miss dozens of notes in a performance. Herbert L. Clarke relates that he hadn't actually been aware of his inaccurate playing until the day a friend commented on the large number of errors he heard.[5] He revised his practice habits and became the most famous cornetist of all time.

[4] Philip Farkas, ibid.
[5] Herbert L. Clarke, *How I Became a Cornetist* (St. Louis: Joseph Huber, 1934), 50.

FLEXIBILITY

Many players lack the flexibility to slur upward. Others get the upper note by using an unmusical burst of air. Excessive pressure reduces flexibility and contributes to the difficulty of slurring. These players pull the mouthpiece back into the lips. This use of pressure is not entirely wrong, but it should not be used as a crutch to overcome slurring difficulties.

Occasionally the trumpet or horn player must execute a lip trill. The lip trill is nothing more than a fast lip slur usually between notes a whole tone apart.

RANGE

It isn't easy to develop a good high range. The young player always hopes to find a secret that will suddenly empower her to soar flawlessly into the upper registers. Whereas a major scale can be practiced sufficiently in one evening to be played very fast, learning to play high notes takes a great deal of time and progress is usually slow. A good high register results from the combination of good embouchure and a solid airstream, developed through practicing sustained tones and lip slurs in a comfortable register at medium volume. As strength develops, the range and dynamic level may be extended.

High tones are produced by coordinating the breath, lips, and tongue, not by violent physical exertion. The corners of the mouth must be held firmly together to increase tension; the more developed these muscles become the greater is their ability to contract. The player must tense the corners of his mouth with the feeling that the corners of his lips are pressing against his teeth. He must exhale with greater abdominal pressure to increase the speed of the airstream. His tongue should be raised or arched as if forming an "ee" sound—the arch is in the middle of the tongue, not at the back. Tightening or tension in the back of the tongue will close the throat. The lower lip must not be allowed to collapse into the mouth over the lower teeth or behind the upper lip. For the high range, the lower jaw will often rise somewhat so that the lip and teeth opening becomes smaller. Some horn players hold the head back to alter the angle of the flow of air entering the mouthpiece; a more acceptable alternative is to draw the lower lip back so that it is *slightly* under the upper lip, keeping the lips together, and sending the stream of air downward. The brass player using the pivot system does the same thing. For the upper limits of the range, suddenly expelling the air with greater speed will help produce the higher pitches. Students attempting to increase their upper range should play softly in that register—this approach aids the student in distinguishing between the speed and the volume of the air. Even a very soft, slight squeak (played with little mouthpiece pressure) is fine at first; a baby crawls before it walks and walks before it runs.

Learning to play in the high register demands practicing in the high register, but accompanied by care, frequent rest, and alternate practice in the low register. Playing in the high register is developed gradually by adding one step at a time and playing as high as possible without excessive mouthpiece pressure. Progress may be inconsistent, but over a period of time the range will be extended. One cannot maintain a correct embouchure for the high range without strong facial muscles. The higher the notes, the greater the air pressure—muscles must be able to retain their position against it. With insufficient strength, the player will blow open her lips and the corners of her lips will tire quickly.

ARTICULATION

As the term is defined in most dictionaries, articulation is how sounds are connected, that is, not only how a sound is started but how it ends. This definition is important since many wind players are adept at starting a pitch using the tongue, but far too many use the tongue to end the note. Many instrumental music teachers take the time to teach students how to start a note, but fewer teach them how to end one. Use of the tongue to end a note not only results in an unpleasant sound but handicaps the player in fast passages or long, soft, tapered phrase endings.

Brass players may learn in the earliest stages of their music instruction that notes can be started and stopped without any use of the tongue. Unfortunately, they may also learn that high notes can be played by blocking the embouchure with the tongue, building up excessive air pressure behind it then quickly removing the tongue, resulting in a very explosive and unmusical yet fairly high sound. Proper use of the tongue for articulations should be learned before these gross and unpleasant sounds become a substitute for correct upper-register pitches. Too early a demand is placed for upper-register pitches arrangements used by high school marching and jazz bands.

For attacks, the tongue is used merely to clip off the "wind sound" at the beginning of each tongued note (i.e., the milliseconds between the point that the air is released and the point that a standing wave in the instrument produces a tone). Beginning brass players should be introduced to tonguing first by having them start pitches without the aid of the tongue while trying to make the note "speak" as quickly as possible after releasing the air. Next, they should experience the difference in tongue placement when vocalizing: "tuh," "duh," "thuh," and "kuh" (used in double-tonguing, but used here to demonstrate various ways one can start a tone). While tongue placement for the vowel sound is the same for each of these syllables, the tongue is used differently for each of the consonant sounds (the vowel "ah" is often used, but because it involves movement by the jaw it can lead to associating jaw movement with tonguing. Use of the "oo" sound may be more appropriate for trumpet and horn players while "oh" is most frequently used by low brass. The tip of the tongue touches the teeth the farthest forward on "thuh," and the middle of the tongue touches the roof of the mouth for "kuh."

The cleanest beginning of each note is achieved by letting the tongue touch the roof of the mouth just behind the upper teeth. Some students will have better success if they use the syllable "duh," since it is slightly less explosive than "tuh," although every brass player will eventually face an articulation that requires an explosive attack.

The tongue stays out of the way when the player is inhaling and during the actual time the tone is being produced. It rises very quickly, touches the roof of the mouth where the consonant "d" is vocalized, then quickly returns to the bottom of the mouth (as if vocalizing "uh"). Teachers must be careful in working with students who choke off the airstream; too much emphasis on keeping the tongue at the bottom of the mouth can result in tension and poor articulations. In general, students should be directed to keep the tongue relaxed and to tongue using the least amount of tongue movement. If teachers emphasize the appropriate vowel sound in vocalizing exercises and melodies, the tongue will respond properly. The rule of thumb (or tongue) is that the shorter the distance the tongue must move, the greater the control, the quicker it can move, and the less fatiguing rapid and prolonged passages will be.

Most pitches are stopped *only* when the air is stopped; they should not be stopped abruptly with the tongue except for many jazz articulations. One of the most difficult concepts for a beginning brass player to understand is that notes are connected unless the music indicates something different. The words in this sentence are printed with spaces used to separate them; when vocalized or read aloud, however, the words run together and the vowel sounds are articulated by consonant sounds. Students must understand that notes in a musical phrase are analogous to the vowel sounds when speaking and are separated when tongued only by the consonant used at the beginning of each note, a sound which quickly disrupts the airstream. In very fast passages, the tongue starts and stops tones with the same motion.

The most difficult note for most brass players is the first one, the attack. Starting the note exactly when desired, with exactly the right sound and on pitch, is no easy task for a beginning brass student—and few professionals consider the attack an easy task. A good attack requires the lips, air support, brain and tongue to be perfectly coordinated and synchronized. If any one of these four factors is off, the result will be less than musical. A common problem among eager young brass players is to position the tongue at the "ready" position; this procedure builds up air pressure and results in an explosive attack. Comparing the tongue's movement with a fine symphonic percussionist striking a note pianissimo on a timpani is a useful analogy.[6]

A second common articulation problem is for students to hold the air until time to play the note. Holding the air prior to an attack will guarantee tension in the throat, neck, and chest and make it difficult to "restart" the airstream with control. To counter this habit, the mouthpiece should be placed on the lips (which should be relaxed and completely at rest), the breath taken through the corners of the mouth "around" the mouthpiece and released with *no* hesitation. At the instant the air is released, the lips form the proper embouchure for the desired pitch (from memory), and the tongue moves to touch the area just behind the top teeth. The placement of the tip of the tongue must be the same for the same style articulation whether the note is loud or soft, and regardless of register. The player should blow *through* the note, not just *at* it; golfers and musicians refer to this concept as *follow-through.*

The adjustment of the lips from a position of rest to a correct embouchure for any given note is accomplished in milliseconds. Practice and more practice will develop the player's memory to dictate exactly how the embouchure should feel for a particular pitch at a particular dynamic level. Students who attempt to set their embouchure too early prior to attacking a pitch will usually set for a pitch higher than the intended one. The brain, over a period of time, will learn how to set the embouchure for the desired pitch and dynamic level.

Important to all wind players is speed of tonguing and evenness of rapid tonguing. Students should see, through demonstration, that taking a proper breath and vocalizing "duh, duh, duh, duh" will result in no movement in the face or jaw. If the students blow or vocalize as if playing a long tone and repeat "duh," the tongue will slightly and properly disrupt the air flow without stopping the air.

When controlled and accurate tonguing becomes a habit, and as demands in the music require, the student can gradually be introduced to the variety of articulations used by brass players. Syllables such as "luh, luh, luh" are appropriate and commonly used for legato passages; "tuh, tuh, tuh" is often used for marcato passages. Brass players (and flute players) also have the advantage of being able to easily double- and triple-tongue.

Double-tonguing is done by "rocking" the tongue so that the tip alternates with the middle of the tongue in touching the roof of the mouth: "tuh–kuh, tuh–kuh" or "duh–guh, duh–guh" (Figure 15–1). In learning multiple tonguings it is much easier to vocalize these syllables than to use

[6]Keith Johnson, *The Art of Trumpet Playing* (Ames, IA: Iowa State University Press, 1981), 108.

Figure 15–1   Stages for Double-Tonguing

them in playing an instrument. The student should practice by starting a long tone, then very slowly articulate that pitch over and over by placing the tongue in the positions for the consonants "duh–guh" (unfortunately, at such a slow tempo there is no "need" to double tongue). This exercise should be repeated slowly until the articulations become even sounding, which may require separate practice just on the "guh" syllable, and flow easily. The tempo should be increased gradually.

Only when the student begins to feel comfortable with the task of double-tonguing and a moderate to fast tempo is achieved should use of the valves be added to the task (Figure 15–1, second exercise). Finally, difficult passages may be introduced that require much greater coordination of lips, tongue, embouchure, and also the fingers (third exercises). Each of these types of exercises should be single-tongued, then practiced only using the "guh" articulation, then slowly double-tongued, striving for evenness and a good tone quality.

In triple tonguing, the tongue makes a somewhat circular motion, repeating "tuh–duh–kuh, tuh–duh–kuh." Again, the same technique of starting slowly and gradually increasing speed and accuracy is used; this technique is followed by stages of adding valves, then the actual coordination of the embouchure, tongue, air, and fingers together.

Brass teachers may find that other series of syllables work well for triple-tonguing and seem to be more natural for some players. The syllables most experienced teachers agree are not useful are "tuh–kuh–tuh, tuh–kuh–tuh." "Tuh–kuh–tuh" seems natural for many students who learn to double-tongue first, and try to add another "tuh" after the double-tongued notes, but these syllables make it virtually impossible to play the notes evenly.

Multiple tonguings should be introduced only after the brass player can consistently single-tongue smoothly, cleanly, evenly, and accurately. Younger students have many aspects of brass performance to practice; yet multiple tonguings must be learned before the actual need for them arises. As it takes at least several months to become proficient at double- or triple-tonguing, the player should be introduced to these articulations in the year before the high school ensemble, with its more demanding literature, is encountered. Multiple tonguings are a required weapon in every brass player's arsenal of articulations; to wait until the literature requires them is too late.

Slurring is moving from one note to another without breaking or disrupting the airstream (with the possible exception of trombone playing). Valve slurs are more common than lip slurs and are executed by keeping the air moving and changing the valve combinations or slide positions. Common problems with valve slurs and slide adjustments include trying to adjust the embouchure too much, not moving the valves or slide quickly enough, and not blowing *through* notes but *at* the notes. As with lip slurs, young students frequently have difficulty blowing a fast airstream without blowing more air. This error causes the lips to blow open, thus making upward slurs difficult or impossible. The student should be encouraged to keep the corners of his embouchure tight and tighten them further when slurring upward without pinching or stretching the corners of the mouth.

TONE

Plenty of wind (air) and a strong embouchure are essential for good tone quality on all brass instruments. The quality of tone is also affected by the physical properties of the equipment itself: (1) the size of the rim, cup, and throat of the mouthpiece; (2) the shape of the tubing within the instrument; (3) the relationship of the cylindrical to the conical part of the tubing; (4) the shape of the bell; and (5) the thickness of the walls of the tubing. Embouchure and the student's physical condition also affect breath support and the resulting tone.

A fuzzy tone is common among both beginners and more advanced players. A common cause is improper mouthpiece contact with the lips, which can result from:

1. Too little or too much mouthpiece pressure.
2. Too much saliva.
3. Lips tired or swollen from overpractice.
4. Improper pivoting.
5. Tonguing in the wrong place within the mouth.
6. An uncentered mouthpiece.
7. Lips that are sensitive or sore for any of a variety of reasons.
8. Weak muscles at the corners of the mouth.
9. The vibrating parts of the lips being too dry.
10. Trying too hard.

Other factors in fuzzy tone production may include any of the following: the aperture of the embouchure is too large; the mouthpiece may be unsuited to the lip, teeth, and jaw structure of the player; the instrument or mouthpiece is dirty; the player isn't breathing properly—shown by puffed cheeks or bulging veins and muscles in the neck; the player's tongue may be at the wrong level, usually too high; the player's sloppy posture may be inhibiting the flow of air or causing him to use wrong muscles; the valves of the instrument are worn or leaky, a worn cork is on the water key, a tube connection has loosened; the player may be overcompensating for an instrument tuned too sharp; the player's head may be held too far forward, causing the throat to contract; or the player may try to keep his teeth together while playing. A player may produce a dark, stuffy tone by pursing his lips too far into the mouthpiece (usually identified by a bunched-up chin), a thin tone by doing the opposite (identified by the corners of the mouth stretched toward the ears).

Another common detriment to good tone is the presence of rattles and obvious overtones (a "doublebuzz," especially with low brass players). These are almost invariably due to involuntary lip vibration brought on by performance fatigue. Performance fatigue and its corollary, lip fatigue, often appear in overenthusiastic beginners who want to do more than they are physically able to do. Fatigue is caused by:

1. Failure to warm up.
2. Too many high notes for the player's embouchure development.
3. Fortissimo playing without proper warm-up.
4. Too much practice on one type of exercise or too much playing without resting.
5. Too much mouthpiece pressure.
6. Reversing the natural pivot or over-pivoting.

7. A shifting mouthpiece due to improper seating or moving about when breathing.
8. Improper tonguing.
9. Chin or lip vibrato rather than more preferable types.
10. Too frequent change of mouthpieces or instruments when the player must double on one or more instruments (rare).
11. The skipping of a proper warm-down the previous day or playing session.

A thin tone may be due to one or a combination of several things:

1. Too shallow a cup or too small a throat on the mouthpiece.
2. Placing the mouthpiece too low on the embouchure, which will produce a thin tone especially on the horn and trombone and be more noticeable in the low register.
3. Playing above the tonal center to gain the proper intonation on a flat instrument.
4. Blowing improperly.
5. Aperture of the embouchure too small or too flat.
6. Using a smile-type embouchure.

A repeated grunting sound may sometimes occur. Grunting sounds are often due to lack of proper breathing, a tight throat, placing the tongue too high in the mouth, or breathing from the chest rather than allowing for a full, natural breath.

A tight or constricted throat is the most common culprit in producing a thin, strained, or fuzzy tone. The most common analogy, used by many teachers, is for the student to feel a yawn sensation when playing. The following exercise to help open the throat should be included in the intervals warm-up: This exercise consists of playing long notes (such as whole notes) starting on an open or first position note (i.e., no valves used) in the most relaxed and comfortable register of the instrument, then lipping the note down as far as possible without its cracking, then lipping back to the starting pitch. After a brief rest (several seconds), the player repeats the passage and attempts to lip the pitch down even farther. The object is to open the throat. While playing the exercise, the student feels and hears the difference an open throat and lowered jaw make; this sensation can then be simulated while using the valves.

This technique will be successful *only* if plenty of air is used. Students may close and tighten the throat to compensate for a lack of air. Assuming that the throat is relaxed, opening the throat is actually done by lowering the back of the tongue and raising the soft palate.

Brass players have other weaknesses in common: faulty intonation, lack of sustaining power (especially with the higher brass), muddy articulation, uncertainty and inflexibility of attack, failure in dynamic control, and dry mouth. The teacher whose students have these problems need not feel unique; these are problems to be expected but not neglected. Cotton-mouth, in which the dryness in the mouth is so great that a satisfactory sound cannot be produced, is caused by nervousness, an overdosage of medicines such as cold remedies, bad diets, or playing too soon after eating.

INTONATION

There is no such thing as an instrument that is perfectly in tune. Keyboard instruments are tuned to the tempered scale, a compromise to make per-formance in all keys feasible, and one to which we have become accus-tomed. Wind instruments are not exactly in tune with the tempered scale and must be played in tune through careful listening and pitch adjustment.

Two of the primary factors in intonation of a brass instrument are (1) the harmonics of the overtone series and (2) valve combinations. As stated earlier, every note produced on a brass instrument has overtones that can be made to sound instead of the fundamental by tightening the corners of the mouth and increasing the speed of the air. The overtone series, being a "natural" phenomenon, does not conform to the rules of the tempered scale; certain pitches are higher or lower than their equivalent in the tempered scale. In relation to the tempered scale, partials five and ten are somewhat flat; partials seven, eleven, thirteen, and fourteen are severely flat; and partials three and six are sharp. When these partials are used, the player must make pitch corrections to play in tune with other instruments using the tempered scale. The fingerings commonly used by valved instru-ment players are suggested specifically to avoid these partials or to compen-sate for out-of-tune partials.

When valved instruments are constructed so that the notes played with a single valve are in tune, notes played by the valves in combination are not in tune: valve combination 1–2 is a little sharp, combination 1–3 is quite sharp, and combination 1–2–3 extremely sharp, by at least a quarter step. To counteract this intonation problem, the valves are not constructed exactly in tune with each other; the third valve slide is a little too long (when used alone it produces a flat note), but it compensates for the sharpness of combination 1–3 and 1–2–3. The compromise leaves combi-nation 2–3 a bit flat on some instruments, but makes 1–3 and 1–2–3 more tolerable, though still sharp.

Nearly all instruments are made so that the slides must be pulled slightly to be in tune. The tuning slide should be pulled, and for the valved instruments all the valve slides may be pulled, especially those of the horn. The general rule is to pull the first slide twice as much as the second, and the third slide three times as far as the second. This tuning is useless unless the player listens and uses the embouchure to make fine adjustments when playing. Many trumpets and cornets are designed with a ring on the third-valve slide, which is adjusted by the ring or middle finger on the left hand. Other brass instruments use a fourth valve, and the trombone has a trigger. Most professional-line and many middle-line trumpets have similar devices on the first-valve slide.

Pitch normally rises for brass instruments during playing due to the warming up of the instrument and rising temperature in the hall. These same conditions may cause piano and string instruments to go flat. The player may go sharp from muscular constrictions and tension of embouchure (especially when compensating for fatigue), throat, or tongue, or a combination of these. He may go flat because of nervousness or inadequate breathing. Performance anxiety affects brass players' pitch in different ways. Mutes tend to sharpen the pitch (they in effect shorten the tubing). Brass instruments often go flat in cold temperatures; for example, in a marching band, and the larger the instrument the greater the change in pitch due to weather extremes.

The brass player can alter pitch by changing the position of his lips or tongue, the direction of the airstream, or the amount of air pressure. The general rules are these: To raise the pitch, tighten the muscles at the corners of the lips; arch the middle of the tongue slightly by thinking "ee," as though moving to a higher register; increase the amount of air pressure (using the abdominal muscles) to increase the speed of the airstream; focus the airstream at an angle rather than straight into the mouthpiece. To lower the pitch, loosen the muscles at the corners of the lips; lower the tongue and jaw by thinking the syllable "aw," as though moving to a lower register; in the lower registers, direct the stream of air down into the mouthpiece. In the higher registers any angling of the airstream will sharpen the pitch, but in the low register a downward direction of the air can help flatten the pitch.

Students must be taught to listen for pitch discrepancies and taught how to fix them.

Good intonation is the result of accurate listening *and hearing*. The student should practice with a tape recorder and work with small ensembles, as all group work on chorales, scales, and intervals can improve a player's ability to hear accurately. Good tone quality goes hand in hand with good intonation; each enhances the other and both are required for outstanding performances.

DYNAMICS

After good tone quality, the factor that can most enhance the music is dynamic control. The player who has developed the complete dynamic range from pianissimo to fortissimo approaches professional standards.

Whereas the amateur often has little besides an ear-shattering fortissimo and an ever-present mezzoforte, the professional seems to have every graduation from a whisper to a *sforzando*, all produced with a consistently fine tone.

Dynamic control depends on breath support and control, a responsive and flexible embouchure. Powerful tone requires more air, soft tone requires less air. To develop volume, the student practices inhaling a large amount of air and getting rid of it rapidly. To play softly, she inhales the same amount of air, but exhales it more slowly, making it last for a much longer time, and increases her control to avoid wavers, quavers, and bends. More muscular control is necessary for soft playing; more embouchure control is necessary for loud playing, as an increase in the air pressure tends to force the lips open.

To maintain a pianissimo tone, the lips should be relaxed and close together, the throat open and relaxed, and the air blown with intensity as a small, thin, steady stream. If the lips are too far apart the tone may break. The ability to attack and sustain a note played pianissimo can be developed by practicing whole notes as softly as possible and alternated with whole rests. The player should remove the mouthpiece from her lips on each rest and make a fresh start for each tone. A common problem in playing softly is the tendency to "hold onto" the air, even on soft passages. The tone must be projected and constant air support maintained. A valuable mental concept is to project the soft note to the back of the auditorium.

Various articulations at a fortissimo dynamic level should also be part of the daily routine. The only muscles that should work harder in fortissimo are those used for breathing. One good practice approach is to play exercises at several dynamic levels: mezzoforte, pianissimo, and fortissimo. A valuable exercise involves attacking a note as softly as possible, crescendoing to as loud as possible with a good tone quality, then gradually decrescendoing and fading to silence, holding the pitch steady. Practice on such exercises increases the two extremes of the exercise with improved control: softer and softer attacks, a fuller and fuller fortissimo, and softer and more controlled tapered phrase endings.

THE MOUTHPIECE

The mouthpiece on a brass instrument influences intonation, tone quality, and response, and it is a factor in accuracy and endurance. In short, the mouthpiece is probably the single most influential factor among the physical aspects of brass playing. Fortunately, mouthpieces are sturdy. If the player finds one that pleases him, he has it forever. Finding the right one can be a problem, as the mouthpiece can cause half-a-dozen playing faults. Professionals may try and discard literally dozens of mouthpieces before settling on one.

Even the very best mouthpiece will not solve all playing problems. The wisest course of action is to select a good mouthpiece from a reputable manufacturer, one that has been recommended by an expert, then develop the embouchure for that mouthpiece. The reason to change a brass mouthpiece is more often physical growth than a stronger embouchure.

The dimensions of most mouthpieces are identified by number and letter. The same numbering system is *not* used by the three most popular manufacturers, so it is necessary to give both size and brand name when speaking of mouthpieces. With the Bach and Giardinelli, the low numbers indicate a larger cup diameter as measured across the inner edge of the rim, (a Bach 3 is larger than a 7), whereas the opposite is true for Schilke numbers. The depth of the cup is indicated by a letter. The Bach A cup is the deepest, models without letters have medium-deep cups. Bach B cups are medium deep but slightly more lively than the unlettered cup, and the C cup is medium shallow.

There are four critical areas to consider in selecting a mouthpiece. They are the rim, cup, throat, and backbore (see Figures 15–2, 15–3, and 15–4).

The Rim

A medium-wide rim offers good flexibility without cutting off blood circulation to the lips. A wide, flat rim provides greater endurance by spreading the pressure from the embouchure toward the mouthpiece over a greater area, but at the expense of flexibility and accuracy. Rounded outer and

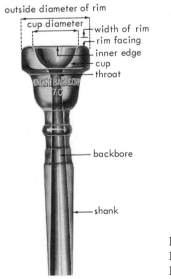

outside diameter of rim
cup diameter — width of rim
— rim facing
— inner edge
— cup
— throat

backbore

shank

**Figure 15–2 Mouthpiece for Brass Instrument
Photo furnished through the courtesy of
H. & A. Selmer, Inc.**

SCHILKE MOUTHPIECE
LABELING SYSTEM

Example:

9C3c (trumpet mouthpiece)

9   refers to the CUP DIAMETER
        Smallest numbers have smallest
        diameters

C   refers to the CUP VOLUME
        A. Small Cup
        B. Medium-small
        C. Standard (medium size)
        D. Medium-large
        E. Large

3   refers to the RIM CONTOUR
        1. ⌒ Roundest
        2. ⌒ Semi-round
        3. ⌒ Standard
        4. ⌒ Semi-flat
        5. ⌒ Only slightly rounded

c   refers to the BACKBORE

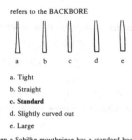

        a   b   c   d   e

a. Tight
b. Straight
c. Standard
d. Slightly curved out
e. Large

When a Schilke mouthpiece has a standard backbore, rim and cup only the cup diameter (first number) is shown on the mouthpiece. In the example above only the #9 is necessary to identify the mouthpiece because the 'C' is the standard cup volume, '3' is the standard rim, and 'c' is the standard backbore. Whenever measurements differ from the standard sizes, the alterations are shown on the mouthpiece.

**Figure 15–3   Schilke Mouthpiece Labeling System.
Chart furnished through the courtesy of Schilke Music Prod. Inc.**

inner rims reduce the amount of flat surface coming in contact with the lips, tending to reduce endurance but enhancing flexibility. Wide-rimmed mouthpieces coupled with a round rim and a large cup diameter may result in a poor high register and less lip flexibility.

The rim of the mouthpiece may have a fairly sharp inner edge, often called a "bite"; a rounded inner rim will give more comfort, but at the expense of control of articulation and accuracy. Of the two most popular brands of brass mouthpieces, Bach and Schilke, probably the most significant difference is that Bach mouthpieces have more bite than Schilkes. On the horn, a sharp bite facilitates clean attacks but hinders the production of clean slurs; a rounded rim produces the opposite effects.

The Cup

Vincent Bach recommends the use of the largest possible cup diameter, since the player is then forced to use her lip muscles correctly rather than pinching out the high tones. A narrow and shallow cup favors the upper harmonics, producing a sound that is thin, shrill, and almost nasal. If the dimensions are both shallow and small, the tone is choked, hard, and stuffy, and a good tone is hard to produce (although it may be easy to get "a sound"). A deep, big cup gives increased volume and tone in the low and middle registers, but carried to extremes results in a dull, unfocused tone. The smaller sizes are recommended for players who have weaker embou-

Size
indicated by model numbers

LARGE CUP DIAMETER
A large cup produces a large volume and reduces the risk of cracking tones.

SMALL CUP DIAMETER
A small cup requires little strength. It limits the tone, and also inhibits embouchure development.

Depth
indicated by model letters

SHALLOW CUP
The shallow cup, designed for brasses in high keys, also makes it easier to play in the high register.

DEEP CUP
A deep cup improves the tone, especially in the lower register.

Shape
described in model listings

WIDE RIM
A wide rim increases the player's endurance, but limits his flexibility.

NARROW RIM
A narrow rim helps players who must cover a wide range of pitch.

ROUNDED RIM
Crooked teeth may require a rounded rim contour at the expense of clean low-register attacks.

SHARP RIM EDGE
A sharp inner edge on the rim produces a brilliant metallic tone, and makes attacks more reliable.

Figure 15–4 Brass Mouthpiece Cups and Rims

Diagram used courtesy of Schilke Music Products, Inc.

chures. In short, the deeper the cup, the darker the sound, and usually the more difficult the upper range.

With the horn, true euphonium, and tuba mouthpieces, the shape of the cup from the rim to the bore can be nearly straight or only slightly bowl-shaped. The bowl-shaped cup will produce a somewhat darker and more resonant tone; the straight will result in a less resonant but smoother, lighter tone. This difference is caused by the angle of the edge where the cup joins the throat.

The Throat

Tone quality is also determined by the size of the throat opening in the mouthpiece. Larger throat openings enable the player to produce a darker or more mellow sound and to play louder without overblowing or distorting the tone; at the same time the larger throat often reduces control at softer dynamic levels. A large throat demands more muscular strength in the embouchure and greater endurance. Small-sized throats make the sound more brilliant and make playing in the upper register easier, but the sound usually becomes more and more shrill as the range is extended upward. For the average player, a mouthpiece with a large throat is not recommended because her lips are not in shape for long hours of playing.

The Backbore

The backbore of the mouthpiece must be related to the instrument as well as to the size of the rim, cup, and throat. If the backbore is small, notes in the high register can usually be played more easily but tend to be stuffy; if too large, there is insufficient resistance in the instrument, resulting in poor endurance and airy, spread tones. Most mouthpieces are made with medium-sized bores for average players. The standard Schilke mouthpiece is made with a larger backbore than the Bach; the Bach is often bored out by advanced players.

General Considerations

The best mouthpiece for beginning students is a compromise of all the available sizes in the four parts of a mouthpiece; that is, a medium-sized cup with a standard rim on a medium-sized throat and backbore. As the student develops his embouchure and the teacher observes the player's strengths and weaknesses, a mouthpiece can be selected to help remedy any weaknesses that cannot be remedied by good playing habits.

Students who have a tendency to play with excessive tension and a squeezed tone and cannot seem to relax the sound may benefit from a mouthpiece with less resistance. Conversely, those with a tendency to overblow may be helped by a more open mouthpiece. Split tones or a strident, thin sound are often a sign of too small and too shallow a mouthpiece.

After the student has chosen a mouthpiece, he should stick with it. There is no such thing as a mouthpiece that will make a poor player into a good player.

CARE AND CLEANING

All brass instruments accumulate a certain amount of dirt and grease. Brass instruments can be washed by pouring warm (not hot), soapy water through them, followed by a rinse in clear water to remove all the soap. Running clear, warm water through the instrument every few days is recommended. The outside should be dried with a soft cloth. Piston valves and slides should be removed to clean them. When using a swab, the student should be certain the metal end is covered with a soft, lint-free cloth to prevent scratching the soft valve casings. The valves must be handled carefully because even a tiny bump can cause them to jam. The valves and valve casings should be carefully wiped without the fingers touching them, since dirt, perspiration, and acid from the hands slow valve action. After cleaning, the valves are returned to the instrument with the numbers of the valves matching the numbers of the casings. Valve slides (*not* trombone slides) should be slightly lubricated with petroleum jelly or slide grease.

Most of the dirt accumulates in the mouthpiece and leadpipe. A small flexible brush or cloth along with lots of warm water should be used to clean these areas regularly. The leadpipe can be cleaned by removing the main tuning slide and using a flexible brush and flushing with water. Placing the mouthpiece in boiling water may be necessary if it is extremely dirty. When mouthpieces become stuck in the horn, they may be extremely dirty, the student may have driven the mouthpiece in with his hand, the horn may have been dropped, or the shank may be bent. If the mouthpiece does become stuck, it should not be removed by force, tugging, or wiggling it back and forth. Almost any repairperson can recite tales of expensive damage to instruments at the hands of well-meaning but uninformed students and parents. The use of a mouthpiece puller or the services of a repairperson are required. Proper preventive actions will eliminate this problem altogether. The player should remove the mouthpiece when he is through playing and keep the mouthpiece and receiver clean.

The tuning slides can become as firmly stuck as the mouthpiece, due to a copper precipitate that builds up or to dirt and sludge resulting from saliva passing through the horn. Removing the slides often and keeping them greased eliminates this problem. If a slide becomes stuck, one can sometimes loosen it by inserting a handkerchief or belt through the tubing and exerting pressure. This move failing, it is best to call a repairperson, who has special equipment to loosen these slides.

Daily care is important. The valves must be kept oiled, but too much oil can cause dirt and sludge to accumulate more quickly. Saliva, although effective, should not be substituted for oil, because it is injurious to the valves and contains acids that in time will corrode the valve or casing. One way to oil a valve is to pull the first-valve slide and allow the oil to run through, working the valves up and down and removing the excess oil from the third-valve slide. The valve casing can be cleaned with a chamois cloth. The valve itself should not be cleaned by an amateur; if it is, a lintless paper such as a coffee filter can be used without causing damage.

Another aspect of daily care is to wipe the instrument free of perspiration and finger marks each time it is played. Hand guards made of plastic or leather are available to protect the valve casings against acids from the left hand. A cloth should be used to wipe off the remainder of the instrument. Instruments can be relacquered by a competent repairperson or by returning to the factory.

The dirt that tends to accumulate in the small ports in the valves can be removed by drawing a small cloth through the ports. The cleaning rod should not be used for this purpose as there is danger of denting the valve casings where the star aligns the valves. This dirt can be removed with a toothpick. Threads on caps should be kept clean to ensure their easy removal when needed. The felt at the top of the valves becomes worn and must be replaced occasionally, as is also true of the corks on the valves.

New instruments should be flushed with warm water before they are used, otherwise dust that has worked its way into the instrument during packing and shipping may cause damage to valves or valve casings. Running a small amount of oil through the leadpipe will keep the acid in the saliva from producing a slimy copper precipitate inside the tubing. New valved brass instruments require frequent cleaning and reoiling of the valves until for a three-day period no trace of dirt or grime has appeared on the valves.

The student should not be carrying school books or the day's lunch in the instrument case. If the case has a special compartment, it should be used for accessories such as valve oil, cleaning equipment, lyre, and mutes. All these accouterments should be secure and out of contact with the instrument, for even the smallest dents on the mouthpiece or the shank will affect intonation and tone quality. All braces should be kept soldered to prevent weakening the instrument when held and to prevent the possibility of a buzzing sound caused by the vibration of the instrument.

Sodas, candy, or other sugary foods should never be put in the mouth when playing. Sugar in the instrument can cause valves to stick. Rinsing out the mouth, or better yet, brushing one's teeth, before playing will promote cleanliness of the instrument.

The instrument should never be picked up by grasping the valve slides or a tuning slide. The resulting leverage could spring the slide or even cause a slight buckling of the valve casing near the slide. When this happens, the valves will drag against the warped casings. The instrument should be picked up by grasping it around the valve casings.

Most instrument retailers now offer parents who rent instruments a maintenance contract for a nominal fee. For students who play trombone this is a wonderful option. Beginning trombone students are going to dent their slides regardless of how careful they try to be. Most maintenance contracts cover repair of the instrument.

ACOUSTICAL CONSIDERATIONS

Although more detailed and technical explanations are available, a brief description of the acoustics of brass instruments may be useful for clarifying any misconceptions that future instrumental music teachers may have regarding the family of brass instruments. Although there are many students who would prefer to go to the dentist than read this section, understanding how brass instruments work may enhance one's ability to teach brass players and help diagnose those problems that are due to faulty equipment and those problems that are due to a "faulty" player . . . as well as how the two complement each other in producing music.

A standing wave in a brass instrument is created by exciting the enclosed air column with a steady stream of tiny bursts of air. These tiny bursts of air are created by the performer opening and closing his lips very rapidly (appearing to buzz the lips) and are controlled by the mouthpiece. This air passing through the lips is needed to resupply the vibrating air inside the instrument, since to a large degree friction and to a lesser degree the air projected from the bell produce a damping effect.

The bursts of air pass through the mouthpiece and create a pressure wave inside the brass tubing where air molecules push against each other traveling longitudinally through the horn (as opposed to transverse motion when a violin string is plucked). The longitudinal pressure wave is kept in motion by a stream of tiny bursts of air at an appropriate frequency or speed.[7]

The change of pressure at the bell of a brass instrument causes this pressure wave to be reflected back toward the mouthpiece. Only a slight amount of air escapes the bell of a brass instrument; this phenomenon can

[7] Arthur H. Benade, *Fundamentals of Musical Acoustics* (New York: Oxford University Press, 1976), 406.

be observed by placing one's hand over the bell of a brass instrument being played at a high pitch and at a very loud dynamic level. Pressure waves start at the player's lips, travel through the tubing, are reflected at the bell (by the change in air pressure), and travel back to the player's lips, where the waves are resupplied with air (energy). The resulting waves are called *standing waves*.

If a trumpet player produces air bursts at the speed corresponding to the fundamental resonant frequency of her instrument, the longitudinal sound (or pressure) wave would be twice the length of her trumpet (or a wavelength about 10 feet long). The wave would start at her lips, travel through the instrument, and be reflected at the bell (a point at which longitudinal motion is reversed, called a node). From the bell, it would return to the lips, where it is "recharged" with new bursts of air and sent to the bell again (making one complete wavelength: from the node at the bell back to the node).

Since the lips are more pliable than the reeds used by woodwind players, brass players have more control over the frequency of the tiny bursts of air than do woodwind players. The brass player can create greater tension in her lips to produce a stream of air bursts at twice the fundamental frequency and a new resonant frequency will be heard. This frequency, twice that of the fundamental, is present when the fundamental is played and now becomes the primary pitch that is heard.

As tension is increased or decreased in the lips, the frequency of the tiny bursts of air is increased or decreased. While the buzz sets the air inside the trumpet in motion and also serves to sustain the pitch, the vibration of the pressure wave inside the trumpet (at its resonant frequency) in turn helps the lips buzz at the proper frequency. Students who buzz at a frequency *exactly* between resonant frequencies will get absolutely no sound (which is almost impossible to do . . . intentionally); those who buzz slightly closer to one resonant frequency or the other will splatter or "scoop" the note, but the vibration inside the instrument will help the lips vibrate at a proper speed.[8]

Since the pressure wave inside the brass tubing helps the lips vibrate at the proper speed, brass players are prone to miss the initial attacks in performance. The first tiny bursts of air are sent through the instrument, but the lips must wait for the wave to be reflected at the bell before the pressure wave and lips work together to lock into the desired pitch.

Embouchure adjustment becomes a more serious problem when a musical passage requires frequent and rapid changes between partials.

---

[8] Arthur H. Benade, *Horns, Strings, and Harmony*, 29–39, and *Fundamentals of Musical Acoustics* 94–110; Charles A. Culver, *Musical Acoustics*, 4th ed. (New York: McGraw-Hill, 1956), 156–160; James H. Winter, *The Brass Instruments: Performance and Instructional Techniques* (Boston: Allyn and Bacon, 1964), 3–5; Earle L. Kent, ed., *Musical Acoustics: Piano and Wind Instruments* (Stroudsburg, PA: Dowden, Hutchingson, & Ross, 1977), 180–90.

Only experience and practice can develop the kinesthetic skill required for the brain to set the lips in a position close to that necessary to obtain the desired pitch.

Many students suffer from the misconception that the buzzing of the lips is the actual sound and that the brass instrument actually serves as some sort of amplifier. If this were true, then brass instruments would produce a tone quality considerably less than pleasing and brass choirs would rank somewhere behind the local Shriners' Oriental Band in aesthetic appeal.

REFERENCES

ANDERSON, PAUL G. *Brass Ensemble Music Guide.* Evanston, IL: The Instrumentalist Co., 1978.

BACKUS, JOHN. *The Acoustical Foundation of Music.* New York: W. W. Norton, 1969.

BAINES, ANTHONY. *Brass Instruments: Their History and Development.* New York: Scribner's, 1978.

BELLAMAH, JOSEPH L. *A Survey of Modern Brass Teaching Philosophies.* San Antonio, TX: Southern Music Co., 1976.

————. *A Survey of Teaching and Playing Methods of Leading Brass Authorities.* San Antonio, TX: Southern Music Co., 1961.

BENADE, ARTHUR H. *Fundamentals of Musical Acoustics.* New York: Oxford University Press, 1976.

————. *Horns, Strings, and Harmony: The Science of Enjoyable Sounds.* Garden City, New York: Doubleday, 1960.

Brass Anthology. Revised edition. Northfield, IL: The Instrumentalist Publishing Co., 1980.

FARKAS, PHILIP. *The Art of Brass Playing.* Rochester, NY: Wind Music, 1962.

FOX, FRED. *Essentials of Brass Playing.* Enlarged edition. Pittsburgh, PA: Volkwein Brothers, 1978.

HAZEN, MARGARET, AND ROBERT HAZEN. *The Music Men: An Illustrated History of Brass Bands in America: 1800–1920.* Washington, DC: Smithsonian Institution Press, 1987.

HUNT, NORMAN. *Guide to Teaching Brass.* 3rd ed. Sacramento, CA: W. C. Brown Co., 1984.

JOHNSON, KEITH. *The Art of Trumpet Playing.* Ames, IA: Iowa State University Press, 1981.

KENT, EARLE, ed. *Musical Acoustics: Piano and Wind Instruments.* Stroudsburg, PA: Dowden, Hutchinson, and Ross, 1977.

LEIDIG, VERNON F. *Contemporary Brass Technique.* Hollywood, CA: Highland Music Co., 1960.

LIGDEN, JOHN S. *Physics and the Sound of Music.* New York: Wiley, 1977.

SCHILKE, RENOLD O. *The Acoustics of Inner Brass and the Acoustical Effects of Various Materials and Their Treatment.* Chicago: Schilke Music Products, n. d.

SEVERSON, PAUL, and MARK McDUNN. *Brass Wind Artistry: Master Your Mind, Master Your Instrument.* Athens, OH: Accura Music, 1983.

RASMUSSEN, MARY. *A Teacher's Guide to the Literature of Brass Instruments.* Durham, NH: Brass Quarterly, 1964.

REINHARDT, DONALD. *The Encyclopedia of the Pivot System.* Rockville Center, NY: Belwin-Mills, 1964.

SWEENY, LESLIE. *Teaching Techniques for the Brasses.* Rockville Center, NY: Belwin-Mills, 1953.

WEAST, ROBERT. *Brass Performance: An Analytical Text of the Processes, Problems and Technique of Brass.* New York: McGinnis and Marx, 1965.

WINTER, JAMES H. *The Brass Instruments: Performance and Instructional Techniques.* Boston: Allyn and Bacon, Inc., 1964.

16

The Horn

HISTORY

The horn has been in use throughout Europe and Asia for more time than one would care to imagine—probably about thirty centuries, give or take a few. For all except the last three of these its existence had little to do with music. The ancient "shofar" of Biblical times was used for war and worship; the nearer relative found in the Middle Ages was used for battle and for hunting. The latter was high pitched and brilliant, even raucous, and was carried over the shoulder. The jagertrommet was one of the earlier hunting horns; the trompe de chasse was a later development of French origin that came somewhat closer to the modern horn with its more tapered conical bore, a wider bell, and longer tubing. The waldhorn, the German version of the trompe de chasse, was admitted to the orchestra at the end of the seventeenth century. Lully had used the horn as early as 1664 in the opera *Princess d'Elide*, but for color effects rather than as a real musical instrument.

The characteristic that hindered the use of the horn in the orchestra was not so much its tone quality as its incomplete scale. Having no valves or keys, it was limited to those pitches that could be produced by lip alterations above the fundamental tone. To increase its pitch possibilities, crooks were added around 1718.

Hampel's revolutionary contribution was the use of the hand in the bell. With the hand in a variety of positions in the bell, Hampel could not only mute the tone somewhat, but could change the pitch being produced, thus increasing the pitch flexibility of the instrument. During the latter eighteenth and the early nineteenth century, the hand horn was popular and had achieved its most beautiful tone and appearance. The valved horn was introduced in the early nineteenth century and soon replaced the hand horn, though the latter was still played until the end of the century. The variety of crooks were discarded, and gradually the F horn predominated over those in other keys. As orchestral music demanded increasingly greater power and higher range, the B-flat horn was thought to be the solution, especially for first and third horn parts with their higher tessitura. About 1900, the German firm of Kruspe produced the first double horn, designed to have the advantages of both the F and the B-flat horns.

Musically, the life of the horn began in the late Baroque period in Germany; Keiser used it in an opera in 1705. Bach made much of it, and Handel's writing for the horn is so characteristic as to be almost a trademark. In France, Rameau used it in his 1749 opera *Zoroastre*.

These composers usually used two hand horns. Beethoven added a third horn in his Third Symphony. In the Ninth Symphony, he added the fourth, and composers after him wrote for either two or four, depending on their musical objectives. Schumann was one of the first composers to recognize the advantages of the valved horn.

In spite of the excellence of mass-produced horns, many professionals prefer a horn that has been made for them by a skilled craftsman.

SELECTING THE INSTRUMENT

F Horn versus B-flat Horn

At the outset, the prospective horn player is faced with a choice of which horn to play. There are three horns to choose from, all equally legitimate and all widely used. A choice among the F horn, B-flat horn, and the double horn depends chiefly on the kind of sound desired.

The F horn has the most traditional horn quality. It is about 12½ feet in length, rarely has more than three valves, and has a practical range of approximately F-sharp at the bottom of the bass clef to second-leger-line C above the treble clef (these pitches *sound* a perfect fifth lower). Because the F horn plays in its upper partials rather than the lower partials or the fundamentals, the pitches playable with any valve combination are close together, more so in the upper register. Beginners tend to lose confidence and become discouraged over the difficulty of playing the correct note when the note a step above or a third below is produced with the same fingering and nearly the same embouchure formation.

The B-flat horn is 9 feet long with a range lying a perfect fourth above the F horn. It can usually be played lower because the fundamental of the F horn is so difficult to reach. Compared to the F horn, the B-flat horn is cheaper, slightly lighter to hold, easier to play, and plays the same notes as the B-flat trumpet in beginning method books (though sounding an octave lower). It blends well with the other B-flat instruments of the band both in intonation and in tone color. Because its partials are similar to those of the trumpet, the beginner learns to play with accuracy and confidence. Single B-flat horns have a different quality, a slightly harsher, more open sound than the F horn, but directors who use them are enthusiastic about them. Tradition more than anything else keeps the single F horn popular. Furthermore, if the student later changes to a double horn she will have an advantage because the B-flat side is used more than the F (at least by accomplished horn players). Figure 16–1 illustrates the partials produced on the F horn and the B-flat horn.

The principal difficulty that the B-flat horn causes beginners is tone quality in the low register and often poor intonation on the beginning pitches used in most beginning method books. The single B-flat horn has one built-in disadvantage. When the hand is used to stop the tone and produce hand-stopped sound, the pitch must be lowered three quarters of a tone rather than the usual half step. Because this pitch is impossible to correct by transposing, the hand alone cannot be used for muting. Therefore, some manufacturers have placed a fourth valve on professional-line horns that makes the necessary pitch alteration when the hand is used to play "stopped" horn. Some B-flat horns have a fifth valve that lowers the horn to F. Some foreign-made single B-flat horns have a fourth valve that lowers the pitch a half step to A.

Due to the difficulty of obtaining correct pitch on the F horn, the double horn has become standard in spite of its greater weight and price. The double horn is not a horn put into another key by adding a slide, but is two horns with a common mouthpiece, leadpipe, and bell. The B-flat side of the horn is accessed by a fourth valve (activated by the thumb) that reduces the overall length of the brass tubing to roughly 9 feet (double the length of the B-flat trumpet). The B-flat side of the instrument has the advantage that its partials are not as close together as the F horn (i.e., it plays in a "lower register" of the instrument in order to sound the same

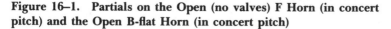

Figure 16–1. Partials on the Open (no valves) F Horn (in concert pitch) and the Open B-flat Horn (in concert pitch)

pitches), and consequently the high register is easier to play accurately. Usually the player of a double horn uses the F horn in the lower register for its tone quality and the B-flat horn in the upper register for its accuracy and tone quality.

When selecting a double horn (whether new or used), it should be played by a horn player and the student herself if she has been playing for several years to verify that both sides are in tune with each other. If there is any question that the player lacks a discriminating ear, or if the player is in the habit of lipping certain notes in tune, it is best to use an electronic tuner for such a task, since stability of intonation is of great importance in selecting an instrument.

Many high school students who play double horns never benefit from the advantage offered by the instrument because they never learn the fingerings for the B-flat side. Actually, much of the F horn sound can be produced on the B-flat side if the player closes her hand somewhat and listens carefully to the tone. There is no unalterable spot at which one should change from one side to the other on a double horn; the right place is that which is the easiest, where the notes speak the best, and where the player can get the most consistent quality. Often this is somewhere between G-sharp and C-sharp in treble clef (Figure 16–2 shows where particular sides of the double horn can be used). Use of the F side results in improved intonation and a sound more closely associated with the natural horn.

Many horn players will purchase used instruments due to the relatively high cost of double horns. As when buying a used automobile, one should question why the owner wishes to part with it. The same concerns apply to all used instruments; the primary additional concern for a used horn is the dents it may have. Because the bell of the horn is so thin, it is very easy to dent; and dents alone can cause intonation problems, while repairs made by an unqualified horn repairperson can increase the intonation problems *and* add tone quality problems. A bell on which the lacquer has worn off is of much less concern. Any repairs to the braces can usually be identified; these can give some indication as to the maintenance and previous damage of the instrument.

A used horn should be inspected for pitted brass where the hands touch the instrument. A certain amount of wear should be expected on the valve stems, but pitted brass can wear through and result in costly damage.

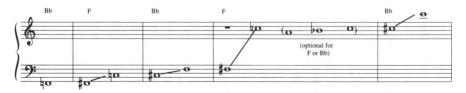

Figure 16–2. Approximate Uses for F and B-flat Sides

Another concern is the cleanliness of the bore. Horns have more resistance than any of the brass instruments—this resistance affects tone quality, flexibility, range, intonation, virtually every aspect of the instrument. But resistance should be constant and a characteristic of the horn itself, not due to years of accumulated dirt. A flexible snake designed for the horn should be pushed through the bore to determine the condition of the inside of the instrument.

The Horn as a Marching Band Instrument

In the early 1970s, when corps-style marching bands began to emerge, there developed a desperate need for a midrange sound in the brass. Consequently, the mellophone, which had previously been used in jazz ensembles such as Ken Stanton's, was improved by several manufacturers and marketed as a marching alternative to the horn. Presently, horn substitutes are labeled mellophones and marching horns; the latter are slightly more conical, use a horn mouthpiece, and have a tone more closely resembling a real horn. Mellophones are designed to use a trumpet mouthpiece, but are commonly available with an adapter for a horn mouthpiece; however, its use seriously affects the already poor intonation of the instrument.

The advantage of mellophones and marching horns is that they are bell-front instruments. Both are normally pitched in F, but an octave higher than regular horns. The written range is the same as a trumpet's, and they use trumpet fingerings; they sound a perfect fifth down from the written pitch. They can easily be played by trumpet players. The upper register of the mellophone can be played with more confidence than on the horn, since the notes are spaced farther apart. The most universal criticism of the mellophone and marching horn is that due to the proportion of conical to cylindrical tubing they are easily overblown, especially by trumpet players. The mellophone has more cylindrical tubing than conical tubing; in order to make up for this ratio and achieve a sound "approximating" that of a horn, the conical portion is made so that it flares sooner (in relationship to length) than other conical instruments. Horn players, who are used to more resistance, are often carried away by their ability to suddenly play as loud as trumpets and trombones, and they diligently strive to do so.

The marching horn is also available in B-flat. It is the same length as the single B-flat horn, the primary difference being reshaped tubing to make it bell front. These instruments use horn mouthpieces and are probably the best choice for marching bands, partly because their use forces horn players to learn and use B-flat fingerings, which can facilitate their playing on a double horn. Like the mellophone, these instruments are easily overblown.

It is essential that horn players continue to practice the horn during marching band season. Among the worst nightmares of instrumental music teachers is that the horn section of the band will sound like mellophones in symphonic band work.

ASSEMBLING THE HORN

The horn is taken from its case by grasping the outside tubing in the vicinity of the valves. Here the tubing is reinforced for precisely this purpose; the rest of the horn is more fragile than one would believe metal to be. The metal is extremely thin—so thin that the bell can be dented by pressure from the fingers. Even the weight of the instrument will dent the metal when it is handled incorrectly.

The single step in assembling the horn is to insert the mouthpiece into the leadpipe with a gentle twisting motion.

HOLDING THE HORN

Some artists recommend sitting on the right corner of a chair at about a 45-degree angle, with the right leg positioned beside the chair and slightly back supporting the horn. The left leg should be directly in the line of vision with the conductor. This position facilitates seeing both the music and the conductor and keeps the player's back well away from the back of the chair. Some younger players may need a book on which to rest their right foot to help keep the horn in the proper position for playing. See Figures 16–3 and 16–4 for examples of playing position while seated.

Horn players also stand to play, especially in solo work, but should not march. The body from the waist up should be in the same position whether sitting or standing, a naturally relaxed and efficient position. The right hand's function is to move in and out of the bell, correcting intonation and altering tone quality; when standing, the player must listen carefully as she uses her right hand partially for support, thus her intonation and tone quality could suffer.

The left hand holds the instrument and operates the valves. The little finger is placed within the hook to support the horn, the three middle fingers rest in a curved position on the valves. The horn uses rotary valves, which are depressed considerably less than the piston valves used by most cornet and trumpet manufacturers, and the horn can be played with a flatter finger position than the trumpet. Because of the grip, horn players must be reminded from time to time not to use excessive pressure on the embouchure. The little finger should not clench and push the mouthpiece into the embouchure. On the single horn, the thumb is placed around the

**Figure 16–3. Sitting Position for
Playing the Horn**

tubing, resting lightly rather than grabbing the tubing. Some single horns
have a hook for the thumb, which may aid in the development of good
habits when that hook is replaced by the thumb valve on a double horn.
The left arm hangs loosely from the shoulder, as relaxed and natural as
possible, with just enough angle or slant to help the fingers perform freely
and rapidly.

**Figure 16–4. Sitting Position for
Playing the Horn.** Note: Both positions
are correct; the exact position depends
on embouchure. The teacher should,
however, make sure that the beginning
horn student holds the instrument in
such a manner as to avoid tilting the
head back.

The placement of the right hand affects both pitch and tone and enables the student to produce the effects desired by the conductor. Because of the wide variety of hand sizes and shapes, it is not possible to be much more specific about its placement, shape, or use. The young student with a small hand will have a different placement than a full-grown player in order to produce the same effects. The right hand can make the difference between a beautiful horn sound and one that is unpleasant. Since habits are so hard to break once set, some hornists recommend positioning the beginner's hand as it will be used when the player reaches maturity, even though the sound suffers temporarily.

Although there are several schools of thought on hand position, only one method is generally used in the United States today. The fingers are close together with no space between them and are extended with the finger knuckles almost straight. The hand is cupped, bending at the knuckles to form an angle somewhat larger than 90 degrees. The thumb lies next to the index finger, fitting flush so that no open space exists between the thumb and the hand. The thumb is bent a little so that the tip of the thumb lies almost on top of the index finger rather than at its side. The hand goes into the horn with the fingers held vertically rather than horizontally; the back of the fingers touches the inside of the bell on the side away from the player. If the player's hand is small, her thumb will not be brought over the index finger but will extend out from the hand, still joined. This formation makes it possible to close off the bell with the heel of the hand by moving the wrist to cup the palm more—the fingers remaining as flat as they can and against the bell. Players are prone to curl their fingers within the bell, but this is not correct. The fingers should be against the side of the bell in a fairly straight position. The more of the bell that is covered, the darker and flatter the pitch.

The player determines how far the hand should be inserted into the bell by listening and adjusting; younger students may benefit from an electronic tuner. The hand is placed at the point where the tone quality is best and the pitch of the horn matches the pitch of the ensemble (examples of right-hand positions are shown in Figures 16–5, 16–6, and 16–7). Horns are manufactured about one-quarter step sharper than other brass instruments to compensate for the placement of the hand in the bell. This affects upper register response and pitch more than lower. One rule is to place the hand in as far as it can go without muffling the tone. The distance will not be the same for any two hands. The size of the hand alters tone as well as intonation, and the player must learn to produce the tone quality she wants with the hand she has. Cupping and straightening the hand must be done gradually to avoid sudden changes of tone quality.

The horn should be held at an angle similar to that used for playing the clarinet. The mouthpiece, not the head, is tilted downward. The horn is held at an angle so that the leadpipe is about 15 to 20 degrees from the

Figure 16–5. Normal Position of the Hand in the Bell

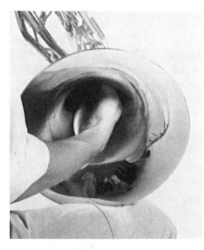

Figure 16–6. Normal Position of the Hand in the Bell

Figure 16–7. Closed Position of the Hand in the Bell

horizontal. Some authorities strongly advocate starting beginning horn players in a standing position to determine a proper relationship of the horn to the body; others feel that standing for beginners adversely affects use of the right hand for tone quality.

The bell should not face directly into the player's body or directly to the side. An angle about half way between the two would cover nearly all correct positions for holding the instrument. The double horn should rest on the right thigh. When the player rests the horn on her thigh and sits on the corner of the chair, the edge of the bell will be more parallel to her leg; if she sits straight forward in the chair, the edge of the bell will form an acute angle with her leg.

THE BEGINNING STUDENT

When the beginner knows that the horn is her instrument of choice, no valid reason exists for starting her on the trumpet. There are, in fact, many reasons for opposing it. Problems of embouchure increase the difficulties of the horn player who has previously played the trumpet, and little evidence can be found that trumpet study contributes to a keener ear or better harmonic sense.

A source of frustration on the part of beginners is the fact that many beginning method books start all wind students on a concert F, a note that is comfortable and easily accessible for most winds but transposes for horn to a C below the staff, fairly low in the F horn's register. Furthermore, most beginning method books progress from that pitch downward. To have the F horn player play up an octave (or a third-space C) is not feasible: this is the eighth harmonic for the horn, and the pitches both one step above and one step below are played with the same fingering, a discouraging task for the beginner. If the teacher does not wish to use a method book that starts the horn on a different pitch from the rest of the instruments, the alternative is to start horn players separately from other beginning wind players.

Certainly the B-flat horn and the double horn can be made accessible to an interested grade school pupil. Starting a student on the single F horn is more easily accomplished at the middle school level because of the student's greater embouchure control and more accurate sense of pitch and intervals.

For students of small stature who have difficulty reaching both the bell with their right hand and the mouthpiece with their embouchure, a *competent, experienced* instrument repairperson can bend the leadpipe to a more comfortable position with little or no effect on the horn or overall tone quality. The leadpipe can be bent back to its original position when appropriate.

EMBOUCHURE

European players use several types of embouchure formation and hand placement; they are all acceptable and successful. In the United States, fairly standard practices have grown up concerning embouchure. One hears frequently about the "einsetzen" and "ansetzen" embouchures; these are graphically and delightfully portrayed in a humorous booklet called *Complete Method for the Waldhorn or the Ventilhorn*, which every instrumental teacher will find amusing.[1] The terms refer to setting the mouthpiece *in* or *on* the embouchure. The einsetzen is rarely recommended, though a surprising number of players without formal instruction apparently feel that it is natural and right, especially for the lower register. It produces a fine tone but is limited in flexibility and upper range. With this embouchure, the mouthpiece is placed in the lips, about midway in the red area of both upper and lower lips. For many it is placed midway "inside" the lower lip with the upper lip shaped for a more traditional appearing embouchure. The outer lip area then curls around the mouthpiece. Since the delicate red area of the lip furnishes support for the mouthpiece, developing endurance is more difficult with this embouchure. Players who use the einsetzen successfully usually have fuller, thicker lips. It is most often used for playing in the lower register.

With the ansetzen embouchure, the mouthpiece is set on the lips after they have been shaped into the proper, pursed formation. Farkas's excellent illustration of this likens the mouth to a drawstring on a bag, drawing the bag tightly shut over a coffee can—the tautness of the bag results from pulling forward and backward at the same time.[2]

The lower lip is turned in a little over the teeth; the chin must not bunch. (It may help to have the beginner exaggerate this slightly.) The teeth are somewhat apart, and the mouthpiece is placed high on the lips. Having the mouthpiece entirely outside the red of the lip seems to prohibit range and produce poor tone; some middle-ground combination of *in* and *on* the lips is probably the most practical approach. If the jaw is flat, the corners of the mouth will not turn up into a smiling position. A correct embouchure is illustrated in Figure 16–8.

TONE QUALITY

Horn tone is produced similarly to tone on other brass instruments except that the horn player has an additional way of changing tone. On all brass instruments, tone is chiefly controlled by the embouchure and breath

---

[1] Erich von Schmutzig, *Complete Method für der Waldhorn oder der Ventilhorn* (Reading, MA: Foster Print Shop, 1949).

[2] Philip Farkas, *The Art of Brass Playing* (Bloomington, IN: Brass Publications, 1962), 17.

Figure 16–8a.   Horn Embouchure

support; the horn player also uses her right hand in the bell to change the sound. Beyond these techniques, the most important factor is the ear. As on all wind instruments, tone quality is primarily determined by the player's mental image. On horn this is especially important, since what the audience hears is different from what the player hears due to the position in which the horn is held and played. Furthermore, the design and acoustics of the room affect horn tone quality more than that of any other wind instrument.

The player should listen to as many horn players and good recordings as she can and choose the kind of tone that she desires. She must then listen to herself as she plays and keep adjusting her embouchure to get closer to her mental ideal. While tone quality of the horn is different from performer to performer, recordings differ in timbre between those performers who play with woodwind quintets and those who play with brass

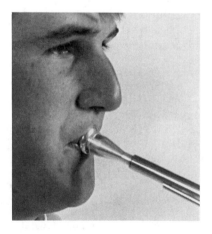

Figure 16–8b.   Horn Embouchure (side view)

quintets. Horn players approach the instrument differently depending on their concept of the desired tonal color, but the best professional horn players can perform equally well with brass and woodwind groups, chamber groups and large ensembles, and as soloists. A professional may play twentieth-century music with a distinctly different tone than that used for German Romantic compositions.

Perhaps the single most important variable in good horn sound is the airstream. Because the horn has the most resistance of all brass instruments, it is quite easy to produce a sound with only a minimum amount of air. The F horn is more than twice as long as a trumpet, requiring that the air must be constantly and consistently supported whether one is playing long lyrical lines or fast technical passages. Too much air, often a sign of too tight an embouchure, will promote overblowing and produce a brassy, uncharacteristic sound (but occasionally useful for special effects).

A common problem among horn players is that they seem to crack more notes than players of the other brasses; this cracking can be blamed on the closeness of the notes with any given valve combination. Young horn players are also late on many attacks. Compared to the shorter brass and woodwinds, the length of the horn requires more time for the pressure wave from the embouchure to create the standing wave that makes the note speak. With experience and continued development of the breathing apparatus, hornists learn to time their attacks. Teachers should be understanding of the beginning horn player's dilemma.

The tone quality is also controlled by the embouchure: the size of the lip opening, the shape of the lips, the amount of mouthpiece pressure on the lips, and the angle at which the air enters the mouthpiece. A high palate and fairly large oral cavity enhance the tone, but these are not within the power of the player to change. A more puckered embouchure, within reason, will give a smoother, mellower, darker sound. Too much pucker can make the tone so dark that it begins to resemble the baritone horn in quality. A more smiling, stretched embouchure will give a bright, brilliant tone that can become brassy and harsh. The term *cuivre* or *schmetternd* designates this brassy, harsh sound, which is used for special effects in orchestral and band literature. In ordinary playing, sufficient pucker is maintained to obtain a tone that is mellow but not overly subdued—the horn tone should have an element of brilliancy to it.

The horn produces a wide variety of tone colors and effects for which there are many foreign labels. For example, *mit dampfer* ("with mute") is often used synonymously with *stopped, stark anblasen, gedampft* with "+" above the note marked forte, *gestopft* with *muted, consordino* or the British *closed*. The player has to remember specifically what each means and then alter the practice with the conductor's wishes.

Some further explanation should be made of the term *cuivre*. Players are often puzzled about whether this term indicates use of a mute. *Cuivre* means to play with a brassy tone; the same sound is also indicated by the terms *schmetternd* and *blechern*. The tone may be produced by forcing too much air into the horn, or it may be obtained by using the mute (cheating) and forcing against it, creating sufficient air pressure to get the brassy quality asked for. If a forte passage is being played and some form of muting is called for, the "cuivre" effect is desired.

There are three primary effects on the horn in addition to the straight horn tone. These are (1) the stopped tone (hand tightly in the bell) used for special effects, (2) the muted tone produced by means of a regular mute, and (3) the brassy tone designated by *cuivre* or *schmetternd*.

The hand in the bell makes the tone more open or more closed. If the tone is too dull and thick, the hand should be withdrawn a little. The closed hand darkens and subdues the tone, while the open hand allows the tone to emit freely. The stopped bell, like the muted bell, is used only for special effects specified by a composer and is not part of normal playing. The position of the bell also affects the sound for listener and player, but that sound is never the same for listener as for player. The player may like the dark tone she gets with the bell turned into her body, but the listener may find it lifeless, dull, and uninteresting.

If the tone is not good, one should check for the following: Does the embouchure have enough of a pucker to get a good cushion on the upper lip? Is the upper lip free enough from pressure to enable it to vibrate? Are the teeth open enough to make a round tone? Think of forming an open vowel; "oo" is usually preferred, or "oh"; and for a brighter tone, "aa" or "ee" may help. Is the embouchure too tight, or too smiling? Does breath come from the diaphragm area through an open throat? Is the tongue bunched up in the back of the mouth?

The horn is so adaptable that it can blend with woodwinds, brass, or strings. It is also a beautiful complement to the human voice. It can be the accompaniment or solo instrument, and by changing the tone quality can be used in nearly every combination of instruments. With all these challenging possibilities, players should never limit themselves to an embouchure that produces only one kind of tone. To play every passage with a dark sound or a light, bright sound is to ignore the musical style and the meaning of the passage. The player who enjoys the instrument the most is the one who widens her range of sounds from dark to light just as conscientiously as those from high to low.

Occasionally it is necessary to change dynamics from those indicated in the music in order to obtain an intended effect. This is because all tone colors are not possible at all dynamic levels, and though many composers are very skillful in their use of the horn, others are less so and must be interpreted rather than taken literally. Lack of complete understanding of the horn is not surprising, since the complexity and wide possibilities of the instrument are coupled with limitations not always realized by even the very knowledgeable composer.

Vibrato

Though at present vibrato is more widely accepted, horn players traditionally have not used a vibrato except occasionally in solo works. The French are an exception; they favor a thin tone with a vibrato, the same speed vibrato for all registers and dynamics. The vibrato seems to destroy the genuine horn quality, giving it a more sentimental, superficial character not in keeping with most of the music written for it. Although some hornists advocate diaphragm vibrato, and some even claim to achieve a controlled vibrato by "wiggling" the fingers of the right hand, the most popular method has been jaw vibrato.

Mutes

Ideally, a commercial mute is used for muted passages, and the hand is reserved for passages calling for hand-stopping. When the hand is used, it goes into the bell of the F horn with the effect of shortening the overall length of the instrument (raising the pitch one half step, or temporarily creating a horn in F-sharp). Normally, in order to play hand-stopped, the hand is inserted about 6½ inches into the bell, but the distance will vary with the size of the hand and the size of the bell. When a commercial mute is used, the pitch obtained will depend on the age of the mute, for the cork wears down and is affected by moisture. Hand-stopping the B-flat horn raises the pitch about ¾ of a step, making transposition a serious problem. Players of double horns normally play muted passages on the F side of the instrument or use nontransposing mutes if the register being performed requires use of the B-flat side of the instrument.

Hand-stopping is often referred to as *stopped horn*; other terms are *sons bouches*, *bouchez*, *chinuso*, and *gestopft*. The hand is useful for this purpose only to about the bottom of the treble clef, since below that it is not powerful enough to resist the air pressure. A small hand may make the pitch too sharp even after transposing down a half step; a large hand may produce the opposite pitch problem. In these cases, the player must use a stopped mute or compensate by altering her embouchure, lipping up or down, or, if the stopped passage is a long one, retuning the slides. Today there are several special mutes available that can be used for the appropriate sound and do not require transposition. These mutes enable the hornist to use both the F and B-flat sides of a double horn. Criteria in selecting a nontransposing mute include good intonation as well as the desired muting effect.

Mutes come in a variety of shapes, materials, and cork sizes with a consequent variety of sounds. Terms commonly used to indicate a mechanical mute are *muted, con sordino, avec sourdine, gedampft,* and *mit dampfer.* The nontransposing mute is appropriate for school use, obviously because transposition isn't required, but also because the mute is placed in the same position in the bell as the hand, eliminating intonation surprises. The transposing "brass mute" requires transposition down a half step but is seldom used, as it is primarily a substitute for hand-stopping.

The use of any mute creates intonation problems because the player can no longer use her hand to bring the pitch into tune. She therefore must listen to the pitch created, make the necessary adjustments on the mute corks when possible, and adjust the pitch with her embouchure. Mutes are manufactured with a screw arrangement by which the player can adjust the mute to assist in intonation. These have not been widely accepted since they take too long to adjust.

FINGERING

The horn is a transposing instrument. Pitched in F, the notes played sound a perfect fifth below. When a player switches to the B-flat side of the double horn, she continues to read the notes for horn in F but uses a different set of fingerings. Consequently these notes also sound a perfect fifth below those read and played, although they are played on a B-flat horn. The fingering chart at the end of the chapter shows the fingerings for both the F and B-flat horns (as well as the double horn). The most common fingerings are marked by an asterisk (although depending on the particular passage, alternate fingerings and even the other side of the horn are frequently used). The chart covers a very broad range of written pitches for the horn; most public school horn players will never see music written to these depths or heights.

INTONATION

Initial tuning utilizing an electronic tuner is done in the following manner. All the slides are pushed in. Then, if the double horn is used, the B-flat side is tuned first, since it contains the main tuning slide, which affects the pitch of both F and B-flat. Usually the main slide will need to be pulled ¼ to ½ inch to bring the B-flat horn down to standard pitch. When the B-flat side is in tune, the player is through adjusting the main slide regardless of how sharp the F side may yet be. The next step is to tune the open tones on the F side by adjusting the F slide. Having the open tones on both sides in tune, the player may then bring the other notes into correct relationship by pulling the other valve slides, those on the B-flat side first and then those on the F side. This entire procedure is to no avail if the right hand is not in the correct position during the tuning. The player must not tip or move her hand, or favor notes during tuning; if she does, she will not tune the instrument correctly. All companies provide excellent booklets on how to tune a horn. Each player should be sure to read one and follow the procedures with patience. This entire procedure will be a waste of everyone's time if the student does not listen carefully and develop an understanding of what she is tuning toward—in performance.

For day-to-day tuning, players are often seen adjusting one valve slide and stopping. When one valve slide is altered, it is almost always necessary to adjust the others to it, and to adjust both sides of the double horn. If only one note is tuned, it will be incorrect when used in combination with others. The player should tune several notes, compare the B-flat and F sides, and adjust when necessary. Again, beginners will require the assistance of their teacher and possibly an electronic tuner—these are both tools for developing the ear and not a substitute.

The double horn has fewer intonation problems than the other valved instruments, providing that it is a standard make, first-quality instrument. Unlike the temperamental woodwinds or even the trumpet, the double horn can be played well in tune on almost all pitches throughout its range. This is not because it is more perfectly designed than the other brasses, but because it is actually two horns. Bad notes on one side can be avoided by playing them on the other side. Since the same notes are rarely out of tune for both the F and B-flat horn, an acceptable scale is possible throughout. In addition to the adequate intonation, the double horn player has numerous devices to help her play in tune: she can adjust the two tuning slides as well as the six valve slides that affect the overall tuning, she can adjust her embouchure while playing to change the individual pitches; and if need be, she can adjust the position of the right hand in the bell. The player of a single horn can adjust pitch in the same way, as she merely has one tuning slide and three valve slides; furthermore, by not having the double horn, she is required to adjust her embouchure and hand position much more frequently.

The hand alters pitch by moving in (cupping more and closing the bell more as if to "catch" the sound) to lower the pitch and darken the timbre and moving out (straightening more and opening the bell as if to let the sound pass "freely" by the hand) to flatten the pitch and brighten the timbre (often described as a "brassy sound"). With all these devices at her disposal, there is no reason for a hornist to play out of tune . . . except for not listening.

Figure 16–9 shows intonation problems of the B-flat and F horns, with particularly out-of-tune notes indicated by asterisks.

Because most of the innate intonation problems are solved by alter-

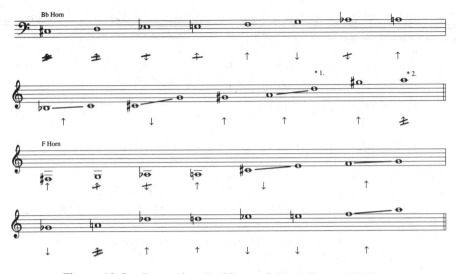

Figure 16–9. Intonation Problems of the B-flat and F Horns

nate fingerings, harmonics, or the tuning processes just described, most of the details will be given in following sections.

One of the unimportant but fascinating idiosyncrasies of the horn and other brass is that a chord may be produced on it. A few players have been able to do this, and there are compositions that call for it. One note is played while another that is a member of the chord built on the first is hummed; this combination produces two other strong partials that are audible, resulting in a four-note chord. We know of no method for learning this trick other than experimentation. Except for the rare occasion when it is called for, this feat may fall into the category dismissed by "things not worth doing are not worth doing well."

WHAT TO PRACTICE

Like every brass player, successful performance depends on the quality and quantity of practice; a positive correlation exists between performance and preparation. For the beginning F horn student, use of supplementary material is perhaps more critical than for any other brass student. Beginning band method books are designed for the majority of the wind class; the first notes are not the best notes for a beginning F horn player and may result in problems for young hornists. Discouragement can beset young horn players who see their colleagues advancing rapidly through the book and find themselves lagging behind often through no fault of their own.

The warm-up for horn players should include long tones at various dynamic levels, and crescendos and decrescendos in all registers of the instrument (the player diligently attempts to keep the pitch and volume from wavering; blasting at the upper dynamic ranges should be avoided). Lip slurs for flexibility and scales for finger dexterity should also be included on a daily basis.

As players develop, most scales and arpeggios should be expanded to cover a full three-octave range. This range improves accuracy (the bane of most horn players), strength of the embouchure, endurance, control, flexibility over a wide range, and intonation.

Attacks are usually a frustrating problem for beginning horn students. Daily practice on attacks should include all dynamic levels and all registers. A valuable study is to write out a series of unrelated pitches (not unlike a tone row), each followed by a rest, and have students attack each note. Emphasis should be placed on the "duh" articulation, as the "tuh" articulation creates an exaggerated explosive sound on the horn and leads to even more cracked pitches. Because of the small size of the mouthpiece and the normally puckered embouchure, tonguing with accuracy is more difficult on the horn than on the other brass. Daily practice should include tongued scales and other technical studies.

The hornist's daily practice should include something she can already play, preferably a lyrical or melodic piece. Emphasis is placed on improving the expressive qualities of this piece every time it is practiced. Continued practice on a piece in which the notes are no longer a problem allows the performer to concentrate on musicianship.

CARE AND MAINTENANCE OF THE HORN

Moisture collects in the horn as in any other instrument. It presents more of a problem, however, because obviously the horn cannot be swabbed out, and the moisture doesn't run out the bottom. The addition of spit valves is becoming more common, and some professionals have several water keys added to their instruments.

Horn players must unwind their instruments at every opportunity— they have enough trouble playing accurately without contending with bubbly notes. The valve slides should be emptied after each playing, more frequently if needed. Running water through the horn or forcing in a small swab is not a good idea—these practices may push the dirt and sludge into some inaccessible spot where it will lodge permanently. Some of the slides are shaped so that they can be cleaned with water or a brush, and a little common sense can indicate which ones these are. Moisture left in the horn will retain dust and grease that in time will change the tone of the instrument. Since cleaning the horn after it becomes dirty is so much more difficult than draining it each time it is used, the latter should be enforced or at least urged on the student.

Removing the slides should be easy. If the horn is cared for properly, the slides are removed often for emptying, adjusted continually for tuning, and shouldn't stick. Since students, however, have been known to fail to accomplish that which they have been asked to do, slides sometimes go for semesters unmoved. In such cases, the slides should not be yanked out by grabbing with the hand and pulling, for the soft metal will yield to the pressure of the hand and take on a different shape than that intended. A repairperson is recommended if any real force is needed. Students often discover that when they pull out a slide they can get a popping sound, and slide pulling can become a favorite pastime. The popping action can result in leaks in the slide or the valve casing; students should be urged to find other amusement. The affected valve should be depressed when removing or returning the valve slide—one slide at a time—which will eliminate the pop and keep the instrument in better condition. The slides should be kept lubricated with *slight* amounts of petroleum jelly or slide grease.

The valves must be oiled regularly, with either special horn oil or regular valve oil. To oil the horn, pull the slides and insert three or four drops of oil onto the slide. Replace the slide, return the horn to playing position, press and release the valve numerous times, then remove the slide and expel the excess oil. Some books suggest letting the oil run down the casing onto the valve, but this is not recommended since the oil picks up dirt and lint on its way and deposits it on the valve. At least weekly the valve bearings should be oiled (top and bottom).

The genuine corks on rotary valves are subject to wear and to hardening and should be replaced with a synthetic rubber cork. Most manufacturers today use a synthetic material. The corks are crucial to valve alignment, which determines pitch and greatly affects tone quality.

The string on the valves needs to be replaced occasionally if breakage is to be avoided, perhaps once a year for players practicing an average amount. Strings do not break often, but when they do it always seems to be at a critical time—the horn player must realize that unless the strings are replaced periodically, they *are* going to break, and if Murphy is correct, it will be two measures prior to her solo at the district band festival. Only one string at a time is removed and replaced. The important thing is to line the valve up at the exact level of the other two. Instruction in how to replace strings on rotary valves is too often ignored by instrumental music teachers.

The finish on the horn is a matter of preference. Many horn performers play an instrument that has been stripped of all lacquer (sometimes just from the bell) or manufactured without lacquer. All student-line horns, however, are finished with lacquer to protect the brass from pitting. The finish can and should be preserved from damage caused by the acids of the student's hands by frequent wiping with a soft cloth. The horn lacquer is as durable as that on other instruments, but the hands come into more contact with the horn, so the possibility of deterioration is greater. Left-hand guards made of plastic or leather help eliminate contact. Leather is preferred because of its greater softness and flexibility. Players like to polish the instrument to a beautiful sheen, but polishing should be done in moderation as the lacquer is so thin that polishing can eventually remove it, particularly on the bell, where it is almost constantly being touched. Some foreign manufacturers do not polish the instrument at all, and a new horn looks as dull as one used for forty years.

TROUBLESHOOTING

EQUIPMENT

sluggish valves
1. Place three or four drops of valve oil into valve slides, replace slides, return to playing position, work valves, expel excess oil from valve slides. Oil valve bearings (top and bottom).

air will not pass through horn
1. Make sure valves are aligned.
2. Inspect for worn corks.
3. Inspect for a dirty mouthpiece.
4. Determine if foreign object is lodged in instrument.

bubbly sound
1. Empty valve slides, unwind horn slowly to pour out excess water from the leadpipe. If left for too long some will pass all three valves and must be poured through bell.

mouthpiece wiggles
1. Shank too long—have competent repairperson remove one section at a time; a mouthpiece shank that is too short causes moderate to severe intonation problems.
2. Shank out-of-round; again to be repaired only by competent repairperson.

buzzing sound
1. Inspect for broken brace(s). Have resoldered.
2. Determine if a recent soaking may have loosened residue inside. Rewash or use flexible brush.

TONE

thin, strident, brassy, or forced sound
1. Teeth together. Drop jaw.
2. Aperture too small; try more pucker. Have student attempt to form a mouth for whistling while buzzing without the mouthpiece, then with mouthpiece.

3. Tongue tense in a possible attempt to keep it "out of the way." Relax tongue.

4. Tension in throat. Drop shoulders, pretend to be a rag doll—limp.

5. Embouchure too stretched. Relax mouth, tighten corners as if "whistling," or buzz without mouthpiece.

6. Mouthpiece too shallow or too cup-shaped (with edge).

7. Aperture too flat. Attempt to get student to pucker more—like a whistle; try a "doo" articulation rather than "dee".

8. Too much upper lip.

9. Right hand too straight or not inserted enough. Cup more; try to cover more bell.

10. Tongue too high. Try articulating "daw" rather than "dee".

11. Practice breathing large amounts of air with the mouth in shape for vocalizing "o–o–o–o–o."

dull, spread, or unfocused sound

1. Lips not buzzing evenly. Buzz without mouthpiece, then with mouthpiece alone.

2. Insufficient air support. Blow slightly faster air.

3. Cheeks puffing. Practice buzzing without mouthpiece.

4. Embouchure too slack. Tighten corners and encourage student to focus pitch—blow a "pencil-thin" stream of air.

5. Aperture too large. Same as for # 3.

6. Mouthpiece too large.

7. Fingers apart. Keep fingers together.

8. Head too high, tilted back. Reposition horn so that student can bring mouthpiece to embouchure at approximately same angle as a clarinet.

9. Too much pucker in embouchure. Buzz without mouthpiece.

stuffy, fuzzy, or airy sound

1. Lips not buzzing evenly. Buzz without the mouthpiece and with the mouthpiece alone. Could also be due to fatigue caused by lack of proper or sufficient warm-up, too much demand on student (e.g., her eagerness to play high notes before she is able), lack of warm-down after previous playing. Tired, swollen lips hurt sound.

2. Embouchure may be spread for the low notes, without keeping corners firm.

3. Too much hand in bell.

4. Pinching the lips together, or the teeth are together. Drop jaw; keep corners of mouth clamped shut firmly to loosen the center.

5. Air pockets behind upper or lower lip. Practice buzzing without mouthpiece—this forces a flat chin and firm embouchure—in the right places.
6. Cheeks puffing. Again, buzz without mouthpiece.
7. Closed throat. Pull shoulders downward.
8. Too much saliva in embouchure or mouthpiece.
9. Improper mouthpiece placement. Correct placement.

difficulty with upper range

1. Excessive playing of low notes. Rely more on air and less on pressure; corners of the mouth should be kept firm, attempt to pull horn and mouthpiece away from embouchure when playing.
2. Mouthpiece too large. Cup diameter and depth.
3. Blow faster air; a "pencil-thin," fast airstream.
4. Fatigue. Lack of proper warm-up or warm-down.
5. Try to direct air slightly downward by rolling in lower lip or tilting head backward slightly.
6. Improper mouthpiece angle. Correct position for holding.
7. Embouchure too tight. Correct embouchure.

ARTICULATION

explosive attacks

1. Building air pressure behind tongue or "holding" onto the air before releasing it. Try for better coordination between air and tongue; inhale to exhale without stopping (try practicing attacks completely without the use of the tongue).
2. Tonguing between the teeth. Work toward a "duh" tongue placement instead of "thuh."
3. Stopping the previous note with the tongue. Practice playing long tones while merely disrupting the airstream with the tongue, notes are connected.
4. Attempting to articulate with lips touching "puh" or "muh." Work on long tones with "big, opened, focused tone" and use slow repeated "duh" articulations.
5. Aperture in embouchure too small. Same as for #4.
6. Head tilted back too far. Reposition horn to keep head at approximately the same angle as clarinet.

scooping notes, facial movements

1. Air starting too slow then increasing to proper velocity. Work on making the inhale-to-exhale one continuous cycle without stopping; sometimes student is timid or fears failure.
2. "Chewing notes"; excessive chin movement. Tongue moving too far; replace "taw–taw" with "duh–duh." Practice long tone *and* lip slurs up and down in front of mirror to hold chin still.

3. Head tilted back too far. Reposition horn.

4. Jaw too closed. Try opening jaw and teeth more at all times; inhaling, tonguing, exhaling.

5. Too much lip in the mouthpiece. Practice forming an embouchure and buzzing without the mouthpiece, then try to establish the same sensations when playing.

difficulty with lip slurs

1. Try directing air slightly downward for upward slurs.

2. "Lean" into lower note for upward slurs, followed by upper pitch played slightly softer.

3. Increase air speed when going to upper pitch.

4. Too much upper lip.

5. Head tilted too far backward. Reposition horn.

6. Too many long tones in daily practice schedule.

7. Mouthpiece rim too wide.

REFERENCES

Texts

BARBOUR, JAMES M. *Trumpets, Horns, and Music*. East Lansing, MI: Michigan State University Press, 1964.

BERV, HARRY. *A Creative Approach to French Horn*. Bryn Mawr, PA: Theodore Presser Co., 1977.

BUSHOUSE, DAVID, and JAMES D. PLOYHAR. *Practical Hints on Playing the French Horn*. Melville, NY: Belwin-Mills, 1986.

COAR, BIRCHARD. *The French Horn*. Ann Arbor, MI: B. Coar, 1947.

FARKAS, PHILIP. *The Art of French Horn Playing*. Evanston, IL: Summy-Bichard Publishing Co., 1956.

FITZPATRICK, HORACE. *The Horn and Horn Playing in the Austro-Bohemian Tradition: 1680–1830*. London: Oxford University Press, 1970.

GREGORY, ROBIN. *The Horn: A Guide to the Modern Instrument*. 2nd ed. London: Faber and Faber, 1969.

LaBAR, ARTHUR, ed. *Horn Players' Audition Handbook*. Melville, NY: Belwin-Mills, 1986.

MORLEY-PEGGE, R. *The French Horn*. London: Ernest Benn Limited, 1960.

SANSONE, LORENZO. *French Horn Music Literature with Composers' Biographical Sketches*. New York: Sansone Musical Instruments, 1962.

SCHULLER, GUNTHER. *Horn Technique*. London: Oxford University Press, 1962.

TUCKWELL, BARRY. *Horn*. New York: Schirmer Books, 1983.

YANCICH, M. *Practical Guide to French Horn Playing*. Rochester, NY: Wind Music, 1971.

Journals

The Horn Call. Semiannual journal of the International Horn Society. Paul Mansur, Editor, Dean, School of Arts and Letters, Southeast Oklahoma State University, Durant, OK 74701.

Studies

Easy—Beginning (elementary or junior high)—all start in range from low C to second-line G

BERV, HARRY. *A Creative Approach to the French Horn* (Chappell).
CLEVENGER, DALE, MARK McDUNN, and HAROLD RUSCH. *The Dale Clevenger French Horn Methods*, Books I and II (Kjos).
CLODOMIR, PIERRE. *Methode Elementaire* (Alphonse Leduc).
FEARN, WARD. *French Horn for Beginners* (Theodore Presser).
GETCHELL, ROBERT W. *First Book of Practical Studies* (Belwin-Mills).
GOLDSTEIN, A. *Book of Exercises* (Cor Publishing).
HILL, DOUGLAS, and JAMES O. FROSETH. *Introducing the French Horn* (includes recording) (G.I.A. Publications).
HOWE, MARVIN. *Method for French Horn* (Marvin C. Howe).
MOORE, RICHARD. *French Horn Method*, 2 vols. (Mel Bay).
MUSSER, JOHN, and E. DEL BORGO. *Modes in Contemporary Music* (Alfred).
———. *Rhythm in Contemporary Music* (Alfred Music).
———. *Tonality in Contemporary Music* (Alfred Music).
SINGER, JOSEPH. *Embouchure Building for French Horn* (Belwin-Mills).
TUCKWELL, BARRY. *50 First Exercises* (Oxford University Press).
———. *Horn Tutor* (Oxford University Press).
YANCICH, M. *Method for the French Horn* (Wind Music).

Medium (advanced junior high or high school)

BELLOLI, A. *8 Studies* (International).
———. *24 Etudes* (Sansone).
BORRIS, S. *Studies and Pieces*, Vols. 1 and 2 (C. F. Peters).
BROPHY, WILLIAM R. *Technical Studies.* (Carl Fischer).
———. *Legato Studies* (Belwin-Mills).
CONCONE, GIUSEPPE. *Lyrical Studies* (Brass Press).
GALLAY, J. *30 Etudes* (Sansone).
———. *12 Grandes Etudes Brilliantes* (Sansone and Elkan-Vogel).
———. *Unmeasured Preludes* (Sansone).
GETCHELL, ROBERT W. *Second Book of Practical Studies* (Belwin-Mills).
HORNER, A. *Primary Studies for the French Horn* (Theodore Presser).
LEBAR. *Horn Player's Audition Book.* (Belwin-Mills).
MAXIME-ALPHONSE. *40 Etudes Facile* (Alphonse Leduc).
———. *70 Etudes Tres Facile* (Alphonse Leduc).
MIERSCH, *Melodious Studies for the French Horn* (Carl Fischer).
MUSSER, JOHN, and E. DEL BORGO. *Modes in Contemporary Music* (Alfred).
———. *Rhythm in Contemporary Music* (Alfred).
———. *Tonality in Contemporary Music* (Alfred).
PARES, G., and E. CLAUS. *Daily Exercises and Scales for the French Horn* (Carl Fischer).
POTTAG, MAX. *Daily Exercises* (Belwin-Mills).
———. *Preparatory Melodies to Solo Work* (Belwin-Mills).
POTTAG, MAX, and ANDRAUD. *335 Selected Melodious, Progressive and Technical Studies*, Vols. 1 and 2 (Southern Music).

SHOEMAKER. *Legato Etudes for Horn* (Belwin-Mills).
SINGER, JOSEPH. *Embouchure Building for French Horn* (Belwin-Mills).

Advanced (high school or college)

BITSCH, MARCEL. *12 Etudes* (Alphonse Leduc).
BOZZA, EUGENE. *18 Etudes en Forme d'Improvisation* (Alphonse Leduc).
_____. *Graphismes* (Alphonse Leduc).
DUFRENSE and VOISIN, R. *Develop Sight-Reading* (Colin).
FALUX, J. *20 Virtuoso Studies after Bach* (Elkan-Vogel).
_____. *25 Progressive Studies* (Elkan-Vogel).
FEARN, W. O. *Exercises for Flexibility* (Elkan-Vogel).
GALLAY, J. *30 Etudes* (Sansone).
_____. *12 Grandes Etudes Brilliantes* (Sansone and Elkan-Vogel).
_____. *Unmeasured Preludes* (Sansone).
KLING, HENRI. *40 Characteristic Etudes for French Horn* (Southern Music).
_____. *24 Horn Studies* (Israel Brass and Woodwind Publications).
KOPPRASCH, C. *50 Etudes for French Horn* (Southern Music).
_____. *60 Selected Studies* (Carl Fischer).
MAXIME-ALFONSE. *40 Etudes Moyenne Force* (Alfonse Leduc).
_____. *20 Etudes Difficiles* (Alphonse Leduc).
MUELLER, B. E. *34 Studies*, Vols. 1 and 2 (International).
_____. *22 Studies* (International).
REYNOLDS, VERNE. *48 Etudes for French Horn* (G. Schirmer).
SANSONE, LORENZO. *A Modern Method for French Horn*, Vols. 1 and 2 (Sansone).
SINGER, JOSEPH. *Embouchure Building for French Horn* (Belwin-Mills).
VANDER-WOUDE, MARY. *French Horn Studies* (Summy-Birchard).

FRENCH HORN
Fingering Chart

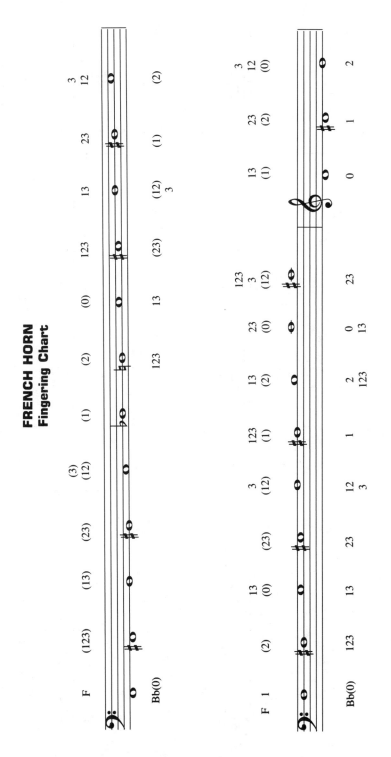

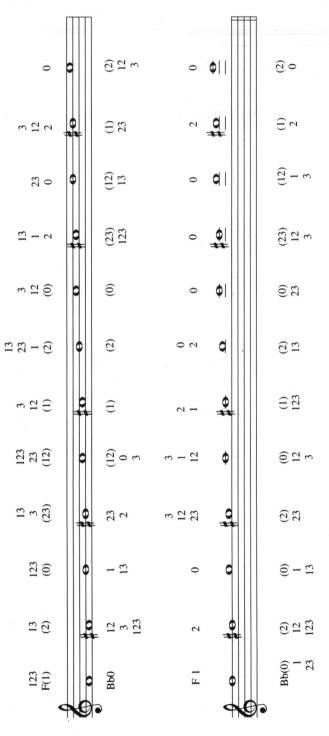

17

The Trumpet
and Cornet

HISTORY

The history of the cornet or trumpet is very old if the instrument is viewed as related to the first lip-voiced instruments such as a shell or elephant horn of the prehistoric era. More directly related is a trumpet made of wood, mentioned in Sumerian texts from about 3000 B.C. The Swiss alphorn and Jewish shofar of the present are descendants of this early instrument. Various horns of different lengths and shapes can be found throughout history. They were generally connected with war or ceremonial events. Some historians trace the rivalry between the cornet and trumpet back to earliest times. There had been for centuries a fluctuation of preference for either the conical or cylindrical instrument, depending on the situation and sound desired. Actually the trumpet was preferred until about A.D. 1400. It was the more effective in the primary use of such instruments, that of causing fright or awe.

The first instrument that could be fingered was the cornett or zink, traced to the Persians as early as A.D. 77, but not used widely until the Middle Ages. It was a conical instrument with a cup mouthpiece and holes in the body comparable to the clarinet of today. This instrument culminated in the serpent, ophicleide, and keyed bugle of the nineteenth century. The trumpet has undergone fewer changes than any other instrument, and only the addition of the valve has had any lasting effect on its basic design. It was throughout history the instrument of royalty; even as late as the Stuarts of England the unauthorized possession of a trumpet was a serious offense. The trumpet was favored by both Bach and Handel as well as other late Baroque composers. The Classical composers, however, did not like its shrill sounds, and not until Beethoven used it in his Third Symphony did it come to be a standard part of the orchestra.

The keyed bugle was invented by Kolbel of St. Petersburg in 1760. It was soon replaced, around 1815, by an instrument with a piston valve, the invention of Blumel, an oboe player from Silesia. Stolzel, who purchased the patent, added a second valve. By 1830, Muller added the third valve so that the scale was complete above the second partial, as we use it today. Although the valve trumpet was used by Halevy in *La Juive*, Wagner is generally considered the first composer to write well for the instrument. Wagner's use of the trumpet occurred almost simultaneously with the rise of the band and the great cornet virtuosos such as Levy, Smith, Bellstedt, and Goldman. Throughout the early part of the twentieth century, the cornet was associated with bands, the trumpet with orchestras and dance bands. Today, in the hands of master players the cornet and trumpet have very small differences in sound, but definite opinions are held as to the superiority of each.

The question of whether the beginning student should purchase a cornet or a trumpet was debated for decades. The cornet was preferred as the beginning instrument for many years because it fit the average fourth- or fifth-grade student better than the trumpet. The trumpet, however, has become the instrument of choice.

SELECTING THE INSTRUMENT

The length of the B-flat cornet and the trumpet is the same: approximately 4½ feet. The trumpet is approximately two thirds cylindrical with only one basic winding while the cornet is about 70 percent conical and the tubing has two windings. Technically the difference lies in the degree of taper. The tubing of the cornet tapers from the mouthpiece opening throughout its entire length except for the valve and tuning slides. The trumpet is slightly larger at the mouthpiece opening and gradually becomes larger. The trumpet tubing is primarily cylindrical and is smaller than the cornet tubing for much of its length. The sound is different in that the cylindrical bore instrument (trumpet) enhances the higher partials while the conical bore (cornet) enhances the fundamental and the lower partials. Many teachers have described the difference in sounds as analogous to the difference in a floodlight (cornet) and a spotlight (trumpet).

It matters little on which instrument a student begins instrumental music, so the child should select the instrument with which he will be happiest. In addition to different-sized bores, instruments are obtainable with different-sized bells. A large-bore instrument with a small bell produces brilliance rather than a broad tone. A broad tone can be obtained from a medium-bore instrument with a large bell if a mouthpiece with a medium to large cup is used. The bore size is measured at the second valve port and the bell size immediately before the flare. Bells are made of various materials: most are of the same brass alloy as the rest of the instrument, but some professional-line manufacturers offer the player a choice of alloys for the bell. Opinions differ as to the value of these various brass alloys; many find no difference whatsoever between them. The effect, if any, seems to be in the degree of brilliance.

The metal of the horn is important for tone quality, and most companies presently use a satisfactory grade. A lacquer finish is the most common; silver is preferred by most professionals. Silver-plating becomes a part of the instrument itself instead of simply a coating; silver is thinner than lacquer finishes and results in a darker tone quality. Unfortunately, silver is much more expensive than lacquer. Many student-line instruments are nickel-plated. These wear better and usually produce a slightly more brilliant sound. Most repair shops, however, do not have the facilities to replate nickel. A number of professionals prefer a "raw brass" finish (or lack thereof), which produces the darkest tone quality.

There are also other details of construction to look for. Top-valve spring action is superior for all small piston brass. The instrument should be tight (that is, no banging around when shaken) and the valves freely moving. It should give the desired response in a playing test.

When inspecting a used instrument for possible purchase, one should inspect the valves for undue wear at the bottom of each valve. A poor playing habit is to press the valves at a slight angle rather than straight down, a motion that creates wear and tear on the alloy coating on the valves. If this coating is worn off one can expect serious trouble from the instrument. Valves should also be tested to see if they "wiggle" in the valve casing, an additional sign of excessive wear, or if they bounce when pressed and then released—valves with good springs should not bounce up and down at the top of the stroke. And finally the outside of the instrument should be inspected for pits. Some players have excessive acid in their perspiration, and frequent handling of the instrument without wiping it off after playing can damage and pit the brass, especially around the valve casings.

All valve combinations should be checked with an electronic tuner to determine if they are inordinately out of tune; the open tones should be played first and then the valves. Compression can be checked by pulling a valve slide, then depressing the valve and listening for the pop. Students should know that normally the valves must be depressed in order to pull slides; for example, the first valve should be pressed before adjusting the first-valve slide. One of the most common problems among beginning trumpet players is the inability to remove saliva through the third valve slide water key, a frustration due to not pressing the third valve while blowing air through the instrument.

Detailed instructions for breaking in a trumpet should accompany a new instrument. Especially good instructions come with instruments manufactured by the Selmer Corporation. The instrument being purchased should play responsively in all registers and not have too much or too little resistance. Since most beginners find instruments with greater resistance easier to play, a parent should seek assistance from an advanced trumpet player in selecting an instrument.

Whether to purchase an instrument with an easily adjustable first- or third-valve slide is generally a matter of personal preference and cost, but all high school calibre trumpet players should have an adjustable third-valve slide. Trumpets designed with this adjustment are manufactured with the third-valve slide slightly shorter, bringing the low E-flat and all A-flats into tune. With this instrument the third valve alone can be used in lieu of first-and-second-valve combinations because of the improved intonation. Some trumpets and cornets employ a trigger-operated device on the first valve slide; the more common "hook" or "saddle" is preferred since it has no mechanism to break and makes removing the slide to drain water easier. If the first valve slide is short enough to bring fourth-line D and third-space C-sharp in tune, certain first and second valve combinations are sharp (such as the bottom-line E). The professional-quality trumpet offers the player a choice of using either the first-valve slide or third-valve slide to adjust the most out-of-tune notes, low C-sharp and D. Which slide to use depends on the situation, fingering patterns, and technical difficulty. Decisions on which of the two tuning devices to use also depend on the range of the music.

ASSEMBLING THE TRUMPET OR CORNET

Assembling the trumpet should not present any problems. It consists of merely putting the mouthpiece in. Mouthpieces for brasses can be damaged if they are forced or jammed into the instrument. Some players give the mouthpiece a slight turn after it is inserted to ensure proper seating. Wiggling the mouthpiece back and forth to work it in can damage both the end of the mouthpiece and the leadpipe, allow air to leak, and affect intonation and tone quality.

HOLDING THE TRUMPET OR CORNET

The correct hand position for playing the trumpet is shown in Figure 17–1. The trumpet is held with the left hand. It is grasped with the fingers around the third-valve casing and the thumb around the casing of the first valve. It is important that the thumb not be too high, or the student may

Figure 17–1. Hand Position for Playing the Trumpet

support the instrument with his wrist. The wrist should be as straight as possible and in line with the forearm. If the wrist is bent, the wrist muscles will soon tire from supporting the weight, which should be sustained by the entire arm. If the instrument is held so that the valves are slightly tilted to the player's right and the left wrist kept straight, the weight will be carried by the arm. It is then necessary for the player to experiment to find the point of balance of the instrument for maximum comfort. Most modern trumpets are balanced at or near the third valve, so when properly held the point of balance in the left hand will be near the point where the bell tubing rests on the upper joint of the first finger.

If the trumpet is held in balance and tilted slightly to the right with both wrists held straight, both elbows will be about even, comfortably away from the body so as not to hamper breathing, but not out so far as to require real effort to hold them up. The head rests easily on the shoulders without bending. The wrists are straight and the arms form an angle of approximately 60 degrees when viewed from the front. Proper posture is complete when the student rests both feet on the floor and sits or stands tall (see Figure 17–2). Bad posture inhibits correct breathing and contributes to muscular tension.

Whether the player should hold the trumpet parallel to the floor is a question over which there is disagreement. Vincent Bach says, "Hold the instrument in horizontal position or slightly above—without leaning your head backwards. . . . Push the lower jaw forward so the lower teeth are in line with the upper ones."[1] Donald Reinhardt says, "Please do not take too seriously the greatly overrated mid-Victorian phrase, 'hold the instrument in a horizontal position at all times.' Forget this nonsense and hold your instrument to conform to your type of jaw."[2] The great jazz trumpeter

[1] Vincent Bach, *Embouchure and Mouthpiece Manual* (Elkhart, IN: H. & A. Selmer, n.d.). Reprint of *Genuine Bach Mouthpieces* (Mt. Vernon, NY: Vincent Bach Corporation, 1956), 11.
[2] Donald S. Reinhardt, *The Encyclopedia of the Pivot System* (New York: Charles Colin, 1964), 9.

Figure 17–2. Sitting Position for Playing the Trumpet

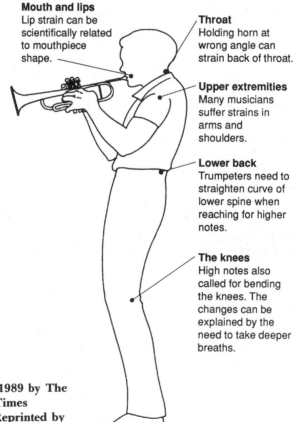

Mouth and lips
Lip strain can be scientifically related to mouthpiece shape.

Throat
Holding horn at wrong angle can strain back of throat.

Upper extremities
Many musicians suffer strains in arms and shoulders.

Lower back
Trumpeters need to straighten curve of lower spine when reaching for higher notes.

The knees
High notes also called for bending the knees. The changes can be explained by the need to take deeper breaths.

Snooky Young and the great symphonic player Vincent Cichowicz both play with their instruments pointed slightly downward. The best approach to the problem is to keep in mind that a slightly downward tilt is desirable and to experiment with the tone by moving the instrument in an arc from horizontal to the floor while keeping the head erect and relaxed. The position that gives the best sound should be adopted. Poor hand position can tip the bell downward, putting pressure on the lower lip, changing the angle of the air and jaw, and resulting in a dead tone. Conversely, although less likely, poor hand position in tilting the bell upward results in poor endurance in the upper register. Students with an overbite will probably find they obtain a better sound by holding the instrument somewhat below the horizontal.

The right hand should be placed so that the fingertips curve in a relaxed manner above the valve buttons; the right hand should not help hold the trumpet. If the fingers are too flat, if the wrist is bent, or if the right hand is too low or too close to the instrument, the valves will be pulled down rather than pushed. For example, if the trumpet is held with the valves exactly perpendicular to the floor, the right wrist can be kept straight only by holding the elbow high and far away from the body; the left wrist can be kept straight only by keeping the left elbow jammed into the left rib cage. Playing should be done on the fleshy balls of the fingers, not on the knuckles or on the extreme tips of the fingers.

The right thumb should rest under the leadpipe so that it comes between the first- and second-valve casing. This position is important because it places the fingers properly above the valves, allowing better use of the weak ring finger. The position of the thumb (1) provides support for fingers when they depress the valves, (2) aids in keeping the fingers up, (3) prevents the hand from drooping inward toward the side of the instrument, and (4) can be used to play and control vibrato.

The finger ring or hook should not be used. The little finger should remain free to respond in sympathy with the third finger. The third finger is the weakest and should not be inhibited by a restricted little finger. The finger hook is used only when the player needs to hold the instrument with the right hand, as in turning pages or placing a mute in the bell. Using the hook may also lead to excessive and damaging pressure on the lips. Some players use the hook as an aid to the upper register, but the added pressure results in a stuffy tone quality and limited range because there is only so much pressure the lips can stand. Clamping the lips between the mouthpiece and teeth also restricts flexibility.

One can demonstrate to students the technique problem caused by using the finger ring: ask the student to hold out his right hand and wiggle his fingers, then grasp and hold his little finger, completely restricting it from moving, and then ask him to wiggle his fingers—the resulting action is not only less comfortable, but the fingers simply cannot move as freely.

Because so many of the elements of trumpet playing are equally valid for the other brass instruments, numerous topics of importance to trumpeters were discussed in Chapter 15. Those items are not repeated here.

THE BEGINNING STUDENT

The discussion of physical characteristics and their importance in trumpet playing is heard over and over, yet there are many exceptions to the rule. The older idea of thin lips for a trumpet player and thicker lips for playing the larger brass instruments has been largely abandoned; if such a rule was held in every case, both Snooky Young and Vincent Cichowicz would have probably become bassoon players. Physical differences that may be considered are the following:

1. Uneven teeth make if difficult for the player to seat the mouthpiece properly on the lips, although teeth that are only slightly irregular are not necessarily detrimental. Many good players have overcome a minor irregularity by placing the mouthpiece rim slightly to one side. The muscles of the face and tongue are sufficiently flexible so that with practice small variances can be overcome. When the player places the mouthpiece very much off-center, however, he has unequal muscular control. This position imposes a strain on the embouchure muscles, limits range and endurance, and allows an uneven vibrating surface and improper position of the tongue that impedes tonguing. Two simple tests to determine whether the prospective player can place the mouthpiece in the center of his lips are to have him whistle to see if the whistle aperture is in the center of the lips, and to have him produce a buzzing sound with the lips alone.

2. A severe malocclusion (overbite or underbite) or failure of the jaws to come together evenly results in strain and prevents the mouthpiece from receiving correct support. A small degree of malocclusion is normal. Pointing the chin corrects some overbite. Philip Farkas states that if the student is unable to align his jaws as though he were biting a piece of celery, he is not a brass player.[3]

3. A player whose lips are considerably longer or shorter than his front teeth may have trouble. Lips that are long in relation to the teeth tend to roll inward too much. If the upper lip alone rolls in too far, it is injurious to both endurance and range. Lips short in relation to the teeth may not come together sufficiently at the center to form a proper embouchure.

4. Front teeth that slant inward prevent the lips from providing a firm support for the mouthpiece.

[3] Philip Farkas, *The Art of Brass Playing* (Bloomington, IN: Brass Publications, 1962), 7.

5. Unusual defects such as injured facial muscles, harelips, and large scars should be carefully considered before allowing a student to begin on trumpet.

EMBOUCHURE

To assist the formation of a correct embouchure, the student may be asked to place his lips in the position for vocalizing the syllable "em." Then he can place the instrument to his relaxed lips and vocalize "pooh." This procedure will naturally produce a sound with a tone quality considerably short of that by Maurice Andre, but it will have immediate results. At this point in producing a sound, the student should be asked to form his lips as if vocalizing "em," then tighten the corners of the mouth and buzz the lips until a tone of sorts is produced. Practice and careful instruction in shaping a proper embouchure along with proper breathing will result in rapid improvement.

Students who have initial difficulty in producing a tone on the trumpet should buzz with the mouthpiece only, and buzz their lips without the instrument or the mouthpiece. While buzzing the lips alone, the teacher can touch the student's chin to determine if the air is being directed too far downward. If so, the student should be reminded to extend his chin a bit more forward. Buzzing without the mouthpiece is also useful for those students who have a tendency to puff out their cheeks, as buzzing strengthens these muscles; it is virtually impossible for one to puff out the cheeks when buzzing without a mouthpiece, just as it is impossible to bunch up the chin.

A correct embouchure is shown in Figures 17–3, 17–4, 17–5 and 17–6. The mouthpiece should be centered on the lips horizontally and placed vertically so as to use one-third upper lip and two-thirds lower lip, which when observed using a mouthpiece visualizer is actually closer to half-and-half inside the mouthpiece. A "half-and-half" distribution of the lips' visual appearance (which means even more upper lip) may be acceptable. The corners of the mouth are tightened and pressed against the teeth. The center of the lips sympathetically tighten just enough to provide a fleshy cushion that vibrates when the air stream passes through it. Tightening the corners of the mouth also helps to keep the chin drawn flat.

Mouthpieces

The trumpet has attracted more mouthpiece manufacturers than any other brass instrument. Many "gimmick-type" mouthpieces are available, most often advertised as extending the upper range and capable of doing half the work for the trumpet player. The student should select a mouth-

Figure 17–3.   Trumpet Embouchure

piece from a reputable company (e.g., Bach, Schilke, or Giardinelli) and secure his upper and lower range by developing the embouchure and breathing apparatus. If one were to select the single best, all-around mouthpiece for beginning trumpet students, it would probably be the Bach 7C.

As the student grows physically and the embouchure muscles grow stronger, he should consider moving to a larger mouthpiece. A larger mouthpiece (at least with regard to cup diameter and depth) allows for a richer, darker tone quality. A larger cup diameter allows the aperture of

Figure 17–4.   Trumpet Embouchure (side view, playing low C)

Figure 17–5. Trumpet Embouchure (side view, playing middle C)

the embouchure to open more, with more of the lip vibrating, resulting in a clearer tone. For students who have not developed a strong embouchure, a larger mouthpiece will hurt the upper range. They should not resort to bad habits in order to play in the upper register; therefore the teacher must be careful of the demands placed on these developing trumpet players.

Figure 17–6 Trumpet Embouchure (side view, playing high C)

INTONATION

Intonation requires practice and good listening habits. Trumpet players in most ensembles are given a brief opportunity to tune their C or B and the rest of the pitches are assumed to be in time. Intonation on any instrument can be improved by knowing the natural tendencies of the instrument—this is especially true with the trumpet, as most trumpets share common intonation flaws. Figure 17–7 shows the intonation flaws of the majority of B-flat trumpets manufactured as student-line and professional-line instruments. The medium- or professional-line instruments with devices to extend the first- or third-valve slides help correct many of these problems. Developing players should use these devices consistently in warm-ups and drills.

Trumpet students should also be made aware of their personal intonation tendencies. Many students play slightly flat in the upper register when fatigue begins to set in and become quite sharp as they become more fatigued and pinch for the high notes. Ideally, the fatigued trumpet player should immediately warm-down and put the instrument away, but during the spring concert this response may not please the audience, conductor, or the rest of the section. Temperature and performance anxiety also affect intonation.

The ear is the best judge. Good intonation is the most neglected aspect of beginning trumpet instruction. Far too many teachers wait until immediately before the concert to ever mention it. Since it goes hand-in-hand with good tone quality it should be a matter of daily attention.

The notes comprising the seventh harmonic are so flat that they are completely ignored; these notes are played by using valve combinations that lower the eighth harmonic.

TONE QUALITY

The trumpet may well be the most versatile instrument in the brass family. Tone quality varies among professional players and even more so among students, but the trumpet student is going to sound only as good as his mental image of the ideal tone. Often the young student is so caught up in technique and range that tone quality is neglected. It matters little how fast a trumpet player can double-tongue or how many major and minor scales can be ripped off; if the tone is unpleasant the effort has been lost. Good tone quality depends on the student's ability to mentally conceive of a good trumpet sound, to listen critically, and to evaluate the tone produced.

A fine teacher can encourage students to produce a better sound by demonstrating good and poor examples, for example: (1) a focused, centered sound in which the tone does not spread on crescendos or become

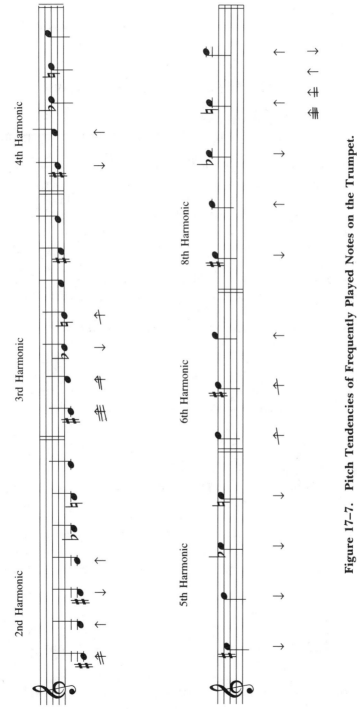

Figure 17–7. Pitch Tendencies of Frequently Played Notes on the Trumpet.

pinched on decrescendos; (2) excessive edge in the sound caused by over-blowing, a mouthpiece that is too small or too shallow or one that has too prevalent an edge where the cup meets the backbore; and (3) a relaxed sound, not forced, relying on the embouchure with plenty of wind as opposed to excessive mouthpiece pressure to make up for lack of air or a developed embouchure. A trumpet has a great range of dynamics. The student should practice in all dynamic ranges and make dynamic changes when practicing for focused and clear tones. Long tones are a useful tool and can be made exciting to the student by an understanding and inspiring teacher.

Keith Johnson in *The Art of Trumpet Playing* discusses the importance of imagination and experimentation in playing the trumpet. His emphasis is on imagination, allowing the student to produce new ideas from existing information. He emphasizes that for a player to improve his sound, he must have existing information, that is, a firm grasp on how successful trumpet players sound, even though he may not want to emulate that exact sound.

This need for a model can be satisfied in several ways. (1) The music teacher can provide an example. This option is limited by the teacher's ability. (2) Private lessons may be the most common means for providing young students with models. (3) The better-sounding high school players may be used. (4) For high school players, master classes taught by professional musicians or college students can provide entire sections a role model for good tone quality. Also, master classes as models do not have to be on trumpet. A young trumpet student can learn much and begin conceptualizing a good tone quality by listening to a professional flute player. As Johnson observes:

> "Musical imagination, if properly used, is beneficial in several ways. First, it ensures receptiveness to new ideas that can be gained from listening to music of all types and sources. Trumpet players can gain unlimited ideas from fine singers, pianists, string players, and others. New ideas should be incorporated into one's playing. Occasional alterations in vibrato, increasing or decreasing the volume level for certain passages, or modifying an articulation in some subtle way will enhance the musical interest of any performance. . . .
>
> In the process of acquiring new ideas, players should not be afraid to experiment. Many students are so conditioned to "right" and "wrong" judgments that they become overly cautious and afraid of making mistakes. . . . Fear of mistakes is a threat to imaginative, creative playing. . . .
>
> For substantial improvement to occur the student must be able to imagine a better sound than he has played previously,

and in order to implement this new sound he must be willing to experiment. . . . The teacher should direct and encourage the student, guide his experimentation, and comment on the results with understanding and accuracy. . . . Any skill, artistic or otherwise, is learned through trial and error."[4]

Vibrato

Vibrato is often used for lyrical solo passages. Those who believe vibrato was invented to hide intonation problems are greatly mistaken; vibrato compounds intonation problems—there is hardly anything lovely about ten to sixteen trumpets all using different types and speeds of vibrato in an attempt to cover intonation problems.

The most common method of vibrato for trumpet, and the easiest to develop, is hand vibrato. Hand vibrato is created by using the thumb of the right hand, which rests gently under the leadpipe between the first and second valve casings, to move forward and backward making subtle pulsations in the pitch (about 7 per second). The pulsations should be even and the pitch not noticeably affected. Many jazz trumpet players use a wider, broader vibrato, especially on phrase endings of ballads. Again, students should listen to recordings or live performances of successful trumpet players, then let the ear determine what is most appropriate. Acceptable vibrato changes depending on tessitura and style of the music. Some styles of music are best played with no vibrato, for example, Classical orchestral literature.

Many trumpet players also use jaw vibrato, achieved by playing a straight tone and moving the jaw slightly as if vocalizing "wah–wah–wah" rapidly. Jaw vibrato can usually be done more subtly than hand vibrato but affects endurance and also flexibility in slurs (especially lip slurs). Whole treatises are written on vibrato. When Adolph Herseth was asked how he produced a vibrato he said he didn't know. After a pause he said "I guess I just wiggle my lips and blow."

Mutes

Mutes in general tend to raise the pitch of the instrument in the lower register. They also make the instrument harder to play and less responsive. Students should not practice excessively with mutes. Because they add resistance, they are considered by many teachers to be a viable means to build the embouchure, but it is impossible to work on tone quality when the

[4] Keith Johnson, *The Art of Trumpet Playing* (Ames, IA: University of Iowa Press, 1981), 15–16.

instrument is muted, and tone quality is, after all, the most important characteristic. For complete information on using mutes with brass instruments, one should obtain a copy of the thesis by Martin Kurka published by the F. E. Olds Company.[5]

Straight mutes, except for the plastic variety, tend to raise the pitch. The straight mute produces a brighter tone but a thinner sound; the tone seems to be affected most in the lower register, somewhat less in the high register, and least in the middle register. The most popular straight mutes are the metal mute and a hard-board, "stone-lined" one. The former sounds a bit more raspy and is preferred by jazz musicians. The stone-lined mute produces a softer, smoother sound and is preferred by many due to its less expensive cost. Plastic mutes enjoyed a brief period of popularity because they were extremely inexpensive and never leaked as metal mutes can if handled roughly or dropped; but the corks tended to come off, which rapidly diminished their popularity.

Cup mutes, used primarily in jazz ensembles, lower the pitch in the middle register. Tonal color cups, however, lower the pitch in the upper register. Use of the cup mute gives a velvety tone quality with the tone attenuated most in the lower register and less as the pitch rises.

Wah-wah and harmon mutes tend to raise the pitch in the middle register and lower it in the high register. These mutes produce a piercing or strident tone. They thin out the tone more in the extremities than in the middle range but are adjustable using the stem projecting from the center. Since these mutes fit snugly inside the bell of the instrument and the cork completely surrounds the mute, the trumpet player must blow slow, warm air into (or onto) the bell to create a layer of water vapor to keep the mute in place.

A general rule to follow is to play one dynamic step louder when using all mutes except the wah-wah, where one should play two steps louder. Mutes cannot be expected to fit the horn exactly. In order to obtain a proper fit and achieve the best sound, the player may have to sand the corks.

FINGERING

The basic fingerings on brass instruments are much easier to learn than those for the woodwinds. The student should understand the function of the valves as described in Chapter 15: Tubing is added to change the overtone series. If the principle is understood, it is quite easy to memorize the seven valve combinations used.

[5] Martin J. Kurka, *A Study of the Acoustical Effects of Mutes on the Wind Instruments* (Fullerton, CA: F. E. Olds Music Co., 1961).

Good hand position is important in developing fingering skill. The player should learn to push the valves down firmly and feel a slight impact when the valve cap hits the valve top.

Technique comes with practice. Scales and studies are indispensable for gaining technique, but they should not be the entire substance of the student's musical diet. Tasks such as learning to play scales fast can be learned over a relatively short period of time; other tasks such as good tone quality, extended upper range, and endurance require much more practice and should not be neglected during any stage of the trumpet player's development.

Common and alternate fingerings are shown at the end of the chapter. Alternate fingerings should not be ignored, for they are needed for tuning and technique. Some passages are almost unplayable without the use of alternate fingerings. Alternate fingerings help to clear up intonation worries. Alternates can best be learned through application.

A few illustrations of the use of alternate fingerings may serve to clarify the discussion.

1. Valves 1 and 2 equal valve 3. Passages involving an awkward movement from 1–2 should be tried with 3 used as a substitute; for example, a passage where low D (1–3) to bottom-line E (1–2) is repeated rapidly. It is much easier to "trill" between these two notes using only the index finger.
2. Valve 3 is sometimes preferable to 1–2 for intonation. For instance, first-line E is often too sharp when played with 1–2. It can be played with 3 (a little flat) and lipped up to pitch. The same substitution may make high A more in tune.
3. On some good trumpets (especially C trumpets), a preference is given to finger fourth-space E with 1–2 and fourth-space E-flat with 2–3.
4. Many quickly moving articulated passages are played more cleanly using alternate fingerings. A very simple example, but one with which young students can readily identify, are bugle calls played without valves or using any single valve or combination of valves.

WHAT TO PRACTICE

One of the things that discourages youngsters from studying an instrument is boredom. Confinement to a single instruction book is guaranteed to create boredom. There are many excellent books to which students may be exposed. Those listed at the end of the chapter are not intended as a comprehensive survey, but are indicative of the variety of material available.

The psychological principle of working on a single problem at a time is sound, and certain materials are better than others for solving problems, developing confidence, and accuracy. Any of the complete methods offers a vast source of control studies. For instance, the single-tonguing and the interval studies in Arban's should be practiced very slowly part of the time, emphasizing the perfect placement of each tone and the absolute evenness of each tongued note. When the student is certain he can usually play any interval without error, he has come a long way toward developing assurance and control.

Daily practice should include long tones while crescendoing and decrescendoing and maintaining the same dynamic level; flexibility studies (lip slurs) to ensure continued embouchure development; studies on various articulations; technical studies to develop finger facility; and lyrical studies or melodic passages to promote expressive playing. While this routine may appear somewhat long for first-year players, the teacher should remember that a beginner's lip slurs may only be between two notes for each valve combination; their various articulations may only consist of long tones, quarter notes tongued, and slurs; and their technical studies may consist of one half of their C and F major scales. Young students should frequently play pieces they already know. Familiar pieces build confidence and musicianship and enable one to concentrate on musical aspects of playing.

One should never dismiss the value of "doodling around." Such playing by ear helps develop listening skills and technical facility and often keeps students interested. Good instrumental music teachers encourage their students to play by ear.

CARE AND MAINTENANCE OF THE TRUMPET OR CORNET

In general, brass instruments present fewer maintenance problems than woodwinds, strings, or percussion instruments. The primary task of the young trumpet or cornet student is to keep the instrument clean. Care of the instrument on a daily basis should include wiping it off with a rag to remove acidic perspiration left by the hands, which can destroy the finish and pit the brass over a period of time.

As with all brass instruments, students must always be reminded to treat their trumpets with care; not to leave them unattended lying on chairs or on the floor, not to bang the music stand when bringing them to playing position, and not to play rhythms or "tunes" by popping the mouthpiece with the palm of their hand. Dents in the leadpipe, valve or tuning slides, and valve casings cause serious problems in tone, intonation, and technique.

TROUBLESHOOTING

EQUIPMENT

sluggish valves

1. Place several drops of valve oil into first valve slide, holding instrument so that it runs down; work the three valves up and down; expel excess oil out third-valve water key. As students gain experience in playing the trumpet, they should be taught to oil the valves correctly—that is, remove, wipe, and reoil, then replace in the correct valve cylinder.
2. Make sure student is pressing valves straight down and not at an angle.
3. Remove valves, and clean them and the casing with lint-free cloth, oil well, and replace.
4. Student may have the instructions backward: petroleum jelly is for the slides, oil for the valves.

air will not pass through horn

1. Make sure valves are in correct casings and the tabs are in the slots. For those valves with two tabs, they may be backward.
2. Inspect for clogged leadpipe or bell. Mouthpieces and pencils fit very snuggly in the bell.
3. Inspect for a dirty mouthpiece or leadpipe.

gurgling sound but water key will not expel any water

1. If water gurgles without valves pressed, inspect for clogged water key. Remove tuning slide and dump. Unwind trumpet to pour out of bell section.
2. If water sounds with valves pressed, remove valves to expel. Many students forget that the third valve must be pressed for the third-valve water key to work effectively.

mouthpiece wiggles

1. Shank too long—have competent repairperson remove slight sections at a time. A mouthpiece shank that is too short causes moderate to severe intonation problems.
2. Shank out-of-round. Again to be repaired only by competent repairperson.

instrument leaks air

1. Inspect and if necessary replace cork (water key).
2. If around valve casing, have resoldered by competent repairperson.
3. If a new trumpet, have retailer replace it.

buzzing sound

1. Inspect for broken brace(s); have resoldered.
2. Determine if a recent soaking may have loosened residue inside. Rewash or use flexible brush.

TONE

thin, strident sound

1. Teeth together. Drop jaw.
2. Aperture too small. Try buzzing without mouthpiece (pitches, scales, or tunes), then with mouthpiece, then with trumpet.
3. Tongue tense in a possible attempt to keep it out of the way. Relax tongue.
4. Tension in throat. Drop shoulders, pretend to be a rag doll—limp.
5. Embouchure too stretched. Relax mouth, tighten corners, buzz without mouthpiece.
6. Mouthpiece too shallow or backbore too tight.
7. Aperture too flat. Attempt to get student to pucker more—like a whistle; try a "doo" articulation rather than "dee."
8. Too much lip in the mouthpiece. Try a larger mouthpiece or keep corners tighter.

dull, spread, or unfocused sound

1. Lips not buzzing evenly. Buzz without mouthpiece, then with mouthpiece alone.
2. Insufficient air. Blow "fast" air.
3. Cheeks puffing. Practice buzzing without mouthpiece.
4. Embouchure too slack. Tighten corners and encourage student to focus pitch—blow a "pencil-thin" stream of air.
5. Aperture too large. Same as for #3.
6. Mouthpiece too large. Try a smaller rim diameter without using a more shallow cup.

forced sound with too much edge

1. Mouthpiece too shallow, or throat or backbore too tight.
2. Throat too tight. Try relaxation exercises.
3. Dirty mouthpiece or leadpipe. Clean thoroughly.
4. Too much lip in the mouthpiece. Buzz without mouthpiece and with mouthpiece only.
5. Embouchure too stretched, which flattens aperture. Attempt to pucker more; plenty of buzzing without mouthpiece and with mouthpiece alone.
6. Tongue is too high. Try articulating with "daw" rather than "dee."
7. Practice breathing large amounts of air with the mouth in shape for vocalizing "o–o–o–o."
8. Excessive pressure. Attempt to play while pulling mouthpiece away from embouchure.

9. Work toward mental image of warmer airstream. Demonstrate by having student blow a cold then warm airstream against his hand.

10. Often due to mouthpiece being too low on embouchure.

stuffy, fuzzy sound (airy)

1. Lips not buzzing evenly. Lots of buzzing without the mouthpiece and with the mouthpiece alone. Could also be due to fatigue caused by lack of proper or insufficient warm-up, too much demand on student (e.g., his eagerness to play high notes before he is able), lack of warm-down after previous playing; tired, swollen lips hurt sound.

2. Too much lip in the mouthpiece. Correct embouchure or try larger mouthpiece.

3. Pinching lips together, or keeping teeth together. Get student to drop jaw; keep corners of mouth clamped shut firmly to loosen the center.

4. Air pockets behind upper or lower lip. Practice buzzing without mouthpiece—this forces a flat chin and firm embouchure in the right places.

5. Cheeks puffing. Again, buzz without mouthpiece.

6. Closed throat. Pull shoulders downward.

7. Too much saliva in embouchure or mouthpiece.

8. Improper mouthpiece placement. Correct placement.

difficulty with upper range

1. Excessive mouthpiece pressure. Rely more on air and less on pressure. Corners of the mouth should be kept firm, attempt to pull horn and mouthpiece away from embouchure when playing.

2. Facial muscles weak. Practice buzzing intervals, tones, etc., without the instrument *or* the mouthpiece.

3. Mouthpiece too large. Cup diameter too large.

4. Blow faster air; a "pencil-thin," airstream.

5. Fatigue; lack of proper warm-up or warm-down.

6. Try to direct air slightly downward by rolling in lower lip or tilting head backward slightly.

7. Too much bottom lip in mouthpiece.

8. Try practicing in the low register; try playing pedal tones—many believe it opens throat, which has a tendency to close when trying high notes.

ARTICULATION

explosive attacks

1. Building air pressure behind tongue or "holding" onto the air before releasing it. Try for better coordination between air and tongue; inhale to exhale without

stopping—we all know from physics that for an instant it *must* stop to change direction; so it is at that instant the tongue is used.

2. Tonguing between the teeth. Work toward a "duh" tongue placement instead of "thuh"—moving tongue to roof of mouth.

3. Stopping the previous note with the tongue. Practice playing long tones while merely disrupting the air-stream with the tongue, notes are connected.

4. Attempting to articulate with lips touching "puh" or "muh." Work on long tones with "big, opened, focused tone" and use slow repeated "duh" articulations.

5. Aperture in embouchure too small. Same as for #4.

scooping notes, facial movements

1. Air starting too slowly then increasing to proper velocity. Work on making the inhale-to-exhale one continuous cycle—without stopping. Sometimes student is timid—fear of failure—get him to take a chance.

2. "Chewing notes"; excessive chin movement. Tongue moving too far; replace "taw-taw" with "duh-duh." Practice long tone *and* lip slurs up and down in front of mirror to hold chin still.

3. #2 is usually accompanied with a bunched chin. Try buzzing without mouthpiece to force chin flat.

4. Too much lip in the mouthpiece. Practice forming an embouchure and buzzing without the mouthpiece, then try to establish the same sensations when playing.

difficulty with lip slurs

1. Try directing air slightly downward for upward slurs.

2. "Lean" into lower note for upward slurs; follow by upper pitch played slightly softer.

3. Increase air speed when going to upper pitch.

4. Avoid excessive pressure on upward slur; tighten corners of mouth instead.

5. Not enough lower lip in mouthpiece can make upward slurs difficult.

6. Do not let tone spread on downward slurs. Bad habits sometimes develop since it is almost impossible to "undershoot" the lower note.

7. Too many long tones in daily practice schedule.

8. Mouthpiece rim too wide.

9. Steady airstream to avoid breaks.

difficulty with valve slurs

1. No embouchure change if valve slurs are within the same open partial (i.e., there should be absolutely no movement or change when slurring from a second-space A to fourth-line D—air should move in a fast, thin stream).

2. Too many long tones in daily practice schedule.
3. Slam valves to exaggerate the change of pitches.
4. Steady airstream to avoid breaks.

ENDURANCE

lacking

1. Too much pressure. Try holding the trumpet away from embouchure when playing, try holding it between thumbs, try holding it with the left hand placed under valve casing.
2. Facial muscles weak. Buzz lips without mouthpiece.
3. Fatigue from too demanding a practice or rehearsal session without periods of rest.
4. Lack of proper warm-up or warm-down.
5. Not using corners of mouth properly (these are the strongest muscles in the face).
6. Mouthpiece placement may need correcting.
7. Tonguing may be improper or too tense.
8. Anxiety. Relaxation and the realization that mistakes *are* going to happen—but it's not the end of the world.

REFERENCES

Texts

AUTREY, BYRON. *Basic Guide to Trumpet Playing*. Chicago: M. M. Cole, 1963.

BARBOUR, J. M. *Trumpets, Horns, and Music*. Ann Arbor, MI: Michigan State University Press, 1964.

BATE, PHILLIP. *The Trumpet and Trombone*. 2nd ed. New York: W. W. Norton, 1972.

BLACK, LARRY. *The Trumpet Performer*. Atlanta, GA: Atlanta Symphony Orchestra, 1972.

BUSH, IRVING R. *Artistic Trumpet Technique and Study*. Hollywood, CA: Highland Music Co., 1962.

DALE, D. A. *Trumpet Technique*. London: Oxford University Press, 1965.

JOHNSON, KEITH. *The Art of Trumpet Playing*. Ames, IA: The Iowa State University Press, 1981.

MATHIE, GORDON. *The Trumpet Teacher's Guide: A Bibliography of Selected and Graded Etudes*. Cincinnati, OH: Queen City Brass Publications, 1984.

MENDEZ, RAFAEL. *Prelude to Brass Playing*. New York: Carl Fischer, 1961.

MENKE, WERNER. *History of the Trumpet of Bach and Handel*. London: W. Reeves, 1934. Reprinted Nashville, TN: The Brass Press, 1985.

NOBLE, CLYDE. *The Psychology of Cornet and Trumpet Playing: Scientific Principles of Artistic Performance*. Missoula, MT: Mountain Press, 1964.

REINHARDT, D. S. *The Encyclopedia of the Pivot System*. New York: Charles Colin, 1964.

SHERMAN, ROGER. *The Trumpeter's Handbook*. Athens, OH: Accura Music, 1979.

SMITHERS, DON. *The History and Music of the Baroque Trumpet*. Syracuse, NY: Syracuse University Press, 1973.
TARR, EDWARD. *The Trumpet*. Portland, OR: Amadeus Press, 1988.

Journals

Journal of the International Trumpet Guild. Quarterly from the International Trumpet Guild, School of Music, Florida State University, Tallahassee, FL 32306–2098.

Studies

Easy-Beginning (elementary and junior high)

ARBAN, J. B. (ed. Goldman and Smith). *Complete Conservatory Method* (Carl Fischer).
BALASANIAN-MUSSER. *25 Easy Studies* (Belwin-Mills).
BEELER, WALTER. *Method for the Cornet*, 2 vols. (Warner Brothers).
CLARKE, H. L. *Elementary Studies* (Carl Fischer).
CONCONE, G. (ed. Sawyer). *Lyrical Studies* (Brass Press).
FULLER, R. *Complete Beginning and Intermediate Method Chamber Music* (Chamber Music).
GETCHELL, ROBERT. *Practical Studies for Trumpet*, Book I (Belwin-Mills).
HERING, SIGMUND. *The Beginning Trumpeter* (Carl Fischer).
LITTLE, LOWELL. *Embouchure Builder* (Pro-Art).
MUSSER, W., and DEL BORGO, E. *Modes in Contemporary Music* (Alfred Music).
_____. *Rhythm in Contemporary Music* (Alfred Music).
_____. *Tonality in Contemporary Music* (Alfred Music).
SCHLOSSBERG, MAX. *Daily Drills and Technical Studies* (M. Baron).

Medium (advanced junior high and high school)

ARBAN, J. B. (ed. Goldman and Smith). *Complete Conservatory Method* (Carl Fischer).
BOUSQUET, N. *36 Celebrated Studies* (Carl Fisher).
CLARKE, H. L. *Technical Studies* (Carl Fischer).
CLODOMIR, PIERRE. *70 Petits Exercices* (International).
CONCONE, G. (ed. Sawyer). *Lyrical Studies* (Brass Press).
DAVIDSON, LOUIS. *Trumpet Techniques* (Louis Davidson).
DUFRENSE, G., and ROGER VOISIN. *Develop Sight-Reading* (Colin).
GETCHELL, ROBERT. *Practical Studies for Trumpet*, Book II (Belwin-Mills).
HERING, S. *The Advancing Trumpeter* (Carl Fischer).
_____. *28 Melodious and Technical Studies* (Carl Fischer).
MUSSER, W., and DEL BORGO, E. *Modes in Contemporary Music* (Alfred Music).
_____. *Rhythm in Contemporary Music* (Alfred Music).
_____. *Tonality in Contemporary Music* (Alfred Music).
POTTAG, M. *Preparatory Melodies to Solo Work* (Belwin-Mills).

SCHLOSSBERG, M. *Daily Drills and Technical Studies* (M. Baron).
SMITH, WALTER. *Lip Flexibility on the Cornet or Trumpet* (Carl Fischer).

Advanced (high school and college)

ARBAN, J. B. (ed. Maire). *Celebre Methode Complete*, Book 3, French Arban (Alphonse Leduc).
_____. (ed. Goldman and Smith). *Complete Conservatory Method* (Carl Fischer).
BARTOLD, GABRIEL. (ed. Voisin). *Orchestral Excerpts*, Vol. 1 through 5 (International).
BITSCH, M. *20 Etudes* (Alphonse Leduc).
BORDOGNI, N. *24 Vocalises* (Alphonse Leduc).
BRANDT, W. (ed by Vacchiano). *34 Studies and 24 Last Studies* (International).
CHARLIER, THEODORE. *36 Etudes Transcendantes* (Alphonse Leduc).
CHAVANNE, H. *Etudes de Virtuosite* (Robert King).
CLARKE, H. *Characteristic Studies* (Carl Fischer).
_____ *Technical Studies* (Carl Fischer).
COBIN, C. *Advanced Lip Flexibilities* (Colin).
DAVIDSON, LOUIS. *Trumpet Techniques* (Louis Davidson).
DUFRENSE, G., and R. VOISIN. *Develop Sight-Reading* (Colin).
LONGINOTTI, P. *Studies in Classical and Modern Style* (International).
MAXIME and ALPHONSE. *20 Etudes Tres Difficules* (Alphonse Leduc).
SABARICH, R. *10 Etudes* (Edition Selmer).
SACHSE, E. *100 Etudes for Trumpet* (International).
SCHLOSSBERG, M. *Daily Drills and Technical Studies* (M. Baron).
SMITH, WALTER. *Studies for Embouchure Development* (Carl Fischer).
TOMASI, HENRI. *6 Etudes for Trumpet* (Alphonse Leduc).
VOISIN, R. (ed.) *Orchestral Excerpts*, Vols. VI through X (International).

TRUMPET
Fingering Chart

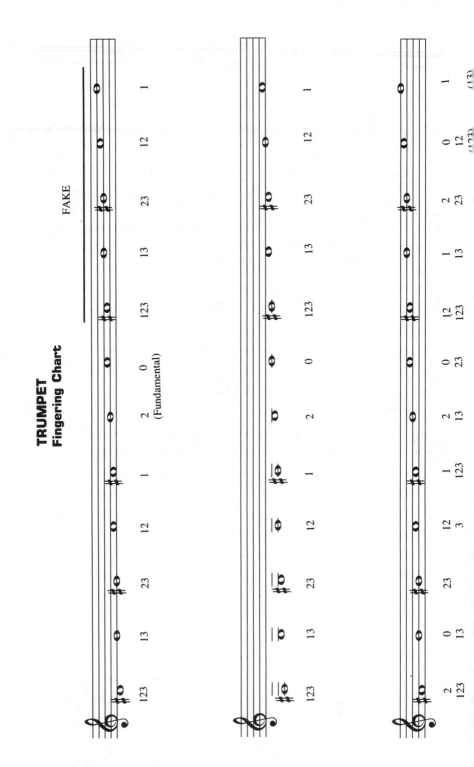

Common and Alternate Fingerings for the Trumpet (Note: Parentheses indicate the seventh partial—always a bad note [very flat] and best played with another fingering)

18

The Trombone

HISTORY

The Roman armies marched to the calls of brass instruments, among which were those named *buccina*. This instrument, about 12 feet in length, vaguely resembled the trombone, although it was shaped more like the letter C. The Romans seemed to have mastered the art of bending metal tubing, but this art was lost with the fall of Rome and not rediscovered until the Middle Ages; with the disappearance of this skill, the buccina also disappeared.

In the fourteenth century, a definite ancestor of the trombone was used, bearing the unpoetic name of *sackbut*. It appears in paintings before 1500, and by the end of the sixteenth century it was found in several sizes and ranges—a family of sackbuts similar to the family of stringed instruments, according to the common practice. These were useful instruments, for they could play the first four semitones below the open tone, so that with the use of overtones most of the notes of the chromatic scale could be obtained, a rare feat for a wind instrument. In the early 1500s, the fifth semitone was added, which made the complete scale available except for one or two low tones at the bottom of the range.

The sackbut was especially prominent in the tower music of Germany and in the church music of the Gabrielis, Monteverdi, and others of the Venetian school. The early concept of the trombone as a sacred instrument for use in the church remained prominent for many years. In spite of this, it found its way into one of the first operas, *Orfeo* by Monteverdi. It was used thereafter in opera and ensemble music continuously, more for color effects than as a legitimate member of the orchestra. Mozart's extraordinary sense of the potentialities of the trombone is shown in its use in the *Requiem, Don Giovanni,* and *The Magic Flute,* but only with Beethoven's Fifth Symphony did it find a place in symphonic music. The possibilities of the trombone seem to have been better understood following Berlioz' *Treatise on Orchestration* (1844), and since that time it has been a standard member of the brass family.

SELECTING THE INSTRUMENT

The trombone is a cylindrical brass instrument (approximately two-thirds cylindrical, one-third conical) pitched one octave below the B-flat trumpet. Although both are B-flat instruments, only the trumpet transposes (it sounds one step below the written pitch). The trombone is not a transposing instrument; it sounds the pitch that is read. Like the trumpet, the trombone plays in the register encompassing its second to ninth or tenth partials.

In selecting a used trombone, one should look for the following:

1. Possible leaks. These may be located by removing the tuning slide, stopping the smaller of the exposed tubes, and blowing smoke through the leadpipe. Leaks can also be identified by immersing the slide in water and stopping one end with the hand while blowing in the other; bubbles will pinpoint the leak. A leak at the point where the slide section screws onto the bell section will be evident if condensation forms on the player's left hand.
2. Obvious wear. This is indicated by badly worn lacquer and, more serious, worn chromium plating on the inner slide. Worn plating will cause sticking due to brass rubbing against brass.
3. The alignment of the slide and valve alignment. The slide may stick and appear to be well-worn in spots, indicating an alignment problem. The valve alignment may be checked by removing the valve cap and examining the position of the notches. The F attachment valve can be either a string valve, a mechanical rotary, or ball and socket.
4. Loose braces and worn corks. Bass trombones occasionally leak at the valve; this may be checked by removing the F tuning slide, pushing the trigger, and blowing into the mouthpiece while holding the hand over the open tubes.

The F attachment is a device consisting of extra tubing that is switched into the basic length of the instrument by means of a thumb-operated valve or trigger. It makes accessible six pitches at the bottom of the range. The F attachment also adds a multitude of possible slide positions, offering alternatives for intonation, trills, and other technically difficult passages. Why aren't all trombones made with F attachments? Purists insist that the attachment distorts the basic proportion of two-thirds cylindrical plus one-third conical, thus harming the tone quality. Furthermore, it creates a noticeable difference in tone quality when passages use the F trigger on only a few interspersed notes. The characteristic trombone sound is to be desired; anything that militates against it is undesirable. A recent invention, an improved axial-flow valve provides improved response and definition. Presently this valve is not used by any trombone manufacturer and must be installed by a brass repairperson.[1]

The B-flat (tenor) trombone is designed to play seven different fundamental positions. With the F attachment, only six positions are available because the positions are farther apart on the slide. The B-flat trombone with F attachment is identical to the bass trombone in range and playing techniques, but the difference in the size of the bore produces the difference in the sound.

The bore of the B-flat trombone is approximately .468 to .547 inch; the bass trombone has a large bore, about .560 inch or larger. The larger bore makes the lower tones more accessible and of better quality as, conversely, the tenor trombone is better suited to playing in the upper register. Because of the larger bore, the bass trombone needs a larger bell and larger mouthpiece to produce its best efforts. Many players who transfer from the higher to the lower instrument keep their old mouthpiece, which will fit the bass trombone with the use of an adapter shank; however, to do this destroys much of the true bass quality and makes intonation unpredictable at various dynamic levels. A better solution is to order two identical mouthpieces, one with a tenor trombone shank and the other with a shank for bass trombone. Both larger cup size and deeper throat are needed in order to obtain the volume and richness desired from the bass trombone.

The bass trombone has no low B-natural on the conventional model. Low B can be obtained by pulling out the F tuning slide, but this is an awkward maneuver and produces a low B that is unusually sharp. The C above it is also sharp. A solution to the problem of low B is an F–E mechanism—two separate attachments. The second attachment adds more tubing and has an additional thumb valve to open both the F attachment and the extra tubing. The result is a complete chromatic scale without the nuisance of manipulating the tuning slide.

The valve trombone has virtually disappeared from existence. While many may consider this fortunate, the instrument is most useful in jazz bands, especially when one of the trombone parts must be covered by a trumpet or baritone player. With the advent of corps-style marching bands, brass manufacturers have produced in addition to the mellophones and

---

[1] Marketed by O. E. Thayer Company.

marching horns, marching trombones, marching baritones, and the hybrid flügelhorn. Different manufacturers use different labels, but generally the labels refer to the bore size and the proportion of conical to cylindrical tubing. Like mellophones, these instruments are easily overblown but are preferable to slide trombones in marching band. Furthermore, these instruments sound more like trombones and baritones than mellophones sound like horns. Shaped like a large trumpet, they do not suffer damaged slides nor do they snag on plumes in close quarters. Unfortunately they are costly, especially in view of their limited use.

ASSEMBLING THE TROMBONE

There are three parts to the trombone: the slide, the bell, and the mouthpiece. The slide and the bell are assembled by resting the bottom of the slide on the floor, being careful not to grasp the slide in the middle of both tubes (squeezing the tubing will ruin the alignment), taking the bell in the right hand and carefully fitting it into the slide, then screwing the two together. The angle at which the two sections fit together is 90 degrees or less, varying with the individual player. The angle is usually less with the F attachment. The slide can be dented by the slightest knock or bump, impairing intonation and slide movement. When removing the parts from the case and in assembly, care should be taken that the slide does not strike anything. Bumping a music stand often occurs when young students raise their trombones to play. With older trombone players, it normally occurs when aiming a low C at the saxophone player sitting in the row in front.

The mouthpiece should be inserted with a slight clockwise twisting motion and removed by a simple counterclockwise twist; forcing will cause damage. If the mouthpiece does not fit securely in its compartment in the case, it should be kept in a vinyl or rubber mouthpiece pouch so that it does not bounce about inside the case and damage the trombone.

HOLDING THE TROMBONE

The player sits in an upright but relaxed erect position, bringing the instrument to her lips in such a way that mouthpiece pressure is distributed evenly between the upper and lower lip. During the early stages, the trombone should be held to the left side of the music stand so that the student can see "around" the bell and not hit the music stand with the slide.

The left hand holds the trombone by grasping the braces of the slide and bell section, the thumb around the brace of the bell section nearest the mouthpiece, the lower three fingers around the top brace of the slide and the slide receiver. The left index finger rests on the shank just behind the mouthpiece or leadpipe (the size of the student's hand, consequently, will determine the angle at which the bell section and slide are secured together). The entire weight of the instrument is borne by the left hand and arm. The wrist must be straight, or tension will cause it to tire quickly. On a good trombone, a weight is usually placed in the back brace of the tuning slide to balance the instrument in first position. The farther the slide is extended, the more the left hand must grip to keep the balance. Balance is often difficult for the beginner; if forced to hold the instrument in playing position too long, she may develop bad habits such as propping her elbows on her waist.

The right hand manipulates the slide, grasping the slide brace lightly between the thumb and the first two fingers. The most control seems to occur when the thumb and middle finger are closer to the lower than to the upper part of the slide. The right hand and arm must be relaxed and loose. If the hand, wrist, or elbow is tense, flexibility will be limited. The palm of the right hand should be kept facing the player rather than turned toward the bell. Correct hand position for playing the trombone without an F attachment is shown in Figure 18–1.

Due to the weight of the trombone and the mere presence of metal so close to one's head, many students develop the habit of tilting the head, which occasionally results in the bell section's resting on the player's shoulder. Tilting the head will affect the airstream and consequently tone quality, range, flexibility, and articulation. The student should be encouraged to hold her head up straight, sit or stand tall, and bring the trombone to her, not stoop to the instrument (Figure 18–2).

The hand position for a trombone with the F valve is slightly different (Figure 18–3). The weight of the trombone is supported primarily by the

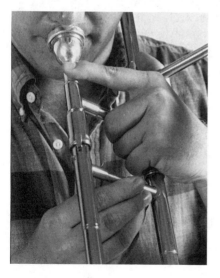

Figure 18–1. Hand Position Without Using the F Attachment for Trombone

Figure 18–2. Sitting Position for Playing the Trombone

lower three fingers of the left hand and the index finger, which is placed over the leadpipe to help the balance. The thumb remains free to operate the valve mechanism.

THE BEGINNING STUDENT

The most important physical characteristic in a beginning trombone student is adequate size. Smaller students have difficulty reaching sixth posi-

Figure 18–3. Hand Position Using the F Attachment for Trombone

tion on a trombone. Although many method books avoid introducing sixth-position notes, teachers tend to begin with the B-flat major scale, thus forcing the beginning trombone player to go from first to sixth position on the first two notes of the scale. Because of cost, most beginning trombone students do not have the F attachment; it is handy for the beginner, however, for with it the extreme position can be avoided. Starting beginners on tenor trombones with F attachments can also help avoid the problems the more advanced trombonist will have in learning to use the device.

Among the most difficult tasks for the beginning trombone player is simply holding the instrument, even one that has a counterweight. The first lessons should not require the student to hold the instrument in playing position too long. The muscles to hold the instrument must be developed. First lessons should be spent having the student buzz with and without the mouthpiece. To use the mouthpiece, grasp the end of the shank with thumb and index finger only. Buzzing the simple tunes and exercises that appear early in most method books helps the beginner focus on pitches, especially useful for the young player who must quickly learn to use her ear.

The trombone has the potential for being the only wind instrument with perfect intonation, and by the same token, it has the potential for having the worst. Buzzing without the mouthpiece reinforces the development of the embouchure, preventing cheeks from puffing, keeping the corners of the mouth firm, keeping the chin flat. Buzzing on the mouthpiece reinforces good intonation and pitch placement, but adding the trombone to the end of the mouthpiece makes it an entirely new task. To encourage in-tune playing, emphasize a focused, well-centered tone.

EMBOUCHURE

A correct trombone embouchure is illustrated in Figure 18-4. The mouthpiece is usually placed to utilize two thirds of the upper lip and one third of the lower lip in the embouchure. This is not a hard and fast rule; some trombonists play with about half upper and half lower lip. For young players with small faces, the mouthpiece may fit tightly against the nose and cover part of the chin also.

Ideally the trombone player should have a fairly square facial structure, so that the large mouthpiece has a firm support. Young players with a more V-shaped jaw or a somewhat pointed chin will find the mouthpiece less well adapted to their facial conformation.

To form the embouchure, the player adjusts her lips to a position as in vocalizing "em." This adjustment separates the teeth and aligns the upper and lower front teeth. The corners of the mouth are then tightened

Figure 18–4. Trombone Embouchure

or pressed against the teeth leaving the lips suitable for buzzing. The upper lip should be out slightly over the lower, an automatic occurrence if the student buzzes her lips without a mouthpiece. The trombonist alters the direction of the airstream more than any other brass player. Normally for the lowest pitches, the airstream is directed somewhat straight through the mouthpiece; the higher the pitch, the more downward the airstream is directed. The basic embouchure formation is similar to that for most brass instruments—lips relaxed across the front of the teeth, corners of the mouth clamped tightly and anchored firmly against the teeth. There must be sufficient lip in the mouthpiece. After the mouthpiece is set against the lips, the player can pull them back and out of the cup by clamping the corners of the mouth together if necessary, but she can't push more lip into the cup. A rigid embouchure should be avoided, as occasional adjustments are necessary for flexibility.

The lower jaw is dropped more in the correct trombone embouchure than for a trumpet or horn embouchure. Consequently the teeth are slightly farther apart.

The mouthpiece should be centered horizontally. When the player watches the slide to avoid striking music racks or other players, she tends to pull it to one side, usually to the right. Moving the slide may move the mouthpiece on her embouchure unless she turns her head with the slide. When young players with short arms attempt the sixth or seventh position they often slide the mouthpiece to the right side of their face; rarely does the mouthpiece recenter when the arm returns to a closer position.

Playing the first, second, and third overtones can help expose embouchure faults. A good sound cannot be produced in this range with a bad embouchure. Some of the more common embouchure faults are these: (1) Excessive mouthpiece pressure, detrimental to the tone and also to the lips. Some pressure is necessary to produce a seal between the lips and the mouthpiece, but excessive pressure will restrict the circulation of the blood and cause fatigue, restrict range, and severely limit flexibility. Excessive pressure is caused by an overly tense left arm, but some left-arm tension is necessary to hold the instrument steady against the movement of the slide. Practice and experimentation are necessary before the player learns to adapt the position and tension of the arm to the most comfortable setting. The instrumental music teacher must be on the alert for fatigue in the left arm. Demands on the young player to hold up the instrument for long periods of time will result in bad habits as well as frustration. (2) Substitution of mouthpiece pressure for air pressure. The teacher has to be alert for indications of too little air support, and she should stress at every opportunity the importance of blowing air *through* the instrument. (3) Shifting the mouthpiece to the right. This may not be harmful, but a centered position is better for the vast majority of players. (4) Pinching the lips together. The student should think of the teeth as being apart (about the width of a penny or nickel), the tongue at the bottom of the mouth as if vocalizing "taw." This tongue position helps relax the throat and allows for an open sound. Most accomplished trombone players feel that they perform with an open embouchure, that is, that the center of their lips never touch.

In short, the two greatest embouchure faults are (1) stretching the lips too much, forming an aperture that is too flat and possibly too wide, which creates a harsh, edgy, or thin tone; and (2) too much lip jammed in the mouthpiece, causing an uneven aperture that creates a stuffy or thick tone. Both problems are difficult to identify because the trombone mouthpiece covers such a significant portion of the student's mouth.

Mouthpieces

The mouthpiece is critical for a quality trombone tone. It is possible for a trombone to play "sweet and lyrical" (the sound made famous by the jazz trombonist Tommy Dorsey) or with great edge and projection. The mouthpiece can enhance either of these two extremes; proper mouthpiece selection for most students must consider the player's strengths, weaknesses, and desired tone, or what would best enable her to perform in a variety of styles.

A small cup diameter coupled with a shallow cup facilitates the upper register—especially when attached to a narrow backbore—but the tone may become edgy at a lower volume. A larger cup in rim diameter and depth enhances the lower register, increases volume, and provides a deep, dark tone. Its restrictions include making the upper register more difficult and reducing flexibility and endurance for those players with poorly developed embouchures. Many trombonists prefer a more funnel or V-shaped mouthpiece that produces a richer, more mellow sound and eliminates all edge from the tone quality.

As with all brass students, a compromise mouthpiece is the best selection. The most popular student mouthpieces are the Bach 12 and 12C, and the Conn Remington model. Many players with more developed embouchures switch to a Bach 6½ AL or 7, or for the bass trombone, a Bach 3G or 4G.

TONE QUALITY

The trombone has a brilliant sound. The desired trombone quality has progressively darkened during this century, and many players mistakenly copy the mellow sound of the euphonium rather than develop the instrument's own potential. A good trombone sound is produced by playing with enough breath support that the tone is in danger of cracking. If the player will practice cracking the tone (which most will do with great delight), then learn to stop just short of this, she will get the large, projecting sound characteristic of the symphonic trombone. By no means, however, should the tone be crude and obnoxious.

Absolutely essential to producing good tone quality on any musical instrument is a well-developed mental image of what the tone should sound like. This is perhaps most critical for the young trombone player, who hears a wide variety of trombone tone quality in rock and funk tunes, Muzak, jazz, and new wave recordings. Without a mental goal for which to strive, the student trombonist is severely handicapped.

Choice of equipment has an important bearing on tone. The jazz trombonist is not likely to favor the large-bore instrument with a 10-inch bell used by the bass trombonist in a symphony, and the symphony player would probably hesitate to face the wrath of the conductor should she appear for rehearsal with a narrow-bore, small-bell trombone. The four physical factors influencing the degree of brilliance possible for any trombone are (1) size of bore, (2) size of bell, (3) type of metal used, and (4) mouthpiece. Larger bore, bell, and mouthpiece produce larger, deeper sounds. The sound closest to a real symphonic sound is achieved by most school musicians only on a bass trombone and not on a tenor trombone with an F attachment, even though many professional symphonic trombone players do use large bore tenor and alto trombones. The average school player does not practice enough to develop a good upper register on a large-bore instrument. Famous players of the past were noted for their individual sounds. According to the reports of those who thrilled to his performances, Arthur Pryor used a small-bore trombone that he played with the utmost in virtuosity. The students of the late Emory Remington, famed trombone teacher at the Eastman School of Music, are almost unanimous in their choice of a large-bore, large-bell trombone.

Legato playing, although related to tonguing, has a direct bearing on beauty of tone. Tommy Dorsey taught the world that a trombone can sing. This quality, long forgotten, was a predominant characteristic of the very early Renaissance trombones used with voices in the music of the church. Today, the development of a true legato style is a must for the trombonist.

A fine legato depends on the player's mastery of lip slurs, legato tonguing, evenness of sound, and rapid pitch change. Lip slurs are used for two kinds of musical situations: (1) a slow contrary-motion slur for when the interval ascends and the slide extends, or the interval descends and the slide moves up; and (2) slurs for two pitches played in the same position, for instance B-flat down to fourth-line F.

Vibrato

The trombone may be the easiest instrument on which to produce vibrato and among the most difficult on which to control it. Vibrato has traditionally been achieved by gently rotating the right wrist similar to a string player playing with vibrato with her left hand and wrist. The trombone player's right hand moves the slide slightly raising and lowering the pitch. Unfortunately, many young players attempt to play with vibrato before developing the fine muscular control required to play tastefully. More recently, jaw vibrato has become increasingly popular and preferred by most conductors and professional players.

Jaw vibrato is appropriate for most twentieth-century compositions other than jazz, and for solos appearing in band and orchestra literature. Either type of vibrato must be used in moderation.

Mutes

The same mutes mentioned for the trumpet are commonly used with the trombone. Buddy Baker and other professionals use "the plumber's best friend," the plunger, when called for. Straight and cup mutes are the most frequently required. Although mutes sharpen the overall pitch, the trombone slide makes the intonation problems easy to correct.

SLIDE TECHNIQUE

The new *Harvard Dictionary of Music* defines *portamento* as "a continuous movement from one pitch to another through all the intervening pitches, without, however, sounding them discretely. . . . *glissando* remains the prevalent term for this effect in musical scores. Some writers have preferred to restrict the meaning of *glissando* to the motion in which discrete pitches are heard, reserving *portamento* for continuous variation in pitch, but musical practice is not consistent in this respect."[2] "The glissando is a continuous or sliding movement from one pitch to another. In piano playing, for example, the nail of the thumb . . . is drawn over the white keys or the black keys."[3] When a trombone player starts on an open tone and extends the slide to seventh position, she is actually playing a portamento, not a glissando. Legato tonguing is needed for all slurs for which the slide moves to avoid a smear or portamento effect. A soft "doo" or "dee" syllable is used for legato tonguing. This syllable is coordinated exactly with the action of the slide so that the sound is clean and the slide movement is not heard. If the slide is moved too slowly, the tonguing will not be able to cover the portamento effect. Usually the legato tongue is better than the lip slur for slurs in rapid tempo—the effect will be cleaner and clearer.

The feeling of legato is one of a constant flow of air, as in playing a long tone. The embouchure changes are necessarily minimal and smooth. Pitch changes should come from adjustments in the lips and in the airstream, never from tensing the throat. One school of brass playing favors the use of vowel singing ("tuh–ee") to produce an ascending slur. The other holds that vowel singing causes tension in the throat, so should be avoided. As the trombonist advances, the music contains greater demands for slurs in the upper register; using "aw" to "ee" syllables will help focus the air. All slurred passages on trombone should be treated as a legato tongue.

The slide always moves at the same rapid speed whether the notes are close or far apart, the music fast or slow. A common bad habit for young trombone players as well as high school trombone players is moving the slide slowly during slow passages. Rapid movement of the slide must be taught early, from the first lesson, for the habits of slow motion are hard to break.

There are at least three viewpoints as to proper slide technique. One states that the slide should move the shortest distance in fast passages. In the higher register, for example, nearly all notes can be played in adjusted

[2] Don Randel, *The New Harvard Dictionary of Music* (Cambridge, MA: Belknap Press, 1986), 648 and 342.
[3] Ibid., 342.

positions one, two, and three, thus necessitating very little slide movement and requiring only a flexible wrist. A second viewpoint advocates a circular motion, in which the slide continues to move in the same direction as long as possible. This continuous movement in one direction is smoother, avoiding the jerkiness that may come from changing slide direction. Greater evenness of tone quality is possible, since the use of all seven positions offers a wider variety of alternate positions. If the player plays in only a few positions, she will use both high and low partials, and these vary greatly in richness. The third viewpoint is a compromise, playing as many notes as possible in a phrase within the same overtone series. Slide movement is of less concern; matching tone quality is the deciding factor. For example the opening music for *Der Rosenkavalier* would be:

School 1		6	6	7	6		6	6	6
School 2		6	2	1	3		4	4	6
School 3		6	2	1	3		1	2	2
with F attachment	1	2	b4	3		1	#2	2

Figure 18–5. Four sequences of slide positions for one passage covering a major 13th.

To be able to select the best method, the player must know all possible positions of every note, something not generally taught. Most method books present the higher notes in the first three or four positions rather than in all seven. Beginning students are seldom taught that slide positions are closer together near the bell than they are toward sixth position. Far too many students are instructed to either "look" or "feel" for the slide positions such as feeling for the edge of the bell to locate third position. Such instruction and practice does nothing for developing the student's ear or technique. The chart at the end of the chapter contains the most frequently used slide positions for the B-flat trombone as well as the most useful alternate positions; slide positions for the B-flat trombone with the F attachment are given below the regular positions. The trombone has harmonics that are out of tune and slide positions that are sharp. The trombone player is expected and encouraged to develop her ear to hear these problems and correct them immediately. Use of the altered slide positions for certain notes should become a habit.

INTONATION

Playing in tune depends primarily on two things: first, tuning the instrument properly with whatever mechanical means are available, and second, listening. The general practice is to tune the instrument in first position by pulling the tuning slide to the exact intonation. For beginners, first position should be tuned slightly sharp. Many quality instruments have a spring in the slide receiver that allows first position to be tuned normally and allows pitches such as D above the staff to be brought into tune by depressing the spring slightly. However, the advanced player usually tightens her lips for first position, enabling her to mechanically tune exactly and still have the slide vibrato available. If the instrument has an F attachment, there is a second tuning slide for the attachment. The procedure for tuning with the F attachment is as follows. Adjust the B-flat tuning slide, then tune the F tuning slide by playing fourth-line F on both the B-flat and the F trombone. After both slides are satisfactorily in tune, flicking the trigger that opens the extra tubing should produce a pitch matching the F in sixth position on the B-flat horn.

The trombone has the greatest potential for good intonation of any of the wind instruments, but few high school trombonists achieve this potential. The cause is failure to listen. Proof may be had by simply watching young players as they measure pitch with their thumbs outstretched in a vain search for third or fourth position, or bump the slide against their teeth as they return to first position. "The ear should dictate the slide placement of any pitch to the trombonist."[4] Different partials have different pitch characteristics: two or three pitches played in the same position may each need a slightly different adjustment of the slide. One famous trombonist argues there are at least fifty-one positions on the trombone, not seven.[5] The trombone slide can be moved to the exact pitch, the player should therefore learn to play each tone as well centered, focused, and in tune as possible. Other brass players humor pitch by adjustments in the embouchure, but this is neither necessary nor correct for the trombonist.

High school players will play second and third position flat, and fifth, sixth, and seventh positions sharp. Teachers can remedy these pitch problems by pointing out that the difference between slide positions increases as the positions increase—the difference between first and second position is slightly less than the difference between fifth and sixth positions. Most beginners have difficulty locking in on specific pitches. Experienced music teachers will testify that beginning trombone players routinely play A-naturals too flat and A-flats too sharp. To develop the ear and help distinguish

[4] Edward Kleinhammer, *The Art of Trombone Playing* (Evanston, IL: Summy-Birchard Publishing Co., 1963), 90.
[5] Mark R. McDunn and Clifford Barnes, *Trombone Artistry* (Kenosha, WI: Leblanc Publications, 1965), 2a.

different slide positions, it is advisable to have students play on a daily basis passages similar to that in Figure 18–6.

On most bass trombones, F below the staff is very flat and C below the staff is sharp; the F is tuned flat in an attempt to get C low enough. The best remedy is to play F in sixth position on the B-flat side. The double valve, the F attachment plus an E attachment, prevents the low B from being so sharp. The double valve puts low B in tune and the player adjusts the rest of the pitches. Instruments with these attachments are very costly; few schools use them, and even fewer high school players own one.

WHAT TO PRACTICE

No matter how elementary or advanced the student trombone player may be, the technical aspects of trombone performance must be reviewed every day. The mental attitude necessary to successful trombone playing includes the motivation to practice and improve.

After a warm-up of buzzing without the mouthpiece, then on the mouthpiece alone (to develop the facial muscles and improve the ear), the daily practice session should include (1) long tones to promote centered, focused pitches played in tune at various dynamic levels and while crescendoing and decrescendoing; (2) lip slurs for increased flexibility; (3) various types of articulations on repeated notes (fast and slow); (4) melodic material to develop good phrasing and other expressive traits; and (5) technical passages, including scales and technical studies. The last element of the trombone practice session is especially important, because the slide presents problems not found on any other wind instrument. Daily drill on the following will develop slide technique:

1. Place slide in position and play the written tone.
2. Move slide to the new position quickly before starting the new tone.
3. Play one to two octave scales slowly in tenuto style and listen critically, striving to play each pitch in tune with the preceding note.
4. Practice in front of a mirror to be certain that the slide does not move before a tone ends or after a new one begins.

Figure 18–6. Beginners Tend to Play the E-natural and the E-flat in the Same Position; They Should Strive for Correct Pitches and Slide Positions

5. In fast tempos, practice playing without stopping the slide at each tone. Learn to tongue in coordination with the slide so as to "pick off" each tone as it goes by. This is especially helpful for developing the ear and ridding one of the habit of feeling for third and fourth positions.

6. Practice playing all possible tones at one slide position from the fundamental up to the highest partial possible before moving on to the next position.

Practicing portamentos is also desirable. To play them properly, the student must use breath support and fill the instrument with air. The widest portamento possible on a trombone is an augmented fourth—six half steps—because there are but seven slide positions, each one a half step higher than the previous one. Shorter portamentos are possible when the notes permit a single slide motion or when they are in the same harmonic series. Arrangers and composers may write out all the notes in a portamento, or they may put down only the terminal notes with the marking *gliss.* between. Arrangers seem to be somewhat uncertain of the actual portamento possibilities of the trombone, so occasionally music contains notes impossible to play; the F attachment can be used to open up entirely different overtone series.

For more advanced players, pedal tones are a means for improving range and tone quality. Pedal tones are the lower fundamentals, virtually impossible to play on the upper brasses due to the narrow bore. Pedal tones are the most difficult notes to play with control, good tone quality, or clarity; therefore, striving to perform the notes in this register can greatly improve the embouchure. Working toward playing the pedal tones with a focused, centered, full, rich sound increases overall strength and power beyond developing the embouchure. Pedal tones are also useful in a trombone player's warm-down.

CARE AND MAINTENANCE OF THE TROMBONE

The care of the trombone is a problem of some dimension. Beginners, both young and old, are inclined to drop the slide. The slide is remarkably delicate, with a wall thickness as small as six thousandths of an inch or about the equivalent of three human hairs. The clearance between slides is even less, being only the width of a single hair or of a single sheet of bond writing paper.

With this in mind, the following rules for care of the trombone will assume proper importance.

1. Keep the slide locked except when playing the trombone.
2. Assemble the instrument with care, so that hitting the slide is avoided. The case should remain on the floor and not on the lap.

3. Handle the case with care and always open it from the middle. Opening the case from one end puts a strain on the slide. The slide is in the lid and twisting the lid can damage the slide.
4. Never assume the slide is locked. Pick up the trombone by the two side braces.
5. Do not put objects that might damage the trombone in the case.
6. Keep a rubber tip on the bumper knob to prevent the instrument from slipping during rest periods.
7. Never leave the instrument balanced on a chair.
8. Be sure there is plenty of playing room so that the slide does not hit objects when extended to the lowest positions.

The slide is usually lubricated with cold cream or slide cream and water, or with oil, but never with both. The slide cream–water combination is good when the instrument is used every day; if the instrument is not used it becomes gummy and the slide sticks. There are now a number of commercially prepared cold creams for trombone slides (e.g., Superslick) that have less tendency to gum-up than face creams.

Oil is probably better for beginners, but in applying it the player should be careful not to touch the glass dropper to the slide, for tiny particles of glass may come off which will then be rubbed into the metal by the slide motion. To add water to the slide cream, use a clean spray bottle such as that used to contain household cleaning products, and use clean water. A little water goes a long way, and in the case with most trombonists, it will go all the way to the clarinets, flutes, trumpets. . .

In cleaning the trombone, this procedure should be followed:

1. Fill the assembled slide with warm (not hot) water.
2. Clean the slide with a flexible wire cleaning brush and flush again with water. Do not use a cleaning rod, for it can easily damage the fragile inner slide.
3. Take the slide apart and place the inner slide/mouthpiece section in a safe place while working on the outer slide.
4. The outer slide may be cleaned with the cleaning rod wrapped in unbleached muslin, but when the rod is used it must always be followed by the flexible brush to move out any dirt or lint that has become lodged in the curve of the slide. Because this is true, it is easier and nearly as thorough to simply use the flexible brush. Always hold the side of the slide that is being cleaned—never hold one side while cleaning the other.
5. After cleaning, lubricate with oil or slide cream. Between cleanings, wipe the inner slides periodically and spray with water as needed. Avoid working the slides when they are dry.
6. The cork barrel next to the slide brace accumulates dirt that can get

into the area between the slides and foul the action. Clean the barrel with a pipe cleaner.

7. Clean the tuning slide the same way the slides are cleaned, using a flexible brush and warm water, not the rod. If the tuning slide becomes dirty and begins to stick, even the use of a cloth to help pull it out may dent it. When adjusting the tuning slide, use equal pressure in both directions from the middle of the two tuning braces.

When the trombone is taken outside for football games or parades, dirt is invariably blown on the slide. It should have a thorough cleaning before it is played again, because dust and cinder particles on the slide will scratch it as it is moved. Often there are microscopic metal filings left over from manufacture that can scratch and damage the slide.

Trombones with one or two rotary valves require some additional care—a drop of oil applied beneath the valve cap each week. The valve should be dismantled annually and thoroughly cleaned. A repairperson should handle this, or an older player may do it herself.[6]

TROUBLESHOOTING

EQUIPMENT

slide moves slowly

1. Place several drops of slide oil onto slide, expel excess oil through water key.
2. Make sure student is keeping right arm, hand, and fingers relaxed.
3. Inspect slide for slide cream-oil mixture (thoroughly clean and use either oil or slide cream–water).
4. If student uses slide cream, spray with water until the water beads up on the slide.
5. Remove slide and lay on table; the slide should lie flat; one raised "corner" indicates alignment problems.
6. Inspect slide for edges rubbing the tubing inside the slide. Worn plating will cause brass against brass friction and excessive wear.
7. Interrogate student to determine if she was only half listening when you explained petroleum jelly on *tuning* slide.

air will not pass through horn

1. If F attachment, inspect for correct alignment.
2. Inspect for clogged leadpipe or bell (mouthpieces fit very snuggly in the bell).
3. Inspect for a dirty mouthpiece

[6]Kleinhammer, op. cit., 11.

mouthpiece wiggles	1. Shank too long. Have competent repairperson remove short sections at a time; a mouthpiece shank that is too short causes moderate to severe intonation problems.
	2. Shank out-of-round. Again, to be repaired only by competent repairperson.
instrument leaks air	1. Inspect and if necessary replace cork on water key.
	2. If around F valve casing, have resoldered by competent repairperson.
	3. If new trombone, have retailer replace it.
	4. If leak is around the slide it is a very serious problem, try slide cream–water solution; replating is a costly alternative.
buzzing sound	1. Inspect for broken brace(s). Have resoldered.
	2. Determine if a recent soaking may have loosened residue inside. Rewash or use flexible brush.
	3. Inspect for loose receiver spring.
	4. Be sure that the receiver screw connects bell to slide tightly.

TONE

thin, strident sound	1. Aperture too small. Try buzzing without mouthpiece (pitches, scales, or tunes), then with mouthpiece, then add trombone.
	2. Tongue tense or possibly too high. Relax tongue or try pushing against the back lower teeth; use "taw" syllable.
	3. Tension in throat. Drop shoulders; drop tongue as in yawning.
	4. Embouchure too stretched. Relax mouth, tighten corners, buzz without mouthpiece.
	5. Mouthpiece too shallow or backbore too tight.
	6. Aperture too flat. Attempt to get student to pucker more—like a whistle. Try a "doo" articulation rather than "dah" or "duh."
	7. Too much lip in the mouthpiece. Keep the corners tight or try to think "em" with corners tight.
dull, spread, or unfocused sound	1. Buzz without mouthpiece, then with mouthpiece alone.
	2. Not enough air support. Blow "fast" air.
	3. Cheeks puffing. Practice buzzing without mouthpiece.
	4. Embouchure too slack. Tighten corners and encourage student to focus pitch—blow a fast, "pencil-thin" airstream.
	5. Aperture too large. Same as for #4.
	6. Mouthpiece too large in diameter.

7. Chin may not be stretched flat. Keep corners firm and teeth apart to flatten chin.

forced sound with too much edge

1. Mouthpiece too shallow, or throat or backbore too small.
2. Throat too tight. Relaxation exercises.
3. Embouchure too stretched. Attempt more pucker.
4. Too much bottom lip. Try two-thirds upper.
5. Embouchure too stretched, which flattens aperture. Attempt to pucker more; buzz without mouthpiece, then with mouthpiece alone before adding trombone.
6. Tongue is too high. Articulate with "daw" instead of "dee" or "dah."
7. Practice inhaling and exhaling large amounts of air with mouth in shape for vocalizing "o–o–o–o–o" and without "holding" the air.
8. Attempt to play while pulling mouthpiece away from embouchure.
9. Work toward mental image of warmer airstream.
10. Dirty mouthpiece or leadpipe.
11. May try a more funnel- or V-shaped mouthpiece.

stuffy, fuzzy sound

1. Too much lip in the mouthpiece. Try a larger mouthpiece or keeping corners of mouth tighter.
2. Pinching the lips together.
3. Teeth together. Drop jaw as in "aw."
4. Air pocket behind upper or lower lip. Keep corners of mouth firm and practice buzzing without and with only the mouthpiece.
5. Cheeks puffing. Buzz without mouthpiece.
6. Closed throat. Pull shoulders down; drop tongue like there's a hot potato in your mouth.
7. Head tilted to left.
8. Fatigue. Relax embouchure by "flapping" lips like a horse; buzzing without and on the mouthpiece alone; work on pedal tones with a focused sound. Lips may not buzz evenly when they are tired or swollen; this can be caused by lack of proper warm-up, trying for too many high notes too soon, or simply by a demanding practice session.
9. Too much saliva in mouthpiece or embouchure.

difficulty with upper range

1. Excessive mouthpiece pressure. Rely more on air and less on pressure; corners of embouchure must be kept very firm.
2. Blow air faster, a "pencil-thin" airstream.

3. Fatigue. Lack of proper warm-up or warm-down on previous day.
4. Mouthpiece too deep or diameter too large.
5. Try to direct air downward by rolling in lower lip.
6. Too much bottom lip in mouthpiece.
7. Extensive work on pedal tones to open throat, keep air moving without excessive demand on embouchure endurance.
8. Embouchure may be too immature. Be patient and work on lip slurs for strength.

ARTICULATION

explosive attacks

1. Building up air pressure behind tongue prior to attack. Coordinate breath and tongue, eliminating holding the air.
2. Tonguing between the teeth. Work toward a "duh" articulation to replace "thuh."
3. Stopping air with tongue. Keep notes connected, each note continues into the next with the tongue merely disrupting the air flow during long tones.
4. Articulating with a "pah" or "mah" syllable.
5. Aperture too small. Practice for a big, rich, full, but *focused* sound in all registers. Flexibility exercises to keep from "closing down" when going into upper register.

scooping notes, facial movement

1. Air taking too long to reach appropriate velocity. Full breaths and complete diaphragm support.
2. "Chewing notes"; excessive chin movement. Tongue moving too far; replace "taw-taw" with "doo-doo."
3. Inspect for chin bunching up. Buzz without mouthpiece; stress keeping corners firm.
4. Sometimes caused by students playing timidly. Explain that mistakes are expected—encourage brass players to take a chance.
5. Slide not working smoothly. Keep it well lubricated.
6. Drop back of tongue.

difficulty with slurs

1. Smears. Use legato tongue for all slurs: "duh" or "dah" articulation.
2. Teach alternate slide positions.
3. Move slide very quickly.
4. Do *not* change embouchures if pitches are on the same harmonic series (i.e., slurring from a middle-line D to a fourth-line F uses the identical embouchure).
5. Slide not working smoothly. Keep it well lubricated.

difficulty with
lip slurs

1. Try directing air downward for slurs going up.
2. "Lean" into lower pitch for slurs going up; followed by the upper pitch played slightly softer.
3. Increase air speed when going to upper note (but not volume).
4. Avoid excessive pressure on upper note; tighten corners of mouth instead and *let* air do the work.
5. Roll in lower lip for upper pitch.
6. Do not let tone spread on lower pitches (an easy habit to fall into since it is almost impossible to "undershoot" a low pitch).
7. Too many long tones on a daily basis.
8. Mouthpiece rim too wide.
9. Keep airstream steady to avoid breaks.
10. For ascending slurs arch tongue "tah–ee."

ENDURANCE

lacking

1. Too much pressure from mouthpiece onto embouchure. Loosen grip in left hand; try using only a few fingers on left hand to hold instrument.
2. Fatigue from too demanding practice sessions without enough rest periods.
3. Lack of proper warm-up or warm-down.
4. Not using corners of mouth properly (the strongest muscles in the face) and not relying on the air to do most of the work.
5. Mouthpiece placement may need correcting.
6. Anxiety.
7. Lacking *full* intake of air.

REFERENCES

Texts

ARLING, HARRY J. *Trombone Chamber Music.* An Annotated Bibliography. 2nd ed. Edited by Stephen L. Glover. Nashville: Brass Press, 1983.

BAKER, DAVID N. *Contemporary Techniques for the Trombone.* New York: Charles Colin, 1974.

BATES, PHILIP. *The Trumpet and Trombone: An Outline of Their History, Development and Construction.* New York: W. W. Norton, 1966.

FINK, REGINALD H. *The Trombonist's Handbook: A Complete Guide to Playing and Teaching the Trombone.* Athens, OH: Accura Music, 1977.

GRIFFITHS, JOHN R. *The Low Brass Guide*. Hackensack, NJ: Jerona Music Corp., 1980.

GUION, DAVID M. *Trombone: Its History and Music, 1697–1811*. Gordon and Breach, 1988.

KLEINHAMMER, EDWARD. *The Art of Trombone Playing*. Evanston, IL: Summy-Birchard Co., 1963.

KNAUB, DONALD. *Trombone Teaching Techniques*. 2nd ed. Athens, OH: Accura Music, 1977.

MCDUNN, MARK, and CLIFFORD BARNES. *Trombone Artistry*. Kenosha, WI: Leblanc Publications, 1965.

REINHARDT, DONALD S. *Pivot System for Trombone: A Complete Manual*. Philadelphia: Elkan-Vogel Co., 1942.

WICK, DENIS. *Trombone Technique*. 2nd ed. London: Oxford University Press, 1984.

Studies

Easy—Beginning (elementary or junior high)

BEELER, WALTER. *Method for Trombone*, Books 1 and 2 (Remick).
CIMERA, JAROSLAV, and NILO HOVEY. *Method for Trombone* (Belwin-Mills).
ENDRESEN, R. M. *Supplementary Studies* (Rubank).
FINK, REGINALD. *Studies in Legato* (Carl Fischer).
GOWER, WILLIAM, and HIMIE VOXMAN. *The Rubank Method Series* (Rubank).
LONG, NEWELL. *Elementary Method for Trombone and Baritone* (Rubank).
YOUNG, LUCILLE. *Elementary Method for Trombone or Baritone* (Carl Fischer).

Medium (advanced junior high or high school)

ARBAN, J. B., and S. MANTIA. *Method for Trombone* (Rubank).
BLAZHEVICH, VLADISLAV. *Clef Studies for Trombone* (Leeds).
————. *Sequences 26 Melodic Studies* (Carl Fischer).
BLUME, O. *36 Studies for Trombone*, 3 vols. (Carl Fischer).
CAMPBELL, CHARLES J. *30 Contemporary Etudes* (Sam Fox).
CIMERA, JAROSLAV. *55 Phrasing Studies* (Belwin-Mills).
————. *170 Studies* (Belwin-Mills).
FINK, REGINALD. *Introducing the Alto Clef* (Accura).
————. *Introducing the Tenor Clef* (Accura).
————. *Studies in Legato* (Carl Fischer).
GREGORIEV, B. *78 Studies* (International).
HARVEY, RUSSELL. *Method for Trombone and Baritone* (Belwin-Mills).
KOPPRASCH, C. *60 Studies*, Vol. 1 (Carl Fischer).
OSTRANDER, ALLEN. *Bass Trombone and F Attachment for Tenor Trombone* (Ostrander).
PARES, G. *Scale Etudes* (Rubank).
REMINGTON, EMORY. *Warm-Up Exercises* (Rochester Music).
ROCHUT, J. *Melodious Etudes*, Book I (Carl Fischer).
SCHLOSSBERG, MAX. *Daily Drills and Technical Studies* (Baron).

SHUMAN, DAVIS. *Preparatory Studies for Trombone* (Leeds).
SLAMA, ANTON. *66 Etudes in All Keys* (International).
VOXMAN, HIMIE. *Selected Studies* (Rubank).

Advanced (advanced high school or college)

ARBAN, J. B., and S. MANTIA. *Method for Trombone* (Rubank).
BACH. J. S. *Six Suites for Unaccompanied Violoncello.*
BLAZHEVICH, VLADISLAV. *Clef Studies for Trombone* (Leeds).
————. *Sequences 26 Melodic Studies* (Carl Fischer).
COLIN, CHARLES. *Progressive Technique* (Colin).
KOPPRASCH, C. *60 Studies*, Vols. 1 and 2 (Carl Fischer).
LA FOSSE, *Methude Complete de Trombone a Coulisse* (Alphonse Le Duc).
MANTIA, SIMONE. *Trombone Virtuoso* (Carl Fischer).
MILLER, R. *Clef Studies* (Carl Fischer).
MUELLER, ROBERT. *Technical Studies* (Carl Fischer).
OSTRANDER, ALLEN. *Bass Trombone and F Attachment for Tenor Trombone* (Ostrander).
REMINGTON, EMORY. *Warm-Up Exercises* (Rochester Music).
ROCHUT, J. *Melodious Etudes*, Books II and III (Carl Fischer).
SCHLOSSBERG, MAX. *Daily Drills and Technical Studies* (Baron).
SHAPIRO, AARON. *Modern Universal Method for Baritone and Trombone* (Cundy-Bettoney).
TYRREL, H. W. *40 Progressive Studies in the Tenor Clef* (Boosey & Hawkes).

TROMBONE
Position Chart

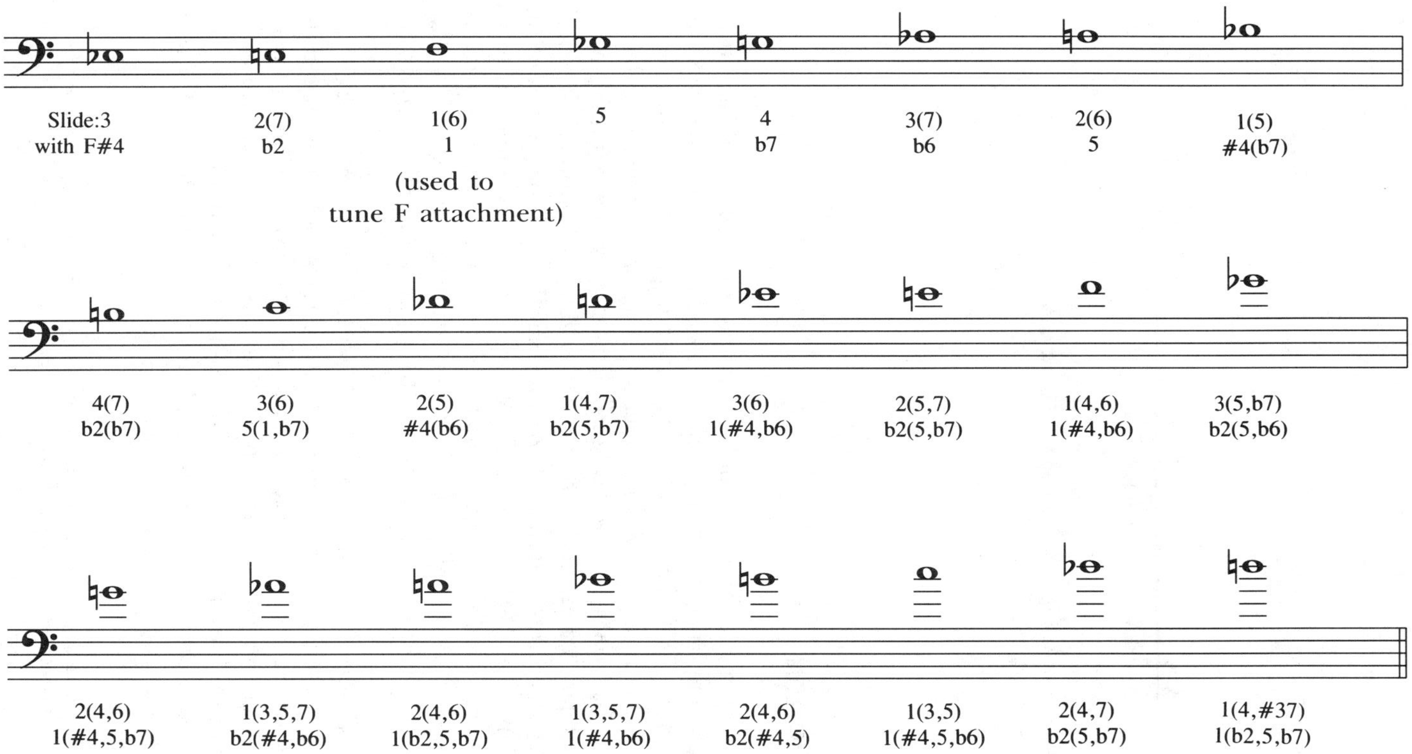

Slide:3
with F#4
2(7)
b2
1(6)
1
(used to
tune F attachment)
5
4
b7
3(7)
b6
2(6)
5
1(5)
#4(b7)
4(7)
b2(b7)
3(6)
5(1,b7)
2(5)
#4(b6)
1(4,7)
b2(5,b7)
3(6)
1(#4,b6)
2(5,7)
b2(5,b7)
1(4,6)
1(#4,b6)
3(5,b7)
b2(5,b6)
2(4,6)
1(#4,5,b7)
1(3,5,7)
b2(#4,b6)
2(4,6)
1(b2,5,b7)
1(3,5,7)
1(#4,b6)
2(4,6)
b2(#4,5)
1(3,5)
1(#4,5,b6)
2(4,7)
b2(5,b7)
1(4,#37)
1(b2,5,b7)

19

The Baritone and Euphonium

INTRODUCTION

The baritone and euphonium hold a unique place in band literature. Students playing baritone or euphonium often have been those who, due to embouchure or facial characteristics that impaired their success on trumpet (or because they didn't practice), have transferred to a larger instrument. Baritones and euphoniums normally are not required in the high school jazz band, and with a few notable exceptions are seldom required in orchestras; neither is there an abundance of solo literature for these instruments. Due to its relatively large bore in relationship to its length, combined with a relatively small bell, the euphonium can produce the most beautiful tone quality of all brass instruments. In the hands of an accomplished performer, it can play virtuosic lines as well as any of the brasses.[1]

The baritone is often equated with a valved trombone. When this occurs, the baritone players attempt to emulate a trombone sound, and the trombones sound too much like a baritone. The instruments are completely different and should not sound alike; they normally play different types of musical lines in wind ensemble compositions and transcriptions. They fulfill two distinctly separate needs in the overall timbre of a well-balanced band.

---

[1] Selections such as Ravel's orchestration of *Pictures at an Exhibition*, Strauss' *Don Quixote*, and Holst's *The Planets* have euphonium parts.

428

SELECTING THE INSTRUMENT

The baritone and euphonium are both brass tubes that are approximately two-thirds conical and one-third cylindrical. Their appearance is similar, and with beginning students their tone quality is similar.

The baritone horn is more common and is the preferred instrument for beginners. The range, acoustical properties and tone quality of the baritone has roughly the same relationship to the trombone as the cornet has to the trumpet. The baritone has a more mellow sound than the trombone; the euphonium is even more mellow. Like the trombone, the "unwrapped" baritone is approximately 9 feet in length, pitched in B-flat, and is a nontransposing instrument. Its fundamental is the same as that of the trombone, with three (occasionally four) valves lowering the pitches in the overtone series in a fashion identical to those on a trumpet. The instrument is a true bass instrument, and players should learn to read bass clef, as most serious music is written in bass clef for these instruments.

The euphonium has a larger bore and requires a larger mouthpiece than the baritone horn. The baritone has an average bore size at the second valve port of approximately .504 inch; the bore of the euphonium averages .571 inch. The euphonium bell is approximately three inches larger than that of the baritone. Most euphoniums come with a fourth valve that lowers the fundamental to F below the bass staff. On the euphonium the fourth valve is also essential for good intonation. A few euphoniums have a low-E extension (like a slide within a slide) on the fourth valve slide, with the compensating systems becoming more common. The fourth valve affords an extension of range to low B-flat, with the exception of the low B-natural, which is not available unless the fourth valve slide is pulled to E. The famous euphonium soloist Brian Bowman suggests that an instrument can be tested to determine if it is a true euphonium by reversing the tuning slide; the main tuning slide of a baritone will fit the instrument reversed due to its greater proportion of cylindrical tubing, the tuning slide of a true euphonium will not fit reversed since one end is larger than the other.[2] The baritone is also available with upright bells and four valves like most euphoniums, and euphoniums are available with only three valves like most baritones.

Most euphoniums are provided by the school, whereas the baritone can be rented by parents at affordable rates. This situation frequently leads students to keep their baritones at home to practice and leave the euphonium at school for band rehearsals, making it difficult to develop appropriate tone quality and control on the euphonium. Since the euphonium has a

[2] Brian L. Bowman, *Practical Hints on Playing the Baritone (Euphonium)* (Melville, NY: Belwin-Mills, 1983), 23.

larger bore, larger mouthpiece, and even less resistance than a baritone, much is lost if the student practices on one instrument and is expected to perform on the other.

The baritone is the preferred instrument for beginners because its smaller mouthpiece and smaller bore require less air, making it more responsive and easier to control. Most baritones are bell-front, whereas the euphonium is usually made with an upright bell. Consequently, the baritone has the more projecting and focused tone quality of the two, with the euphonium responding more easily in the low register.

Guidelines to follow in selecting a new or used instrument are:

1. Consider if the partials are reasonably in tune.
2. Check the instrument for any air leaks.
3. On a used instrument, inspect the valves for tightness of fit (i.e., do the valves "wiggle"?) and for excessive wear at the bottom edge of the valves.
4. Check compression by pulling the valve slides then pressing the valve and listening for a "pop."
5. Listen for whether the instrument has similar response and tone quality in all registers. The compensating device found on professional-model instruments is probably not worth the extra cost. A fourth valve, however, is worth the extra cost and is used much more often.

Like all brass instruments, a choice of finishes is available. Lacquer is the most common for baritones. Most professional-model euphoniums are silver plated because this is the finish preferred by most professional brass players.

ASSEMBLING THE BARITONE OR EUPHONIUM

Assembling the baritone should present no problem except for its weight and size. The instrument should be removed from its case by grasping it through the thumb ring with the right thumb and carefully lifting; the left hand assists in steadying the horn by holding the bell section. The mouthpiece should be inserted with a slight twisting motion.

HOLDING THE BARITONE OR EUPHONIUM

The euphonium and baritone are held diagonally across the chest in an upright position, resting against the crook of the left arm (Figures 19–1 and 19–2). The left hand should be extended across the body of the

Figure 19–1.   Sitting Position for Playing the Baritone

instrument so that the left thumb reaches the ring of the tuning trigger (as in Figure 19–2) or grasps the side or bottom tubing wherever it is most comfortable (as in Figure 19–1). This position puts the weight of the instrument on the bones rather than on the muscles and helps reduce fatigue.

Correct hand positions are shown in Figures 19–3 and 19–4. Some euphoniums have the fourth valve mounted on the side where the left hand holds the large tubing, thus a finger on the left hand manipulates the fourth valve. Players who have instruments with the fourth valve next to the third valve occasionally hold their horn to manipulate the fourth valve with a finger on the left hand.

The right hand and arm should bear no weight, as the fingers must be free to operate the valves with maximum speed. As with the trumpet, the fingers of the right hand are slightly curved. The instrument should not rest in the player's lap when he is playing. Many players use a small pillow or cushion on their lap to support the instrument (as is the player in Figure 19–2).

Good posture is essential for proper breathing, good tone, and intonation, whether the student is standing or sitting. Young baritone players

Figure 19–2. Sitting Position for Playing the Euphonium

Figure 19–3. Hand Position for Playing the Baritone

Figure 19–4. Hand Position for Playing the Euphonium

may get into the habit of playing with poor posture if they twist about to reach the mouthpiece; the player brings the mouthpiece to the embouchure rather than bringing the embouchure to the mouthpiece.

THE BEGINNING STUDENT

If there is any physical criterion for starting on the baritone, it would be size of the student. If the desire is present, however, physical size is less relevant. Lung capacity can be developed.

The procedures used to produce the initial sound on trumpet (Chapter 17) can be applied to starting baritone players. The baritone player may not be required to blow the air as fast as a trumpet player, but he must provide plenty of air support. The teeth should be farther apart for the baritone—articulations of "doe" or "toe" are substituted for "duh" and "tuh."

When students are transferred from trumpet, careful instruction on tone production is necessary. Trumpet players initially play the baritone with a more "stretched" embouchure than is appropriate. Left unchecked, this embouchure results in a thin, cold tone quality and often a strident sound. Furthermore, although the baritone is easier to play due to less resistance, former trumpet players are often satisfied with a thin tone, failing to breathe deeply and to project a thick, broad, lush sound. Baritone players who start on trumpet _must_ learn to read bass clef.

Starting promising students on baritone is a better practice than relying solely on students who are "less than successful" on trumpet. These beginning baritone players can later be successful if they switch to euphonium or tuba.

EMBOUCHURE

Because the baritone is a conical instrument, the proper embouchure is closer to that of the horn than that of the trombone. The embouchure is slightly more puckered than for a trombone.

The mouthpiece is centered horizontally with two-thirds upper lip and one-third lower lip. The instrument offers so little resistance that the aperture may be too large, causing the embouchure to "cave in." This in turn can lead to bad habits if the student tries to create resistance by tightening the throat. The solution is patient buzzing on the mouthpiece and practice on the instrument to develop muscular strength, along with plenty of air from a supported, full airstream passing through a relaxed upper torso and neck. A correct baritone embouchure is illustrated in Figure 19–5.

Next, ask the student to vocalize "toon" into the instrument. This will

Figure 19–5. Baritone Embouchure

usually result in a first tone. The teacher who encourages a well-focused and centered pitch will be rewarded with students who quickly develop good tone quality.

An open, buzzing sound should be emphasized when practicing with the mouthpiece alone. A common fault among young baritone players is a tight sound resulting from a pinched embouchure or an aperture that is too closed or too flat. Occasionally students try to play with more tension toward the center of their embouchure than at the corners of their mouth. This bad habit can be detected by air leaking out of the corners and is often the result of a smile embouchure rather than a puckered one.

When increasing the range upward, baritone and euphonium players should try to maintain a focused airstream. If the student closes the aperture in his embouchure by stretching the lips (smiling), the resulting sound is a distorted tone. The air must move faster through the instrument, not just into the mouthpiece. Because increased air velocity is accompanied by greater air pressure, the lips have a tendency to "blow open." Students must be encouraged to be patient while their embouchure strengthens. A beginner can learn to play two or three scales in one evening; he cannot go home and learn to play to a high B-flat in one evening. Practice on pedal tones will help loosen the embouchure after demanding practice in the upper range and will keep the throat relaxed and open. Practice on pedal tones also helps to place embouchure tension at the corners of the mouth, where the embouchure should be firm.

Mouthpieces

The mouthpiece provided with many student-line instruments is identical to the trombone mouthpiece; the mouthpieces for both instruments fit both leadpipes. Ideally, however, the baritone should have a deeper mouthpiece than the trombone to help promote a warmer, darker sound. Beginners should start on a medium-sized mouthpiece such as a Bach 9 or 11, switching to a Bach 5 or 6 or to a Schilke deep-cup when the embouchure becomes more developed.

The euphonium requires a mouthpiece with a larger shank than that for a baritone. Mouthpiece manufacturers make a mouthpiece with a euphonium shank and baritone dimensions; this should be avoided. When the student moves from a baritone to a euphonium, the larger mouthpiece should be used to enhance the tonal characteristics of the euphonium.

INTONATION

The baritone and euphonium have built-in intonation problems, many of which are solved with the fourth valve. The fourth-valve slide is slightly longer in length than the 1–3 valve combination, so it can be tuned to play those pitches accurately, whereas the 1–3 combination is always sharp. Similarly, the 2–4 combination can be substituted for the 1–2–3 valve combinations. The fourth valve also serves to extend the lower register. Many baritones and euphoniums are equipped with devices for quickly altering the valve slides (like the rings or saddles found on many trumpets). When the school purchases a euphonium, it is wise to invest in a top-of-the-line model with a fourth valve.

The ideal broad, rounded sound of the baritone must not be misinterpreted as a spread, unfocused sound, a quality that produces very poor intonation. Good intonation depends on good tone quality.

Notes on the baritone that are occasionally out of tune can be improved with alternate fingerings. Figure 19-6 and the fingering chart at the end of the chapter should be consulted and compared for pitch problems and alternate fingerings. When alternate fingerings are used, the tone

Figure 19–6. Pitch Tendencies of Certain Notes on the Baritone and Euphonium (arrows show tendency of sharp or flat)

quality should remain unchanged. Practice with an electronic tuner is useful for students to develop the habit of automatically lipping certain notes in tune as well as developing a good overall sense of pitch. Practicing intervals with the mouthpiece alone and checking intonation with a piano are also beneficial for developing the ear and for controlling intonation.

TONE QUALITY

The baritone player should strive for a "wide," full sound; a helpful mental image is that of the sound filling up the bell and radiating throughout the auditorium. The projecting, "pencil-thin," fast air concept used for trombone players is not appropriate for the baritone player. It usually results in too much edge.

The student should constantly be reminded to strive for a "euphonium" sound. In beginning method books, the trombone and baritone will play identical pitches and lines, but the tone quality should be different.

Vibrato

The baritone and euphonium player uses vibrato more than any other brass instrument, partly because they play many lyrical lines in wind literature. As with other instruments, baritone vibrato should be subtle, not distracting, enhancing not dominating. The preferred method of vibrato is jaw vibrato.

The student must first establish and be able to maintain a well-centered, focused sound, then use the embouchure to create vibrato by forming "wah–wah–wah" without using the jaw as much as when these syllables are actually vocalized. The student should begin with slow metered pulses and gradually speed them up.

Mutes

Mutes are seldom used on the euphonium or baritone, yet when notated they are very important (e.g., for Persichetti's Symphony No. 6 for Band). The shape of the mute depends on the shape of the bell; mutes are available for bell-front baritones and upright baritones and euphoniums.

The muted baritone or euphonium is useful for covering essential bassoon parts when a bassoon is not present. Although band directors usually attempt to cover bassoon parts with tuba, the muted euphonium can play these woodwind parts more delicately and with greater control. With the fourth valve, the euphonium has a similar range to the bassoon. As with most brasses, the mute tends to raise the pitch of both the baritone and euphonium.

FINGERINGS

Good hand position is essential for technique. Proper curvature of the fingers is even more important for baritone players than for trumpet players because the piston stroke is longer for the lower brass. Students should develop the habit of pressing the valves all the way down. Many students allow their fingers (especially the third finger) to rest under the valve buttons or between the valve stems; they should keep the fingers ready, resting lightly on top of the valves.

WHAT TO PRACTICE

The young baritone player should spend time daily on lip flexibility studies, scales, and technical studies, as well as the chromatic scale and melodic passages. Long tones are helpful for developing good tone quality and pitch as well as building endurance. Warm-ups should begin in the instrument's middle range and extend upward and downward; the warm-down should incorporate pedal tones to relax the embouchure and throat.

Students often get in the bad habit of using different embouchures depending on the register in which they are playing. Young baritone players are especially prone to this habit because they play music written in the upper as well as the lower extremes, now doubling the horn part, and then doubling the tuba part.

CARE AND MAINTENANCE OF THE BARITONE
OR EUPHONIUM

The care of the baritone and euphonium is similar to that for the trumpet. A spray-type furniture polish can be used on the outside of the baritone to preserve its lacquer finish. This polish should be sprayed on a rag, not on the instrument, then wiped over the lacquer, avoiding getting it on any valves or inside a tuning or valve slide. Most baritone and euphonium cases have a strap to secure the instrument within the case; the strap should always be used—that's why it's there.

TROUBLESHOOTING

EQUIPMENT

sluggish valves
1. Oil valves separately by loosening retaining cap and carefully lifting from valve casing.
2. Make sure student is pressing valves straight down and not at an angle.

3. Remove valves and clean them and the casing with lint-free cloth, oil well, and replace.

4. Interrogate student to determine if he understood the instructions: petroleum jelly on slides; oil on valves.

5. If horn is well used, try stretching springs or rotating springs between valves.

6. Mix a slight amount of olive oil in valve oil to make the oil stick to the valve longer (most brass instruments are constructed so that the leadpipe goes directly into the first valve; consequently, much oil is washed off by condensation).

air will not pass through horn

1. Make sure valves are in correct casings.

2. Inspect for clogged leadpipe or bell (mouthpieces fit very snuggly in the bell).

3. Inspect for a dirty mouthpiece.

gurgling sound but water key will not expel any water

1. If water gurgles without valves pressed, inspect for clogged water key. Remove tuning slide and dump. Rotate baritone to pour out of an open slide tube, leadpipe, or bell section.

2. If water sounds with valves pressed (especially a problem with the euphonium second valve), remove valves and slides to expel; tilt baritone to pour (many students forget that the third valve must be pressed for the third-valve water key to work effectively).

mouthpiece wiggles

1. Shank too long. Have competent repairperson remove slight sections at a time; a mouthpiece shank that is too short causes moderate to severe intonation problems.

2. Shank out-of-round. Again, to be repaired only by competent repairperson.

instrument leaks air

1. Inspect and if necessary replace cork (water key).

2. If around valve casing, have resoldered by competent repairperson.

3. If new, have retailer replace it.

buzzing sound

1. Inspect for broken brace(s). Have resoldered.

2. Determine if a recent soaking may have loosened residue inside. Rewash or use flexible brush.

3. Determine if mouthpiece shank is too small. Purchase proper mouthpiece.

TONE

thin, strident sound

1. Lack of air and air pressure.

2. Teeth together. Drop jaw.

3. Aperture too flat. Try buzzing without mouthpiece (pitches, scales, or tunes), then with mouthpiece, then with baritone—aperture should be more rounded than for the trumpet or trombone.

4. Tongue tense in a possible attempt to keep it out of the way. Relax tongue.

5. Tension in throat. Drop shoulders, pretend to be a rag doll—limp.

6. Embouchure too stretched. Relax mouth, tighten corners, buzz without mouthpiece.

7. Mouthpiece too shallow or backbore too tight.

dull, spread, or unfocused sound

1. Lips not buzzing evenly. Buzz without mouthpiece, then with mouthpiece alone.

2. Insufficient air support.

3. Cheeks puffing. Practice buzzing without mouthpiece.

4. Embouchure too slack. Tighten corners and encourage student to focus pitch.

5. Mouthpiece too large.

6. Aperture in embouchure too large.

forced sound with too much edge

1. Mouthpiece too shallow, or throat or backbore too tight.

2. Throat too tight. Relaxation exercises.

3. Dirty mouthpiece or leadpipe. Clean thoroughly.

4. Too much lip in the mouthpiece. Buzz without mouthpiece and with mouthpiece only.

5. Embouchure too stretched, which flattens aperture. Attempt to pucker more; plenty of buzzing without mouthpiece and with mouthpiece alone.

6. Tongue is too high. Try articulating with "doe" rather than "dee."

7. Practice breathing large amounts of air with the mouth in shape for vocalizing "o–o–o–oh."

8. Excessive pressure. Attempt to play while pulling mouthpiece away from embouchure.

9. Work toward mental image of warmer airstream. Demonstrate by student blowing a cold then warm airstream against his hand.

10. Often due to mouthpiece being too low on embouchure.

stuffy, fuzzy sound (airy)

1. Lips not buzzing evenly. Lots of buzzing without the mouthpiece and with the mouthpiece alone; could also be due to fatigue caused by lack of proper or sufficient warm-up, too much demand on student (e.g., his ea-

gerness to play high notes before he is able), lack of warm-down after previous playing; tired, swollen lips hurt sound.

2. Too much lip in the mouthpiece. Correct embouchure or try larger mouthpiece.

3. Pinching the lips together, or the teeth are together. Get student to drop jaw; keep corners of mouth clamped shut firmly to loosen the center.

4. Air pockets behind upper or lower lip. Practice buzzing without mouthpiece—this forces a flat chin and firm embouchure in the right places.

5. Cheeks puffing. Again, buzz without mouthpiece.

6. Closed throat. Pull shoulders downward.

7. Too much saliva in embouchure or mouthpiece.

8. Improper mouthpiece placement. Correct placement.

9. Aperture in embouchure too large.

difficulty with upper range

1. Excessive mouthpiece pressure. Rely more on air and less on pressure. Corners of the mouth should be kept firm, attempt to pull horn and mouthpiece away from upper lip when playing.

2. Mouthpiece too large (cup diameter and depth).

3. Blow faster air; a "pencil-thin" airstream.

4. Fatigue. Lack of proper warm-up or warm-down.

5. Try to direct air slightly downward by rolling in lower lip or tilting head backward slightly.

6. Too much bottom lip in mouthpiece.

7. Try practicing in the low register; try playing pedal tones—many believe it opens throat, which has a tendency to close when trying high notes, and it forces the tension in the embouchure to the corners of the mouth.

ARTICULATION

explosive attacks

1. Building air pressure behind tongue or "holding" onto the air before releasing it. Try for better coordination between air and tongue. Inhale to exhale without stopping—we all know from physics that for an instant it *must* stop to change direction—it is at that instant the tongue is used.

2. Tonguing between the teeth. Work toward a "duh" tongue placement instead of "thuh."

3. Stopping the previous note with the tongue. Practice playing long tones while merely disrupting the airstream with the tongue, notes are connected.

4. Aperture in embouchure too small. Correct embouchure, keep center of lips relaxed and jaw lowered.

scooping notes,
facial movements

1. Air starting too slow then increasing to proper velocity. Work on making the inhale-to-exhale one continuous cycle—without stopping. Sometimes student is timid: fear of failure; get him to take a chance.
2. "Chewing notes"; excessive chin movement. Tongue moving too far; replace "taw–taw" with "duh–duh"; practice long tone *and* lip slurs up and down in front of mirror to hold chin still.
3. #2 is usually accompanied by a bunched chin. Try buzzing without mouthpiece to force chin flat.
4. Too much lip in the mouthpiece. Practice forming an embouchure and buzzing without the mouthpiece, then try to establish the same sensations when playing.

difficulty with
lip slurs

1. Try directing air slightly downward for upward slurs.
2. "Lean" into lower note for upward slurs, followed by upper pitch played slightly softer.
3. Increase air speed when going to upper pitch.
4. Avoid excessive pressure on upward slur; tighten corners of mouth instead.
5. Not enough lower lip in mouthpiece can make upward slurs difficult.
6. Do not let tone spread on downward slurs (bad habits sometimes develop since it is almost impossible to "undershoot" the lower note).
7. Too many long tones in daily practice schedule without a sufficient balance of flexibility studies.
8. Mouthpiece rim too wide.
9. Steady airstream to avoid breaks.

difficulty with
valve slurs

1. Minimize embouchure change if valve slurs are within the same open partial (e.g., there should be absolutely no movement or change when slurring from a second-space A to fourth-line F).
2. Too many long tones in daily practice schedule without a sufficient balance of flexibility studies.
3. Slam valves (i.e., press them very quickly).
4. Steady airstream to avoid breaks.

ENDURANCE

lacking

1. Excessive pressure. Try holding the horn away from embouchure when playing, try holding it between thumbs, try holding it with the left hand placed under valve casing. Try more of a "cushion" embouchure.
2. Fatigue from too demanding a practice or rehearsal session without periods of rest.

3. Lack of proper warm-up or warm-down.
4. Not using corners of mouth properly (these are the strongest muscles in the face).
5. Mouthpiece placement may need correcting.
6. Anxiety. Relax and realize that mistakes *are* going to happen—but it's not the end of the world.

REFERENCES

Texts

Bowman, Brian. *Practical Hints on Playing the Baritone (Euphonium)*. Collaboration with James Ployhar. Melville, NY: Belwin-Mills, 1983.
Griffiths, John R. *The Low Brass Guide*. Hackensack, NJ: Jerona Music Corp., 1980.
Rose, William. *Studio Class Manual for Tuba and Euphonium*. Houston, TX: Iola Publications, 1980.

Studies

Easy-Beginning (elementary or junior high)

Archmede, Ales. *Foundation to Baritone Playing* (Carl Fischer).
Beeler, W. *Walter Beeler Method*, Book I (Warner Brothers).
Getchell, Robert (ed. Hovey). *First Book of Practical Studies* (Belwin-Mills).
Long, Newell. *Elementary Method for Trombone or Baritone* (Rubank).
Young, Lucille. *Elementary Method for Trombone or Baritone* (Carl Fischer).

Medium (advanced junior high or high school)

Arban, J. (ed. Randall and Mantia). *Complete Method* (Carl Fischer).
Archmede, Ales. *Foundation to Baritone Playing* (Carl Fischer).
Clark, H. L. *Technical Studies* (Carl Fischer).
Endreson, R. M. *Supplementary Studies* (Rubank).
Fink, Reginald H. *From Treble Clef to Bass Clef Baritone* (Accura Music).
————. *Studies in Legato* (Carl Fischer).
Gower, William. *Rubank Advanced Method*, Book 1 (Rubank).
Harvey, Russell. *Method for Trombone and Baritone* (Belwin-Mills).
Langely, Otto. *Practical Tutor for B-flat Euphonium (four valve, Bass Clef)* (Boosey and Hawkes).
Long, Newell. *Elementary Method for Trombone and Baritone* (Rubank).
Pares, Gabriel. *Pares Scales* (Rubank).
Remington, Emory (ed. Hunsberger). *Warm-Up Exercises* (Accura Music).

SCHLOSSBERG, MAX. *Daily Drills and Technical Studies* (M. Baron Music).
VOBARON, EDMOND. *34 Etudes Melodiques* (Costallat).
WEBER, FRED. *Tunes for Technique* (Belwin-Mills).

Advanced (high school or college)

ARBAN, J. (ed. Randall and Mantia). *Complete Method* (Carl Fischer).
CONCONE, G. (ed. Shoemaker). *Legato Studies* (Carl Fischer).
BLUME, O. *36 Studies* (Carl Fischer).
BORDOGNI, M. (ed. Rochut). *Melodious Etudes*, Book 1 (Carl Fischer).
SCHLOSSBERG, MAX. *Daily Studies and Technical Drills* (M. Baron Music).
SLAMA, ANTON. *66 Etudes* (Carl Fischer).
VANDERCOOK, H. A. *Vandercook Exercises* (Rubank).

BARITONE AND EUPHONIUM

Fingering Chart

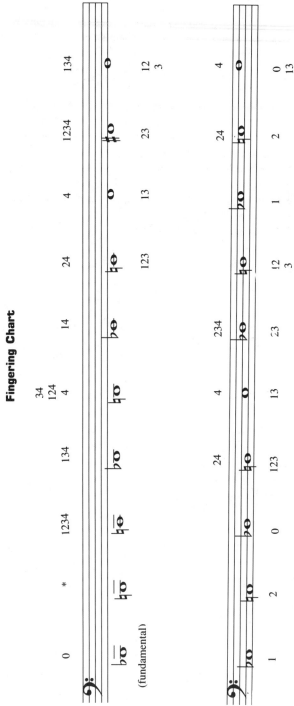

Figure 19–7. The most frequently used fingerings and alternate fingerings for Baritone and Euphonium; where they differ, fingerings for three-valved instruments are below the staff—fingerings for four-valved instruments are above the staff

20

The Tuba

HISTORY

The tuba is the lowest pitched of the brass instruments; its name, although applied specifically to one instrument, is a basic name for those bass-pitched brass instruments that are held in the vertical position rather than the horizontal. Tubas include alto horns, baritones, and euphoniums as well as the contrabass tuba. The tuba as we know it was invented in the early nineteenth century and has no direct ancestors with the same general characteristics and appearance. One might consider the serpent, invented by Guillaume about 1590, to be an early forebear of the tuba, although the similarities between the two are not great. The keyed serpent, or *ophicleide*, appeared in the early 1800s. Originally pitched in B, two octaves and one half step below middle C, it was soon built in a variety of pitches. The helicon may also be considered an ancestor of the tuba. Known as the "rain catcher" because its bell opened upward, it was carried in an upright position, wrapped around the body. In Germany, the helicon was called *bombardon* and was built in B-flat, F, or E-flat, with a wide, semiconical bore. According to Berlioz, the bombardon differed from the bass tuba in having only three valves and an inferior tone quality. There is no connection between the present-day tuba and the old Roman tuba, which was more like a cornet or bugle with a conical bore and a cup mouthpiece.

The question of who actually invented the tuba is unsettled. Stolzel and Moritz have both been credited with inventing the instrument and both actually received patents for the tuba. The date for its invention is often given as 1835, but it was first used before 1835 by Wilhelm Wieprecht in the Trompeteer Corps of the Prussian Dragoon Guards in Berlin. It was an instrument in F with five valves, held in an upright position. For a short period, a version of this instrument was produced that was held over the shoulder so that infantry marching behind the band could hear it adequately. The piston valve was added, and the first BB-flat bass was brought out by Cerveny of Koniggratz in 1845. Around 1848, Sax produced the E-flat and B-flat upright bass tubas similar in most respects to those of the modern orchestra, with a conical bore like the French horn and the oblong shape and cupped mouthpiece of the trumpet.

The Wagner tubas were developed for use in the *Ring* cycle, where the horn sound was needed at low ranges. They were made in at least two keys, B-flat and F. They had a narrow conical bore and were played with a funnel mouthpiece like the horn. They were more mellow and more agile than the regular tuba, but their sound failed to blend with the rest of the brasses.

A bass tuba similar in construction to the euphonium existed for awhile but was gradually replaced by the inventions of Adolph Sax, the double E♭ and B♭ instruments. These two have remained in use to the present, although the EE-flat is rarely found outside the brass band today. The BB-flat tuba is used in the band, while the CC and F are preferred for orchestral work. The F instrument is found largely in German and French orchestras.

The sousaphone is a form of helicon bass tuba developed by Conn just before the turn of the century. The earliest sousaphones had a bell that opened upward; the bell-front version appeared about 1908. The sousaphone rapidly replaced the helicon and has remained popular to the present, particularly in high school bands.

SELECTING THE INSTRUMENT

This lowest-pitched brass instrument has two basic forms, quite different from each other in appearance and tone quality. The upright model is the tuba. Because of its weight and size, it is impractical for marching bands. A harness is made so that the tuba can be used in marching, but it is little used. The tone quality of the tuba is superior to that of the sousaphone and is consequently favored for concert playing.

The sousaphone has been the more common public school instrument because of its versatility, although many schools are now replacing it with convertible tubas. While the sousaphone can sound better than many convertible tubas, the "over-the-shoulder" instruments, as in Figure 20–1, are usually easier to carry and generally more attractive visually (and as the old adage in marching bands goes, "Everybody can see, but not everybody can hear"). Several companies have released convertible tubas since 1990 that are of excellent quality.

Figure 20–1.   Convertable Tuba in Marching Position

Most better-quality tubas have rotary action valves similar to the horn, a highly efficient action that is both fast and silent. Unlike the horn, the rotary valves on most tubas do not use string but rather a mechanical linkage made of brass or similar alloy. Ordinarily the mechanical rotary valve is slightly slower than piston action due to added resistance; however, the Mirafone tuba is an example of an instrument with mechanical rotary valves that are satisfactory. European tubas commonly use a mechanical rotary action that has a shorter "stroke" than American rotary valves but is slower and tends to become noisy with wear. Because of the added resistance, legato playing is more difficult with this valve type.

The rotary action permits the tuba to be tilted slightly to the left, making the right-hand position more comfortable, but it has the disadvantage of taking up space. Piston valves such as those used on trumpets and most baritones require the instrument to be held upright, making the right-hand position more clumsy but keeping the instrument directly in front of the player. The worst feature of piston valves on the tuba is their long stroke which hampers technique. The majority of tubas constructed with rotary valves have a fourth valve similar to the fourth valve on the euphonium. Any new purchase, whether with rotary or piston valves, should include the fourth valve.

The sousaphone is comparatively easy to carry in marching. It rests on the left shoulder and its weight is carried by the entire body. Where budget limitations do not allow purchase of both tubas and sousaphones or convertibles, the convertible tubas may be the best choice. All three instruments, although very different in appearance, consist of conical tubing of practically the same length (18 feet for BB-flat), bore, and taper. Three piston valves are the norm for the sousaphone and convertible tuba. The advantage of rotary valve tubas over piston valve tubas, even those with short-stroke valves, makes it worthwhile for schools to invest in rotary valve instruments. The middle-line Mirafone 186-8 and Yamaha YBB641 instruments are quite good for most school programs.

All possible attempts should be made to purchase concert tubas as well as tubas for marching. During marching season, the students keep the concert instrument at home for practice, then reverse the instruments during concert season. Few parents are willing to purchase a tuba, and even fewer students will be willing to lug it home for nightly practice.

The concert tuba is made in two versions, upright bell and, less common, bell front. The upright bell produces a brighter sound and cleaner articulation; the front model spreads the sound and is less brilliant. Characteristics of the concert stage may make the upright bell disappointing; for example, if the stage ceiling is too high, the sound from the upright tuba will go straight up and never reach the audience. Experimentation with moving the tuba section to various positions on the stage may produce good results. The upright bell has the definite advantage of cleaner articulations; it diffuses the sound more than the more directional bell front.

The tuba is made in several keys. The BB-flat tuba, pitched one octave below the baritone and trombone, is the most common school instrument. The CC, the B-flat, the E-flat, and F are used. The French make a small, light tuba in C, which might be considered the top of the range, and at one time Conn made a BBB-flat that required the player to stand to reach the mouthpiece. Two other varieties of tuba are available: the "recording tuba," a modernized tuba built with side or top action, usually in BB-flat; and a double tuba similar to the double horn combining the F and BB-flat tubas.

The E-flat tuba was widely used at one time as it was small enough for younger students. It was also a good transfer instrument for trumpet players because it could be played without learning new fingerings. Music for the BB-flat tuba could be read as if it were in the treble clef, three sharps added, and played on the E-flat tuba with trumpet fingerings—an early form of instant tuba. Presently Mirafone, Premier, and Yamaha make a relatively inexpensive small-bore BB-flat tuba for younger students that has replaced the single E-flat and single B-flat instruments.

The F tuba has become the principal solo and chamber music instrument in the United States. For orchestral playing, with its greater demands on the low register, the CC-tuba is the preferred instrument. Compared to the BB-flat, the CC instrument has a better tone quality, greater flexibility, and better intonation, and is generally more full and powerful. The ease and certainty of the CC's high range give it an additional advantage in orchestral works. Wagner, for example, wrote for E above the staff and higher, in which case it is handy to have the CC or an F tuba.

An excellent practice is to buy a companion instrument with each BB-flat tuba or sousaphone, a used baritone in good condition for the beginner. This purchase will avoid the necessity of parents' buying the smaller instrument for their youngster and later having to sell it at a loss when the pupil graduates to the tuba or sousaphone. Experience on the baritone also provides the tuba player with opportunity to perform melodic lines, a practice that should continue when he switches to tuba. Many students who switch to tuba find themselves playing "oom-pah" on the tonic–dominant for the rest of their public school music tenure. Such practice reflects bad teaching and is unfair to the students and to the entire program. The supplemental material at the end of this chapter should be used to provide a more complete musical experience for tuba players.

ASSEMBLING THE TUBA

Like the other brasses, assembling consists of inserting the mouthpiece. It may also include attaching the bell or putting the instrument in its stand. On school instruments, even putting on the mouthpiece may not be necessary, for it may not have been removed for years.

HOLDING THE TUBA

The upright tuba may be placed on a chair stand, in which case the stand is adjusted to fit the player's height. If a stand is not used, the instrument is held with the left hand in a position comfortable for the embouchure to meet the mouthpiece. The instrument may rest on the chair between the player's legs (see Figure 20–2 for the correct position for holding the tuba). Adjusting the angle of the mouthpiece is important; the two mouthpiece bits are for this purpose. The player should not need to strain or put her head or neck in an unnatural position to get to the mouthpiece; she should adjust the angle so that it is comfortable for her as she sits in a relaxed, upright position or slightly forward. She may have to sit on books straddling the tuba (resting on the chair) or possibly straddle the tuba that is resting on books or a cushion—in either event, it is important that the student experiment to determine the correct height of the mouthpiece to her embouchure.

With a large instrument, the player often has a tendency to move her face and lips to the instrument. The player who adjusts herself to the horn asks for trouble: her posture will be poor, she will develop unnecessary tension, have trouble getting adequate breath support, produce a poor tone, and become easily fatigued. If the player holds the tuba, she must

Figure 20–2. Sitting Position for Playing the Tuba

shift the instrument to the place where the mouthpiece meets her embouchure comfortably.

The proper position for holding the sousaphone is even simpler. The
player gets into the instrument, rests the upper part of the circular tubing
on her left shoulder, and adjusts the mouthpiece for her comfort (see
Figure 20–3). Sponge pads for the left shoulder are desirable for carrying
the sousaphone any distance and may also be used when the player is
seated.

THE BEGINNING STUDENT

Picking the player by his size to fit the size of the instrument is unwise.
Those big fellows picked in grade school to play the tuba very frequently
turn out to be the football heroes in high school, and the band loses its tuba
section for the football season.

Figure 20–3. Sitting Position for Playing the Sousaphone

The best criterion for selecting a student to play tuba is desire, followed closely by the second criterion, a good ear. A teacher can point out the importance of the bass line, the essential part that the bass plays in all wind and symphonic literature, and the necessity of having bright students with accurate listening skills to establish the foundation of the wind ensemble. The best approach seems to be to start the beginner on a baritone horn if she wishes to eventually play the BB-flat tuba—she can use a regular BB-flat bass book with the identical fingerings. When transferring to the tuba she need only change the size of the mouthpiece and learn to hear the instrument an octave lower.

There may be a definite advantage in starting the new tuba player on the mouthpiece only—success on the mouthpiece alone may build confidence and perhaps courage before the student tackles a large brass pipe sometimes as big as herself. Buzzing on the mouthpiece also helps the student use the air more efficiently and helps develop the ear.

EMBOUCHURE

The embouchure for the tuba (Figure 20–4) is similar to that for all brass; the reader should review Chapter 15 carefully. The placement of the mouthpiece is less critical for the tuba because less pressure is needed. Still, the player needs to experiment until she finds the placement that gives the best results. Because the mouthpiece and the bore are larger, the upper and lower teeth are farther apart and less mouthpiece pressure is used. The additional space between the teeth is necessary to create a larger mouth cavity for the escape of air. A wider portion of the lips vibrates, so more air must be projected to set the lips in motion. A problem developed by some students is an embouchure with more tension toward the center of the lips than toward the corners of the mouth. A smile-type embouchure or air leaking at the sides of the mouth may be an indication of this problem.

Because the mouthpiece is larger, size may enter once again into the selection of a bass player and gauging her capacity for success. The mouthpiece requires enough distance between the mouth and nose to use two-thirds upper and one-third lower lip in the mouthpiece, which appears to be about half-and-half when viewed with a mouthpiece visualizer. Mouthpiece placement is not as critical with such a large mouthpiece. Comfort and placement for the best control should dictate actual tuba mouthpiece placement.

The embouchure can be strengthened and developed more quickly if one buzzes on the mouthpiece with regularity. The most common problems among young tubists are (1) lips too tight, which especially affects flexibility; (2) too much puckering often accompanied by a bunched-up chin; (3) chewing each note; (4) teeth too close together (occasionally a piece of 1.5 cm cork can be held between molars to keep them apart); and (5) the tongue too high in the mouth.

Figure 20–4. Tuba Embouchure

The beginner often has difficulty finding enough air to support the tone. Less pressure is required than for the higher brasses, but more air must be moved through the instrument since its bore is considerably larger than the upper brasses. Although more of the lip vibrates, only the inner edge of the lip is involved, as on other brass instruments. A smile-type embouchure makes the lips too thin and destroys the cushion necessary for good tone. The cushion does not imply loose, flabby lips. A dull or airy tone will result from loose lips that push too much into the mouthpiece cup. On the lower pitches from about B-flat below the staff down, the lips do thicken and actually extend into the mouthpiece. For pitches above this, the tension must be adequate at the corners of the mouth to keep the lips from bunching up in the mouthpiece. Since the mouthpiece covers such a wide area of the lips and face, many students often drop the entire lower lip from the mouthpiece to inhale larger amounts of air required for good tone on the tuba.

With transfers from other instruments, the problem is usually not one of too much relaxation but of too much lip tension. Former trumpet players have difficulty realizing that the teeth should be fairly far apart and that little embouchure pressure is required for producing the tone. To open the teeth sufficiently and produce a rounder tone, McMillen suggests using the syllable "toe," first spoken, then blown, then blown through the mouthpiece, and finally blown into the horn. Use of "toe" tenses the corners of the mouth slightly but at the same time keeps plenty of cushion in the center of the lips. The embouchure will change for the lower pitches, the jaw dropping and moving slightly back as the pitches descend. The lips are relaxed for the low notes, forming a shape closer to "pooh." The movement of the jaw in descending passages is enough to be noticeable. A rule sometimes given is that for B-flat below the staff, the teeth are open wide enough to allow the first knuckle of the index finger to be placed between the teeth. For lower notes the opening becomes even wider. The corners of the mouth do not change and remain slightly tense, even though the center of the lips is relaxed. In the middle and upper range, the syllable formed by the lips is "too," with "tee" for the extreme top of the register.

When the embouchure is too loose and relaxed or there is insufficient breath support, the tone will be airy and fuzzy. If the embouchure is too tense and not open enough, the sound will be raspy, cracked, or explosive.

Some young tuba players get in the habit of letting their jaw move when playing. This habit may in part be due to dropping the jaw for a note, then relaxing the embouchure and letting the lower teeth move back to a more "natural" position. The results include poor articulation, unstable pitch, and notes resembling those by a wah-wah guitar. The embouchure should be set in position and held except for breaths. Many high school tubists play slightly above the "center" of the pitch, the resonant pitch for each valve combination, and need to relax and open up the oral cavity.

Critical to embouchure development is the angle at which the tuba is held. As the student plays the mouthpiece alone, the teacher should observe carefully the angle at which she holds the mouthpiece to her embouchure, then help her duplicate that angle when the instrument is held.

Mouthpieces

Mouthpieces are as much a problem for the tuba player as for the other brass players, and even greater when one considers the cost. The Bach mouthpieces, such as models 18, 22, and 25, are generally accepted as the most satisfactory.

An experimental, funnel-shaped mouthpiece, similar to that for the horn, was produced commercially for a few years, but without success. It increased range and ease of playing, but was unreliable for intonation and tone quality.

While the tuba mouthpiece is certainly the most expensive mouthpiece of any wind instrument, parents must realize that these mouthpieces are certainly less expensive than the instruments purchased by the parents of other wind instrumentalists. Students should be required to purchase their own mouthpieces since they do not have to purchase their own tubas, if for no other reason than to promote pride of ownership.

INTONATION

Good pitch is an essential aspect of good tuba playing. It is also a very difficult task, and problems include: hearing intonation discrepancies in the low register; control of pitch with such a large embouchure opening; lack of control when so much air is needed; and, frequently, problems associated with neglected school-owned instruments. Yet good intonation is required of the tuba player and tuba section for a well-tuned band or orchestra. The perception involved in listening to the pitch of any chord is based on the bottom pitch.

Notes below the staff, those most difficult to hear, are also the most troublesome in intonation. Because the overtones are different for differently pitched tubas, intonation difficulties will arise when they are played together. Figures 20–5 and 20–6 show pitches that are commonly flat or sharp for one tuba and adequately in tune for another.

Good intonation begins with an instrument that is in good shape. Due to the size of the tuba, it is usually not cleaned as often as it should be. In addition, intonation depends on good tuning. The bass player must work toward achieving control so that a steady, clear pitch—that is *reliable*—can

Figure 20–5. Intonation Problems on the CC, E-flat and BB-flat Tubas

be played. Good intonation is the student playing in tune with the ensemble as well as herself.

Several things can be done to improve intonation. First, the tuning slides may be used. Besides the general tuning slide, each valve has its own slide, similar to the other valved brasses. Because of the length of the tubing and the low range of the instrument, the slides must be pulled much farther than on the higher instruments to change the pitch. An inch or more is not uncommon, and the player should pull the slide boldly—if she makes too great a change she can adjust it, but she may never get to the correct pitch if she timidly pulls little by little. The tubist must learn to alter the first-valve slide while playing to flatten those pitches that require adjustment, then push that slide back in for other notes that use the first valve.

Second, the tuba, like all brass instruments, becomes sharper with increased temperatures, but does so at a pace nearly twice that of the higher instruments. Therefore, if the temperatures are likely to be markedly warm (during a concert, for instance), tuning the rest of the group slightly sharper than normal will allow for the tuba's rise in pitch. The tuba cannot pull the slide sufficiently to match pitch if the tuning standard remains at A440.

Third, vowel formation or the position of the tongue and lower jaw can affect the pitch somewhat. As on other instruments, a more closed vowel causes the pitch to rise slightly; a more open vowel lowers the pitch. Consequently, the tuba player is always struggling to maintain a consistent tone quality and centered pitch between the different registers of the instrument. This consistency requires the practice of long tones in different registers, and a copious number of hours working with an electronic tuner. If the sound is somewhat choked, then it will also be sharp. This sharpness can be remedied by pulling a slide or two, but this procedure for tuning does not help the tone quality. The student should attempt to open up the vocal cavity and throat, and drop the tongue; each alteration will require the student to breathe properly. The immediate change will be a flatter, more open sound. The sound will be better and the flatness can easily be fixed by adjusting the tuning slide.

A fourth help for intonation is a trigger on the first valve slide. The player can also push the slide down for any note she needs to make sharper. When the slide is released, it will immediately return to its normal position. The spring mechanism is easily controlled with a flick of a left

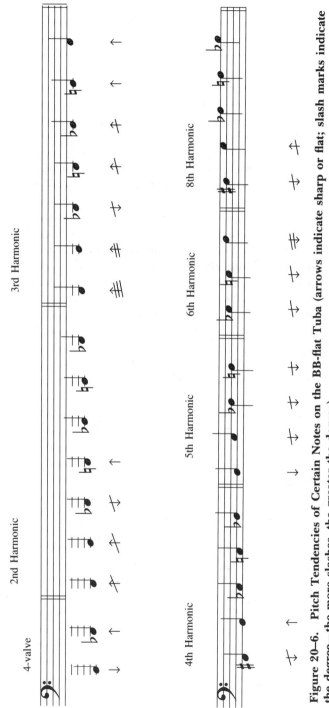

Figure 20–6. Pitch Tendencies of Certain Notes on the BB-flat Tuba (arrows indicate sharp or flat; slash marks indicate the degree—the more slashes, the greater the degree)

finger. This trigger is an expensive item and unfortunately is rarely found on school horns.

TONE QUALITY

The element having most influence on the tone is plenty of air, plus support for that air, and a relaxed throat and jaw. The more open the throat, the better the tone, provided there is adequate breath support from the diaphragm. Most players try to tighten the lips too much. They defeat the purpose by putting forth too much effort. The cheeks should not puff out, as this detours the air on its way from diaphragm to instrument. If the lips and jaw are relaxed, there will be less danger of air in the cheeks. "One problem unique to the tuba, due to the long way the air has to travel, is the time lag between initiating the tone and its sounding. The tuba, as foundation of the band, must be precisely on the beat, so the tuba player must anticipate the beat slightly. The bass drum also has this problem of a time lag; both tuba and bass drum control the beat of the ensemble. If they lag or are not together, the director will find it impossible to obtain a precise, crisp, synchronized sound from the group. This problem is further aggravated if the student has difficulty with response—the bane of many tuba players. A proper warm-up is essential for control and for a responsive embouchure.

A fuzzy tone results from too much relaxation of the embouchure or diaphragm. A raspy or cracked tone may be due to a tongue that is arched too high in the middle, or to insufficient breath support. It may also be due to jaws that are clamped shut restricting the air flow. A more open throat and jaw help eliminate rasping and cracking. On the other hand, a cracked or blasting sound may be due to the player's taking a breath for each note. Beginning players may feel that they cannot play more than a single note on one breath and thereby develop the habit of breathing more frequently than needed. Breathing with the phrase should be habitual. If the problem is difficulty with sounding the very low notes, the solution is more air support and a more open jaw and throat. For the lowest pitches, one can hardly get the lips and throat too open, as long as the corners of the mouth stay firm.

Most tuba players at all stages of development need to practice in the lowest register of the instrument. Long tones with crescendos and decrescendos help. Playing in the low register, including pedal tones, helps the student's breathing and helps to establish good playing habits such as opening the throat and dropping the jaw.

Vibrato

Vibrato is seldom used by tuba players in ensembles as the tuba establishes the pitch for the entire group, whether it is a band or brass quintet. Most fine tuba soloists use jaw vibrato for solo literature.

Mutes

Mutes are little used in tuba literature, though they are not completely unknown. In certain selections, such as Persichetti's Symphony for Band, tuba mutes are required. There are straight mutes available, made in shapes to fit either an upright bell model or bell-front tuba. Band directors may find the primary use for tuba mutes when there are no bassoons in the band and the tuba plays bassoon parts or bassoon cues. As with other brasses, tuba mutes tend to sharpen the overall pitch.

FINGERINGS

The fundamental that sounds when no valves are depressed is easily produced owing to the wide bore of the tuba. The entire low range is very sonorous because of the limited number of harmonics. When the fourth valve is added, it is a substitute for valves 1 and 3 and it improves the normally sharp intonation of this valve combination and the 1–2–3 combination, which can be played 2–4. The fourth valve also extends the range an additional fourth, since it can be used in combination with the other valves to reach even lower pitches. The chart at the end of the chapter contains the common fingerings as well as alternate fingerings for three- and four-valved tubas.

A fifth valve is sometimes added solely to help solve intonation problems. It produces a pitch between a major second and a minor third so that much adjustment of intonation is possible.

Music for the tuba is often badly written and may need to be altered to achieve musical results. Among the common changes a director may expect to make are these: (1) The part may need to be moved up or down an octave. (2) Rapid slurred passages are often impossible for the entire section to play clearly and precisely (especially with piston valves); the usual solution is to have only the first chair play the passage as written, with the others tonguing every note or a combination of tonguing and slurring; (3) Orchestral transcriptions frequently contain passages originally written for the string bass which make unreasonable demands on the tuba player. These should be simplified, not only for the player's morale but also for the sake of musical clarity and accuracy.

Solo literature for the tuba is limited in quantity and even more in quality, although an increasing number of pieces are being written and transcribed every year. One solution is to use cello, bassoon, string bass, and even horn literature. Careful editing is necessary in most cases to accommodate the music to the tuba's possibilities without violating the composer's original intent.

The number of tubas for a well-balanced organization is a matter open to debate. There is a tendency to l.ave large numbers, perhaps because they do not play as well as other members of the band, or perhaps because an entire row of sousaphones looks good in the marching band and the school name can be spelled out on the bell coverings. One viewpoint says that having too many tubas makes a thick, muddy sound; three is plenty for the average band and probably never more than five should be used, even with a 120-piece organization. The other viewpoint is that of E. F. Goldman, who at one time said that he believed 10 percent of the band should be tuba. Stauffer states it is better to have too many than too few. The kind of sound the director wants and the competency of his players will be the deciding factor.

WHAT TO PRACTICE

Like other brass players, the tuba student should practice on long tones, flexibility studies, and technical studies, including scales and arpeggios, and melodic passages. All too often, tuba players are switched to the instrument in a junior high band situation, in which the extent of the tuba player's participation is the stereotypical "oom-pah" oscillation between the tonic and dominant with the subdominate thrown in for occasional variety. These easy parts do little to encourage the tuba player to practice other literature.

Tuba students should also include breathing exercises as part of their daily schedule to learn to control the air and to use their limited air supply more efficiently. Exercises such as taking a slow, long, deep breath followed by several short, quick breaths ("packing it in") helps increase the lung capacity if practiced with a relaxed chest cavity. Exercises such as playing long tones as long as possible, trying to increase the time in seconds each week, help control the efficient use of the air supply. Long tones should be practiced with a tuner as much of the time as possible.

Tuba players require as much warm-up as any other brass player. Occasionally teachers see a demand for a careful warm-up by the first trumpet player but overlook the critical demands of the tubist. Since the instrument is so large and the student blows a "large" airstream into a "cavernous" mouthpiece, control is more difficult to acquire on the tuba than on any other brass instrument. Breathing exercises followed by long tones started (held, and tapered to the end) at all dynamic levels from ppp to ff and in all ranges are essential. Perhaps the most difficult "lick" on tuba is to enter on a whole note at a pp dynamic level.

Pedal tones and slurring exercises going from the middle register to the lower register help the player keep the large amounts of air required moving in the low registers. Young tuba players also invariably have difficulty with technical passages. First, they seldom encounter them. When they finally play Grade VI band literature and are faced with sixteenth note runs, they often have difficulty even knowing how to practice. The long stroke of the piston valves on the tuba is a serious handicap for playing with good finger facility; rotary valves are a definite advantage. Technical passages should be practiced very slowly for evenness and correct pitches, the tempo then slightly increased with phrasing and dynamic changes added, then the entire passage speeded up to the appropriate tempo and even slightly faster. Patience on the part of the music instructor is of primary concern, as the tuba players see far fewer moving passages than any other instrument in the band.

CARE AND MAINTENANCE OF THE TUBA

For general care of the tuba, consult the section on care in Chapter 15. The tuba is normally a relatively maintenance-free instrument. The most important and often neglected aspect is cleaning the inside of the instrument. The tuba should be taken apart like the other brasses and soaked in a bathtub of very warm water at least once a year. The teacher should either do this task or make it *very* clear to the student that 18 feet of brass tubing filled with water is extremely unmanageable. Cleaning involves removing the slides, the bell section if possible, and piston valves if they are used. A flexible, "snake" brush should be used to clean the leadpipe and slides. Brass rotors can be left in the instrument while soaking. Once a year, however, they should be removed and cleaned. All moving parts will require lubrication; valves may need oiling on a daily basis. Due to the nature of rotary valves and their expense, players may want to leave this maintenance task to a competent repairperson.

Additional items of importance for the tuba are the following: The mouthpiece bits as well as the mouthpiece should be cleaned weekly. The bits should not be boiled if they are lacquered, as boiling will remove the lacquer finish. Warm water and a brush are sufficient. The mouthpiece should not be left on the instrument for decades; it should be removed when the tuba is not being played and stored in a mouthpiece pouch (vinyl or leather) to protect the rim from nicks and scratches.

Many band rooms have hooks for storing the sousaphone, but these are often the kind that the instrument can be knocked off of by a careless passerby. Many schools do not buy sousaphone cases because of their expense and their infrequent use. Schools that have purchased cases often find the time required to assemble the rather bulky instrument detracts from rehearsal time, so the cases are not used on a daily basis. Carefully wrapping the instrument in heavy blankets protects it adequately for trips. The use of separate instruments—the sousaphone for out-of-doors and the tuba for concert work—alleviates damage to the tuba. The use of newer materials such as fiberglass in the sousaphone has greatly reduced the problem of dents in the bell and large tubing; however, the valves, valve tubing, mouthpiece, and bits are still delicate. Most structural problems invariably occur in places where the plastic materials are joined to the metal pieces.

Quality cases for a concert tuba are a must. Why spend thousands of dollars on a brass instrument and then try to save money on a $300 case?

The tuba or sousaphone should never be placed on the floor with the bell down. The weight resting on the bell can cause a dent or bend in the bell. For storing, the instrument should be placed on its side in a level spot, and away from traffic.

TROUBLESHOOTING

EQUIPMENT

sluggish valves

1. a. Rotary valves: Place several drops of valve oil into first-valve slide, holding instrument so that oil runs down; work the three or four valves up and down; expel excess oil out third-valve water key; oil the front bushing and remove the valve cap to oil the back bushing—*using rotary valves that are not oiled can quickly ruin the valves.*
   b. Piston valves: Carefully remove each valve separately and oil well; if the leadpipe leads directly into the first valve, olive oil may be added to the valve oil to make it stick longer.
2. Make sure student is pressing piston valves straight down and not at an angle.
3. Remove piston valves and clean them and the casing with lint-free cloth, oil well, and replace.

air will not pass through horn

1. Make sure valves are in correct casings.
2. Inspect for clogged leadpipe or bell (mouthpieces fit very snugly in the bell).
3. Inspect for a dirty mouthpiece.
4. Inspect bell section for paper, method books, etc.

gurgling sound but water key will not expel any water

1. If water gurgles without valves pressed, inspect for clogged water key (remove tuning slide and dump); unwind tuba to pour out of bell section.
2. If water sounds with valves pressed, remove valves to expel (many students forget that the third valve must be pressed for the third-valve water key to work effectively).

mouthpiece wiggles

1. Wrong size shank for tuba—tubas do not have a standard-sized shank as do most trumpets and horns; call instrument dealer to find out correct mouthpiece size and order one.

2. Shank out-of-round. Have repaired only by competent repairperson.

instrument leaks air

1. Inspect and if necessary replace cork (water key).
2. If around valve casing, have resoldered by competent repairperson.
3. If around any tubing or joints, have repaired by a competent repairperson.

buzzing sound

1. Inspect for broken brace(s). Have resoldered.
2. Determine if a recent soaking may have loosened residue inside. Rewash or use flexible brush.

TONE

dull, spread, or unfocused sound

1. Teeth too far apart in an attempt to play in the low register. Correct embouchure.
2. Lips not buzzing evenly. Buzz without mouthpiece, then with mouthpiece alone.
3. Insufficient air support. Blow "fast" air.
4. Cheeks puffing. Practice buzzing without mouthpiece.
5. Embouchure too slack. Tighten corners and encourage student to focus pitch—blow a "pencil-thin" stream of air.

stuffy, fuzzy sound

1. Teeth too close together. Lots of buzzing without the mouthpiece and with the mouthpiece alone.
2. Lips too puckered (buzz without mouthpiece).
3. Pinching the lips together, or the teeth are together. Drop jaw; keep corners of mouth clamped shut firmly to loosen the center.
4. Air pockets behind upper or lower lip. Practice buzzing without mouthpiece—this forces a flat chin and firm embouchure in the right places.
5. Cheeks puffing. Again, buzz without mouthpiece.
6. Closed throat. Pull shoulders downward.
7. Too much saliva in embouchure or mouthpiece.
8. Improper mouthpiece placement. Correct placement.

difficulty with upper range

1. Excessive mouthpiece pressure. Rely more on air and less on pressure. Corners of the mouth should be kept firm, attempt to pull horn and mouthpiece away from embouchure when playing.
2. Not enough lip in the mouthpiece.
3. Blow faster air, a "pencil-thin" airstream.
4. Fatigue. Lack of proper warm-up or warm-down.
5. Try to direct air slightly downward by rolling in lower lip or tilting head backward slightly.

6. Try practicing in the low register; try playing pedal tones.

ARTICULATIONS

explosive attacks

1. Building air pressure behind tongue or holding onto the air before releasing it. Try for better coordination between air and tongue. Inhale to exhale without stopping.
2. Tonguing between the teeth. Work toward a "duh" tongue placement instead of "thuh."
3. Stopping the previous note with the tongue. Practice playing long tones while merely disrupting the airstream with the tongue, notes are connected.
4. Attempting to articulate with lips touching, "puh" or "muh." Work on long tones with big, open, focused tone and use slow repeated "duh" articulations.
5. Aperture in embouchure too small. Same as for #4.

scooping notes,
facial movements

1. Air starting too slowly then increasing to proper velocity. Work on making the inhale-to-exhale one continuous cycle without stopping. Sometimes student is timid and fears failure; get her to take a chance.
2. "Chewing notes"; excessive chin movement. Tongue moving too far; replace "taw–taw" with "duh–duh." Practice long tone *and* lip slurs up and down in front of mirror to hold chin still.
3. #2 is usually accompanied with a bunched chin. Try buzzing without mouthpiece to force chin flat.
4. Too much lip in the mouthpiece. Practice forming an embouchure and buzzing without the mouthpiece, then try to establish the same sensations when playing.

difficulty with
lip slurs

1. Try directing air slightly downward for upward slurs.
2. "Lean" into lower note for upward slurs followed by upper pitch played slightly softer.
3. Increase air speed when going to upper pitch.
4. Avoid excessive pressure on upward slur; tighten corners of mouth instead.
5. Not enough lower lip in mouthpiece can make upward slurs difficult.
6. Do not let tone spread on downward slurs (bad habits sometimes develop since it is almost impossible to "undershoot" the lower note).

difficulty with
valve slurs

1. No embouchure change if valve slurs are within the same open partial (e.g., there should be absolutely no movement or change when slurring from a second-space A to fourth-line F).

2. Too many long tones in daily practice schedule.
3. Slam valves.
4. Steady airstream to avoid breaks.

response
1. Mouthpiece too large.
2. Bore of instrument too large.
3. Something obstructing the inside of the instrument.
4. Not enough air—or a tentative release of the air.
5. Lack of a systematic warm-up.

ENDURANCE

lacking
1. Too much pressure. Try holding the instrument away from embouchure when playing.
2. Fatigue from too demanding a practice or rehearsal session without periods of rest.
3. Lack of proper warm-up or warm-down.
4. Not using corners of mouth properly (these are the strongest muscles in the face).
5. Mouthpiece placement may need correcting.
6. Tonguing may be improper or tongue too tense.
7. Anxiety. Relax and realize that mistakes *are* going to happen—but it's not the end of the world.

REFERENCES

Texts

BELL, WILLIAM. *Foundation to Tuba and Sousaphone Playing*. New York: Carl Fischer, 1931.

BEVAN, CLIFFORD. *The Tuba Family*. London: Faber and Faber, 1978.

CUMMINGS, BARTON. *The Contemporary Tuba*. New London, CT: Whaling Music Publishers, 1984.

GRIFFITHS, JOHN R. *The Low Brass Guide*. Hackensack, NJ: Jerona Music Corp., 1980.

LITTLE, DONALD. *Practical Hints on Playing the Tuba*. Melville, NY: Belwin-Mills, 1984.

MASON, J. KENT. *The Tuba Handbook*. Toronto: Sonante Publications, 1977.

MORRIS, R. WINSTON, ed. *Tuba Music Guide*. Northfield, IL: The Instrumentalist Co., 1973.

ROBINSON, JACK. *Advanced Conditioning Studies for Tuba*. New London, CT: Whaling Music Publishers, 1985.

ROSE, WILLIAM. *Studio Manual for Tuba and Euphonium*. Houston, TX: Iola Publications, 1980.

STEWART, M. D. *Arnold Jacobs: The Legacy of a Master.* Northfield, IL: The Instrumentalist Co, 1987.

Journals

T.U.B.A. Quarterly journal of the Tubist Universal Brotherhood Association, Paul Ebbers, School of Music, Florida State University, Tallahassee, FL 32306.

Studies

Easy—Beginning (elementary or junior high)

BEELER, WALTER. *Method for Tuba* (Remick).
BELL, WILLIAM. *Foundation to Tuba and Sousaphone Playing* (Carl Fischer).
ENDRESEN, R. M. *BBb Tuba Method* (also *Eb Tuba Method*) (Rubank).
————. *Supplementary Etudes* (Rubank).
GETCHELL, R. (ed. Hovey). *First Book of Practical Studies* (Belwin-Mills).
HINDSLEY, M. *Basic Method for Eb or BBb Tuba* (Carl Fischer)
HOVEY, NILO. *Elementary Method*, 3 vols. (Rubank).
KUHN, and JAROSLAV CIMERA. *Method for Tuba* (Belwin-Mills).
RYS, GILBERT. *50 Easy Studies* (Alphonse Leduc).
UBER, DAVID. *25 Early Studies* (Southern Music).
————. *Warm-Up Procedures* (Colin).
VASILIEV, A. *24 Melodious Etudes for Tuba* (Robert King).

Medium (advanced junior high or high school)

BACH, J. S. *Bach for Tuba*, Book I (Western International).
BEELER, WALTER. *Method for Tuba* (Remick).
BELL, WILLIAM. *Foundation to Tuba and Sousaphone Playing* (Carl Fischer).
————. *Tuba Warm-Ups* (Colin).
BLAZHEVICH, VLADISLAV. *70 Studies for BBb Tuba*, Vol. 1 (Robert King).
BLUME, O. *35 Studies*, Book I (Carl Fischer).
BORDOGNI, M. (ed. Roberts). *43 Bel Canto Studies* (Robert King).
FINK, R. *Studies in Legato for Bass Trombone and Tuba* (Carl Fisher).
GETCHELL, R. (ed. Hovey). *Second Book of Practical Studies* (Belwin-Mills).
OSTRANDER, ALLEN. *Shifting Meter Studies* (Robert King).
REMINGTON, E. (ed. Hunsberger). *Warm-Up Exercises (Accura).*
ROCHUT, J. *Melodious Etudes* (Carl Fischer).
SLAMA, ANTON. *66 Etudes* (International).
UBER, DAVID. *30 Studies for the Bass Tuba* (Southern Music).
VASILIEV, A. *24 Melodious Etudes for Tuba* (Robert King).

Advanced (high school or college)

BACH, J. S. *Bach for Tuba*, Book II (Western International).
BELL, WILLIAM. *Tuba Warm-Ups* (Colin).
BLAZHEVICH, VLADISLAV. *70 Studies for BBb Tuba*, Vols. 1 and 2 (Robert King).
CIMERA, JAROSLAV. *73 Advanced Tuba Studies* (Belwin-Mills).
GALLAY, J. F. *30 Studies* (Robert King).
GRIGORIEV, BORIS. *78 Studies for Tuba* (Robert King).
KOPPRASCH, C. *60 Selected Studies* (Robert King).
KUEHN, DAVID. *60 Musical Studies* (Books 1 and 2) (Southern Music).
RYS, GILBERT. *50 Finishing Studies for Tuba* (Alphonse Leduc).
TYRRELL, H. W. *Advanced Studies for BBb Bass* (Boosey & Hawkes).

TUBA Fingering Chart

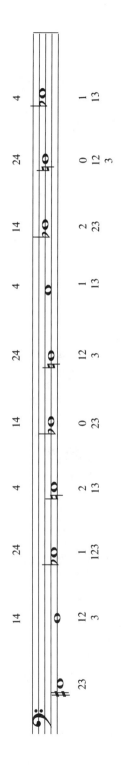
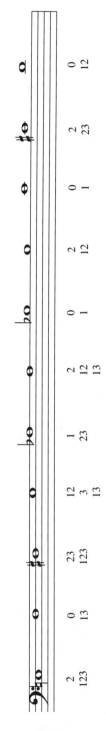

21

Percussion
Instruments

HISTORY

Idiophone, autophone, plate, and *bar group* are the terms used to designate percussion instruments. *Membranophone* is used to indicate the drum family. Together these contain the most ancient and primitive instruments known. Humans learned to rub and strike objects together before they learned to blow into a hollow reed or pluck a taut string. Idiophones, including castanets, cymbals, sticks, clappers, and other similar instruments, are as a class more venerable than the drum. Stick clappers date back at least to 3000 B.C., rattles to 2500 B.C., and cymbals to 1100 B.C. These went under the general name of *sistra* and were found in many varieties.

The possible origin of the more sophisticated percussion instruments makes stimulating food for thought. Often the original was a far cry from its present-day descendant. For example, the chimes grew out of a stone slab that was suspended and struck; the xylophone was once nothing more than a wooden slab or two placed across the legs and struck. Some instruments reached a high degree of beauty and refinement early in their history; the Peking bell in China is over 4,000 years old. Drums as a class are somewhat more sophisticated than the idiophones, for making a head to a drum out of stretched skin or hide demands some previous thought and planning rather than simply accidental discovery. Opinion is that drums probably were invented rather than found by chance; they were used very early as signals and may have been created for that purpose.

In the historical era, most of the percussion entered the orchestra as late as the Classical or Romantic period. Kettledrums, or timpani, were the earliest to be admitted. They date from A.D. 600 in Persia and came into

Europe with the Crusaders about 1300. They entered the orchestra about 1675 in connection with operatic effects. For many years, the timpani were tuned to the trumpets, but Beethoven broke this tradition with the Eighth Symphony, in which he tuned them in unison with the bassoon. Although the tambourine is spoken of as early as Genesis and Exodus, called there *tabret* or *timbrel*, it was not until Weber used it that this instrument was put into the symphony. Gluck had used the triangle as early as 1779; Haydn in *The Seasons* introduced a number of programmatic sounds including thunder, the whistle of a quail, gunshot, and the chirp of a cricket; Wagner and Tchaikovsky used the broom beating the edge of a drum. In almost every case, these were introduced for a programmatic effect, but once used this way they began to be utilized for strictly musical effects and gradually became legitimate members of the percussion section. Contemporary music has made great use of them and has invented some new ones, such as brake drums and kitchen chairs, instruments that would have astonished even Papa Haydn.

In spite of their ancient age, the percussion instruments have not been quite respectable until recently. They had no literature of their own, no good texts or method books, and no systematic approach for learning the necessary techniques. Merv Britton, Michael Colgrass, and Jack McKenzie demonstrated the musical worth of the percussion instruments by writing solos and ensembles that go beyond mere noisemaking and have artistic merit.

Most percussionists do not develop real musical skills; they do not have melodic lines to follow or harmonic parts to fit into. They should be able to count accurately, but many cannot. An added deterrent to musical growth is the tendency toward specialization. Snare drummers play only snare drums, timpanists play only timpani, and so forth. This makes the student desultory and unoccupied. If she were expected to play all the percussion instruments, she would have occasional melodic parts (in addition to the rhythmic), she could double on instruments in the same composition, and she might even practice to improve her skill in using sticks and mallets.

To help provide real learning situations and also motivation for the percussionist, the percussion ensemble has been organized. Music for percussion ensemble can offer challenging parts and demand real knowledge of the players.

SELECTING THE INSTRUMENT

In spite of their ancient age, it has only been since 1950 that percussion instruments have gained the serious attention of musicians. Beginning with Paul Price and his students and extending into the 1990s with composers such as Mark Ford, Cirone, Kraft, and dozens of others, the body of literature for percussion ensemble and solo percussion has become extensive. Band and orchestra composers are using more and varied percussion instruments for coloring effects. The days of assigning a student with a bad ear to drums is over. Modern day *percussionists* (not drummers) must be able to count, as any band work in a complex meter usually relies heavily on percussion; to read both treble and bass clef as well as the abbreviations used by composers for rudiments and special effects; to command technique, as keyboard mallet playing makes it virtually impossible to look at both the music and the instrument; and to listen carefully, as most percussionists are positioned behind the ensemble, making listening for balance more difficult.

Percussionists can benefit as much from small ensembles as the brass and woodwind players who form quintets. Percussion ensembles provide added motivation and a chance to develop performance skills on the many percussion instruments.

Cook's excellent text on teaching percussionists categorizes percussion instruments into five large groups: membranophones, idiophones, chordophones, aerophones, and electrophones.[1] Membranophones are those instruments commonly labeled drums; their sound is produced by the vibration of a leather or synthetic head stretched over a resonating chamber (a shell or bowl). Timpani and the Indian tabla are the only membranophones producing specific pitches. Idiophones are those many instruments whose sound comes from the vibration of their entire body. The marimba, xylophone, vibraphone, bells, and genuine gongs are tuned idiophones; triangles, cymbals, temple blocks, woodblocks, claves, castanets, guiros, and so on, are idiophones that can be played in "graduated" pitches, such as temple blocks from low to high, but produce undefined pitches. Chordophone sound comes from a vibrating string over a resonating chamber, such as a piano; and aerophones are those wind instruments that do not play specific pitches and are used for special effects, such as sirens, slide whistles or bull roars. Electrophones include the new body of drum machines that are becoming increasingly popular.

One of the greatest problems facing the modern percussionist is performing the notation. This problem results from the varying degree of damping by percussion instruments. A single quarter note played by a snare drummer will be much shorter than a quarter note played by a timpanist, and a quarter note for crash cymbals will last even longer than that of the timpani unless the player dampens the instrument. These problems of interpretation of notation are discussed in the following sections.

---

[1]Gary D. Cook, *Teaching Percussion* (New York: Schirmer Books, 1988), 10–12.

The Percussion Section

Percussion instruments can be expensive so that purchase of these items is restricted by budget considerations. With care and regular maintenance, however, percussion instruments can last many years. Students must be convinced that marimba covers are just as important as an oboe case, that timpani are not to be used as coffee tables, and that only percussionists (*not* the trombone players) are to club the percussion instruments.

It is not unreasonable to have the players provide their own sticks and mallets. Piano instruction is of value to all instrumentalists, but it probably benefits percussionists more than other members of the band or orchestra.

The equipment that should be on hand in the middle school program, listed by priority, includes:

1. Two snare drums (5 × 14 inch and 6 ½ × 14 inch) with stands
2. One bass drum (16 × 32 inch) with a tilting stand rather than the more commonly found metal "cradle"; skin heads are preferred but plastic will suffice
3. One pair of medium crash cymbals (16–18 inch) with leather straps and special stand for holding crash cymbals
4. Two suspended cymbals (one medium 18 inch and one thin 16 inch) with stands
5. One 2½ octave bells (steel or aluminum) with stand (a set of marching bells may be available)
6. One 3-octave xylophone (the type used for marching bands is usually the least expensive—resonators are not necessary)
7. One marimba—student-line instruments are available and are less expensive than those designed for marching bands (which are less expensive than those designed for concert use)
8. Tenor drums—these can be an expensive item but are often required (snare drums with the snares off can be used or marching tenor drums from the high school can be used—a concert stand is required)
9. Timpani (at least a pair of 26- and 29-inch drums, then a 32-inch, then a 23-inch as funds allow)
10. Tam-tam (commonly but erroneously called a gong—24 to 28 inch) with stand
11. Accessory percussion—the collection should include several triangles (6 and 10 inch, possibly also an 8 inch) with clips, 10-inch tambourine, ratchet, cowbell, woodblock, claves, maracas, guiro, sleigh bells, castanets, and trap table storage table

The middle school should supply a large, general bass drum beater as well as two smaller ones for rolls, and thick and medium triangle beaters.

Each student should purchase during the course of the year his own snare sticks, brushes, and tuning key, a pair of hard rubber or plastic mallets for bells and xylophone, a pair of soft and hard timpani mallets, and several pairs of soft rubber and yarn mallets for marimba and suspended cymbals. With careful planning, the director can have different students purchase different types and strengths of mallets thus equipping the section with every type from soft yarn to hard phenolic mallets and the many in between.

Every attempt should be made to invest in professional-quality instruments. The high school should have:

1. Snare drums (one 3, 3¼, 3½ × 13 or 14 inch piccolo, one 5 inch, one 6½ × 14 inch, and one marching band snare with the pitch lowered—as a field drum)
2. Bass drum (one 18 x 36 inch) with a suspended stand that can be tilted, skin heads on both sides require care and should not be used in the marching band pit
3. Two pairs of medium crash cymbals (18 inch medium heavy and 20 or 22 inch medium heavy) with leather straps (lighter weight cymbals used in marching band can also be used for "higher" pitched crash cymbals)
4. Two suspended cymbals (16 inch and 18 inch can be used from the cymbals commonly played in marching bands)
5. One 2½ octave steel bells (with brass mallets or very hard plastic)
6. One full size xylophone (rosewood or kelon)
7. One full size marimba (rosewood or kelon)
8. One 3-octave vibraphone with variable speed motor
9. One set of chimes (with 1½ inch tubes)
10. Tenor drums (tom-toms) (at least four drums between 6 and 16 inch, no more than 2-inch graduation; for example, 8, 10, 12, 14 inch)
11. Timpani—(a set of four: 23, 26, 29, and 32 inch)
12. Tam-tam—30 inch with stand (additional tam-tams may be borrowed as needed)
13. Accessory percussion—all those listed above for the middle school plus additional ones of different sizes and more: temple blocks, bell trees, wind chimes, finger cymbals, sirens, slide whistles, and whip-cracks.[2]

Again, students should supply their own mallets. With the proper motivation, percussionists can take great pride in selecting the proper mallet for each instrument to achieve the desired articulation and dynamic level.

[2] Ibid, 21–26.

SNARE DRUM

Purchase

A good quality drum will have these characteristics: ten tension lugs; a snare release; individual snare-strand tuning; and gut, wire, or nylon snares. The shells may be made of a synthetic material, wood, or metal, with metal producing the most brilliant sound. Ten tension lugs have become standard for most concert snare drums. The snare release is essential to prevent the drum from "buzzing" due to sympathetic vibrations when winds or strings are playing and to enable the snare to be used as a tom-tom. Gut snares are generally more articulate than wire snares, making them important for marching snare drums, but wire snares are fine for concert work. Most student-line snare drums have wire snares.

The size of the drum is determined by the use for which it is intended and the number of accompanying drums. Drum sizes are indicated by the depth of the shell and the diameter of the head. If the drum section is fairly large, a smaller drum will be preferable; the 5 or $5\frac{1}{2} \times 14$ is probably the best choice, as it will give enough but not too much volume and will retain a crisp sound. Larger concert drums like the 8×15 or 8×14 are fairly common but not as appropriate. They are noisy and require careful attention when matching heads. Larger drums are less satisfactory in metal than in wood; while the $5\frac{1}{2} \times 14$ is perfectly acceptable in metal, the 7×15 should be wooden. The field drum used exclusively for marching should be 12×14; some prefer the larger 12×15 size. The type of shell seems to make little difference as long as it is properly made and holds its shape. Drums in different sizes are shown in Figure 21–1.

A heavy stand for all concert drums is a necessity. Stands should be adjustable and have deep, covered guide arms to hold the drum in place. Cases should be purchased for all drums. There should be large wooden storage areas in the rehearsal room in which to put drums so that they do not stand out in the room for experimentation by every hopeful amateur.

Heads and Sticks

Snare drumheads are available in either plastic or calfskin. While professionals prefer a skin head, plastic heads are generally used for school groups. They require less maintenance, are unaffected by weather, and are cheaper. The snare head should be as thin as possible, the batter head of medium thickness. Plastic snare heads are usually made transparent for easy identification, but this is due only to custom and has no effect on the tone or quality of the head. The batter head must be thick in order to wear well.

Figure 21–1. Three sizes of commonly used snare drums, from left to right: 15 × 12 inch field drum, 15 × 5 inch concert drum, 13 × 3 piccolo drum

The head is made with an outer attached ring called a flesh hoop. On virtually all drumheads these are made of metal. The method of attaching the heads to the flesh hoop varies from manufacturer to manufacturer. Percussionists must learn how to tighten the drum head without having the head pull out of the flesh hoop. Heads for snare drums vary from .002 inch to .015 inch; they are found in various plys, coatings, and special reinforcing material. The coating is necessary for brush playing. Heads are held onto the shell by a metal counterhoop through which the tension rods are placed and evenly tightened.

The most common muffler found on snare drums is a felt pad that is raised to touch the head, thus eliminating unwanted ringing and increasing the damping time. The pad should be adjusted to barely touch the batter head and not push up to create a small mountain. A knob is used to raise and lower the muffler; adjustment is made with the snares off in order to hear the ring. Several kinds of batter heads are available with "dots" to help eliminate both the ringing overtones and the muffler.

The stick appears to be the simplest piece of equipment used for making music, but it comes in a variety of sizes, shapes, weights, and materials, and the knowledgeable player needs to understand what these differences will do for her playing. The parts of the stick are tip, neck, shoulder, shaft, and butt (Figure 21–2). Since different weight and shape sticks are appropriate for different musical situations, the drummer should have a variety from which to choose. The entire snare drum section, however, should use the same type of stick unless each drummer is playing a different part.

Generally, the more useful stick is one with a short taper. A short taper places the balance point farther forward, as there is more weight left in the tip end. A long taper facilitates the playing of the long roll up to

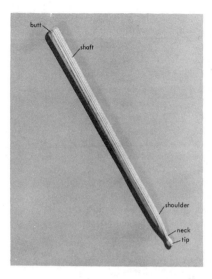

Figure 21–2. Drumstick

about mezzo forte, but does not have the weight at the tip to achieve a good fortissimo. Tips are usually acorn or ball head, with acorn preferred by most experts.

According to Cook, the size of the head is among the most important elements of the stick's effect on the drum. A smaller head results in clearer articulations but a softer sound; a larger head helps in playing loud passages but is more difficult to play clearly.[3]

Sticks were once classified with a letter and a number, the larger number usually indicating a larger stick. Today there are many types of drumsticks and each company uses its own designation for length, taper, headsize, material, and weight.

Too light a snare drumstick should be avoided even though students seem to prefer them. A heavier stick is easier to control and generally has a wider range of usefulness. When buying wooden sticks, the player will find straight-grained hickory to be the best, but she must be sure in selecting them that she chooses a balanced pair. With wood, the factor of weight always has to be considered. Plastic sticks can be chosen with somewhat less care because the manufacturer controls the weight and balance. Plastic sticks are fine for light to average work, and with further improvements can be expected to surpass wood in balance and control (See Figure 21–3).

Brushes

Two faults often occur in using brushes. The first is that the brush is fully extended, making too large a fan and producing a spread, uncontrolled sound. The brush should be pushed out only far enough to leave about ½

[3] Ibid, 25–26.

Figure 21–3.   Snare sticks, from top to bottom: Vic Firth "Echo" (for light, delicate passages), Vic Firth "Bolero" (for soft to medium dynamic levels), Vic Firth "Combos" (for small jazz groups), Tom Gauger (multi-purpose), Vic Firth "5-B" (nylon bead; for medium drum set), Vic Firth "Slammers" (for heavy drum set), Vic Firth "Generals" (all purpose), W.H. Reamer custom made "field drum sticks," Vic Firth "Swizzle Sticks" (multi-purpose stick with felt ball for suspended cymbal, tom-toms, etc.)

inch of the handle showing at the other end of the metal rod; if the handle is pushed all the way in, there will be more brush than desirable for good playing. The second fault is to make an overly large pattern. The player should keep the brush in a fairly small area to achieve the proper flare. Usually the right hand plays the rhythm while the left hand engages in a circular motion.

Position for Holding Sticks

There are generally two types of grips: the traditional and the matched grip. The traditional grip (Figure 21–4) resulted from the angle at which drums were played by military drummers. Although timpanist and keyboard mallet players have always used matched grip, when concert snare stands were invented they were made to hold the snare drum at an angle to facilitate traditional grip. Since 1975, the matched grip (Figure 21–5) has become almost universally accepted.

The first element in playing all percussion instruments is the height of the instrument in relationship to the body. For matched grip, the drum is placed 8 to 10 inches from the body, about waist high. Most stands for

Figure 21–4. Traditional Grip Position for Playing the Snare Drum

snare drum can be adjusted rather low, but not all can be adjusted very high.

For timpani and keyboards, some players must elevate the instrument by using small wooden blocks. Conversely, younger players may need to stand on several boards or a riser to play marimba. The timpanist may need to sit on a stool to lower her upper torso to the drums and to facilitate using the feet for tuning.

Figure 21–5. Matched Hand Position for Playing the Snare Drum

The height of the instrument should be such that the player's fore-arms are parallel to the floor. With the sticks or mallets resting on the instrument, the elbows should be at the players side or slightly forward.[4]

The essential element in holding the sticks is to locate the balance point, that spot which when held around the fulcrum will enable the sticks to rebound freely several times. If the stick stays on the head or rebounds just once or twice, it is held too far back and too much weight is in front of the fulcrum. If the stick strikes the head only once and then remains in the air, it is held too far forward with too much weight behind the fulcrum. The balance point is where the stick bounces the most; that point can be marked with a pen or piece of tape. Most percussionists hold the stick at the balance point.

The stick is held between the thumb and the first curve of the index finger, which wraps around the sticks. The remaining fingers fold around the stick and are used to help control it. There should be little tension in the thumb and index finger. If the percussionist starts using the fingers for control too soon, he may develop tension that will hinder facile and smooth technique.

Rudiments

Teaching the snare drum has been organized into rudiments, which vary in number according to the expert's view. Price gives two basic rudiments, the stroke and the tap. Buggert believes the number to be three: the stroke, tap, and rebound. Berryman gives four: stroke, tap, double stroke, and press. Each of these is made with a different motion. The stroke is made with the full arm, the tap with a motion of the wrist. The rebound can be made with either a stroke or a tap, but successive rebounds depend on the tap. The press is like the stroke except that the stick is held in contact with the drumhead until the momentum stops. The double stroke is like the press except that the stick is lifted after it has hit once and bounced once.

Continual use of the tap tends to create tension and stiffness. Greater accent and intensity in faster passages can be made with the stroke because it has the weight of the arm behind it. The additional rudiments, number-ing either thirteen or twenty-six depending on the classification, are all combinations of these basic rudiments.

Playing

The skillful drummer is careful to equalize the bounces of the sticks to give his playing a smooth, even sound. One of the first things he observes is to keep the striking area small, within a diameter of 3 to 3½ inches. Striking

[4] Ibid, p. 44.

area is important, because the head sounds different when struck in different areas. The center of the head gives a clear, dry sound, the area near the rim sounds more resonant. The generally accepted place to strike is about halfway between rim and center, although rudimental drummers often play in the center for volume. If one compares the wild flailing so common among high school drummers to the controlled sound of a professional, the evenness created by playing in a very small area is immediately apparent. A clean snare drum sound has identical spacing between bounces. Spacing is facilitated when the sticks match each other in size and weight and are held at right angles.

The motion of playing snare drum can be equated with bouncing a rubber ball. Most motion is in the wrist, with the forearm held still and without the wrist rotating. Initial strokes should start with the stick several inches above the batter head, then raised. The stick is used to "stroke" the drum, with the stick rebounding freely. The player should develop the mental image of strokes rather than "hits," of the *tone* following the stick, and of a rich, resonant, full sound.

Among the common faults of snare drummers are the following:

1. Incorrect stick grip—excessive use of fingers and too tight a grip.
2. Incorrect hand position—hand turned out or in too much.
3. Uneven balance in sound between sticks due to uncontrolled height above the drumhead.
4. Wrist bent because the arm is not held at the right angle, resulting in tension and lack of relaxation.
5. Using too much arm rather than wrist, thus producing large movements when small, agile ones are required.
6. Not using a firm blow in the stroke.
7. Not hitting the correct spot on the head for the sound desired.
8. Not matching sounds—one stick hitting in a different spot than the other stick.

Tuning the Snare Drum

Snare drums need to be tuned to approximately the same pitch. Therefore, it is wise to have the same size drums in the section. Most of the tension should be on the batter head for a good lively bounce. If the center of the head can barely be dented with the forefinger, the proper tension has been achieved. Too much tension will make the drum sound above the entire band or orchestra; too little tension will result in loss of clarity. The snare head should be tuned higher than the batter head. Though it sounds higher, pressure from the finger will usually indicate that it is actually looser (remember it is much thinner).

Care and Maintenance

About twice a year, the snare drum should be taken apart to be oiled and cleaned. All the movable parts should be oiled with a light, all-purpose oil such as 3-in-1. About one drop for each rod thread is enough. Any dirt between the flesh hoop and the counterhoops should be removed. Marks on the head may be erased with an art gum eraser. All loose screws and nuts should be tightened.

After use, the snare drumhead should be left at the same degree of tension, neither loosened nor tightened, and the snares should be left "on" when the drum is stored. If the drum is not in use and buzzes when other instruments are played, a coffee filter can be inserted between the snares and snare head when the drum is stored.

BASS DRUM

After the snare drum, the bass drum (Figure 21–6) may be the most frequently used percussion instrument. A stand to suspend the drum prevents extraneous vibrations and enables the drummer to adjust the angle of the instrument to direct the sound. Drums do direct their sound, with the bass drum perhaps the most crucial. A padded cradle type stand is adequate but not preferred.

The player stands somewhat to the right of the drum, not directly behind it, with the head directed to where most of the sound is to be projected, seldom toward the audience. The beater should be held with the

Figure 21–6. Bass Drum

right hand using the same basic grip as for the snare drum. The arm should be flexible and the wrist relaxed. The blow used most of the time should be an upward stroke slightly outside the center of the head, a compromise between a glancing and a direct blow. The slightly glancing blow will be used most frequently. The extreme glancing blow, the perpendicular, hammerlike stroke, and the arc-like stroke are used for special effects. The sharp, perpendicular blow to the middle of the head produces a staccato sound and the maximum tone; the straight approach is useful in slower tempos to pull out the tone. The slightly glancing blow is used for fast tempos and on the march.

Special effects can be made on the bass drum, not only by different strokes but by various kinds of beaters, muffling effects, and by striking it in different places on the head. These effects should all be part of the drummer's repertoire. They will all be useless, however, if the drummer cannot play on the beat. A good bass drummer must be able to slightly anticipate the beat. The bass drum is sluggish in response, and if the player actually plays with the conductor's beat, he will always be a fraction behind, sending the conductor rapidly toward a nervous breakdown.

At least four different beaters should be available: lamb's wool, hard felt, a large timpani stick, and a wooden beater. Some professionals like a short, double-end lamb's wool beater. There is nothing wrong with this if the player is sufficiently proficient to control it. But what is good enough for the professional is often too good for the amateur, and the player must use what he can master well. Often with school-age drummers, the double-headed mallet is too difficult to balance. It is preferable to play well with a less sophisticated beater than to be handicapped by a fancy gadget.

Most playing is done in the area about one third to one half of the distance to the center. Other areas of the head are used only for special effects. Rhythmically active figures should be played closer to the center of the head, where there is less ring to muddy the articulations. Conversely, long tones are struck near the rim. The bass drum is played for dynamic as well as rhythmic effects; it will be struck harder and lighter and in different spots on the head.

Many players strike too close to the rim, obtaining a high, thin sound. Striking too close to the center also produces an unattractive sound—dull, monotonous, and without resonance. On a 36-inch drum, for example, playing 6 inches from the center produces a sound that is resonant, moderate in length, and easily varied in volume; 12 inches from the center gives a thin tone that lasts longer and cannot be articulated successfully. The player should work with the drum to learn what type of sound he will get in what area, then play intelligently and musically rather than booming away in happy ignorance. Rhythmic passages and marches will usually require a different spot on the drum than overtures or symphonic transcriptions. Contemporary music for band calls for considerable experimentation and dexterity and cannot be played thoughtlessly or in routine fashion. The bass drummer must be a musician just like any other member of the organization.

Muffling can be accomplished by use of the left hand (Figure 21–7), the right hand, the right knee, or a manufactured muffler for internal or external muffling. The right knee used against the batter head (Figure 21–6) and the left hand touching the left head are effectively used for applying pressure to raise or lower the pitch. In using the hands for muffling, the fleshy part of the fingers is placed on the drum, not the entire finger or the palm. Some of the more commonly used effects are achieved as follows:

1. Accents are played closer to the center.
2. Pianissimo passages are played with harder, heavier sticks to achieve clarity and avoid muddiness.
3. A sharp staccato, a crack, or shot are produced by using a hard beater or a timpani stick and striking in dead center of the head.
4. A thud can also be made by striking the center, but with a soft mallet.
5. A roar is produced by striking very hard with a woolen beater near the rim.
6. The thump sound is made by striking softly with a hard stick in the middle of the drum, then muffling immediately.
7. The roll is best accomplished on a bass drum by using two sticks. The double-headed beater is not good for a roll, as it is designed to produce two different sounds. A more resonant roll can be made by using bass drumsticks rather than timpani sticks.

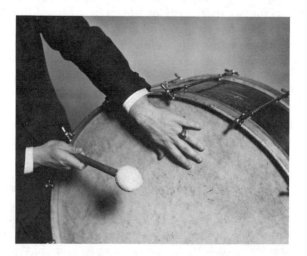

Figure 21–7. Left Hand Muffle Position for the Bass Drum

There should never be more than one bass drum in a concert band or orchestra—if the drum does not furnish adequate sound, a bigger drum may be used, but not an additional one. It should not be necessary to continually use the knee for muffling. If a player feels it necessary to keep his knee on the drum because the drum has too much ring to it, the drum should be replaced or a pad secured for it.

Care and Maintenance

The bass drum is played with a relatively loose head, the batter head being somewhat tighter than the muffler head. When the heads are equally tight, an excessive roar and rumble occurs, interfering with the real drum sound. A medium tension for the muffler head and slightly more for the batter head will create the desired sound. Because the head is relatively loose in playing, it should be tightened about two steps or a third higher after playing in order to keep the collar on the head. Plastic heads are common, but calfskin heads are best and should be used on the playing head. When the drum has a calfskin head and is to be left without playing for two or three days, tightening is essential; the only exception to this is when the equipment is old and the room subject to changes of humidity and temperature. In this case, the hoops may warp unless the head is loosened. Warped hoops should be replaced as soon as possible.

Cleaning should be done twice a year, the rods oiled once every year. The nuts and screws on the tension rods work loose and fall into the inside of the drum; they should be tightened frequently enough to prevent this. Some players are greatly tempted to stuff things into the airholes of the drum, a capital offense in many ensembles.

Purchase

The width of the shell rather than the diameter of the head is the determining factor in volume. Shell width can vary from a minimum of 12 inches to 18 or 20 inches. A 16-inch drum is useful for junior high bands; an 18-inch width is necessary to produce adequate volume for high school organizations—18 $\times$ 34 to 38 is best. A drum that is too small will have a tenor quality and be unable to produce the boom desirable in a bass drum. Within the limits of 14 to 18 $\times$ 30 to 38 inches, any good quality drum will be satisfactory depending on what the school can afford.

Overall, it is best to remember that the lower the sound the better. Furthermore, with the help of mallets, a larger bass drum can be played with a good, soft tone quality more easily than a small bass drum can be played loudly with good tone.

TIMPANI

The timpani are considered by many to be the chief or most exalted member of the percussion family. Nonetheless, it is the one instrument that almost no percussionist ever purchases or has at home to practice. It is also the only percussion instrument that requires students to tune as they play.

There are two accepted ways of holding the timpani sticks, each with advantages and disadvantages. One way is vertical to the drumhead, the thumb on top of the stick and the four fingers cupped directly underneath, often called the *French grip*. This grip produces rotation action. The second way is labeled the *German grip*. The thumb is on the side of the stick, the palm down, the hand, wrist, and forearm making a straight line. This matched grip results in what is called *hinge action* similar to that used with the snare drum or mallet instruments. The advantage of the first position is that it gives the beginning student a better timpani sound; he is able to more easily get the idea of a sharp perpendicular attack and a fast getaway, both necessary to timpani playing. The disadvantage is that the vertical palm feels somewhat unnatural and wrist tension easily develops. Tension militates against a good roll, which depends on a loose, relaxed wrist. The second, hingelike approach has the advantage of being natural and encourages flexibility in the beginner. However, the student playing with this position invariably uses a glancing blow or a modification of it rather than the straight, perpendicular blow correct for timpani. In both positions, the stick is held closer to the end of the shaft than to the center, usually about an inch below the balance point. The stick is held with the thumb and first finger, the middle and ring fingers are used for control. The little finger is never used. Examples of hand position for playing the timpani are shown in Figures 21–8 through 21–11.

Figure 21–8. Hand Position for Playing Timpani

Figure 21–9. Hand Position for Playing Timpani (French grip)

The player stands relatively close to the instruments, which are positioned approximately 8 inches below the waist, so he can comfortably strike about 3 to 6 inches in on the head. The timpani must sit close together but not touching, the largest drum to the left, smallest to the right. The height of the timpani is about 33 inches from the floor.

Heads and Mallets

Striking in different areas of the head will produce different sounds. The most generally accepted area is about 4 to 6 inches from the rim. Soft

Figure 21–10. Playing the Timpani (German grip)

Figure 21–11.   Cross-Hand Position for Playing the Timpani

passages are played closer to the rim, but even extremely loud passages are not struck closer to the center than the normal playing area. Beyond the 6-inch limit, the tone tends to lose its quality and becomes a tubby, unmusical sound. Most timpani come with plastic heads and they are, as for the other drums, entirely satisfactory, being durable and untemperamental, as well as economical. The normal range of the timpani is a fifth, although an occasional extra note beyond this is possible.

The timpanist constantly changes the pitches of her instruments, hence she must be a sensitive musician with an acute ear. Tuning the timpani is more difficult than most other instruments due to their extremely low pitches. Furthermore, the timpani must often be tuned during a piece so the ear must be both keen and practiced. The beginning timpanist should start training her ear immediately. Scales, arpeggios, and simple tunes should be learned and memorized to help her find pitches and intervals (e.g., "Taps" begins with a perfect fourth).

Mallets come in an assortment of sizes and materials, each with a specific purpose. Because the instrument relies largely for its expressive character on the type of mallet used to strike it, its musical effect is lost when mallets are used inappropriately. Mallet heads vary in size from ½ to 3 inches and in consistency from soft to very hard. Mallet handles are of wood, bamboo, metal, or some type of rattan, and should be at least 12 inches long in order to have resiliency. Longer ones are satisfactory if the player can handle them. In order to elicit a good tone from the head, the center of the stick head is of some noncompressible material, regardless of the exterior. Harder mallets are needed for higher passages. The heavier stick is used not only for higher pitches but also to produce a more sustained, resonant legato. Most players use sticks that are too large, too fluffy, and too fat, where a firmer, smaller stick head would produce better results. New sticks should be saved for loud work, as playing wears them down quickly and gets them in shape for softer playing. It is surprising how frequently a student timpanist will play an entire number or even an entire concert with the same pair of mallets. When this happens, it clearly indicates that the player has not learned the essentials of her art (See Figure 21–12).

Playing Techniques

The timpani are attacked with a short, sudden, perpendicular stroke. The stick should bounce off the instant it touches the surface of the head. Both forearm and wrist are used in making the stroke. Once struck, the sound will ring for a long time unless cut off, so each note must be stopped as well as started. The tone is stopped by placing the fleshy area of the fingertips on the head. If all the fingers are placed on the head at once, an unattractive and unmusical slap is created at the end of the tone. Avoid this sound by starting with the little finger and dropping the fingers on the head with a rapid rolling motion, getting the fingers on the head nearly together, enough to avoid the slap.

Single-sticking is used for equal notes of slow or moderate value; hand-to-hand sticking is used for more rapid notes. Single strokes appear to be simple enough, but the appearance is deceptive. When speed is desired, more control must be exercised to ensure that (1) the left hand is used exactly like the right and (2) that the strokes for both hands are of the

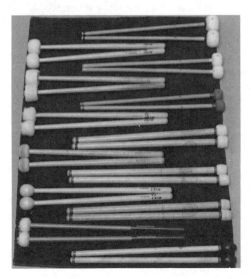

Figure 21–12. **Commonly used timpani mallets (top to bottom): Andrew Feldman (soft; purple trim), Vic Firth "Custom General," Feldman (medium hard; green trim), Firth "Cartwheel" (general purpose— especially appropriate for Classical music), Feldman (extra-hard; red trim), Firth "Generals" (general purpose), Fred Hinger (soft; yellow trim), Firth "Ultra-Staccato," Hinger (medium hard; green trim), Firth "Woodball", Hinger (hard; red trim), American Drum medium, Hinger woodballs (red trim).**

same weight and height. The left hand is naturally weaker with right-handed people and needs special attention to keep the beat at the same strength as that of the right hand. Daily practice in hand-to-hand single-stroking is obligatory. Rolls are usually played faster on the higher-pitched drums and slower on the lower drums. Most rolls, either fast or slow, should be held over to the beat following the last written note; the exception to this is the short eighth note roll, which should be played exactly as written. Advanced students may play fast rolls without the wrists, using only arm and fingers, the ring fingers and the middle fingers controlling the motion. This technique is successful only when a relatively large amount of force is exerted by the arm; it is therefore useful only with passages of at least mezzoforte volume. A delicate roll produced only with the fingers is used for extremely soft symphonic passages. This specialized technique is needed infrequently.

Variations in volume result from variations in the height of the stroke, the distance the stick falls, and the speed of its descent. Arm action is combined with wrist action to achieve a rapid drop to the stick and an immediate release or withdrawal. By exerting different pressures with the thumb and first finger, different intensities and tone qualities can be created. For instance, a crisp staccato needs a tighter grasp by thumb and forefinger than does a legato. A more intense tone will also need more finger pressure than a relaxed, peaceful tone quality. A different type of blow from the perpendicular will occasionally be needed. An extreme legato can be produced by a glancing blow. Timpani sticking, like snare drum sticking, is partly learned by hearing what fine professionals do. Hard-and-fast rules are not as useful as listening for what sounds right. A few common sense practices illustrate this point. Although alternate sticks are usually used, there are passages for which more musical sense would be achieved by using the same stick. Crossing of sticks is done to reduce movement and thus gain greater control; therefore, the crossing stick should pass over the stationary stick if efficiency is to be gained. The lasting ring of a note that has been struck should be allowed to fade out naturally whenever possible, because it makes a more musical effect than stopping the tone with the fingers. But even when long notes are written in the music, it is frequently better to stop them earlier than their notation indicates lest they create unintentional dissonances with other parts. Composers are not always careful about timpani writing; the player must use her ear to determine a note's proper length to fit with the rest of the music. In forte–piano rolls, the player should wait briefly after the forte note is struck before beginning the piano roll so that the forte will have time to fade. Because the area closer to the rim is better for soft playing, crescendo passages should begin in that area and move out to the usual playing spot. For diminuendo passages, the reverse should take place; sticking starts at the usual spot and moves in toward the rim as the sound diminishes. For forceful playing, the thumb on top of the stick produces good effects. All other variations of position from horizontal to vertical can be used after the basic techniques are understood and learned, but the important thing is to pull the tone *out* of the drum, not pound it *in*.

Placing a handkerchief or chamois on the head at the spot directly opposite the beating area mutes the instrument. *Coperto* means to put this cloth or felt on the head to produce a distant sound; *S Coperto* means to remove it. Muffling is accomplished by the last three fingers of the hand placed lightly but firmly against the head.

Care and Maintenance

Plastic heads are durable and require little maintenance. Their disadvantage has been a weak fundamental and excessive ring. More care is required if one is fortunate to obtain quality calf- or goatskin heads. The best preventive measure is to tune the drums before putting them away at the end of rehearsal or practice, thus leaving them with sufficient tension to maintain the collar and springiness of the head. Timpani should be tuned at least half way in their playing register, or a little tighter. For the 25- and 28-inch timpani, this means leaving them at the pitches A and D, respectively, or even B-flat and E-flat if conditions are somewhat dry. The range of the 28-inch drum is F to C; B-flat to F for the 25-inch drum (Figure 21–13).

Calfskin timpani heads will generally last several years before needing to be replaced. Plastic should be replaced every one to three years; excessive scratches will affect tone quality. While changing pitches on timpani tends to stretch the heads, it is abuse that usually necessitates their replacement. The public school rehearsal rooms seem to offer opportunities for the timpani heads to become scratched, torn, or dented.

Covers should be available for the timpani heads and should be used each time the drums are put away. The heads should occasionally be wiped with a damp cloth to get rid of accumulated grease from fingers and dust from the air. Nothing should be placed on the timpani head, certainly no books, instrument cases, and sharp objects. Plastic heads are satisfactory and durable but still deserve care. Students are prone to lay the sticks down on the heads, which really doesn't hurt the heads but does violate the rule.

28-inch   25-inch

Figure 21–13. Ranges of Timpani

Other elements of care include getting rid of an occasional "creak" or "crackle" that occurs with the use of the pedal. This sound indicates that the bowl of the kettle needs cleaning: the head should be removed, the rounded underside cleaned with a fine emery cloth, and the edge that touches the rim of the kettle rubbed with paraffin wax, petroleum jelly, or talcum powder. The head is then replaced.

Dents in the bowl may be straightened with a rawhide or rubber hammer. The procedure is to tap gently, holding a piece of wood as a bevel against the outer side of the bowl. Dents most frequently come from careless pushing of the drums. Students should be taught to drag the drum behind them rather than push it ahead of them. This helps ensure its remaining upright.

Tuning

Tuning is done either by means of tension handles around the head of the drum or by a foot pedal. If the foot pedal is used, some timpanists feel the player should sit to play rather than stand so that she can have her feet free for tuning purposes. When additional drums are used, they are the 30-inch and the 23-inch. The 23-inch has E-flat as its lowest note, the 30-inch, D. Each drum has a normal compass of a perfect fifth.

The composer usually indicates at the beginning of the work what notes will be required of the timpani. A change of tuning is indicated in the music by *change* or *muta*. In using either hand tension or pedal tension, the basic notes are always tuned by hand, turning two opposite handles the same number of times at the same time in order to keep the opposing tension equal and the head centered. When there is a moderate and even pressure on the drum from the tension screws, the head is settled by gently pressing down with the palm of the hand in the center of the head. The pitch is tested by tapping lightly with the finger or drumstick in the playing spot, then checked around the head near each lug at the approximate playing distance from the rim (4 to 6 inches). Any further adjustments in tuning are then made by using the pedal or the tension handles. The head is settled once more before playing.

When pedal timpani are used, the drum is tuned not to the first note of the piece but to the lowest note of its range. This is done by pushing the heel of the pedal all the way down to the off position to release all pedal tension, then tuning to the desired pitch by hand, using the tension screws. The pitch may then be raised to any higher note in the drum's range by pressing the toe of the pedal.

TENOR DRUM AND TOM-TOMS

The term *tenor drum* is a carry-over from early marching band days. The instrument is actually quite old and is referred to as tamburo, cassarullante, caisse roulante, tambourin roulant, or ruhrtrommel, all indicating a field drum of approximately 12 × 15 to 18 inches with snares off, and tuned considerably lower than modern-day marching snare drums.

In modern marching bands, the tenor drum has been replaced with "triples," "quads," "quints," and so on, seemingly all the drums that one's spine can carry. These multiple drums were adapted from tom-toms used in concert work; they provide marching percussionists with a wide range of pitches.

Tom-toms differ from tenor drums in that they have only one head. Most band and orchestral pieces that call for tom-toms require four different sizes; many percussion ensemble works call for six to eight.

CYMBALS

Cymbals are rarely given the treatment that their importance to an organization warrants. Directors look on them as noisemakers that anyone can bang together,—no care is given to their purchase or their playing, so the cymbal sound degenerates. The cymbal has a contribution to make to the sound of the band and orchestra; if this were not so it would have met its demise 2000 years ago. There are techniques of playing and levels of quality in the physical characteristics that can make it either an asset or a detriment.

Selection of good cymbals is important. Nothing can destroy a fine-sounding musical piece faster than to have in a climactic moment the clanging together of two pie plates from the kindergarten rhythm band. A poor cymbal is hardly better than a pie plate.

Most companies make acceptable or even good cymbals, but the name Avedis Zildjian stands for top quality in this area. Most of our references are to the Zildjian product; its characteristics are a measure for other brands. Quality of cymbals is judged by the quality of tone produced, the rapidity with which the cymbal reaches full vibration, and by the lack of a single predominant pitch. The best cymbals do not produce one dominant pitch. They produce overtones of such size that they create the desired ringing crash rather than a specific pitch. Nevertheless, a certain amount of pitch in each cymbal is necessary for the sound to be musically pleasing. Pairs are made so that the pitch produced by one is a second or a third from the other.

Cymbals come in various sizes, weights, thicknesses, and pitches. They also come in a choice of materials, beaten brass or coiled wire. Beaten brass has the better tone and is more widely used in good organizations.

Size does not determine the pitch. Small cymbals can be lower in pitch than large ones. Size does determine the proportion of noise produced from striking the two instruments together. There is bound to be some noise in striking, but the larger the cymbal, the less noise and more tone produced. For this reason, directors have tended to purchase larger and larger instruments, to the extent that they become unmanageable in the hands of student players. A variety of sizes will offer flexibility of sound and avoid limiting the organization to the gonglike quality of the oversized cymbal.

Seven weights of cymbals are available, ranging from paper-thin to extra-heavy. Medium and medium-heavy cymbals are the most popular. Too light a cymbal may sound better at close range, but it lacks the overtones and carrying power of the thicker instrument. It should therefore be listened to from a distance before any decision is made concerning its acquisition. Contrary to what one might expect, thin cymbals are lower in pitch than thick ones. A danger with lighter and thinner cymbals is that a fortissimo crash will turn them inside out because they lack the weight to resist the blow; this is a fairly common occurrence and the cymbals can be popped back into position easily, but once they have been turned wrong side out they will tend to do it again each time a heavy blow is struck. It is therefore poor economy to buy a thin cymbal in the larger size unless its only use is to produce a gonglike tone. The best instrument for the longest life and for the widest range of effects should be selected. A heavier cymbal of reasonably good quality is the best choice. The thinner and smaller the cymbal, the faster it will speak, this property being determined by the total amount of metal in the instrument.

What should be bought? If the school can afford it, three pairs of matched cymbals should be part of the basic equipment of the band and orchestra, one pair of 14 to 16-inch, one pair of medium-heavy 17 to 19-inch (probably 18), and one pair of extra-large, medium-thin 20 to 22-inch cymbals. Besides these three pairs, two or three suspended cymbals are required, at the minimum a small 13 to 14-inch size and the larger 17 to 18-inch size.

For the drum set and for special effects that fall into the category of traps, any number of other cymbals may become a part of the group's equipment, depending on the budget and the interest. Hi-hat, crash, be-bop, ride, and sizzle cymbals are some of the more common ones.

Wooden handles continue to be used year after year in spite of widespread condemnation by authorities. Wooden handles detract both from the quality of the sound and from the life of the cymbal. They deaden the tone, eliminating almost all of the overtones and leaving only an uninteresting, plain sound rather than the rich welter of conflicting partials that the good cymbal offers. In addition, they tend to crack the cymbal in the area near the bolt attachment. Good cymbals should be equipped with leather straps.

Playing

The cymbals are held by gripping the strap with the thumb on top and the other fingers underneath, most of the pressure being exerted by the thumb and forefinger. This position gives the most opportunity for fingertips, knuckles, and wrists to be used for control. It is tiring when the cymbals must be held for a long period without relaxing the grip, so for marching the hand can be inserted into the strap. The fingertips and knuckles should be utilized for control, thus a small felt pad is preferable to the large lamb's-wool pad in common use on cymbals today. The lambs wool pad makes it impossible to bring the hand in contact with the reverberating metal to help control it. It also muffles the tone by interfering with the full range of overtones.

The left cymbal is held almost stationary. The right cymbal is moved against it. This is the standard approach for right-handed players; left-handed players may wish to reverse it. A straight blow is unsatisfactory; rather than producing a ringing crash, it traps the air inside the two cymbals as they come together and results in a muffled "pop." A glancing blow is more effective, but this also can be carried to extremes because the sound will be too delicate and fragile if the blow is too glancing. The best sound is produced when the cymbals are held fairly close together with the right cymbal a little below the left (Figure 21–14), and struck by moving the right cymbal up in a modified glancing blow which begins hitting the left cymbal at a point about three inches from the top as the left cymbal starts down (Figure 21–15).

The right cymbal begins to move first and makes a more vigorous movement; the left cymbal moves down to meet it. After a crash, the cymbals are opened and turned toward the audience so that the sound moves directly to them as shown in Figure 21–16. A good crash cannot be made if the cymbals are too far apart at the start. A long running start is unnecessary to produce a huge sound; a vigorous push and a short stroke will suffice. When several crashes in a row are demanded, the left hand remains perfectly still. When successive blows are called for at a moderate or slow speed, the right hand will start the first one and then the hands

Figure 21–14. Position for Playing the Cymbals

Figure 21–15.   Normal Follow-through for Cymbal Crash

alternate for each blow after that, the hand that has moved down in the preceding blow being in position to start up for the next one.

Whenever possible, the cymbal tone should be allowed to ring until it dies of its own accord. When the music calls for short sounds from the cymbal, it must be stopped before the ring is over. Stopping the sound is done by placing the cymbal edge against the chest or upper torso at the precise moment the tone is to cease.

For soft crashes, only the edges of the cymbals are used. The soft crash is difficult to perform with any control or cleanliness to the sound;

Figure 21–16.   Position for Ring after Cymbal Crash

striking the inside facing of the left cymbal with the right as in loud crashes is necessary, but when the force behind it is decreased to make the sound a soft one, it loses some of its overtones and is thinner in quality. The two-plate roll, also called the double-cymbal roll, is made by placing the cymbals together about an inch or two off center so that air will not be trapped between them. A fast clapping motion is then made with both hands and arms, resulting in a loud, harsh sound. The swish, also called angels' wings, is achieved by rubbing the edge of one cymbal lightly across the inside face of the other. A similar effect is produced by rubbing only the edges of the cymbals together.

The suspended cymbal (Figure 21–17) can be struck in many different places and with nearly every object imaginable to obtain a variety of effects. It may be struck directly or with a glancing blow on the edge, middle, two edges at once, and so on, with wood sticks, nails, knife blades, saw blades, coins, and soft mallets. Regardless of the effect desired, the cymbal, like the gong, is slightly set in motion with the fingers before striking. A glancing blow is better for the instrument than a direct one, since the direct blow tends to warp the edge. When regular sticks are used, it is recommended that the blow be struck down and out with the thick part of the stick or a felt-tipped mallet. The roll is produced by striking with small, rapid, alternate blows on either side of the cymbal, equidistant from the center so that a balance can be maintained with the suspended disc. Fairly hard timpani sticks are most successful. Loud crashes are made by striking the edge a glancing blow with a stick. Nonmetallic sizzling sounds are produced by placing a snare drumstick under the cymbal and striking the top of the cymbal with another stick; metallic sizzling is made by placing

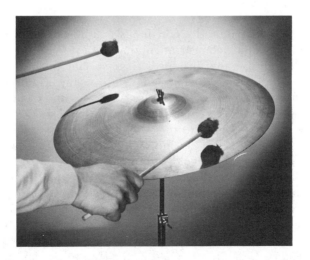

Figure 21–17. Position for Playing the Suspended Cymbal

metal filings or keys on top of the cymbal and striking with a padded stick. Debussy, for example, wanted a metal coin scraped on the surface for a specific effect in "Fêtes." The only limiting factor to the cymbal's use seems to be the imagination of the player and teacher.

The player will not be able to tell at first reading how long to let the cymbals ring and when to stop them. After the number has been played a couple of times, she will know what follows the cymbal crash and how long a ring is appropriate.

A suspended or mounted cymbal of any type should not be screwed too tightly to its holder. It must be left free enough to vibrate well and to avoid the danger of cracking around the center hole.

Care of the Cymbals

Cymbals must not be left in excessive heat or in the direct rays of the summer sun. They are tempered with heat, and when they become extremely hot for any length of time dead spots will result. The edges are relatively fragile and can be chipped—being dropped on the floor or knocked together does not help them.

Dirt and sediment dampen some of the overtones, so cleaning will help retain the brilliance of tone. Cymbals should never be buffed with a buffing wheel. The heat caused by the friction will destroy the temper of the instrument and dead spots will result. Cymbal polish can be purchased if a high sheen is desired.

TAM-TAM

The term *gong* has been used synonymously with *tam-tam* for generations. In truth, a gong is a pitched instrument that has a very pronounced tone. A tam-tam is a large disc that produces a nonspecific pitch.

The spot for striking the tam-tam will probably be a little off-center, but the best approach is to test the entire surface to find the area that gives the best sound. Tam-tams are hammered out by hand and will therefore be thicker in some spots than in others. Before being struck, the tam-tam should be set in motion by touching it inaudibly several times with the hand. Otherwise, the tone is cold with little staying power. For best resonance, the tam-tam should be hung with a gut double-bass string; if possible, it should be positioned at the height where either the knee or the free hand can be used to dampen the sound after the tam-tam is struck—this will usually be about 3 feet off the floor. Like the cymbal, the tam-tam can produce different effects by being struck in different spots with a variety of beaters. It is often scraped with a coin to produce a mysterious effect.

Since the tam-tam has a delayed response, there has been great disagreement as to its use. Cook indicates that the tam-tam should be played before the sound is desired in order to have the instrument sound at the proper time; McBeth indicates that modern composers are aware of the delay and that this is the sound they want, that is, the instrument played as notated with the sound 250 and 600 milliseconds delayed.[5]

MALLET INSTRUMENTS

The major keyboard percussion instruments are similar in their playing techniques and are discussed together. They are the xylophone, marimba, and vibraphone, all of which exist in a variety of ranges. On the xylophone the sound is produced by the vibration of hard wooden blocks of different pitches. Many xylophones have resonators; on those that do not, the volume is limited to what can be obtained from the blocks themselves. A marimba is a keyboard of softer wooden blocks which always has resonators to enlarge the sound and offer a wider dynamic range. The vibraphone, or vibraharp, is a metal keyboard with resonators that produce a vibrato. Revolving fans, electrically powered, open and shut the resonators and create the pulsation or vibration. Recommended is a variable-speed motor that allows the player to select the speed of the vibrato.

All three instruments are played with the same position and use of mallets. The player should stand near the center of the instrument, a few inches from the edge of the bars. The height should be about 6 inches below the player's waist. The mallets are held similarly to timpani sticks: between the thumb and the curved joint of the first finger with the thumb on the side of the stick, the fingers well turned under and almost touching the palms, as shown in Figure 21–18. The hands are level, palms down, with as much relaxation as possible, but a firm pressure from the thumb on the mallet handle for control. Single mallets are fairly short, for rapid playing. For three- or four-mallet playing (Figure 21–19), the handles need to be longer, but even here very little stick protrudes beyond the back of the hand. The shoulders are never moved, and the elbows rarely. The hands are held low over the keyboard; wrist action is used to make the stroke. The sticks should be at about a 45-degree angle to each other and should generally strike the center of the bars for the best sound. Striking where the string passes through the bar will result in a dead sound, but rapid playing will necessitate varying the striking area. When many accidentals are used, the front row is struck farther back to keep the mallet head close to the back row of bars for economy of movement. The back bars are struck on the letter name about ½ inch from the tip.

[5]Cook, op. cit., 74 and Francis W. McBeth, *Effective Performance of Band Music.* (San Antonio, TX: Southern Music Co., 1972). 291–93.

**Figure 21–18. Two-Mallet Position for Playing a Mallet
Instrument**

The playing technique for these keyboard instruments is identical
with that for the timpani. Technique is developed by practicing single
strokes, three or four strokes to each note for wrist flexibility; scales on the
front row of bars and both rows; and interval practice to develop accuracy.

Xylophones and marimbas come in a variety of sizes, and the vibraphone in two models. The xylophone can be obtained in ranges from
2½ to 4 octaves. The standard is 3½, extending from a sounding pitch of F

**Figure 21–19. Four-Mallet Position for Playing a Mallet
Instrument**

above middle C to C. Marimbas are designed with a 2½-octave range for beginners, a 3-octave range, a 3½-octave range, and the most common, a 4-octave range, from bass clef C to C. The large, orchestral size has 4¼ octaves, from A (bottom space, bass clef) to C. Bass marimbas exist but are not common. Vibraphones are either 2½ or the more standard 3 octaves, F below middle C to F above the treble clef.

The bars for both xylophone and marimba are made from Honduran rosewood. The xylophone is made from the hard core of the log, the marimba from the softer outer part. Sometimes pine or boxwood is used, but these do not match the quality of rosewood. The width of the bar has no effect on the pitch. Length and thickness alter frequency, and both are used in matching the bars of marimba and xylophone. The size of the resonators on the marimba is less important than whether the resonator is in tune with its bar.

Mallets

Because of the difference in the wood, harder beaters may be used on the xylophone than on the marimba, where a hard mallet will detract from the tone quality and do permanent damage to the fragile wood. For xylophones, three or four pairs of mallets are the minimum equipment. These should include one pair of hard ebonite white plastic or wood, one of vulcanized rubber, one of medium rubber, and one of soft rubber. The handles should be about 9 inches for regular playing and 12 inches for four-mallet work. (see Fig. 21–20.) Fiberglass handles are excellent, being

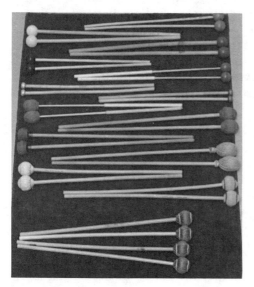

Figure 21–20. Commonly used keyboard mallets (top to bottom): Malletech plastic xylophone (blue, rattan, hard), Musser plastic xylophone (white, rattan, med.), Hinger rubber xylophone (dark green, rattan, extra hard), Firth plastic bell (black, rattan, hard), Musser rubber gen. purpose (red, two-step, med.), Balter brass bell, Balter aluminum crotale, Musser yarn gen. purpose (blue, two-step, med.) Musser yarn gen. purpose (red, birch, hard), Firth plastic gen. purpose (black, birch, hard), Malletech yarn marimba (khaki, birch, med.), Balter chord vibe (yellow, rattan, hard), Balter chord vibe (silver, rattan, hard), Balter chord vibe-marimba (green, rattan, med. hard).

durable and nonwarping, and rattan is acceptable. Some xylophones are barred with aluminum or steel; the latter can take much harder mallets than the former—brass-headed mallets are quite effective on steel bars but will dent aluminum.

More mallets are needed for the marimba, but the best tone is produced with medium and hard felt mallets, or medium and soft rubber. Three-quarter hard rubber and various weights of yarn-wound mallets should be available. Hard rubber and plastic mallets are not used.

Music for the keyboard instruments is not always within the instrument's playing range, because composers are occasionally unfamiliar with the exact compass of the keyboards. The music is often incorrectly written and must be played up or down an octave. The percussionist must experiment to determine what sounds the best.

The mounting cords on the keyboard instruments wear thin and break after much use, so they should be checked periodically. Bars should be inspected for cracks, checked for intonation, and, if desired, polished with appropriate polish.

Bell-lyra

The bell-lyra is a set of chromatic bells built in a lyre-shaped frame. It has a 2-octave range; the low note is second-space treble clef A. In concert the bell-lyra may be placed in a specially designed floor rack, which can be used vertically or tilted down to a horizontal position. It may also be set on a heavy table, in which case it is played like the other keyboard instruments. In marching, the bell-lyra is traditionally carried by means of a heavy leather strap that has a cup at the bottom into which the bottom of the lyre is placed. The left hand grips the rod at the bottom to help support the instrument and the free hand does the playing. Hard celluloid white plastic or nylon hammers are generally used.

Most bell-lyras are tuned to 440 or 442 at the bottom, but to 444 at the top. Because players of wind and string instruments tend to go sharp in the higher registers, the bell-lyra is tuned to account for this tendency.

Orchestra Bells

Orchestra bells are expensive, and most directors substitute the bell-lyra. The difference in sound is appreciable and the substitution should not be made unless absolutely necessary. The reason orchestra bells are so expensive is that they are hand-hammered. In securing secondhand bells, one should check for chips in the plating of the bars. The only maintenance required is occasional adjustment of the cord that holds the bars in place and checking for proper padding under the bars. Thus, a set will last a lifetime. Orchestra bells usually have a range of 2½ octaves, sounding G above the treble staff to C.

Chimes

Chimes are a set of long, tubular bells, covering a chromatic range of about 1½ octaves from middle C to F. They are suspended by a gut string and struck at the very top of the tube by a rawhide mallet. The most common mallet weighs about 6 ounces. It is usually too hard, and may be softened by making cross cuts on the striking end or by covering the end with chamois or other soft leather. Playing technique involves striking a chime with the mallet and simultaneously dampening the previously struck chime with the free hand. Some chimes have a damper pedal, which is used with chord changes. The hand is used for dampening the notes in normal melodic playing.

Tuning the chimes is difficult because the prominent tone is not the fundamental but the fourth overtone. The instrument is heard most accurately at a distance of about 75 feet; when one is closer than this, other partials are strong enough to interfere with hearing the sounding pitch. The player should not expect the octaves to sound perfectly in tune. The upper chime sounds the fourth overtone of its fundamental, and the lower octave sounds the fifth overtone (sixth partial). This irregular overtone series sounds too far out of tune to permit effective use with harmony unless heard from a great distance, where the overtones are less discordant.

If the chimes seem to actually be more out of tune than is proper, they may be sent to the factory for some alterations. Any other attempt at altering them will result in damage.

TAMBOURINE

The tambourine is an interesting instrument, capable of being played in a half dozen ways for as many different sounds. The 10-inch and 8-inch sizes are the most common, with both larger and smaller sizes available. Tambourines are presently made of metal, plastic, and wood and can be found with and without heads. A true tambourine has a skin head and is made of wood (metal is heavy and produces a different sound, and plastic is not very durable).

Little upkeep is necessary, but the pins that hold the jingles should be examined occasionally, as they work loose with much playing. If the head becomes slack, it can be moistened with a wet cloth and allowed to dry out slowly.

Playing

The tambourine is held in one hand and struck with the other. The instrument is held immobile, and the striking hand moves, so that extraneous jingles resulting from moving the instrument can be kept to a minimum. For a right-handed person, the instrument is held in the right hand with the thumb on the outside of the rim and the four fingers gripping the inside and muffling the head. The center may be struck with the fleshy part of the fingertips (Figure 21–21), the heel of the hand, the knuckles, or on the knee (Figure 21–22). The rim may be struck with the fingers, timpani sticks, or snare drum sticks. It may be shaken, played with the thumb, or muted with a handkerchief. Most of these are for specific purposes, but some are left to the discretion of the player.

Loud playing is usually accomplished by striking with the fleshy part of the first three fingertips, or with the knuckles, in the approximate center of the head. This technique is adequate for moderate or slow passages at forte volume. For rapid rhythmic passages, a different technique is necessary. Here the knee and the knuckles are used: the foot is placed on a chair so that the knee is bent, the tambourine is held head down just above the knee. The instrument is then moved up and down in the rhythm required, alternately striking the knee and the knuckles at the speed and volume required. In this fashion, complex rhythms can be played forte with considerable precision.

Soft, fast passages are played by setting the tambourine head down on a soft pad and using timpani sticks on the wood of the rim. Slow to moderate rhythms played piano are produced by placing the tambourine,

Figure 21–21. Normal Playing Position for the Tambourine

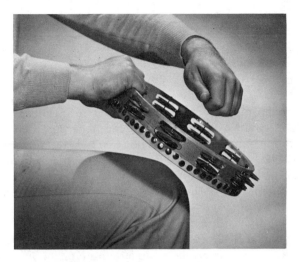

Figure 21–22. Knee Position for Playing the Tambourine

head down, on a soft cushion or on the knees and striking the rim with the flat part of the fingers of both hands. Soft passages are sometimes played by holding the tambourine parallel to the floor, head down, just as though the instrument were resting on a pad or cushion, and striking the rim with fingers of the other hand. Faster passages require both hands to produce the rhythm, so this is practical only for slower passages. For any speed or any dynamic level, articulations are generally cleaner when the head is parallel to the floor. Muffling may be appropriate for any situation and is done by placing a handkerchief on the inside of the head.

Long rolls are produced by shaking the instrument back and forth with a rotating action of the hand and wrist. A short, quiet roll of one or two counts may call for the thumb roll, which is a way of vibrating the jingles by means of friction between the thumb and head. The thumb is wetted, then rubbed around the edge of the head close to the rim with the tambourine tilted toward the empty hand. The friction sets the jingles in motion. This is a somewhat hazardous practice, as the player is never sure when the thumb is going to suddenly become dry. Some players use powdered rosin rather than wetting the thumb. An even more secure solution is to use wax around the edge of the head or to glue a thin strip of emery paper around the edge of the head. Regular sandpaper is less satisfactory; it begins to wear the skin of the thumb away if many rolls are required.

If the tambourine is to be played with a snare drum stick, it should be placed on a cushion with the head up.

TRIANGLE

The pitch of the triangle is determined by its size. Three triangles varying from 4-inch to 10-inch are considered adequate for most playing needs. As with all other instruments, they should be of good quality. The use of a poor-quality triangle is hardly preferable to having none at all; the tiny sound of a cheap piece of metal will make its use ridiculous.

Triangles come supported with twine or string. This should be replaced with a fine gut string and attached to a holder. Old music clips make excellent triangle holders—the triangle can be grasped with the thumb and forefinger of the left hand without the palm and fingers getting in the way of the instrument. When the triangle needs to be suspended from the music stand, the clip fastens on with a secure grip. The triangle should be suspended when not in use, and also when both hands will be required to play it. See Figure 21–23 for proper playing position for the triangle.

In sound, a tinkle is preferred to a definite pitch. Since some strikers produce more specific pitches than others, the sound varies with the striker used. The regular triangle beater should be at least 10 inches in length and from $1/16$ to $3/8$ inch in diameter. Other strikers include heavy nails, medium-sized metal nailfiles, pieces of wire coathangers, and the wire handles from telescoping snare drum brushes. Most of these are for special effects, of course, and the triangle beater is more frequently used than the others. See Figure 21–24 for proper playing position for special effects.

The beater, of whatever nature, should be held about 3 to 4 inches in from the butt end—if it is held too close to the end it produces a harsh sound. The player should hold the triangle in front of his body at a height where he can see both the music and the conductor without strain. For

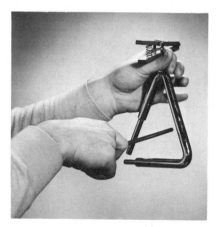

Figure 21–23. Normal Position, Single-Stick Rolls, and Fast Rhythmic Patterns on the Triangle

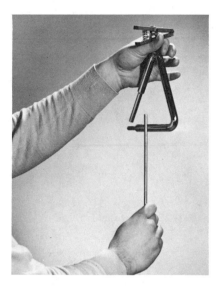

Figure 21–24. Single Stick Position for Special Effects on the Triangle

single-stick rolls and fast rhythmic patterns, the beater should be approximately 2 inches through the triangle in playing; that is, 2 inches should extend on the far side of the instrument.

Most playing is done by placing the beater inside the triangle and striking the base about one third of the way in from the closed lower corner. A single beat is often played outside, either on the closed face of the triangle or on the base, but rhythmic patterns are easier to control when the beater is placed inside and played on the base. This applies to slow and moderate rhythms, both loud and soft. Faster rhythms require use of both base and side. An extremely fast passage may necessitate the use of two beaters, one in each hand, with the instrument suspended. Triplets also are more successfully executed with two beaters. They tend to sound like a roll when a single beater is used.

The sound is dampened by gently touching the triangle near the top with the playing hand. This must be done carefully in order to avoid a "clunk" noise as the sound ceases.

Rolls are performed by using a single beater and moving it rapidly back and forth between the base and the closed side. Softer rolls will be played close to the angle, so little motion is required. Louder rolls will be wider, played farther away from the angle so that the greater motion can allow more vigor and produce more volume. Rolls are started on the base rather than on the side.

Figure 21–25. Castanets

CASTANETS

Castanets come in two models, single or double, in addition to the castanet machine. The single has one pair of blades, or clappers, attached to a wooden handle that is also the sounding board. The double has two sets of clappers. They are held by gripping the handle with the bottom three fingers, the thumb resting lightly wherever comfortable, and the index finger furnishing control. Three fingers of the opposite hand strike the handle to produce the sound, as in Figure 21–25.

The castanet machine allows the player to use her fingers to obtain more precision. Slower passages make use of the double castanet at dynamics from mezzoforte to fortissimo. Softer passages in moderate or slow speeds will use the single, which may be struck in the normal manner— on the open palm, on the knuckles of the closed fist, or on the leg (Figure 21–26).

Fast, loud passages require two sets of single castanets, one in each hand, struck on the leg slightly above the knee or on the thigh. Fast but soft passages are played by holding the top clapper down against the handle with the index finger so that it does not vibrate, and striking the instrument softly against the knee.

Rolls are produced in the following ways: (1) pianissimo to mezzoforte by using the single instrument, striking rapidly against the knee; (2) from mezzoforte to fortissimo by a well-controlled shaking motion using the double castanets; or (3) alternating two castanets against the knee or shaking. Tremolos are produced by using a set in each hand.

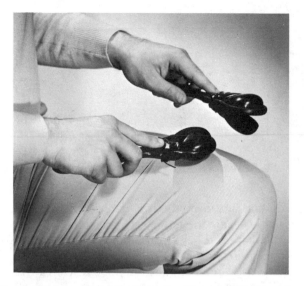

Figure 21–26. Knee Position for Playing the Castanets

LATIN AMERICAN RHYTHM INSTRUMENTS

There are many minor percussion instruments whose chief use is in Latin American dance rhythms. The instruments used on the conga should be conga drums, timbales, and cowbell. On the samba, the snare drum is used with the regular drumstick in the right hand and the wire brush in the left. The right hand plays the first note on the edge of the drum like a rim shot, and the left hand plays the second note near the center. The snares should be off. The tambourine may be used to double the snare, and maracas should be used on quarter notes. The characteristic bolero rhythm is a triplet on the second half of the first beat. In Latin American music, the bolero is simply a slow rumba, but all of its other specific characteristics have dwindled in importance until the only one left is the triplet rhythm. Don't improvise the tango. When substitute players are used for an augmented percussion section, the drummers should be kept on the timbales and maracas because these demand more percussion skill; the nonpercussionists can play the claves, guiros, and cowbells.

Maracas

Two maracas are used, one a little larger than the other (Figure 21–27). The left hand is in front of the body holding the lower-pitched instrument;

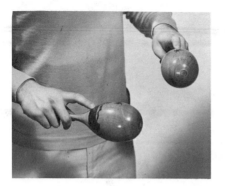

Figure 21–27. Maracas

the right hand alternates over the top of the left hand. They are usually played with a single beat in the left hand and a double beat in the right. For soft passages, the maraca is held with thumb and bottom three fingers and the base is tapped with the index finger.

Maracas are used for mambos, guarachas, Cuban boleros, rumbas, and beguines. They are used on tangos, congas, and paso dobles. The rumba rhythm is even, as in Figure 21–28.

Temple Blocks

These are Korean blocks, each made of one piece of balsa wood and painted. They are very fragile and chip easily, and they should be played near the edge with medium-hard rubber or yarn marimba mallets. They usually come in sets of five, although many more are available.

Woodblocks

The woodblock is related to the temple block but is oblong in shape. It is struck with the end of a regular drumstick or hard rubber mallet, never with a metal beater. For the best sound, the long tone slot should face the player and be at the top of the block rather than at the bottom. A holder gives the best effect, although the woodblocks may be placed on a pad on any flat surface. At least two should be available, a high and a low. Playing on the solid and on the hollow sides of the block will produce different sounds.

Figure 21–28. Typical Maracas Rhythm

Figure 21–29. Claves

Claves

These are two small, round sticks of rosewood or grenadilla, played by clicking them together (Figure 21–29). They are the most important instruments in the rhythm section for Cuban rhythms. The smaller one is placed on the partially closed knuckles of the fingers as the palm is turned upward, held gently in place with the thumb. It is struck with the larger one, held loosely in the right hand. They furnish a steady beat in the mambo, Cuban bolero, rumba, and beguine. They are not used in the conga, samba, or paso doble. Typical claves rhythms are illustrated in Figure 21–30.

Cowbells

A regular cowbell is used with the metal striker removed. It is played with a snare drumstick. The cowbell is particularly useful on fast rumbas, congas, and the montuno. Two bells of different pitches are used on the conga and the montuno. The bell is held in the flat of the left hand and struck with the tip of the stick or the thick shoulder, depending on the sound desired. Muffling with adhesive tape is done to produce a dead tone. This muffled bell is often called a *concerto* and is used for the Conga and the montuno.

Figure 21–30. Typical Claves Rhythm

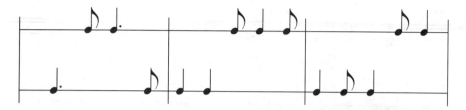

Figure 21–31.   Cowbell Rhythm Using Both the Flat and Edge of the Bell

Figure 21–31 illustrates the use of both flat and edge, the lower note played on the edge, the upper on the flat of the bell.

Conga Drum

The conga drum is a deep, barrel-shaped drum made of coco wood, with a head of mule hide. It may be slung over the shoulder with a strap for playing, or rested on a stand. Two should be available, approximately 27 inches in size. They should be capable of being tuned. To play, the right hand slaps the center of the head with flat fingers or the flat palm. The left hand plays rim shots with flat fingers, holding the fingers against the head after striking.

Bongo

Bongo drums are played in pairs of different sizes, the most common pair being a 5½ × 6 or 8 and a 10 × 6 or 8. They are made with a goatskin head and are used principally for boleros, rumbas, mambos, and similar dance types. The smaller instrument plays predominantly; it should be placed on the left. Only the tips of the fingers and the left thumb are used, except for rim shots, which are struck flat on the edge. The drums are not played alternately; the smaller one is used more.

Timbales

In France the term *timbales* indicates the timpani; in the United States it refers to two small tom-toms on a single stand. The player must be sure of his directions and select the right instrument.

Timbales are larger than the bongo drum, usually 6½ × 11 or 6½ × 13, and give more volume. They can be wooden or metal (metal is preferred), and are played in pairs. Either sticks or hands are used in playing; if hands, the center of the head is struck with the right hand while the left hand strikes over the edge of the rim at the same time. When sticks are used, they are either small snare drumsticks or straight rattan. The right-hand stick is held in the usual grip, while the left-hand stick is held over the drum, palm down. The timbales are commonly used in beguines, in which they serve to heavily accent the first afterbeat as is typical of beguines. Different areas of the drum are used for various effects: shell, rim, center, and so forth.

Cubaza

The cubaza is very much like a maraca, except that the rattlers—small hard beads—are on the outside rather than the inside, strung on a ribbon that wraps around the ball. It is held by the handle with one hand and struck on the palm of the other. It is effectively used in sambas.

Guiro

The guiro is a gourd-shaped instrument with a corrugated surface that is scraped with a small piece of wood, wire, or bamboo. A wooden guiro produces the best sound. Guiros are used principally in the rumba.

Chocalli, Ganza, Tubes, Shaker

These are similar, all being some type of sealed tin can, cylindrical in shape, filled with stones or gravel. They are held with both hands and shaken.

OTHER TRAPS

The list of items usable in percussion effects is nearly endless, depending on the originality of the composer and the inventiveness of the player. The following list suggests the scope of possibilities; it is not inclusive by any means. It is presented as an indication of what may be done: wind machine, anvil, steel drums, whistles, brake drums, rattles, slapstick, bird whistles, Quijada, agogo bells, talking drums (three), log drums (two), calypso maracas, 14-inch ka-me-so, sleigh bells mounted on handles (all sizes), tablas, and cabasa.

MARCHING PERCUSSION

The emphasis on percussion as an integral (and expensive) component of the high school marching band has grown steadily since the mid-1970s. High school band directors have borrowed many concepts and techniques from drum and bugle corps, such as staging the performances to the audience rather than the end zones, use of adjusted step, and greater reliance on auxiliary groups for visual elements to choreograph the music. A major factor in the growth in popularity of marching bands was percussion—after all, the models were not called *bugle* and drum corps.

To fully treat the complex and ever-changing area of marching band percussion is beyond the scope of this text. References that provide more detailed guidance are listed at the end of Chapter 8, "An Overview of Woodwind and Brass Instruments."

The role that marching band plays in the instrumental music program will influence the size of the percussion section. It is not easy to determine that a band of x size should have a percussion section of y size with z instrumentation. To illustrate: Most high school marching bands will have some trumpets, some trombones, some flutes, and some saxophones. But a marching band can have anywhere from one to twelve snares; one to six triples, quads, or quints; one to five pairs of cymbals; two to nine bass drums; and a virtually unlimited array of percussion in the pit: timpani, tam-tam, suspended cymbals, concert vibes, marimbas, xylophone and bells, tom-tom, chimes and so on. The tremendous variance between percussion sections may require an arranger to alter the percussion scoring of many band scores. Although almost any band has the wind instrumentation to play the published stock arrangements, percussion parts often must be augmented or simplified to conform to the instrumentation and expertise of the performers.

It seems to have been the trend during the last decade to include as many percussionists as possible in the drumline. In some programs this enlarged percussion section has been to the detriment of the clarinet and flute sections. It is much better to have three good bass drummers playing precisely and synchronized than to have five weak ones. By the same token, the majority of marching band adjudicators will testify how pleasant, refreshing, and unusual to hear a good *band* sound from a marching band—which of course implies the blend of adequate brass and woodwinds with percussion.

The percussion section is largely responsible for creating the musical energy and rhythmic drive of the marching band (the color guard may add to the visual energy and rhythmic drive by popping flags and such on the musical accents). An ideal piece of music for marching band might have predominately long notes in the winds to facilitate a variety of dynamic levels, intonation, and articulation, giving the percussion all of the rhythmic aspects. For example, a piano score of a popular, top-40 type of song often has repeated notes in the bass line that many experienced arrangers will transcribe for the tubas. A better sound is achieved by letting the tubas play half notes or whole notes and writing the articulation or rhythm for the bass drums.

As in all good music, however, contrast is essential. The driving rhythm provided by the percussion should always be contrasted with sections in an arrangement, or at least sections of the show, with the drums tacet. And clearly, all the percussion do not need to be playing all the time.

Each of the primary areas of the marching band drumline is discussed briefly below: snare drums, multiple drums, bass drums, cymbals, and the pit.

Snare Drums

Snare drums are the foundation of the marching band percussion section. Most teachers place their best percussionists on snare because it plays the most intricate music and because the use of several snare players increases the need for precision.

Among the manufacturers of marching snare drums, Yamaha and Pearl are known to be dependable in quality control. The newest company on the market, Stingray, has introduced a snare drum with a fiberglass shell, which may set the industry standard in the 1990s. This was the first drum guaranteed against structural damage when fitted with a Kenlar drumhead.

Marching snares are generally found in two diameters, 14 and 15 inch, the former preferred because it is somewhat lighter and can be tuned higher (which enhances projection). The depth of the shell is standard for all good quality marching drums. The shell on the fiberglass Stingray is slightly shorter to compensate for its heavier weight.

Most percussion companies make marching snare drums in a variety of levels of quality and prices. As has been advocated throughout the previous chapters on winds, directors should make every attempt to purchase the best-quality marching snare drums—and to keep them in good playing condition. With marching snare drums, for example, this will usually mean features such as individually adjustable snares on the snare strainer. Such items seem to intimidate directors, who are convinced that their drummers will never learn to adjust each single gut snare to the proper tension and tune the drums to the same pitch. . . . If students can learn to adjust reeds, they can certainly adjust snares, and if trumpet players can learn to play with good intonation, then clearly snare drummers can also.

The number of snare drummers needed in a marching band is difficult to determine. Many directors overestimate the number required to balance the brass—simply because they consider only the loud volume levels and not the softer levels. On the other hand, extra snare drummers allow each individual player to play more softly and so with more control. A rule of thumb is to field one snare drummer for every eight to ten brass players (assuming a nearly equal number of woodwind and brass players).

The most difficult task for the marching band snare drummers is precision. In any given arrangement, drummers probably average 100 notes for every note played by the first trumpet. With ten to twelve students playing these lines in unison, precision of the ensemble is a formidable task. With the visual elements of stick heights, stick angles, drum angles, and any gimmick-type stick visuals added, the task can become extremely time consuming. When the marching formations and maneuvers are added to the playing, the role of marching band percussionists may be the most difficult of any in the high school marching band.

Most successful marching drumlines spend time each day warming up. Marching snare drum exercises are available in a number of sources (some of these are listed in the chapter references and the references at the end of Chapter 7: Rehearsal Techniques). Most of these exercises are simply based on repeating sixteenth-note patterns over and over while alternating one of the sixteenth notes with a double (thirty-second notes with the same stick), then a double substituted for several of the sixteenth notes, and so on. Examples are shown in Figure 21–32.

Most good snare lines will play an exercise like this thousands of times trying to achieve a precision comparable to a single, individual concert snare drum player.

Multiple Drums

The band director who is enlarging the marching band drumline must decide whether to purchase triples, quads, quints, or some other multiple percussion. Then he must determine the sizes. This same dilemma confronts the arrangers and publishers of commercial marching band arrangements.

The first notable use of multiple percussion in a marching group was in the 1960s when the now-famous drum and bugle corps director Bobby Hoffman carried a pair of timbales as a marching member of the Hawthorne Cabeleros. Since that time, drum and bugle corps (and bands) have attempted to "carry" as many drums as possible onto the field.

The most efficient multiple drums are quads: a mounted arrangement of 8-, 10-, 12-, and 14-inch (or similar graduated increments) cutaway drums for projection and for reduced weight. When a fifth drum is added, often the most useful is a 6-inch "gocker" tuned extremely high and used like a rimshot on snare drum (See Figure 21–33).

The decision as to what sizes to purchase is guided by pitch. Conceptually, the multiple drums are used to "fill the gap" between the snare drum and bass drums. If the snare drums are using older 15-inch drums that cannot be tuned as high as 14-inch drums with Kavlar heads, then one may wish to use quads in 10-, 12-, 14-, and 16-inch sizes. 16- and 18-inch bass drums are growing in popularity, and the pitch of the 16-inch drum

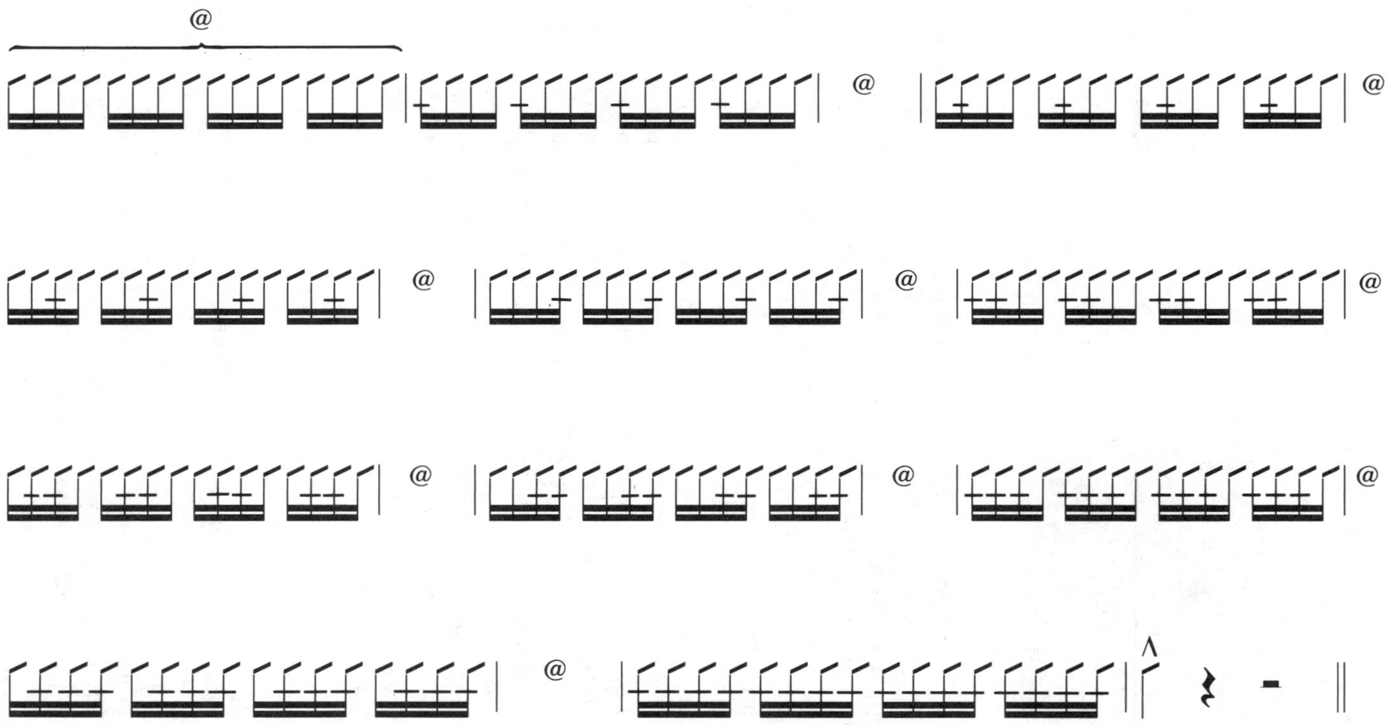

Figure 21–32. Drumline Warm-Up Exercises

Figure 21–33. Quint line, each carrying 6-, 10-, 12-, 13-, and 14-inch drums

may "bleed over" into the pitch range of the bass drums. A compromise must be sought.

Multiple drums are generally expensive. And one should never cut cost on the carriers. Due to the mounting arrangement of multiple drums, a quality carrier is important to prevent the mounts from breaking and more important, to prevent the student from breaking.

Several points in favor of triples are reduced cost, less concern with those pitched drums "bleeding over" into the snare or bass drum ranges, and lighter weight. The negative aspect is greater limitation for playing musical lines. Depending on the budget, a viable route is to purchase triples (10, 12, 14 inches) and good carriers initially (CMI carriers may be the best) and add a fourth and possibly a fifth drum later. Most commercial arrangements are written and scored to be played by triples, quads, or quints.

The general rule of thumb is to field one multiple player for every two or three snare drummers. Smaller drumlines may have only one multiple player and one snare player; this arrangement usually provides much greater musical contrast, interest, and ensemble support than would an arrangement using two snare drums.

Bass Drums

Traditionally the marching band bass drummer has been the most singled-out, fussed-at, unappreciated musician in the ensemble. Two reasons can be given: first, band directors have often assigned one of their weakest players to this seemingly simple instrument; and (yet) second, it is one of the most important instruments in the ensemble.

Happily, bass drummers have come to enjoy a status once reserved for only the snare line. Bass drumlines comprised of three to nine tonal bass drums have impressed audiences throughout the country in the last decade. The most common line is five drums: 22, 24, 26, 28, and 30 inches. Some directors prefer to replace the 30-inch drum with a 20-inch; some directors have also used an 18-inch drum instead of the 28-inch drum for an 18-, 20-, 22-, 24-, and 26-inch combination. Advantages of such an arrangement include lighter equipment and less expensive equipment (cost increases with bass drum size).

There are, however, many marching percussion specialists who advocate larger drums, such as a 36-inch drum, especially useful for special effects. The largest drum used successfully in recent years has been the 42-inch Pearl custom-made bass drum for the Garfield Cadets. It was not carried, but mounted in the pit. Unless needed for a visual effect the 36-inch drum also belongs on the sideline.

The smallest number of tonal bass drums that can be used effectively is three, although occasionally marching bands use only one or two. The best arrangement for a three-drum combination is a 22, 24 and 28 inch. The next addition would obviously be a 26-inch drum, followed then by a 20-inch bass drum.

The largest drumlines have normally fielded 18-, 20-, 22-, 24-, 26-, 28-, 30-, 32-, and 36-inch bass drums. Such an array provides opportunity for a few spectacular moments in a marching band show as well as a tremendously powerful visual element. An array of white drum heads can be visually striking (See Figure 21–34).

As for the other marching percussion instruments, it is important that good quality bass drum carriers be purchased. There are a number of padded, nonpadded, high-rise, and other carriers available that are of good quality.

Yamaha, Ludwig, and Pearl are among the best bass drum manufacturers. Bass drums made of fiberglass manufactured prior to 1991 have not proved light enough to be satisfactory, and the translucent bass drums popular for a few years proved to be too lightweight.

Figure 21–34. Bass drumline of 16-, 18-, 20-, 22-, 24-, 26-, 28-, and 32-inch drums

Cymbals

Generally the cymbals selected for use in marching band are of lighter weight than those used for concert band. Weight becomes especially important when the cymbal players are required to hold the instruments extended to allow the snare players to play side cymbals. Whereas the lamb's wool pad is usually removed for concert use, these pads generally protect the marching cymbalist's knuckles. Most players are also more comfortable when wearing lightweight leather gloves. The newest innovations have been cymbals manufactured by companies such as Paiste in a choice of colors. These merely provide an unusual visual effect for the marching band.

The Pit

In 1975 Drum Corps International altered their rules to allow tonal mallet percussion instruments on the field. For several years, drum and bugle corps students marched around the field carrying bells, marching xylophones and marimbas (both smaller than concert instrument), and even chimes. A few years later, DCI allowed those percussionists to "ground" their equipment; several years later, it became legal to place percussion equipment just off the sideline and allow it to remain stationary throughout the show. Band directors followed the model, lagging several years behind—although the band marched bell-lyras for decades before drum corps did.

Presently, drum and bugle corps and most corps-style bands utilize a tremendous range and variety of stationary instruments on the sideline near the drum major's podium. All provide new sounds to enhance a band's overall musical performance; all are limited, however, and most are expensive.

The most beneficial are the mallet instruments. Use of the pit enables a concert marimba, with Kelon brass, to be rolled and secured on the sideline. Bells, xylophone, and vibraphone are also useful—in that order. Great care must be taken to keep these instruments in good repair; rolling these instruments from the rehearsal room to the practice field on a daily basis will reduce their span of usefulness regardless of how carefully they are treated.

Also commonly found in the pit are Latin instruments: timbales, bongos, chimes, cowbells, shakers, and others. Although these instruments are much less costly than keyboard instruments, their usefulness is more limited. Marching bands have made good use of Spanish or Latin tunes for years, as these are favored by both students and audiences. Latin instruments add a great deal to this style of music, but have little use otherwise.

Tenor tom-toms (mounted on a concert stand), timpani, tam-tam, suspended cymbals, all can provide beautiful colors to any musical ensemble and especially to the marching band. But, again, these instruments are expensive and difficult to move. Relatively few instrumental music programs can afford a set of timpani for concert work and a set for marching band. Still fewer programs can provide the personnel required to move two to four timpani, four keyboard mallets, a dozen Latin instruments, tom-tom, tam-tam, and so forth, on and off the field for every rehearsal and performance.

When marching bands have attempted to utilize all percussionists in the pit, they have suffered from phrasing, balance, and percussion problems to such an extent as to make these attempts unsuccessful.

Instrumentation

The minimum marching drumline should have six people—one snare, one triple or quad, three bass drums, and one cymbal player—and available equipment. Common sense should help one decide where to add the seventh player, then the eighth, and so on (See Figure 21–35).

Most directors will have a minimum of three snares, one quad, four bass drums, and two cymbal players before adding a pit percussionist. This single individual on the sideline, however, can cover a variety of instruments. Each should enhance the total ensemble, not be used simply to demonstrate that the school owns three or four keyboard percussion instruments.

Drum Solos

During the late 1970s and 1980s, marching bands often included drum solos as a component of their half-time or competition shows. This component, like so many others in modern marching bands, was borrowed from

Figure 21–35. **A common instrumentation for high school drum lines (bass drums are 18-, 22-, 26-, and 30-inch drums)**

drum and bugle corps. Trends in the 1990s indicate that rather than a separate drum solo in a show, most successful marching bands are featuring the percussionists in portions of other selections.

REFERENCES

Texts

AKINS, T. N. *The Musical Timpanist*. Delevan, NY: Kendor Music, 1974.

BAJZEK, DIETER. *Percussion: An Annotated Bibliography*. Metuchen, NJ: The Scarecrow Press, 1988.

BARTLETT, HARRY R. *Guide to Teaching Percussion*. 4th ed. Dubuque, IA: W. C. Brown, 1983.

BENVENGA, NANCY. *Timpani and the Timpanist's Art: Musical and Technical Development in the 19th and 20th Centuries*. Goteborg, Sweden: Goteborg University, 1979.

BLADES, JAMES. *Orchestral Percussion Technique*. 2nd ed. London: Oxford University Press, 1973.

BLADES, JAMES, and J. MONTAGU. *Early Percussion Instruments from the Middle Ages to the Baroque*. London: Oxford University Press, 1970.

BRINDLE, R. S. *Contemporary Percussion*. London: Oxford University Press, 1970.

————. *Percussion Instruments and Their History*. London: Faber and Faber, 1972.

BUCK, ROBERT. *Precision Marching Percussion Ensemble Method*. Sherman Oaks, CA: Alfred Publications, 1979.

BUGGERT, ROBERT. *Teaching Techniques for the Percussions*. Rockville Centre, NY: Belwin-Mills, 1960.

CIRONE, ANTHONY. *The Orchestral Mallet Player*. Menlo Park, CA: Cirone Publications, 1977.

————. *The Orchestral Snare Drummer*. Menlo Park, CA: Cirone Publications, 1975.

————. *The Orchestral Timpanist*. Menlo Park, CA: Cirone Publications, 1978.

CIRONE, ANTHONY and JOE SINAI. *The Logic of It All*. Menlo Park, CA: Cirone Publications, 1977.

COLLINS, MYRON D. and JOHN E. GREEN. *Playing and Teaching Percussion Instruments*. Englewood Cliffs, NJ: Prentice Hall, 1962.

COMBS, F. M. *Percussion Manual*. Belmont, CA: Wadsworth, 1977.

COOK, GARY D. *Teaching Percussion*. New York: Schirmer Books, 1988.

DENOV, SAM. *The Art of Playing Cymbals*. Rockville Centre, New York: Belwin-Mills, 1963.

HELLER, GEORGE N. *Ensemble Music for Wind and Percussion Instruments: A Catalog*. Reston, VA: Music Educators National Conference, 1970.

HOLLAND, JAMES. *Percussion*. New York: Schirmer Books, 1978.

HOLLOWAY, ROLAND H., and HARRY R. BARTLETT. *Guide to Teaching Percussion*. Dubuque, IA: W. C. Brown Company, 1978.

KIRBY, PERCIVAL R. *The Kettle Drums*. London: Oxford University Press, 1930.

LANG, MORRIS and LARRY SPIVACK. *Dictionary of Percussion Terms*. New York: Lang Percussion Company, 1977.

LEACH, JOEL. *Percussion Manual for Music Educators*. New York: Henry Adler, 1964.

LUDWIG, WILLIAM F. *The Development of Drum Rudiments*. Chicago: Ludwig Drum Company, n.d.

MACCALLUM, FRANK. *The Book of the Marimba*. New York: Carlton Press, 1969.

MASONER, ELIZABETH. *Reference Guide on Percussion Publications*. Minneapolis, MN: Typist Letter Co., 1960.

McCORMICK, R. *Percusion for Musicians: A Complete Fundamental Literature and Technique Method for Percussion*. Melville, NY: Belwin-Mills, 1983.

MOORE, STEPHEN. *Percussion Playing*. London: Paxton, 1959.

MOTT, VINCENT L. *Evolution of Drumming; Textbook of the Snare Drum*. Paterson, NJ: Music Textbook Co., 1957.

MUELLER, K. A. *Teaching Total Percussion*. West Nyack, NY: Parker Publishing Co., 1972.

PAPASTEFAN, JOHN J. *Timpani Scoring Techniques in the Twentieth Century*. Mobile, AL: University of South Alabama, 1978.

PAYSON, AL. *Techniques of Playing Bass Drum, Cymbals and Accessories*. Park Ridge, IL: Payson Percussion Products, n.d.

PAYSON, AL, and JACK McKENZIE. *Music Educators' Guide to Percussion*. Rockville Centre, NY: Belwin-Mills, 1966.

————. *Percussion in the School Music Program*. Park Ridge, IL: Payson Percussion Products, n.d.

PEINKOFER, KARL, and FRITZ TANNIGELE. *Handbook of Percussion Instruments*. Translated by Kurt and Else Stone. London: Schott, 1969.

Percussion Anthology. Evanston, IL: The Instrumentalist Co., 1977.

PETERS, GORDON. *Treatise on Percussion*. Rochester, NY: Masters thesis, University of Rochester, 1962.

————. *The Drummer Man: A Treatise on Percussion*. Wilmette, IL: Kemper-Peters, 1975.

PRICE, PAUL. *Percussion Corner*. Urbana, IL: Music Extension, University of Illinois, 1961.

RAPP, WILL. *The Visual Drum Line*. New Berlin, WI: Jenson Publications, n.d.

SNIDER, LARRY. *Developing the Corps Style Percussion Section*. Oskaloosa, IA: C.L. Barnhouse Co., 1980.

SPINNEY, BRADLEY. *Encyclopedia of Percussion Instruments*. Hollywood, CA: Hollywood Percussion Club and Clinic, 1959.

SPRINGER, GEORGE H. *Maintenance and Repair of Wind and Percussion Instruments*. Boston: Allyn and Bacon, 1976.

SPOHN, CHARLES. *The Percussion Performance and Instructional Techniques*. Boston, Allyn and Bacon, 1967.

STEVENS, LEIGH HOWARD. *Method of Movement for Marimba*. New York: Marimba Productions, 1979,

TAYLOR, HENRY W. *The Art and Science of the Timpani*. London: John Baker Publishers, 1964.

VOSE, DAVID. *Developing Musicianship in the Contemporary Marching Percussion Ensemble*. Lebanon, IN: Studio P/R, 1981.

WHITE, C. L. *Drums Through the Ages*. Los Angeles: Sterling Press, 1960.

Studies

Easy-Beginning (elementary or junior high)

BROWN, THOMAS. *Combination Method for Snare Drum and Mallets* (Belwin-Mills).

COFFIN, JAMES. *The Performing Percussionist*, Book 1 (C. L. Barnhouse).

FELDSTEIN, SANDY. *Mallet Technique for Bass and Treble Clef, : Two Mallets* (Belwin-Mills).

FIRTH, VIC. *Vic Firth Snare Drum Method*, Book I (Carl Fischer).

GREEN, GEORGE HAMILTON. *George Hamilton Green's Instruction Course for Xylophone* (Meredith Music).

HOULIFF, MURRAY. *Play at First Sight* (Kandor).

LA ROSA, MICHAEL. *Contemporary Drum Method*, Book 1 (Somers Music Publications).

McMILLAN, THOMAS. *Percussion Keyboard Technique* (Belwin-Mills).

PAYSON, AL. *Beginning Snare Drum Method* (Payson Percussion Products).

————. *Elementary Marimba and Xylophone Method* (Payson Percussion Products).

PETERS, MITCHELL. *Developing Dexterity for Snare Drum* (Mitchell Peters).

WHALEY, GARWOOD. *Basics in Rhythm* (Meredith Music).

————. *Primary Handbook for Mallets* (Meredith Music).

Medium (advanced junior high or high school)

BECK, JOHN. *Flams, Ruffs and Rolls for Snare Drum* (Meredith Music).

BELLSON, LOUIS and GIL BREINES. *Modern Reading Test in $\frac{4}{4}$* (Belwin-Mills).

————. *Odd Time Reading Test* (Belwin-Mills).

BERLE, ARNIE (ed. Feldstein). *Mallet Independence* (Belwin-Mills).

BREWER, HARRY. *Harry Brewer's Mallet Solo Collection* (Alfred).

CIRONE, ANTHONY J. *Portraits in Rhythm* (Belwin-Mills).

COFFIN, JAMES. *The Performing Percussionist*, Book 2 (C. L. Barnhouse).

DELECLUSE, JACQUES. *30 Etudes*, Books I through III (Alphonse Leduc).

————. *20 Etudes* (Alphonse-Leduc).

FIRTH, VIC. *Mallet Technique—38 Studies for the Marimba, Xylophone and Vibraphone* (Carl Fischer).

GOLDENBERG, MORRIS. *Modern School for Xylophone, Marimba and Vibraphone* (Hal Leonard).

GREEN, GEORGE H. *George Hamilton Green's Instruction Course for Xylophone* (Meredith Music).

HOULLIF, MURRAY. *20 Bach Chorales* (Music for Percussion).

KRAUS, PHIL. *Phil Kraus—Modern Mallet Method, Book 1* (Belwin-Mills).

LANG, MORRIS. *15 Bach Inventions for Mallet Instruments* (Belwin-Mills).

————. *14 Contemporary Etudes for Mallet Instruments* (Belwin-Mills).

McMILLAN, THOMAS. *Basic Timpani Technique* (Belwin-Mills).

————. *Masterpieces for Marimba* (Belwin-Mills).

PODEMSKI, BENJAMIN. *Podemski's Standard Snare Drum Method* (Belwin-Mills).

WHALEY, GARWOOD. *Audition Etudes for Snare Drum, Timpani, Keyboard, Percussion, and Multiple Percussion* (Meredith Music).

_____. *Musical Studies for the Intermediate Mallet Player* (Meredith Music).

_____. *Primary Handbook for Timpani* (Meredith Music).

_____. *Solos and Duets for Timpani* (Meredith Music).

Advanced (high school or college)

ALBRIGHT, FRED. *Contemporary Studies for the Snare Drum* (Belwin-Mills).

_____. *Rhythmic Analysis for the Snare Drum, with Introduction to Polyrhythms* (Award Music).

BURTON, GARY. *Four Mallet Studies* (Ludwig).

CIRONE, A. J. *Portraits in Rhythm* (Belwin-Mills).

DELECLUSE, JACQUES. *30 Etudes*, Books I through III (Alphonse Leduc).

FINK, RON. *Sight Reading and Audition Etudes* (Fink).

_____. *Timpani Tuning Etudes* (Fink).

GATES, EVERETT. *Odd Meter Duets* (Sam Fox).

GOLDENBERG, MORRIS. *Modern School for Snare Drum (with a Guide Book for the Artist Percussionist)* (Hal Leonard).

_____. *Modern School for Xylophone, Marimba and Vibraphone* (Hal Leonard).

GREEN, GEORGE H. *George Hamilton Green's Instruction Course for Xylophone* (Meredith Music).

KRAUS, PHIL.—*Modern Mallet Method*, Vols. 2 and 3 (Belwin-Mills).

PAYSON, AL, and JAMES LANE. *Concert Etudes for Snare Drum* (Payson Percussion Products).

PETERS, MITCHELL. *Advanced Snare Drum Studies* (Mitchell Peters).

STEVENS, LEIGH HOWARD. *Method of Movement for Marimba* (Marimba Productions).

STOUT, GORDON. *Etudes for Marimba*, 2 Vols. (Paul Price Publications and Alfred).

Index